D1218922

Two Masters and Two Gospels Volume 1

TWO MASTERS AND TWO GOSPELS VOLUME 1

THE TEACHING OF JESUS VS. THE "LEAVEN OF THE PHARISEES" IN TALK RADIO AND CABLE NEWS

J. MICHAEL BENNETT, PH.D

 Akribos Press

ISBN: 978-1-952249-03-7

Published in 2020 by Akribos Press, 1020 Kellyn Lane, Hendersonville, TN, 37075

Find us on the World Wide Web at www.akribospress.com

Cover design by GlitschkaStudios.com

To my father, who modeled the love, patience and integrity of a Heavenly Father; a mother who was not only my biggest cheerleader but also the catalyst for my concern for the outsider, disadvantaged and the stranger; friends Adam and Micah who believed in my pursuits and cajoled me to complete this maiden voyage; Ginny, Greg, Beau and the gang at Radio Free Nashville, who gave me a voice; Steve and Bill, two strangers to each other but who each waited patiently for many years for my writing to bear fruit while they faithfully helped with my website and other expenses; Von, Martin and Sean, old friends who played key roles; my long-suffering wife Ginger who toiled and supported my (income-free) quest without complaint or condition; and a Carpenter who still shows me how to live life, while also helping others collectively make it to the next one

For Those Who Have Ears To Hear

Contents

AN IMPORTANT PRELIMINARY WORD
FOR THE READER

The following manuscript was not originally planned to be written. I, an aspiring but amateur, dabbling writer (what golfers call a "duffer"), was previously focused on completing a very lengthy book series begun in late 2011 entitled, *The Holy War Chronicles—A Spiritual View of the War on Terror*. It currently comprises 12 or more lengthy volumes on the different facets of how the religious convictions of our Judeo-Christian ancestors (in particular Christians, like myself) have historically led to aggressive and eventually violent confrontations with those in whom they disagree, which explains the curious and strident behavior of American Christians today towards the Muslim community during the War on Terror, and as a glimpse of the nature of Christians' faith, based upon their words and deeds. However, I also try to stay generally abreast of current social and political developments, and I could not help but be struck by the "Trump phenomenon," and the societal association of his success with the staunch support of the bulk of the evangelical and Religious Right community. I also pondered the implications of what it suggests about how evangelicals and other Religious Right leaders and the rank and file really think, how this impacts their perception by the greater public and their success in their supposed devotion to Christ's Great Commission. I began to post a few entries on my blog I use to keep tabs with my listeners to my old *Future Quake* radio show (www.futurequake.com) as well as other followers, as a site to let them know I am not "dead" during my long underground work in finishing my lengthy book series. Several of these posts were in essence my "coming out" to them of my evolving social and political thinking, informed by my more in-depth consideration of Christ's teachings in the Gospel and elsewhere in the Bible recently (resulting from my Bible-based studies for my earlier book series, as well as merely keeping an eye on current events and pondering its implications). As I began to mull over more implications of how my Christian friends began to think this way, and about who is influencing them, I quickly proceeded to document further thoughts and discoveries I made on the issue as an aside, and under roughly ten months later I had compiled the manuscript you now hold in your hands (along with most of two following volumes). *I hope this "preliminary word for the reader" will help you to better understand me before you read this controversial work, and thus I can hopefully and legitimately get on the reader's "good side" in advance.*

For any readers unfamiliar with me and my background, I was born in 1964 in Louisville, KY, and raised in a two-parent, blue-collar home that was significantly involved in a small Southern Baptist church. As such, I was raised as a conservative evangelical, and remained very involved in serving in churches at various locations where I have lived up until now. Having now reached my mid-50s, it has also included some lay teaching and leadership from time to time (I currently serve in such manner in a conservative, small Calvary Chapel along with my wife today). An encounter with the Bible prophecy classic *The Late, Great Planet Earth* in our local K-Mart in 1976 led my older brother and I into a renewed revival of interest in God's work in the world and prophetic subject matter, fed by access to other prophecy ministries then coming available on religious cable television programming. It brought with it a natural support for Zionism and a conservative geopolitical outlook. Although my immediate family had not served in the military, after I completed my Bachelor's and Master's degrees in Mechanical Engineering at the University of Louisville, I took a job as a scientist at the U.S. Air Force Research Labs at Wright-Patterson Air Force Base, Ohio, where I served my entire full-time employed life of sixteen years, while being exposed to a military mindset of aggressive foreign policy and patriotism that fit well with my conservative religious upbringing and Bible prophecy passion. When my Alabamian wife desired to move south to better tend to her aging parents (shipping out the day I received my Ph.D in engineering from the University of Dayton), I was able to continue and expand the moonlighting work I had been permitted to do as a consultant, and more importantly to sell two sets of high-tech patents (of the twenty four I had eventually obtained, most them for private activities) to two small companies to help bring them to market in the intervening years, having developed an appreciation (and realistic view) of small business enterprises, entrepreneurship, venture capital and the risks and rewards of innovation.

By 2005, the recent move to Nashville led me to a chance encounter with an ad in the back of the local newspaper (for all of the two weeks or so we subscribed) asking for volunteer programmers for a new community radio station ("Radio Free Nashville," WRFN-FM) trying to get off the ground. Having always had a Walter Mitty-style dream of a radio talk show stint like the late-night local hosts I enjoyed growing up, I submitted the one-page proposal requested, which reflected my other dream of a secondary career as a "futurist" consultant, who sees where society and technology is going, and provides advisement to their clients. I was shocked to find that my proposal for the *Future Quake* radio show from this neophyte was selected to air. When I first met with the radio organizers and volunteers, I was confronted with a people I had never encountered—exotically dressed, culturally, racially and ethnically diverse, with various sexual orientations, and all with a hard-left, progressive perspective. I also learned for the first time that these kinds of people, so different from my culture, did not seek money or other benefits, and seemed sincerely to care about the less fortunate. I was surprised that my wife found it intriguing as well, and as we helped get the small radio station room attached to a mobile home built, and assisted in manually raising the 75-foot tower—manned by volunteers from Japan, Ecuador and nationwide who endured freezing rain in pup tents and had no other motive other than to see that real people had a voice—I saw their devotion in cooperation under difficult circumstances. I also witnessed an attitude of joy amongst strangers, which we were not seeing in our classic, well-financed Baptist church we were attending. It would be an understatement to say we learned a few lessons from these devoted "hippies" and counter-cultural types who "put their money where their mouth is" and expended effort to provide "low power to the people," free of charge and without corporate, big business oversight.

Soon after I began broadcasting *Future Quake* live on Tuesday nights, this person with no radio training had a chance to interview Alvin Toffler, the "original futurist" and author of the best-seller *Future Shock*, the colleague of Indian activist legend Russell Means and others in independence movements (whom I interviewed while under the desk as a tornado was touching down), *Fox News* star Judge Andrew Napolitano, *World Net Daily* chief Joseph Farah, Sheriff Joe Arpaio, Sen. Rand Paul, Alex Jones, Jess Ventura, the founder of the Minutemen, and many other celebrities. I also began to have offbeat, non-mainstream but interesting and thoughtful Christian and other religious voices on air. This led to my attendance at one of the most perspective-changing events I have ever experienced—at the 2005 "Ancient of Days" Christian conference on possible Biblical explanations of aliens and similar phenomena, held in Roswell, New Mexico, at the 48th anniversary of the supposed famous sighting, during their UFO Festival. There I encountered some of the most fascinating Christian people I ever met, most of them far out of the mainstream, but thought-provoking, and a big leap in helping me think "out of the box." Not only was I invited to speak there years later on some of my research, but my hosting on air of a clerical leader of a United Nations NGO (non-government organization) on religion and spirituality led me to give an invited address at a subsequent United Nations conference on religion and spirituality in Montreal (alongside astronaut Edgar Mitchell and many other famous figures in the *Coast to Coast*/Art Bell radio and paranormal circles), in a distinctly non-Christian environment, while giving a foundational Christian worldview talk.

These experiences and many more (including speaking opportunities at exceptional and unique conferences of truth seekers such as the grass-roots "Politics of Religion" Conference) led me to the process of, for once, starting to think for myself, while remaining true to what I viewed to be a solid Christian and Biblical worldview. However, my views were now influenced by a greater interaction with those outside my original small religious circle, debunking many cultural myths along the way, and using my educational skills and knowledge of the world to harmonize my own understanding. The unique and inspiring spiritual Christian figures and thinkers I met along the way—many with little following, or "boutique" celebrities with a small but loyal cult of supporters—took the radio show and my thinking into new territory, as our audience began to grow into an eclectic global assembly of diverse thinkers, who found *Future Quake* as an early home for free and open thinking about spiritual matters in a nurturing and irreverently upbeat and sometimes whimsical setting.

In actuality, it probably became too religious for some of the radio station management and their broader mission, and more so concerning some guests featured there, who in my naiveté included some whose extreme politics I explored out of curiosity, but whom I would later formally renounce. Thus, it led to my departure from Radio Free Nashville in 2008 after three years, thinking that this would bring an end to my foray in radio. However, due to some unique circumstances and a little initiative, I was able to transfer from a low-power FM station to an AM regional Christian station, with the enviable 4 PM daily drive time. This was amazingly made available to this un-credentialed and untrained lay person, still with no pay but no broadcast airtime or production expenses either, requiring I produce the show in my bedroom and upload it for airing. It was broadcast daily through the airwaves to multiple states, right after a rogue's gallery of hard-right religious celebrities such as Janet Parshall. This phase actually began a "golden age" of the show, with an audience of at least an estimated 70,000 (over the air and online) with a strong global online reach as well, and a surer footing as my thinking definitely began to galvanize. Some of the seminal experiences that at least indirectly influenced my evolving worldview were the disturbing implications raised after attending a "9/11 Truth" Conference led by the controversial Alex Jones (eventually a guest on my show, before his later antics led to a backlash to his operations) and hosting radio guests such as quirky wrestler/politician Jesse Ventura (who said he could now like Christians since he met us), and many others (some with good ideas, others without) who began to force me to exercise my wider understanding, discern better and distill out the good data from the bad—eventually rejecting many of their views as I sought a Biblical philosophy, but thankful for the "mental stretching" their hard questions produced.

Nothing lasts forever, and with a radio station sale, that chapter came to an end (the show continued online for over a year afterwards until February 2012). I then began to feel a call to take what I was starting to learn from my own research and hearing from others, and devote myself to in-depth research and writing on focused topics for which I had a passion, and which I felt I could serve God best at this phase of my life. God had blessed my patented technology ventures, although usually rocky and tenuous in the experience while being quite an adventure, enough to let me devote my full time to this quest, as my last consulting gigs wrapped up by 2009. This allowed me to jump into writing what was planned to be a simple book, but which now stands as a series of twelve-plus lengthy unpublished manuscript volumes (to date), entitled *The Holy War Chronicles—A Spiritual View of the War on Terror*. It was catalyzed by my observations that Christians, particularly in the 2010–2012 period for some reason (some of whom have reasoned as a backlash to the Obama presidency), were becoming more strident in their attitudes towards Muslims in their paranoia of their threat, including many conservative Christians that worshipped alongside me or amongst family and friends, that I suspected were exhibiting symptoms of a far deeper spiritual problem. What I thought might stretch into a small book with a focused scope on the War on Terror has led me deep into religious history (of Jews and Christians), political history, social sciences, and theology, to name a few areas. One might fairly say that I practically reflect a "everything relates to everything" mode of thinking, as evidenced by my scope, but although exhausted by the daily writing process for years without positive feedback affirmation (except for a few dear friends and readers of my blog), I still feel I have something to say (however clumsy), and that I am being led by God to speak out, and see this as my way today to serve Him.

This work you have in your hands, never intended to be written and a type of "distraction" to my agenda of my planned book series of another subject, but for which I felt compelled to document albeit in an unpolished fashion, will be seen to exhibit a pretty strong and forceful tone, of which I am aware. It may sound a wee bit prophetic in tone (I think what they call a "jeremiad" these days, after the dear prophet, in my understanding). Although it uses strong, neutrally-biased academic and other high-quality references for its data underpinnings (or published works and direct quotations of its subjects), I know it is overall a subjective work that uses this data to present a strong perspective on the significance of the information from a spiritual perspective, with the intent to promote positive change, unlike other high-quality historical or sociological works. It presents me in the position of my "sitting on my high horse," as my kinfolk used to say, and I know that when I have taken such forceful positions in the past, God has humbled me by having me eat many of those very words, and this exercise may turn out no different. It may sound very judgmental, particularly of popular and revered Christian leaders, and many readers may be offended of such, and in cases where I am later found out to be unfair, extreme or wrong, I will be certain to apologize to those figures personally when we reach "the other side," because like the Apostle Paul I "see through a mirror darkly" now. I prefer a more gentle, measured, fair-minded and indirect style, presenting data and letting readers draw the inferences, but I find as of late that my dear Christian friends have been drawn into a type of "spell" of torpor or clouded thinking, fed by talking points by media figures, that requires a "clanging cymbal" or garbage can banging in the barracks to get their attention—*in fact, that reality was the motive for writing this entire book.*

While many readers may not just be offended by my characterization of the Christian leaders I profile in this work, they may also erroneously extrapolate my views to extend to Christian leadership in total, the entire Christian community, or the Christian message in general. *In reality, nothing could be further from the truth.* I am well aware that there are many good Christian leaders and pastors, and indeed I am blessed to be ministered to by such a one in my own local church. Many local pastors and lay servants effectively minister to the spiritual, psychological/emotional, and physical needs of those placed under their care in their communities, and the bottom line is that they do a lot of good. It is far more difficult to find such sincere, dedicated and untainted "saints" on the national stage, where the pressure to raise funds to underwrite large non-profits and charities, and the ambitions and hidden agendas of its figureheads and backroom operators, make it a place more common for rogues and scoundrels—*but each should be evaluated case-by-case, on their own merits.* Even amongst those leaders for which I have critical words, it should be conceded that not everything these leaders do or say is wrong, and it is often commendable, but just as you would not drink a glass of water with just a drop of sewage in it, we should expect good words and deeds from these well-compensated figures and set high standards, and take special note when any of their actions and statements are not becoming of a witness of Christ. They often have public relations assistance and many controls on their operations to conceal their deeds, assets and sources, so when disturbing data comes to light, it should be assumed that they are but the tip of the iceberg.

Many believe that such criticisms are not only unfair, hypocritical and falsely elevate the critic, but may also give the church at large a "black eye," and thus set back the agenda of the Church and its Great Commission to make disciples. I would alternatively assert that "the world" usually already knows about these hypocrisies and sins of these religious figures, and that members of the Church are usually the last to know or admit them (often because they do not veer from their own fawning Christian press, or avoid reading serious secular investigative reporting). Thus, the resulting cynicism is already "baked in the cake," and awaits a credible Christian admittance of wrong doing, denunciation and even ostracizing of the perpetrators (with overtures of prudent restoration offered for the sincerely humble repentant, for "a broken and a contrite heart, O God, thou wilt not despise" (Psalm 51:17)), for the sake of the integrity of the Gospel message and the ones who proclaim it. I have a personal creed that states, "That which we do not critique, we worship," *for to worship any person or ideology is to no longer critique it, but rather use it as a standard to judge everything else.* I believe Jesus Christ, as expressed by His words and nature as revealed in the Gospels, to be the "cornerstone" (even measuring and "squaring" the foundation of the words of the apostles and prophets (Eph. 2:20)) by which to judge every idea, incident, ideology, statement and belief I encounter. Therefore, when I critique my most precious heritage, traditions and beliefs as expressed in my church culture, leadership, denominations, doctrines, creeds, political party affiliations and ideologies, to distinguish what in them differs from His expressed nature, *it is in effect an act of worship of Jesus Christ, which I intend this written work to represent,* so as to "remove those things that are shaken," so "that those things which cannot be shaken may remain" (Heb. 12:27).

I have given my background in classic, conservative evangelical thinking and culture, and my continued devotion to Jesus Christ, the Gospel and the Bible as my rule and guide, to assuage any fears my conservative Christian readers might have, if they dare to read this work, that I have "gone off the rails"; please give me the benefit of the doubt as to where my heart is and motives, and I think we'll learn something together, as my radio listeners have done alongside me on our journeys. I particularly want to salute those readers that do not ascribe to any particular religious faith or that of another, or of a diverse cultural or political persuasion from my own, as those whom I really respect and admire for picking up a tome of this subject matter, and investing the time to investigate it. I hope you are rewarded with an eye-opening narrative as well, showing that *those who follow Jesus are not monolithic in their manner or worldview, and that the core of Jesus' thinking and teaching is probably not all that different than what you know to be good and decent in your heart and mind already, and that the core of the Gospel and His views often contrast sharply with what you see from the most ubiquitous Christian media public personas.*

I also use an relatively-untrained writing style that reflects my obtuse style of long, complex sentences with a smorgasbord of punctuation, which is a book publisher's nightmare; I feel that the subjects I discuss are complex and that the sentences should reflect those interactive relationships, rather than a handful of "dumbed down" simple (and misleading) declarative sentences. I feel that independent publishing might be the last bastion of true "liberty" in public discourse with which to "break" rules, and I fully flex my own personal style with long sentences, long passages and highly personal views, without the merest touch of an editor/butcher—I hope this eccentric expression does not get in the way of your ability to meditate on the significance of the important issues and thoughts raised here, regardless of my limitations. This work, like my others, reflects who I am—a witches' brew of the supremely serious and goofy, comical and grim, culturally relevant and "old school," and hopefully all sincere. Anyone who has encountered me on air or in writing knows what they're getting, and I thank you for letting me "be myself." Christian friends I know have looked at the length of the works I write (including this one) and say, "No one will ever read it," because in this age of short attention spans from two minute YouTube "documentaries" and Facebook and Twitter rant statements, slogans and "bumper stickers" of 140 characters or less, in not only a video gaming, stimulus-overload society but a texting one where people grunt indecipherably as cavemen (or with license-plate phonetics) without complete sentences, no one will commit to a length of time to consider an important topic to that depth, or the attention span to stay focused. That may be true, but if it is, *it is the very nature of what has led us into this state of demise, and no "right thinking" and solutions will ever help unless Christian people commit adequate time to considering complex explanations and solutions, if they really mean to be of legitimate help in society.* My full works may not be read by many, but *they are intended to restore the public standing and "saltiness" of the Christian community and reinvigorate the Great Commission offer of a better Kingdom, by whatever "nudge" my little individual influence can give, and I encourage you to do the same.*

I close by offering a repeated apology for any I offend here in this work; I only ask you to not fling it aside, but "stick with it" and withhold judgment in a teachable spirit, and by the end, see if at least some of its points give you pause and food for thought and consideration. If you would like to consider further other topics for which I have interest, I encourage you to check out the archived audio files of interviews from my old *Future Quake* radio show, currently online at www.futurequake.com (note that its seven-year run was a lengthy time of education for me, and thus the views and guests near the end of its run often vastly differ from my earlier, more naïve yet inquisitive period). I also sparingly update my blog to (as I said) let everyone know I'm not dead; its site is www.twospiesreport.wordpress.com (named after the two dissenting spies from Canaan, as a type of "Christian Minority Report"). I view all of my works in these spiritual topics as my attempt, as a child, to scribble a picture of Jesus with my crayons; I usually go outside the lines, and my mess bears little resemblance of Him, but I give it personally to Him, for Him to smile and display it on His refrigerator, bragging on the seismic blob to His visitors—I write only to Him and for Him, but I invite everyone to lean over His shoulder and read away. I warn you again, friend, that in all such works that I do, on air or in writing, that "there is something there to offend everybody."

J. Michael Bennett, Ph.D
Nashville, TN
November, 2019

INTRODUCTION: "KINGDOM CONFUSION," AND THE SPIRITUAL "RAT POISON" OF TODAY'S TALK RADIO AND CABLE NEWS

"No servant can serve two masters; for either he will hate the one and love the other, or else he will be devoted to one and despise the other. *You cannot serve God and wealth.*" Now the Pharisees, *who were lovers of money,* were listening to all these things and were scoffing at Him.
JESUS OF NAZARETH, LUKE 16:13–14, NEW AMERICAN STANDARD BIBLE (EMPHASIS ADDED)

I am amazed that you are so quickly deserting Him who called you by the grace of Christ, for a *different gospel;* which is [really] not another; only there are some who are disturbing you and want to *distort the gospel of Christ.* But even if we, *or an angel from heaven, should preach to you a gospel contrary to what we have preached to you, he is to be accursed!* As we have said before, so I say again now, *if any man is preaching to you a gospel contrary to what you received,* he is to be accursed!
APOSTLE PAUL TO THE CHURCH AT GALATIA, GALATIANS 1:6–9, NASB (EMPHASIS ADDED)

I first began to contemplate on this topic when I was in line voting at the 2016 presidential election. I noticed that the traditionally-conservative older people in my "red hat" state of Tennessee had come out in force. When I asked one of them in line how he thought things were going on in our country today, he exhibited the grim determination on his face like the rest of his peers, and replied, "It's best that I not speak about that." Given that it is likely from his demographic and presence in my neighborhood that he was the typical "church-goin', Bible believin'" sort here in the buckle of the

1

Bible Belt, I wondered how my neighbors here, and those of similar upbringing who were playing this election "for keeps," chose to rally around a presidential candidate known for cheating on his wife while she was nursing their newborn on numerous occasions, lying about the incidents then caught red-handed when the payoff checks emerged, said juvenile and vulgar things about women, those of other ethnicities, and even POWs and physically disabled people, all in front of cameras, and who did not apologize for his remarks.

Even more remarkable, I watched how our Religious Right leaders in our nation, whom I grew up respecting as models of righteousness and decency and the promotion thereof, debased themselves with this casino magnate, such as Liberty University head Jerry Falwell Jr. standing (along with Falwell's wife) with Trump in Trump Tower, in front of a fake Playboy cover emblazoned with Trump on the wall (with such sleight-of-hand Trump has been often wont to do, such as pretending to be a "Mr. Baron" on talk radio for years to promote "Mr. Trump," and his using of his own charitable foundation to auction and then buy Trump's portrait paintings at a high price to promote his image[1]). I see these leaders such as Falwell Jr. invite Trump to speak at his Christian university to influence the impressionable young minds for which many a Christian parent has saved for years to pay the exorbitant tuition to make sure their precious children go to a "Christian school," only to see Trump mock them by holding up his grandmother's Bible in pandering to their simple gullibility, quoting "Two-Corinthians" and refuting the Jesus of the Sermon on the Mount, and extolling the virtues of "getting even" there. Whether he exhorts his thuggish rally attendees to beat up protestors like an early-era Hitler, telling them to "beat the hell out of them" and "I will pay your legal bills," to his veneration of torture, overlooking the actions of white supremacists and even his bragging of sexually molesting women because of his celebrity status on recordings, I have grieved to see prominent Religious Right leaders contort themselves, and with it their commitment to the truth and Biblical values of decency, purity and humanity, in firmly justifying his statements and actions. They have even gone so far as to construct some kind of perverse theology that rather sees this vulgar, childish and character-less man as some kind of reincarnation of King David, or Cyrus the Great — statements they will one day have to apologize to those great figures about, if they are so lucky to eternally reside in the same zip code.

I recognize that this is not a revelation about Trump himself; to his credit, he has always consistently been an a_s. But it does expose a whole lot of the *real* nature of the "Moral Majority" crowd I grew up respecting, and a majority of the folks in the pews. Trying to understand their priorities when they enter the voting booth, I have to wonder *if they really understand what kingdom they are a citizen of.* Do they listen when their preachers preach from the Gospels? Do they really take Jesus seriously in the things He taught?

I have been told by certain readers of my internet blog (mostly just one) and even family members and old friends that for even asking these questions, I have recently "changed sides" and they imply I have become the one thing more diabolical than a devil-worshipper—a *liberal.* I was accused on a holiday visit with my loved ones recently that I "loved Muslims and the poor," as a serious vice (*I only wish it were more true!*). A recent visit with old dear Christian friends of mine informed me of an additional short-sightedness of mine that I did not recognize—regarding the "truth" that all "the poor" and those of non-white ethnicities were all lazy and taking advantage of us working whites, mocking us and taking away our jobs and promotions (leading them to propose starting (as they had retired "just in time") an association "for the advancement of white people"). To my knowledge, I have never extolled the virtues of Hillary Clinton, Nancy Pelosi or even the Democratic Party, but all my talk of "the poor," "refugees" and being kind to the "stranger," and even being so bold as to cite the "Golden Rule," has earned me a status as an "outsider" of dubious motives, progressing from being a "golden boy" in my evangelical circles to (with the exception of a very small circle of friends) being a pariah. It's just like when a fundamentalist church I briefly attended once shunned me (even as a young member whom they could previously count on to serve faithfully there) when I read Colossians 2 verbatim in their singles group (as I was asked to do) which talked of the "false form of humility" resulting from artificial dress or food restrictions, or another fundamentalist church who isolated me on the church bus because I defended the Christian status of charismatics (of whom I am not one).

I still see a lot of confusion in Christian circles as to what kingdom we really belong to, what its agenda is and our duties in it, and how it affects how we respond as American citizens, and even at the voting booth. I admit that it does get a little more confusing today because (a) we live in a Christian era when God has prescribed a kingdom for us that is not the one in which we now physically exist, (b) we live in a unique age as a select set of Christians that have a participatory role in the selection of our leaders, and their resultant decisions (and responsibility for them), and (c) we do not live in a theocracy (by design), and must recognize that secular government has a legitimate agenda that is NOT identical with the Kingdom of Heaven, but through which we should non-coercively provide "salt and light," and "love our brothers." However, if a Christian today will sit down with their Bible for an evening or two and focus on this topic, they could quickly be a lot more informed and achieve some clarity on the subject. Since we live in the Information Age with a relatively high degree of literacy, there is really no excuse for such darkness of ignorance, *other than that the state of being informed on a Biblical opinion on the topic is not a priority for average Christians*, and what little time they dedicate to it usually comprises their mere acceptance of the directives of strangers, such as evangelical leaders in the media, or the unbelievers they listen to on talk radio and cable news.

Even with what little Abraham knew about God, and having been given an earthly inheritance of land with fixed physical demarcations and the respect of his neighbors in the land, he still recognized that he was a pilgrim and nomad in that very same land, and, like other "people of faith" like him, actually looked for

> a city which hath foundations, whose builder and maker [is] God. ...and confessed that they were strangers and pilgrims on the earth. For they that say such things declare plainly that they seek a country. But now they desire a better [country], that is, an heavenly: wherefore God is not ashamed to be called their God: for he hath prepared for them a city...Wherefore we receiving a kingdom which cannot be moved, *let us have grace, whereby we may serve God acceptably with reverence and godly fear.* (Heb. 11:10, 13–14, 16, 12:28)

Thereafter Joshua, leading a nation that understood itself to be a sole earthly expression of God's nature, agenda and presence, fell for the "tribalism" view common in Christian circles today, in that a follower of God is either with their movement and circle, or otherwise an "enemy of God"; in our circles today, it would be in the Republican party, with the "heathen" in the alternative Democratic Party. However, God never felt the need to carry the same "buckets" of our preferred tribes, be they political parties, ideologies (left or right, capitalist, communist or socialist), nation-states, or any other affiliation. In turn, as a "jealous" God, He is not too thrilled when we carry any other identification in our own "buckets" except with Jesus, as the "cornerstone" of which whose teachings all other ideologies have to be measured against (given that they may be suited for a secular kingdom but without the same agendas as the Kingdom of Heaven), and certainly not when we compromise our most core Christian values from the Kingdom of Heaven taught by Jesus, to accommodate and justify such affiliations. In practice, those ideologies which have a veneer of overt "righteousness" are actually the most seductive and dangerous. Here's what happened when Joshua and the Hebrews confronted another of God's men:

> Now when Joshua was near Jericho, he looked up and saw a man standing in front of him with a drawn sword in his hand. Joshua went up to him and asked, "Are you for us or for our enemies?" *"Neither,"* he replied, "but as commander of the army of the LORD I have now come." Then Joshua fell face down to the ground in reverence, and asked him, "What message does my Lord have for his servant?" (Joshua 5:13–14, New International Version (NIV))

Joshua wisely recovers from this incident, re-orienting himself to humbly ask what direction God now has for him, rather than directing this other servant of God to get in line with his movement. *You might ask me if I have difficulty in realizing that God is not obligated to get behind my own "spiritual" direction or ideas at any time, and my answer is yes, I do have a difficulty with that, and it is perpetually humbling to me to realize it; we should continuously be measuring our directions against that of the "Cornerstone" before we get too far down any road.*

Daniel served in a pagan kingdom and government, and did not curse them, but humbly and gently tried to help the spiritual condition of his pagan leaders and their people, even when threatened with harm. His denouncements of sin were not directed towards the people and cultures different than him (unlike Mordechai), but *rather at those of his own culture and faith*, and for that, Gabriel said he was "greatly beloved" in heaven in Daniel 9, and also "greatly beloved" in a visitation in Daniel 10, possibly by Jesus Himself.

In an upcoming section (which will describe these matters more fully) we will be considering and will see that the commandments of God, either by His own voice or through the prophets or other saints, were for His people and their nation (to be enforced by their kings and rulers, as well as the priests, as a form of national law) to be kind to the "stranger" of another kind of faith within their society, because "you were once strangers in Egypt" as a religious and ethnic minority yourself. They command also to take care of the poor, to make sure the vulnerable (fatherless, widows and orphans) are provided for, to make sure the poor get justice in the courts which are not controlled by money, and that the wealthy and businessmen do not take over the less wealthy with debt or confiscating their sources of income ("tools"), and by regulating the marketplace to fight exploitation by means of fraudulent "dishonest weights and measures" there. They not only prevent excessive capitalistic exploitation of natural assets due to repetitive harvesting and rather leave residual profits (or ungleaned ripe produce and grain) as a free entitlement for the poor, but even insist on a civil statute to forcibly "redistribute wealth" through the Year of Jubilee and avoid its concentration in the hands of the wealthy, and to leave private lands fallow (i.e., their sources of income and provision) as an environmental provision to restrict greed and "free enterprise" by letting the land "rest." Its other primary purpose is for the expressed use of the "wild," uncultivated fruit and grain naturally occurring to available to the poor as a state of a God-enforced form of "welfare" of one-seventh of a seven-year yield, or approximately a 14% "income tax" dedicated for the poor and needy, *in addition to the tithes and alms given for religious activities,* such as for Temple and religious institution operations. Sadly, the Jews evidently never seemed to comply with this compulsory command from God, for which He said they were sent to exile for. *When is the last time you heard politically-active Christians or media outlets make these issues a priority in the political debates and candidate evaluations, even though God makes it clear it is a priority for Him?*

As another way to understand how God intended the secular nations (like our own) and their leaders and decision makers to faithfully fulfill their duties to their people, let's hear how God rebukes the "sons of God" assigned at the Tower of Babel to administer over the "seventy nations" of earth (as referred to when "When the Most High gave to the nations their inheritance, when he divided mankind, he fixed the borders of the peoples according to the number of the sons of God. But the LORD's portion is his people, Jacob his allotted heritage" (Deut. 32:8–9, Septuagint (LXX), English Standard Version (ESV)); for further explanation, see textual expert Dr. Michael Heiser's academic paper on the topic for *Bibliotheca Sacra*[2]), and how they oppressed their own subjects and became objects of idolatrous worship of their peoples, and how He will judge them in the Last Days:

> God has taken his place in the divine council; in the midst of the gods he holds judgment: "How long will you judge unjustly and show partiality to the wicked? Give justice to the weak and the fatherless; maintain the right of the afflicted and the destitute. Rescue the weak and the needy; deliver them from the hand of the wicked"...I said, "You are gods, sons of the Most High, all of you; nevertheless, like men you shall die, and fall like any prince." Arise, O God, judge the earth; for you shall inherit all the nations! (Psalm 82:1–4, 5–8, ESV)

How many times have you heard these elements of God's agenda for the secular nations also be the agenda of America's politically-active Christian leaders today?

A lot of these commands are directed towards the leaders of nations, which gives many Christians a quick "Whew!," thinking that they are not obligated to such responsibilities. However, the majority of historic believers of God, like all peoples, were subjects of outside reigning powers, or otherwise not able to elect leaders or influence their decisions, and therefore not responsible for their decisions. However, when God brought His children to the Promised land, He set them up as a decentralized federation of tribes, with its leaders chosen by the people, where at the end of the Book of Joshua, "everyone did what was right in their own eyes"—certainly a heresy to control-freak Christians who want to control behavior from the top down, but a libertarian's dream that God seemed to intend as His permanent plan. However, the Hebrews soon wanted a king to control them, like the other nations had, because it looked "cool" (they were dazzled by strong men and celebrities and "heroes," like Christians today) and projected power; they gave up their freedom by acclamation, and God explained to Samuel that they had really rejected Him. God gave them what they wanted—a dashing man a head taller than the rest of them, with a shining spear, but reckless in his personal behavior and character—*thank goodness God's people have gotten beyond such short-sightedness and immaturity!*

However, the age of citizen-influenced government rose again, this time amongst the pagan Greeks and Romans, since the Jews rejected it. It has been further refined, with setbacks and dormant ages, up to the period of the American experiment. This is relevant to Christians today, I believe, because we now live in a period of alleged "self government," where we collectively choose "representatives" as our proxies to rule based upon our own agendas and preferences, and replace them if they don't. Thus, we have in effect become our own leaders, which generations of Christians before us, under kings (even "Christian" ones), could not imagine. Therefore, since we now reportedly have the right to rule ourselves, *I believe we have each also earned the responsibilities the Bible has said are the responsibilities of earthly rulers. This includes an obligation to protect the poor and other vulnerable people, and make sure justice is available for all (yes, even "social justice")—if we take God and His Word seriously. Heaven help those who take our Lord's expectations lightly! We are in fact "our brother's keeper," and that crown of responsibility rests on each of our brows, and in particular toward the "strangers" within our gates, outside the gates wanting in, and the refugees from beyond (but within our reach) who are crying out for mercy from God.*

As a Christian who was groomed to vote as a good Republican through my upbringing, which I did until the last few national elections (having voted third party), I understand how Christians were seduced by them with a veneer of righteousness and Christian virtue. This was backed by Christian leaders I used to trust, but in actual practice we were being led to accept the party's priorities not for the unborn or other issues of Christian mercy, but rather tax cuts for big businesses and business handouts, and paying for the "warfare state" (and the windfall of profits and welfare for defense contractors) rather than for the poor and medically needy, or the refugee. A classic example is President Trump, who suckered people into a tax plan "for the middle class" which increased the standard deduction (which people who itemize for home mortgage or charitable gifts cannot use) while taking away their valuable exemptions, and only giving temporary citizen tax deductions, while making permanent the almost halving of business taxes. This has led to a huge increase in the annual deficit and adding national debt to necessitate a further reduction to programs for the needy—*all with Christian support.* One of his first acts as president—less than two weeks after his inauguration—was to sign an executive order (# 13772, Feb. 3, 2017) *to eliminate the need for financial advisors paid for by individuals to act in their fiduciary interest, or disclose that their recommendations serve the best interests of the financial firms and their products rather than their paying client.*[3] I see Christians today primarily concerned with what they think is their own pocketbook (not necessarily a bad thing, to keep in check a gluttonous government budget spent on cronies and businesses rather than the needy), and in the end get fleeced by the far-savvier business scoundrels they put in office or in advisory roles that they greedily trusted to help them "get rich quick," while further adding to the suffering of those less fortunate, who are not even part of the conversation. *It is key to understand that in the Religious Right community today, they are not worried about the people better off than them getting their money; they are only concerned about those worse off than them getting their money.* Jesus of Nazareth, whom American Christians reportedly say they follow and heed His commands, had the following advice for them:

> Do not store up for yourselves treasures on earth, where moths and vermin destroy, and where thieves break in and steal. But store up for yourselves treasures in heaven, where moths and vermin do not destroy, and where thieves do not break in and steal. For where your treasure is, there your heart will be also... No one can serve two masters. Either you will hate the one and love the other, or you will be devoted to the one and despise the other. You cannot serve both God and money. (Matt. 6:19–21, Luke 16:13, NIV)

Jesus made clear to the secular government official Pilate that His movement was not about seizing the "seven mountains of culture" or government, or overcoming those who think differently than them, or any rule here whatsoever, but rather laying the groundwork for a future kingdom, based in another sphere, that poses no necessary threat to secular powers in this age. He said,

> My kingdom is not of this world. If it were, my servants would fight to prevent my arrest by the Jewish leaders. But now my kingdom is from another place...the reason I was born and came into the world is to testify to the truth. *Everyone on the side of truth listens to me.* (John 18:36–37, NIV) (emphasis added)

Sadly, most professing Christians today don't listen to Him.

Paul understood this. He also understood that God's people should not only decline to fight physical "holy wars" to try to overcome secular governments (like the Zealots, or the Maccabeans before them), but also not even "culture wars" against their fellow citizens outside the church, as moral crusaders. He had to address this regarding sexual immorality inside the church, which many Christians tolerate or overlook today in their Christian leaders if they are charismatic enough. He writes:

> I wrote to you in my letter not to associate with sexually immoral people—*not at all meaning the people of this world who are immoral, or the greedy and swindlers, or idolaters. In that case you would have to leave this world.* But now I am writing to you that you must not associate with anyone who claims to be a brother or sister but is sexually immoral or greedy, an idolater or slanderer, a drunkard or swindler. Do not even eat with such people. *What business is it of mine to judge those outside the church? Are you not to judge those inside? God will judge those outside.* Expel the wicked person from among you. (1Cor. 5:9–13, NIV) (emphasis added)

The Christian "culture wars" are the exact opposite of Paul's admonition.

Paul would remind us that we are citizens of another Kingdom, where our real interests lie, and with a Great Commission to be "fishers of men," particularly by demonstrating our love for our neighbors. To most fully accomplish this, our necessary political participation is an element, while not certainly the main agenda, but its approach geared towards an expression of love toward the downtrodden, and not the control of others. We are indeed "ambassadors" of a foreign nation, as Paul writes:

> For we know that if the earthly tent we live in is destroyed, we have a building from God, an eternal house in heaven, not built by human hands... Since, then, we know what it is to fear the Lord, *we try to*

persuade others. What we are is plain to God, and I hope it is also plain to your conscience...*For Christ's love compels us,* because we are convinced that one died for all, and therefore all died... So from now on we regard no one from a worldly point of view. Though we once regarded Christ in this way, we do so no longer. All this is from God, who reconciled us to himself through Christ and gave us the *ministry of reconciliation:* that *God was reconciling the world to himself in Christ, not counting people's sins against them.* And *he has committed to us the message of reconciliation.* We are therefore Christ's ambassadors, as though *God were making his appeal through us. We implore you on Christ's behalf: Be reconciled to God.* (2 Cor. 5:1, 11, 14, 16, 18–20, NIV) (emphasis added)

Does this sound like our Christian politically-active leaders today, and their front-burner agendas? It is an agenda with the world which will always have a political component in any social interaction, based upon *compelling love, gentle persuasion, lack of worldly judgment, and far-reaching forgiveness and reconciliation, in its emphasis, tone and overall spirit, as opposed to judgment and adversity, much less selfishness.*

Paul set a good example for us American Christians. He was privileged to have Roman citizenship, as well as citizenship at Tarsus. He did not use his rights to feather his own bed for financial enrichment or other privileges, to oppress others, or change Rome for his own group's agenda or betterment. He did use his legal rights to facilitate a heavenly agenda to preach the Gospel in Rome and along the way, rather than die short of the goal in Jerusalem and the hands of Romans and Jews. *His rights of citizenship were not a tool for his own personal use or to look out for his interests or that of his fellow Christians, but only to complete his Kingdom of Heaven assignment, which did not restrict (for the Golden Rule still applies) but only blessed others.*

Paul gave one other similar admonition to "keep our eyes on the prize," and also warning that there will be those around us who don't "get it" (probably even some professing Christians in our circles, whose recent elected official choices may show that "their god is their stomachs" and as such, embrace leaders who, with them, do "glory in their shame"):

> *All of us, then, who are mature should take such a view of things.* And if on some point you think differently, that too God will make clear to you. Only let us live up to what we have already attained. *Join together in following my example, brothers and sisters, and just as you have us as a model, keep your eyes on those who live as we do.* For, as I have often told you before and now tell you again even with tears, many live as enemies of the cross of Christ. Their destiny is destruction, their god is their stomach, and their glory is in their shame. *Their mind is set on earthly*

things. But our citizenship is in heaven. And we eagerly await a Savior from there, the Lord Jesus Christ. (Phil. 3:15–20, NIV) (emphasis added)

I will leave my thoughts on this topic at this, but thinking of being "ambassadors" of another kingdom, maybe we should consider Christ's teachings of the Kingdom and the Sermon on the Mount, and the amplification of the Apostles, to love our enemies and be a neighbor to those of other faiths and cultures in need (like the Good Samaritan), and in exhibiting mercy and forgiveness as "agents of reconciliation" to "rescue the perishing," and eating with "sinners," *as our Christian "foreign policy" on behalf of the Kingdom (also seen in our politics as well as personal behavior and interactions).* Meanwhile, we exhort our fellow Christians to lives of love, purity, holiness, prayer, faithfulness, encouragement, wisdom, learning, and body ministry *as our "domestic policy" of the Kingdom,* all devoid of outside political parties or ideologies (or evolved doctrines) and their influence, or any other kingdom to which we should otherwise not owe any allegiance.

Having said that, many Christians have spent uncountable years in innumerable sermons and heard Christian teaching on Christ's Kingdom and its ways as we just documented, *yet typically do things far counter to it in their public statements and political activity.* So what leads them to proudly take opinions and views demonstrably counter to the clear teachings of Christ? To try to solve this mysterious contradiction of cognitive dissonance, we will indulge in some statistics, and reflect on the significance of the effect of conservative media on the public positions of evangelical Christians (as evidenced by their tangible actions at the ballot box), it being possibly their most overwhelming philosophical influence.

First of all, according to those who keep track,[4] the U.S. population currently in 2018 stands at around 327.5 million. According to exit polling of Edison Research of the 2016 Presidential election,[5] of which 136,669,276 Americans voted, 26% were "white evangelical or born again" Christians, comprising 35,534,012 people. Of those, *81 percent of those voting evangelical Christians voted for Trump,* or 28,782,550 people. *Remember the scale of this number.* According to the prestigious, conservative Christian-oriented Pew Research Center,[6] 25.4 percent of Americans are "evangelical Christians," which shows that evangelicals vote in same proportion as the total U.S. population, and which would make the full evangelical population total 83.2 million. It also shows that roughly a third (34.6 percent) of all identified evangelicals voted for Trump, which would also exclude the young, many of the very old, those unable to get to the polls, and the many who are too lazy or self-absorbed to bother to go, *of the 57.3 percent of evangelicals who did not or could not vote, in addition to those who voted against him.* Not only does this third of the evangelical population represent its most engaged and activist portion, which presumably listens to some news somewhere to motivate itself enough to get to the polls, but also *represents an overwhelming segment that very publicly embraced Donald Trump and his values. It also presents to the outside world of skeptical unbelievers what evangelicalism is all about, on behalf of the other two-thirds of evangelicals who did not vote for him, and thus impacts all of their abilities in evangelizing and outreach.* These evangelical Trump voters also represent 21 percent of the total voting electorate, and almost 46 percent of all Trump voters, whereas less than 34 percent of voting non-evangelicals (and 14 percent of all non-evangelicals) voted for Trump; *in other words, everyone recognizes that Trump is our president because of the evangelicals (the "activist" variety, at least), as "their" candidate.*

Let's look now at the numbers of people who listen to a few conservative media outlets, which we can assume produce virtually all of the Trump votes. First of all, a July 2018 report in *Forbes*[7] on Sean Hannity's nightly *Fox News* TV show reported that he was hosting almost 3.4 million viewers nightly at the time. The April 2019 data from *Talkers* Magazine[8] shows that Sean Hannity receives 15 million weekly unique radio listeners, Rush Limbaugh 15.5 million, Michael Savage 7.5 million, Glenn Beck 10.5 million, Mark Levin 11 million and Mike Gallagher 8.5 million (data for August 2018[9] adds Laura Ingraham at 8 million and conservative firebrand Alex Jones at 5.9 million)—almost *all the dominant voices (top 10 or more) are all hard-core conservatives.* This data does not include the 30 million subscribers to Sirius XM,[10] as of mid-2016, many of whom listen to talk radio. Since sometimes these shows overlap in their time periods, are on one or no radio stations in many markets, and listeners can only hear one show at a time in their limited in-car time, it is likely that the listener overlap between these individuals is very limited. *This means that many tens of millions of conservative listeners listen to these heavily-opinionated (and many extreme) worldview formers as a "captive audience" every day in their cars, with their focused attention during their 30 to 60 minute drive times each day, as well as being on the radio at work, or shuttling kids.* Those interested in such talk would primarily be those with enough interest to go out and vote—easily covering the 62 or so million Trump voters, and the 27 million evangelicals in his camp. I routinely hear the "talking points" and terms originating from many of these shows, either sent to them by communications officials from the Trump administration or ginned up themselves (sometimes forwarded back to presidential communications officials, and in Trump's case, when he watches them in the mornings), coming verbatim from the mouths of my friends, such as the "Democratic mob" memes trotted out not long ago.

In contrast as a competing source of ideological influence, that of our pulpits (local churches, not the televangelists and other Christian media), in 2015 Pew Research reported[11] that 58% of all evangelicals (48.2 million) attend some church event at least once a week in 2014 (but is quickly declining annually), which may or may not include a sermon (and if so, it may be a single 30 minute or less variety) in one week. I still tend to view this as a large overestimate, based upon what I have observed in our church pews; otherwise our churches would be bursting at the seams, rather than featuring a lot of empty seats, and people who attend "when they feel led to." Other reports like those by *Outreach* Magazine[12] suggest those numbers are grossly over-estimated, and are actually much less. *In any case, I wonder how many of those people are listening carefully in the pews, based upon their public behavior and voting, and I doubt (with some exceptions, such as in many popular churches) that these parishioners are being exposed to as extreme and concentrated a direct political messaging operation as they get with corporate-paid talk radio during the week.*

The punch line of this data is that American Christians are getting 14 or more intense political "sermons" of extended length each week, with motives coming from unknown people with unknown agendas paying for them, except that we know they do not comprise the non-profit, unselfish views of a Bible and a Christ that is not selling anything, which would otherwise promote sacrifice, putting others before oneself, turning the other cheek, and the pursuit of reconciliation and a future kingdom driven by love, mercy and forgiveness—all items that just would not "sell" on radio or TV, and certainly not get good ratings. With this ratio of messaging and high-dollar public relations behind it, the poor pastor and his measly half-hour weekly sermon has no chance to offset the psychological conditioning of conservative talk radio during the week, which has become the real "church" of most conservative Christians, and where they form their real world views, as dictated by advertisers and corporate sponsors. This is a problem that I have not seen identified anywhere that I have observed, and I think that pastors and Christian leaders (those not totally "in the can" with these hard right media outlets) need to acknowledge that they have a formidable rival for the hearts and minds of active Christians, as opposed to "usual lineup of suspects," such as the "godless universities," movies and "the devil weed." This does not even consider the formidable influence of online political news, with The Drudge Report reporting 33 million reads daily and about one billion a month, YouTube (with five billion videos watched each day[13]), Facebook (1.4 billion active users), Yahoo News (175 million unique monthly visitors[14]), Google News (150 million), and Huffington Post (110 million)—as a juggernaut which will envelop these other media, as people in younger middle age and even younger rely almost exclusively on online and social media, and can listen to it 24/7. The era of people coming to hear an oration and speaker has ended a generation ago; people now prefer the "intimacy" of a recorded voice speaking close to their ear, sometimes while they are further distracting their low attention span by doing another task, and receiving much of the message thus subliminally.

An example case in point is what you will hear conservative Christians believe about Hillary Clinton. While I am certainly no fan of hers, rather seeing her as a Washington insider (although she paid her dues as a legal activist), I am shocked to see the degree to which normally loving Christian people I know truly despise her, but when I ask for details of specific, proven things she has done that warrant such feelings, they are hard pressed to give specifics, rather than just "impressions," from unknown sources. They truly would deal with any "devil" to oppose her, as the last election testifies. In fact, I have seen repeatedly that there was no criterion or "line drawn" where they would hesitate to support a person, if they opposed Hillary and could beat her, with their votes being merely an "anti-Hillary" vote. When I ask which specific policies of hers that she has promised to pursue that they oppose, they are also hard pressed to give specifics.

One thing many of them seem to know: that she is a bona-fide witch who operates a pedophile ring under a Washington pizza parlor—albeit without any tangible evidence to confirm such a far-fetched yarn. These are some of the same people—many of whom I previously thought were pretty wise—who take seriously the mythical "Q Anon" legend, much like Paul Bunyan, and fashion him into whatever Guy Fawkes-type resister they want him to be (or what influential online fearmongers suggest). Meanwhile they plead ignorance of the fact that similar secretive "whistle blowers" like Guccifer 2.0 were "outed" as Russian operatives, and not who they suggested they were, some time ago, trying to sow general discord within the gullible American public. My dear, normally-wise and loving Christian friends cannot seem to realize that they have been conditioned to have these irrational thoughts without vetting—which all of us online are vulnerable to—and subject to "psy ops" via the mass media in conservative talk radio, just as elsewhere, and sadly Christian online media in particular. It's similar to how the same conservative media has demonized the term "liberal" to mean the vilest of all (although the Bible says that God gives to men liberally (James 1:9), and the King James Version of the Bible passages of those described as "liberals" (such as Isaiah 32:8) are alternatively translated at "generous" or "noble"), as well as "socialist" being another term just below "devil worshipper," *although many of our Christian brethren in Europe happily live in socialist countries, and have no desire to leave.*

This phenomenon of conservative media on the public, and its Christian community, is certainly nothing new, and was built on earlier foundations, although it has certainly "amped up" in the last quarter century. You could say that some of its early origins were amongst the Sanhedrin, who were concerned that "If we let him [Jesus] thus alone, all *men* will believe on him:

and the Romans shall come and take away both our place and nation" (John 11:48)—*a true priority of a conservative, to conserve the public order and status quo of power and class.* They also made false accusations of Jesus for violating conservative "traditions," with Jesus in turn asking them, "Why do ye also transgress the commandment of God by your tradition?" (Matt. 15:3)—*which would make Him not a good, tradition-loving conservative.* They also used their early mass media to give "fake news" about Jesus not only in the courtroom, but among the crowds, to make him an anti-tradition, anti-conservative who needed to be stopped. Conservatives' use of the public's fears and base instincts was also common among the Romans and Greeks—where the term *demagogue* originated—always finding a scapegoat outsider to blame for their mismanagement and woes, or even false-flag attacks, such as the Christians blamed (as a feared minority religion, having had many lies told about them) for the fires in Nero's Rome.

Conservative Christian leaders were used to colluding with power structures, such as with Constantine in Rome, to then anathematize many of their brethren having slightly different views of disputable and mysterious theological issues, and thus eliminate rival priests and help Constantine galvanize power and use Christianity to cement and stabilize the empire and control. They worked within the Catholic Church to humble independent kings (and Popes themselves by the cardinals), and provoke the masses into crusades not only against Muslims, but even rival Christian sects. Conservative Lutherans and Calvinists soon got into the act, while those deemed liberal, like the Quakers, were seen as pacifists and non-violent, and thus the object of their scorn. Conservative, unyielding and uncompromising Christians of all stripes in Europe kept the continent in flames in religious wars, with the less fundamentalist folk caught in the crossfire. Some Christian groups were persecuted by their fellow conservatives, like the Puritans by the Anglicans, to which they fled to the New World to do some fundamentalist persecution of their own, against Baptists and Quakers. Conservatives justified the institution of slavery, while the liberal denominations fought it. The Protestant sects participated in a wave of anti-Catholic, anti-Mason and anti-immigrant persecution over the eighteenth and nineteenth centuries in the U.S., while at the same time the liberal Christian groups began to address poverty and social injustice.

However, conservative media and influence came into its own in the Twentieth Century, with the development of mass media, in addition to print. Some of the early stars, like Father Coughlin, had audiences in the millions, and focused on pro-fascist and anti-semitic positions. Others continued in the anti-Catholic tradition. Many took up the anti-Communist cause, and some transitioned into anti-education, anti-science, or anti-socialism. *Do you detect a trend here?* We should not forget the Klan, who by the 1920s had already compiled the basic modern conservative Christian agenda of prayer in schools, the Ten Commandments in the court room, mandatory church attendance, and the promotion of "Christian soldiers," *as roughly fifteen percent of all white, Protestant men in the U.S. (4–5 million) were members of the Klan by 1925.*[15] One thing they did take a positive position on was money—free enterprise and capitalism, and big business, and sacredized it—leading to today's Christian emphasis on these principles (with them being in the statements of purpose at Liberty University), helping big business while in their overseas missionary ventures, like Dole in Hawaii and United Fruit Company in Central America, and setting the stage for the "name it and claim it," "prosperity gospel" and televangelists in the latter part of the century. Alternatively, they took a hard line against Roosevelt's "New Deal" welfare and jobs assistance for those suffering during the Great Depression, and "welfare cheats" and "deadbeats" ever since.

There ultimately became various strains of conservatism, soon after it took root in history. One strain stood behind tradition—in power structures and the divine right of kings, whose followers would be known as monarchists or royalists later, and protected the widespread power of the king, and the wealthy noblemen and aristocrats supporting them, and despised democracy. Another strain soon supported tradition in religion, and its existing power structures—not only in Rome, but also in Canterbury or Constantinople, and opposed any independent expression, or resources not centralized under the hierarchy, or attempts to fill the populace with "dangerous ideas," such as from the Bible, which would have been seen as quite liberal and progressive, and certainly not "traditional." Another strain would be the military, comprising military members and veterans who wanted a strong military not answerable to anyone, and an adventurous foreign policy. Yet another would be "money class," comprising bankers and big business, based upon the earlier Knights Templar and Rothschild templates, and typified in the City of London and later Wall Street, and *arguably the most powerful segment of conservatism, with its wealth ultimately buying and controlling its rival segments,* and with a justifiable argument to be made that it strongly influences the CIA, with Goldman Sachs and hedge fund managers now the most important elements.

Beyond these, we have the "fringe" elements, which can be influential at times, and often comprise hybrids of these established groups, like the John Birch Society, founded in 1958 as an anti-Communism movement often seen as a conspiracy-theory group that distrusts all global entanglements, and now sees a secret Illuminati cartel or cabal even above that of International Communism. In contrast, the banker conservatives tend to be internationalists (for there is money to be made and controlled globally), and mainstream conservatives like Eisenhower would be viewed as potential Communist collaborators by the "Birchers." The Religious Right is another "fringe" group that is not so fringe in size, and is essential for conservative political victories, but usually ends up on the short end of the stick when getting payouts for their hard work in driving their rank and file to the polls. For example, for 28 or more years of Republican power since Roe V. Wade, they did not do much to curb abortions at all, as is always promised every election cycle, although to be fair the Religious Right groups did not originally oppose abortions, including the Southern Baptists, until the Religious Right groups first formed to stop Christian school integration, and adopted the anti-abortion platform more into the 1980s.

William F. Buckley, Jr. was the standard bearer of the "blue blood," aristocratic Ivy League conservatives, with his *Firing Line* show (on public television, no less) being the main conservative mass media forum from 1966 until 1988, with the rise of Rush Limbaugh. Rush took his conservative "with an attitude" radio show national in 1988, as "Bush 41" was getting ready to be elected, and he virtually invented talk radio as a force of societal change, and is still going strong thirty years later, with no liberal rival. Sean Hannity then became a similar force, beginning in national talk radio and with the first conservative cable news network, *Fox News*, in 1996, in the middle of the Clinton Administration. Around that same time, Matt Drudge began to perform the same revolution on the Internet, initially seeming more even handed in his criticism, but as he aged became more sympathetic to right-leaning positions, as well as the spinoff project by his longtime associate Andrew Breitbart (as a home for the more extreme fascist and younger-oriented "alt right," and the oversight of senior Trump advisor Steve Bannon), as well as hard-right conspiracy trouble-maker Alex Jones. So one can see, there is a long legacy of conservative conditioning of the public, for which the evangelical community appears most vulnerable and gullible.

Based upon these documented observations, I conclude that outlets such as *Fox News* (with their veritable "HeeHaw Honeys" anchors, with their short skirts and low cut blouses that only feature attractive, mostly young women, talking about "family values" (and which makes no surprise that the organization was rife with infidelity and sexual harassment)), Sean Hannity and their ilk, talking about (a) despising immigrants, (b) encouraging war and intimidation, (c) justifying torture and secret detainment without trial (or secret trials without defendant rights), (d) supporting the cause of the powerful institutions (like the police) always over a populace that might have been wronged, (e) having suspicions of those of different faiths, (f) the love of money and the powerful, and (g) veneration of big business as the saviors of society while denigrating public servants if not in the military, all with a big dose of swagger and bullying, *is in effect a "rat poison" that kills the conscience, morality, character, circumspectness, mercy, humility and love for others that is essential for well-functioning Christians, and has done more to handicap the Christian cause and reputation in America than any Communist or liberal professor could ever do.* It took a long time to purge that "poison" out of my system, and I encourage all readers to take a *Fox News* and talk radio "break" for an extended time, instead reading the words of our Lord, and see if you don't start having the same second-thoughts that I did—*if our consciences aren't already seared.* So—do the ancient words of the Bible have any concept to express this line of thinking, wrapped up in religion? We'll see in the next chapter.

The "Leaven of the Pharisees" Ideology Explained, As the Ancestor and Taproot of Modern Conservatives and Religious Right Narratives

In the last chapter I began to make some provocative claims and associations, to the extent of referring to right-wing talk radio and cable news as a type of "rat poison" that brings harm, and can even kill the sensitivity, compassion, gentleness, and empathy of American Christians for the weak, vulnerable, and needy in society. These latter attributes reflect the perspectives their Savior, "The Good Shepherd," would otherwise have for these "lost sheep," as One who called to them (as well as to many of us), "Come to me, all ye that labour and are heavy laden, and I will give you rest" (Matt. 11:28). Regardless of the debate of the role that government has in addressing their needs versus that of other societal institutions, the coarseness, hatred, bigotry, paranoia and ambivalence of the suffering of others now exhibited from a large portion of American Christians, both from the top spheres of the Religious Right leadership down to our kitchen tables and local church fellowships, reflects the slogans, memes, talking points and narratives written not from most of our better pulpits, but actually from the "sermons" of the talk radio and cable TV "priests." They dispense their dogma for hours on end all week to captive listeners, Christian and non-Christian like, who sit commuting in their vehicles, and watching the cable news shows during and after dinner, with such creeds written by Lord-knows-who (usually financial and business interests who richly sponsor these spokesmen, and sometimes themselves), for agendas sometimes alluded to in their financial and tax records, but *rarely shared with their listening audience.*

At this point it might be helpful, particularly for the practicing Christian readers whom I assume are the bulk of the audience here, but maybe also Jews, Muslims and other monotheists, or other readers interested in the religious angle, to cast this phenomenon in light of an ancient religious and historical context from the Bible era. I make the assertions in this chapter as a layperson and not an academic expert or a theologian, and I am sure someone will dispute some of its finer points and as such I encourage the reader to use this discussion to spur them to do their own due diligence of the subject, but much of its points are mere recitations from the Biblical record. As any simple reader of the Bible during their life (even Sunday School or Vacation Bible School) can attest, the main opponents of Jesus Christ and His teachings and mission, as evidenced in the four Gospels, were the pious Jewish fundamentalist group in Palestine known as the Pharisees, and to a lesser extent their Jewish rival group the Sadducees. In Volume 3 of my soon-to-be-published *Holy War Chronicles* book series, I give a crash course on these groups, and other facets of post-Exilic (i.e., when the nation of Judah was exiled into the Kingdom of Babylon for roughly seventy years) Judaism, and how they subsequently perverted Judaism from its original premise as established by God before that time. It was this earlier pre-Exilic Jewish religion and culture (fantasized as a "Camelot" in its Biblically-prescribed form that was never fully historically practiced) for which we evangelical Christians cling to, in "Disneyfied"-style, to project onto modern Jews and Judaism, which has far departed from its original pre-Exilic, Old Testament moorings today.

In fact, in that book I make the pithy observation that, after their return back from Babylon, "the Jews may have left Babylon, but Babylon never left them." From the era of Ezra forwards, a dramatic change in Judaism began to occur that emphasized a departure away from the sacraments and lessons of the Temple sacrifices to a concentration on Torah study, and to further a lawyerly-like culture of refining and defining the legal finer points of the Mosaic Law, with the "lawyers" a newly defined class of people known as the "rabbis," in contrast to the priests of the original Mosaic sacrificial system. These self-appointed gate keepers of religious observance (and in fact, the observance of every minute facet of personal life) not only used their personal views and hunches of how to define the trivial and marginal issues of Torah observance, but even produced the concept of an "oral law," presumably passed down by Moses but with no paper trail, that not only rivaled the written code in the Torah, but in practice replaced it.

The Sadducees were the elite aristocrats that came from the priestly caste (in fact, their name is derived from the "sons of Zadok" that administered the sacrifices in the Temple as priests), and were known for their wealth and secular power and status emphasis, performing many of the administrative duties of the vassal state and interacting with Rome. They did not believe in the resurrection or other supernatural beings, and believed in earthly rewards and experiences only. Within the world of conservatism, they would align with the secular Northeast "Rockefeller Republican" elites, like the old Bush family, coming from the business and financial worlds with old money, Yale education and Foreign Service experience. They also see themselves as the patriarchal "caretakers" of their nation over the generations, and do not get into the finer points of religion, rather seeking a more patriotic and generic "civil religion." In contrast, the Pharisees were more like the Religious Right side of the Republican Party, in their obsession with taking the purity rituals of Temple religious worship, and extending them to every aspect of individual life, with them as the mutually-appointed gatekeepers and referees. Like Reformed Calvinists with Calvin's *Institutes* doctrines, Catholic canon law or the traditional doctrinal views of evangelicals, Pharisees placed more emphasis on the religious-culture "traditions of their fathers" as expressed in the "Oral Law" that was a paraphrased interpretation of the meaning of the words of scripture, much as many Christians do today with their pet doctrines and "presuppositions."

They held contempt for the "unwashed" masses of Jews throughout Palestine who did not acknowledge their self-appointed supreme position as rabbinic "sages" and authorities (particularly in Christ's Galilee area of His youth). They derived such important religious innovations that they must have thought impressed God Himself, such as the fact that one could carry a grape on the Sabbath, but no more, and how many feet one could traverse on that day, or the exact way to ritually wash your hands. They saw most people as "unclean," vulgar, and unworthy of association. Historians of Judaism agree, however, that Pharisaism was the one strand of Judaism that *survived* the fall of Jerusalem and the Diaspora, and thus forms the basis of modern orthodox Judaism, with their oral law eventually compiled into a written Talmud that is emphasized over the Bible itself, with interpretations from their sages at the time of its beginning compilation (not long after the era of the Apostle Paul) and a few centuries afterwards. (It should be noted that these attributes do not describe the significant minority branch known as modern Reform Judaism today.) In contrast, the Sadducees disappeared with the fall of their nation and the Temple in 70 CE, whereas the Pharisees evolved as a rabbi-led culture and religion that could continue outside Palestine, as Judaism had done during the Exile.

Jesus said a very curious thing about the Pharisees (and to some extent, the Sadducees) in a warning to His followers. Like most of His followers today, He was instantly misunderstood by His disciples in what He said, necessitating Him to repeat it and "pin it on the end of their nose" to make it blatant, as their simplistic understanding that did not appreciate the deeper communication via metaphor (my fellow Christian hyper-literal fundamentalists have the same problem, as many of us do). This is what He said (repeated in three of the four gospels), as they were being watched by, and sometimes interacted with, the Pharisees in their journeys:

> And Jesus said to them, "Watch out and beware of the leaven of the Pharisees and Sadducees....How is it that you do not understand that I did not speak to you concerning bread? But beware of the leaven of the Pharisees and Sadducees." Then they understood that He did not say to beware of the leaven of bread, but of the teaching of the Pharisees and Sadducees. (Matt. 16:6, 11–12, NASB)

This is a strong and uncommon statement by Jesus, to "beware" anything, and I am certain He still holds that imperative to any of His followers today. The mysterious allegorical statement raises two clarifying questions, if we are to properly understand and apply His warning today: (1) why did He compare their teachings to "leaven," and (2) what were, and are the actual teachings of the Pharisees and Sadducees? Firstly, leaven was no different then, than it is today. It comprises active bacterial cultures of yeast, which ferment and spread. It thus has the following properties, which relate to Christ's warnings about their teachings: (1) Even though it looks small, it can get big, unknowingly until it is too late, (2) it does take some time to grow and make its impact felt throughout the mass, (3) it does not look like it, but it is a "living" thing, (4) a little bit reproduces on its own, living on its host, and secretly spreads throughout its host, (5) It puffs up its host it is placed within, and fills it full of gas, and (6) it has to be purposely put in place, for cultivation under the proper conditions to intentionally grow and produce its results. *Always remember these six attributes when considering the "leaven" teachings of Pharisees and Sadducees, which I assert have found new life today in talk radio and cable news, in how they operate and irreparably modify their "host" in the Christian heart, as we will consider as a thesis throughout this work.*

Some fermented, "leavened" dough was always kept as a "starter" to jumpstart a new batch of dough by spreading again through a new and larger mass of dough, just as it is often practiced today. Similarly, the "leaven" of the Sadducees and Pharisees, which I assert is thriving today in our world and in Christian thinking here, is actually "old" thinking and ideas, which have been preserved over the ages through various extremist groups, and are now re-implanted via mass media and find new intellectual and cultural "dough" to permeate. One of the primary observances of Judaism, that of Passover, has a central tenet that not only may leavened bread or other leavened agents not be consumed, but also no trace of it can be left in the house. Vigorous and formal efforts are scheduled before each annual Passover observance to carefully "sweep" the house and every nook and cranny within it for tiny traces of it; any that is found must be burned, or possibly sold. (Even today, resorts, hotels and cruise ships undergo a similar deep cleaning before Passover to be certified as "kosher" for their Jewish customers). The most obvious meaning of this ritual is the remembrance that the Hebrews had to evacuate quickly after Pharaoh permitted them to leave Egypt after the slaying of the firstborn in each house (before he shortly changed his mind), but Jewish and other scholars also recognize the old association of leaven with corruption, as a foreign agent added to modify a natural substance. It should be noted that non-living, chemical rising agents, such as baking soda, are not forbidden under such ceremonies.

As regarding our second question, let's consider and confirm the actual teachings of the Sadducees and Pharisees, which in turn act as "leaven" throughout the minds of God's people. A review of the Sadducees' comments and beliefs in the Bible reveals in Matthew 22 that the Sadducees not only thought any resurrection to be absurd, but also displayed their historical proclivity for preserving paternal lineage of property, when they posited a nearly ridiculous thought experiment of who a seven-time widowed woman would be married to in the resurrection amongst her seven brotherly past husbands. Jesus responded to this farce in appropriately strong fashion, stating about these priestly "experts" of the Law, "Ye do err, not knowing the scriptures, nor the power of God," acknowledging their simplistic presupposition that marriage would be an institution that continued in a heaven in which they did not believe; *would we be similarly bold and confident in our denunciation of such religious authorities today?* When Peter and John preached about Jesus at the Temple when prompted by the people there who had witnessed a healing, the Sadducees and the priests were grieved that they taught about Jesus and the resurrection of the dead, and imprisoned them. The next day the judges of Jesus, Caiaphas and Annas the high priests had them tell the court by what "power" or "name" they had done this, and could only merely threaten them since they could not retort against what their eyes had seen (Acts 4). They again ran afoul of Sadducees shortly thereafter (Acts 5) when too many were being healed in town, and Paul used the deep dissentions between the Sadducees and Pharisees in the Sanhedrin, in particular their dispute on the resurrection and afterlife, to escape their clutches in a riot (Acts 23). *Many of the media figures alluded to in this work have used their platforms in talk radio and cable news, while often exhibiting some form of religious piety, to promote political positions directed against others (particularly the poor and disadvantaged) that must suggest they do not believe in any accountability to God and His Biblical prescriptions in the afterlife either.*

While they were often rivals in the Sanhedrin and in Jewish debates, the Sadducees and Pharisees often formed a unified front when their privileged place of power was threatened, such as by a poor carpenter's son "who had no place to lay His head," due to the power of His message, and His influence and respect amongst the common people. This collaboration even began to confront His predecessor, the "voice crying out in the wilderness," John the Baptist, who referred to these respected and influential religious leaders as a "generation [or society] of vipers," and of their precious historical religious pedigree and heritage that "God is able of these stones to raise up children unto Abraham" (Matt. 3:9). Later, they both demanded that Jesus seek their approval of authenticity by performing a sign from heaven, to which He refused to act as their trained seal, and said that a "wicked and adulterous" community would seek such (Matt. 16:4)—*such "adultery" being a deceptive unfaithfulness to the God to which their phony religious persona was publicly devoted.*

The Pharisees were those who paraded around most publicly amongst the people (not flaunting their aloof aristocracy of governing like the elitist Sadducees), but with a religious elitism that they used to browbeat the public and cement their esteemed position, and thus encountered Jesus in the streets more often, and with more strident opposition. Jesus was very clear early in His ministry on what He thought His Father thought about the religious state of the Pharisees, when He said in His famous Sermon on the Mount that "except your righteousness shall exceed the righteousness of the scribes and Pharisees, ye shall in no case enter into the kingdom of heaven" (Matt. 5:20). *Do we similarly have an obligation to set higher standards for ourselves than the Christian celebrities and leaders we observe in our religious media?*

Just as we will see with the Religious Right leaders and their conservative henchmen, the Pharisees placed a premium upon "keeping up appearances" by refusing to have dialogue with or associating with the "riff-raff" that did not meet their pedigree or standards or purity or piety. When they asked Jesus why He and His followers ate with "publicans" (the dreaded secular government collectors of infernal taxes, as enablers of the State) and "sinners" (like the gay community or transgendered are considered by them today), He responded that "They that be whole need not a physician, but they that are sick. But go ye and learn what [that] meaneth, I will have mercy, and not sacrifice: for I am not come to call the righteous, but sinners to repentance" (Matt. 9:12–13). When Jesus earned a reputation of compassion on the poor, destitute, and helpless and diverted His agenda to provide relief when they pleaded to Him, like many in the Religious Right leadership today the Pharisees grew to envy the devotion He had from the people who did not grovel at their own feet, since the Pharisees had been found to be impotent in dealing with the problems "on the streets" in their day. Rather than seeking to learn from Him to "up their game" in humble fashion, they sought to slander and criticize Him as an "outsider" using their position of influence, saying ridiculously that "He casteth out devils through the prince of devils" (Matt. 9:34), *which certainly didn't further endear them to the "unwashed" public any more than it does for the Religious Right today.*

The things the Pharisees complained about were not that Jesus' followers sought to interfere with the Pharisees' own religious convictions, nor even challenge the fundamental "holy books" of their faith, but rather that *His followers did not feel subject to the narrow religious (conservative) traditions the Pharisees' culture had produced to practice it, and thus the Pharisees felt challenged and incensed that they wouldn't live in obeisance to their customs. This is similar to the posturing of the Religious Right today, who have not been threatened by others or the government to impose homosexual practice on themselves or other behaviors for which they object, but rather see that their inability to impose their convictions on other people as a threat and instance of "Christian persecution."* They accused Jesus' letting His disciples eat ears of corn on the Sabbath as being "unlawful" (Matt. 12:2)—*not because "the law" (Torah) said it was unlawful, but rather the "hedge" of conservative, traditional restriction of its principle they had cultivated was different, having thus confused the public on what God's Word actually forbade, and put the authority on the "gatekeeper" religious leaders as opposed to the flexible and common-sense Law itself. The Religious Right community today similarly gets confused on the differences of the traditional "Bible Belt" Religious Right social culture and norms, versus the explicit restrictions within the broad liberties the New Covenant provides and celebrates.* Even in my era of upbringing, "drinking, dancing and card playing" were still taboo in many religious circles, or the use of pants by women or short sleeves; since then, it has been "rock music," birth control and "smoking," and now may focus on tattoos, "vaping" or hip-hop music. Jesus saw this enforcement of "conservative" cultural hedge-building as a danger, and amusingly corrected these "experts" of scripture by using simple stories from the Bible itself, adding that "if ye had known what this meaneth, I will have mercy, and not sacrifice, ye would not have condemned the guiltless" (Matt. 12:7); *this kind of talk by Jesus is "fighting words" and blasphemous to Religious Right culture today, and not part of their vocabulary.*

Christ made His condemnation of them more explicit, and threw their supposed piety and "devotion" to God's Word back in their face, when they further condemned Jesus for letting his disciples "transgress the tradition of the elders" by not washing hands when they eat (not a Mosaic Law requirement, but a Pharisaic one), retorting to them directly, "Why do ye also transgress the commandment of God by your tradition?" (Matt. 15:3). He then gave them an example of how, as the "lawyers" fundamentalists tend to be, they had contorted a legal interpretation that let them avoid the common-sense command to take care of one's parents by designating the funds through another tax code-like loophole, which had "made the commandment of God of none effect by your tradition" (v. 6). He further quoted the prophet Elijah's words from God to show that their "tradition" was actually trying to consistently deceive God while trying to appear outwardly pious, with His father having said that "This people draweth nigh unto me with their mouth, and honoureth me with their lips, but their heart is far from me. But in vain they do worship me, teaching for doctrines the commandments of men" (vv. 8–9). When His disciples sheepishly (or alarmingly) told Jesus that the Pharisees were offended by this, Jesus responded with the description of them that might well fit many in our nationally-famous Religious Right leadership today, stating that "Every plant, which my heavenly Father had not planted, shall be rooted up. Let them alone: they be blind leaders of the blind. And if the blind lead the blind, both shall fall into the ditch" (vv. 13–14).

Just like the Religious Right leaders' devotion to President Trump today as evidence of their real commitment to "family values," the Pharisees showed their "family values" by criticizing Jesus for not acknowledging the allowance in the Law (which they blamed on Moses) of the provision to divorce women, to which they cleverly added to the text (as religious leaders are wont to do) the phrase, "for every cause" (Matt. 19:3). This addition was selfishly used by them as sexists to dump the wives of their youth and to obtain a young "trophy wife" when they became well established. Jesus then pointed out a reality of His Father's interaction with mankind, which the Pharisee "experts" should have known (or acknowledged), and which most Christians do not understand, when He said that "Moses because of the hardness of your heart suffered you to put away your wives; but from the beginning it was not so" (Matt. 19:8). *In other words, rather than God's commands and nature being an immutable, eternally rigid edifice (as many believe, to the verge of idolatry), Jesus confirms that His Father reveals Himself and His commands in a form that is suitable and realistic to accommodate the people with whom He has relationship, and their nature, weaknesses and proclivities. Thus, the "vengeful" God of wrath with "fire on the mountain" in the Old Testament—a nature abhorrent to many critics and seemingly inconsistent with His New Testament representation through His Son, may have been a necessity to earn respect from the Hebrews and their neighbors, particularly since the Hebrews were "prone to wander" to even more brutal gods whom they evidently respected more, such as Molech with his sacrificial requirements of their children.*

When Jesus told the parable of the householder's son, who was killed by the vineyard husbandmen (who had also beat and killed his earlier servants) because they wanted to "seize on his inheritance" (Matt. 21:38), the chief priests and Pharisees "perceived that he spake of them" (v. 45). This is interesting, because Jesus had also said to them that "The kingdom of God shall be taken from you, and given to a nation bringing forth the fruits thereof" (v. 43). *For those "Christian" leaders who seek to take "dominion" over today's kingdoms that are the inheritance of Christ, or even serve as stumbling blocks to Christ's real and plain teachings, do they realize what tenuous situations they are in?* The Pharisees were also able to combat their perceived ideological rivals and threats by confusing the narrative and debate for the observing populace, just like that routinely performed by talk radio and cable news today, to obfuscate issues and cloud the moral bearings of choices to make; the Bible says regarding Jesus that these conniving rhetorical mad geniuses the Pharisees "took counsel how they might entangle Him in his talk" (Matt. 22:15).

Jesus then had an extended conversation talking about the Pharisees in Matthew 23, which sounded like an apt description of many of the most popular Religious Right leaders today (particularly in this era of their fawning adoration of President Trump and his "Christian" leadership), when He said,

> The scribes and the Pharisees sit in Moses' seat: All therefore whatsoever they bid you observe, [that] observe and do; but do not ye after their works: for they say, and do not. For they bind heavy burdens and grievous to be borne, and lay [them] on men's shoulders; but they [themselves] will not move them with one of their fingers. But all their works they do for to be seen of men: they make broad their phylacteries, and enlarge the borders of their garments, and love the uppermost rooms at feasts, and the chief seats in the synagogues, and greetings in the markets, and to be called of men, Rabbi, Rabbi...

But woe unto you, scribes and Pharisees, hypocrites! For ye shut up the kingdom of heaven against men: for ye neither go in [yourselves], neither suffer ye them that are entering to go in. Woe unto you, scribes and Pharisees, hypocrites! For ye devour widows' houses, and for a pretence make long prayer: therefore ye shall receive the greater damnation. Woe unto you, scribes and Pharisees, hypocrites! For ye compass sea and land to make one proselyte, and when he is made, ye make him twofold more the child of hell than yourselves. Woe unto you, [ye] blind guides, which say, "Whosoever shall swear by the temple, it is nothing; but whosoever shall swear by the gold of the temple, he is a debtor!" [Ye] fools and blind: for whether is greater, the gold, or the temple that sanctifieth the gold? and, whosoever shall swear by the altar, it is nothing; but whosoever sweareth by the gift that is upon it, he is guilty. [Ye] fools and blind: for whether [is] greater, the gift, or the altar that sanctifieth the gift?

...Woe unto you, scribes and Pharisees, hypocrites! For ye pay tithe of mint and anise and cummin, and have omitted the weightier [matters] of the law, judgment, mercy, and faith: these ought ye to have done, and not to leave the other undone. [Ye] blind guides, which strain at a gnat, and swallow a camel. Woe unto you, scribes and Pharisees, hypocrites! For ye make clean the outside of the cup and of the platter, but within they are full of extortion and excess...Woe unto you, scribes and Pharisees, hypocrites! For ye are like unto whited sepulchres, which indeed appear beautiful outward, but are within full of dead [men's] bones, and of all uncleanliness. Even so ye also outwardly appear righteous unto men, but within ye are full of hypocrisy and iniquity. Woe unto you, scribes and Pharisees, hypocrites! Because ye build the tombs of the prophets, and garnish the sepulchres of the righteous, and say, If we had been in the days of our fathers, we would not have been partakers with them in the blood of the prophets. Wherefore ye be witnesses unto yourselves, that ye are the children of them which killed the prophets. (Matt. 23:2–7, 13–19, 23–25, 27–31)

There is much to unpack here, but just like our Religious Right today and all their moralizing about sexual purity and fidelity, yet making excuse after excuse for their standard bearer President Trump, Jesus begins by noting that even then the well-known religious leaders talked a good game, but their example and priorities totally belied their message. They weighed people down with guilt and overly-confining lifestyle expectations, but did not use their supposed wisdom and understanding of Biblical knowledge to "ease" the burden and liberate them with liberating and wise counsel. Like those today, they liked to be recognized and given distinguished positions (and honorary doctorates from Christian diploma mill schools), and pictures praying next to the President, and titles bequeathed to them. Both groups make followers as confused and in the dark spiritually as they are, and exploit widows and other destitute and easily-manipulated followers, "devouring their homes" in fundraising pleas, and talk more about riches, even in the house of God, whether it be the gold in the temple or the private jet owned by the "ministry," being more obsessed with the riches rather than the worship made possible there.

Finally, both the Pharisees and Religious Right leaders today "major in the minors," fixating on the amount of spices to tithe, or gay marriage or the "war on Christmas," and the Ten Commandments down at the courthouse, but both ignore, and *both even dispute the concept of,* "the weightier [matters] of the law, judgment, mercy, and faith." They see talk of "justice" and such as just "liberal talk" of the "socialists" and "social gospel," and *sadly they are right, in that these last two groups may be the only ones talking about it, as well as mercy. They cannot conceive of the idea that God has "front burner issues" and "back burner issues," and rather perceive that He is as one-dimensional as they are; if they did conceive it, it would reveal that they have totally missed the point of God's priorities and agenda, and they would have to admit it.* As such, they become "blind guides," straining at gnats and "swallowing camels." Both parties would be greatly offended at being described as "dead" and "unclean," and full of hypocrisy and iniquity. Furthermore, they arrogantly suggest that they, as "enlightened ones" but of the same ilk and views as their religious forbearers, would not have made their predecessors' tragic mistakes, whether it be killing the prophets, honoring corrupt kings, slaughtering Indians and giving them cholera-filled blankets, wielding crusader blood baths against different believers or of other faiths, and even hosting Klan and eugenics sterilization recruitment drives on Sunday morning within the doors of the church; *Jesus suggests that He knows better.*

These religious leaders are not publicly known for contrition or repentance, unless they are caught red-handed in heinous acts and can no longer deny it, and must feint repentance to salvage their ministry and its income and lifestyle. Similarly, the Pharisees rejected the baptism of repentance of John (Luke 7:30), and resented when "sinners" like tax collectors were liberated when they did comply. This trait may explain why they can easily follow a president who publicly stated in an interview that he had nothing to ever ask God for forgiveness about. One thing that Pharisees could be relied upon, just like their Religious Right descendents, was their condemnation of religious rivals and groups that were known to cavort with those of unsavory reputations (at least the "upstanding" religious leaders did it discreetly in the shadows!). When a Pharisee admirably hosted Jesus for a meal, he was incensed that a woman of ill repute interrupted them by emotionally debasing herself in cleaning Jesus' feet with her tears, and using expensive ointment on them (Luke 7:38). Jesus explained to him that these types of people will be shown to be the most devoted people to Jesus in the Kingdom, and that religious leader snobs would thus miss out on seeing God's hand work to build His kingdom and fill it with the greatest sinners that were the most forgiven, and most devoted.

One other aspect the Pharisees had in common with their Religious Right progeny today is their skills at self-promotion and their own public relations. Luke 18:9 says that Jesus "spake this parable unto certain which trusted in themselves that they were righteous, and despised others." Telling the story of the Pharisee and the publican praying in the Temple, the Pharisee humbly confessed in all sincerity to God that "God, I thank thee, that I am not as other men [are], extortioners, unjust, adulterers, or even as this publican. I fast twice in the week, I give tithes of all that I possess" (vv. 11–12). *One unmistakable trend one will notice on Christian talk radio and programming is their emphasis on the sinfulness of others, and not on their own sinfulness or limitations or mistakes, or those within their own ranks; in fact, that is true of conservative media in general, which will not acknowledge the mistakes of their community and its leaders or past decisions, and certainly not of America, for to acknowledge them would make them part of the "Hate America" crowd, and certainly not a proud American if they apologize for every offense.* In contrast, the publican smote his chest and dwelt on his own inadequacy, merely proclaiming, "God be merciful to me a sinner" (v. 13). Although this man made no sophisticated theological confession, creed or catechism, knowing only to address his need to God, and take full responsibility and to hope that God's love might forgive him, Jesus said he went home justified—in essence, a saved man, even though he "flunked" an average theologian's laundry list of recitations to obtain such a status.

To be fair, there is a notable exception to the typical "leaven" of the Pharisees—at least a few of them—and it belies the assumptions that the animosity between the Pharisees and Jesus' teaching and movement was inevitable, and had to clash and fight to the bitter end, and illustrates the overtures made by Jesus and others to use the period for needed reforms; *this can be a glimmer of optimism and hope when we see the perilous position and late hour of the conservative Religious Right leadership community today, in terms of its ability to retain its mission to be "salt" and "light."* John chapter 3 recounts a discreet, late-night visit by the Pharisee ruler Nicodemus, privately with Jesus out in the field. *This meeting was so unique, and the secrecy of its communications possibly supernaturally silenced and encrypted outside their presence*, such that it provided the only (in my understanding) full, blatant disclosure in those days, in unvarnished fashion, of Jesus' status as the *only begotten* (of same substance) Son of God, rather than merely one of the celestial "sons of God"; which "none of the *archons* (whom I understand to be the principalities and powers, or 'sons' of God ruling over the seventy nations) of this world knew, for had they known it, they would not have crucified the Lord of glory" (1 Cor. 2:8). If this understanding is true, then it might possibly explain why Paul wrote in Colossians that Christ soon thereafter was "blotting out the handwriting of ordinances that was against us, which was contrary to us, and took it out of the way, nailing it to his cross; [And] having *spoiled principalities and powers*, he made a shew of them openly, triumphing over them in it" (Col. 2:14–15).

The passage says that first of all, rather than merely talk about him like we see in the Sanhedrin deliberations and in much of Religious Right and conservative radio about liberal "boogeymen" with which they do not have dialogue or clarification, Nicodemus left his Sanhedrin delegation to "hear from the horse's mouth" (whether all or any of his fellow members knew of his mission or not), and to get real answers, as opposed to merely excuses to bolster their eradication campaign. His nightly visit may have been to protect his reputation, maintain the aloof status of the Sanhedrin, or preserve "plausible deniability" of the interaction if needed later. Regardless, Nicodemus regarded Jesus as "rabbi"—a term that acknowledged His status as a legitimate (if disputed) teacher of God's word and will by this Sanhedrin leader. He further made a shocking statement about the secret position of the Jewish leaders themselves, when he added that "we know that thou art a teacher come from God; for no man can do these miracles that thou doest, except God be with him" (John 3:2).

This is further confirmed by the deliberations of the chief priests and Pharisees after they heard reports that Jesus had raised Lazarus from the dead, as recounted in John 11. They state in the meeting that they were afraid that if they did not impede Jesus, everyone would "believe on Him" and "the Romans shall come and take away both our place and nation." Again, this portrays religious leaders that are most worried about their own careers and economics threatened by someone whom God has anointed, as well as their influence and privileges from the government; *much like I suspect many Religious Right leaders fear now if President Trump is not re-elected.* Most importantly, their own high priest Caiaphas (who later presided over the trial of Jesus to sentence Him to death) in their ranks not only asserted there that "one person should die for the people," and "prophesied that Jesus should die for that nation; and not for that nation only, but that also he should gather together in one the children of God that were scattered abroad" (vv. 51–52); as a result "from that day forth they took counsel together for to put him to death" (v. 53). *This shows that this counsel of the top Jewish leaders did not oppose Jesus out of zeal for their faith or misunderstanding of what God was doing, but rather were supernaturally informed through their most distinguished member what God was up to, and they chose to knowingly rebel against God and His plan, which might not only supplant their favored status and control, but even permit non-Jews outside Judea to share in the favored status of deliverance. I assert that this behavior is seen in our many Religious Right leaders today, in their public pronouncements in the media and even newsletters, attacking those outside their ranks who seem to resonate with the people, or who espouse issues as followers of Christ that they are not willing to sincerely reconsider. They further oppose any movement outside their own ranks that might overshadow them, even to the point of high degrees of aggression to intimidate and accomplish this (often manipulating civil legislation, police or even our military to enforce their national or international agenda, just as the Sanhedrin did with the Romans, all fully aware of what they were doing).*

In contrast, Jesus responded to the evidently inquisitive Nicodemus with legitimate seriousness (He did not answer the Sanhedrin later, for they had no interest in answers, and had already made their minds up), and told him the secrets of being "born again," as a mystery which not everyone else was privy to as of yet. In turn, Nicodemus did not leave in response to Jesus' seemingly absurd answer, and it is not even clear that he replied in a mocking tone, but rather in total confusion and perplexity to the response. Jesus clarified that Kingdom of Heaven immigrant applicants must be reborn in the Spirit and, as opposed to the strict bureaucracy and regulations of piety of the Pharisees, or the Religious Right or other denominational or ecclesiastical authorities, the "wind bloweth where it listeth" and "canst not tell whence it cometh" for those "born in the Spirit" (John 3:8), and thus were not controllable by these authorities. Jesus said Nicodemus should be surprised, as a "teacher" of Israel, that he didn't understand these things already. Jesus then blatantly explained to him the Father's plan to save the "world" that He "loved," not just Jews, and that Jesus came "not to condemn the world" but to save it (vv. 16–17). *The fact that God loves and seeks to save more than the self-designated "elect" religious elites, and that God was really not about condemning, but saving, flew in the face of the Pharisees and their "leaven," and it flies in the face of the Reformers and the Religious Right today.*

The message must have stuck, because Nicodemus later spoke up about Jesus in a subsequent meeting (John 7). Then at that time the chief priests and Pharisees had chided the Temple guards for not arresting Jesus because of His presence, calling them "deceived" (v. 47) and added that Jesus couldn't be so great if the religious leaders had not believed him *(a peer pressure tactic much like the Religious Right and other ecclesiastical leadership (including Roman Catholic and Orthodox) has used to keep people in line, belittling them and their ability to see what is right in front of them and have experienced)*. As their elitist rebukes extended even to the point of calling the people "cursed" (v. 49) for not knowing the law like them *(much like the Religious Right does for those believers who even suggest we should have a conversation about the status of fellow worshippers willing to commit to monogamous gay marriage covenants, as just one example)*, Nicodemus spoke up. He just (however bravely) suggested that Jesus should be "heard out" and to at least understand what He is about (much as he had admirably done himself). In return they belittled him, as many religious leaders are wont to do, by exhibiting their knowledge in reminding him that no prophet came out of Galilee, as they were absolutely certain where Jesus had His origins (rather than asking and finding out He was born in Bethlehem) (Matt. 7:45–52). Similarly, just as an earlier Pope showed his remarkable knowledge of the Bible to tell Galileo that the Sun moves around the Earth because the Sun "sets" in the Bible, *Religious Right leaders today speak with authority and belittle others because of their remarkable recollection of scripture, but no understanding of the facts on the ground, and how they really relate to them, be they the views of "liberals," "social gospel" activists, civil rights and humanitarian figures, environmental champions, or interfaith dialogue advocates.* Jesus similarly said these leaders can see the signs in the sky and clouds, but "not discern the signs of the times" (Matt. 16:3).

Nicodemus later came and brought ointments to anoint Jesus' dead body *(a risky act of intimate devotion that only some women, and no other prominent male disciples offered)* along with the wealthy Joseph of Arimathaea, who offered his own expensive grave for His body (Matt. 27:60). *This story should remind us that although many of the criticisms I allege against Religious Right activists and other conservative leaders are valid here and show a severe misunderstanding of the basics of Christ's message and an unwillingness to consider their own thoughts and actions, there may well be a remnant of "Nicodemus-types" from their own ranks which are privately pondering their actions today and the mind of Christ, "looking at the signs of the times" with soul searching, and later "defect" from the religious establishment and stand with the humble people and Kingdom of Heaven message, and willing to pay the price to their clerical careers and fortunes, as did Nicodemus and Joseph.* In fact, I believe we will see a few examples of such people at the end of this work. Just like the "leaven" has to marinate for a time to take full effect, often in these people the antidote has to take time to cleanse, and lead to outer repentance.

Just like Billy Graham recommending and submitting his formal proposal to President Nixon that the U.S. should blow up the dams in North Vietnam to drown the villagers[16] (a violation of the Geneva Convention,[17] for which Nazi commissioner over Holland Arthur Seyss-Inquart was hanged at the Nuremberg Trials for offenses including bombing dikes and flooding Dutch residents, under "Count Two—Crimes Against Peace"[18]), or the Hawaiian "Christian missionaries" escorting the Christian Queen out at bayonet-point while waving in the U.S. warships or in South and Central America in helping facilitate the slaughter of villagers by tin-pot dictators, and the many "Christian" leaders today that are fine with water-boarding and other torture tactics at Guantanamo Bay and elsewhere, similarly the Pharisees would join league with or exploit the government or other rivals to consider violent actions to cement their power and objectives. Matthew 12:14 says that, regarding Jesus, "Then the Pharisees went out, and held a council against him, how they might destroy him." (Mark 3:6 says they came in league with the religious/secular "Herodians" in government power to do such.) There are many passages in the Gospels that suggest that the Pharisees and allies sought to kill Jesus, long before the deed was done, leading Jesus to sometimes "lay low" or to even come to Jerusalem unannounced, until that He knew it was "His time."

They threatened not only Jesus and His disciples, but also the people at large who were interested in knowing more. The parents of the man born blind were afraid to speak to the Pharisees "because they feared the Jews [religious leaders]: for the Jews had agreed already, that if any man did confess that he was Christ, he should be put out of the synagogue" (John 9:22). At that time, being thrown out of the synagogue would eventually become a death sentence, because synagogue-worshipping Jews had a waiver on emperor worship, because of all the rebellions they started when coerced; in fact, the Book of Acts says that the Jews often threw the early Christians out of the synagogue, which would expose them then to the requirement of Caesar worship, and martyrdom when they would not. *Sometimes some do not speak up for what they know is right (or who is right), because of what their Christian friends, or pastors (or a senior pastor boss or denominational leader) might say, or its impact on their status or career.* Regarding the Pharisees, "Nevertheless among the chief rulers also many believed on him; but because of the Pharisees they did not confess [him], lest they should be put out of the synagogue: For they loved the praise of men more than the praise of God" (John 12:42–43).

Their threats did not stop there; when the healed man born blind simply and honestly recounted his experience, and furthermore began to question the spiritual ignorance and lack of answers of the Pharisees, they restored their lofty position by accusing him of being "born in sin" because of his low status of being disabled at birth and not a credentialed religious "insider," asking, "dost thou teach us?" *Many Religious Right leaders do not value the spiritual experiences of those not in concert with their views or agenda, and least of all, not being revered as the official conduit to God with all the answers.* However, when Jesus later found this honest spiritual "experiencer" again, whose experience didn't meet the narrative desired by these religious leaders, *the man found his answers directly from Jesus, and not the religious gatekeepers.* In contrast, the Pharisees shockingly asked Jesus if He thought they themselves were blind, to which He replied, "If ye were blind, ye should have no sin: but now ye say, 'We see'; therefore your sin remaineth" (John 9:41). *Even religious leaders today who say they have "all the answers" from their creeds and doctrines that run counter to what people experience and see before their very eyes need to think twice before their attitude of not being open and teachable (even as senior credentialed "gatekeepers" themselves) lands them in the same category.*

This leads us to another primary attribute of the "leaven of the Pharisees" that they deployed, which their fundamentalist and Religious Right descendants continue to execute today, along (to some degree) with their secular conservative leadership and media cousins, of far vaster influence. *It is the collusion with secular power brokers of aligned personal agendas to maintain the religious/governmental power status quo and establishment, in "Faustian bargains" behind closed doors and mutual public advocacy, where violence or aggressive actions are often the end game, the secular arm serving as the coercive punishment "goons" for the religious elite. Most importantly, its most important technique is leading the gullible religious public "sheep" to turn away from their fundamental spiritual values and trusted role models "on a dime" when prodded and "whispered in their ear" by these religious leaders of disguised motives, using "fake news" and secular patriotism (when convenient) to galvanize public support to dispense with those asking hard questions and "upsetting the apple cart."* There are so many prominent examples of this behavior within the Church Age of Christian leadership, I could not list but a wisp of a sample of them here (including many here in "God's country" America in the last hundred years), but many such examples are carefully documented in the various volumes of my *Holy War Chronicles* book series. In fact, we have become so accustomed to them (particularly when the Jim Bakker, Jimmy Swaggart and other televangelists' scandals seemed like daily headlines) that we tend to see them as not worthy of our time to explore (and feel a sense of guilt for not "supporting our team" as Christians). However, *the integrity of the Church is paramount for its Great Commission message, and the exposed public disgrace of such behavior by prominent Christian figures is "all our business," not to leer over their demise and seek their destruction, but to make clear to the "perishing" we seek* to "rescue" that their corruption is not part of the genuine Christ or the Gospel, nor of the masses who seek to emulate Him and further the message. This position of fidelity is only made credible by our public denouncement of these deeds and attitudes, otherwise we are viewed as giving tacit endorsement, or see the corruption as trivial, which tells the world more about our own hearts and integrity, as "guilty bystanders."

The "passion week" of Jesus' entry into Jerusalem, initially met with widespread praise by the Jewish people of "Hosanna!," and "Blessed is He that comes in the name of the Lord!" in His triumphal entry while hailed by the public, until His betrayal, the schemes made against Him by the Pharisees and allies, and His barbaric torture (ahem, "enhanced interrogation") by their hands and exploitation of government figures to assure His grisly (and supposedly permanent) disposal by death, is a classic example of such devilry by the leaders of "God's people" in action. All four gospel writers document the following events, with small details added in each to supplement their eyewitness testimony, based upon their Spirit-supported perspectives and recollection. The Pharisees finally sprung their-long planned private scheme to not only silence Jesus, but to destroy Him, with their plan to co-opt the power and authority of the mighty Roman global empire. They deemed this necessary, since apparently they were afraid of His power, even as a carpenter's son with "nowhere to lay His head," but with the power of righteous condemnation of them like the prophets before Him (whom they also had historically decided they had to kill), and the widespread support of the populace that resented the oppression of the misplaced tyranny of excessive public "piety" the Pharisees imposed on them.

They deployed and corruptly used the Temple guards under their authority (permitted by Rome to maintain order on the Temple grounds and prevent the riots common there by the restless Jews) to do their covert work of arresting Jesus under the cover of darkness, like the KGB and secret police behind the Iron Curtain, but this time "sanctified" for "holy cause," like their Blackwater-type mercenary "guns for hire" for a private agenda. Jesus pointed out their mindset of an expected violent confrontation and had thus secured the "upper hand" with the overwhelming, SWAT-like armament they wielded, while He noted that His crew was known for being defenseless. Popular Christian leaders like retired general Jerry Boykin have actually had the chutzpah to allege that Jesus told His followers to "find a sword" because violent battles would be the normal future course of "spreading the Gospel"; the very fact that Jesus said two swords would "be enough" belies this assertion when He knew the vast weaponry they would encounter, and I suspect He wanted a couple of swords there so He could find cause to publicly declare to "put them *away" to show His real feelings about the use of violence, and that this command would be recorded and preserved for future generations.*

Now a hallmark of today's Christian and conservative media in presenting a misleading record of the messages and statements of those they oppose, the Pharisees used "false witnesses" to put words in Jesus' mouth, in a secret trial after an illegal "rendition" and detainment without legal authority or rights. *This is a technique most Christian conservatives still support today against those whose religious views they disagree with during today's "War on Terror," using an "existential threat" as an excuse, just like the Pharisees did. They worried about Jesus and His handful of followers leading to events that would take away their traditional "place and nation" (John 11:48); today's Religious Right worries about the tiny Muslim community doing the same thing, and recommends the same covert, illegal methods by the secular authorities to use as well to address it.* The "leaven" the Pharisees spread in this case was that both a religious and nationalistic patriotic duty to "save" their "nation" and its traditions (i.e., its traditional power brokers) justified all their underhanded and disguised deeds, and even lies and propaganda "fake news" (not to mention torture, law circumvention and "respectable" institution-blessed terrorism) to maintain the God-honoring "piety" of the nation. *Does this justification sound familiar to those of you who follow Christian and conservative talk radio and media?*

Often, in relatively "civilized" societies such as America, and Imperial Rome beforehand, the civil government retains the authority of violent force and capital punishment, therefore the religious community finds ways to manipulate the government to do its "dirty work" for it, whether against religious rivals such as Muslims in America, or Jesus' movement in the Roman province of Judea. Also, in both cases the civil government often shows greater virtue, fairness, humanity and restraint than their religious community counterparts. The Jewish leaders turned Jesus over to the civil Roman government, because (to their lament) they were not granted the authority to murder their rivals. The Roman governor Pontus Pilate found no reason to justifiably punish Jesus, without clear evidence of His misdeeds, and found an opportunity to avoid an unpopular veto of these officials' will, by exploiting a benevolent provision the Romans had instituted to placate the Jewish officials during the religious season (showing yet again that secular governments will often attempt to accommodate God's people, as opposed to the martyr complex often in Christian circles).

He offered them the opportunity to have released the innocent and non-violent Jesus of Nazareth, or one known as "Jesus Barabbas." The latter was said to be in prison for murder and sedition as a rebel terrorist against the government (Luke 23:19), and a robber (John 18:40), and also termed an insurrectionist (Mark 15:7). Christians today still prefer these types of fellows, like an Oliver North that sells weapons to the Iranians (who had held Americans hostage) in league with the Israelis, and then kept it secret from Congress and the American people, or a master mercenary that heads his own mercenary group Blackwater, or similar politicians like Kentucky Governor Matt Bevin, who told the Value Voters Summit in 2016 (while receiving the "Distinguished Christian Statesman" award) that if Hillary Clinton won the presidency, his own sons might have to shed the "blood of patriots" to water the "Tree of Liberty"[19]—*in essence, suggesting armed sedition to confront a legally-elected "tyrant" Clinton.* Of course, those same violent "patriots" like Barabbas that the Pharisees lauded, who were "so patriotic" (the primary concern of many American Christians) as to commit violent crimes for their cause, would later use their barbaric actions *against their own Jewish people*, who tried to flee Jerusalem when they instigated a major rebellion against Rome.

One thing that differentiates the religious leader from the dreaded "pagan" is that when both do their own immoral "dirty work," the pagan often does it openly while the religious leader does it discreetly while maintaining their public persona of piety. When the Pharisees and priests led Christ to Pilate to finish a violent, unjust act on Jesus, they would not enter his judgment hall, "lest they should be defiled, but that they might eat the Passover" (John 18:28). *This is another case where they prove Jesus right in that these fundamentalist "Bible/Torah believers" do in fact, "strain at gnats, and swallow camels" by focusing on the superficial, trivial matters of outer piety, but do not even recognize what He called the "weightier matters of the law," such as "justice" and "mercy." These last two terms will generally not be heard in Religious Right circles, at the top or within the grass roots, as they rather focus on gay people and their deadly agenda to make all of us to convert, as well as the handful of Muslims in our society and their existential threat, not to mention the dreaded "war on Christmas," but ignoring the plight of refugees, the innocent who are incarcerated, poverty, and the like.*

Furthermore, as they sneer at these Gentile "pagans" who do not meet their theological standards (yet exploiting them when it serves their purpose), they do not realize that these ignorant "unwashed" Gentile leaders understand the nature and motives of these religious fundamentalists more than they do themselves. The Bible says that Pilate, ever the political operative, "knew that for envy they [the Pharisees] had delivered him" (Matt. 27:18, Mark 15:10). This is the root of a lot of railing of the Religious Right today against those they anoint as enemies—envy of their success and popularity, wealth, and devotion and respect from the people. Even Herod, a type of secular Jew who represented them while pursuing his own power trip and hedonistic pleasures, and dispensing with their pesky reformers such as John the Baptist (similar to the role President Trump performs for the Religious Right today), found their shared contempt for this genuine Jesus (whose holy example poorly reflected on all their shared corruption) bound them together. The Bible says that "the same day Pilate and Herod were made friends together: for before they were at enmity between themselves" (Luke 23:12).

The "strange bedfellows" made of the enemies of Christ and His Gospel, as we shall see in the rest of this book and series, will include the most pious Religious Right community snuggled up right in the middle of them, and covering them all with a cloak of public piety and religious justification to "sell them" and their agenda to the simple-minded and deluded sheep in the populace. At that time, Jesus made a comment to Pilate that would be disputed by many Christians today, as it is by Jews who wish to suppress their Pharisee descendants' shared complicity in the death of Jesus (in reality, we all share culpability in His death by our sins that necessitated it) and complain of accurate Passion Play dramas portraying such, when He stated that "he that delivered me unto thee hath the greater sin" (John 19:11). *Similarly, when Jesus sees the Religious Right vote en masse to install "their people" in secular government to oppress religious minorities domestically, provide cover for white supremacists, and contempt for the refugee, immigrant and the poor (and others who are the "face of Jesus"), and on and on, Jesus will remember who is guilty of the "greater sin."*

The key point from this period in the betrayal and murder of Jesus is the marvelous psychological operations and propaganda of their "fake news" dispensation and virus of perverted thinking propagated by the Pharisees at this critical juncture, both to the common people who had just praised Jesus days before, and the "decision maker" Pilate. Towards Pilate they warned him to do their bidding, even though he was governor, by saying that "If thou let this man go, thou are not Caesar's friend" (John 19:12). They knew Pilate's tenuous position with Rome and desire to appease his own superiors, and cagily used it to pressure him. The Religious Right uses the same pressure tactics against their Republican mouthpieces, to make sure they keep up legislation targeting gays and Muslims, as well as Palestinians and their interests, lest there be boycotts of campaign funds or the funding of rivals in primaries; most of all, they appeal to secular patriotism, as opposed to Christ's teaching (which they usually cannot use to justify their acts), to challenge their political puppet's public reputation as a loyal "patriot."

Regarding their own "patriotism," the chief priests revealed their regular cognitive dissonance and hypocrisy by publicly rejecting Pilate's somewhat cynical recognition of their "king" Jesus, by declaring that "we have no king but Caesar" (John 19:15). Not only do they publicly reject their God as King or even Herod, but falsely imply their total devotion to this secular state as loyal "patriots" to serve its agenda, having just moments before called for the release of an insurrectionist intending to overthrow Roman power in their area, but such an indefensible incongruity served their purposes at the moment. *Religious Right leaders and their flock do the same today, appealing to secular "patriotism," and challenging the same of those with which they disagree, while distancing themselves from it in a retreating "bunker mentality" when their party is not in power (while plotting for the Empire to "strike back"). Meanwhile, they act and think as if they are either being ignorant of or more likely ignore Christ's teachings in this incident that "if my kingdom were of this world, then would my servants fight" (John 18:36), and the clear and consistent Bible teaching of Christ's followers being pilgrims in this world, and citizens of a heavenly kingdom.*

The saddest aspect of their "psy-ops" is the effectiveness of how they turned the people 180 degrees to hold contempt for Jesus and the principals He represented. Matthew says that "the chief priests and elders persuaded the multitude that they should ask Barabbas, and destroy Jesus" (Matt. 27:20). They riled the people up into a non-thinking, non-reflective fervor, getting them to continuously chant, "Crucify Him!" as a patriotic chant against a demogogued scapegoat (sounding a lot like chants of "Lock her up!" at the 2016 Republican convention). They ignored even the secular governor's appeal as to the lack of legal charges against Jesus, and the injustice of their claims, to the point in their delirium of proudly claiming (like any Value Voter's Summit frenzy), "His blood be on us, and on our children" (Matt. 27:25). *Even today, Religious Right followers do not care about civil rights, human rights, the downtrodden, justice, laws or even the Golden Rule—all as illustrated by their unflinching support and justification of the scoundrel and law-evader President Donald Trump and his agenda, and his predecessors like Dick Cheney and Richard Nixon—and are ready to use whatever talking points their religious leaders and conservative/big business allies give them to chant, regardless of what it reveals about their Christian walk. This is the job of Religious Right and conservative talk radio and cable news, and they do this job supremely well, because it is like "shooting fish in a barrel."*

Why do they do this? What is the fuel and motivation that undergirds these positions, and all the effort and expense justified to sell them to the Religious Right suggestible flock and others, as the "activating ingredient" of the "leaven of the Pharisees"? The foundation of motivation is revealed in the pages of the Bible, but lightly regarded by most Christians, and almost never reflected upon in explaining their curious positions today versus those of the early church, but which overshadows all the remaining content of this book. After Jesus taught about this topic and its central impact on our thinking and position in the Kingdom, the Bible states that "Now the *Pharisees, who were lovers of money,* also heard all these things, and they derided Him" (Luke 16:14, New King James Version (NKJV)) (emphasis added). The King James translation says they were "covetous"—a state of always wanting more wealth and possessions, including its acquisition of and envy of those who possessed it, as an overarching motivation and preoccupation. *Does any other word better describe our Western/American materialistic, consumerist culture, and the Religious Right community that sanctifies it, or the economic system known as capitalism that makes its societies elevate greed and covetousness as its highest virtues, and provides the means for the elites to pursue it in unabated fashion?*

Since the times of the building of impressive Christian churches and the advent of wealthy (and thus influential) congregations (as in the early Roman church) and the institutional acceptance of Christianity as the "state religion" by Constantine, to the production-obsessed Reformation "Protestant work ethic" and the individualistic, Darwinistic "every man for himself," no-holds-barred economies of the Puritans and early Americans, the Western/American conservative church has allowed this "leaven" to infiltrate and dominate its priorities, and serve as a filter for all its biblical doctrines. *As we shall see, this covetousness and money-obsession dominates or influences almost every domestic, foreign policy, budgetary, economic and even social issue and position espoused by the Religious Right, if one indeed "follows the money" and even its covert, indirect role as catalysts, as the base undergirding the "leaven" of the "gospel" successfully proclaimed in talk radio and cable news.*

This passage and the elements of Christ's teachings that generated this response from the Pharisees arose from His parable of Shrewd Servant. This is arguably the most perplexing of Christ's parables, and His teachings at large, for theologians and Bible students to agree upon as to its intended spiritual principles to universally apply, and the extent to which the lessons were meant to be applicable. It tells the story of a wealthy "lord" who discovered his steward of his resources was incompetent and wasteful of his goods, leading him to declare that his role of steward was to be discontinued imminently. Panicking over his inability to make an honest or humble living, the steward hatches a quick plan to use his final days in the role to at least garner friends amongst the lord's debtors, by using his authority to write down their debts to him, and in return receive favor from them when he was dismissed. Instead of his arrest when the lord discovered this, the lord commended him for his cleverness and wisdom. Jesus added that the "children of this world" are "wiser than the children of light" by means of their practical acceptance of reality and their realistic options (Luke 16:8); *this should serve as a sobering word to coddled, naive and sheltered fundamentalists who cloister themselves and their children in geographical or social "bunkers" of their own kind, thinking they are impressing God by shielding themselves from "pagan" thinking and the realities of surviving in the real fallen world, and in turn living in an unsustainable fantasy world of their internal incestuous religious ideals.* Jesus told the listeners to "make to yourselves friends of the mammon of unrighteousness," knowing that "when ye fail," those whose affections you bought might "receive you into everlasting habitations" (v. 9). Jesus said that if you could not handle "unrighteous mammon" wisely, why would He entrust them with "true riches" (v. 11), nor be given their own wealth if they could not handle someone else's (v. 12). This led Jesus to the seminal statement that "put the period" to the teaching that led to the Pharisees' contempt:

> No servant can serve two masters: for either he will hate the one, and love the other; or else he will hold to the one, and despise the other. Ye cannot serve God and mammon. (Luke 16:13)

One could make some pretty deep inferences from this parable, of wider applicability, to ponder: that the Pharisees and Jewish leaders were given stewardship of the riches of God's law and spiritual guidance, and had failed in managing it with surrounding "debtor" nations and peoples, or (as I like to consider) that we as Christians are given stewardship of the "ministry of reconciliation" of the outside world to God (2 Cor. 5:18), and having been given the Holy Spirit and the authority to forgive sins (John 20:23), we are commended for canceling others' debts to God as if they were our own (and sometimes when they are in fact owed to us). However, in this case we will focus on the most direct reference to the Pharisees and their history with money. Jesus here does not directly address their value of their pursuit of wealth, or means of doing so, but He insinuates that while God may have allowed them to be successful in such endeavors, *they were not even smart enough to use it to make friends amongst the people, by sharing a little bit like Robin Hood.* They were rather known for being tight-fisted and greedy as well as covetous, which further led to contempt of them by the people. This "leaven" of greed and unconcern of others, fed by capitalism and "every man for himself" stratification of wealth, led to the French aristocrats losing everything in the Revolution when they told the poor without bread to "eat cake," when the Russian czar ignored the poor, the excesses of Dickens' London, the Gilded Age robber barons and the Roaring Twenties banks and industrialists as it led to the Great Depression and societal unrest—all incidents where greed and "not sharing the wealth" led them to lose it all, when the commoners were pushed to the wall. *Capitalist conservatives today are of the same mind—turning their backs on sharing the wealth from their business schemes, with the workers and others not blessed with ready capital to bankroll their ventures, and encouraging the increasing disparity of wealth and feudal society, seeking short-term payoffs and ignoring their long-term doom because of their excesses.*

When the Pharisees derided him then, for not only exposing their real love and devotion to accumulating capital, but more so their refusal to share God's blessing of it with others and thus laying the seeds for their future demise, Jesus continued the discussion on the spot in this passage with a story of a "rich man" who was dressed well and ate upscale cuisine every day (Luke 16:19). Conservatives and Religious Right figures today would publicly portray him as a "success story" and "an example of God's blessing and anointing," and one to emulate, having him speak at their pulpits, and sell his "success" books (all best-sellers) in the church bookstore. He likely would be inspiring the Christians at the Value Voters Summit, Tea Party meetings or other Christian political gatherings. Christian filmmakers would likely make his "riches to riches" story a movie to see in theaters and churches. He also followed the official conservative social policies of libertarian/*laissez faire* capitalism and acknowledged that it was not the goal of government to take care of the poor (nor the church to do so either, in their view—particularly those outside their walls), and that the "lazy poor" (i.e., all the poor) should quit scamming the system and rather pull themselves up by their bootstraps, starting their own businesses, getting large bank loans to flip houses at high profits (and establishing a large line of credit to tap), and finding cheap migrant labor of their own to exploit, or sweatshops overseas to get cheap goods. We see he directly employed what conservative icon Ronald Reagan coined as "trickle down economics"—the tactic of giving lots of money, tax credits and breaks, government contracts and foreign stakes for corporations (secured and defended by poor American soldiers), and letting the wealth "trickle down" to the middle class and poor in the furs and paintings the rich supposedly buy from them, the illegal immigrant labor used for their landscaping, and tips for the car washers, doormen and resort cleaning women. *In his case, the "rich man" literally let the crumbs from his table "trickle down" ironically to a pitiful poor beggar,* full of sores, named Lazarus, who was laid at his outer gate, because he couldn't come inside (v. 20).

It is curious to note that from Jesus' telling of the "heaven's eye" view of these affairs, that while in the world (and our own religious circles) the rich man would have had a world-famous name as a celebrity and sought after, while the beggar would be ignored as one of many nameless faces, in Jesus' view the beggar had a real name—"Lazarus"—and was well-known, while the "rich man" was anonymous. The rich man also, unlike the "Good Samaritan" outsider, evidently believed in the conservative philosophy of "privatized" health care, not supplemented by the government because no one is "entitled" to it, therefore the dogs licking Lazarus' wounds were the only "indigent care" or welfare Lazarus was entitled to. We see that in this world—just as the capitalists and their conservative and Religious Right supporters would have it—the rich man and his colleagues held all the cards, but upon Lazarus' death, God sent His powerful angels to personally escort Lazarus to "Abraham's bosom" (v. 22). This was a pre-Atonement place of post-death comfort, awaiting Christ's redemption, whereas the rich man died as well, as both rich and poor suffered the same earthly fate regardless of money, but their destinies were quite different. In opposition to the capitalistic utopia, in the eternal world—*the one that really matters*—the rich man now found himself in torment, and *he himself became a beggar*, asking for Lazarus to have mercy and cool his parched tongue with water. In essence he was asking for "entitlements" and "welfare" for his pitiful, helpless need, but Abraham said that the post-death gulf was too great, *unlike the proximity he could have had to Lazarus in earthly life.* He then appealed to have Lazarus sent to his five brothers to warn them not to follow his uncaring life toward the poor and needy, and its ramifications; Abraham said that if they did not respond to "Moses and the prophets" (Biblical law and prophecy), they would not respond to one from the dead (v. 31). Abraham knew that the warnings of ignoring the poor and needy were throughout both types of Biblical writings, and for today's Religious Right *you can add the Gospels as a testimony of a "dead man" brought back to life, which they also continue to ignore as well.* Some scholars have also pointed out that Jesus may have been referring to Caiaphas and his father-in-law Annas, who both served high priests and judges over the poor Jesus in rigged trials. Annas had five sons (all later high priests) as Caiaphas' "brothers," who persecuted Christians throughout the early church period up to the dawn of the fall of Jerusalem, the last priest unjustly stoning Jesus' brother James (causing the Romans to remove him). The Gospels also reported that the Jewish leaders sought to kill the Christ-resurrected Lazarus (John 12:9–11, 17–19), which would make sense, since his very existence in resurrected form would disprove their Sadducee disbelief in the resurrection or afterlife. If this allusion is valid, even the testimony of the historically-risen Lazarus could not (and did not) prevent the eternal fate of these rich, stubborn, afterlife-denying religious rulers.

One gets the distinct impression from the Bible and other sources that there was a lengthy feud between Jesus and His followers and the "House of Annas" (albeit one-sided from a power and threat standpoint), which extended throughout Christ's ministry and for a number of decades. The sense given from the Bible, and Jewish and secular academic historians is that although the Romans removed Annas from the high priest position, eventually replacing him with his various sons or his son-in-law Caiaphas, Annas' role as a "mafia family don" of the high priest aristocracy, calling the shots through his titular family members, appears apparent, as the Jews still saw him as the "high priest" although they acquiesced to the Romans with having Rome-picked family members as figureheads. The 1906 *Jewish Encyclopedia* entry on "Annas"[20] states that "The Anan family is referred to in the Talmud (Pes. 57a) as having influence, but using it against the interests of the people." Shortly after they sent Christ to his death, Caiaphas was removed from office approximately 37 CE, about the same time Pilate was recalled back to Rome to account for a massacre in Palestine, as he disappeared from the pages of history. The online *Catholic Encyclopedia* entry on "Annas"[21] states that "The 'house of Annas,' wealthy and unscrupulous, is pronounced accursed in the Talmud, together with 'the corrupt leaders of the priesthood', whose presence defiled the sanctuary." The 1915 *International Standard Bible Encyclopedia* entry on "Annas"[22] states (without giving the author's sources) that

> He belonged to the Sadducean aristocracy, and, like others of that class, he seems to have been arrogant, astute, ambitious and enormously wealthy. He and his family were proverbial for their rapacity and greed. The chief source of their wealth seems to have been the sale of requisites for the temple sacrifices, such as sheep, doves, wine and oil, which they carried on in the four famous "booths of the sons of Annas" on the Mount of Olives, with a branch within the precincts of the temple itself. During the great feasts, they were able to extort high monopoly prices for theft goods. Hence, our Lord's strong denunciation of those who made the house of prayer "a den of robbers" (Matt. 11:15–19), and the curse in the Talmud, "Woe to the family of Annas! Woe to the serpent-like hisses." (Pes 57a)

The 1923 edition of the *New International Encyclopedia* entry on "Annas" makes a similar statement about the source of high priest Annas' wealth, stating that "The wealth of 'the house of Annas' was to some extent derived from the booths, where they provided all kinds of materials for sacrifice. By this monopoly they made the temple 'a den of robbers'."[23] The entry on

"Annas"[24] in the 1911 *Hastings Dictionary of the Bible* states that "The immense wealth of these Sadducean aristocrats was, in part at least, derived from 'the booths of the sons of Annas,' which monopolized the sale of all kinds of materials for sacrifice...It was the sons of Annas who made God's house 'a den of robbers'," and cited a source stating that "forty years before the destruction of the temple the Sanhedrin banished itself from the chamber of hewn stone, and established itself in the booths," and that "the booths were destroyed, three years before the destruction of the temple, in the same year in which the younger Ananus was murdered" (evidently during the War with Rome in which Ananus took part). The oft-sided passage from "Pesachim 57a" of the Talmud that allegedly refers to Annas (the senior's name also alternatively spelled as "Ananus" in the literature) and his family was apparently written by a first century Jewish sage prior to the destruction of the Temple, about the high priest dynasty at the time, which certainly would pertain to the "sons of Annas." He writes,

> Woe is me due to the High Priests of the house of Baitos, woe is me due to their clubs. Woe is me due to the High Priests of the house of Ḥanin; woe is me due to their whispers and the rumors they spread. Woe is me due to the High Priests of the house of Katros; woe is me due to their pens that they use to write lies. Woe is me due to the servants of the High Priests of the house of Yishmael ben Piakhi; woe is me due to their fists. The power of these households stemmed from the fact that the fathers were High Priests, and their sons were the Temple treasurers, and their sons-in-law were Temple overseers [amarkalin]. And their servants strike the people with clubs, and otherwise act inappropriately[25]. ["Hanin" supposedly translates to "Ananus" or "Annas" in Greek, and the other names of "houses" pertained to other families of high priests who served from the time of Herod the Great, through Jesus' life and that of the early church.]

While the specific "house of Annas" may have made their wealth from fleecing the religious flock with their spiritual "products" of piety and religious observation (like the "prayer cloths," anointing oils and fetishistic figures, icons and other idolatrous "spiritually blessed" paraphernalia sold by today's religious celebrities on television and elsewhere), the aristocratic wealthy families that comprised the Sadducee priestly caste, abetted by their intermarrying into other wealthy families, already had access to innumerable sources of revenue. This "wealth class" status that controlled the revenue-generating monopolies in their primordial capitalistic societal structure allowed them to maintain an elevation of their elite social status in their economically-feudalistic society (as today's society is rapidly becoming), and to see themselves both as role models and contemptuous of others, and to focus on temporal wealth and luxury and provide religious justification for it. As such, they functioned like a restricted, elite "prosperity gospel" gated community, telling each other the spiritual justification of their elect status and rightful lowly status of the predestined "riff raff" commoners, although today's democratic, "land of opportunity" American variant offers that to all who are willing to buy in (and buy the books, CDs and "faith promises," of course). This is not only reflected in the lavish lifestyles of televangelists, para-church organization leaders and top-tier ecclesiastical leadership; many (but certainly not all) local pastors (from predominantly "mega churches" and similar ilk, but not exclusively to them) and prominent members of their flocks and other religious groups emphasize their physical material assets as evidence of "God's blessings" and affirmations, as "King's kids" who convince themselves and others that they "deserve the best," and the popular "dominionism" teachings that teach the Christian's duty to conquer the "seven mountains" of earthly power—including finance, business and politics—as a rite of earthly domination and destiny, much like their Sadducee forbearers.

The highly-regarded 1906 *Jewish Encyclopedia*, in its online entry concerning the "Sadducees,"[26] has the following to add about their history and nature, saying they

> degenerated under the influence of Hellenism, especially during the rule of the Seleucidæ, when to be a follower of the priestly aristocracy was tantamount to being a worldly-minded Epicurean. The name…became in the course of time a party name applied to all the aristocratic circles connected with the high priests by marriage and other social relations, as only the highest patrician families intermarried with the priests officiating at the Temple in Jerusalem (Ḳid. iv. 5; Sanh. iv. 2; comp. Josephus, "B. J." ii. 8, § 14)….The Sadducees, says Josephus, have none but the rich on their side ("Ant." xiii. 10, § 6)….Among the Rabbis the following legend circulated: Antigonus of Soko, successor of Simon the Just, the last of the "Men of the Great Synagogue," and consequently living at the time of the influx of Hellenistic ideas, taught the maxim, "Be not like servants who serve their master for the sake of wages [lit. 'a morsel'], but be rather like those who serve without thought of receiving wages" (Ab. i. 3); whereupon two of his disciples, Zadok and Boethus, mistaking the high ethical purport of the maxim, arrived at the conclusion that there was no future retribution, saying, "What

servant would work all day without obtaining his due reward in the evening?" Instantly they broke away from the Law and lived in great luxury, using many silver and gold vessels at their banquets; and they established schools which declared the enjoyment of this life to be the goal of man…These two schools were called, after their founders, Sadducees and Boethusians (Ab. R. N. v.)….Representing the nobility, power, and wealth ("Ant." xviii. 1, § 4), *they had centered their interests in political life, of which they were the chief rulers. Instead of sharing the Messianic hopes of the Pharisees, who committed the future into the hand of God, they took the people's destiny into their own hands, fighting or negotiating with the heathen nations just as they thought best, while having as their aim their own temporary welfare and worldly success.* This is the meaning of what Josephus chooses to term their disbelief in fate and divine providence ("B. J." ii. 8, § 14; "Ant." xiii. 5 § 9)…As the logical consequence of the preceding view, they would not accept the Pharisaic doctrine of the resurrection (Sanh. 90b; Mark xii. 12; Ber. ix. 5, "Minim"), which was a national rather than an individual hope. As to the immortality of the soul, they seem to have denied this as well (see Hippolytus, "Refutatio," ix. 29; "Ant." x. 11, § 7)….According to Acts xxiii. 8, they denied also the existence of angels and demons. This probably means that *they did not believe in the Essene practice of incantation and conjuration in cases of disease, and were therefore not concerned with the Angelology and Demonology derived from Babylonia and Persia*….In the New Testament the Sadducees are mentioned in Matt. iii. 7 and xvi. 1, 6, 11, where they are identical with the Herodians (Mark xii. 13), that is, the Boethusians (Matt. xxii. 23, 34; Mark xii. 18; Acts iv. 1, v. 17, xxiii. 6–8). In John's Gospel they simply figure as "the chief priests" (vii. 23, 45; xi. 47, 57; xviii. 3). (emphasis added)

It should be noted that while the Jewish Encyclopedia garners the highest widespread regard for its academic accuracy and rigor, it likely reflects a modern rabbinic view that leans towards the Pharisaic worldview and perspective on history of their spiritual forbearers.

The eminent Jewish historian Josephus also wrote about Caiaphas and the house of Annas, as the primary extra-biblical source of their exploits. He recounts how Ananus' son Ananus II used the change of Roman power locally from procurator Felix to Albinus (en route from Rome) to quickly convene a Sanhedrin illegally to order and conduct the stoning of Christian leader James (brother of Jesus), leading the newly-arriving Roman official to remove him from office[27]. He further writes that the now-deposed Ananus II became one leaders of the rebelling Jewish nation against Rome by the end of 66 CE (p. 290), repairing the walls of Jerusalem, building war-engines and even sending out armies (p. 292), and suggests that he led a people's resistance to the Zealots who had led them into war, driving them into the interior of the Temple as a refuge (p. 317). However, a Zealot spy escaped and was able to raise an army of nearby Idumeans to rescue them (p. 318). Having been led inside the walls, the Idumeans killed Ananus (his corpse left without burial) and thousands more, until they were shown that the Zealots had hoodwinked them, and they returned home (pp. 319–320). *Thus, the parties that had played a collaborative role with the House of Annas in the disposal of Jesus—the Zealots like Jesus Barabbas that Caiaphas sought released and the Idumeans (the people of King Herod)—both betrayed and ended the line of aristocratic rule of their family (and thus plundered and dispersed over a generation of their accumulated ill-gotten wealth), within a generation of Jesus' betrayal.*

Skeptics of Jewish and Christian historical narratives often look on controversial central figures like a "Caiaphas" and their supposed existence or biographic details with a raised eyebrow of suspicion, much like the historical King David and others. However, like the recent archeological findings confirming the details of David, Pontius Pilate and others, recent discoveries strongly support the biblical and other ancient document narratives concerning this man. In 2016 the Israeli newspaper *Ha'aretz* reported[28] that a recent archeological dig had uncovered an opulent (for the time) home of what must have been one of the elite from 2,000 years ago— "most probably the priestly ruling class." It featured an ornate ceiling, multiple bread oven, a *mikveh* ritual bathing pool, and even a private bathtub—a luxury for only the rich in those days, and otherwise "have so far only been found at King Herod's palaces in Masada and Jericho, and in the so-called 'Priestly Mansion' in the Jewish Quarter of the Old City of Jerusalem." They quote the co-director of the excavation Shimon Gibson as saying that "It's clear from the finds that the people living here were wealthy, aristocrats or perhaps even priests...Caiaphas' house has been located. It's up on the hill not far from our site," and the article adds that "A ritual stone cup with a priestly inscription, used for purification rituals, also found there supports the archaeologist's theory that this area was the Priestly Quarter of ancient Jerusalem." A professor (and excavation co-leader) from the University of North Carolina is quoted to say that, concerning its connection to the Annas family of priests, "perhaps these are the homes of that extended priestly dynasty," as the article quotes the Talmudic passages concerning the family we have already discussed, and adds Josephus' observation that Annas was "a great hoarder up of money," and notes the discovery there of unique sea snail shells that indicated the possession there of valuable purple and turquoise dyes extracted from the snails. They add that "The extraordinarily grandiose buildings with towers, gates, barracks and magnificent gardens were all part of the Herodian propaganda endeavor. In fact, Gibson discovered that the floor level of Herod's palace was higher than God's temple on the opposite hill."

In 1992 *The New York Times*[29] and other world newspapers reported on the archeological discovery of what they understood to be the actual tomb of Caiaphas, with his bones housed in an ornately-carved ossuary box. They add that "It was during Caiaphas's reign, the Talmud says, that the Jewish high court, the Sanhedrin, was removed from the Temple Mount, thus weakening its power. And it was Caiaphas, according to the Gospels, who encouraged money changers and the sellers of animals to enter the main court of the Temple, strengthening his control of trade....In the Gospels, Jesus' expulsion of the vendors and money lenders from the temple is a central event: 'It is written, My house shall be the house of prayer,' Jesus is quoted as saying in Matthew 21:13. 'But ye have made it a den of thieves.' This may have provided the crucial conflict between him and Caiaphas."

It is almost certain that this writer is correct, for Jesus definitely "picked a scab" of Annas' family, or a figurative punch right into the nose of their hated religious money-making operation in God's name, when Jesus, unbeknownst to most casual Christian Bible students, apparently "cleared out the money-changers tables" and the "den of thieves" that was economically exploiting the women and poor with inflated prices, *on more than one occasion*. The first incident is reported in John chapter 2 (vv. 13–16), and appears to occur around Passover (the time when the most money was to be made for the required sacrifices then) just after Christ launched His ministry with His first miracle at the wedding at Cana. The ruckus He caused was certain to have put this poor Galilean rabbi on the "bad list" of the Annas-Caiaphas high priest family syndicate, not for rebuking them on theological matters, but hitting them where it hurts many religious leaders the worst—*their pocketbook*. Then, as He experienced His "triumphal entry" into Jerusalem on Palm Sunday, right before His last Passover, He conducted an "encore" by then driving out the money changers again, calling the operation a "den of thieves" (Matt. 21:13, Mark 11:17), after previously having called it a "house of merchandise," and as a result "the scribes and the chief priests heard it, and sought how they might destroy him" (Mark 11:18). Those present knew He was quoting from one of His favorite people, the prophet Jeremiah, who had told these same crowds in Jerusalem centuries before on behalf of their God, "Is this house, which is called by my name, become a den of robbers in your eyes?" (Jeremiah 7:11)—where in the same speech God told them "if ye thoroughly execute judgment between a man and his neighbour; if ye oppress not the stranger, the fatherless, and the widow, and shed not innocent blood in this place," and stay true to Him, "then I will cause you to dwell in this place, in the land I gave to your fathers, for ever and ever" (vv. 5–7). Jesus hit on the two points that would get Him definitely killed when He knew His "time had come," within a week's time at Passion week, by going to see Lazarus at the start of the week (John 12) to reinvigorate interest in resurrection (which the Sadducees hated) and the power of God to come, and to interrupt the money operations at the critical money-making time. While the "Religious Right"-style Pharisees, being pious and "super-religious," were not of the aristocracy (yet) and as blatantly hedonistic as the Sadducees, Jesus exposed what everyone else knew in Israel, that these pious hypocrites were also obsessed with money; Jesus said that one of their operations was to "devour widows' houses" (Matt. 23:14) (possibly by any number of fundraising or service-charging schemes, or creative use of "oral law" to transfer their wealth to those in league with them), and they were "covetous" or "lovers of money" (Luke 16:14), as ambitious "wealth class wannabes."

Many of the leaders of "God's people" still look for money rackets to take advantage of their position (as this and the next book in the series will suggest) as well as the people, and Jesus will continue to expose them and overturn their tables and get in the way of their works, or through those He appoints for this important but thankless mission, which will raise the ire (and maybe lawsuits and threats) from them just as Jesus experienced in His day.

Like many of our Religious Right leaders (and many Christian pastors and their parishioners as well), the Pharisees liked the status and respect that money and social position brought them, and how it was important in religious circles. Jesus said they "love the uppermost rooms at feasts, and the chief seats in synagogues" (Matt. 23:6), and being called "Rabbi" (v. 7), while they "devour widows' houses" (v. 14) like televangelists fleecing the widows for "faith promises," and swear by the gold in the Temple as opposed to the Temple itself, to show what they really valued (v. 16). Jesus showed His zeal in combating economic exploitation by "God's people" and in His Father's name when He overturned the money changers tables in the Temple, possibly because of how deadly such behavior was in impeding the reconciliation of God and man, both in denying the women and the poor a means to affordably purchase the items needed to honor God's law, and due to the cynicism toward religion it understandably bred like a rampant cancer. This mindset and imperative of the Lord may have been foretold by His own mother Mary when she prophesied, "He hath put down the mighty from [their] seats, and exalted them of low degree. He hath filled the hungry with good things; and the rich he hath sent empty away" (Luke 1:52–53). Jesus thought that addressing financial corruption and exploitation by religious leaders was not something to shake one's head over and overlook, or even worse try to ignore, wallpaper over or excuse. He was so adamant that it was as bad as teaching heresy or worship of false gods, that His own disciples saw Him get more animated during these incidents than any other time in His ministry, and the Bible says they remembered the Psalmist in Psalm 69, who said, "The zeal of thine house has eaten me up" (John 2:17), because to Jesus at least, *this was serious business.* It also was serious to the apostles and the early church too; when church members Ananias and Sapphira ran a scam by bringing only part of their asset sale to donate but misrepresented its value (merely frowned on and blamed on tax accountants these days), Peter told them "Satan filled thine heart" and they had lied to God, causing God to strike them both dead. When new convert Simon the sorcerer tried to buy the giving of the Holy Spirit from Peter and John to showcase in his own money-making religious show, they told him, "Thy money perish with thee."

The chief, priests, scribes and Pharisees also used their money not only to elevate themselves, but also to cover up their misdeeds and to discreetly fund operations that would not comport with their pious persona. We all know the story of how they paid the apostle Judas thirty pieces of silver (around $200–$600, or around six weeks' wages—not much difference than Russian intelligence pays some U.S. spies, or the FBI pays would-be terrorists in stings) to lead them to Jesus under cover of darkness, because they were too cowardly to arrest Him in front of the people, with no real charges (much as the Stasi secret police did in East Germany, and elsewhere in authoritarian regimes). Note that they referred to it as "blood money"— that paid by murderers for the privilege of killing victims without further consequence; their own Mosaic Law (Num. 35:31) forbid such a practice for murder, but the Law is usually important to religious leaders only when it affects their public relations image. Scripture also notes that the Sanhedrin paid off the Roman soldiers that guarded Jesus' body, who had told them that an angel had rolled away the stone as He resurrected, so they would rather tell the public that His own disciples stole the body at night (Matt. 28:13); there was no good explanation on how they could overcome Rome's finest, but the Jewish leaders said that they would cover them with their bosses (v. 14).

This is not unique to the ancient Jewish leaders, and not uncommon with Religious Right leaders today, from pastors to para-church ministries and global leaders, with payoffs made to keep mouths shut. In recent days, it was in the news how Liberty University President Jerry Falwell Jr. had Trump "fixer" Michael Cohen (an old friend) take action to get rid of sexually lewd pictures of the Falwells in the possession of someone in Florida, as revealed in secretly taped phone conversations of Cohen (with him describing the pictures as "terrible," and retaining possession of one). While he intimidated the possessor to relinquish them, it is not known if money exchanged hands, but after his success Falwell Jr. enthusiastically endorsed Cohen's boss Donald Trump for President, turning away from his Sen. Cruz endorsement just before the Iowa caucuses, according to *Reuters.*[30] In March 2016, as the presidential primaries were just underway, Liberty University President Falwell Jr. was interviewed by their campus newspaper *The Liberty Champion* about Trump, which can be read online at the time of this writing.[31] He said that he and his family came to campaign with Trump in Iowa before the caucuses when Trump agreed to his demand to pay Falwell's family to get there. He said he had texted Sean Hannity beforehand to get advice on leading his rally, and Hannity gave Falwell the questions to ask. The next day Trump asked him to continue to campaign with him, and offered him a ride on the opulent Trump plane, which really impressed him. He writes, "We went to the airport, and there was Trump's 757 all lit up on the runway…He brought us up front. He's got this big living room with this big screen TV. He's got a master bedroom he showed us. Then he let my son and his wife actually sit in the cockpit to take off because my son's a pilot…Then he put on a concert. He found out that when I grew up in the 70s, I was an Elton John fan. So, he put the concert on the big screen. He was doing it all himself. He was the one serving the food. He was the one waiting on us." (Note that secular artists like the gay Elton John would probably not be allowed to be listened to at the university he presides over.) *He appears to have had no idea, or did not care, that he was being pandered to by Trump to garner the Religious Right vote at a critical time, possibly displaying an example of the "Christian discernment" he wished to teach at his school.* He added concerning Trump that "I think he is what our Founding Fathers envisioned," and that "he has been extremely successful in the private sector," and "thinks Trump's skills will translate into an ability to help the U.S. recover from its almost $20 trillion debt" (although within two years from taking office, Trump's administration *added* $2 trillion to that debt amount (after he had promised to eliminate the entire federal debt in eight years).[32]

Falwell added concerning Trump that "He's perfectly suited to serve as the political leader, and I think that gives evangelicals comfort." The cited article notes that Falwell wrote in *Facebook* in January that "Let's stop trying to choose the political leaders who we believe are the most godly." The campus newspaper adds that "Liberty cannot legally endorse a candidate for presidency and keep its nonprofit, tax-exempt status as a university." They note at the presidential primary voting at the University, of the 1,215 votes cast, 90 went for Trump. Falwell expressed one of his deepest spiritual concerns of the election, beyond economic vitality, when he stated that "If the wrong person is elected this fall, then the Second Amendment will be in jeopardy almost immediately." Ironically, when the sports editor of the same campus newspaper wrote an article noting that Trump's bragging statements of assaulting women were serious, *Falwell Jr. himself had the article removed from the newspaper*, although Falwell had previously released a statement regarding students criticizing Trump that "It is a testament to the fact that Liberty University promotes the free expression of ideas unlike many major universities where political correctness prevents conservative students from speaking out," leading to a letter signed by 2,500 students criticizing Falwell's support.[33]

Earlier reports that the person wielding sexually controversial pictures of the Falwells resided in Florida led me to a hunch that it might be related to the "pool boy" the Falwells had invested in a "gay-friendly" hostel in Miami with (which I had written about in my blog roughly a year ago previously), and a June 2019 article in the *New York Times*[34] appears to bolster that assertion. There they write that the incident "features the friendship between Mr. Falwell, his wife and a former pool attendant at the Fontainebleau hotel in Miami Beach; the family's investment in a gay-friendly youth hostel; purported sexually revealing photographs involving the Falwells; and an attempted hush-money arrangement engineered by the president's former fixer, Michael Cohen. The revelations have arisen from a lawsuit filed against the Falwells in Florida; the investigation into Mr. Cohen by federal prosecutors in New York; and the gonzo-style tactics of the comedian and actor Tom Arnold." They note that in 2012 the Falwells stayed at Miami's Fontainebleau resort, which they explained "was now the stomping grounds of the Kardashians, Paris Hilton and Lady Gaga, known for allowing topless sunbathing and for a cavernous nightclub that one travel guide described as '30,000 square feet of unadulterated fun'." There they became close to the 21-year-old pool attendant Giancarlo Granda, who later joined them for hiking and water skiing in Virginia; in months they helped him start a business in Florida. Some of his other real estate friends found a Miami youth hostel for them to buy, which also had a restaurant and liquor store, which the Falwells agreed to finance, as the Falwells flew Granda to Liberty to meet Trump. They note that at Trump's 2012 Liberty address Falwell stated that Trump was "one of the greatest visionaries of our time" who "single-handedly forced President Obama to release his birth certificate." In turn Trump shared his secrets to winning in business and life to the Christian Liberty students, including the advice to "Get Even" and "Always have a prenuptial agreement," although he added, "I won't say it here, because you people don't get divorced."

They completed the purchase of the Miami Hostel in 2013 (the article noting its sometimes being listed in promotional ads as being "gay-friendly"), but their involvement became public in a 2017 *Politico* article (which I profiled on my blog) written by a Liberty graduate who visited there, noting a sign on the front gate requiring "No Religion" on the premises. Inside he noted pamphlets promoting Tootsie's Cabaret, which featured "74,000 square feet of adult entertainment and FULL NUDITY." A later sign there stated that the hostel was not responsible for accidents, "especially if you are drunk." Of the $4.7 million price paid for it, $3.8 million came from a Virginia bank the Falwells used to finance Liberty University; Falwell claimed that their personal contribution was a $1.8 million loan, while their son Trey Falwell managed the business, with Granda as co-manager, and Falwell's wife as another member of the company. A dispute with other partners led to a lawsuit. Michael Cohen said that he became "like family" with the Falwells by that time, and used Liberty's deputy chief information officer for the Trump campaign, including manipulating the results of two online polls on *CNBC* and the *Drudge Report* to favor Trump, as confessed by the man himself to the *Wall Street Journal.* Most importantly, the earlier lawsuit over the hostel brought to light "compromising photos" of the Falwells held by the litigants. After Cohen's threats, the litigants actually changed their legal names. Cohen told comedian Tom Arnold in a secretly recorded conversation that the photos may have come off of "Jerry's phone" and involving both spouses, and added that "the evangelicals are kinkier than Tom Arnold," and stated that "I was going to pay him, and I was going to get the negatives and do an agreement where they turn over all the technology that has the photographs or anything like that, any copies." Falwell eventually endorsed Trump shortly thereafter at Cohen's request. In turn "Mr. Trump sought to make Mr. Falwell his secretary of education."

An interview Falwell Jr. did for the *Washington Post* at the beginning of 2019 clarified his views further.[35] He explained that "It's a distortion of the teaching of Christ to say Jesus taught love and forgiveness and therefore the United States as a nation should be loving and forgiving." When asked, "Is there anything President Trump could do that would endanger that support from you or other evangelical leaders?," Falwell replied, "No," and then added, "I know that he only wants what's best for this country, and I know anything he does, it may not be ideologically 'conservative', but it's going to be what's best for this country." He also stated, "In the heavenly kingdom the responsibility is to treat others as you'd like to be treated. In the earthly kingdom, the responsibility is to choose leaders who will do what's best for your country." Importantly, he added, *"A poor person never gave anyone a job"* (emphasis added). He closed by saying, "A lot of the people who criticized me, because they had a hard time stomaching supporting someone who owned casinos and strip clubs or whatever, a lot them have come around and said, 'Yeah, you were right.' Some of the most prominent evangelicals in the country have said, 'Jerry, we thought you were crazy, but now we understand'."

Circumstances in 2019 involving Trump led to Falwell revealing more about his internal thinking and priorities. *ABC News* reported[36] that President Trump made an unannounced stop at McLean Bible Church in Virginia, telling reporters just before his arrival that he was coming to "pray for the victims and community of Virginia Beach." He arrived straight from his golf club and joined Pastor Platt, but neither of them mentioned the victims of the Virginia Beach shooting while on stage. When many of his congregants later complained, Platt released an open letter explaining that he had to make a split-second decision, since he was told only minutes before his arrival, and stated that "My aim was in no way to endorse the president, his policies, or his party," noting that "some within the church, for a variety of valid reasons, are hurt that I made this decision." In response, according to *Christian News,*[37] Falwell Jr. tweeted that "Sorry to be crude, but pastors like @plattdavid need to grow a pair," which led to complaints, and Falwell eventually removed it. Ironically, Platt was known for the book *Radical,* *"which discusses abandoning materialism and the quest for the American dream"* (emphasis added). He later asked his congregation, "Would you pray with me for gospel seed that was sown today to bear fruit in the president's heart?" Falwell's tweets on June 4, 2019 still remain, stating to his Christian critics that, "The faculty, students and campus pastor @davidnasser of @LibertyU are the ones who keep LU strong spiritually as the best Christian univ in the world. While I am proud to be a conservative Christian, my job is to keep LU successful academically, financially and in athletics,"[38] and that *"I have never been a minister.* UVA-trained lawyer *and commercial real estate developer for 20 yr*s. Univ president for last 12 years—student body tripled to 100000+/*endowment from 0 to $2 billion and $1.6B new construction in those 12 years"*[39] (emphasis added), *thereby revealing the real materialistic goals he has for his "Christian" university as its leader.*

No public incident better illustrates the contrast between a major conservative American Christian leader becoming a "Nicodemus" and bravely beginning to question the societal positions of his fellow Christian leaders and their departure from the teachings of Jesus and the Bible, and that of his ideological rival, Jerry Falwell Jr., then one that occurred in June 2019. A June 2019 article in the *Washington Post*[40] by David Fouse, a graduate of Liberty University and partner in a public relations firm in Washington, details a twitter spat between Southern Baptist leader Russell Moore and Falwell Jr. He notes that Moore is President of the Southern Baptist Convention's Ethics and Religious Liberty Commission, *a group established to propose public positions on societal issues from a Biblical perspective* (replacing the hard-right Richard Land in 2013, who left after fifteen years for his comments regarding the Trayvon Martin case and his organization's confirmation of his repeated plagiarism), an ordained Southern Baptist minister, senior pastor, and prior provost and dean of Southern Baptist Theological Seminary and an ethics professor at various Baptist seminaries. Most importantly, while he would still espouse what are considered very conservative theological and social positions (a few more so than myself), he has been one of the brave few leaders to denounce his fellow Christian leaders and flock for dispensing with moral standards and ethics in their unabashed defense of Trump and his debased lifestyle and values, and what this will do to the church's societal witness.

Fouse writes that Moore had tweeted that "The reports of the conditions for migrant children at the border should shock all our consciences. Those created in the image of God should be treated with dignity and compassion, especially those seeking refuge from violence back home. We can do better than this." *It is interesting to see in Moore's evolving public stances that, like my own experience, when the "scales come off" of one's spiritual perception and the burden of having to stay "in line" and "behind the line" of recently traditional moral and economic views of our Religious Right culture, rapidly many tolerated social status issues become unacceptable, in domino fashion, and one feels compelled to denounce it as the reality of the situation from a heavenly perspective and bigger picture begins to add up.* Moore also added a news report that the government had moved hundreds of children from a Texas border facility due to being detained in "perilous conditions." In response, Falwell Jr. tweeted, "Who are you @drmoore? Have you ever made a payroll? Have you ever built an organization of any type from scratch? What gives you authority to speak on any issue? I'm being serious. You're nothing but an employee—a bureaucrat." Fouse writes that "As a proud alumnus of Liberty, I was surprised by Falwell's disrespectful and condescending response," and that "As a partner in a public relations firm, I am grieved that a faith leader's right to communicate on societal issues is being challenged based on false authority." *More importantly, it not only shows that Falwell emulates Trump's arguments that the value of a leader is in their ability to raise and oversee money-making operations, but lays down a general religious worldview (that he represents as a "Trump-thinking" Religious Right leader) that employee/servants are contemptible, and virtue is derived from business success, as a means of societal leadership legitimacy.*

Jerry Falwell Jr.'s criticisms, and others' criticisms of himself, have continued to crescendo through the fall of 2019, as he continued to "up the ante," defending himself and his soul-mate Trump. On August 27, 2019, *Reuters* reported[41] that "Jerry Falwell Jr. personally approved real estate transactions by his nonprofit Christian university that helped his personal fitness trainer obtain valuable university property, according to real estate records, internal university emails and interviews." They note that around 2011 Falwell and his wife Rebecca began using a 23-year-old local Liberty graduate Benjamin Crosswhite as their personal fitness trainer. They add that "Now, after a series of university real estate transactions signed by Falwell, Crosswhite owns a sprawling 18-acre racquet sports and fitness facility on former Liberty property. Last year, a local bank approved a line of credit allowing Crosswhite's business to borrow as much as $2 million against the property."

As I had surmised when hearing of this new story, Reuters notes that "The support Falwell provided to the two young men, Granda and Crosswhite, has some parallels. Both were aided in business ventures and both have flown on the nonprofit university's corporate jet." They do add that there is "One difference: when Falwell helped Crosswhite, he used the assets of Liberty," which he had led since 2008. They add that anti-government Falwell's "Liberty depends on hundreds of millions of dollars its students receive in federally backed student loans and Pell grants." They write that "In 2016, Falwell signed a real estate deal transferring the sports facility, complete with tennis courts and a fitness center owned by Liberty, to Crosswhite. Under the terms, Crosswhite wasn't required to put any of his own money down toward the purchase price, a confidential sales contract obtained by *Reuters* shows. Liberty committed nearly $650,000 up front to lease back tennis courts from Crosswhite at the site for nine years. The school also offered Crosswhite financing, at a low 3% interest rate, to cover the rest of the $1.2 million transaction, the contract shows." They add that "Liberty had received the athletic center as a gift in 2011 from a trustee who has since died," and the university told *Reuters* that Falwell "tried to be a business mentor" to Crosswhite. They also note that "As Liberty's leader,

Falwell draws an annual salary of nearly $1 million." They write that in 2011, "Falwell urged other Liberty personnel in an email to cut Crosswhite a 'sweet deal' allowing him to offer private gym training," adding in the email that "Becki and I wouldn't mind working out over there with Ben as a trainer because it is more private." *Confirming my immediate suspicions, Reuters* add that

> *The Falwells brought the trainer along on Liberty's private jet during a 2012 trip to Miami.* Later, Falwell sent an email directing Liberty to lease its gym space to Crosswhite's fitness business, which began a five year lease in 2013. The cost, according to a lease document: *$2,300 per month.* Liberty said *Falwell uses the university-chartered jet to fly every year to his annual physical in Miami. Crosswhite joined him in 2012 "to explain to the doctors Mr. Falwell's diet and exercise program and help document the results,"* the university said. Because Liberty's board requires an annual physical for Falwell, *the president doesn't have to reimburse the university for the corporate jet travel to Miami*, the statement said. *It was in Miami in 2012, as well, that Falwell met Granda, the pool attendant he would later finance in business.* (emphasis added)

Why would Crosswhite need to accompany the Falwells to Miami by corporate jet (Liberty-paid, which means Liberty student, donor and government financial aid-paid) in the days that they were making another deal with another muscular "pool boy" in the same distant town, just to tell his remotely-located doctor about his diet, rather than by phone or email, in the town where the Falwells stayed at a "no holds barred" pleasure-dome resort?

They add that "In 2016, Falwell signed the deal transferring the facility to Crosswhite. The contract says the price is $1.2 million, but notes that the 'Net Purchase Price' is $580,000, because Liberty 'agrees to credit' Crosswhite with rental payments for seasonal use of the site's tennis courts through 2025…Liberty 'agrees to finance the purchase' at a 3% interest rate, the contract says. To help Crosswhite in the transaction, Liberty was lending Falwell's fitness trainer more than half a million dollars to buy its property. The university would receive no cash up front from the sale, the contract shows." They note that school representatives expressed written concern that Crosswhite was not performing contractually required roof maintenance, but Liberty's general counsel, David Corry, responded to them that "Ben Crosswhite enjoys a close working relationship with several LU administrators, including the President," and that anyone communicating with Crosswhite should do so "with knowledge ahead of time that it may be second guessed." They also add that "In 2017, Liberty provided Crosswhite with another $75,000 line of credit to conduct maintenance and repairs, the university said in its statement," and noted Corry sent an email to Liberty's trustees warning them of *Reuters'* inquiries, and "reminded the former trustees they had signed confidentiality agreements," and told them "they were required 'forever' to keep secret what they knew about the university." By 2018, Crosswhite had obtained a $2.5 million credit line from a local bank against its interest in the facility, and a day later Liberty filed paperwork saying that the $576.000 note Crosswhite owed had been paid in full.

As would be expected in these all-too-frequent situations of evangelical hypocrisy exposed to the public like this, we can see those whose actions many Christians would define as "the heathen rage" will ask hard questions and propose speculations that often have some measure of credibility. In this case, the evidently LGBTQ-friendly website "Queery" showed in a September 3, 2019 entry on their website[42] a purported video from Crosswhite's Instagram page (with 2600 followers and mostly "consists of shirtless pics, gym selfies, and photos with his wife and dogs"), and a number of photos of Falwell, and a March 2017 video of Falwell huffing and puffing as he pushes Crosswhite around on a sled, exhorting him to "Come on! Push it!" They show his subtitle to the video says, "Sometimes you have to take it easy and let someone else do all the hard work. Since @jlfjr62 quickly becoming an American sensation with his right hand man @realdonaldtrump, we have to stay looking good for the camera." They show other photos from his site of Crosswhite riding shirtless and bareback on a horse through a lake at Falwell's ranch, saying, "Thanks @jlfjr62" (the latter Falwell's own since-deleted Instagram page), followed by a photo of Falwell himself shirtless and riding bareback on a horse in the same lake, with Falwell saying the venture was an "annual tradition." Beyond these generic suspicions, the following day the same website[43] decided to look further into Falwell's own Instagram page, finding a March 2013 entry of a photograph of a real sky with trees, however with what looks like a brightly colored rainbow drawn in—not realistically but in a comic book style that looks remarkably like common LGBTQ graphics, but without any caption or explanation, and with only Ben Crosswhite's comment added, *"I love rainbows" and a "winking" emoji*. Beyond people's personal spiritual convictions regarding the gay issue, and without knowing whether these observations of their postings have any significance whatsoever beyond being merely eyebrow-raising (assuming they are authentic), with the common harsh and ugly words said about gay citizens and the hypocritical covert behaviors by the public celebrity faces of the evangelical world (with such behaviors usually only exposed by outsiders), *is it no wonder that there is not much success in spiritual fruit borne by evangelicals in the gay community?*

To be fair to Falwell Jr., even in late 2019 he had other pictures of himself bare-chested on his horse, such as one from July 6, which actually shows him *standing on top of the back of his horse as it struggles to keep its head above water*, stating there that later the horse "threw me off three times. I kept crawling back on to teach her who was boss even after she stepped on my leg twice. Never quit!"[44] Meanwhile, on his "trainer" Ben Crosswhite's Instagram site, Jerry Jr. is seen in an April 22, 2019 photo there smiling and holding Crosswhite's big, heavy (apparently Husky) dog uncomfortably off the ground underneath its front legs in a bear hug, while Crosswhite writes, "@jerryfalwelljr terrorizes Kaiya every time he works out. Have no idea why she likes him so much. He also terrorizes his friends and family and just like Kaiya we still like him. This is why he's one of the few people @realdonaldtrump listens to."[45] *I could be completely misreading these snapshots, but to me it smacks of a "bully" who preys on the vulnerable, whether animals within reach or browbeaten students, which is not only consistent with the picture of him that emerges within these pages, but also that of his "hero" Donald Trump in how he treats women, the disabled, and underclasses. Like how common psychopathy and narcissism is associated with animal abuse, such as is described in a Psychology Today article,[46] I am not surprised that Falwell, Jr. would at least revel in giving discomfort, if not abuse, to innocent animals he can overpower without consequence.*

On September 9, 2019, *Politico* again reported[47] on Liberty president and chancellor Falwell Jr., interviewing and quoting more than two dozen senior Liberty officials and Falwell advisors, who admitted they secretly talked amongst themselves "when he does stupid stuff," but said "they won't rat him out," and either talked to the article author or provided documents. He says that in interviews over the recent eight month span, the associates explained how Falwell and his wife Becki consolidated power at the school, and directed the school into financial dealing to assist their friends, including giving his son Trey management over a shopping center the university owns, and Falwell awarding university contracts to his friends, as evidence "why they don't think he's the right man to lead Liberty University or serve as a figurehead in the Christian conservative movement." They quote one senior official saying that "We're not a school; we're a real estate hedge fund….We're not educating; we're buying real estate every year and taking students' money to do it." The employees interviewed detailed Falwell's behavior, "from partying at nightclubs, to graphically discussing his sex life with employees." They add to *The Wall Street Journal's* earlier report that Trump's Michael Cohen hired Liberty employee John Gauger to manipulate online voting polls for Trump, in that *Falwell's young son Trey (a vice president at the University) traveled on the flight to New York with Gauger to receive payment from Cohen*, where *"Trey posted a now-deleted photo on Instagram of around $12,000 in cash spread on a hotel bed,"* which Trey refused to comment about. Falwell did respond to some of the questions submitted to him by *Politico*, however admitting that answering them would "simply not make any difference" and "will only result in more questions," and declined to answer the rest.

They note that despite the controversy, "Falwell has never had his position seriously challenged," during the period where it is "thriving financially" with an enrollment over 110,000 students—most enrolled online—as construction continues on the expanding campus. The author notes that the members of Liberty's board of trustees, senior officials and staff members who work with Falwell provided information to *Politico* because, while still believing in the university's mission, Christian tradition and conservative politics (with many still supporters of Trump), they felt they had to speak out (the author himself was a graduate of Liberty). He writes that members of the Liberty community are normally reluctant to speak out because "The school uses nondisclosure agreements to prohibit many university employees or board members from openly discussing what they've seen Falwell do. ('All trustees sign a confidentiality agreement that does not expire at the close of Board service', Liberty's attorney told board members in an email that was sent earlier this month…)." The author added that "tenure and its protections are not available to Liberty faculty members outside the law school," and they must first get permission from Falwell's office before any faculty speaks to the media, because without it they could be subject to dismissal, which one employee described as "a dictatorship." Another employee stated, "Everybody is scared for their life. Everybody walks around in fear," and who only agreed to talk after purchasing a "burner" phone, "fearing that Falwell was monitoring their communications." They note that even Lynchburg residents not attached to the school are reluctant to talk and go on the record, "fearing Falwell would take revenge upon them and their families," with one former senior university official saying, "Fear is probably his most important weapon"; however, one longtime current employee stated, "someone's gotta tell the freakin' truth."

They note that Jerry Falwell made provisions after his tenure to give the University helm to Jerry Jr., and Thomas Road Baptist Church to his other son Jonathan—running it like a family business rather than a non-profit charity, or *rather, like a family Mafioso syndicate*. Employees claimed that after Senior died, both Junior and his wife Becki demanded further respect and obeisance from the employees there, as Becki would assert herself in complaints to executives, insisting on their taking actions against minor employees for their online complaints for petty issues like insufficient campus parking, prompting them to place late-night calls to the accused—in this latter case to a person no longer employed there. Accusations were also made of Becki attempting to reduce brother-on-law Jonathan's role at the university, the latter being seen as attempting to keep the spiritual moors of the institution. They report that Jerry Jr. bought out all the Thomas Road Church properties and other properties of Jonathan out from under him. They do note that under Junior's tenure at the school from 2007, where it then listed assets of $259 million, by 2018 it had assets of over $3 billion. These assets have been benefiting the Falwells personally; in 2012, Falwell informed university executives that his son Trey (actually Jerry Falwell III, the vice president of the school) was starting a new company to manage all the school properties, including the shopping center. The article gives numerous other examples of businesses the Falwells gave university business to, in which they had a financial stake, to the point of promoting the businesses on the university website, as well as huge university loans to individuals and their businesses connected to the Falwells. This included family friend Robert Moon (who frequently hosted the Falwells on his boat) and his Construction Management Associates, Inc. (CMA), noting that "previously unreported is the fact that Liberty gave Moon a loan of $750,000 to form the company before awarding it more than *$130 million in contracts* and selling it land owned by the university" (emphasis added), to cover all construction projects, paying them $62 million over two years even though senior officials have expressed concerns about their high quotations and cost controls. Pertaining to the infamous "Miami trip" of 2014, he writes that

> In July 2014, Falwell, Trey and Moon traveled to Miami together. Falwell said in his statement that he recalls "discussing University business" on the trip. During the trip, photos were taken of Jerry and Trey Falwell partying at a Miami nightclub—photos that multiple Liberty University officials said Jerry Falwell tried to make disappear. On July 19, 2014, popular Swedish DJ John Dahlbäck performed at Wall, a nightclub in Miami Beach, Fla. That night, the club happened to have a photographer on-site to grab candid shots of the revelry. The photos were shared online by World Red Eye, an outlet that documents Miami's nightlife scene, and Jerry and Trey Falwell were visible in some of the pictures—the outlet identified Trey by name. In a statement on August 21, Jerry Falwell denied the existence of any photo of him at the club. "There was no picture snapped of me at

WALL nightclub or any other nightclub," Falwell wrote…When told that I had obtained a photo of him for this article, Falwell said I was "terribly mistaken." "If you show me the picture, I can probably help you out," he wrote. "I think you are making some incorrect assumptions, or have been told false things or are seeing something that was photo-shopped." After I sent him the photo, as well as a photo of Trey at Wall, Falwell responded: "I never asked anyone to get rid of any pictures on the internet of me and I never have seen the picture you claim is of me below. If the person in the picture is me, it was likely photo-shopped." In a second email sent 23 minutes later, Falwell wrote: "But the bigger question, Brandon, is why would I want a picture like that taken down if I had seen it?" According to several people with direct knowledge of the situation, Falwell—the president of a conservative Christian college that frowns upon co-ed dancing (Liberty students can receive demerits if seen doing it) and prohibits alcohol use (for which students can be expelled)—was angry that photos of him clubbing made it up online. To remedy the situation, multiple Liberty staffers said Falwell went to John Gauger, whom they characterized as his "IT guy," and asked him to downgrade the photos' prominence on Google searches.

The article includes pictures of the wild club, with Falwell Jr. circled in the middle of the dancing crowd, as well as a clear close-up photo of him and a posed picture of Trey and his wife, who sports some margarita-styled drink glass. The article notes that officials said they were surprised at the rapid promotion of the "nobody" Gauger to the university's deputy CIO (Chief Information Officer) position (the same man whom Cohen used to rig the Drudge and other polls for Trump), and they "describe Gauger as a sort of fixer for Falwell, a man promoted because he would do what Falwell asked of him without complaint." While an employee, his RedFinch LLC also did "lucrative contract work for Liberty," getting paid almost $125,000 in 2016. The article states that "In an email from August 2013 obtained for this article, Falwell asked Gauger to defend him in the comments section of a local news article that Falwell felt reflected too negatively on him. Falwell even emailed Gauger the exact wording to post," and stated how Gauger said he could turn opinion around there. They state that "At Liberty, Gauger reports to Trey, and Trey answers only to his dad." They state that in 2014 and 2015, Cohen hired Gauger and RedFinch to rig online polls to repeatedly vote for Trump there, paying him the $12,000 that Trey evidently spread out on the bed in New York, as previously cited. They add that "Liberty officials also pointed to a tweet sent out by the university's Twitter account on January 23, 2014, linking to one of the polls that the *Wall Street*

Journal reported Gauger had rigged," showing the actual Liberty tweet that said "our friend" Donald Trump had been nominated as one of CNBC's top 25 businessmen of the last 25 years, and which Falwell Jr. confirmed to the author he had directed to be sent.

Cohen also helped Falwell Jr. deal with "racy photos" of himself and his wife that someone had obtained, while Falwell Jr. told Todd Starnes regarding the issue that "This report is not accurate…There are no compromising or embarrassing photos of me," while sending Cohen to take care of the matter with the possessor of the pictures. The author adds that "Longtime Liberty officials close to Falwell told me the university president has shown or texted his male confidants—including at least one employee who worked for him at Liberty—photos of his wife in provocative and sexual poses. At Liberty, Falwell is 'very, very vocal' about his 'sex life,' in the words of one Liberty official—a characterization multiple current and former university officials and employees interviewed for this story support. In a car ride about a decade ago with a senior university official who has since left Liberty, 'all he wanted to talk about was how he would nail his wife, how she couldn't handle [his penis size], and stuff of that sort'." The author added that "on at least one occasion, Falwell shared a photo of his wife wearing what appeared to be a French maid costume, according to a longtime Liberty employee with firsthand knowledge of the image and the fallout that followed. Falwell intended to send the image to his and Becki's personal trainer, Ben Crosswhite, as a 'thank you' for helping his wife achieve her fitness goals, the employee said. In the course of texting, Falwell accidentally sent the message to several other people, necessitating a cleanup," although Falwell denied it.

The article adds that in 2017, "after Trump was invited to deliver the school's commencement address, Becki Falwell asked university counsel Corry to look into whether Liberty could 'permit third-party vendors to sell t-shirts and hats [on campus] during commencement weekend'." She replied to Corry and to other officials with concerns about violating their existing clothing contracts that "It's great advertising for Liberty to be on products with Trump's name," and "In a follow-up email to the Liberty officials, Becki wrote, 'I spoke to Michael Cohen and he said to make sure any shirts we buy are made in America!' " The article states that "The school ended up printing and selling Trump T-shirts and hats. The shirts, in MAGA red with white type, read 'TRUMP' in large block letters and 'Liberty University Commencement 2017' in a much smaller font size. Another design, used on both hats and T-shirts, borrowed Trump's campaign slogan and signature style: an all-caps 'Making America Great Again', then in a script font: 'One degree at a time',", and the article showed pictures of these products that the non-profit university sold. They add that " 'Liberty University actually benefited by having President Donald Trump speak at commencement and by associating his brand with the University's brand,' Jerry Falwell said in a statement, expressing his disappointment that the emails were shared"—*a 501 (c)(3) organization evidently participating in forbidden political campaigning.*

In response to Falwell Jr.'s assertion that any pictures of him in a Miami nightclub were probably "photo-shopped," on September 10 the World Red Eye website, the originator of the photos it regularly takes of Miami nightlife, produced a response via an online post,[48] whereby author Seth Browarnik provides identification of the Falwell family members in each of the nightclub photos (including Trey, Jerry Jr., Becki and Wesley Falwell), and also wrote,

> For 21 years, I have maintained an impeccable reputation for documenting Miami Beach's storied social scene. We wholly reject Jerry Falwell Jr.'s baseless allegation in yesterday's *Politico* report by Brandon Ambrosino that one of our pictures was "photo-shopped" or manipulated in any fashion. We, in fact, did not know *Politico's* purpose for licensing the image and were as surprised as anyone to discover that Mr. Falwell was among the partygoers we photographed on July 19, 2014 at WALL Lounge. As a result, we reviewed all the images we have from the event and discovered an additional four photos that include Mr. Falwell and two more of his son.

Falwell's crowd and supporters didn't take the *Politico* expose sitting down. On September 10, the Liberty twitter site ran a link to a critique of the piece on the "getreligion.org" website, with a quote evidently from it, stating, "Sorry, but *Politico's* long expose on Jerry Falwell Jr. lacks adequate named sources to be taken seriously. I'm no Falwell fan myself…the writer relies almost entirely on anonymous sources."[49] The actual piece itself, by a Bobby Ross Jr.[50] at the "Get Religion" site, predominantly takes offense to the fact that the insider Liberty staff sources *Politico* uses are anonymous. The author does acknowledge that *Politico* alleges the sources stated their fear of legal retribution if their names were made known, and "Certainly, it should be stressed, too, that *Politico's* piece contains a fair amount of on-the-record material that seems to support its case that Falwell is a greedy hypocrite more in love with power and politics than a crucified savior who washed people's feet," but then adds, "as an old-school journalist, I just can't get past the lack of sourcing." The commenters to the story at the site also reiterated the extenuating circumstances above, as well as the myriad of sources of email and photo evidence materials, much of which Falwell directly refuted until it was produced in convincing fashion. Soon thereafter, Liberty University itself posted on their website a nineteen-page rebuttal of the assertions about Falwell and Liberty based upon recent reporting of not just *Politico*, but also *Reuters* and *The Washington Post*, with rationales at first glance that appear to be mostly just extended explanations of those already briefly summarized in the offending articles.[51]

In the flurry of reports at that time, the press inquiries about Falwell Jr. were not limited to his autocratic management on campus, or his dalliances with young virile men with his wife in the party scene of Miami. On September 12, 2019, *Reuters* again reported[52] that "In emails to his colleagues over the years, Liberty University President Jerry Falwell Jr. has denigrated students and staff at the Christian university he runs, referring to one student as 'emotionally imbalanced and physically retarded' and calling the school's police chief a 'half-wit'," revealing screenshots of the emails themselves. They add that "Falwell said this week he has asked U.S. federal authorities to investigate whether former board members and employees at the nonprofit university may have broken the law and divulged internal school documents to journalists....Falwell told the *Associated Press* on Tuesday that he had contacted the Federal Bureau of Investigation and that the email disclosures constituted an 'attempted coup' aimed at securing his ouster from Liberty, where he has served as president since 2008." They write that "The several dozen emails reviewed by *Reuters* span nearly a decade-long period starting in 2008. In the emails, Falwell insults some Liberty students, calling them 'social misfits'. In others, he blasts faculty members and senior Liberty staff," such as calling the dean of the engineering school a "bag of hot air" who "couldn't spell the word 'profit'," and the campus police chief a "half-wit and easy to manipulate" that shouldn't be allowed to speak publicly, as well as other examples, and when Falwell was asked to comment on them, Liberty's general counsel David Corry said they wouldn't respond. The emails also show a condescending tone toward parents of Liberty students, such as deriding them for pleading not to tear down their children's dorms in their freshman year to move them off campus, and attacking students for using off-campus parking to avoid its high fees, telling them "These students need to learn to play by the rules or they can go to another college. I am tired of this crap." He called the Liberty students who wanted to work out in the Liberty off-campus gym "social misfits" in 2013, because "The email shows Falwell wanted to bar students from working out in that gym, where he and other top Liberty executives wanted to train in private."

As key evidence that these Liberty board and staff whistleblower complaints, made anonymously under threat of prosecution as Falwell had them all tied up under non-disclosure veils of secrecy like North Korean officials, weren't just made up by these press accounts, is the fact that *Falwell Jr. himself acknowledged that they were being made by those resistant to him on the "inside," as part of what in his autocratic self-status deemed an "attempted coup."* The aforementioned September 10 report by the *Associated Press*[53] states that "Liberty University President Jerry Falwell Jr. said Tuesday that he is asking the FBI to investigate what he called a 'criminal' smear campaign orchestrated against him by several disgruntled former board members and employees. Falwell told *The Associated Press* he has evidence that the group improperly shared emails belonging to the university with reporters in an attempt to discredit him. He said the 'attempted coup' was partially motivated by his ardent backing of President Donald Trump." They note that Falwell Jr. said he is "going to civil court," and referred to the *Politico* reporter as a "little boy"—*very reminiscent of his "brother from another mother," Donald Trump and his reference to "little Marco Rubio," "little Adam Schiff," etc.* He further added that Liberty has hired "the meanest lawyer in New York." While they quote Falwell Jr. that "every email sent on our server is owned by Liberty and if anybody shares it with anybody outside Liberty, it is theft. And so that's the underlying crime," the article's cited cybercrime expert calls the position "insane," because "ex-board members and employees can share emails with reporters as long as they had authorized access to them and didn't hack into someone else's account."

While the watchdog secular media began to circle around "blood in the water," we see Falwell Jr. quickly run into the nurturing, non-judgmental arms of the evangelical media. By September 12, Falwell Jr. was giving an interview to the charismatic community party organ, *Charisma*, and reiterating his same complaints of the *Politico* "hit piece," without any evidence disputing its findings.[54] The *Charisma* article author reiterated the charges against Falwell and the university without disputing them as well, but Falwell retorted that the complaints were just from a small disgruntled set of current and former employees, whereas most students and employees felt otherwise—*a group, I surmise, that naively prefer not to know "the details," or gullibly simply refuse to believe them, like most of my fellow evangelicals I have known who do not wish to adjust their "Disney-fied" worldview to comport with the facts, and whose faith is so tenuous as to be intertwined with and dependent upon a corruption-free view of the evangelical heroes they have set up and adopted, living in cognitive dissonance when a long list of them like the Bakkers, Swaggart and many others have similarly been exposed by secular truth-seekers and subsequently fallen.* Falwell repeated that "There's nothing in any of those emails….This has been going on for a year and a half. We've answered every question with everything squeaky clean"— *sounding just like his role model Donald Trump, who used similar "gaslighting" phraseology as he obstructed other fact-finding, and conducted witness tampering and threats during the Muller investigation and subsequent Ukraine impeachment inquiry.* He focuses on their financial heft as the mark of their virtue, saying that "we pulled ourselves up by our own bootstraps, never need help from anybody"—not mentioning the critical funding his father secretly secured from Rev. Moon and the Unification Church to keep the school afloat, as we explore in detail in the next volume.

Most importantly, he cleverly (at least enough to be swallowed by their immature followers) wraps his misdeeds and diverts inquiry into a larger "persecution" of Trump and his henchmen in general (i.e., trying to hold them accountable for their well-hidden malfeasance), and how he views Jesus' support for the "corporation" and its interests, regardless of the truth, when they report that

> Falwell admits that this course of action may not look like turning the other cheek to some people. But he believes *Jesus taught that His followers must do what's in the best interest of the government or corporation they are part of…*'I believe in Jesus' teachings to do what's in the best interest of the corporation, just like Donald Trump has a job to do. It's in the best interest of the nation. So that's my take on it all. And I'm glad to go to war. I just actually enjoy it probably a little too much.' Falwell says he's not the only one facing intense scrutiny right now. In fact, he says others who support Donald Trump have also wrestled with media backlash. (emphasis added)

While Falwell Jr. dismisses criticism on campus as coming merely from the few (and who really knows how the rank and file feel, from those staunchly in his corner, to those who care not to get involved and just get their degrees, or prefer to not disturb their idyllic evangelical utopia at Liberty), evidently a few young students felt the moral urge to make a statement (which could cost them their enrollment at school, grief from their parents, etc.), while their senior-official mentors cower in fear of their high-dollar jobs. On September 13 the *Associated Press* reported[55] that "Students at Liberty University in Virginia gathered Friday to protest in the wake of news reports containing allegations that school president Jerry Falwell Jr. improperly benefited from the institution and disparaged students in emails," with about 35 students being involved. While one 20-year-old student reportedly said, "I couldn't stay silent anymore" and wanted to see an investigation done to see if the allegations were true, particularly offended by Falwell emails reportedly calling a fellow student "mentally retarded," another had a sign saying, "I TRUST JERRY." One was shown with a sign with a quotation from Falwell Jr.'s father, saying, "If it's Christian, it ought to be better," and they quoted another student who said, "I am a Christian....We didn't come out here to be angry or militant. We honestly just wanted to show the student body that there are people like them who care and who want to see this place be the best it can be."

Ultimately, the theme of this book series is that all these religious phenomena in America cited here and those like it can be often understood in terms of the almighty dollar and its influence. In Falwell Jr.'s case, he is a textbook example of one whose "just win, baby" rationale, used by his political twin Donald Trump, in that the accumulation of major assets, by whatever means, constitutes a "winner" and thereby makes one deserving of support and forgiveness of one's unethical means, lamentably appears to be the "spiritual criteria" of a majority of America's Religious Right. To provide more data which crystallize this persona in terms of Falwell Jr., Pro Publica, the site normally associated with publishing non-profits' tax filings (at least for my use), co-published with *The New York Times* in April 2018 an expose of how Falwell Jr. built Liberty University into a multi-billion dollar enterprise, on the backs of thousands of distance learners—and federal government dollars.[56] They note the current $40 million football stadium upgrade underway, as well as the construction of the new Freedom Tower, which at 275 feet will be the tallest structure in Lynchburg. They state how that all Republican presidential candidates now see a trip to Liberty as essential, and that many Liberty graduates end up working in Republican congressional offices and think tanks. In terms of its financial largesse, it noted that at the time the university had swelled up to roughly 100,000 remote-site students via distance learning, and that by 2015 Liberty had become the second largest provider of online education in the United States.

So where does Falwell Jr. and Liberty University get their money? Well, the article documents that "By 2017, Liberty students were receiving *more than $772 million in total aid from the Department of Education*—nearly $100 million of it in the form of Pell grants and the rest in federal student loans. Among universities nationwide, it *ranked sixth in federal aid*. Liberty students also received Department of Veterans Affairs benefits, some $42 million in 2016," and adds that "a vast majority of Liberty's total revenue that year, which was just above $1 billion, came from *taxpayer-funded sources*" (emphasis added). They quote a former Liberty professor who said the school broke even on residential students, but that the online students were funding the school, where they were making a "killing." They note that Jerry Sr. began distance learning there via videotapes to paying customers in the mid-70s, which were accredited a decade later. The article describes how Liberty University Online, which resided in an old mall (since, "like much commercial real estate in Lynchburg, it is majority-owned by Liberty University"), has now moved to a Nationwide Insurance building. The key facet is the 300 phone recruiters who work two shifts from 8 AM to 8 PM, calling people they obtained from lists of inquirers on online college investigation sites, as they race to beat Phoenix University and other rivals, usually calling inquirers mere minutes after they fill out a generic college inquiry online. They note that *Liberty paid Google $16.8 million* for "admissions leads generation" in 2016, based upon tax records. Phone operators get no more than 45 seconds between calls, and each of the 300 recruiters tries to sign up at least eight students a day, while those signing up four or less are subject to disciplinary action, and the best performers can get a small raise to their *$30,000 base salary.* A separate division of sixty people focuses on courting members of the military, "who have access to even greater federal tuition assistance," and they note that *more than 30,000 online students are from the military or military families.*

They quote costs to students on a cost per credit, not class, so it sounds lower, and do not clarify that students will have to come to an on-site orientation until they agree to apply and sign up for their classes, including the three required Bible classes. They note that any grade point average above 0.5—*equivalent to a D-minus record*—is accepted for admission, although they make it sound competitive to applicants on the phone. They note that students can't normally transfer credits from Liberty to other schools, which discourages dropping out or transferring. Being a non-profit religious school, it is spared many of the new regulations, such as a threshold percentage of graduates being able to attain "gainful employment," or that they could get no more than 90 percent of their revenue from federal sources; the crackdown on their for-profit rivals actually helped out Liberty, as facts which Falwell Jr. confirmed. In contrast, they report that Liberty only spends $2,609 per student on instruction expenses in 2016, for the online and regular school combined, a fraction of most other schools; in 2013 on their audited financial statement, *they received $760 million in tuition and fees but spent only $260 million on instruction, academic support and student services.* In 2016 they reported $216 million in net income on nearly $1 billion in revenue, "*making it one of the most lucrative nonprofits in the country*"; they add that "Falwell, *whose Liberty salary is nearly $1 million,* does not apologize for those margins" (emphasis added).

They add that "*U.S. News and World Report* clumps Liberty in the lowest quartile of institutions in its 'national universities' category." Students on campus stated that they took some classes online because "they're a joke" and they use Google when they take their quizzes, and make their minimum participation on discussion boards. Even a quoted Liberty instructor (who taught his English class online and in classroom right after his Bachelor's degree) noted that "As an online instructor…he was not expected to engage in the delivery of any actual educational content," being rather done by "course designers and editors," leaving the instructors little to do in the eight-week courses, aside from handling emails and grading—the 2,400 nationwide adjunct and local professors getting paid $2,100 per online course. Falwell Jr. acknowledged to the authors that the Liberty faculty feared the degradation of academic standards with the increasing online program, but that "The big victory was finding a way to tame the faculty." The remainder of the lengthy article reveals the horrible experiences of many online students, including many older adults rebuilding their lives, who were met with confusing requirements, lost assignment submissions, and "help" from adjunct teachers that usually consisted of religious bromides such as "pray more." They also note that Falwell Jr.'s affiliation with Trump may have permitted the former to influence the relaxation of standards for schools like his through Education Secretary Betsy DeVos. Falwell Jr. is quoted regarding his Christian university, whose motto is, "Training Champions for Christ," that "What I will say is that we've always operated from a business perspective. We've treated it like a business."

Falwell has another reason to be proud—in 2014 he was the second highest paid college president in Virginia, getting *$926,634 annually at the time (while not knowing how much more he is paid in 2019 since Liberty's meteoric growth),* while the national average was $512,987; in comparison, the president of Virginia's other major Christian university, Regent University and its Chancellor, Pat Robertson, was paid $72,635.[57] *This "Jerry Falwell, Jr." and Liberty University we have profiled in the last twenty pages or so is the same one many of my church members, past and present, as well as Christian family and friends, have aspired to go to, either themselves or to provide for their precious children the purest form of Christian education and role model they could find or imagine (ironically, I was offered a first-year scholarship there as a high school class valedictorian/salutatorian, but declined, seeking a more prestigious and credible engineering education at the time). These people sacrificed much to satisfy the steep costs of the "enriching" Liberty evangelical elite experience, although all of us taxpayers paid a very steep bill to bankroll them as well, even though most students still leave with steep, lifetime student loans, and often a difficult time of job placement. Falwell and his school probably well represent the "evangelical elite* *wealth class," augmented by the prosperity gospel preachers and the local mega churches, as the "Scarlet Woman who rides the Beast" of the Great merchant city of Babylon. His own unique, clever religio-capitalistic "racket" of exploiting humble worshippers and their zeal to serve God by charging exorbitant prices for the privilege by means of his university (augmented by government subsidies and veterans' benefits) is certainly a syndicate that would make Caiaphas and the House of Annas very proud, as well as the "leaven of the Pharisees" taught at his school.*

To be fair to Falwell Jr., he is not the only major evangelical leader to have the mindset of wealth and lead a privileged life, even beyond those of the televangelists and "prosperity gospel" preachers. For most evangelicals and many other American Christians, the only person one should *never* critique (aside from Jesus Himself) is the late Rev. Billy Graham, as an iconic figure usually mentioned in hushed tones, and of a very unique cultural status, with any questions raised about him being "fighting words." In one of my volumes of my *Holy War Chronicles* book series, I analyzed some of his lesser known attributes and activities. They include his animosity towards Martin Luther King in many aspects, as well as the Vietnam War student protestors (whom he accused of being aligned with the Communists and "giving aid and comfort to the enemy"), and his missionary trips aboard that were coordinated with the CIA and used as intelligence gathering exercises under the guise of ministry and confession from foreign heads of state. They also included his actions as an "unofficial cabinet member" of the Nixon administration, along with his formal proposal for the U.S. military to bomb North Vietnamese dams to drown the civilians, which was declassified some time ago. However, this humble servant, a public denouncer of unions or any anti-business sentiment, had a lifestyle that became very lucrative, apart from his public image.

Money magazine had one of the broadest analyses of Rev. Graham's finances after his death.[58] They write that by the time of his death at 99 years of age, he was down to his last *twenty-five million dollars* (certainly an essential sum needed for a man of that age). They note a *Beliefnet.com* study that placed him as one of America's eight richest pastors, being equal to Rick Warren but lower than Joel Osteen ($40 million) and Kenneth Copeland (*$760 million – that's lots of "widow's mites"!*). They report that two of the major non-profits affiliated with Billy Graham (and now both run by his son Franklin Graham, as an example of nepotism and perception as the "family business" resembling similar arrangements at many a local church, and even the Trump family) posted annual revenues of *$635 million* in 2016 for Samaritan's Purse, and revenues of *$101 million* for the Billy Graham Evangelistic Association in 2010. They write that Franklin Graham "received a whopping total of *$1.2 million in 2008 and $880,000 in compensation in 2014 for running the two charities,* according to the *Charlotte Observer*" (emphasis added). They also note that "In 2005, *Forbes* listed Billy Graham as the highest-earning employee at the Billy Graham Evangelistic Association, with annual compensation slightly over $450,000."

They add that "Graham and the Billy Graham Evangelistic Association have purchased vast acres for various museums, libraries, and religious training centers, and spent tens of millions in their construction. The Billy Graham Library, opened in Charlotte in 2007, was built at a reported cost of $27 million. In 1972 the association bought more than 1,000 acres in North Carolina's Blue Ridge Mountains, where the Billy Graham Training Center at the Cove now stands." They note that his biographer wrote that Graham found his talent as a door-to-door Fuller Brush salesman, calling him a "natural" and the most successful salesman in two states. Graham later wrote about "selling anything—including the Christian plan of salvation," and told *Time* in 1954 that "I am selling the greatest product in the world; why shouldn't it be promoted as well as soap?" They do quote him as saying (as a man himself who accumulated many millions), "Greed causes a great deal of harm. Our hearts aren't satisfied by materialism....*That's why you see someone who has made millions driven on to make more millions,*" but added that "Money represents your time, your energy, your talents, *your total personality converted into currency*" (emphasis added).

In a story run shortly after Graham's passing by the conservative Christian publication (edited by the Southern Baptist's president emeritus of its Ethics & Religious Liberty Commission, Richard Land) *The Christian Post*,[59] they also added that "Graham was a wealthy man and left behind not just millions of supporters but also millions in real estate holdings and book royalties." They also note that "There were some reports that Billy prioritized his evangelization over his own family, and his children grew up barely knowing who their father was. In a 2005 interview, daughter Ruth claimed her father has always had an awkward relationship with their family. 'Because he has two families: BGEA and us. I always resented that', she shared. 'We were footnotes in books—literally. Well, we're not footnotes. We are real, living, breathing people'." The reader should importantly understand that this murky disclosure of the finances of the Graham family and its organizations is very limited due to the limited government oversight permitted of religious charitable organizations (at least limited to the data released to the public, (sometimes including) their major contributors and board members, etc.) *As would be common in similar situations and arrangements of well-to-do families and organizations, many of the "assets" of the family, such as the family houses, real estate and other holdings may be in the name of the religious organizations themselves, so we really have no idea the full extent of the assets to which the Grahams and their lifestyles are privy, with some or many merely assigned to their business entities and on their ledger, like Kenneth Copeland and his luxury jet, and the schemes of other "servants of God."*

The earlier referenced story in the *Charlotte Observer*[60] in 2015 has the following narrative:

Six years ago, Franklin Graham decided to give up his pay as head of the Billy Graham Evangelistic Association. "I feel that God has called me to this ministry and that calling was never based on compensation," he wrote then in a memo to the BGEA staff. But since 2011, at the urging of the Charlotte-based ministry's board of directors, Graham has been receiving a salary again. That's in addition to the more than $620,000 he receives for his other full-time job, leading Samaritan's Purse, an international relief agency based in Boone. *His 2013 compensation from Samaritan's Purse alone made him the highest-paid CEO of any international relief agency based in the U.S.*, according to data provided by GuideStar, the world's largest source of information on nonprofit organizations. Graham's total compensation last year from the two charities was more than *$880,000, including $258,667 from BGEA. That total is less than the $1.2 million he received in 2008,* but it's still more than some nonprofit experts consider appropriate. Graham, 63, inherited [like a family business] the BGEA from his famous father—Charlotte-born evangelist Billy Graham, now 96—and has led Samaritan's Purse since 1979. In 2009, questions raised by the *Observer* about Graham's rising financial compensation during tough economic times prompted the evangelist to announce he would—"for the time being"—give up future contributions to his retirement plans from both BGEA and Samaritan's Purse. This came after BGEA's revenues dropped 18 percent and it laid off 10 percent of the staff. Graham acknowledged to the *Observer* then that, whatever the explanation, his compensation total "looks terrible" and that "people won't understand it." (emphasis added)

But his decision to give up a salary at BGEA lasted only one year. In 2011, he was paid $100,000....By 2014, his retirement, health care and insurance compensation from BGEA accounted for an additional $149,390....Graham spokesman DeMoss told the *Observer* in an email that Graham "never said he would give up his pay forever. He chose to give up his salary and retirement benefits for a season, in part because of the national economy in 2009."...Several nonprofit experts, though, said Graham should have stuck with his decision to forgo pay from BGEA. "It gives the appearance that he went back on his word and can't be trusted," said Ken Berger, a nonprofit consultant and former CEO of Charity Navigator, which evaluates nonprofits for donors. "It's worrisome. It appears sneaky." Pablo Eisenberg, a senior fellow at the Georgetown University Center for Public & Nonprofit Leadership, agreed. "It doesn't matter that some board members wanted him to get money again," Eisenberg said. "He's a big boy. He could have said, 'no'." DeMoss' reply: "This organization has earned the trust and prayers of those who support it with their financial and prayer support for more than 60 years and continues to be as transparent as possible."

Nonprofit watchdogs raise questions about the size of Graham's overall compensation and whether one person should do—and get paid for—two full-time jobs. Those are the same two issues that sparked controversy in 2009. Graham's pay is "definitely an outlier for the nonprofit sector," said Sandra Miniutti, Charity Navigator's chief financial officer. "When you start getting compensation above a half million dollars," she said, "it's probably not appropriate for the nonprofit sector."...Gail McGovern, the CEO of the American Red Cross, had $597,061 in total compensation in the fiscal year ending in June 2014. That was lower than what Graham got from Samaritan's Purse, even though the Red Cross' budget is about $3 billion—about seven times larger than Samaritan's Purse's. Three other Graham family members also sit on the 14-member BGEA board—Graham's son Will, his sister Anne Graham Lotz and his cousin Melvin....Certainly, a lot of corporate CEOs make much more. But many philanthropy experts say it's unfair to compare salaries in nonprofit organizations with those in the for-profit world. That's because nonprofits get substantial tax breaks—a form of public subsidy. In exchange, they're expected to keep salaries lower.

While Graham gets high marks for international relief work—Samaritan's Purse also runs Operation Christmas Child, which sends holiday presents to poor children around the world—his leadership of the BGEA has made him a polarizing figure. As head of that organization, he speaks—through publications, broadcasts, events, and most recently Facebook postings—to hundreds of thousands of evangelical Christians. He's been outspoken in his criticism of Muslims, the Obama administration and the move to make same-sex marriage legal in all 50 states. He's also been accused of using the religious nonprofit as a megaphone for conservative politics. In 2012, he took out ads that effectively endorsed Republican Mitt Romney in his race against President Barack Obama. Recently, some evangelicals joined Muslims in denouncing Graham's call on Facebook to bar Muslims from emigrating to the United States. 'We should stop all immigration of Muslims to the U.S. until this threat with Islam has been settled,' Graham wrote after four U.S. Marines were gunned down by a Muslim in Chattanooga, Tenn. "Every Muslim that comes into this country has the potential to be radicalized—and they do their killing to honor their religion and Muhammad."

Translation: when the poor widows and others give their gift to Samaritan's Purse to save the most destitute children near starvation with probably $1 a day or so of life-saving food, responding to Franklin's desperate appeal to Christians, roughly 620,000 of those children went to bed without food because that amount was the "cut off the top" of the sacrificial contributions that went to first supplement the investments, assets and estate of Mr. Graham.

The man whom many regarded as the most unassuming and humble minister in the world was honored by a Christian denomination (the one I was raised in) historically known for eschewing magnificent cathedrals and opulent clerical vestments, or the trappings of "state church" riches. They did it in a commemorative way very unique for a "radical reformer" body known for disregarding the authority or veneration of high level clerical officials, and rather relying on the "priesthood of the believer," with no clerical hierarchy and humble independence. In June 2005 the *Baptist Press* reported[61] that "The Southern Baptist Convention will unveil a bronze statue honoring the life and ministry of evangelist Billy Graham at the 2006 annual meeting….The sculpture, which will depict Graham under a cross offering an evangelistic invitation with uplifted hands, will be produced by Wyoming artist and pastor Terrell O'Brien." Since then, that nine-foot-tall statue of Graham has been a fixture in downtown Nashville, Tennessee, and had been mounted for most of its "life" in front of Lifeway, the organization originally known as the "Baptist Bookstore" and owned by the Baptists, downtown. *This was only one-tenth the height of the similar metal "image" of Nebuchadnezzar in Babylon (Daniel 3:1); it is not known what the downtown dwellers in Nashville were to do when they heard "the sound of the cornet, flute, harp, sackbut, psaltery, dulcimer, and all kinds of musick" (v. 5).* What did occur is that something was discovered about the statue when attempts were made to move it in 2016 to the Graham's resident North Carolina when Lifeway moved their headquarters to more modern digs, with a truly ironic metaphoric ring—*the statue was found to have a faulty, mysterious and problematic foundation and base.* At the time, *The Christian Post* wrote[62] that "LifeWay

Christian Resources announced Wednesday that the removal of a large bronze statue of the Rev. Billy Graham from its Tennessee headquarters to its new home at Ridgecrest Baptist Conference Center in North Carolina has been delayed due to unforeseen circumstances. In an 'editor's note' on LifeWay's newsroom page, the organization explained: 'LifeWay has delayed the removal of the Billy Graham statue because it was *attached to the ground differently than expected* " (emphasis added).

Speaking of Nebuchadnezzar's statue, Nashville, my home town for roughly the last two decades, is as much of an enigma of cognitive dissonance of outer Christian piety yet with a dark underbelly, as much as the Christian leaders profiled in this book series. *Road and Travel Magazine* describes Nashville this way[63]: "As 'The Buckle of the Bible Belt,' Nashville boasts 800 houses of worship; and with most area residents practicing Protestant religions, it's also been termed 'the Protestant Vatican'." Nashville is home to the headquarters of a good number of the largest Protestant denominations in America, including the Southern Baptists, United Methodists, National Baptists, Free Will Baptists, and African Methodist Episcopal Church, and major Christian print and music publishing houses such as Gideons International, Thomas Nelson, LifeWay, and the Gospel Music Association, as well as a large assortment of prominent Christian universities. Beyond the Billy Graham monolith, the city is even more famous for another iconic structure and statue of even greater magnanimity. The reference *Religions of the World: A Comprehensive Encyclopedia of Beliefs and Practices*, writes in their entry on "Athens"[64] that

> In 1897, the city of Nashville, Tennessee, had a full-scale replica of the Parthenon built as part of its celebration of the centennial of the state of Tennessee…In 1920, the city voted for the resources to have the building reconstructed of modern permanent materials. It was reopened in 1931….In 1897, the front of the original replica building was the site of a large mega-statue of Athena, now destroyed. In 1982, the city commissioned Alan LaQuire to reproduce the statue of Athena that had once been inside the original Parthenon….The final reproduction was completed in 1990 and *its gold gilding added in 2002. It stands 42 feet, 10 inches, and is the largest piece of indoor sculpture in the Western world it is now the largest statue of a Pagan goddess.* (emphasis added)

While rabbis have warned in the Israeli press[65] in recent days that those vile Muslim Arabs in the UAE (actually, a multi-national group of scientists) have constructed a model of an Athena statue from Syria (recently destroyed by ISIS) to display at the United Nations building, as a sign that the UN is promoting paganism tied to Islam (?) and fulfilling Talmudic prophecies of the "End of Days," meanwhile The Parthenon has become THE iconic image of the city of Nashville, located in a central downtown location, being of comparable dimensions and looks to the original in Athens. Within it is housed, within a sacredly lighted, solemn area, the idol/cult image (as this unique statue is often described in the literature) as an exact replica of that originally housed in the Parthenon in Athens, with lifelike flesh tones, but whose tunic, shield, spear and crown are covered in dazzling gold, to astonish visitors who witness it as worshippers were who came to worship it in the ancient world. She features strange (but historic) additions such as the head of Medusa on her chest, and *an enormous golden serpent hidden behind her shield.* Money was raised from Nashville-area schoolchildren and visitors to pay for the full-size pagan idol to be built. A tourist site online called "RoadsideAmerica.com" wrote[66] that a donation box in the Parthenon was used to fund the statue, which was covered in "real gold" in 2002, and that

> After more than a hundred years, work finally ended at the Parthenon. "At the time," said [Parthenon Director] Wesley, "some people said it was just a horrible thing for this pagan statue to be in a city park"....But, she added, *we could not have bought such great publicity. Our critics spread the word far and wide.*" Athena stands 42 feet tall—the tallest indoor statue in the U.S.—and with *her giant companion snake and crazy eyes she's an eerie sight in the temple gloom. Visitors lower their voices in her presence*....Tosh Williams, a docent who was overseeing Athena's hall when we visited, told us that *pagan visitors sometimes lay flowers at the statue's feet.* A woman, who Tosh guessed was not pagan, *once backed away in horror when she saw Athena.* Another woman, whose husband held a Bible, wanted to sing hymns to counteract the statue's pagan juju.

A website entitled "InterestingAmerica.com" provides a very lengthy and detailed history[67] of the 1896 Centennial Exposition in Nashville, the role of The Parthenon and the Athena statue as parts of it, and the revivals of those structures later in the Twentieth Century and beyond. Regarding additional details about the current Athena display itself, it mentions that numerous mythological figures surround or are attached to Athena herself, as she wears a breast plate given by Zeus that gives "magical powers" and having eleven snakes on them, and a giant snake Erichthonios residing behind her seventeen-foot-tall shield, as "Athena's shield protects the snake." They claim the Athena statue, complete with a 36-foot-tall spear, is 42 feet, 10 inches in height, and weighs an estimated 12 tons. Ironically, they also note that an enormous Christian nativity scene was constructed and displayed annually in the front of the pagan Parthenon building from the mid- to two thirds mark of the Twentieth Century, as a curious juxtaposition of the traditional American Christian culture intertwined with the pagan, as is not uncommon in Western cultures, particularly since *it accomplished the "higher calling" of Western sacred (Great City Babylon) belief of bringing in tourist dollar money and revenue, regardless of the spiritual inconsistency of "whatever works" to accomplish it.* This bizarre pagan building and statue was not constructed merely for the amusement (and tourist dollars) of visitors alone. Nashville once hosted elaborate mythological-era dramas in 1913 and 1914 in front of the Parthenon, as newly-written dramas with classic legendary sagas of death and rebirth, which could be best described as "mystery plays" like the ancient secret Eleusinian or Dionysian cult mystery plays, with deeper spiritual meanings behind the poetry (as the author intended), and at that time were probably very similar to the plays written and conducted at the mysterious and secretive "Bohemian Grove" for society's elite power-brokers deep in California's massive great sequoia forests at the same time. They made headlines and drew in attendees from across the country, being written by one of Nashville's most world-famous yet now-forgotten literary figures, the mysterious occultist author Sidney Mttron Hirsch. This central figurehead of the influential "Fugitives" literary movement and poetry journal, whose circle included those such as Robert Penn Warren, and who has been variously described as an occultist, Cabbalist and Rosicrucian by various historians is explained, as well as his central role in the legacy of the Parthenon lore and definition of Nashville's history, as attested by the following narrative from the same cited historical source:

Of the many events staged in the old, slowly deteriorating plaster Parthenon were the Spring Pageants of 1913 and 1914. The 1913 pageant's immense theatrical production of *The Fire Regained* used a *cast of about 600*, and *attracted audiences from surroundings states, who traveled to Nashville with specially discounted rail tickets.…The Fire Regained* had a mythological storyline. In the present age of motion pictures, it is difficult for audiences today to envision the kind of outdoor visual spectacles which were held in the late 19th and early 20th centuries. Both of these shows featured extraordinary displays as diverse as *chariot races, huge dance numbers, the release of thousands of doves and set pieces that shot flames*, all set against the backdrop of the Nashville Parthenon. *The Atlanta Constitution* of May 5, 1913 (page 9) reported that, "An elaborate Greek pageant will be produced in Nashville this week, beginning tomorrow night. The play is the work of Sidney M. Hirsch, a local author, and is entitled 'The Fire Regained.' The pageant will have as its background a reproduction of the famous Greek Parthenon and will be staged outdoors at Centennial Park. *Five hundred persons, the majority of them women and girls, will be in the cast."* (emphasis added)

The author, Sidney Mttron Hirsch (1883–1962), eccentric autodidact and scion of a prominent Jewish family in Nashville, was a *Rosicrucian mystic* who…ran away to join the U.S. Navy.…During a two-year tour of duty in China, he studied Oriental philosophy, *Rosicrucianism, mystical numerology, astrology, and "the more recondite passages of ancient Hebrew texts,"* wrote John Lincoln Stewart. A self-styled Greek scholar, it was reported that he had spent three years in Athens, though in reality he left Nashville to briefly visit Paris, where he did some *modeling for Rodin and met Gertrude Stein*. From Paris he journeyed to New York, where he also modeled by posing for sculptures for Gertrude Vanderbilt Whitney.…shortly after returning to Nashville in 1913, he managed to get his verse play *The Fire Regained* produced for the May Festival, *sponsored by the Nashville Art Association and the Board of Trade*, and which made good use of the full scale replica of the Parthenon. (emphasis added)

As John Lincoln Stewart described the epic in his book, *The Burden of Time* (page 7): "A *cast of 600* spent three months in rehearsal.… Professional drivers were engaged to race chariots drawn by four white and four black horses. Huge papier-mâché wings were prepared for the stallion representing Pegasus. *Three hundred sheep and 1,000 pigeons were made ready*. The railroads reduced their fares for out-of-town visitors drawn to Nashville by full-page advertisements inviting them to see 'The Flight of a Thousand Doves, the Revel of the Wood Nymphs, the Thrilling Chariot Race, the Raising of the Shepherd from the Dead, the *Orgy of the Flaming Torches'."* The Fire Regained tells a dramatic story concerning the *ordeals endured by one of the vestal virgins, guardians of the sacred flame*, who has been accused of "disloyalty to her trust"—unjustly accused of having allowed the sacred fire to die out upon the altar sacred to Pallas Athena (*Athena was played by Lucy McMillan, wife of Tennessee's governor*) and which was supposed to have originally been kindled by the gods themselves. *The young woman is tried by various ordeals* such as by the direction of a flight of doves, by a chariot race between white horses and black ones, *by being bound upon the back of a sacrificial bull, and by the words of a sacred oracle uttered by its fume-intoxicated priestess*. (emphasis added)

The stupendous production of *The Fire Regained* was *later staged in Washington, D.C., starting on Saturday night, May 16, 1914.* As reported by the May 17, 1914 edition of the *Washington Post* (page 57), the Grecian pageant drama that "opened auspiciously last night at the amphitheater at Sixteenth and V streets, will be continued every night this week at 8:20 o'clock. The great spectacle will be given in its entirety with its *1,500 participants* taking part in the colossal pageant of ancient Grecian times. A monster reproduction of the Parthenon of old Athens has been constructed..." And as reported by the January 13, 1914 issue of the *Washington Post* (page 2), *Joseph R. Wilson, President Wilson's brother, had seen the pageant in Nashville....*As Mark Royden Winchell wrote, "This production created such a stir that the *U.S. State Department seriously considered staging it on the Acropolis in Greece as an international gesture of goodwill.*" This idea was foiled by the start of World War I. The performances of *The Fire Regained* brought Hirsch the celebrity for which he yearned, but he was never able to build upon his success. His next play, for the 1914 Nashville May festival, *The Mysteries of Thanatos* [the Greek personification of "Death"], also had a mythologically-based plot (a copy of the script is on file at the Nashville Public Library), but it was shorter than *The Fire Regained* and seemed to get better reviews....Hirsch's later plays such as his one-act *The Passion Play of Washington Square* was performed briefly in Washington, D.C., then fell by the wayside. (emphasis added)

Sidney Mttron Hirsch could very well have remained an obscure *28-year-old aesthete* living with his father and stepmother, but by chance his apparent *all-knowing worldly sophistication and knowledge of the exotic and esoteric* (broad but not very deep), began to attract a group of young intellectuals and poets of Vanderbilt University that expanded into what became known as "The Fugitives" (see sidebar) which met for informal philosophical and literary discussions at the Hirsch family home on Twentieth Avenue near the Vanderbilt campus. It was Hirsch who both suggested publishing the poetry produced by the group and came up with the title for its magazine—*The Fugitive.*

One might say that these were merely yet another two ancient Greek plays (albeit newly written) performed as a tribute to Greek contributions to society, religion, philosophy and the arts. However, Hirsch was widely known as an esoteric student of the occult, to emphasize the *deeper meanings* behind the basic narrative in legendary sagas of verse or prose, and structured these productions as if timeless "mystery plays" which conveyed *deeper occult meanings to the enlightened priesthood and acolytes.* Furthermore, while Christian leaders, politicians and many grass-roots figures have portrayed the

United States as an embodiment of the "Christian destiny" of the world as a "chosen nation" (such notions largely constructed in government board rooms in the mid-1940s and 50s, as we soon shall see), its traditional elites have also reflected the love of Greek and Roman culture and philosophy as inherited from the Enlightenment, which had overcome the prior de-paganizing (although often compromising nature) of the "triumphant Church" in the centuries after Constantine, and which was promoted by our deist Founding Fathers. This throw-back to pagan Greek values, and mythological and real figures is reflected in the architecture and pagan idol statues present in the most foundational buildings of our nation's capital (including the Capitol Building), *similar to many pagan temples*, while no prominent statues or structures dedicated to Christian themes or figures are generally found. *This "mixing of dissonant cultures" (while justifiably respecting the non-religious contributions such as democracy) is prominent in the Western and particularly American Christian public culture (with famous Christian leaders even extolling the warmongering, pederasty-practicing Spartans), which is accustomed to simultaneously serving "two masters and two gospels."* The "sidebar" mentioned by the previous citation further reinforces these assertions. Within it they write: "America, the world's great premier democracy, gave testimony to how it— and indeed western civilization in general—had inherited the legacy of Greek culture, filtered down to us in a form profoundly influenced by the Romans." They add that "George Washington was compared to Cincinnatus, an early Roman hero of virtue and simplicity…When Thomas Jefferson pondered the prospective design for Virginia's Capitol building at Richmond, he settled on the look of the first century B.C. Roman temple in Nîmes, France….Thus, the new American Republic could symbolically connect via architecture to the ideals of the classical past, in this case the Roman Republic."

The "sidebar" also concisely describes the influential "Fugitives" literary group in the following way: "A group of writers, poets and intellectuals at Vanderbilt University in the early 20th century known as 'The Fugitives' (representing the poetic archetype of the outcast character, *imbued with mysterious and sacred wisdom* who wanders the world), such as the English professor John Crowe Ransom (*whose great-uncle was James R. Crowe, who co-founded the Ku Klux Klan in Pulaski, Tennessee on December 24, 1865*), William Yandell Elliott, Sidney Mttron Hirsch…and Robert Penn Warren, employed classical allusions in their work" (emphasis added). Portions of the book cited in this last reference, entitled, *The Burden of Time: The Fugitives and the Agrarians*, are available online,[68] and shed additional light on the nature of Mr. Hirsch and his motivations. The author, John Lincoln Stewart, writes that Mr. Hirsch's curious middle name "Mttron," is explained that "Mttron comes from the Kabbala, wherein it is the name of an archangel of immense and spiritual powers associated with the sun" (p. 3)—actually the highest divine entity second only to God, Metatron, supposedly the transformed nature of the biblical character Enoch, according to Jewish magical texts, the Kabbala and Talmud (where his status as the "second power of heaven" is debated), but not mentioned in either the Hebrew Bible (Tanakh) or Christian Old or New Testaments. Stewart writes, "Without Sidney Mttron Hirsch contemporary American letter would not be quite the same. Though he published only one book, a verse-play called *The Fire Regained* which appeared nearly fifty years ago and has since been wholly forgotten, he put his mark on our literature and literary studies" (p. 3). He adds that "no contemporary group has made such a lasting impression as have the Fugitives, and without Sidney Hirsch this group would never have come into being....[and] their work would not have had its singular and cumulative influence on our culture" (p. 3).

Based upon his studies in China, Stewart writes that "Hirsch began a course in self-instruction in mysticism of all forms…[including] *Oriental philosophies, Rosicrucianism, mystical numerology and etymology, astrology, the more remote passages of Hebraic lore*—these and countless other matters were jumbled together in the vast warehouse of his mind, waiting to be brought forth to baffle or amuse his listeners" (p. 5) (emphasis added)—*a description of an almost identical man from England who would similarly spellbind America's Christian clergy from the 1930s to 1960s with his own amalgam of esoteric sources, as we shall soon see.* Studying more mysticism in Korea and India, he stopped off at his place of birth, Nashville, then continued on to Paris, and as an Adonis-type figure he served as a male model for famed sculptor Auguste Rodin, while meeting writer Gertrude Stein. Writer and mystic "A. E." there "urged him *to look below the surface for even the most ordinary poem for the true meaning which might be unrecognized by the author himself*" (emphasis added)—*which his Parthenon "mystery plays" likely reflected*—and "with his predilection for the esoteric," taught himself ancient Hebrew, Babylonian, Chaldean, Arabic, Sanskrit and ancient Egyptian" (p. 5). As such, his studies and associations led him to claim that "the Trojan horse is the esoteric and symbolic horse," and that "hermetic meanings, which he was not free to divulge, were present in the term *hamlet*," much of which he discovered by "intuition" (p. 6), in true New Age fashion.

He adds that "From Paris he went to New York, where he became the model and friend of the sculptress Gertrude Vanderbilt Whitney. With her patronage he was able to push on with his studies of the occult." He soon returned to Nashville, where the Board of Trade was planning the Exposition, and who "wondered if the Festival would do as well as the New Orleans Mardi Gras at pulling in out-of-town shoppers," and that "The pageant chosen to launch what all hoped would become an annual affair was Hirsch's *The Fire Regained*" (p. 7). Stewart described the play, seen by 5,000 for its six performances, as largely "incomprehensible," which concerned a shepherd who is told by Athena that he must rescue a vestal virgin guarding the sacred Athenian flame who is accused of negligence; however he dies and is buried, but resurrected by Eros (pp. 7–8). By Act 2, one of the virgins becomes hysterical, suggesting her own guilt, and leading her to undergo 'trials by ordeal that involve the pigeons" and others, which prove her guilt and she is led to the flames. Fortunately, the god of Hell, Hermes, appears to rescue her with "servants of the chthonian gods," while the shepherd bearing Athena's shield (which can turn beholders to stone) arrives, which "calcifies the enemy" and sets the maiden free, which turns out to be helmeted Athena herself (p. 9). In its aftermath, "Newspapers called the pageant 'the most significant production ever given in the South or the entire country'," while he received an ovation at the third performance, and a movie was made there to show nationwide (p. 10). Stewart writes that in 1914 " 'The Fire Regained' was staged in Washington *with the aid of 600 Marines* and caused even more of a sensation than it had in Nashville" (emphasis added). Later in Nashville, Stewart notes that Hirsch believed that "there are scattered in widely different parts of the world seven mystic seers to whom are given insights denied other men and that he was one of the seven then living. These men might not publish their knowledge. They were obliged to wait for those who deserved to learn to seek them out" (p. 20).

Thus, my hometown is defined by two statues—both religious icons, one representing passion (Graham) and one representing wisdom (Athena), with both adored by millions of religious adherents over time; religious historians might call her a "consort" to the other if both were found buried in older lands. As Graham made his money in "old time religion" and fever-pitched revivals (long before his current public perception), bolstered by an organization of religious intercessors and intermediaries, so did Athena in her cult, as "old time religion" in temples like hers in her day featured sleight-of-hand techniques in the ceremonies to stir the passions of the flock as well. *Thus, Nashville (like old Ephesus) is a town built on the "business of religion," with money flowing in from the faithful like the "booths of Annas" of old, represented by religious icons gilt in gold, that sometimes covered a heart of stone.*

Reflecting back to our original Pharisees of interest, as we all know a certain stigma, not only of the Pharisees but of Jews in general with money, carried over historically into anti-semitic tropes of medieval times and beyond, justifying cruel pogroms and persecution, but with these Biblical warnings we can see how some tried to justify these views. The rabbinic teachings to charge usury to Gentiles but not fellow Jews, and the dependence of desperate Gentiles on their local Jews for "loan shark"-rated loans (as Jews of the land-detached Diaspora had few career options outside of the banking and mercantile fields) when money was not available elsewhere, inevitably fed the animosity, and the replacement of the Knights Templars with families like the Rothschilds as Europe's "money supply" perpetuated the association. We'll close this discussion with a final admonition by Christ, and His Apostle Peter, to warn the members of Christ's Church not to fall into the "deceitfulness of riches," and the greed of always wanting more, obsession with protecting one's stockpile, and stinginess to share with those less fortunate. Jesus clearly warned of such when He said, "Beware, and be on your guard against every form of greed; for not [even] when one has an abundance does his life consist of his possessions" (Luke 12:15, NASB).

When Jesus told His disciples directly, "Take heed and beware of the leaven of the Pharisee and the Sadducees" (Matt. 16:6), they could not grasp that concept then any more than Christians can today, thinking He was talking about literal bread. However, what have we documented here as elements of their "leaven" of doctrines, which I assert comprise the foundation of the message now given in conservative and Christian talk radio and cable news? The following is a (somewhat) succinct summary of what we have just pointed out from scripture itself as the doctrinal "leaven of the Pharisees and Sadducees" that it foists upon all exposed to it:

(1) Followers of God should listen to and trust less in their own daily interactions with Him, their God-given conscience, common sense or even their own reading of the ancient, timeless sacred texts, and rather rely upon their religious leaders as clerical "gate keepers" and self-appointed authorities over them, and the leaders' personal interpretations (from their own private "oral law") of how the people should comply with God's wishes and understanding of Him, and not ponder if they have their own hidden motives or agenda,

(2) Purity rituals intended merely for special public sacramental acts to preserve a reverential sense of sanctity of the interactions between God and mankind, should be applied (as prescribed without question by the Pharisees) *to every action large and small of daily life*, as a "yoke" beyond that

required by the Law or commandments, as a means of control and to further separate out the elite outwardly pious and compliant from others, focusing on "what goes into a man" without revealing their inner heart, or "what proceeds out of them,"

(3) Its ingrained status as the religious and cultural "establishment," and the wealth and complicity with secular powers of intertwined agendas of power preservation that comes with it, as "conservatives" of the existing power holders of religious and public society like the Sadducees (with their inevitable de-emphasis on an afterlife or Kingdom of Heaven agenda and accountability), while the Pharisees "conserved" their hold on cultural and piety "family" issues like the Religious Right, often combating each other but often colluding with each other to stop righteous usurpers with "disruptive teachings" like Jesus,

(4) Jesus stated these religious leader "experts" of God's commandments "err, not knowing the scriptures, nor the power of God" (Matt: 22:29); *when we see their views expressed through talk radio and cable news, in contrast to the clear teaching of Jesus, we will see how true His assertion is,*

(5) Like the Sadducees, their actions and contempt for the poor and disadvantaged suggests that they either do not believe God's views on the matter in scripture, or they don't believe they will be accountable for their disobedience in an afterlife,

(6) Being publicly lauded and recognized for their piety and godliness is important, in their recognition in the media and at conferences, the awards and honorary doctorates they receive, and the public support as evidenced by contributions to their non-profit organizations and their salaries,

(7) Refusing to have interactions with ones that do not recognize their religious values or authority, and shunning them as "unclean" (particularly government tax collector workers), rather than engaging in respectful and constructive dialogue as Jesus did with Zacchaeus,

(8) Feeling that a lack of submission to their religious customs and artificial boundaries (what they called the "hedge around the law"), and to their authority over it, was in fact an act a rebellion against God Himself,

when it was merely a deviation from their religious culture and traditions,

(9) Their use of religious law, creed, confession or code to beat up other devoted adherents they see as rivals, while using their expertise in it to find legal "loopholes" to permit their own lifestyle proclivities, or more importantly their financial coffers,

(10) Their preaching of "dominion" and "kingdom now" to enact a theocracy under their leadership, in effect in opposition to a future kingdom under the authority of Christ (which they see as a rival),

(11) Their religious talk and values that show a conservative, capitalistic premium on the value of money, prosperity and protecting it from the needs of others, and esteeming those successful in business and banking, like the Pharisees who swore upon the gold in the Temple and the monetary gift on the altar as the things of value, rather God's Temple and His altar itself,

(12) Not grasping that God actually recognizes "weightier matters of the law," and that they actually comprise justice and mercy, which they see as "socialistic" words and not part of their vocabulary, having "majored in the minors" ("straining gnats and swallowing camels") and not acknowledging the greater things God prioritizes when they conflict with secondary devotional procedures,

(13) An emphasis on outer cleanliness and purity as opposed to that inwardly, or not part of their public persona or where the public can't see,

(14) Commonly are associated with hypocrisy,

(15) They often "devour the houses of widows" and other common folk with their alarmist and manipulative fund-raising pleas for their lucrative non-profits,

(16) They preach the need for repentance of others, but almost never exhibit self-introspection and soul-searching to consider the need for their own repentance of that of their own culture, or its legacy and history of insensitive misdeeds towards others,

(17) They denounce other religious leaders that cavort with those they think are of unsavory character or lifestyles, and who have dialogue with them and listen rather than just preach damnation upon them,

(18) They fear rival Christian movements that might expose them and threaten their hypocrisy and risk their privileged position of power and wealth within the religious community and even government and business circles, and they furthermore ridicule them if they don't understand them and "certify" them,

(19) They resent any expression of God's plan that would care about or save any more than a small elite group of "elect," led by themselves,

(20) Their judgment of others is often based upon misinformation, either of their subject of derision or the biblical statements on the matter, or both,

(21) They have no problem with secretly allying with other societal institutions (like the government, law enforcement or others) to secure their interests and attack their enemies, even though they may attack these "frenemies" in public and denounce their wickedness or corruption,

(22) They often blame the poverty or misfortunes of others as due to their "sins" or those of their family and culture, without really knowing the true circumstances,

(23) They do not validate the spiritual experiences or wisdom of others (even Christ-proclaiming) if they do not "toe the line" of their own narrow ideologies or traditions, including and specifically their political implications,

(24) They have no problem using violence or recommending violence to maintain their pious position in society and to remove any threats (justified as patriotically "saving the nation" and its "traditions"), including spiritual ones, encouraging the deployment of the power of the State via police and the military (which serve Caesar, in essence) to serve their agendas,

(25) They will gravitate to violent military heroes and mercenaries with blood on their hands as their patriotic religious "heroes," regardless of their murky pasts, as opposed to non-violent, meek but convicting "truth-tellers" that proclaim "uncomfortable truths,"

(26) They will use political intimidation to keep their secular allies and politicians in check, and "fake news" to rapidly shift the views of the god-fearing populations (via mass communication) away from their high regard for true religious reformers, to then embrace immediate distrust and open contempt for them,

(27) Their devotion to money, wealth, and the lifestyle and respect it brings are of paramount importance to them, and undergirds almost all of their actions and strategies, as a foundation of their values and means of self-preservation, doing it even in their very temples and churches, and covering up their own misdeeds with hush money, while admiring the secular wealth of others,

(28) They resist sharing their wealth and plenty with those in need and even their supporters, with the same short-term exploitation mindset of capitalism which will eventually lead to their demise,

(29) They see the poor as a nuisance and lazy exploiters, and do not see the duty of government (or anyone) to meet the basic needs of the ill and destitute, such as the basics of food, shelter and basic health care,

(30) They are often too cowardly to do their deeds in public, or with public scrutiny, and

(31) They seek to silence critics that call them to task, even amongst young voices within their own religious tradition.

According to Peter, the Pharisees' descendants in the Church Age will continue spreading their "leaven." Peter seemed to have envisioned the rise of the televangelists, the "prosperity gospel" hucksters and the Religious Right and their money-raising, fear mongering para-church activists of today, when he warned that even in his times within the church that

> ...false prophets also arose among the people, just as there will also be false teachers among you, who will secretly introduce destructive

heresies, even denying the Master who bought them, bringing swift destruction upon themselves...and in [their] greed they will exploit you with false words; their judgment from long ago is not idle, and their destruction is not asleep...having eyes full of adultery that never cease from sin, enticing unstable souls, having a heart trained in greed, accursed children; forsaking the right way, they have gone astray, having followed the way of Balaam, the [son] of Beor, who loved the wages of unrighteousness; but he received a rebuke for his own transgression, [for] a mute donkey, speaking with a voice of a man, restrained the madness of the prophet...For speaking out arrogant [words] of vanity they entice by fleshly desires, by sensuality, those who barely escape from the ones who live in error, promising them freedom while they themselves are slaves of corruption; for by what a man is overcome, by this he is enslaved. (2 Peter 2:1, 3, 14–16, 18–19, NASB)

Today, do we need more "mute donkeys, speaking with a voice of a man" who "restrained the madness of the prophet," the money-obsessed Balaams in the church, and will other "donkeys" join me in that assignment?
Now that we have established and summarized the facets and elements of the "leaven of the Sadducees and Pharisees" and its tactics and operations, in the next section we will see how this "leaven," embedded and empowering the narratives and ideologies of right-wing talk radio and cable news, and in particular its Christian, Religious Right variant as a reflection of their real beliefs, thus establishes their views of each pertinent societal issue today, issue by issue, and contrast it with the plain teaching of Jesus of Nazareth as recorded in the Gospels, and by the other saints in the holy writ of the Bible. *The provocative and disturbing contrast we will see is the fulcrum of the argument of this work, and its central point of emphasis for the reader to comprehend, ponder and then decide what ideological, spiritual, political and lifestyle responses and changes are warranted for them with such an enlightenment.*

The Gospel of Jesus Vs. the "Gospel" of Hannity, Fox News, and Conservative Talk Radio and Cable News—Issue by Issue

In this chapter I will demonstrate the damage wrought and deception accomplished by the teachings and "catechism" of the "leaven of the Pharisees" pronounced by conservative and Religious Right media sources in talk radio, cable news and online outlets, to those who profess to follow the teachings and basic human and societal positions of our risen Lord. To best pinpoint the areas where such deviations exist, we will need to compare the published and preserved teachings from the Gospel of Jesus Christ, as well as the Biblical saints (which we will note by the symbol [J]), with what I will call the "Gospel of Conservatives, Fox News and Hannity" (denoted as [CFNH]), although we all know this latter category would also apply to "fellow traveler" conservative media figures such as Michael Savage, Laura Ingraham, and the deep well of regional conservative celebrities. As such, we will contrast the two, issue by issue, for a large number of issues that are "front burner" subjects that consume most the discussion time in conservative circles. I need to first acknowledge a disclaimer, in that these views expressed here are my views of not only what Christ and the other saints of the Bible taught on these various matters, but also what I grasp are the general consensus views of most conservatives on these topics, in a generalized form, both from what I have intently heard from them for years, and also what I believed for years as a card-carrying member of the conservative clan. Any reader could debate the finer points of any of the generalizations I make, in particular those that are specialists in certain topics, but I think that regardless of that, a subtext and picture will emerge that will be undeniable to most. With that explanation, let's begin, issue by

93

issue, comparing the "gospel" of Jesus and the saints taught in our Sunday Schools, Vacation Bible Schools and sermons, and the "gospel" taught to us by conservative media, week in and week out, starting with the following topics:

American Exceptionalism

CFNH: American exceptionalism, through a rationale that is vaguely Christian in its presumed foundation but totally unsubstantiated in its holy texts (in essence being "love of self," as a "respecter of persons"), and a historical narrative of the messianic goals of a number of the early European residents and colonists of the New World (with additions to the narrative largely back-constructed and promoted by the U.S. government in the early Cold War), in essence asserts that the United States has inherited some divine role that is unique from all other nations, and thus plays by a different set of "rules." Its own self-defined agenda to dictate the nature of the global order to fulfill its own manifest destiny and personal interests is expected to be accepted without question by the other nations and citizens of the earth. If any other nations or individuals object or have competing personal or corporate agendas within their spheres, they are considered to be "enemies" of the United States and thus worthy of any measures to neutralize them, using the unparalleled military, economic and political muscle of the U.S. If such protests come from resident Americans (including those within the Christian or other religious communities), they are considered to be part of the "Hate America" crowd (much as Zionist Jews consider their Jews of another view as "self-loathing Jews"), and possibly worthy of surveillance.

This position permits the United States to ignore, and not even acknowledge its past sins of exploitation of others or history of slavery and oppression of indigenous peoples, immigrants, minorities, or those in lands that it has occupied, while using similar behavior by other nations as due cause for intervention, and often their overthrow and occupation. It justifies the placement of hundreds of American military bases off of its own shores, often without the approval of the citizens at their locations, and covert or overt American military actions within their lands without any need to seek sanction. It particularly despises willing coalitions of nations that seek mutually-respectful solutions and deliberations of nations on a more equal footing, such as the United Nations. To be fair, the promotion of this selfish ideology is not limited to conservative media and politicians; it is wholeheartedly endorsed from the pulpits of a large portion of evangelical churches and their para-church organizations, and much of their Christian community has openly embraced it.

J: Although the Bible narrative is filled with the perspectives of a nation who felt God owed His allegiance to them, and persisted in a perceived divine state of inherent superiority over the "heathen" and beholden to special blessings by right regardless of their obedience or virtues (with later groups such as the Sanhedrin, priestly class, and many of its rulers also sharing this view of special status unfettered by its own obligations), in actuality the consistent message from Jesus Christ and His Father was one of one's value being given by grace, but sustained by one's devotion and humble service to God and others, rather than inherent genetic or cultural merit. Christ's apostle Peter stated this clearly,

> Then Peter opened [his] mouth, and said, Of a truth I perceive that God is no respecter of persons… (Acts 10:34)

His apostolic peer Paul made similar statements:

> For I say, through the grace given unto me, to every man that is among you, not to think [of himself] more highly than he ought to think; but to think soberly, according as God hath dealt to every man the measure of faith. (Romans 12:3)

John the Baptist warned against God's people thinking that their special national and religious status afforded them any special dispensation or unique, irreplaceable position:

> Bring forth therefore fruits worthy of repentance, and begin not to say within yourselves, We have Abraham to [our] father: for I say unto you, That God is able of these stones to raise up children unto Abraham. (Luke 3:8)

God often referred to people that had such a view of their own self-importance and "exceptional" privilege as the "proud" (with "pride" being itself an irreplaceable patriotic self-description amongst most conservative Christians), and described them as such:

> The LORD will destroy the house of the proud: but he will establish the border of the widow. (Prov. 15:25)

Every one [that is] proud in heart [is] an abomination to the LORD: [though] hand [join] in hand, he shall not be unpunished. (Prov. 16:5)

Wherefore he saith, God resisteth the proud, but giveth grace unto the humble. (James 4:6)

Pride [goeth] before destruction, and an haughty spirit before a fall. (Prov. 16:18)

Thy terribleness hath deceived thee, [and] the pride of thine heart, O thou that dwellest in the clefts of the rock, that holdest the height of the hill: though thou shouldest make thy nest as high as the eagle, I will bring thee down from thence, saith the LORD. (Jer. 49:16)

Behold, this was the iniquity of thy sister Sodom, pride, fullness of bread, and abundance of idleness was in her and in her daughters, neither did she strengthen the hand of the poor and needy. [Ezek. 16:49)

The Spiritual Holiness of Capitalism

CFNH: The concept of capitalism, whereby those already with money (capital) hold the keys to wealth making and creation of jobs and resources over everyone else, with the abilities and agenda to hoard and collect evermore stockpiles for their personal use, justifies their insurmountable leverage over working people whose families subsist on weekly wages (with only unions providing minimal mitigation) and the masses at large (even family, small and medium businesses). It is a society designed to be run and organized by the banking and financial houses, hedge funds and venture capitalists, transitioning to such around the time of the Medici and Italian merchant city-states and the City of London, and finding its biggest "Vatican" of its sacred veneration on Wall Street. In America it created the robber barons and a generation of aristocrats who became the "idle rich" (without the need for European peerage and nobility, and estate endowments) and not required to earn a living for generations, buying politicians and their tax codes, becoming government contractors and war profiteers. Meanwhile their families held opulent parties in places like "Millionaires Row" in Newport, Rhode Island (ironically, also a center of the American slave trade), literally having sandboxes full of diamonds and rubies at their parties, in the Gilded Age. With the United States having become the global flagship of capitalism (having supplanted their British and other

European capitalistic descendants), they and their bought politicians have created an environment whereby the nation's wealth has indisputably transferred from the poorer to the richer, as judged from overwhelming data that supports the trend for probably a century or more.

An article in *The Washington Post* in December 2017[69] stated that "The wealthiest 1 percent of American households own 40 percent of the country's wealth, according to a new paper by economist Edward N. Wolff. That share is higher than it has been at any point since at least 1962." The author adds that "from 2013, the share of wealth owned by the 1 percent shot up by nearly three percentage points. Wealth owned by the bottom 90 percent, meanwhile, fell over the same period. Today, the top 1 percent of households owns more wealth than the bottom 90 percent combined. That gap, between the ultra-wealthy and everyone else, has only become wider in the past several decades." They state that

> In 2010, Michael Norton and Dan Ariely surveyed more than 5,500 people to find out how they thought wealth should be distributed in this country....On average, respondents said that in an ideal world the top 20 percent of Americans would get nearly one-third of the pie, the second and middle quintiles would get about 20 percent each, and the bottom two quintiles would get 13 and 11 slices, respectively. In an ideal world, in other words, the most productive quintile of society would amass roughly three times the wealth of the least productive....[In reality, they found that] the top 20 percent of households actually own a whopping 90 percent of the stuff in America....The fourth quintile of households gets literally nothing: no pie. But they're still doing better than the bottom 20 percent of households, who are actually in a state of pie debt: Their net worth is underwater, meaning they owe more than they have. Combined, the average net worth of the bottom 40 percent of households is - $8,900....There's the top 1 percent, gobbling up an astonishing 40 slices of American pie. The next 4 percent split 27 slices between them, while the next 5 percent take another 12 slices (a little over two slices per person)....The top 1 percent in the U.S. own a much larger share of the country's wealth than the 1 percent elsewhere. The American 1 percent gobble up twice as much pie (40 percent) as the 1 percent in France, the U.K., or Canada.

In October of 2017 *The Business Insider*[70] reported that, within the U.S. alone, "The top 0.1% of households now holds about the same amount of wealth as the bottom 90%." In November 2017 *CBS News* reported[71] that "The top 1 percent of global citizens own 50.1 percent of all household wealth, up from 45.5 percent in 2000, the [investment bank Credit Suisse] study found." They add that "the wealth gap recently spurred credit rating agency Standard & Poor's to warn that worsening inequality could hamper long-term economic growth by dampening social mobility and creating a less-educated workforce." In terms of total amount of wealth increase, the *London Guardian* newspaper reported[72] in December 2017 that "The richest 0.1% of the world's population have increased their combined wealth by as much as the poorest 50%—or 3.8 billion people—since 1980....The report, which drew on the work of more than 100 researchers around the world, found that the richest 1% of the global population 'captured' 27% of the world's wealth growth between 1980 and 2016. And the richest of the rich increased their wealth by even more. The top 0.1% gained 13% of the world's wealth," and has garnered "as much of the world's growth since 1980 as the bottom half of the adult population," the report said. It also stated that, "Conversely, income growth has been sluggish or even nil for the population between the global bottom 50% and top 1%." They add that "The economists said wealth inequality had become 'extreme' in Russia and the US. The US's richest 1% accounted for 39% of the nation's wealth in 2014 [the latest year available], up from 22% in 1980," with much of that going to the top 0.1 percent. The economists note that one of the main remedies of the ever-widening gap between the one percent and the middle classes globally is a more progressive tax bracket structure, but admits that *its ability is minimized since ten percent of the world's wealth is protected in offshore tax shelters.*

In 2017 *The Huffington Post* reported[73] that "New research suggests that the top 0.01 percent—households with over $40 million in wealth—are manipulating trusts, offshore bank accounts, and various other opaque mechanisms that mask ownership to evade 25 to 30 percent of what they owe in personal income and wealth taxes." Importantly, they add that "Our current estimates on wealth inequality in the United States come largely from tax data. These estimates, given the billions upon billions the wealthy are hiding from U.S. tax collectors, now appear to grossly underestimate how much wealth actually sits concentrated at America's economic summit."

Another report[74] revealed that 70% of the world's population in 2017, with a net worth under $10,000, owned 2.7% of the world's wealth, while the 0.7% worth $1 million or more controlled 46 percent. They report that 56% (and rising) of the world's population is considered "low income" (make less than $10 a day), and another 15% as "poor." The biggest wealth disparity they show is in the United States, where "the median top 5% household wealth has more than 90 times the wealth of the median U.S.

family." Because of this, the middle class in the U.S. has half the proportion of national wealth of their peers in other industrialized nations, as well as half the net worth of the median family there. Yet another report[75] stated that "If established trends in wealth inequality were to continue, the top 0.1% alone will own more wealth than the global middle class by 2050." Even the hard right, libertarian Alex Jones' website reported[76] that "more than 40 percent of households cannot afford the basics of a middle-class lifestyle, including rent, transportation, childcare and a cell phone," finding "a wide band of working U.S. households that live above the official poverty line, but below the cost of paying ordinary expenses."

This trend continued on into 2018, well into the Trump administration, along with his types of tax cuts and other economic steps. In September 2019 *The Washington Post* reported[77] that new Census Bureau data reveals that income inequality in the U.S. in 2018 was higher than it has been in any year since they started tracking it in 1967—*over half a century* ago—while it has been under the longest economic expansion in history, with record low unemployment. They use the Gini Index which scales wealth inequality from zero (total equality by household) to one (one household holds all the nation's wealth), by proportion. They note the inequality has been accelerating in recent decades; in 1967, it was 0.397; in 2018, *it rose to 0.485; in contrast, no European country had a Gini index greater than 0.38—even in that cesspool of liberal socialist countries, where life satisfaction ratings by citizens are far higher than in the U.S., including those predominantly Christian in religion.* They add that the federal minimum wage of $7.25 has not been raised in more than a decade, and cite a Rice University professor who identifies it as one of the biggest reasons for the widening gap. The trend is present across diverse sections of the country, in states like Alabama and Arkansas, as well as California, Nebraska, New Hampshire and Texas. They also note that the median household income of $63,000 is the same as it was twenty years ago, adjusting for inflation.

This trend continues on into 2019. In November 2019 the financial site *Bloomberg* reported[78] that "The U.S.'s historic economic expansion has so enriched one-percenters they now hold almost as much wealth as the middle- and upper-middle classes combined. The top 1% of American households has enjoyed huge returns in the stock market in the past decade, to the point that they now control more than half of the equity in U.S. public and private companies, according to data from the Federal Reserve....The very richest had assets of about $35.4 trillion in the second quarter, or just shy of the $36.9 trillion held by the tens of millions of people who make up the 50th percentile to the 90th percentile of Americans—much of the middle and upper-middle classes."

This state of affairs, and the inevitable direction it is taking us, according to the data, is the natural "fruit" of capitalism. The wealthy in our capitalistic systems have bought the government that is using its powers to help redistribute the wealth from the poor and middle class to the rich, not the other way around as our wealth class-paid media tells us, by means of tax loopholes for wealthy businesses and individuals, as well as lucrative defense and other profitable contracts, energy and technology credits, and international trade policy favoring big business. Not only has the wealth class bought our government and our media, in most cases it has also, in one way or another, bought our pulpits, by selling and defending the coercive power of unregulated banking and commercial interests, and either directly or indirectly favoring a "prosperity gospel" that at least measures church "success" by means of the size of its facilities and budget, and top religious leaders with their own Lear Jets. "The American Way" and unbridled capitalism is taught as coming from the very mouth of God, with "socialism" (whereby the community or citizenry operate the mission-critical utilities of basic services for a mutual benefit) deemed to be the ultimate evil. A case in point can be seen in the "Statement of Mission and Purpose"[79] of the most famous and influential evangelical university in America—Jerry Falwell's Liberty University—which states that the university will promote an understanding of "the importance of the individual in maintaining democratic and free market processes." It is more directly stated in their "Ten Liberty University Distinctions," with a 2015 copy of their web page[80] stating (in a statement by Jerry Falwell himself) that Liberty will teach "an absolute repudiation of 'political correctness,' a strong commitment to political conservatism, total rejection of socialism, and firm support for America's economic system of free enterprise." *This is the agenda of the school that Christian parents sacrifice for, paying high tuition, to send their children to get a "Christian" education.*

With some Religious Right leaders and their followers, their fawning over the ways of the successful and the wealthy can sometimes lead to unintended consequences of revealing other aspects of their darker subconscious thoughts, even leading enthusiastic Christian Zionists to fall into old anti-Semitic tropes. As an example, in April 2014 the *Jewish Telegraphic Agency* news wire reported[81] that

> Televangelist Pat Robertson said Jews are too busy "polishing diamonds" to do weekend chores. Conservative activist Rabbi Daniel

Lapin appeared on the "700 Club" Monday with Robertson to discuss what makes Jews successful. "What is it about Jewish people that make them prosper financially? You almost never find Jews tinkering with their cars on the weekends or mowing their lawns. That's what Daniel Lapin says and there's a very good reason for that, and it lies within the business secrets of the Bible," Robertson said in introducing the rabbi. Lapin was on the show to promote his book "Thou Shall Prosper," which, according to his website, discusses "why Jews throughout the ages flourish economically," and "how you can benefit from this Jewish wisdom." "When you correctly said in Jewish neighborhoods you do not find Jews lying under their cars on Sunday afternoons, no, I pay one of the best mechanics around to take care of my BMW, I'd be crazy to take my time doing it myself," Lapin said during the interview. *Robertson followed Lapin's explanation with the remark that Jews were polishing diamonds instead of fixing their cars."* (emphasis added)

Like Kenneth Copeland and Falwell Jr., Robertson has been known for his own speculative business ventures on the side while presumably running his religious media empire full-time, and thus values other businessmen and high-stakes big business capitalism in his theology, although their endless greed and ambition (being virtues in capitalism) eventually leads them into corrupt and questionable ventures, regardless of the ambivalence of their followers. In 2010 *The Nation* reported[82] that in the war crimes trial of deposed Liberian President Charles Taylor, convicted in 2012 in the first international tribune since Nuremberg of murder, rape, sexual slavery, inhumane acts, enslavement and pillage (with the use of "blood diamonds" and atrocities in the Sierra Leone Civil War), and sentenced to fifty years in prison, *was also involved in business dealings with Pat Robertson.* They write that "Robertson used to mix his missionary work in Africa with efforts at developing mineral wealth. First he financed a diamond-mining venture in Zaire, and then he pushed for a gold mine in Liberia through a Cayman Islands company he owned called 'Freedom Gold'. That's when President Charles Taylor gave Robertson's company a gold-mining concession." The author revealed a "Mineral Development Agreement" signed by both parties on April 22, 1999. He adds that "The contract gives Robertson the right to mine gold in a southern site—and potentially make millions of dollars. And what did Robertson do to win the mining lease? It is unclear. What is true is that the evangelist used his TV pulpit on Taylor's behalf. Robertson turned out to be a vocal supporter of Taylor in the rather obscure debate over US foreign policy interests in Liberia. Taylor was a strange person to champion:

he had been trained by Col. Muammar Gaddafi after escaping a US prison, and was known, worldwide, to be a dictator presiding over one of the poorest countries in the world. The United States was pushing economic sanctions and there was a UN arms embargo going back to 1992." They add that Taylor "provided some insight earlier this year during his trial when he testified that he believed Robertson could push Washington to get on his side. He even said he believed Robertson had lobbied George Bush on his behalf."

Robertson's statements have also impacted his other religious business dealings that could have been used to generate significant Christian tourism profits, as part of the large but quiet profit-sharing of Christian ministries and the Israeli government, of dollars shaken from naïve Christian pilgrims that fills the coffers of U.S. ministries and the tourism income and political objectives of the atheist nation-state of Israel. In 2006 *CBS News* reported[83] that

> Christian broadcaster Pat Robertson has sent a letter apologizing for suggesting that Ariel Sharon's massive stroke was divine punishment for pulling Israel out of the Gaza Strip. Robertson's comments drew widespread condemnation from other Christian leaders, President Bush and Israeli officials, who canceled plans to include the American evangelist in the construction of a Christian tourist center in northern Israel....Despite the apology, it was doubtful Robertson would be brought back into the fold of the proposed Christian Heritage Center in the northern Galilee region, where tradition says Jesus lived and taught. The exclusion carries a special irony for a preacher who helped define television ministries: The planned complex is to include studios and satellite links for live broadcasts from the Holy Land....
> "But, of course, we continue full engines ahead to construct it because the Christian community around the world—the evangelical community—are friends," said Levi, who is responsible for coordinating tourism contacts between Israeli groups and other faiths around the world. Christian groups, particularly evangelical congregations from the United States, have become an important source of revenue and political influence. Evangelicals funnel millions of dollars each year to Jewish settlers in the West Bank and provide aid for those evicted from Gaza. They also represent an essential component of the estimated $4 billion in tourist revenue expected this year....The complex will include an amphitheater and broadcast facilities near key Christian sites, including Capernaum, the Mount of the Beatitudes, where Jesus delivered the Sermon on the Mount, and Tabgha on the shores of the Sea of Galilee, where Christians believe

Jesus performed the miracle of the loaves and fish. Hirchson had predicted it would draw up to 1 million pilgrims a year, generate $1.5 billion in spending and support about 40,000 jobs. Robertson was leading a group of evangelicals who have pledged to raise the $50 million needed to build the site.

[J]: Jesus, and His prophets before Him and apostles after Him, had a different view as to the innate virtues of big business and their agendas as the "messiahs" of society, to bring it to a utopia of big houses and bank accounts, the latest consumable goods and big retirement assets. The prophets Isaiah and Ezekiel, for example, recorded the views of God regarding the crowns of global capitalism and big business in their day (the "Wall Streets," if you will, like those hedge fund managers selected by our president to run the Treasury and other departments), and the control they demonstrated not only over the world's trade of commodities, but over the welfare and fate of men themselves:

> Who hath taken this counsel against Tyre, the crowning [city], whose merchants [are] princes, whose traffickers [are] the honourable of the earth? (Isa. 23:8)

> Javan, Tubal, and Meshech, they [were] thy merchants: they traded the persons of men and vessels of brass in thy market. (Ezek. 27:13)

Jesus and His angels proclaimed that the Great City Babylon, which has operated since mankind first organized under central control on the plains of Shinar and is led by the supernatural "Cosmic Rebels," exhibits an ultimate control over The State ("the kings of the earth") and the business establishment ("the merchants of the earth") by means of supernatural powers of deception and charming ("sorceries"), and also utilizing public relations firms, advertising, lobbyists and paid politicians and non-profit interest groups. It is a willful bondage that unites all of the world's people regardless of their worldview, ideology (Communist, fascist or democratic), culture or religious tradition to the spirit powers behind the money machine that runs them all:

> For all nations have drunk of the wine of the wrath of her fornication, and the kings of the earth have committed fornication with her, and the merchants of the earth are waxed rich through the abundance of her delicacies...for thy merchants were the great men of

the earth; for by thy sorceries were all nations deceived. (Rev. 18:3, 23)

There are other attributes of the "wealth class" and elites and the bankers, aristocratic families and business titans that many Christian leaders and Christians at large idolize, including exploiting others, which both the prophets and Jesus make clear:

There is that maketh himself rich, yet [hath] nothing: [there is] that maketh himself poor, yet [hath] great riches. (Prov. 13:7)

Whose possessors slay them, and hold themselves not guilty: and they that sell them say, Blessed [be] the LORD; for I am rich: and their own shepherds pity them not. (Zech. 11:5)

The attributes God sees of the typical wealth elite makes it hard for them to have the meekness and others-centeredness required to enter the Kingdom of Heaven (although they make exciting dinner and Sunday morning pulpit speeches with their bold exploits and ambitions), according to Jesus:

Then said Jesus unto his disciples, Verily I say unto you, That a rich man shall hardly enter into the kingdom of heaven. And again I say unto you, It is easier for a camel to go through the eye of a needle, than for a rich man to enter into the kingdom of God. (Matt. 19:23–24)

But woe unto you that are rich! for ye have received your consolation. (Luke 6:24)

The Apostle Paul tried to give instruction on how the rich might still enter, following a behavior that will not earn them the adoration of the crowds:

But they that will be rich fall into temptation and a snare, and [into] many foolish and hurtful lusts, which drown men in destruction and perdition....Charge them that are rich in this world, that they be not high minded, nor trust in uncertain riches, but in the living God, who giveth us richly all things to enjoy. (1 Tim. 6:9, 17)

However, unlike the "heaven's eye view" that values the poor, humble "simple people," God's people fawn over the financially "successful," even electing them president, and worry that those of lower economic strata will steal their wealth (having been conditioned by politicians and media to believe that is their sole agenda), *while not worrying about those in the higher wealth strata stealing it:*

> Hearken, my beloved brethren, Hath not God chosen the poor of this world rich in faith, and heirs of the kingdom which he hath promised to them that love him? But ye have despised the poor. Do not rich men oppress you, and draw you before the judgment seats? (James 2:5–6)

> I know thy works, and tribulation, and poverty, (but thou art rich). (Rev. 2:9)

The capitalistic, materialistic Laodicean church felt self-sufficient, and saw no need to plug in and work collectively with others for mutual benefit, selfishly trusting in their own wealth, but Jesus had another view:

> Because thou sayest, I am rich, and increased with goods, and have need of nothing; and knowest not that thou art wretched, and miserable, and poor, and blind, and naked. (Rev. 3:17)

Do the wealthy businessmen (and those who inherited wealth) that we church people idolize publicly express their dependence on God for their wealth frequently, or rather on their business savvy, as expressed in the latest book they are hawking?

> And thou say in thine heart, My power and the might of [mine] hand hath gotten me this wealth. But thou shalt remember the LORD thy God: for [it is] he that giveth thee power to get wealth. (Deut. 8:17–18)

> They that trust in their wealth, and boast themselves in the multitude of their riches; None [of them] can by any means redeem his brother, nor give to God a ransom for him. (Psalm 49:6–7)

Capitalism diminishes the value of labor itself as a wealth generator, and rather sees it as a resource to exploit from the wage-earning pool; it regards capital (either inherited or by other means, or speculation) as the means to avoid the exertion of one's own personal labor to advance oneself (or even avoiding the military draft, if needed), and alternatively buying the labor cheaply on the marketplace from those not blessed with such capital. God sees the merits of labor in a different way:

> Wealth [gotten] by vanity shall be diminished: but he that gathereth
> by labour shall increase. (Prov. 13:11)

God knows that wealth can buy "friends," including politicians and preachers, whereas the poor have few venues for assistance, with little marketable assets to offer:

> Wealth maketh many friends; but the poor is separated from his
> neighbour. (Prov. 19:4)

Since the synagogue or church has been around, there have been problems with God's people giving preferential treatment and regard for the well-to-do, and never more so than today—look at the church and Christian conference speaking rounds, and what's on the Christian bookstore shelf:

> For if there come unto your assembly a man with a gold ring, in
> goodly apparel, and there come in also a poor man in vile raiment;
> And ye have respect to him that weareth the gay clothing, and say
> unto him, Sit thou here in a good place; and say to the poor, Stand
> thou there, or sit here under my footstool: Are ye not then partial in
> yourselves, and are become judges of evil thoughts? (James 2:2–4)

Business Regulations

CFNH: The conservative, including those of a Christian persuasion, reviles government in general and in particular regulations on private businesses. They see government, and its demand for safety and environmental safeguards, as a scourge. They have been conditioned (by the wealth class and big business-paid talk radio) to believe that regulations that provide consumer protections and protections of our air, water and public spaces (as well as wildlife, such as in Alaska) are somehow evil and a roadblock to the virtuous and job-creating goals of big business, while ignoring the steady stream of stories of businesses whose operations have harmed wildlife, environmental and city living spaces, as well as consumers and those living nearby their operations.

J: God is much more realistic than the average American Christian, and knows that in the eyes of many big merchants and corporations, the welfare of their neighbor is their least concern, in comparison for their need for ever-bigger profits. The act of deceiving or exploiting consumers (i.e., the biblical "false balances" to weigh out goods bought in the marketplace) is an old and steady technique amongst the merchants, and judging by the quantity of citations by God, is probably more important than gay marriage and similar "culture war" issues to Him:

> [He is] a merchant, the balances of deceit [are] in his hand: he loveth to oppress. (Hosea 12:7)

> A false balance [is] abomination to the LORD: but a just weight [is] his delight. (Prov. 11:1)

> A just weight and balance [are] the LORD'S: all the weights of the bag [are] his work. (Prov. 16:11)

> Divers weights [are] an abomination unto the LORD; and a false balance [is] not good. (Prov. 20:23)

> Thou shalt not have in thine house divers measures, a great and a small. [But] thou shalt have a perfect and just weight, a perfect and just measure shalt thou have: that thy days may be lengthened in the land which the LORD thy God giveth thee. (Deut. 25:14–15)

> He hath shewed thee, O man, what [is] good; and what doth the LORD require of thee, but to do justly, and to love mercy, and to walk humbly with thy God?...Shall I count [them] pure with the wicked balances, and with the bag of deceitful weights? For the rich men thereof are full of violence, and the inhabitants thereof have spoken lies, and their tongue [is] deceitful in their mouth. (Micah 6:8, 11–12)

The merchants (even the religiously observant ones) still try to find loopholes around just protocols and policies, while simultaneously looking pious:

> Hear this, you who trample the needy and do away with the poor of the land, Saying, When will the new moon be gone, that we may sell corn? and the sabbath, that we may set forth wheat, making the ephah small, and the shekel great, and falsifying the balances by deceit? (Amos 8:5)

This control over the essential staples of life to hang men's lives in the balance, as recounted on a global scale by international banking cartels in *Confessions of an Economic Hit Man* that bring entire nations to their knees, will not be forgotten by God, and will be dealt with, as they crescendo into ever-worsening behavior and control:

> When the Lamb opened the third seal, I heard the third living creature say, "Come!" I looked, and there before me was a black horse! Its rider was holding a pair of scales in his hand. Then I heard what sounded like a voice among the four living creatures, saying, "Two pounds of wheat for a day's wages, and six pounds of barley for a day's wages, and do not damage the oil and the wine!" (Rev. 6:5–6)

People will gravitate to a wealthy person even if they have a reputation of exploiting others, for the chance they might "get lucky" and have their wealth rub off on them without work, by means of their flattery, whereas the poor cannot garner such an entourage:

> The poor is hated even of his own neighbour: but the rich [hath] many friends. (Prov. 14:20)

God will deal with the "slum lords," bankers and others, even if they are a President and have fed the addictions of the poor, such as by gambling in their casinos or exploiting their economic vulnerability in other ways, if the world itself does not bring them low beforehand:

> He that oppresseth the poor to increase his [riches, and] he that giveth to the rich, [shall] surely [come] to want. (Prov. 22:16)

The inherent deceit and unhealthy motives in many of the economically powerful (and their political allies) necessitates that their tremendous powers of coercion must be tempered by the collective society of citizens:

> As a cage is full of birds, so [are] their houses full of deceit: therefore they are become great, and waxen rich. They are waxen fat, they shine: yea, they overpass the deeds of the wicked: they judge not the cause, the cause of the fatherless, yet they prosper; and the right of the needy do they not judge. (Jer. 5:27–28)

> For the rich men thereof are full of violence, and the inhabitants thereof have spoken lies, and their tongue [is] deceitful in their mouth. (Micah 6:12)

> Thy princes [are] rebellious, and companions of thieves: every one loveth gifts, and followeth after rewards: they judge not the fatherless, neither doth the cause of the widow come unto them. (Isa. 1:23)

Her heads judge for a bribe, Her priests teach for pay, And her prophets divine for money. Yet they lean on the LORD, and say, "Is not the LORD among us? No harm can come upon us." (Micah 3:11, NKJV)

Thou shalt not wrest the judgment of thy poor in his cause. (Ex. 23:6)

Thou shalt not pervert the judgment of the stranger, [nor] of the fatherless; nor take a widow's raiment to pledge. (Deut. 24:17)

Big Business as the Saviors of Society

CFNH: The "Hannity"-types and Fox News-outlet types, and their allies in the Religious Right, tout the "success" of the wealthy businessmen and celebrities, and whose "success" books they promote, marveling at their jumbo jets and trappings of wealth. They assert that big business will save America, if we merely burden them with negligible taxes to pay and non-existent regulations to impact their bottom line, nor banking regulations to tamp down speculative actions and lucrative high risk loans and investments, as corporate "deliverers" who are seen to make "everyone rich," like in the Roaring Twenties. They suggest that removing their societal burdens will make them "job creators" (the conservative public having been conditioned to accept that "whopper" by big business-paid media outlets), and that these ambitious and otherwise selfish and hard-nosed robber barons will instinctively use their ever-greater wealth for public good, which will somehow "trickle down" its blessings to those of us who built their empires—*unfortunately, "trickling down" like the crumbs from the rich man's table to the beggar Lazarus.* We will see that the turning of the Christian community away from concern for the poor and societal decay to the veneration of the wealthy and big business was a premeditated, specific effort by key big-business figures directed toward our nation's Christian clergy earlier in the Twentieth Century, as we will document later.

J: Jesus and His saints had a much more skeptical eye toward the rich, even suggesting that their wealth, and the attitudes and character it often generates, would make it hard for them to enter the Kingdom of Heaven, unless they radically became "poor in spirit." The following are some further attributes they associate with the wealthy:

Be not thou afraid when one is made rich, when the glory of his house is increased; For when he dieth he shall carry nothing away: his glory shall not descend after him. Though while he lived he blessed his soul: and [men] will praise thee, when thou doest well to thyself. (Psalm 49:16–18)

Labour not to be rich: cease from thine own wisdom. (Prov. 23:4)

Better [is] the poor that walketh in his uprightness, than [he that is] perverse [in his] ways, though he [be] rich. (Prov. 28:6)

He that hasteth to be rich [hath] an evil eye, and considereth not that poverty shall come upon him. (Prov. 28:22)

The sleep of a labouring man [is] sweet, whether he eat little or much: but the abundance of the rich will not suffer him to sleep. (Ecc. 5:12)

Redistribution of Wealth

CFNH: Along with a carefully orchestrated effort to demonize previously respected terms by Christians such as "socialism" and "liberal" that transformed their meanings to be synonymous with "devil worship" since the early days of conservative talk radio, the moneyed banking and business interests behind the conservative media and their clergy and para-church henchmen (and who are paying their bills and opulent lifestyles) have also successfully waged another psychological operation on the conservative-leaning citizenry. They have associated any efforts to formally address the decaying social structures and environments of society and the vast gulf in the sharing of the wealth of capitalism between the money/capital class and the workers who build society for a wage as being a nefarious effort to steal, by "redistributing wealth" from hard-working CEOs, multi-generational "idle class" rich families and Wall Street banking and speculative venture capital firms and hedge funds to "lazy" working-class people who do nothing but breed, drink and eat, according the public relations image they have cultivated. In reality, as we previously documented from hard historical statistics of wealth distribution, what has occurred in reality has been *a redistribution of wealth from the poor and middle class to the rich,* which has gone on for a long time, but has accelerated in recent generations. It will lead to disastrous results if it is not remedied by immediate significant actions to stymie this natural by-product of capitalism, which will lead to civil war, major loss of life, and social upheaval with an overreaction and massive destruction of property and resources by a desperate people with nothing to lose, as illustrated by the French Revolution and other populist rebellions in feudalistic societies.

While the wealthy have been ostensibly vulnerable to a varyingly progressive income and corporate tax, there have always been plentiful loopholes available to neutralize its apparent impact, with an army of well-paid CPAs and tax firms to perpetually find such bypasses (and also serving the wealthy politicians who created the loopholes themselves, which they exploit during their terms and in their cushy corporate positions and assets afterwards). The wealth class also receives more tangible benefits from the government taxation system and oversight, with lucrative high-profit contracts to spend the tax money, credits and other incentives to pursue certain industries, and regulations to protect and provide cover for American business rather than regulate and restrain them.

Not only have working class people been disparaged as lazy and exploitative people (rather than a mix of hard-working and lazy, conscientious and exploitative, amongst both the poor and wealth classes as well as middle), but also the American tax code is perpetually excoriated as an oppressive means to redistribute wealth and rob the hard working, with big business and the banks potentially leading us to a Promised Land of universal prosperity (as measured by high levels of disposable income and materialistic increase in consumer goods accumulation) if only the tax rates were dropped below the current extreme levels, whatever they are at the time. In reality, many people do not realize how benign income and corporate tax rates are now in comparison to past times in the last century, even as America boomed during those high-tax periods.

To debunk many of the myths told by the "Church of Hannity/Limbaugh/Fox News" and their allies in the media and clergy regarding our tax history, we should first point out that the personal income tax is not a new phenomenon, and not invented with the 1913 federal law establishment of an income tax at the time. In 1862 Congress established the first income tax, the Revenue Act of 1862, which also included sales and excise taxes, and which also heavily impacted private citizens. Not surprisingly, this income tax (as well as other income tax increases) was justified by the Civil War and other subsequent wars (which is all the more ironic, given that many common folk and Christians in particular are quick to look for and then rally around wars, not thinking how it will be used as a means to confiscate their wealth). The big-defense business interests that would promote such taxes (to ultimately feed back to their coffers) and their government allies began then the perpetual strategy of securing the support of clergy to argue for the spiritual merits of war, and the taxes required to pay for it (or more debt for the grandchildren and later generations), by exempting clergy from many of the tax implications themselves (as in early tax provisions). Unlike the common folk (who actually fought in and died in the wars to secure markets in the South and overseas for big business), big business itself actually profited from the wars and taxes raised to partially pay for it, since it was another venue for money to be taken from the common folk by the government to in turn be channeled and paid to business to build the armaments, supplies and construction to support the wars, with their material destruction providing a sustained market source by "planned obsolescence." Big companies like Dupont blossomed as major war profiteers, and later Ford, Dupont-affiliated General Motors and IBM were later accused of being paid and supporting both sides in making Hitler's Blitzkrieg war machine possible, and the concentration camps.

This tax continued long after the Civil War was over, although it expired in 1873, but was reinstituted in 1894, as a tax on the wealthy to offset tariff reductions. A year later it was declared unconstitutional, and was not in force until the Sixteenth Amendment approved its use in 1913. By 1917 the top rate had increased to 67 percent, again to finance the war, but was as high as 15% a year before. The following years it climbed into the 70s in percent (until 1921), and remained at or above 50% until the second half of the 1920s, during a period when the U.S. Gross Domestic Product took off, *evidently not hurting industrial production.* In the latter half of the 1920s and through 1931, the top tax rates were reduced to 25%; *the cumulative effect was not a sustained boom, but rather the Great Stock Market Crash, Black Tuesday and the Great Depression, and a result precipitous drop in GDP.* This economic bust occurred under the policies of pro-business Republican Herbert Hoover, but *by 1932 the pro-business Republican had drastically raised top tiers of taxes to 63% as well as instituting a number of government jobs and other "socialistic" domestic social investment programs, and almost immediately thereafter the GDP began to rise again, continuously until World War II,* with top tier tax rates going up to 79% by 1936, and then *up to the low to mid 90s through 1964, during the greatest economic boom in world history.* It then remained in the 70s of percent until the early 80s, well into the Reagan administration, tapering off into the 50s until the end of Reagan's second term, with a second boom in the 1990s as top tier taxes approached 40 percent.

Regardless of these high tax rates, the "robber barons" and other wealthy families and institutions found other means of avoiding the impact of the new income tax, using means not available to the average individual, and thus still continued the transfer of wealth from the poorer to richer in unabated fashion. As one technique, the Carnegies sheltered their money by means of public interest foundations, such as the Carnegie Foundation (founded in 1911), followed by the Rockefellers in 1913, and the notoriously spendthrift Fords in 1936, thereby creating institutions whose quiet agendas eclipsed that of the federal government itself in defining social policy and the world we live in today. Another major means of sheltering income by the rich, as well as big business, was through their myriad of tax loopholes and shelters, as they profited mightily even through periods of much higher corporate tax than today. National corporate tax began as a modest 1% in 1909, and remained in the modest low to mid-teens through to the eve of World War II. It climbed to the 40s and 50s during and after World War II, and remained such throughout the U.S. post-war boom and ascendance until the late 1980s, taping off to near 40 percent throughout the remaining boom period, until President Trump successfully argued for the need to drop the rate almost in half due to the tremendous "suffering" of American business during this boom period.

Thus, one can see that taxes historically in the U.S. in the 20th century have been much higher than they have in recent years of supposedly "crushing" taxation, and during the periods of highest taxation and government programs, the Gross Domestic Product and other economic measures have boomed and blossomed. Thus, the argument made by conservative media, their bag men in the clergy, and the super-wealthy who fund them all and pay the PR firms to make the pitch that taxes are evil and crushing to economic prosperity (as well as using those funds to help the less fortunate), is yet another effort of conditioning Christians to feel contempt for the poor and to fear the lower economic classes taking their wealth, while ignoring the efforts of the wealthier classes to take their wealth, as the lengthy and recent historical data confirms.

J: As discussed in a recent post on my personal blog concerning the *Anawim* (a Hebrew word for the "lost and forgotten ones" of low economic means and political clout that God says has His heart and attention), it was documented that that God instituted amongst His people, as a lesson for the surrounding nations, a law-enforced economy with at its centerpiece an enforced, regularly-scheduled *redistribution of wealth*, which most Christians today have been conditioned by media and sermons to be the evil "socialism" that is ungodly and "liberal," for the benefit of the "lazy poor" who are welfare whores and burdens to society. God established the essentiality, for Israel under Mosaic Law, the regularly-practiced Sabbath

Years and Years of Jubilee (every fiftieth year). It allowed the hard-working land to "rest" from cultivation one year out of seven (just like the Lord), which also allowed the people to be given a generous rest by God, who promised to increase their previous years' yield to give them a year's vacation (promising enough for years six, seven and eight during planting until harvest). It also allowed the poor and alien (immigrants) and others to feed from the wild fruit and yield on the land then (as well as wild animals), and the canceling of debts and servitude. It also instituted a fiftieth year of Jubilee to return all land to its original historical owners, with intervening year land transfers being fairly pro-rated in value, with the knowledge of the future year of restitution.

God knew that in any long-established economy (even an agrarian one), the trade and prosperity of the most ambitious and sometimes lucky would inevitably steamroll into the situation of all the land and assets falling into the hands of the few (as they have vectored in every society since then), with His wise provision with these statutes to prevent such economic tyranny. God's main warning against the central government the Israelites wanted with a king was that they would not only confiscate taxes for their own pet projects and enrichment, but would also conscript their children into needless wars to enrich their own personal treasuries, and that of the other wealthy noblemen. This Sabbath Year "rest" was instituted on the Day of Atonement with a "trumpet blast of liberty"—*God's definition of "liberty" not being a libertarian negation of government or law, or low taxation, but rather a "liberty" from economic tyranny and servitude.*

When one thinks about this, God not only expected the tithes (tenths) of their income and yield to go to overtly spiritual endeavors and their expenses (such as Temple worship, sacrifices and teaching, in their instance), but also an additional fourteen percent (one-seventh) of the land's perpetual yield to go to the poor and alien immigrant, on top of the leftover gleaning after each year's bulk harvests, which the land owners were forbidden to go and get via a second gleaning, *rather leaving it for the poor and stranger, as God designed the amount to be left behind. As New Covenant "heirs with Christ" who claim to have taken on the "mind of Christ," do we Christians have a right to be indignant if ten percent of our income goes for direct Kingdom business (soul winning and missions, spiritual ministry and counseling, worship, etc.), and an additional 14 percent minimum dedicated for the taking care of the less fortunate, whether by the Church, or the State if the Church proves inadequate to the task, as at least a minimum?* In contrast, according to 2012 data from the Center on Budget and Policy Priorities,[84] roughly ten percent of the U.S. federal government's annual budget for welfare goes to the non-working poor, at around $200 billion, mostly comprising food stamps and some Medicaid, and which is *5% of the entire federal budget*, the rest goes to the elderly, blind, severely disabled, or to the working poor. Since welfare reform provisions were enacted by President Clinton in the mid-1990s, *60% of welfare recipients got off the welfare rolls.* More data concerning the real numbers of federal tax dollars used for public assistance will be covered in the next section.

Not surprisingly, this critical mandatory requirement of the Sabbath years and jubilees was ignored by the Israelites, who were as greedy as we are, and the poor and middle class suffered as a result, as well as their wealth-generating land. Thus, God showed how serious He was by abiding by His earlier warning that *they would be taken in exile away from the land for every year they ignored the Sabbath Year, so that the land would rest and the poor would benefit*, as it did when the pagan king Nebuchadnezzar took over administration of the region. As God said through the prophets:

> I will scatter you among the heathen, and will draw out a sword after you: and your land shall be desolate, and your cities waste. Then shall the land enjoy her sabbaths, as long as it lieth desolate, and ye [be] in your enemies' land; [even] then shall the land rest, and enjoy her sabbaths. As long as it lieth desolate it shall rest; because it did not rest in your sabbaths, when ye dwelt upon it. (Lev. 26:33–35)

> And them that had escaped from the sword carried he away to Babylon; where they were servants to him and his sons until the reign of the kingdom of Persia: To fulfill the word of the LORD by the mouth of Jeremiah, until the land had enjoyed her sabbaths: [for] as long as she lay desolate she kept sabbath, to fulfill threescore and ten years. (2 Chron. 36:20–21)

Ironically, the pagan king Nebuchadnezzar was the one who not only honored Jeremiah by raising him from the latrine his Jewish leaders had thrown him into, but *also re-distributed the wealth and property to the poor Jews remaining in the land; no wonder God called pagan Nebuchadnezzar "my servant," and gave him the land (Jer. 27:6).*

This mindset intended for God's people was not intended to die or be retired with the Jews, the Old Covenant and the Mosaic Law, even though the particulars of the Law were not relevant to those of the New as far as enforcement. If anything, the New Covenant "joint heirs" of the Church were far more generous and caring of those less fortunate, as judged from their early behavior as documented in the Book of Acts. It was written there that their behavior was far more "socialistic" than today's conservative Christians would ever be comfortable with:

> And the multitude of them that believed were of one heart and of one soul: neither said any [of them] that ought of the things which he possessed was his own; but they had all things common. (Acts 4:32)

Assistance for the Needy

CFNH: The "gospel" of the Hannity/Limbaugh/Fox News conservative media preaches that the lower income people are lazy, duplicitous, expecting something for nothing, and looking to only exploit hard working upper and middle class Americans. They only desire to breed, buy steaks and booze with food stamps, and do drugs and stay at home, and commit crimes (honestly, this I have heard since I was a kid). No distinction is made between those who have life-controlling/addiction issues or are mere exploiters, and those who are trying hard, but have dealt with severe misfortune such as a loss of a parent or bread winner, physical ailments, or some other devastating financial setback, not to mention those dealing with severe psychological issues. No distinction is made between the low income working poor (in a land where the minimum wage is a joke) or those who can work, but refuse to do so. If they find a single example of a person exploiting the system and having many children, the media will exploit it to death, showing it repeatedly and suggesting it is indicative of all low-income people, just like they do when they hear an immigrant has committed a crime.

They see the poor as a "blight" and unworthy of the excess discretionary income of the well-to-do, which cuts into their budgets for the latest gadgets or fashions, or other disposable consumer goods they will soon forget, or ephemeral items of fashion and status symbols of "success." They also present alarmist stories that the poor are taking over by "voting themselves the treasury" to bankrupt the hard-working bankers and other people, and are already receiving the bulk of the annual federal budget for lazy slackers who will not work, and using their huge sums of welfare money for fancy cars, T-Bone steaks and other amenities, on your dime, as they scheme for much more. However, it might be wise to "sanity check" the image the conservative media conjures of people receiving public assistance, in how much they actually receive, how they receive it and with what restrictions, for how long, and how wide a berth amongst the populace are those who have the indignity of being "freeloaders." We have all known the pain and frustration of "freeloaders" in our own circles who simply refuse to "get their act together," and none of us wants to promote any more of them than is practically possible, but how many really exist amongst our ranks, how much is their real impact, and how does it come home to reflect on even some of us?

According to the U.S. Department of Health and Human Services,[85] the average household monthly welfare payment (TANF (Temporary Assistance for Needy Families)) has *decreased* from $238/month in the late 70s, to $154/month in 2006, although since the Great Recession of 2008, the resultant upheaval has caused an increase in payments since then. In perspective, military spending comprised 54 percent of all federal discretionary spending, of $598.5 million in 2015.[86] The 2015 budget totaled $3.8 trillion, with $1.11 trillion in discretionary spending (of which over half is defense), which also includes Head Start education, while roughly 60% of the budget is dedicated to "mandatory" spending, of which the bulk comprises Social Security and Medicare (of which virtually everyone benefits from, with the former comprising one third of mandatory spending and 23 percent of the total budget (over $800 billion), and the latter 23 percent of mandatory spending and 15 percent of the total federal budget (roughly $600 billion)), as well as food stamps, federal transportation/infrastructure spending, and the like, with $104 billion going to "food assistance," and $63 billion to "Housing & Community."[87] The same reference shows that special "tax breaks" to benefit certain parties (including much of it to the rich) over what would be normally collected in annual taxes with the tax code is estimated to comprise *$1.22 trillion* in 2015—*more than all discretionary spending*—and do not have to be approved each year by Congress, and thus stay on the books much longer than their original intended purpose.

The Washington Post also provides some interesting statistics as to the nature of government benefits, in their 2012 article.[88] They note that about *49 percent of the U.S. population lives in a home where at least one resident receives direct financial benefits from the federal government, with about 27 percent of households (32 million households) benefiting from a "means-tested" poverty program.* They note that many of the homes have retirees. They further break down that 29 percent of households received Medicare benefits, and 31.6 percent received Social Security. Of the 27% of households benefiting from poverty assistance, 19.5 percent received Medicaid for health care help, food stamps were received by 12.7 percent, and subsidized lunches by 11.2 percent; 5 percent of households received public housing assistance, 4 percent unemployment, and 2.6 percent veteran's compensation, *with only 7 percent receiving cash assistance, such as welfare.* They also note that three quarters of entitlement benefits go to the elderly or disabled. According to their data, *about 9 percent of entitlement benefits go to non-elderly, non-disabled households without jobs* (with most of that being health care assistance and unemployment insurance). They also note, most interestingly, that *most of the entitlement benefits go to middle class households (58% to the middle 60% of the public by income), with 32% of benefits to the lowest 20 percent income group and 10% to the highest 20% income group.* This includes school lunch programs, welfare, unemployment insurance, the Child tax Credit and Earned Income Tax Credit. They also note that 60 percent of Americans receive more benefits than they paid in taxes, with the middle class receiving $1.15 for every $1 in taxes they paid, and the top 10% (wealthy) receiving $0.43 for every $1 they pay; *many of these recipients include angry Christians who despise the government and its "handouts."* They also note that most people who receive such benefits are temporary in nature (two years or less), like the Earned Income Tax Credit, and then later pay more income tax as they move up the income ladder. Meanwhile, cost saving tax benefits such as the mortgage-interest deduction or employer health care deduction benefits the wealthier households predominantly.

A study by the University of Maryland[89] in 2017 found that cash or near-cash transfer programs to low-income families comprise less than 5 percent of the federal budget, with the *TANF (welfare) program amounting to 0.54 percent of federal outlays*, in comparison to the 1.63 percent for the Earned Income Tax Credit for low-income workers. Furthermore, TANF is time-limited to a *lifetime limit of 60 months for a family* (with some states stricter). They note that in 2017, 2.6 million individuals received TANF benefits a month, with cash payments limited to children or adults with child dependants. The program also has strict work requirements, with exemptions only for the elderly, ill or incapacitated, or expectant mothers in their third trimester. Only one third of TANF spending results in actual cash assistance. They note that the *average benefit for a family of three in 2012 is $427—not quite the "king's ransom" for lavish living that conservative media leads us to believe.* The stricter guidelines put in force in 1996 by the Clinton Administration have been shown to lead to higher actual employment rates by single mothers. They also report that the Supplemental Nutritional Assistance Program (SNAP), commonly known as "food stamps," results in 2 percent of federal outlays of $76.1 billion, providing food vouchers to an average of 45.8 million people a month. *The average benefit for recipients is $126.81 per month.* Adults without dependents are restricted to three months of benefits in a three year period when they are not working or in a 20 hr. per week training program.

The Supplemental Security Income (SSI) program comprises 1.42 percent of federal outlays, benefiting over 9 million people, of which almost half are under the age of 18 or over the age of 65, with the applicable groups comprising the elderly or blind or disabled children or adults. The Social Security Disability Insurance (SSDI) program comprises 3.89 percent of federal outlays, and assists almost 9 million people. Only people who have paid into Social Security for a lengthy period of time (hence withdrawing their contributions), and can prove they are permanently disabled, can qualify for the SSDI; even then, around 60 percent of applications for coverage are denied. *The average monthly cash benefit for a disabled worker was $1,165 in 20*15. To qualify for the SSI, one must be either over 65, legally blind, or have a disability, and *have less than $3000 in assets.*[90] To qualify for SNAP (food stamps), the household may have no more than $2,250 in assets ($3,500 if one resident is 60 or older), with an allowable monthly net income for a two-person household of $1,355 (illegal and many legal immigrants do not qualify for food stamps, and childless unemployed adults only receive three months of benefits every three years; benefits are reduced by 30% of the household's monthly income[91]).

A 2016 article in the *Des Moines Register*[92] also adds that the 1996 welfare/entitlement reforms enacted by Clinton put a lifetime cap of five years on any such types of benefits. They state that in 2015 in Iowa, there were the lowest numbers of families receiving cash welfare since the late 1960s, with about 11,000 families receiving benefits in a state of 3 million people, with 45 recipients dropped each month due to the five-year limit. They add that the number of children in Iowa living in poverty had increased 44 percent since 2000, with the average monthly welfare benefit for Iowans of $130 per person or $320 per family. The typical family is led by a single mother of young children, and a parent with two children must make less than $5,112 to qualify, and collects it on average for less than two years. They add that the average food stamp benefit for Iowa families is $108. His story led a writer to respond that the average American taxpayer making $50,000 per year paid $36 a year towards the food stamps program and $6 a year for the rest of the social safety net programs, *but many still complained that it was too much.*[93] Furthermore, in 2015 the business publication *Forbes* reported[94] that welfare recipients received *an average of $24.77 a day.* As to the adequacy of this "largesse," the business writer states that "It's not entirely obvious that this is an injustice crying out to the very heavens for vengeance, is it?"

The National Priorities Project added that in the decade since 2001, military spending has increased 50 percent, while non-military spending has grown by 13.5 percent.[95] Republicans complain that they cannot make honest critiques of other racial cultures or women because of "political correctness," but in turn they forbid anyone give an honest assessment of our degree of veneration of our military community and institutions, deeming it "off limits." I think we can all agree that there are a proportionally small number of U.S. military members through the years who have made an ultimate sacrifice on behalf of their buddies and some for an ideal they believed in, or more who went to deployments with a primary intention of making their neighbors safer or the world at large, with many of them experiencing varying levels of discomforts, and others experiencing severe or traumatic physical or psychological injuries, for which they may or may not partially recover. For all of the above, they deserve the proper proportionate amount of respect, appreciation, deference and assistance for the degree to which they have sacrificed. However, it is also true that the overwhelming number of citizens enter the military ranks to receive special training or an expensive undergraduate and graduate college education paid for by Uncle Sam (i.e., the taxpayer) while they earn a salary, to build a resume with world travel and experiences, and a lucrative retirement eligible at a young age, with a lifetime of health benefits, tax benefits, free housing and even resort lodging for dollars a day on post, as well as low-cost commissaries and access to low-cost golf courses.

I worked for almost two decades around Air Force officers in a more typical environment of file cabinets and meetings, with the rare chance for them of a short term deployment, and a peacetime overseas assignment or two in their careers; this contrasted with the picture painted in conservative media that all our military members are virtually engaging in trench warfare or hand-to-hand combat on a daily basis and thus above any sort of critique, rather than it being true for a select few who voluntarily choose such assignments, and usually eagerly anticipate them after an extended period of specialized training and with the latest in high-tech weaponry. What I observed is that the military I worked with were very typical of people I have met elsewhere—some were very conscientious and dedicated, and some were not. What I did realize is that when considering the bloated defense department budget with which I became very familiar, very little of that money went to the lower ranks of the enlisted troops (however being financially incentivized to have large families for the government to pay their health care, housing and schooling). The overwhelming bulk of the earmarked funding largess was dedicated to the mid and upper-level military officers and (to some extent) civilians, and defense contractors all making six figures in salary and well above, as well as obscene profits on government contracts for which they performed. For all their busyness, their activities produced no community goods or services, did not build community infrastructure, nor directly helped the quality of life of their fellow citizens, although it could certainly be argued that the most basic efforts of defense against invading forces performs an essential task, but for which a major portion of those funds, as really used, made it hard to justify as such. I heard some of my co-workers call it a "high-paying form of government welfare," but when considering all the expensive travel, offices, overhead and fringe benefits, often doing work that had no direct aspect of protecting Americans, I think it is not too heretical to ask why we think it is forbidden to point out the large sums paid out in lucrative fashion to those who produce no discernible community work, yet fret about a couple of hundred dollars a month given to our fellow citizens for their essential food and survival needs.

J: Jesus and the other saints showed a dangerous liberal or socialist tendency to favor the poor and the worker over that of the elite wealth ruling class, as the following Biblical examples attest:

> He hath filled the hungry with good things; and the rich he hath sent empty away. (Luke 1:53)

> Then said he also to him that bade him, When thou makest a dinner or a supper, call not thy friends, nor thy brethren, neither thy kinsmen, nor [thy] rich neighbours; lest they also bid thee again, and a recompense be made thee. But when thou makest a feast, call the poor, the maimed, the lame, the blind: And thou shalt be blessed; for they cannot recompense thee: for thou shalt be recompensed at the resurrection of the just. (Luke 14:12–14)

Jesus warned that in eternity, the "wretched" poor that the Hannity's and *Fox News* teach Christians to despise as burdens and exploitative, will actually prosper well, while the "wealth class" elites they use as role models will have the tables turned, and spend eternity as beggars for the most basic of staples, like water:

> But Abraham said, Son, remember that thou in thy lifetime receivedst thy good things, and likewise Lazarus evil things: but now he is comforted, and thou art tormented. (Luke 16:25)

Even James warned Christians to not be suckers of such thinking, and to remember the reversal of fortunes God foretells:

> Hearken, my beloved brethren, Hath not God chosen the poor of this world rich in faith, and heirs of the kingdom which he hath promised to them that love him? But ye have despised the poor. (James 2:5–6)

Job and his own concerns suggest he is a liberal or socialist in his thinking, in terms of what he fears he will be judged for by God:

> If I did despise the cause of my manservant or of my maidservant, when they contended with me...Did not he that made me in the womb make him? and did not one fashion us in the womb? If I have withheld the poor from [their] desire, or have caused the eyes of the widow to fail; Or have eaten my morsel myself alone, and the fatherless hath not eaten thereof;...If I have seen any perish for want of clothing, or any poor without covering;...If I have lifted up my hand against the fatherless, when I saw my help in the gate: [Then] let mine arm fall from my shoulder blade, and mine arm be broken from the bone. For destruction [from] God [was] a terror to me, and by reason of his highness I could not endure. If I have made gold my hope, or have said to the fine gold, [Thou art] my confidence; If I rejoiced because my wealth [was] great, and because mine hand had gotten much... (Job 31:13, 15–17, 19, 21–25)

Paul himself made it clear that we were not made as Christians for capitalistic selfishness and greed, and would flunk as an Ayn Rand libertarian due to his concern more for the wealth and prosperity of his neighbor:

> Let no man seek his own, but every man another's [wealth]. (1 Cor. 10:24)

Job described those who "know him not" (Job 24:1) regarding God, but who act like some Christian businessmen in their ruthless regard for their workers and those who fall victim to their exploitative finance and business competition tactics, while their worker victims huddle together, and cannot share in the wealth they create for their master:

> [Some] remove the landmarks; they violently take away flocks, and feed [thereof]. They drive away the ass of the fatherless, they take the widow's ox for a pledge. They turn the needy out of the way: the poor of the earth hide themselves together. Behold, [as] wild asses in

the desert, go they forth to their work; rising betimes for a prey: the wilderness [yieldeth] food for them [and] for [their] children....They cause the naked to lodge without clothing, that [they have] no covering in the cold...They pluck the fatherless from the breast, and take a pledge of the poor. They cause [him] to go naked without clothing, and they take away the sheaf [from] the hungry; [Which] make oil within their walls, [and] tread [their] winepresses, and suffer thirst...they are of those that rebel against the light; they know not the ways thereof, nor abide in the paths thereof. The murderer rising with the light killeth the poor and needy, and in the night is as a thief. (Job 24:2–5, 7, 9–11, 13–14)

The psalmist believes at least God will not forget the lowly *anawim*:

Arise, O LORD; O God, lift up thine hand: forget not the humble. (Psalm 10:12)

But the meek [*anawim*] shall inherit the earth; and shall delight themselves in the abundance of peace. (Psalm 37:11)

God will come again, not to save the money barons, generals and kings, but rather those they (and even some Christians) have exploited:

When God arose to judgment, to save all the meek of the earth. (Psalm 76:9)

The LORD lifteth up the meek: he casteth the wicked down to the ground. (Psalm 147:6)

God promises blessings when we have the same regard as Him in blessing the poor with our resources (and taxes too, I surmise):

He that despiseth his neighbour sinneth: but he that hath mercy on the poor, happy [is] he. (Prov. 14:21)

God would rather see us place the poor as role models and guest speakers in our pulpits, rather than the rich and famous "success stories" and celebrities, and as those we seek to emulate and associate with, rather than those who "made it big":

Better [it is to be] of an humble spirit with the lowly, than to divide the spoil with the proud. (Prov. 16:19)

God says that even in "rich America" we will still have people He views as the poor and needy, no matter how many Christians claim there are only "fat poor" in our nation with big screen televisions and steaks bought with food stamps as opposed to the "myth" of the truly needy, and thus God expects us to share the wealth:

> For the poor shall never cease out of the land: therefore I command thee, saying, Thou shalt open thine hand wide unto thy brother, to thy poor, and to thy needy, in thy land. (Deut. 15:11)

This includes the expectation by God for fair wages and decent working conditions for the working class, including immigrants, as provisions not just invented in recent generations by "the unions":

> Thou shalt not oppress an hired servant [that is] poor and needy, [whether he be] of thy brethren, or of thy strangers that [are] in thy land within thy gates [i.e., "undocumented workers"]: (Deut. 24:14)

Job said in his town he was once well-respected by everyone and received their blessings,

> Because I delivered the poor that cried, and the fatherless, and [him that had] none to help him. The blessing of him that was ready to perish came upon me: and I caused the widow's heart to sing for joy. (Job 29:12–13)

American Christians may not think much about the poor and needy (or rather, hold them in deep contempt, based upon what I hear on the street), but at least God gives them His attention, and at least He will intervene:

> But I [am] poor and needy; [yet] the Lord thinketh upon me: thou [art] my help and my deliverer; make no tarrying, O my God. (Psalm 40:17)

> He shall judge the poor of the people, he shall save the children of the needy, and shall break in pieces the oppressor...For he shall deliver the needy when he crieth; the poor also, and [him] that hath no helper. (Psalm 72:4, 12)

God even commanded the "sons of God" administering the nations of earth (whom some have referred to as the "Divine Council" from the ESV version of Psalm 82:1) to emphasize the defense and protection of the vulnerable, as a judgment on all nations one day:

> Defend the poor and fatherless: do justice to the afflicted and needy. (Psalm 82:3)

We similarly are to be the advocates for the poor and vulnerable, who are otherwise "ripe pickings" by the world:

> Open thy mouth, judge righteously, and plead the cause of the poor and needy. (Prov. 31:9)

It seems like it has always been natural for societies to oppress, rob, and otherwise economically exploit the poor, stranger (immigrant) and the vulnerable:

> The people of the land have used oppression, and exercised robbery, and have vexed the poor and needy: yea, they have oppressed the stranger wrongfully. (Ezek. 22:29)

The Bible says that man is unreliable, but God Himself will help the hungry, oppressed, broken families, and even those incarcerated:

> Which executeth judgment for the oppressed: which giveth food to the hungry. The LORD looseth the prisoners...The LORD preserveth the strangers; he relieveth the fatherless and widow: but the way of the wicked he turneth upside down. (Psalm 146:7, 9)

Jesus voluntarily took on poverty, so they could identify with Him and vice versa, and for others to be blessed:

> For ye know the grace of our Lord Jesus Christ, that, though he was rich, yet for your sakes he became poor, that ye through his poverty might be rich. (2 Cor. 8:9)

Peter, James, John, Paul and Barnabas disagreed on a number of things, but there was one thing that they all readily agreed upon:

> Only [they would] that we should remember the poor; the same which I also was forward to do. (Gal. 2:10)

Jesus said we would be better off emulating the poor for the sake of the Kingdom of God, rather than despising them:

And he lifted up his eyes on his disciples, and said, Blessed [be ye] poor: for yours is the kingdom of God....But woe unto you that are rich! for ye have received your consolation. (Luke 6:20, 24)

Immigrants and Those of Other Cultures and Ethnicities Are Up to No Good and are to be Distrusted

CFNH: The Gospel of Fox News and Hannity consistently portrays immigrants as being up to no good, with hidden agendas of crime and terrorism, riddled with disease and ultimately bringing a reduction in material standard of living to the former descendents of immigrants in America such as you and me. They are portrayed as only seeking to obtain our welfare and will not work and thus burden our systems, bring in foreign customs and religions, and generally be filthy and degenerate. Their diversity is seen as weakening the strength of a white European Aryan-dominated "traditional" America. Their pilgrimage from civil war, danger and persecution is not recognized generally, nor is the fact of how immigrants have been persecuted throughout America's history (including Jews, Irish Catholics, and Chinese), even though history has shown they have made innumerable contributions to American life, and even shed their blood in defense of it when called upon.

On November 1, 2017 *The Washington Post* reported[96] that President Trump was hurriedly rushing 10,000 seasoned professional troops to the border to stop the immigrant caravan "barbarians at the gate," but by that time the exodus of Honduran and other refugees fleeing deadly civil war had comprised around 4,000 persons, of which a large portion were women and children; it is not known how many of these hungry people without shelter, food or medicine will make it all the way to the U.S. border. Also, the Mexican government, far below the U.S. in wealth and standard of living, graciously offered asylum and jobs for many of them—*maybe Mexico has a better claim to being a "Christian nation" than our own*. They also note that the assembly of the poor and largely affirmed would have to march non-stop, without sleep or rest, to make the remaining 870 mile journey in ten days.

Nevertheless, President Trump urgently sent U.S. military forces to confront them (intentionally to publicly position them as a PR stunt before the mid-term elections at the time), whether it violated the fundamental Constitutional prohibition known as *Posse Comitatus* or not, and disregarding the preferred suitability of the National Guard, if not the Border Patrol. They also report that late at night on Oct. 31 Trump told reporters that he may send as many as 15,000 U.S. Troops—*each an "Army of One" and the most sophisticated, capable and deadly military force in the world.* The article as well as other sources notes that the number of these troops would be *roughly equal to the number of U.S. troops now deployed in Iraq and Afghanistan, combined*—the places we were told were the center of the War on Terror and threatened our very way of life. In those places, we were previously told that overwhelming numbers of troops would guarantee a "quick and decisive victory," leading President Bush to quickly declare "Mission Accomplished." After almost two decades of heavy troop deployments and untold repeated tours by our soldiers—*after seventeen years in Afghanistan and fourteen years in Iraq, as of 2018*—we are still struggling to maintain some semblance of control, and regularly stamping out new insurgence movements like ISIS or the Taliban. How much worse would it be if our "Christian nation" were not an overtly militant one in its identity, rivaled only historically by ancient Sparta? According to the budget-hawk Peter G. Peterson Foundation,[97] *our current annual military budget is greater than that of the seven next biggest global military budgets combined, including those of China, Russia, France and the United Kingdom.* Meanwhile, wealthy industrialized Western nations like the Netherlands spend a relatively imperceptible part of their wealth on defense, *yet they remain relatively peaceful and unmolested.*

On November 1, it was reported that President Trump gave a speech in the White House directing the deployed soldiers as Commander-in-Chief that if "they [the children and other refugees] want to throw rocks at our military, our military fights back," and that if they do throw rocks, "I say consider it a rifle," and thus a justification for deadly force—*not only a policy that Prime Minister Netanyahu of Israel approves for addressing stone-throwing children in the Palestinian Occupied Territories, but also reminiscent of the American policy towards Indian refugees at Wounded Knee.* Like some other American and other leaders before him, Trump would love for such a confrontation to be triggered (much as what started the Mexican War previously), and it would be a political goldmine to energize his evangelical and white-supremacist base at the polls.

An unarmed group of largely sickly children and women, desperate and cornered, would obviously be no match for the deadliest and best armed and trained military in the world, as a show of "proportionate force" (at least "proportionate" in terms of Trump's true agenda). And, judging by his statements regarding the "rapists and murderers" comprising these souls escaping civil war both recently and since he first began his presidential campaign, his agenda indeed is to teach these immigrant refugees and the watching world a "lesson about America, and who we are and what we are about"—*and sadly, it will indeed do that very thing.*

It's not that Trump is totally against immigrants, any more than he was against using illegals as workers for the Trump Organization, or in his lucrative resorts. He revealed his "benevolence," "America-first" style, in the RAISE Act he endorsed (and which was designed with the assistance of White House advisors Stephen Miller and Steve Bannon), and was submitted as a Senate bill in 2017. It created a merit-based requirement for immigrants to enter the U.S., based upon a points system that requires earning 30 "points" to even justify submitting an application for submission. I have heard many thoughtful and reasonable souls who have been willing to consider a "wall" or some equivalent, in order to facilitate an orderly and controlled processing of immigrants, *if* it is paired with a generous provision of substantial processing and acceptance of a large pool of lawful immigrants, which is actually needed to support our economy—*particularly at this time with low unemployment and the need for a low-cost workforce.* However, the RAISE Act would reduce the number of green cards by 50 percent, and refugee allowances of those persecuted down to 50,000. It would also reduce the ability for family members to join those already immigrated—*at least consistent with Trump's policy to rip children from their mothers at the border.* Ironically, *NBC News* reported[99] that the Wharton School of Business at the University of Pennsylvania—*the very school who taught Trump his business acumen, and the degree for which he is most proud*—announced that the enactment of RAISE *would cost 4.6 million jobs and lower national GDP through 2040.*

The "VISA GUIDE" website, known as the "Worldwide Visa Travel Guide," provides an online primer of the point system provisions of RAISE,[100] which certainly reflects the values of personal worth of Donald Trump. It notes that the points-based visas will now be limited to 140,000. You are not allowed to get points if you are 17 or younger, or older than 50, with high points given to twenty-somethings. High points are given for those possessing doctorates, with only one point of the 30 given if you only have a high school degree. High points are also given for a demonstrated high proficiency in English in the tests (probably tests many Americans would flunk). Most interestingly, a "Nobel Laureate or comparable recognition in a field of scientific or social scientific study" would automatically get 25 of the 30 points needed, while those with an "Olympic medal or 1st place in an international sporting event in which the majority of the best athletes in an Olympic sport were represented in past 8 years before submitting the application" would get 15 points. 13 points are available for an applying immigrant who has been offered a lucrative job that is 300 percent of the median household income in the U.S., and 200 percent of median household income jobs would get 8 points—*thus keeping natural U.S. citizens from those high-paying jobs, but leaving more menial jobs for native-born Americans than currently.* You can also buy your way here to be a "good American"; if you are "Investing the equivalent of $1,800,000 in a new commercial enterprise in the U.S and maintain such investment for at least 3 years," you get 12 points, while if you are "Investing the equivalent of $1,350,000 in a new commercial enterprise in the U.S and maintain such investment for at least 3 years," you get 6. They add that "If you have less than 30, then you should not apply because your application will not be reviewed," and to apply, you must provide a "Birth certificate or a government-issued document for your age," "Diplomas and degrees for your education," "Official test scores for English proficiency," "Extraordinary achievement proof if applicable," "Official job offer letter with compensation," and "Documents which prove you will start a commercial enterprise in the U.S and the investment," as well as "a $160 application fee for processing."

I doubt that many of the refugees fleeing terror in the Honduran civil war brought all these documents with them. Regardless, I guess they would not likely qualify anyway. Neither would almost all of our ancestors that first came to these shores, as well as most of those who came through Ellis Island and past the Statue of Liberty, or even Plymouth Rock or Jamestown, with many fleeing persecution or deprivation with no more than the shirt on their backs, but while even not knowing our language, they built the strong and advanced nation that we now live in. However, scapegoating immigrants for any current problems in our nation at any time has long been an election winner in America, and with the evangelicals of 2016, it would be no different.

In the inspirational, war-selling 1943 Hollywood movie *This is the Army*, it made its final pitch for American citizens to sign up for the war with their final stage number "This Time," which can be seen at *YouTube*.[101] It features a stage production entertaining the audience with soldier-performers with their bayonets extended forward in a Mayday-like march, declaring they are "dressed up to win!" to "finish the job" that they didn't do in the previous war, "so we'll never have to do it again." Of course they said the same thing in the "War to End All Wars" in 1917, which led to the even-deadlier World War II and atomic devastation and "total war" on civilian populations, which just led to the Cold War, and with the Afghanistan phase leading to the War on Terror. *Will this deployment of intimidating force against these feeble refugees, as fellow North Americans on our own continent, have any different result?* Will our long-standing militant policy of "the beatings will continue until morale improves" actually lead to immigrants not seeking safety within our shores, or revenge when we turn them back to their likely death, as we refuse to share our blessings? Will we ever learn that unless we are our "brother's keeper" and try to *help them where they live*, we will only alternatively have to cut them down in waves by our machine guns, and what happens when we run out of bullets, or they counter with comparable weapons in more desperate fashion? *Will they at least still believe we are a "Christian nation"?*

J: Jesus and His Father had a LOT to say about the "stranger," or the alien immigrant that was not a native Hebrew but was generally in their midst. Unlike the Gospel of Hannity and Fox News, they highly regarded the stranger, did not speak of them in contemptible terms, and rather looked after their well-being, self-worth and rights, and saw them of equal value to native-born Hebrew/Jews, as the following exhortations attest—a point lost on the Jews, evangelical Christians and Hebraic Roots hybrids. God reminded His people constantly that they came from a history of being strangers in the foreign land of Egypt themselves, and God took care of them there and expects them to return the favor to the strangers in their midst, *as God expects Americans and its Christians, who were all immigrants in their origins and taken in by America in earlier days.*

> One law shall be to him that is homeborn, and unto the stranger that sojourneth among you. (Exod. 12:49)

> Thou shalt neither vex a stranger, nor oppress him: for ye were strangers in the land of Egypt. (Exod. 22:21)

> Also thou shalt not oppress a stranger: for ye know the heart of a stranger, seeing ye were strangers in the land of Egypt. (Exod. 23:9)

God believed the stranger truly should have equal rights and be seen as native-born (unlike the Trump administration and Republicans fighting birthright citizenship), and even worthy of love rather than distrust and contempt:

> And if a stranger sojourn with thee in your land, ye shall not vex him. [But] the stranger that dwelleth with you shall be unto you as one born among you, and thou shalt love him as thyself; for ye were strangers in the land of Egypt: I [am] the LORD your God. (Lev. 19:33–34)

God told His people who listened to Him to not resist social assistance to the less fortunate alien immigrant "stranger" in their midst:

> And when ye reap the harvest of your land, thou shalt not make clean riddance of the corners of thy field when thou reapest, neither shalt thou gather any gleaning of thy harvest: thou shalt leave them unto the poor, and to the stranger: I [am] the LORD your God. (Lev. 23:22)

> Ye shall have one manner of law, as well for the stranger, as for one of your own country: for I [am] the LORD your God. (Lev. 24:22)

> And if thy brother be waxen poor, and fallen in decay with thee; then thou shalt relieve him: [yea, though he be] a stranger, or a sojourner; that he may live with thee. (Lev. 25:35)

> One law and one manner shall be for you, and for the stranger that sojourneth with you. (Num. 15:16)

God says we should emulate Him in looking out for the "stranger" in our midst:

> He doth execute the judgment of the fatherless and widow, and loveth the stranger, in giving him food and raiment. Love ye therefore the stranger: for ye were strangers in the land of Egypt. (Deut. 10:18–19)

Even those immigrants of historical "bad blood" are to be treated well; this would also apply to a generous watch care over the American Indian, since the European Christians now dominant in America were once "strangers" in his land:

> Thou shalt not abhor an Edomite; for he [is] thy brother: thou shalt not abhor an Egyptian; because thou wast a stranger in his land. (Deut. 23:7)

> When thou cuttest down thine harvest in thy field, and hast forgot a sheaf in the field, thou shalt not go again to fetch it: it shall be for the stranger, for the fatherless, and for the widow: that the LORD thy God may bless thee in all the work of thine hands. When thou beatest thine olive tree, thou shalt not go over the boughs again: it shall be for the stranger, for the fatherless, and for the widow. When thou gatherest the grapes of thy vineyard, thou shalt not glean [it]

afterward: it shall be for the stranger, for the fatherless, and for the widow. (Deut. 24:19–21)

When thou hast made an end of tithing all the tithes of thine increase the third year, [which is] the year of tithing, and hast given [it] unto the Levite, the stranger, the fatherless, and the widow, that they may eat within thy gates, and be filled. (Deut. 26:12)

Cursed [be] he that perverteth the judgment of the stranger, fatherless, and widow. And all the people shall say, Amen. (Deut. 27:19)

Solomon declared before God before he dedicated the Temple, that it was not to be a place of exclusivity for his Jewish people, but rather a refuge for the alien stranger to come and talk to and hear from God, and be blessed; and certainly not a place for the Jews to see themselves as superior in any way:

Moreover concerning a stranger, that [is] not of thy people Israel, but cometh out of a far country for thy name's sake; (For they shall hear of thy great name, and of thy strong hand, and of thy stretched out arm;) when he shall come and pray toward this house; Hear thou in heaven thy dwelling place, and do according to all that the stranger calleth to thee for: that all people of the earth may know thy name, to fear thee, as [do] thy people Israel; and that they may know that this house, which I have builded, is called by thy name. (1Kings 8:41–43)

God said through His prophets that His intention was not that the immigrant be left out from prosperity behind a wall, but rather that they be invited to join in, and experience full citizenship both nationally and spiritually, and fully share in God's blessings. This included the "sons of the stranger," whom President Trump and the Republicans are trying to deny them their citizenship:

Neither let the son of the stranger, that hath joined himself to the LORD, speak, saying, The LORD hath utterly separated me from his people: neither let the eunuch say, Behold, I [am] a dry tree....Also the sons of the stranger, that join themselves to the LORD, to serve him, and to love the name of the LORD, to be his servants, every one that keepeth the sabbath from polluting it, and taketh hold of my covenant; Even them will I bring to my holy mountain, and make them joyful in my house of prayer: their burnt offerings and their sacrifices [shall be] accepted upon mine altar; for mine house shall be called an house of prayer for all people. (Isa. 56:3, 6–7)

[If] ye oppress not the stranger, the fatherless, and the widow, and shed not innocent blood in this place, neither walk after other gods to your hurt: Then will I cause you to dwell in this place, in the land that I gave to your fathers, for ever and ever. (Jer. 7:6–7)

Thus saith the LORD; Execute ye judgment and righteousness, and deliver the spoiled out of the hand of the oppressor: and do no wrong, do no violence to the stranger, the fatherless, nor the widow, neither shed innocent blood in this place. (Jer. 22:3)

Most Christians don't know or acknowledge that God even told the Jews *to share the inheritance of the precious land of Israel with the "strangers that sojourn among you,"* much like the Palestinians who seek the same today:

And it shall come to pass, [that] ye shall divide it by lot for an inheritance unto you, and to the strangers that sojourn among you, which shall beget children among you: and they shall be unto you as born in the country among the children of Israel; they shall have inheritance with you among the tribes of Israel. And it shall come to pass, [that] in what tribe the stranger sojourneth, there shall ye give [him] his inheritance, saith the Lord GOD. (Ezek. 47:22–23)

God puts those who economically exploit the working man and immigrant, right up there with the sorcerers and adulterers in terms of His judgment:

And I will come near to you to judgment; and I will be a swift witness against the sorcerers, and against the adulterers, and against false swearers, and against those that oppress the hireling in [his] wages, the widow, and the fatherless, and that turn aside the stranger [from his right], and fear not me, saith the LORD of hosts. (Mal. 3:5)

Jesus so identifies Himself with the "stranger" that He calls Himself one, and said that those who do not "take them in" will be subject to His judgment:

I was a stranger, and ye took me not in: naked, and ye clothed me not: sick, and in prison, and ye visited me not...Then shall he answer them, saying, Verily I say unto you, Inasmuch as ye did [it] not to one of the least of these, ye did [it] not to me. (Matt. 25:43, 45)

The Use of the Military to Extend Influence

CFNH: The Hannity and Fox News crowd elevates the military beyond that of a "necessary evil" in a fallen world of selfish individuals and collectives, with service members comprised of real humans including those both heroic and some not-so-heroic (regardless of a uniform they wear and medals), and with a distasteful task of murdering in the cause of nationalism, both military and civilians at times (thus motivating efforts by persons of conscience to prevent such conflicts at all possible costs). The Hannity/Fox News conservative tribe rather views today's professional killer/soldier, armed with the deadliest weapons and technology in the world, as the pinnacle of cultural virtue and in essence an object of sacred worship because of their being held beyond any critique of their deeds by their conservative worshippers. Sadly, this sacredization or idolization does not promote the timely, realistic and sober-minded respect and appreciation due for the humble soldier who truly displays an unselfish motive in protecting the lives, often by endangering their own, of their comrades, civilians, or even the enemy when killing could be avoided, or the soldier or intelligence agent who stops acts of torture or abuse by an ally, enemy or even our own forces.

In effect, the conservative leaders (and by extension, their Christian followers) exploit these military members for their own "feel good" pep rallies and nationalistic fantasies, and as the endangered "tip of the spear" placed in harm's way to conduct their economic and geopolitical adventurism on foreign soil on their behalf, while they cheer from a safe distance. These soldiers comprise many naïve, well-meaning teenagers and young adults of varying maturity and understanding, groomed by mass media and their communities to glamorize war and military service, as well as older members of multi-generational military families who have defined virtue itself as requiring the wearing of a uniform and sometimes taking life or risking one's life as the only meaningful life's calling, as well as an inevitable assortment of ne'er-do-wells who use the authority for violence and institutional incompetence and excess as a secure harbor for their dark vices, in addition to a core of self-reflective and conscientious soldiers. As such, the military as an institution and its members are not only seen as society's idolized model, but that budgets for their ever-skyrocketing financial needs (many times greater than the other nations of the world), actually to be directed to wealthy defense contractors and senior officers, can never be capped and only raised each year to meet a new threat foisted upon the public each year by the media, and compensation raised for lucrative retirements and other fringe benefits, thus requiring severe cuts to aid for the underclass and downtrodden. This Spartan-like militaristic value system of American conservatism is given religious sanction in many conservative pulpits, who see the war-hero as the highest martyr and saintly example, even overlooking their tainted backgrounds, such as convictions of accepting illegal gratuities and lying to Congress about his secret arms sales to enemy Iran (who had just held Americans hostage beforehand), as in the case of Oliver North, an annual "inspirational" speaker at a prominent local Nashville church.

J: Jesus and His Father have never suggested to His people that they put their security in strong military forces. He says that people who have real faith in Him will recognize and act upon the fact that their real security is in the power and faithfulness and protection of their Lord:

> For I will not trust in my bow, neither shall my sword save me. But thou hast saved us from our enemies, and hast put them to shame that hated us. (Psalm 44:6–7)

God also explained that a more authoritarian leader like a king, which usually has some appeal for God's people (including American Christians) unlike the more libertarian-style federation God had set up for the tribes of Israel, would lead to the leaders conscripting their sons into "patriotic wars" in the true guise of expanding their own personal wealth, and to take them away from working on their family farms to help their own financial needs, to rather become defense contractors to build the leader's war machines to build his own wealth:

> And Samuel told all the words of the LORD unto the people that asked of him a king. And he said, This will be the manner of the king that shall reign over you: He will take your sons, and appoint [them] for himself, for his chariots, and [to be] his horsemen; and [some] shall run before his chariots. And he will appoint him captains over thousands, and captains over fifties; and [will set them] to ear his ground, and to reap his harvest, and to make his instruments of war, and instruments of his chariots. (1 Sam. 8:10–12)

The leaders of God's people usually gravitate to military might and strategic foreign policy (usually yoked (often secretly) with ungodly nations) to achieve their objectives, rather than focusing on cultivating godly ethical cultures and dependence upon God, the former strategy of which *actually causes wars* according to God, rather than deterring them, with those of God's servants who warn of such militarism being punished severely to prevent the exposure of such leaders as being out of God's will:

> And at that time Hanani the seer came to Asa king of Judah, and said unto him, Because thou hast relied on the king of Syria, and not relied on the LORD thy God, therefore is the host of the king of Syria escaped out of thine hand. Were not the Ethiopians and the Lubims a huge host, with very many chariots and horsemen? Yet, because thou didst rely on the LORD, he delivered them into thine hand. For the eyes of the LORD run to and fro throughout the whole earth, to shew himself strong in the behalf of [them] whose heart [is] perfect toward him. Herein thou hast done foolishly: therefore from henceforth thou shalt have wars. Then Asa was wroth with the seer, and put him in a prison house; for [he was] in a rage with him because of this [thing]. And Asa oppressed [some] of the people the same time. (2 Chron. 16:7–10)

The psalmist concisely summarized the difference between those of God's people who focus on their nation's military might, versus those who rely on their spiritual heritage:

> Some [trust] in chariots, and some in horses: but we will remember the name of the LORD our God. (Psalm 20:7)

While in many American churches the blood-stained hands of the soldier grant them an honored place in the pulpit dedicated to the Prince of Peace, in God's instance a man of war cannot undergird and represent His own house of worship—the Temple—even if that man is a "a man after God's own heart," King David:

> David said to Solomon: "My son, I had it in my heart to build a house for the Name of the LORD my God. But this word of the LORD came to me: 'You have shed much blood and have fought many wars. You are not to build a house for my Name, because you have shed much blood on the earth in my sight. But you will have a son who will be a man of peace and rest, and I will give him rest from all his enemies on every side. His name will be Solomon, and I will grant Israel peace and quiet during his reign. He is the one who will build a house for my Name. He will be my son, and I will be his father. And I will establish the throne of his kingdom over Israel forever'." (1 Chron. 22:7–10)

All these great military leaders we admire in America and elsewhere will one day gather to band together to fight the returning Lord Himself and the saints:

> Then I saw the beast and the kings of the earth and their armies gathered together to wage war against the rider on the horse and his army. (Rev. 19:19)

They, along with their rich and ruling class peers, will show their cowardice when their deeds are judged one day:

> Then the kings of the earth, the princes, the generals, the rich, the mighty, and everyone else, both slave and free, hid in caves and among the rocks of the mountains. (Rev. 6:15, NIV)

National Interests Vs. Interests of Other Humans

CFNL: The Hannity and Fox News Gospel sacredizes the United States as being of special and unique status of God's favor (rivaled only by Israel) and with a divine mission as a specific tool of God's overall plan of mankind's redemption (while all of scripture actually suggests neither, but it is accepted without question by most, "sola scriptura," "bible-believing" Christians), and thus easily sells the primacy of nationalism ("patriotism") to confused Christians, beyond their basic biblical commitment to their neighbor to seek their well-being and be their "brother's keeper." Skillful politicians of aggressive foreign policy over the years have successfully recruited Christians to a nebulous definition of "national interest" that our historians have shown is usually defined as in the economic interests of big business overseas in oil, commodities and defense sales, with the latter also served stateside. This approach is usually to the detriment of the well-being of other nations or their peoples, which Christians have self-justified, even if those nations have their own Christian communities, although it should not matter in either case.

This privileged status of the United States has been used to justify actions that exploit smaller nations as pawns in the Cold War or War on Terror, or simply economic rivals or with enviable natural resources, and has understandably raised the ire of nations around the world, who are accused by conservatives of "hating freedom" or are envious of our wealth and power. Americans, including its own Christian community, have an international reputation of not thinking internationally (despising "globalism") in terms of how their actions can poison or harm the environment (including the spiritual environment with their exported Hollywood movie/TV morality), exploit overseas workers, or have multi-generation economic impacts, nor regarding the well-being of others or being willing to cooperate in agreements to regulate each other for mutual benefit. Their citizens are known as the "Ugly Americans" for their dismissal of world cultures, often refuse to learn or use their languages, or learn the history of other nations, cultures and values and recognize those which are admirable, or otherwise show respect.

J: While most conservative Christians have been taught or intimated that God loved only Israel or its New Covenant corollary the Church, even a casual reading of scripture will show that God has always loved the peoples of other nations, and even those currently not under His covenant or active in worshipping Him in the way in which we are familiar. He cares about their welfare and future destiny, and expects His children to have the same global perspective, because "Jesus loves the little children, all the children of the world, red and yellow, black and white, they are precious in His sight."

God told the prophet Jonah, who in many ways is a representative of the scripturally revealed mindset of Israel itself (and sometimes God's other children) and who was disappointed that God accepted the repentance of "evil" Nineveh and that He had tarried in His judgment of others, that He is not only concerned about the well-being of the many citizens of this feared pagan empire, but even the CATTLE that could be innocently vulnerable to any such judgment:

> And should I not have concern for the great city of Nineveh, in which there are more than a hundred and twenty thousand people who cannot tell their right hand from their left—and also many animals? (Jonah 4:11, NIV)

God's view was never clearer than in what is known as the most famous Bible verse in the world, which shows how wide His arms are:

> For God so loved *the world*, that he gave his only begotten Son, that whosoever believeth in him should not perish, but have everlasting life. (John 3:16)

Even in the Old Testament era, they knew of the sin of poor regard for one's "neighbor"—and that includes our "neighbors" across our border and overseas:

It is a sin to despise one's neighbor, but blessed is the one who is kind to the needy. (Prov. 14:21)

This command to not only highly regard your neighbor and have compassion on them, but also to "love your neighbor as yourself," is deemed by God to be one of only two "Greatest Commandments," on which Christ says rests all the law and prophets:

The second is this: "Love your neighbor as yourself." There is no commandment greater than these. (Mark 12:31, NIV)

Love does no harm to a neighbor. Therefore love is the fulfillment of the law. (Romans 13:10, NIV)

Do our actions and attitudes regarding fellow humans outside our borders reflect the "mercy" expected from God's people in order to be good "neighbors"?

"Which of these three do you think was a neighbor to the man who fell into the hands of robbers?" The expert in the law replied, "The one who had mercy on him." Jesus told him, "Go and do likewise." (Luke 10:36–37, NIV)

God further reminded His people, who thought they had a special lock on God's graces and relationship, that He not only has regard for, but also a relationship with and a planned destiny for those outside their ranks, and thus they better seek their good graces:

And I say unto you, That many shall come from the east and west, and shall sit down with Abraham, and Isaac, and Jacob, in the kingdom of heaven. But the children of the kingdom shall be cast out into outer darkness: there shall be weeping and gnashing of teeth. (Matt. 8:11–12)

Even the Apostle Paul understood and told the foreign pagan peoples in Athens that they were all of "one blood," and that God had a plan for each of them and a nation for which He wanted them to live, with the goal that they would seek Him because even they can "feel" Him, and He is very close to them already:

God that made the world and all things therein, seeing that he is Lord of heaven and earth, dwelleth not in temples made with hands;...And hath made of one blood all nations of men for to dwell on all the face of the earth, and hath determined the times before appointed, and the bounds of their habitation; That they should seek the Lord, if haply they might feel after him, and find him, though he be not far from every one of us. (Acts 17:24, 26–27)

God further stated through the prophet Isaiah His intention as He earlier discussed with Solomon, that the "stranger" (alien immigrant) would be encouraged to come to His house, the Temple, and fellowship directly with Him:

These I will bring to my holy mountain and give them joy in my house of prayer. Their burnt offerings and sacrifices will be accepted on my altar; for my house will be called a house of prayer for all nations. (Isa. 56:7, NIV)

The Dangers of Progressivism

CFNL: "Progressivism" is a new four-letter-word in conservative circles. In their talk radio and cable news outlets, they contort it to represent anything that is evil, and use it as a label to quarantine people and discussions like the Scarlet Letter. They insinuate that it violates cherished conservative values by letting new ethnic, gender, religious and cultural groups sit at the table of shared economic, financial, cultural and political power of the diverse, secular nation, and thus may threaten "traditions" of society and the "conservation" of the status quo of White European Protestant Male domination at the centers of power. Progressives may let those of other views participate in society unmolested (and thus not "threaten" conservatives, regardless of what they think), and don't feel the burden to "conserve" established views and biases, and shockingly think that things could be "better" in any way other than only a nostalgic, Disney-fied view of American society of the 1950s, or of the Puritans and Founding Fathers. The conservative media ignorantly (either innocently or intentionally) do not acknowledge that, regarding blights on the American legacy such as slavery and civil rights, those who tried to advance beyond those barbaric views in "Christian" America of that time were considered dangerous "progressives" and "liberals," *even by Christians regarding their fellow Christians.* "Liberal" and "Progressive" Christians also tried to prevent child labor and slavery, and horrible living and working conditions of their neighbors, and have been distrusted and libeled ever since. A large portion of Christians are so yoked to conservatism (to the extent of veritable idol worship) and tradition over a progressive view, that they have convinced themselves that God's relations with His people never change, and any assertion of such is tantamount to blasphemy; many of them go so far as to suggest that God still intends us to follow the Mosaic Law of the Old Covenant, regardless of the bulk of the New Testament stating otherwise.

J: A clear-minded and objective reading of scripture, both through Old and New Testaments, will reveal that God is indeed "progressive" in His interactions with man, and gradually advances His people into deeper understandings of His intentions and objectives, and His plans for their operations and manner. In fact, the deployment of the Holy Spirit into the very hearts and minds of believers is the clearest indication that He desires to raise children to "think on their feet," led and guided by His Spirit, with guidance and example by the Word, and not an ironclad yoke of decrees like the Pharisees, that does not truly advance the Kingdom any more than they did. God has indeed proclaimed that He intends to "progress" man and his thinking, through the sanctification of His mind, to one day judge angels, and reign one day as the new "sons of God" over creation under their Creator, in the place of the current principality overlords. To do so, He is "renewing their minds" to take on the mind of Christ to judge as new issues arise, as a "new creature."

The clearest and most indisputable example is that of the centerpiece of the Bible itself, the progressive revelation of the New Covenant, with its foretelling in the Old Testament and primary emphasis in the New, being brokered by Christ Himself under the priesthood of Melchizedek. Though Jews still today reject any notion that any work of God could supplant the Mosaic Law (and that of many professing Christians too, I might add), God told them long beforehand under their prophets that He would be about a "new work":

> Behold, the days come, saith the LORD, that I will make a new covenant with the house of Israel, and with the house of Judah: Not according to the covenant that I made with their fathers in the day [that] I took them by the hand to bring them out of the land of Egypt; which my covenant they brake, although I was an husband unto them, saith the LORD. (Jer. 31:31–32)

> In that he saith, A new [covenant], he hath made the first old. Now that which decayeth and waxeth old [is] ready to vanish away. (Heb. 8:13)

And to Jesus the mediator of the new covenant, and to the blood of sprinkling, that speaketh better things than [that of] Abel. (Heb. 12:24)

In the same way, after the supper he took the cup, saying, "This cup is the new covenant in my blood, which is poured out for you." (Luke 22:20, NIV)

Paul elaborates that this "progressive" work is to be directed not by regulations and decrees, but by Spirit-filled and led men and women, which will lead to true righteousness versus the written Law:

He has made us competent as ministers of a new covenant—not of the letter but of the Spirit; for the letter kills, but the Spirit gives life. Now if the ministry that brought death, which was engraved in letters on stone, came with glory, so that the Israelites could not look steadily at the face of Moses because of its glory, transitory though it was, will not the ministry of the Spirit be even more glorious? If the ministry that brought condemnation was glorious, how much more glorious is the ministry that brings righteousness! (2 Cor. 3:6–9, NIV)

Isaiah himself told them it would be a "new thing"—*a very definition of progression!*

Remember ye not the former things, neither consider the things of old. Behold, I will do a new thing; now it shall spring forth; shall ye not know it? I will even make a way in the wilderness, [and] rivers in the desert. (Isa. 43:18–19)

This is God's nature to create "new things." God will soon do His ultimate "progressive" act, leaving the conservative's embrace of the past to be left behind:

For, behold, I create new heavens and a new earth: and the former shall not be remembered, nor come into mind. (Isa. 65:17)

An example of this progressive mindset is that exhibited by the Council at Jerusalem, comprising the apostles and other church leaders in the Book of Acts, who themselves debated and worked out the fundamental issue of Gentiles coming to the Kingdom of God and their need to obey the Mosaic Law (they decided they didn't), *without citing scriptural commands as justification,* but rather seeking the new guidance of the Holy Spirit and their renewed minds:

> It seemed *good to the Holy Spirit and to us* not to burden you with anything beyond the following requirements... (Acts 15:28, NIV)

The Danger of Other Religions

CFNL: Even though outlets like Fox News are rife with senior management and top on-air figures that have been exposed as flagrant sexual harassers and on-air female cast who have been widely known for dressing provocatively, within a greater conservative media community where infidelity is not uncommon while a specific religious piety is, and where a general money-centered materialistic and status culture is prevalent, nevertheless they often place an emphasis, for the sake of its paramount level of emotional and psychological motivation, on the use of "family values" and "Judeo-Christian heritage" (an association largely disconnected in the New Testament) to emphasize the supremacy of Christianity in American culture, and a special status to Judaism. Of course, those who currently feel the brunt of this superiority in recent decades are the American Muslim community, routinely accused of a myriad of preposterous schemes, practices and crimes, much like the Jews in 1930s "Christian" Germany. The Western Christian community has long used those of other religions as a menacing threat to justify wars of conquest and plunder, or even domestic persecution and confiscation, the most historical of these being the Crusades, first justified against Middle Eastern Muslims, then European and African Muslims and even the Eastern Orthodox Church (of whom they purportedly intended to "save" from Muslim invasion, but plundered anyway), and eventually against pagan Europeans and even rival Christian sects. American history is replete with the scapegoating of other religious sects which have shown themselves over time to be harmless, such as Jews, Quakers, Catholics, Mormons and Sikhs. Nevertheless, religious bigotry and fearmongering is a prime engine of conservative energizing in this age of the War on Terror.

J: While God is often portrayed in American Christian discourse as an angry God from the "fire on the mountain" (as in the most famous American sermon, "Sinners in the Hands of an Angry God"), who harbors no forbearance for those whose understanding of Him varies from any form which a Christian sect in power at the time declares as orthodox (of an orthodoxy that America's Christians can't even decide upon), scripture actually reveals that God normally tries to get His children to tone down the superiority and demeaning view of others outside their faith tradition, and often debunks the old assumptions of them that He remains angered and estranged from those different than them.

In one case, Jesus and His Apostles had to pass through the adjacent region of Samaria to get to Jerusalem. According to the Jews, the Samaritans are their "half brothers" as those earlier Jews from northern Israel who were enslaved, forced to intermarry with Gentiles and then repopulate Israel by the Assyrians, while the Samaritans themselves say otherwise, claiming that they retained the original faith that their Jewish peers discarded due to the apostasy of the biblical priest Eli. Nevertheless, the Jews seemed to hate the Samaritans worse than they did the worst pagan, and their worship that was virtually identical to theirs, but conducted at a different site than the Temple. They refused to interact with Samaritans, and normally not pass anywhere near them, and eventually the animosity apparently became mutual. When some Samaritan cities rebuffed Jesus and His party of apostles, because of their destination towards Jerusalem (while it should be noted that other Samaritan towns warmly embraced Him, such as those near the Woman at the Well), the Apostles acted towards these despised religious rivals as most American Christians do today, but they were surprised that their Lord did not feel the need to endorse their Phineas-like stern religious superior zealotry, as they expected:

> And it came to pass, when the time was come that he should be received up, he steadfastly set his face to go to Jerusalem, and sent messengers before his face: and they went, and entered into a village of the Samaritans, to make ready for him. And they did not receive him, because his face was as though he would go to Jerusalem. And when his disciples James and John saw [this], they said, Lord, wilt thou that we command fire to come down from heaven, and consume them, even as Elias did? But he turned, and rebuked them, and said, Ye know not what manner of spirit ye are of. (Luke 9:51–55)

Even Peter, the "Apostle to the Jews"—the man who later had to be reprimanded by Paul for refusing to congregate with Gentile believers—was humbled by God for his strict adherence to the fine print of the holy book's written code, yet missing the major points about his God's nature and His destiny for others, as He later showed him in a vision that one's strict piety and religious commitment should not lead to us viewing outsiders as "common or unclean." God thus prepared Peter for his imminent interaction with the Gentile Cornelius and his household, who were shocked that a Jew would even enter their house, leading Peter to make a stunning statement about God's view of others outside of their religious community:

> And he said unto them, Ye know how that it is an unlawful thing for a man that is a Jew to keep company, or come unto one of another nation; but God hath shewed me that *I should not call any man common or unclean*...Then Peter opened [his] mouth, and said, Of a truth I perceive that *God is no respecter of persons: But in every nation he that feareth him, and worketh righteousness, is accepted with him.* (Acts 10:28, 34–35) (emphasis added)

The Use of Government to Enforce Christian Principles

CFNL: The Fox News and Hannity gospel emphasizes a vague Judeo-Christian "civil religion," which has a veneer of religious truth and devotion, but is vague enough to permit greed, materialism and even infidelity amongst its celebrity practitioners, while meaning to generally promote a cultural superiority of those from the White European Protestant clan, and give second-class status to those that do not embrace it and the capitalism/colonialism principles that undergird it. It believes that government laws can be used to promote Christianity within the military academies and battlefield as well as the schoolhouse, with the Ten Commandments in the courtroom and a nativity scene in the courthouse square, with "Merry Christmas" festooned in city decorations, all paid for by taxpayers, including Jews, Muslims and secularists.

J: Jesus and the saints portrayed the use of the State (or "the king") to promote the agenda of the "kingdom of heaven" as becoming the Mystery Babylon woman riding the "beast" of government, which not only perverted her (or promoted her darker perversities), but also ultimately betrays her and leaves her destitute. Many (including myself) saw this begin in earnest when the pagan Caesar Constantine declared Christianity the "state religion" (although he was content to worship pagan gods as well), allowing him to co-opt the church for political aims to unify the kingdom (as he further meddled in spiritual matters at the critical Council of Nicaea for political aims), and as the church began to attack itself and anathematize its former colleagues to please him, having pagans flood within their ranks to be in good standing with the State, and the temptation of institutional wealth that caused them to lose favor with the people.

Jesus did not see the collaboration of church and state as spiritually beneficial, as opposed to older era Catholics, Eastern Orthodox through the ages, the Puritans and many fundamentalists today, and rather emphasized it as the tension between competing "masters" (including the "mammon" that comes with state collaboration):

> No servant can serve two masters: for either he will hate the one, and love the other; or else he will hold to the one, and despise the other. Ye cannot serve God and mammon. (Luke 16:13)

The Apostle Paul showed that what Christians need to fulfill the Great Commission was not the coercive power of government (which would only breed resentment rather than true conversion), but rather the persuasive power of the appeals of a Spirit-filled believer, while respecting the same free will of choice of others that God does with them as well:

> Since, then, we know what it is to fear the Lord, we try to persuade others. What we are is plain to God, and I hope it is also plain to your conscience. (2 Cor. 5:11, NIV)

Jesus also differentiated the agenda and kingdom (and jurisdiction) of the worldly sphere of power and government (or "Caesar"), and that of His Kingdom, and recommended living in both, but not confusing the nature or environment of both:

> Then saith he unto them, Render therefore unto Caesar the things which are Caesar's; and unto God the things that are God's. (Matt. 22:21)

Jesus saw that perpetually trying to fight the government for its own sake (rather than merely resisting injustices when they arise that hurt innocent parties), including the resistance of paying taxes for some proposed spiritual reason, was in actuality a distraction that would hinder our labors in advancing the Kingdom and its business. He demonstrated a willingness to give the State what it needs, if not His heart, to "manage" it and minimize its distractive impact on the true work:

> But so that we may not cause offense, go to the lake and throw out your line. Take the first fish you catch; open its mouth and you will

find a four-drachma coin. Take it and give it to them for my tax and yours. (Matt. 17:27)

Traditions of Society and Status Quo

CFNL: In the conservative belief system, "tradition" is interlinked with conservatism and what is being conserved, in terms of a mindset, values and way of life, embodied over generations in fixed rituals. These are often described as a "Judeo-Christian" tradition. In the American "civil religion" of conservatives, it might include patriotic observance of the Fourth of July, saying "Merry Christmas" and nativity scenes at the courthouse, veneration of the military, and multi-generational practices within the "gun culture" and hunting, and even more modern practices such as unrestricted tobacco and alcohol consumption (or even certain processed foods), or motorcycle riding, or other lifestyle practices for which citizens can draw meaning, and thus resist any attempts to regulate or restrict the bounds of such practice, such as for public health and safety, animal welfare or environmental protection.

This practice of assigning meaning to such lifestyle elements and practices is clearly inherited from old religions such as Judaism and Christianity, in which over millennia certain ritual observances have supplanted Bible teaching and the simple, practice guidance from Christ and the Apostles. Such tradition does not limit itself to the ornate robes and headgear, and incense and arcane mystical sacraments of Catholic, Orthodox and mainline Protestant strains; evangelicals have their own rituals, thinly connected to the Biblical instruction they claim to solely follow with their "sola scriptura" convictions, such as church membership, professional clergy, ornate churches and government affiliation as tax-free, and even their styles of music or orders of worship. Amongst the elites of America, "tradition" dictates the leadership of America's power centers in Washington and Wall Street by the aristocratic families groomed for power at Yale and Harvard, and thus directed to the levers of societal control; Christians have their own "grooming centers" for leadership at the prominent seminaries and Christian universities. These traditions and their observance within these culturally-stratified bounds thus serve the conservative cause to "conserve" the status quo of who controls and dictates the levers of power and influence in American society, and who does not. When those of non-white races, women, those of "non-traditional" religions (or none at all), cultures or communities (including the inner cities) or even those of other lifestyle practices who have not had access to such influence suddenly vie for such positions, conservative media (and their henchmen in many of America's pulpits and parachurch organizations) will suggest that "American values and traditions are under attack," as a euphemism for xenophobia, racism, sexism and other phobias that expose their intentions to maintain the status quo of power within a narrow band of the American demographic.

J: Jesus was born into a culture bound by religious (and thus lifestyle-rigid) traditions, as dictated by the "tradition police," the Pharisees, who had taken the actual commands by God for ritual purity by the priests when performing sacrifices, and extended its demands to all of society. They claimed an "oral law" which they asserted to the rest of the Jewish population that they had been given alone to preserve, generation to generation, and thus they were to take their word for it that they knew of such "secret" commands. These commands were not only far greater in number, but also much more intrusive and confining than the original Mosaic Law in the Torah, which turned them into self-appointed lawyers and judges to define the intent of each command for everyone. As such, they were widely despised by the population for their reign of terror, even beyond that of the Sadducee priesthood. It became obvious in time that these self-written "traditions" or "customs" of daily lifestyle practice were far more important to them than the Mosaic Law itself, much less the real meaning and intentions of God behind the original commandments, and what He wanted to instruct His children about concerning His nature through them. It should be noted that the Pharisaic sect of Judaism prevailed in the subsequent fall of Jerusalem and the diaspora of Jews from Palestine, evolving into today's rabbinic Judaism. However, Jesus plainly told them what He thought of their "traditions," and even unlike many of His followers for millennia afterwards, He did not take a kind eye toward these "traditions," with their tendency to obfuscate or distract from God's original intentions, further burdening the people, and actually serving as a roadblock to man's relationship to God.

Even His follower, Stephen the Deacon, was subject to the common accusation by their Jewish accusers, not of breaking the Torah or defying God, but rather belittling their precious Pharisaic national and religious traditions:

> And Stephen, full of faith and power, did great wonders and miracles among the people...For we [synagogue false witnesses] have heard

him [Stephen] say, that this Jesus of Nazareth shall destroy this place, and shall change the customs which Moses delivered us. (Acts 6:8, 14)

Even *the church leaders in Jerusalem* were concerned that Paul was leading disciples to forsake the "customs" of their faith:

And they are informed of thee, that thou teachest all the Jews which are among the Gentiles to forsake Moses, saying that they ought not to circumcise [their] children, neither to walk after the customs. (Acts 21:21)

Jesus was routinely accused by the Pharisees of directing His followers to violate the ritual traditions, to which Jesus said that their "tradition" actually caused the people to "transgress the commandment of God" in order to follow it, and thus expressed what He thought about the merits of "traditions of men" and its dangers—even "Christian" ones:

Then the Pharisees and scribes asked him, "Why walk not thy disciples according to the tradition of the elders, but eat bread with unwashen hands?" to which Jesus replied, "For laying aside the commandment of God, ye hold the tradition of men, [as] the washing of pots and cups: and many other such like things ye do. And he said unto them, Full well ye reject the commandment of God, that ye may keep your own tradition....Making the word of God of none effect through your tradition, which ye have delivered: and many such like things do ye." (Mark 7:5, 8–9, 13)

Likewise Paul warned believers to be wary of religious "tradition," which is really worldly in nature:

Beware lest any man spoil you through philosophy and vain deceit, after the tradition of men, after the rudiments of the world, and not after Christ. (Col. 2:8)

Conservatives Think Consideration of Others is a Weakness

CFNL: Conservatives, reflecting the Gospel of Hannity and Fox News, get really bugged by protests from anyone concerning their broad characterizations of sectors of the public, with their being held accountable for their statements and their accuracy (or degree of hurtful crassness) being labeled as another case of "political correctness." Since they revere "tough guys," either real ones like Special Forces members who can kill with their bare hands, or imaginary movie action heroes, who shoot from the hip and spare no feelings, speaking with bravado and swagger, they have no empathy for those who are demeaned or spoken of with a broad brush. In other words, they have no value for gentleness, respect for those who are different, meekness or consideration, or "loving their neighbor." Those who are labeled as wagers of political correctness, and point out the demeaning statements and attitudes and potential to offend themselves or others, are now labeled with the further demeaning title of "snowflakes," seen to be so fragile because they care about the dignity and feelings of others.

J: The Gospel of Jesus and His saints does not align with the view that everyone who is different is worthy of contempt and ill wishes, and suspicion of mal intent. This version of "klanism" that only sees virtue in one's own perceived "klan," and suspects the motives of others, or shows open contempt for their feelings or rights to be themselves, is a supremacist attitude that is foreign to the teaching of Jesus.

Jesus said that His followers would actually love people who are different than themselves (counter to many Western Christians today, whom only want to provide aid to overseas Christians, or address the persecution of Christians only). Jesus plainly says that such "klanism" thinking is no better than the pagan or any immoral person:

> For if ye love them which love you, what reward have ye? do not even the publicans the same? And if ye salute your brethren only, what do ye more [than others]? do not even the publicans so? (Matt. 5:46–47)

Jesus didn't think that "lowliness of mind" was wimpy, defeatist thinking, by "weak" people. He said we should be talking about how other people are better than us, not that we or our "klan" is better and more admirable than others, nor patting our own backs while turning our backs on the needs of people who are different, and the Apostle Paul felt the same way:

> [Let] nothing [be done] through strife or vainglory; but in lowliness of mind let each esteem others better than themselves. Look not every man on his own things [interests], but every man also on the things [interests] of others. (Phil. 2:3–4)

In its most basic form, we must regard others in light of the Golden Rule, in blatant opposition to the Gospel of the conservative Hannitys and Fox News crowd:

> So in everything, do to others what you would have them do to you, for this sums up the Law and the Prophets. (Matt. 7:12)

Paul affirms this, and that we should be looking out for the rights of people that are different than us in society, and not that of our own kind:

> No one should seek their own good, but the good of others. (1 Cor. 10:24, NIV)

In one of the most famous Bible chapters, Paul explains that real Godly love is known for its "kindness," humility ("it does not boast"), lack of good old American "pride," and "does not dishonor others," and does not look out for its own crowd, nor gnash its teeth at others, or seek to pursue others over perceived prior slights:

> Love is patient, love is kind. It does not envy, it does not boast, it is not proud. It does not dishonor others, it is not self-seeking, it is not easily angered, it keeps no record of wrongs. (1 Cor. 13:4–5, NIV)

God is not impressed with the "tough guy" Christian, talking tough and showing off their masculinity and making threats; He rather says the meek are the ones with the bright future:

> Blessed are the meek, for they shall inherit the earth. (Matt. 5:5, ESV)

Paul makes it clear that thinking too highly of oneself and one's own kind is a real danger, as opposed to "sober" thinking that perceives fairly and accurately, and it is dependent upon the amount of faith that God gives every person, which none of us can boast in comparison to others:

> For I say, through the grace given unto me, to every man that is among you, not to think [of himself] more highly than he ought to think; but to think soberly, according as God hath dealt to every man the measure of faith. (Rom. 12:3)

Conservatives Think Sustainability and Environmental Care Are Subversive

CFNL: Conservatives typically view those who speak of environmental protection and sustainability as pagan earth-worshippers, or gullible bleeding hearts who have no concept of the economic impact of their "do-gooder" environmental adventurism and crusades. They see people who look out for endangered species such as "snail darters" or unspoiled wilderness such as in Alaska, or even opponents of strip mines, as fools who impede our economic progress, which affects the profit potential of corporations. They also see lifestyles that emphasize "sustainability" that try not to consume valuable natural resources faster than they can be replenished, or reduce their production of waste, pollution and greenhouse gas emissions (to preserve such resources for future generations) as misguided and foolish, as well as efforts to commit the United States and other industrialized nations to agree together to reform their economies to prevent environmental damage in a fair and unified manner.

J: Contrary to the long-held beliefs of conservative Christians, God does not believe that the protection and watch care over Earth's finite resources is merely a plot of Satanic "earth worshippers." In fact, the Bible record makes it clear that mankind was created *for the express purpose* of taking care of and managing the creation:

> And the LORD God took the man, and put him into the garden of Eden to dress it and to keep it. (Gen. 2:15)

His charge to "dress it and keep it" uses Hebrew words, with the former (*abad*, Strong's H5647) that is ironically normally used in the Bible to denote "servitude" or "bondage," such as to describe the Hebrews "bondage" in Egypt! The latter word to "keep," the Hebrew *shamar* (Strong's H8104), means to "have charge of," "ward, protect, save life" and "preserve." The principle here is that God created man for the express purpose of husbandry, so that man could cultivate creation to be fruitful, and protect it for the long haul; in other words, God creates from nothing, and man was created to sustain that creation (he was further given the privilege of creatively naming the animals and thus putting his creative input on them, and probably intended for further creative enhancements as God chooses). Sadly, most conservative American Christians reject any such God-given responsibility to preserve creation, viewing "sustainability" as a liberal God-denying Earth worship, much less environmental protection or ecology. Since God's people reject their first and primary assignment (and their follow-up responsibilities to be "fishers of men" by exhibiting Christ's love, acceptance and forgiveness in concert with proclaiming His "good news"), *is it no wonder that God has refrained from giving us further directives on His behalf?*

Meanwhile, Hannity, Limbaugh and their conservative Christian followers actually brag and gloat about driving their big gas-guzzling SUVs that belch out large amounts of pollution and carbon dioxide, and ridicule their more responsible fellow citizens who realize the impact their lifestyles have on their fellow citizens, either in the U.S. or the other side of the world. These latter virtuous souls do not flaunt their wealth and economic ambivalence, but rather make decisions of conscience that are considerate of others, and are willing to adjust their lifestyles and standard of living to minimize pollution (including climate-affecting varieties) and preserve precious natural resources for our descendants, *even when they do not recognize the God of the Bible, but simply know it's the responsible and considerate thing to do.* At least conservatives are consistent—they similarly squander the financial resources of future generations with their current tax cuts and the enormous annual deficits and rapidly expanding national debt, which will be paid dearly by our descendants with crushing taxes to meet the interest payments, in a polluted land of greatly diminished natural resources, for which the unfortunate offspring can thank today's selfish older generation.

To accomplish this task over creation, God gave man the privilege (and responsibility) of "dominion" over the living things of the earth:

> And God said, Let us make man in our image, after our likeness: and let them have dominion over the fish of the sea, and over the fowl of the air, and over the cattle, and over all the earth, and over every creeping thing that creepeth upon the earth. (Gen. 1:26)

Anyone knows that to honorably wield "dominion" over any subjects within any domain in this world, requires those exercising dominion to rule *with a regard for the well-being of its subjects, seeking their prosperity so that their regent can prosper as well,* and with a duty for their watch care if such regent is themselves subject to God, and/or God's representative the Church on earth. However, many conservative Christians have little regard for public policies that seek the well-being of aquatic animals, birds or other land creatures, if they are told by the big-business lobbyists in the conservative media that it could have any remote impact on their standard of living, lifestyle or conveniences, though in reality it is usually only at risk to the ever-expanding quarterly profits of corporate entities. God made the animal kingdom totally dependent upon mankind for their well-being and prosperity. *If God sent His own people into captivity for seventy years because they missed seventy years of letting the land rest, then what will He do for our mistreatment and poor stewardship of the animal kingdom?*

We may in fact have a glimpse of what God eventually has in mind for those who have abused his creation, both in the animal and plant kingdom, in the future events foretold in the Book of Revelation. Earlier in the events of this book, all the animals of earth and the rest of creation praise the Lamb who died to redeem creation after Man's fall, and then sits as Judge to avenge the victims of the misdeeds of others. Thus, at the end of time God does indeed avenge those who not only abused mankind, but also the rest of His creation:

> And the nations were angry, and thy wrath is come, and the time of the dead, that they should be judged, and that thou shouldest give reward unto thy servants the prophets, and to the saints, and them that fear thy name, small and great; and *shouldest destroy them which destroy the earth.* (Rev. 11:18) (emphasis added)

Conservatism and Survival of the Fittest

CFNL: The conservative culture values physically or economically strong men, who have the ability to coerce others (sometimes violently or lethally), and have no compunction against using it. This explains the preponderance of the military commando, athlete and action movie star as the heroes that fill their pulpits and conferences as guest speakers. They do not spend too much time worrying about third world nations (or what their "favorite-son" current president calls, "sh_t-hole countries") slowly dying from famine, disease and civil war, refugees who slowly die from exposure and whom are refused refugee status in the Western world, or "losers" in the geopolitical Cold War or its War on Terror replacement, caught in the crossfire of battles between rogue and autocratic nations on both sides, as pawns in the "great game." They also don't worry much about inner city children and teens killed by rampant gun violence and gang activity, as long as it stays out of their neighborhoods, or the current epidemic of opioid-related deaths nationwide, unless it touches their own families. They are not concerned about unhealthy environments in our prisons, or even the likelihood of many innocent parties rotting in the prisons because they were too poor to afford high-rent legal counsel to buy their way out of prison time, or could be exonerated in many cases with the proper DNA tests. They even do not care much about the epidemic of childhood obesity in the West, affecting all classes but particularly the lower economic strata, due to the paucity of urban grocery stores with fresh produce and vegetables, and media and advertising's emphasis on unhealthy processed foods.

These attitudes exist because conservatives generally embrace a Darwinian "survival of the fittest" mentality, consistent with their embrace of cut-throat, unregulated economic markets, and "gunboat" diplomacy over lesser powerful nations, where the "Golden Rule" means that "he who has the gold, makes the rules." They do not want to inhibit their standard of living or disposable income in any way to potentially preserve any of these disadvantaged groups to any appreciable degree, and are rather relieved to see them go away. Prophecy buffs are even entertained when they see bombs dropping on villages in the Middle East, even using online emojis showing "popcorn eating" (believe me, I have seen them many times) on prophecy boards as they see the bombing raids hit villages, enjoying the "show" and speculating over its "prophetic significance." This attitude is also very libertarian in its darkest representation, and reflects an adherence to the Ayn Rand school of thinking, which is basically a Satanic value system that has absolutely no regard for anyone except for the welfare of oneself, as do the Church of Satan and Aleister Crowley's school of Thelema magic. Conservative Christians do not temper these base, fleshly impulses amongst their own by being "salt and light" and preaching a call to "love their neighbor," but rather give spiritual sanction to the self-centeredness. They have gone so far as to often justify AIDs deaths as "God's judgment" of the gay community, and the expunging of Muslims in the West or elsewhere as an "improvement to the neighborhood," just as their Christian forbearers in America did concerning the eradication of the American Indians, or enslavement and importation of Africans as property, as some Biblical fulfillment of "Ham's prophecy" or an amillennial expression of Biblical "dominion" and "manifest destiny" over the non-white "savages" who stood in the way of the expansion of white, European Christians toward the East.

J: Jesus, His Father and the saints had a different view about the weak and powerless, or who scripture calls the "anawim" or often described as the "lost and forgotten ones." In fact, Jesus said that they would inherit the eternal Kingdom of Heaven, and only others who pretend to be like them (i.e., "poor in spirit") had any chance to join them.

In both the Old and New Testaments, God gave a mandate for His children to embolden the weak and to assist them in their infirmities:

> Strengthen ye the weak hands, and confirm the feeble knees. (Isa. 35:3)

> I have shewed you all things, how that so labouring ye ought to support the weak, and to remember the words of the Lord Jesus, how he said, It is more blessed to give than to receive. (Acts 20:35)

> We then that are strong ought to bear the infirmities of the weak, and not to please ourselves. (Romans 15:1)

This will require the elimination of the warfare state, and our fetishization of the weapons of war, and those who wield them, to raise up and not eliminate the weak:

> Beat your plowshares into swords, and your pruninghooks into spears: let the weak say, I [am] strong. (Joel 3:10)

God will in fact to use these same "weak" that are the bane of the conservative community to stop the "mighty" right in their tracks:

> But God hath chosen the foolish things of the world to confound the wise; and God hath chosen the weak things of the world to confound the things which are mighty. (1 Cor. 1:27)

Restricting one's actions or "liberties" out of regard for those "weaker" in spirit is not the sign of being an over-sensitive, politically-correct "snowflake," but rather sound wisdom from Biblical admonition:

> But take heed lest by any means this liberty of yours become a stumbling-block to them that are weak. (1Cor. 8:9)

The "weak" should not be viewed with contempt or eliminated or left to deteriorate naturally, but rather *embraced and even emulated*, with the intention to redeem and elevate them, for Christ's glory:

> To the weak became I as weak, that I might gain the weak: I am made all things to all [men], that I might by all means save some. (1 Cor. 9:22)

Paul further advised us with the charge to actively comfort the "feebleminded," and to "support the weak," and extend patience to everyone—even those supposedly widespread "lazy, good-for-nothing welfare cheats":

> Now we exhort you, brethren, warn them that are unruly, comfort the feebleminded, support the weak, be patient toward all [men]. (1 Thess. 5:14)

Apologizing for America or Anything Cultural is a Sign of Weakness and Subversion

CFNL: One of the main clarion calls of the conservative community is that any criticism of America's actions in the world, either currently or concerning its historical actions, inevitably comes from the "hate America" crowd. Examples of such topics include America's treatment of Indians, African slaves, natives in colonial territories, business policies overseas, domestic civil rights abuses, or America's actions in war (both top-level-policies and acts by deployed troops), including massacres and torture of civilians or combatants. The common victims of such labeling often include esteemed academic historians who are long-established experts in certain fields, ministers and civil rights activists. One of things conservatives must value in being Americans is their innate "pride" and never apologizing for anything, past or present, and besmirching introspective, soul-searching political opposition in political debates, while insinuating their lack of "patriotism" (or even subversion) for raising such questions is a common tactic. A countless stream of conservative politicians build a foundation of their campaign slogans on being "proud" conservatives who will "never apologize for America." They will make sure that America (through its political leaders) never publicly denounces the nation's past actions or apologize for erroneous actions, much less seek forgiveness and offer any retribution, particularly in any international forum.

J: Jesus, His Father and the saints have a different attitude regarding pride and a refusal to admit one's error, or otherwise express humility, even as a collective society. They not only portray humility as an expression of one's recognition of true reality, but also a sign of strength and genuineness. Alternatively, pride is seen as in the possession of those of less than pure motives, alongside selfishness and a lack of true introspection, and a trait of those who will inevitably fall prey to the destruction of their own self-worship.

Jesus said that a truly circumspect person will know and acknowledge that shortcomings are often more prevalent (and to a greater degree) in themselves than in those of whom they are critical:

> And why beholdest thou the mote that is in thy brother's eye, but considerest not the beam that is in thine own eye? (Matt. 7:3)

God goes so far as to suggest that the only ones who will dwell in His lofty heavenly residence are those of a "contrite (deeply repentant) and humble spirit":

> For thus saith the high and lofty One that inhabiteth eternity, whose name [is] Holy; I dwell in the high and holy [place], with him also [that is] of a contrite and humble spirit, to revive the spirit of the humble, and to revive the heart of the contrite ones. (Isa. 57:15)

Jesus suggests that the ticket to greatness is to be humble in nature, to then be lifted up by God in due course (this would also be true on a national level as well):

> And whosoever shall exalt himself shall be abased; and he that shall humble himself shall be exalted. (Matt. 23:12)

God further stated that if a nation wants to be stronger and healthier, the antidote is not to emphasize its pride and rightness, but rather a public recognition of its failed actions, and efforts to remedy its sinful behavior:

> [Yet] if they shall bethink themselves in the land whither they were carried captives, and repent, and make supplication unto thee in the land of them that carried them captives, saying, We have sinned, and have done perversely, we have committed wickedness... (1 Kings 8:47)

The Apostle Paul suggested that the Church itself had enough to do in introspectively pointing out its own shortcomings (and indeed a mandate to do so), rather than to spend its time as a "culture warrior" in pointing out those of the outer world, which was actually God's business:

> What business is it of mine to judge those outside the church? Are you not to judge those inside? (1 Cor. 5:12)

Conservatives Love Their Tough Guys

CFNL: The "heroes" of the conservative movement are the cigar-chomping, brash figures wearing a uniform, or toting a gun, or whipping bad guys in the movies, or politicians and political commentators with swagger, a smirk and "tough talk," all whose pithy and prideful bromides they listen to with rapt attention, looking for spiritual insight.

J: God is not impressed with their braggadocio, or see anything there that should be emulated. Sometimes God makes it very clear:

> To the arrogant I say, 'Boast no more,' and to the wicked, 'Do not lift up your horns. (Psalm 75:4, NIV)

> The eyes of the arrogant will be humbled and human pride brought low; the LORD alone will be exalted in that day. (Isa. 2:11, NIV)

Even the apostle Paul had to be on the lookout on how these people were infiltrating the church in his day:

> But I will come to you very soon, if the Lord is willing, and then I will find out not only how these arrogant people are talking, but what power they have. (1 Cor. 4:19, NIV)

Conservatives Think Social Justice is of the Devil

CFNL: Conservative leaders have re-invented the meaning of the term "social justice" to be a subversive, destructive practice, rather than what has been its natural and historical meaning, in terms of helping "society" at large, and providing "justice," which no person of good intentions should want to deny to anyone. (One of the most influential media figures to impress this upon Christians is the Mormon media titan Glenn Beck.) They have portrayed the expression itself as "code words" for those unregenerates who are trying to sneak in civil rights to marginal figures in society, such as immigrants from different cultures, or those whose lifestyles, while privately practiced, are different with ours. They warn that these malevolent figures (comprising civil rights activists, journalists and volunteers), if their deeds are left unexposed and unabated, will result in the horrific net effect of everyone being treated equally. "Social Justice" is clearly shown to be a fundamental opponent to the values of moralistic and Christian people everywhere.

J: Alternatively, a perusal of the entire scriptural record will show that social justice is a foundational component and imperative for God's Kingdom, and to be a primary pursuit of its residents here and now, which is not a substitute for the preaching of the Kingdom of Heaven coming in the future, but *as a means to encourage others to take it seriously and to join in.*

In the Old Testament, societal justice, particularly for the underclasses, was a centerpiece of God's message through the prophets, and what He would judge their nation for:

> He hath shewed thee, O man, what [is] good; and what doth the LORD require of thee, but to do justly, and to love mercy, and to walk humbly with thy God?...Shall I count [them] pure with the wicked balances, and with the bag of deceitful weights? For the rich men thereof are full of violence, and the inhabitants thereof have spoken lies, and their tongue [is] deceitful in their mouth. (Micah 6:8, 11–12)

Jesus quoted Isaiah 61:1, emphasizing both a future (as demonstrated by His teaching of the Kingdom) and present (and evidenced by His immediate spiritual warfare) spiritual and physical deliverance (as evidenced by His healing and feeding of the multitudes) of the downtrodden when He stated,

> The Spirit of the Lord is upon me, because he hath anointed me to preach the gospel to the poor; he hath sent me to heal the brokenhearted, to preach deliverance to the captives, and recovering of sight to the blind, to set at liberty them that are bruised. (Luke 4:18)

Jesus emphasized a point that Christians (particularly those of the pro-Ten Commandments, pro-Law, or Hebraic Roots variety) or other fundamentalists routinely miss, is that there is such a thing as the "weightier matters of the law," which are the "front burner" issues God seeks us to focus on, particularly when in a difficult dilemma, such as when the demands of different commandments of God seem to conflict in approach or agenda in a situation. Sadly, Christians over generations have been conditioned to almost always focus on the "less weighty" matters of the law, and don't ask themselves why, as Jesus attests in His rebuke of their fellow fundamentalists, the Pharisees:

Woe unto you, scribes and Pharisees, hypocrites! for ye pay tithe of mint and anise and cummin, and have omitted the weightier [matters] of the law, judgment [justice], mercy, and faith: these ought ye to have done, and not to leave the other undone. (Matt. 23:23)

God frequently makes it very clear as to His intentions for what should be the primary emphasis and actions of His children:

Defend the poor and fatherless: do justice to the afflicted and needy. (Psalm 82:3)

Many Christians are wary of seeking "social justice" for the downtrodden, evidently thinking that if given such they may become a threat or rival for their comfortable lifestyles. They would rather use the age-old Western Christian tradition of merely giving hand-outs of charity voluntarily as the whim hits them, to whatever level they feel salves their conscience based upon what limited exposure to such need that they come into contact with. In terms of economic injustice or oppression, that concern barely enters their minds, for most conservative Christians. *However, God has clearly stated that the "sacrifice" of periodic hand-outs of financial charity, or even expressions of piety, take a back seat to actual efforts to secure long-lasting solutions to remedy economic and social injustice, and demonstrations of "loving your neighbor" and illustrating God's care and concern:*

To do justice and judgment [is] more acceptable to the LORD than sacrifice. (Prov. 21:3)

The Preacher (Solomon) noted that the "higher ups" in institutions and society have always considered the exploitation of the poor and lack of justice as essential to "conserve" the status quo (in fact, establishment higher officials enforce it), so one should not be surprised and, to in fact, expect its existence, but that does not excuse God's people for not combating it:

If you see the oppression of the poor, and the violent perversion of justice and righteousness in a province, do not marvel at the matter; for high official watches over high official, and higher officials are over them… (Ecc. 5:8, NKJV)

Here are just a few more exhortations of like manner from God, about the lack of social justice for the downtrodden amongst the communities of God's children, and His expectation that they make it a priority, based upon this small sampling of His similar statements, for you to grasp the seriousness of how much God means this:

> None calleth for justice, nor [any] pleadeth for truth: they trust in vanity, and speak lies; they conceive mischief, and bring forth iniquity. (Isa. 59:4)

> Do not deny justice to your poor people in their lawsuits. (Exod. 23:6, NIV)

> Follow justice and justice alone, so that you may live and possess the land the LORD your God is giving you. (Deut. 16:20, NIV)

> Do not deprive the foreigner or the fatherless of justice, or take the cloak of the widow as a pledge. (Deut. 24:17, NIV)

> The LORD works righteousness and justice for all the oppressed. (Psalm 103:6, NIV)

> Good will come to those who are generous and lend freely, who conduct their affairs with justice. (Psalm 112:5, NIV)

> I know that the LORD secures justice for the poor and upholds the cause of the needy. (Psalm 140:12, NIV)

> The righteous care about justice for the poor, but the wicked have no such concern. (Prov. 29:7, NIV)

> Learn to do right; seek justice. Defend the oppressed. Take up the cause of the fatherless; plead the case of the widow. (Isa. 1:17, NIV)

> …to deprive the poor of their rights and withhold justice from the oppressed of my people, making widows their prey and robbing the fatherless. (Isa. 10:2, NIV)

> …but with righteousness he will judge the needy, with justice he will give decisions for the poor of the earth. (Isa. 11:4, NIV)

> The people of the land practice extortion and commit robbery; they oppress the poor and needy and mistreat the foreigner, denying them justice. (Ezek. 22:29, NIV)

> They trample on the heads of the poor as on the dust of the ground and deny justice to the oppressed. (Amos 2:7, NIV)

For I know how many are your offenses and how great your sins. There are those who oppress the innocent and take bribes and deprive the poor of justice in the courts. (Amos 5:12, NIV)

This is what the LORD Almighty said: "Administer true justice; show mercy and compassion to one another." (Zech, 7:9, NIV)

So I will come to put you on trial. I will be quick to testify against sorcerers, adulterers and perjurers, against those who *defraud laborers of their wages*, who oppress the widows and the fatherless, and deprive the foreigners among you of justice, but do not fear me, says the LORD Almighty. (Mal. 3:5, NIV)

…they have grown fat and sleek. They know no bounds in deeds of evil; they judge not with justice the cause of the fatherless, to make it prosper, and they do not defend the rights of the needy. (Jer. 5:28, ESV)

Thus says the LORD: Do justice and righteousness, and deliver from the hand of the oppressor him who has been robbed. And do no wrong or violence to the resident alien, the fatherless, and the widow, nor shed innocent blood in this place. (Jer. 22:3, ESV)

The people of the land have practiced extortion and committed robbery. They have oppressed the poor and needy, and have extorted from the sojourner without justice. (Ezek. 22:29, ESV)

What does this small sampling of Biblical examples suggest to you about how serious God is about the downtrodden receiving social justice?

Conservative Christians Are Always Worried about Their Own Rights or Persecution, and Further Think That Not Controlling the Behavior of Others is "Persecution" Itself

CFNL: Conservative Christians only seem to talk in public forums about the persecution of other Christians, and not people at large. In my experience, most Christians I have heard are only interested in meeting the needs of the destitute or persecuted within the Christian communities in other lands, somehow arguing from the Bible that it only matters how Christians take care of each other, *not noticing the irony of how the Bible says that even the pagan Gentiles and tax collectors take care of their own kind*. Domestically, their focus of concern is on any governmental actions that would restrict their role of dominance religiously over a pluralistic American population. Some recent examples include their worrisome claims of the persecution of unwieldy neighborhood Bible studies with parking situations that violate traffic and zoning codes, or the ability to put Christian displays at the city courthouse or inside it, or Christian songs in state school pageants, or Bibles handed out by outsiders on their state school grounds. They cry "Persecution!" even though such tactics impede on their neighbors, while their neighbors are not imposing their beliefs or lifestyles upon the Christians to force them to practice (even sexual ones). Even more importantly, they seem to have blatant disregard for the civil rights or protections of those who are different, such as Jehovah's Witness, Mormons, Jews, Muslims, New Age and atheists, whose experiences in state settings such as school or even local government can impose others' external beliefs on them as taxpayers that they do not believe, or restrict their religious practice, such as certain dress or dietary restrictions. When they seek First Amendment or other Bill of Rights Protection, the Christians look out for their own skin, and forget to make such initiatives broad enough to protect their neighbors of other faiths or beliefs as well (to also garner their shared support), to "love their neighbor" and follow the Golden Rule.

J: Jesus, His Father and the saints taught that not only are God's people expected to experience trials and persecution because of their faith, but that they are supposed to *embrace it*, because (a) they then get to share in Christ's sufferings in fellowship with Him, (b) it purifies believers to test their faith and reset it to focus on the "main things," (c) it lays up treasures in heaven and a chance to do works of faith, which will not be possible when "faith becomes sight," and (d) maybe most importantly, our graceful response to persecution may entice outsiders to see our faith, and the One we have faith in, as genuine, and be persuaded to join our fold, as many did with the early Church, even joining them at the place of execution. God teaches that His children are to trust the Lord with their own well-being as to the nature of how He wishes to secure it, *while using their own energies to intercede on the welfare of others.*

Jesus warned that those who are greatly offended by persecution are those professing Christians who are in effect "rootless":

> ...And have no root in themselves, and so endure but for a time: afterward, when affliction or persecution ariseth for the word's sake, immediately they are offended. (Mark 4:17)

Paul plainly told us that persecution is not an unnatural state for a truly Christ-like practicing Christian:

Yea, and all that will live godly in Christ Jesus shall suffer persecution. (2 Tim. 3:12)

...so that no one would be unsettled by these trials. For you know quite well that we are destined for them. In fact, when we were with you, we kept telling you that we would be persecuted. And it turned out that way, as you well know. (1 Thess. 3:3, 4, NIV)

Probably the clearest teaching by Christ about persecution is from His Sermon on the Mount:

Blessed [are] they which are persecuted for righteousness' sake: for theirs is the kingdom of heaven. Blessed are ye, when [men] shall revile you, and persecute [you], and shall say all manner of evil against you falsely, for my sake. Rejoice, and be exceeding glad: for great [is] your reward in heaven: for so persecuted they the prophets which were before you...But I say unto you, That ye resist not evil: but whosoever shall smite thee on thy right cheek, turn to him the other also...But I say unto you, Love your enemies, bless them that curse you, do good to them that hate you, and pray for them which despitefully use you, and persecute you...For if ye love them which love you, what reward have ye? Do not even the publicans the same? And if ye salute your brethren only, what do ye more [than others]? Do not even the publicans so? Therefore I say unto you, Take no thought for your life, what ye shall eat, or what ye shall drink; nor yet for your body, what ye shall put on. Is not the life more than meat, and the body than raiment? (Matt. 5:10–12, 39, 44, 46–47, 6:25)

The principle Jesus is espousing here is typified in the "Good Samaritan" of His famous parable. The Samaritan, of a religion and ethnicity despised and derided by the "superior" Jews, did not refrain from blessing the Jewish man injured on the road, even though these Jews persecuted his people, and even as the man's fellow Jews passed by him and didn't want to be bothered. He risked his own life by tarrying on the dangerous, bandit-infested highway, taking the injured man into his care, and transporting him to safety at an inn, personally paying for his recovery and well-being. *How often do you see Christians offering to come to the immediate aid of those who have directly persecuted them in this country, without hesitation and without gloating?*

Paul also makes it clear that the Christian life is not about just looking out for the well-being of fellow Christians, but particularly those also created in God's image who you wish to win over and set free. He writes that Christians should be

> not looking to your own interests but each of you to the interests of the others. (Phil 2:4, NIV)

The epistle writers remind us that persecution is actually an *opportunity*, with many beneficial by-products, that we should not resist by fighting so hard for our own rights:

> Consider it pure joy, my brothers and sisters, whenever you face trials of many kinds, because you know that the testing of your faith produces perseverance. Let perseverance finish its work so that you may be mature and complete, not lacking anything. (James 1:2–4, NIV)

> In all this you greatly rejoice, though now for a little while you may have had to suffer grief in all kinds of trials. (1 Peter 1:6, NIV)

> ...if this is so, then the Lord knows how to rescue the godly from trials and to hold the unrighteous for punishment on the day of judgment. (2 Peter 2:9, NIV)

Don't seek so hard to defend your own rights as a Christian—fight hard to defend the rights of others, as God's agent on their behalf, so in turn they might praise God and seek to know Him better, for God's glory!

In summary, politically conservative Christianity, or the Religious Right, exhibits its regard for the values of the first three "Horsemen of the Apocalypse"—(a) the coercive force of using violence and similar compulsion to bring about their version of the Kingdom of God as enforced in the material world today, using carnal weapons and messianic conquering religious figurehead/ celebrity "heroes" and institutions, as illustrated in the Rider on the White Horse, (b) the veneration of military might and its generals (as the "heroes" often asked to speak from their pulpits) to force a klan/ nation's will onto others by means of deadly force and to confiscate their wealth and labor, and earn their respect by their professional use of weapons of death and of valor in combat as illustrated in the Rider of the Red Horse, and (c) the veneration of the capitalists who control capital by means of banking and corporate business entities, to unilaterally dictate wages, availability of critical resources (food, oil, etc.) and their prices (via unregulated "free" markets, subject to cartels, trusts, and the monopolizing of industries and basic staples and commodities), as illustrated by the Rider on the Black Horse.

Therefore, this "free rein" (so to speak) of these horses leads to the inevitable appearance of the Rider of the Pale Horse, with the periodic incidences of widespread pandemics, famines and environmental catastrophes due to their raping of the resources of their own nations and that of others (leaving strip mines, over-harvested fields, etc.), widespread pollution due to oil spills, deforestation, chemical dumping and air pollution and acid rain, blights on crops due to single-specie cultivation (such as United Fruit Company in the "banana republics"), epidemics of preventable diseases due to the restriction of health care to the wealthiest, black lung and other occupational diseases of the Industrial Age, flu and other epidemics due to wars like World War I, and even chemical dependency such as the drugging of China for the wealth of the British Crown and leading to the Opium Wars. Such is the fruit of unbridled capitalism for the benefit of the elites with inherited capital, or that derived by ruthless, selfish ambition, with controls to protect the environment and worker's lives (both in work environments and standards of living) fought against vigorously (to protect their expected ever-increasing profit margins to meet shareholders' expectations) by not only the wealthy elites, but also the politicians, media and Christian leaders they buy by various means. The latter reveals that their parishioners have lazily and thoughtlessly (and for their own personal enrichment) bought into Laodicean values by "Christianizing" their selfish agendas, without realizing that they are being led like lambs to the slaughter, since it will be found that in the capitalistic Great City Babylon "was found the blood of prophets, and of saints, and of all that were slain upon the earth" (Rev. 18:24).

Each of these four horses receives their own specific judgment by the Lord in the future events of Revelation (The Whore Babylon destruction, Armageddon, The Great City Babylon destruction, and the casting of Death and Hades into the Lake of Fire, respectively). The only admonition in the Book of Revelation for the Christian reader as far as current and future events pertains to their relationship to the Great City Babylon, proclaiming, "Come out of her, my people, that ye be not partakers of her sins, and that ye receive not of her plagues. For her sins have reached unto heaven, and God hath remembered her iniquities" (Rev. 18:4–5). In contrast, the Christian leaders and flock of the Religious Right reject the exaltation and advocacy of the poor, stranger, widow, orphan, and those generally vulnerable to the wiles of capitalistic world system and its exploitation by them and extortion from them—i.e., those figures said to enter into the

"Kingdom of Heaven" and be its future leadership. These Religious Right members rather label such priorities as diabolical schemes such as "socialism" (such as like the Early Church practiced) or "liberal," "bleeding heart" efforts by overly-sensitive (over the feelings and welfare of others) "snow flakes," as opposed to the Special Forces commandos and wealth titans who have the swagger and braggadocio they really admire and seek to emulate. As we have seen, this position is diametrically opposed to that repeatedly illustrated by our Lord, His Son, and their further repetitions from Their prophets and apostles in both the Old and New Testaments of what we Christians consider our "sola scriptura," doctrine-defining holy book.

So—if the repeated scriptural testimony from the Bible is normally diametrically opposed to the conservative agenda, then how did evangelical Christians and their other Religious Right brethren, who pride themselves on their strict adherence to Biblical teachings and lecture others on their deviation from such, come to embrace a pro-wealth and aggressive foreign policy that runs counter to the Bible's tenets, with this cognitive dissonance being rarely acknowledged within the evangelical community? The history behind this phenomenon, intentionally fashioned by specific figures in America in the early 20th century in particular, is a fascinating and little-known story that we will explore in depth in the following chapters.

James Fifield Jr., and the Little Known History of American Clergy "Riding the Beast" of Government, Big Business and Wall Street

In one of my book volumes from my soon-to-be-published *The Holy War Chronicles* on Christianity's history with holy wars, and the American experience of such, I encountered and discussed historical data of how the narrative of America's founding as a Christian nation was conceived, with the Puritans and their "city shining on a hill," Washington praying in the snow at Valley Forge, and the legends of the Continental Congress and Founding Fathers and their miraculous and brave stands on the Christian theology and destiny behind the nation's founding. Such things are told to rapt Christian audiences by Christian opportunists such as David Barton, with even Ronald Reagan telling such a story that originated with occult philosopher Manly P. Hall. In my research, I discovered the work of academic historians, such as Jonathan Herzog, who has a Ph.D from Stanford in American History, and career experience in the Foreign Service and conservative Hoover Institute think tank. In his book *The Spiritual-Industrial Complex*,[102] he wrote that a program was initiated by President Truman, and maintained by President Eisenhower, whose goal was to "invent" a sacred Christian origin and agenda about America's founding, to ennoble American citizens into a religious "holy war" against communism, as the only way it was felt by them to secure the "full measure" of sacrificial devotion from its citizens to counter what they were told would be an existential battle, fought in man-to-man combat fashion, over the fate of civilization. This program employed the use of senior intelligence officials, representatives of USAID (United States Agency for International Development) and other propaganda media arms of the government like

169

Radio Free Europe, and *senior clergy officials*, starting in a conference room with a blank sheet of paper, as they "invented" a history to be told to America about its "divine" destiny. I wish I could quote the entire section I devoted to recounting the many amazing revelations of Dr. Herzog's that I recount in my other book, but that would take scores of pages, so a simple summary must suffice.

He states that our American leaders were concerned at the start of the Cold War that Americans might actually find Communism *desirable* over the unbridled capitalism of the monied interests in America, and thus they felt they had to emphasize its one undesirable attribute—its atheism—to exploit to sway the public. One of its tenets was to sell Communism as a *religion*, and thus worthy of a religious-fueled "holy war" (just as with Islam today). He notes a key event held in May, 1947 at the White House, where CEOs and media moguls met under the auspices of the Justice Department, naming their new group the American Heritage Foundation (p. 81). They proposed to invigorate a generic "faith" (or "civil religion") into the public square to win the Cold War propaganda and psychological conflict. It initiated a "Freedom Train" that carried the nation's founding documents from city to city (much like the "Lenin train" of 1918 that transported Soviet propaganda), while local community organizers were told to host "community rededication weeks" and "Inter-Faith Day." The American Heritage Foundation also wrote the "Freedom Pledge" to be recited en masse as the Train passed through towns; in the New Orleans Sugar Bowl, 75,000 people recited the Freedom Pledge in unison (pp. 81–82). Attorney General Tom Clark and FBI Director J. Edgar Hoover (who, a decade later led the COINTELPRO and other programs to infiltrate American peace and civil rights groups, as *agents provocateur* to instigate violence) helped spearhead the campaign.

Herzog also notes that in 1946, efforts of "sacralization" began in Congress to add God onto currency, the national motto and in the Pledge of Allegiance (p. 87). When Eisenhower was inaugurated, he continued the initiative, even debuting something called "God's Float" in the inaugural parade, which featured sacred symbols and paintings of houses of worship around its perimeter, such as a church and a synagogue, and even a mosque (p. 92) (as he was also famous for saying, that for democracy to work it had to be based upon religion, and "he didn't care what it was"). Herzog notes that Eisenhower soon deployed the United States Information Agency (a war propaganda department, designed to be used for psychological warfare against enemy nations to dishearten and control "hearts and minds") to develop a "blueprint for spiritual mobilization," getting assistance from the

American Legion (who not long before in 1933 had been part of a plot to overthrow and then install a fascist government in America, known as "The Business Plot"), The Boy Scouts, The Advertising Council (recently known before then as the "War Advertising Council," run by Madison Avenue firms to support Wall Street and war dual objectives), and others (p. 96). They released a report fifteen months later entitled, *One Nation Under God,* which stated that there was "the need to weld religion to democracy," and called for "public comparisons between the Bible and America's most revered national documents." President Eisenhower, raised as a Jehovah's Witness, declared in 1953 that "Recognition of a Supreme Being is the first—the most basic—expression of Americanism" (p. 97). His advisors felt that to "sell" the message, he should join a church, so he was subject to the first baptism of a sitting President in history, at the National Presbyterian Church (p. 99).

Soon thereafter, Congress began printing "In God We Trust" on stamps and cancelled letters (p. 101), and took the Pledge of Allegiance, written by the socialist Baptist Francis Bellamy (who gave sermons such as, "Jesus is a Socialist"), with his endorsed form of an extended arm salute to the flag that resembled the Nazi salute, and added "under God" to it in 1954 (p. 102), although a number of Christian denominations opposed it, with debate of it discouraged in Congress as being a sign of "disloyalty." Congress then authorized the printing of 681,000 copies for the public, as the all-time largest government-funded effort of religious indoctrination (p. 106). A Congressional Prayer Room was then built in 1955, with a Bible on the altar and a stained glass picture of Washington kneeling in prayer, portraying him as a religious saint (pp. 106–107). The national motto was changed to "In God We Trust" in 1956, with a House report saying it was of "psychological value" (p. 108). They then decided to make a push within the military to produce "religiously grounded soldiers" to counter the "messianic" nature of Communism (pp. 109–110). Truman had decided to enact *a one-year mandatory universal military training (UMT) program for all high school graduates in 1947, as an ideal laboratory to force these new beliefs onto "captive" recruits, with one million or more handled annually.* He began a pilot program connected to this in 1947 at Ft. Knox, Kentucky, *where "military leaders could engineer a generation of patriotic, virtuous Cold Warriors"—a mujahaddin ("holy warrior") for their purposes* (pp. 112–113). This special project was assigned to Brig. Gen. John Devine (who fought under Patton), to "morally and spiritually engineer the U.S. Army," and to "create a perfect soldier who could ground lethal capability in a religious framework"; it became known as "Father Devine's Heaven" (p. 113).

The protocols for these teenagers under the age of eighteen were for them to first be profiled religiously, and then led to a taxpayer-funded religion conversion decision while in the program, along with hours of personal time with a chaplain and weekly mandatory religious services. They were also adopted by local congregations, while attending mandatory religious classes and lectures during the week, and being told how our nation was founded on "religious principles" (p. 115). Chaplains were asked to be moral police, and forbade alcohol, and recruited local bartenders to be informants; they also forbade "pinup" pictures, yet would not tolerate "prissiness." As a result, over 90 percent of recruits went to church, leading Truman's advisory commission to *recommend mandatory training nationwide* (turning America into a Spartan-like "warrior state"), with the idea supported by eighty percent of the public (p. 116). However, teachers and professors, labor unions and many religious leaders opposed it, leading to a petition of 652 religious leaders who called it an "un-American form of indoctrination." The Republicans opposed the hefty price tag, conceding that the Army would take these teens and "make them soldiers for the rest of their lives," subjecting "American youth to the complete domination of the Government during their most formative period." Regardless, Gen. Devine had been training generals and other high-level officers in the same "Knox Method" regimen, which continued on as the officer-students then later trained their troops. The Knox program became "Character Guidance" in basic training, which included six hour-long lectures on the Ten Commandments, the sanctity of marriage, the relationship of democracy and religion and the dangerous faith of Communism, with soldiers having to attend such lectures monthly afterwards (p. 121). Chaplains then began policing all literature, removed questionable materials from base libraries, and confiscated obscene materials (p. 122).

Regarding the use of psychological warfare on civilians by the government with the use of religion, in 1951 Truman set up the Psychological Strategy Board (PSB), comprising the CIA, Departments of State and Defense, and others, and studied "the potential role of religion in psychological warfare" (p. 126). Their first report stated that "The potentialities of religion as an instrument for combating Communism are universally tremendous. Religion is an established force which calls forth men's strongest emotions…Our overall objective in seeking the use of religion as a *cold war instrumentality* should be the furtherance of world spiritual health." Herzog adds that "The PSB was influenced by the earlier United States Information and Education Exchange (USIE), an overt psychological program authorized by Congress in 1948 to cultivate a favorable image of the U.S. worldwide, which had established a three-person council of religious leaders to investigate the 'moral and religious factors' of psychological warfare....Their report recommended that 'public leaders emphasize the historic and continuing influence of religion on American society, the spiritual roots of U.S. institutions, and the religious component of major holidays'" (pp. 127–128). He also notes that "President Eisenhower also established the United States Information Agency (USIA) and the Operations Coordinating Board (OCB), which in turn created the Ideological Subcommittee on the Religious Factor, charged with the Cold War 'spiritual factor'" (p. 130). By 1952, the National Education Association (NEA) formed the Teacher Education in Religion, beginning programs of religious education in public school, adding prayer after the Pledge of Allegiance, and religious discussions in the classroom. Major newspaper chains similarly followed suit (pp. 142–144).

By 1949 business leaders began using mass media advertising to promote religion, calling Americans to mobilize spiritually. He writes that the Religion in American Life (RIAL) campaign, led by General Electric President Charles Wilson (who called it "spiritual rearmament"), was a cooperation of corporations, religious leaders and government, assisted by the corporate Advertising Council (itself founded as a war marketer), funded by corporate interests to the tune of $3 million for a three week campaign (p. 150). Sports figures, images of Betty Crocker, and J. Edgar Hoover appeared in ads discussing the importance of religion; President Truman himself even appealed to the public, saying that "Each one of us can do his part by a renewed devotion to his religion"; Herzog adds that the RIAL campaign lasted for ten years from 1949 to 1958, with many thousands of towns participating, over 5000 billboards deployed, *almost two thousand newspaper editorials given supporting it, and over 300 television programs focusing on religious mobilization* (p. 151). He also writes that projects like the ringing of church bells nationwide on Independence Day was conducted by the Committee to Proclaim Liberty (CPL), which focused on connecting religion and Americanism (p. 151). Its overseers included men like Bing Crosby, Ronald Reagan, Cecil B. DeMille, Walt Disney, J.C. Penney, Fred Maytag, Conrad Hilton, Norman Vincent Peale, and others. Utilities placed notices of "Freedom Under God" in their customers' bills. The "Freedom Under God" television program, hosted by Bing Crosby and others, featured church choirs and military speeches, calling Americans to go to church on "Independence Sabbath" and re-read the Declaration of Independence while church bells rang. They misled the public by suggesting that Independence Day was originally a religious holiday (p. 153).

A similar organization called the Crusade For Freedom was founded in 1950, involving U.S. senators, publishers like *Time* founder Henry Luce, Hollywood studio heads, business executives, and religious leaders like Reinhold Niebuhr (p. 154). *It wrote to over 80,000 American religious leaders, asking that they preach sermons* emphasizing 'the truth that all human rights are derived from God'; Herzog describes them as yet another organization who "sold religion to Americans, using celebrity endorsements, modern advertising techniques, and Cold War urgency" (p. 154). Meanwhile, other civic organizations got involved; the Fraternal Order of Eagles placed Ten Commandments monuments in city parks and public buildings (p. 155). A Notre Dame law school dean suggested that the American Legion create a "Cold War battle flag," with one side with the inscription "This nation is for God" and the other side related to the Ten Commandments (pp. 155–156). The 2.7-million-member American Legion (the same organization purportedly involved in the 1933 fascist takeover of the presidency) began its "Back to God" program, which expected daily times of prayers after meals and with families, and even offered rides to Sunday School for children, and religious posters for schools (p. 156).

Yet another group, the Foundation for Religious Action in Social and Civil Order (FRASCO), sported members such as Billy Graham, Henry Ford II, Herbert Hoover and others. In Hollywood, John Wayne headed the Motion Picture Alliance for the Preservation of American Ideals, while actors and writers suspected of Communists sympathies were blacklisted from work in the industry (p. 159). Some of their artistic efforts were over-the-top, such as the film *Red Planet Mars*, which shows the Martians broadcasting their support for Jesus of Nazareth and the Sermon on the Mount, leading to the overthrow of conniving Communist Eastern Europe and Russia, to be then led by an Eastern Orthodox patriarch. However, after over a decade of such effort, Herzog notes that by 1962 only 45 percent of people believed religion was expanding in influence, and which dropped to 33 percent by 1965, with even religious people becoming cynical over how religion was being exploited (p. 172). By 1955, even Catholic newspapers were stating that "Far too much loose talk about 'God and America' is heard these days" and schemes that religion "should be cultivated as a potent instrument in the cold war and that the Almighty has enlisted in the army of the 'free world' for the duration" (p. 177).

Professor Martin Medhurst of Texas A&M University, in his 1997 paper "Eisenhower and the Crusade for Freedom: The Rhetorical Origins of a Cold War Campaign" for the *Presidential Studies Quarterly*,[103] adds that the Crusade for Freedom spanned fifteen years (1950–65) and through four presidential administrations (Truman through Johnson). He notes its beginnings, in that a few months after the CIA had successfully (and covertly) stopped the Communists from winning power in Italy in 1948 by means of funding propaganda and parties, it tapped former OSS (the predecessor of the CIA) officer Frank Wisner to head the covert Office of Policy Coordination (OPC) which was placed within the CIA, to provide for the direct intervention in the electoral processes of other foreign governments, and to keep its large budget secret from others in the government, and the public. He set up and funded groups of Communist country exiles in America, as "front organizations" in the U.S. to conceal U.S. government funding, and sought high profile members for them, such as Dwight Eisenhower. One such group was incorporated in 1949 as the "National Committee for a Free Europe," and included the CIA's Allen Dulles and publishers Henry Luce (*Time* magazine) and DeWitt Wallace (*Reader's Digest*). He notes that the purpose of the group was to destabilize Soviet satellite countries and to foment unrest with the use of gray-black propaganda. They formed a radio subcommittee (led by a former OSS agent and New York banker), and with a fundraising subcommittee to set up groups nationwide to raise money for the initiative. These efforts began the start of Radio Free Europe and its fundraising arm, the Crusade for Freedom. *The public fundraising was a cover to disguise the fact that it was actually a propaganda operation already fully funded by the American government.*

The chairman of General Mills (and a former OSS agent) with public relations expertise was tasked with coming up with a plan for this, and he came up with the idea of a public "crusade," and represented by a bell as a symbol; they were also tasked with getting as chairman of the Crusade, General Lucius Clay, who served as a military governor over occupied Berlin—*no doubt an apt choice for one experienced in re-formulating the minds of a defeated people, to accept the agenda of new overlords.* Committees were set up in all fifty states and numerous Eastern European countries. He explains that "the last step was to create the cover—to establish in the collective psyche of every American that Radio Free Europe was a private, grassroots organization devoted to telling the truth to the captives behind the Iron Curtain," and determined they had to pick someone to address the nation to begin this effort that *the public supremely trusted to not lie to them*, and thus they chose Dwight Eisenhower (later he would deceive the American public (and the world) by denying the spy flights over Russia, until the shooting down of pilot Gary Powers exposed the lie to the world). He had operated similar black propaganda operations in World War II, with radio stations pretending to be manned by loyal Germans critical of the Nazi government, but actually operated by the Psychological Warfare Branch of the Army; it was said to mix "verifiable news information with rumors and falsifications," even falsely reporting uprisings in German cities to foment a revolution.

His keynote speech to kick off the Crusade was preceded by an intensive media blitz and promotion, and was covered in thousands of media outlets and all the major radio networks live. Thus began an effort paid for in large sums by the tax-paying public for what in effect was a major psy-ops project *on themselves*. This covert operation, not disclosed as to its nature to the paying public, was ironically said in the speech and afterwards as a "battle for truth," to battle an enemy who "weaves a fantastic pattern of lies and twisted facts," and spreads "lies and misconceptions" about America. Ike declared that America was the symbol of "human happiness," and it has only "peaceful intent and decent motives" based on "the peaceful competition of free enterprise." He stated that Americans who signed the "Freedom Scroll" would support this operation, operated by "private American citizens."

Afterwards, *The New York Times* praised the effort, and presented it as a "private effort," and "neither the *Times* nor any other major American media outlet would question that claim publicly for the next seventeen years." The large bell made for the Crusade began to tour the nation's cities, as local politicians encouraged the citizenry to participate in what was basically a psychological operation and a "battle for men's minds"—*for those within America as well as those behind the Iron Curtain.* The New York Times reported that on "Freedom Sunday" declared at that time, "Sermons on the moral value of freedom will be heard in many churches and congregations will receive invitations to sign the scrolls," and that "Special tables will be arranged for signing the scrolls before and after religious service and voluntary offerings will be accepted to help finance Radio Free Europe, the non-government 'freedom station' "—*our nation's pulpits dutifully taking orders from the State for its agenda, which it did not even fully disclose to its Christian "assets."* It is noted that *by the end of the first year, the Freedom Scroll had obtained almost sixteen million signatures, and received $1.3 million in contributions (in 1950 dollars), and continued for fifteen years.*

Stacey Cone, a doctoral student in journalism and mass communications at the University of North Carolina, wrote in her peer-reviewed paper published in the Winter 1998–1999 edition of the *Journalism History* academic journal entitled, "Presuming A Right to Deceive: Radio Free Europe, Radio Liberty, the CIA, and the News Media,"[104] that, concerning Radio Free Europe (RFE) and Radio Liberty (RL) and their legacy and history in Cold War spy craft, "Poisonings, espionage, bombings, sabotage, murders and a few unexplained employee deaths were some of the hot signs that the Radios were deeply involved in the Cold War." She added that "A comprehensive account of the Radios' past has yet to be published," but if it were it should include "a full recounting of how the established news media covered up information that RFE and RL were CIA conduits," as "the media, often knowingly, propagated illusions, not truth; manipulated public opinion, rather than informed it; and tried to manufacture consent, instead of promoting democratic processes through full and open reporting" (p. 148). Although she notes that the two station networks began broadcasting in 1950 and 1951, the greater media implied they were private initiatives, until the *New York Times* "outed" them in 1967 as CIA-sponsored. She further "names names" of prominent media figures who knew of the CIA connection all along, including Sig Mickelson, President of *CBS News*. She also affirms that the "Crusade for Freedom" was used to raise millions of dollars from the public (including much of it from the allowances of patriotic children, I might add) as an ostensibly private initiative, while concealing the fact it was already fully funded through the CIA; she also affirms that "The men in charge of the Radios and the Crusade were avid propaganda enthusiasts. They believed that propaganda, in combination with other aspects of statecraft, was powerful enough to persuade entire populations that the American way was the right and only true way," and was "aided by journalists" (p. 149).

She writes that "propaganda targeting Americans was communicated largely through the Crusade for Freedom's national media campaign," as the campaign was "unquestioningly deceitful," and it "repeatedly took advantage of American good will" (p. 149). She notes that the media industry donated between $9 and $17 million in advertising and public service announcements for the Crusade; she adds that in 1955, *more than 450 newspapers carried 700 Crusade ads, with 75 percent of major newspapers running supportive articles or editorials* (p. 149). It is important to note that Cone points out that reporters and media executives ignored conflicts of interest and served on the admitted propaganda-based organizing committees and boards, and that it was "in the late 1970s that *news reports and a Senate investigation revealed that a number of journalists had worked directly as agents and as informed conduits for the CIA since the time of the agency's founding*" (p. 150) (emphasis added). She asserts that the two most influential media figures behind the RFE/RL and the Crusade were *Time/Life* founder Henry Luce, a religious missionary's son who believed in America's Christian destiny, and *Time* vice president and *Fortune* president C.D. Jackson, who had been described as a "virtually unknown and uncelebrated publicist" of twentieth-century style political warfare, and "the chief architect of America's psychological warfare effort during and after World War II," having been appointed by the President as one of five men to reorganize America's propaganda program (p. 151). Jackson promoted the idea of the secrecy of the CIA's involvement in RFE/RL, for then they could take "positions for which the United States would not desire to accept responsibility"; he added that "We can play tricks, we can denounce, we can take chances, we can act fast, all things that an official government propaganda agency cannot do" (p. 151). *It should also be noted that Jackson was one of the founders of the Bilderberg secret global elite society.* Cone then recounts the confessions of a number of senior journalistic figures across the media spectrum, who became "witting" to the CIA's involvement once elevated to a higher level of confidence, and then stayed publicly silent, while perpetuating the deception.

As further examples of the "big guns" of industry behind these covert operatives of the collusion of the State, Big Business and Big Religion, a biography of CEO Henry Ford II on the Ford Motor Company website[105] notes that "He was national chairman of the Crusade for Freedom in 1952, and chairman of the board of trustees of the American Heritage Foundation, sponsoring organization for the Crusade, from 1953 to 1955. He remained on the board of the Crusade until May 1956." Herzog further notes that General Electric's President, Charles E. Wilson, led Truman's Religion in American Life (RIAL) program. He asserts that because of Wilson's impressive work with RIAL, Truman tapped him to run the governmental Office of Defense Mobilization (pp. 150–151). He further notes that Wilson not only directed the RIAL committee, but also served on the board of the Freedom Train's American Heritage Foundation and the Crusade for Freedom (p. 162). The biography of Wilson on General Electric's primary website[106] adds that Wilson was tasked by President Roosevelt in 1942 to be vice chairman of the War Production Board, and was later picked by President Truman to be director of the Office of Defense Mobilization at the end of 1950 to take over America's economy and place it on a war footing as the Korean War was spooling up, which they state as "*a job which was described in Washington as second in importance only to the Presidency of the United States*" (emphasis added). The strategy undertaken by President Truman to stop the Communist menace and its goal of centralized state-run economies, production and labor was *to accomplish the same thing right here in the U.S. of A.*, as the following excerpted December 16, 1950 *New York Times* story[107] attests of the new emergency state he imposed at the time—*for a strategic war in which no major enemy had attacked us or threatened our shores:*

PRESIDENT PROCLAIMS A NATIONAL EMERGENCY;
AUTO PRICES ROLLED BACK; RAIL STRIKE ENDS; ALLIES
GIVE UP HAMHUNG; WU REJECTS TRUCE

President Truman proclaimed a state of emergency this morning and
delegated many of his own war powers to Charles E. Wilson, the new
Mobilization Director....Today was a day of action in the White
House, in Congress and elsewhere in the Government as officials
moved to implement the President's declaration to the nation and the
world last night that the United States would meet the challenge of
communism. *The Economic Stabilization Agency canceled the price increases
made by Ford, General Motors and Chrysler in the last few days, and this was
merely the harbinger of many new controls that eventually will encompass the entire
economy.* Industry evinced its readiness to accept any war production
goals, *striking railroad men returned to work,* and the general response
from the public indicated an acceptance of the austerity program
suggested by the President....Mr. Truman took two actions this
morning to start a drastic increase of the mobilization program. He
signed the proclamation of emergency, which unleashed scores of
additional executive powers, and issued an *executive order granting
virtually blanket authority to Mr. Wilson to carry out all aspects of war
production and economic control he deemed necessary.* This *authority received by
Mr. Wilson* will be subject in the Executive Branch of the
Government *only to the veto of President Truman.* (emphasis added)

In his proclamation President Truman declared that conquest of the
world was the objective of "Communist imperialism." He said this
now constituted *a threat to the freedoms guaranteed by the Bill of Rights, to
the free enterprise system and to other rights, like collective bargaining, that free
people had chosen for themselves.*...Mr. Truman called for sacrifices, for
cooperation by state and local officials, *for loyalty to the principles on which
the nation was founded,* and faith in our friends and allies. He expressed
his confidence that the people would not be found wanting in
courage and determination. The President signed the proclamation in
his Oval Room office in the Executive Offices of the White House at
10:20 A.M. Only a few members of his staff and photographers were
present....That quickening of a mood was felt generally in the capital.
The Senate Armed Services Committee approved a national civil
defense program, the Senate Finance Committee met in extraordinary
session to work on the *excess profits bill and the Economic Stabilization
Agency clamped a freeze on automobile prices, the first of many promised
controls...The executive order spelling out Mr. Wilson's powers and
responsibilities appeared to leave out nothing that the industrialist could desire to
tackle his job in an untrammeled way. It had been predicted he would get powers*

exceeding those of James F. Byrnes when Mr. Byrnes was the top mobilizer of World War II, and the document bore this out. "The director," stated the order, "shall on behalf of the President *direct, control, and coordinate all mobilization activities of the executive branch of the Government, including but not limited to production, procurement, manpower, stabilization, and transport activities."* The phrase, *"including but not limited to,"* left open the possibility that *other areas of defense activity would be added.* The fourth paragraph specified that the Director of the Office of Defense Mobilization should report to the President periodically, and established Mr. Wilson's authority over Cabinet members and other heads of Federal agencies where mobilization projects are concerned. Under the original concept of a partial mobilization, geared to what was then believed to be a comparatively small war in Korea, most of the control agencies were dispersed in the Federal departments....*This fourth paragraph gives Mr. Wilson ascendancy in the control of these dispersed agencies, and he is expected to consolidate them as he gets organized. The proclamation of emergency, apart from an important psychological effect it is expected to have on the approach of the average citizen to his part in the crisis, revived scores of powers which have been latent. Some of them had been rescinded by Congress in 1947, and some were enacted since then but could be given life only by the proclamation.* (emphasis added)

With this power invested in one unelected man (a fact unknown to almost all the public today), it is no wonder that at the time the press christened his position a "co-presidency."[108] Michael Hogan, in his book *A Cross of Iron—Harry S. Truman and the Origins of the National Security State 1945–1954*,[109] notes that the debate after World War II and the onset of the Cold War within Congress was if America could become a "military dictatorship," and the nation becoming a "garrison state," whereas Charles Wilson testified there that "an age of total war required a comprehensive program of permanent preparedness" to "mobilize the country's industrial, scientific, technological, and manpower resources" (p. 44). By 1948, Truman wanted universal military training (UMT) and reenacting the draft—all *before* the justification of the Korean War—and all of which was supported by the American Legion, the Veterans of Foreign Wars, as concepts also supported by Wilson. When Wilson was appointed as head of the Defense Production Authority (DPA), simultaneously wage and price controls were enforced onto America's economy (p. 346). Eventually, the government tried to confiscate steel plants when the owners and labor could not agree, and when the Supreme Court stopped the action, Truman *even planned to draft the workers into the military to compel their labor.*

The 1972 *New York Times* obituary on Wilson[110] also adds that Wilson "found time to conduct [a] Sunday School class for young men at the First Baptist Church," and that

> between wars, Mr. Wilson not only concentrated on making G. E. a more productive company but also on operating for the Government the vast Hanford, Wash., atomic energy plant, *which made plutonium for atomic bombs.* He also had charge of *an atomic research facility at Schenectady, N. Y., a city popularly regarded as the principal site of G.E.* He had returned to the company after a dispute with President Truman over a wage rise in steel granted by the Wage Stabilization Board. *He believed that the increase represented a threat to the country's economy. Mr. Wilson's attitude to organized labor was one of general resistance, and many union leaders regarded him as a tough opponent.* Shortly after returning from Washington in 1952, Mr. Wilson left G.E. for W. R. Grace & Co., an international industrial and trading concern. He rose to become board chairman before resigning in 1956....*he acted as a business consultant and chairman of the industries advisory committee of the Advertising Council.* (emphasis added)

This same Charles Wilson, GE chief, practicing Baptist and Sunday School teacher, overtook the "buying and selling," and other rights from America (controlling public rationing and enforcing mandatory production quotas), as well as leading semi-covert business-led projects to exploit America's religious heritage for similar military objectives to coerce sacrifices of the citizenry to win a perceived "Cold War."

The narrative exposed by the powerful figures we have profiled, many of whom are unknown to Americans today as to their role in the "engineering" of America's recent zealotry of religious devotion and the sacredization of America and its supposed "divine mission"—going not back to America's origins but rather to *meet a specific secular foreign policy objective in the board rooms in the middle of the Twentieth Century*—is not the whole story of this unnatural harlotry of Christianity with political conservatism and nationalistic agendas. *It can be further discovered that much of the sincere, dedicated American church was conditioned into what we know today as the Religious Right, in particular its affiliation with the agendas of capitalism and corporate big business interests that distrusts labor and government-run versus corporate entities, for-profit privatization of social welfare and deregulation of big business and consumer and environmental protections, by means of another, older operation from the Twentieth Century, specifically geared to co-opt and motivate the powerful Christian community, without a full declaration of their motives, to rescue a discredited and greedy big business community.*

In 2015, Kevin Kruse, a professor of history at Princeton, published a book I highly recommend that every reader obtain and read carefully, entitled *One Nation Under God: How Corporate America Invented Christian America*. In 2015 he also wrote an article in *Politico* that summarized its findings.[111] This very-lengthy article explains, in an overview fashion, the overall premise of its narrative, an excerpt of which follows:

> In December 1940, as America was emerging from the Great Depression, more than 5,000 industrialists from across the nation made their yearly pilgrimage to the Waldorf-Astoria Hotel in New York City, convening for the annual meeting of the National Association of Manufacturers. The program promised an impressive slate of speakers: titans at General Motors, General Electric, Standard Oil, Mutual Life, and Sears, Roebuck; popular lecturers such as etiquette expert Emily Post and renowned philosopher-historian Will Durant; even FBI director J. Edgar Hoover. Tucked away near the end of the program was a name few knew initially, but one everyone would be talking about by the convention's end: Reverend James W. Fifield Jr....the 41-year-old Congregationalist minister...delivered a passionate defense of the American system of free enterprise and a withering assault on its perceived enemies in Franklin D. Roosevelt's administration. Decrying the New Deal's "encroachment upon our American freedoms," the minister listed a litany of sins committed by the Democratic government, ranging from its devaluation of currency to its disrespect for the Supreme Court. Singling out the regulatory state for condemnation...It all sounds familiar enough today, but Fifield's audience of executives was stunned. Over the preceding decade, as America first descended into and then crawled its way out of the Great Depression, these titans of industry had been told, time and time again, that they were to blame for the nation's downfall. Fifield, in contrast, insisted that they were the source of its salvation. They just needed to do one thing: Get religion. Fifield told the industrialists that clergymen would be crucial in regaining the upper hand in their war with Roosevelt. As men of God, ministers could voice the same conservative complaints as business leaders, but without any suspicion that they were motivated solely by self-interest. They could push back against claims, made often by Roosevelt and his allies, that business had somehow sinned and the welfare state was doing God's work. The assembled industrialists gave a rousing amen. "When he had finished," a journalist noted, "rumors report that the N.A.M. applause could be heard in Hoboken."

It was a watershed moment—the beginning of a movement that would advance over the 1940s and early 1950s a new blend of conservative religion, economics and politics that one observer aptly anointed "Christian libertarianism." Fifield and like-minded ministers saw Christianity and capitalism as inextricably intertwined, and argued that spreading the gospel of one required spreading the gospel of the other. The two systems had been linked before, of course, but always in terms of their shared social characteristics. Fifield's innovation was his insistence that Christianity and capitalism were political soul mates, first and foremost....He and his colleagues devoted themselves to fighting the government forces they believed were threatening capitalism and, by extension, Christianity. And their activities helped build a foundation for a new vision of America in which businessmen would no longer suffer under the rule of Roosevelt but instead thrive—in a phrase they popularized—in a nation "under God."

For much of the 1930s, organizations such as the National Association of Manufacturers (NAM) had been searching in vain for ways to rehabilitate a public image that had been destroyed in the Great Depression and defamed by the New Deal. In 1934, a new generation of conservative industrialists took over NAM with a promise to "serve the purposes of business salvation." The organization rededicated itself to spreading the gospel of free enterprise, vastly expanding its expenditures in the field. As late as 1934, NAM spent a paltry $36,000 on public relations. Three years later, it devoted $793,043 to the cause, more than half its total income. NAM now promoted capitalism through a wide array of films, radio programs, advertisements, direct mail, a speaker's bureau and a press service that provided ready-made editorials and news stories for 7,500 local newspapers. Ultimately, though, industry's self-promotion was seen as precisely that....Even President Franklin D. Roosevelt took his shots. "It has been said that there are two great Commandments—one is to love God, and the other to love your neighbor," he noted soon after the Liberty League's [an associated organization] creation. "The two particular tenets of this new organization say you shall love God and then forget your neighbor." Off the record, he joked that the name of the god they worshiped seemed to be "Property"....When Roosevelt launched the New Deal, politically liberal clergymen echoed his arguments, championing his proposal for a vast welfare state as simply the Christian thing to do. The head of the Federal Council of Churches, for instance, claimed the New Deal embodied basic Christian principles such as the "significance of daily bread, shelter, and security." When businessmen realized their economic arguments were no match for Roosevelt's religious ones, they decided to beat him at his own game.

That's where Revered Fifield came in. Nicknamed "The Apostle to Millionaires" by a friendly writer, Fifield took over the elite First Congregational Church in Los Angeles in 1935. The minister was well matched to the millionaires in his pews. Politically conservative but doctrinally liberal, he crafted an interpretation of the Bible that catered to his congregation. Notably, Fifield dismissed the many passages in the New Testament about wealth and poverty, and instead assured the elite that their worldly success was a sign of God's blessings. Soon after his arrival in Los Angeles, Fifield founded Spiritual Mobilization, an organization whose mission was "to arouse the ministers of all denominations in America to check the trends toward pagan stateism, which would destroy our basic freedom and spiritual ideals." The organization's credo reflected the common politics of the millionaires in his congregation: Men were creatures of God imbued with "inalienable rights and responsibilities," specifically enumerated as "the liberty and dignity of the individual, in which freedom of choice, of enterprise and of property is inherent." Churches, it asserted, had a solemn duty to defend those rights against the encroachments of the state.

Fifield quickly brought the organization into national politics, gaining attention from leading conservatives across America who were eager to enlist ministers in their fight against the New Deal. Former President Herbert Hoover, deposed by Roosevelt and disparaged by his acolytes, advised and encouraged Fifield in personal meetings and regular correspondence….In October 1938, Fifield sent an alarmist tract to more than 70,000 clergymen across the nation, seeking to recruit them in the revolt against Roosevelt. "We ministers have special opportunities and special responsibilities in these critical days," it began. "America's movement toward dictatorship has already eliminated checks and balances in its concentration of powers in our chief executive." Finding the leaflet to his liking, Hoover sent Fifield a warm note of appreciation and urged him to press on.

Within a few years, the minister had the support of not just Hoover but an impressive array of conservative figures in politics, business and religion—"a who's who of the conservative establishment," in the words of one observer….In the mid-1940s, he won a number of powerful new patrons, but none was more important than J. Howard Pew Jr., president of Sun Oil….He had previously been involved in anti-New Deal organizations like the Liberty League and now believed the postwar era would witness a renewed struggle for the soul of the nation. Looking over some material from Spiritual Mobilization, Pew decided the organization shared his understanding of what was wrong with America and what needed to be done. But to his dismay, the material offered no agenda for action whatsoever, merely noting that Spiritual Mobilization would send clergymen bulletins and place advertisements but ultimately "leave details" of what to do "to individual ministers." Pew thought this was no way to run a national operation.

In February 1945, famed industrial consultant Alfred Haake explained to Pew why NAM's own outreach to ministers had failed. "Of the approximately thirty preachers to whom I have thus far talked, I have yet to find one who is unqualifiedly impressed....One of the men put it almost typically for the rest when he said: 'The careful preparation and framework for the meetings to which we are brought is too apparent. We cannot help but see that it is expertly designed propaganda and that there must be big money behind it. We easily become suspicious'." If they wanted to convince clergymen to side with them, industrialists would need a subtler approach. Rather than treating ministers as a passive audience to be persuaded, Haake argued, they should involve them actively in the cause as participants. The first step would be making ministers realize that they, too, had something to fear from the growth of government. "The religious leaders must be helped to discover that their callings are threatened," Haake argued, by realizing that the "collectivism" of the New Deal, "with the glorification of the state, is really a denial of God." Once they were thus alarmed, they would readily join Spiritual Mobilization as its representatives and could then be organized more effectively into a force for change both locally and nationally.

Reverend Fifield worked to make Spiritual Mobilization out of the ranks of the clergy. The growing numbers of its "minister-representatives" were found in every state, with large concentrations in industrial regions like New York, Pennsylvania, Ohio and Illinois. They were overwhelmingly Protestant, though a scattering of priests and rabbis allowed the organization to present itself as part of the new spirit of "Judeo-Christianity." In the previous decade, this innovative "interfaith" approach had taken shape as a way for liberal clergymen to unite in common social causes. Now, in the postwar era, conservative organizations such as Spiritual Mobilization shrewdly followed suit. The organization grew rapidly. In February 1947, Fifield reported that in three years he had expanded the mass of their minister-representatives from an initial 400 members to more than 10,000 in all. He set them to work spreading arguments against the "pagan stateism" of the New Deal. "It is time to exalt the dignity of individual man as a child of God," he urged....Clergymen responded enthusiastically. Many wrote the Los Angeles office to request advertised copies of Friedrich Hayek's libertarian treatise *The Road to Serfdom* and anti-New Deal tracts by Herbert Hoover and libertarian author Garet Garrett. Armed with such materials, the minister-representatives transformed secular arguments into spiritual ones and spread them widely. "Occasionally I preach a sermon directly on your theme," a Midwestern minister wrote, "but equally important, it is in the background of my thought as I prepare all my sermons, meet various groups and individuals." Everyday activities were echoed by special events. In October 1947, for instance, Spiritual Mobilization held a *national sermon competition on the theme "The Perils to Freedom," with $5,000 offered in prize money*. The organization had more than 12,000 minister representatives at that point, but it received twice as many submissions for the competition—*representing roughly 15 percent of the entire country's clergymen*. (emphasis added)

Pleased with his progress, Fifield's backers doubled the annual budget. Pew once again set the pace, soliciting donations from officials at 158 corporations, including *longstanding supporters of Spiritual Mobilization such as General Motors, Chrysler, National Steel, Firestone Tire and Rubber and Gulf Oil.* "A large percentage of ministers in this country are completely ignorant of economic matters and have used their pulpits for the purpose of disseminating socialistic and totalitarian doctrines," Pew wrote in his appeal. "*Much has already been accomplished in the education of these ministers, but a great deal more is left to be done.*" The success of Spiritual Mobilization brought increased funding, but also scorn from progressives. In February 1948, *The Nation* ran an acidic cover story. "A major battle for the minds of the clergy, particularly those of the Protestant persuasion, is now being waged in America," it read. "For the most part the battle lines are honestly drawn and represent a sharp clash in ideologies, but now and then the reactionary side tries to fudge a bit by backing movements which mask their true character and real sponsors. Such a movement is Spiritual Mobilization." The article detailed the scope of its operations, noting its high-rent offices in New York, Chicago and Los Angeles, as well as the hundreds of thousands of pamphlets by pro-business authors it distributed for free. But no one knew who was funding the operation, *The Nation* warned. In this withering account, Fifield came off as a charlatan who prostrated himself before the "apostles of rugged individualism" to secure his own fame and fortune and, in return, prostituted himself for their needs.

In response, Spiritual Mobilization redoubled its efforts, taking an even more aggressive approach to public relations. In 1949, it launched *The Freedom Story*, a 15-minute radio program consisting of a dramatic presentation and brief commentary from Fifield. In the original scripts, Fifield made direct attacks on Democratic programs at home, but his lawyer warned him they would lose the "public service" designation that gave them *free airtime* if he were "too plain spoken" with partisan attacks. Instead, he advised, the minister should make use of foreign examples to illustrate the spreading menace of "creeping socialism" at home. *Fifield's financial backers helped secure free airtime* for these programs across the nation. In 1950, *The Freedom Story* was broadcast on over 500 stations; by late 1951, it aired on more than 800. (emphasis added)

Meanwhile, Spiritual Mobilization launched a monthly magazine, *Faith and Freedom*, showcasing the work of prominent libertarian authors, including Ludwig von Mises, leader of the Austrian School of economics; Leonard Read, founder of the Foundation for Economic Education; and Henry Hazlitt, a founding member of the future American Enterprise Institute. Even though laymen dominated the pages of *Faith and Freedom*, the journal purposely presented itself as created by ministers, for ministers. Spiritual Mobilization had long operated on the principle that clergymen could not be swayed through crude propaganda. "The articulation should be worked out beforehand, of course, and we should be ready to help the thinking of the ministers on it," Haake noted in one of his early musings, "but it should be so done as to enable them to discover it for themselves." *Faith and Freedom* thus presented itself as a forum in which ministers could disagree freely. But for all of its claims about encouraging debate, the journal did little to hide its contempt for liberal ministers. The magazine repeatedly denounced the Social Gospel and, just as important, clergymen who invoked it to advocate for the establishment and expansion of welfare state programs. In a typical article, Irving Howard, a Congregationalist minister, darkly noted the "pagan origin of the Social Gospel" in 19th century Unitarianism and Transcendentalism, claiming it was part of a larger "impetus to a shift in faith from God to man, from eternity to time, from the individual to the group, [from] individual conversion to social coercion, and from the church to the state."

With the Republican gains in the midterm elections of 1950, the forces behind Spiritual Mobilization felt emboldened. In an upbeat letter to Alfred Sloan, the head of General Motors and one of his ardent supporters, Fifield reflected on the recent returns. "We are having quite a deluge of letters from across the country, indicating the feeling that Spiritual Mobilization has had some part in the awakening which was evidenced by the elections….Of course, we are a little proud and very happy for whatever good we have been able to do in waking people up to the peril of collectivism and the importance of Freedom under God." For Fifield and his associates, the phrase "freedom under God"—contrasted with what they saw as oppression under the federal government—became an effective new rallying cry in the early 1950s. The minister pressed the theme repeatedly in the pages of *Faith and Freedom* and in his radio broadcasts of *The Freedom Story*, but he soon found a more prominent means of spreading the message to the American people. In the spring of 1951, Spiritual Mobilization's leaders struck upon an idea they believed would advance their cause considerably. To mark the 175th anniversary of the signing of the Declaration of Independence, they proposed for the week surrounding the Fourth of July a massive series of events devoted to the theme of "Freedom Under God."

To that end, in June 1951, the leaders of Spiritual Mobilization announced the formation of a new Committee to Proclaim Liberty to coordinate their Fourth of July "Freedom Under God" celebrations. Despite its apparent spiritual emphasis, the true goal of the Committee was advancing political conservatism. Its two most prominent members had been brought low by Democratic administrations: Hoover, driven from the White House two decades earlier by Franklin Roosevelt, and Gen. Douglas MacArthur, removed from his command in Korea two months earlier by Harry Truman. These conservative icons were joined by military leaders, heads of patriotic groups, conservative legal and political stars, right-wing media figures and outspoken conservatives from the realm of entertainment, such as Bing Crosby, Cecil B. DeMille, Walt Disney and Ronald Reagan. But the majority came from corporate America. J. Howard Pew was joined by other business giants, including household names such as Harvey Firestone, Conrad Hilton, James L. Kraft, Henry Luce, Fred Maytag and J.C. Penney, as well as lesser-known leaders at giant corporations including General Motors, Chrysler, U.S. Steel and Gulf Oil.

The committee's corporate sponsors took out full-page newspaper ads to promote a pinched version of the Declaration. Dropping the founding fathers' long list of grievances about the absence of effective government in the colonies, the sponsors reprinted just the preamble alone. This approach allowed them to reframe the Declaration as a purely libertarian manifesto, dedicated solely to the removal of an oppressive government. The San Diego Gas & Electric Company, for instance, encouraged its customers to reread the preamble, which it presented with its editorial commentary running alongside…[such as] "all men are created equal…That means you are as important in the eyes of God as any man brought into this world. You are made in his image and likeness. There is no 'superior' man anywhere"…

The Committee to Proclaim Liberty also enlisted the nation's ministers to promote the "Freedom Under God" festivities. Those on Spiritual Mobilization's mailing list received a prefabricated press release that merely needed clergymen to fill in the blanks with their personal information ("The purpose of the Committee," the Reverend _____ declared, "is to revive a custom long forgotten in America—spiritual emphasis on the 4th of July"). *The committee also established a sermon contest, modeled on the wildly successful "Perils to Freedom" competition of 1947. The 17,000 minister-representatives of the organization were encouraged to compete for cash prizes and other rewards by writing an original sermon on the theme of "Freedom Under God" and delivering it to their congregations on "Independence Sunday," July 1, 1951.* (emphasis added) [Note: Is your pastor "preaching for hire" for undisclosed patrons today?]

These sermons were amplified by a program broadcast that same evening over CBS's national radio network. Cecil B. DeMille worked with his old friend Fifield to plan the production, giving it a professional tone and attracting an impressive array of Hollywood stars. Jimmy Stewart served as master of ceremonies, while Bing Crosby and Gloria Swanson offered short messages of their own. The preamble to the Declaration was read by Lionel Barrymore, who had posed for promotional photos holding a giant quill and looking at a large piece of parchment inscribed with the words "Freedom Under God Will Save Our Country." The broadcast featured choral performances of "America" as well as "Heritage," an epic poem composed by a former leader of the US Chamber of Commerce. Gen. Matthew Ridgway interrupted his duties leading American forces in Korea to send a keynote address from Tokyo. He insisted that the founding fathers had been motivated, in large part, by their religious faith.

The "Freedom Under God" festivities reached a crescendo with local celebrations on the Fourth of July. The Committee to Proclaim Liberty coordinated the ringing of church bells across the nation, timed to start precisely at noon and last for a full 10 minutes. Cities and small towns across the country scheduled their own events around the bell ringing. In Los Angeles, for instance, the city's civil defense agency sounded its air raid sirens in the first test since their installation, resulting in what one newspaper described as "a scream as wild and proud as that of the American eagle." As bells chimed across the city, residents were encouraged by the committee "to open their doors, sound horns and blow whistles and ring bells, as individual salutes to Freedom." After the bell ringing, groups gathered in churches and homes to read the preamble together. Both Mayor Fletcher Bowron and Gov. Earl Warren, like their counterparts in many other cities and states, issued official proclamations that urged citizens, in Warren's words, to spend the day reflecting upon "the blessings we enjoy through Freedom under God."

That night, 50,000 residents attended a massive rally at the Los Angeles Coliseum. Organized under the theme "Freedom Under God Needs You," the night featured eight circus acts, a jet plane demonstration and a fireworks display that the local chapter of the American Legion promised would be the largest in the entire country. Fifield had the honor of offering the invocation for the evening ceremonies, while actor Gregory Peck delivered a dramatic reading of the Declaration's preamble. In the end, the Committee to Proclaim Liberty believed, rightly, that its work had made a lasting impression on the nation. "The very words 'Freedom Under God' [have] added to the vocabulary of freedom a new term," the organizers concluded. "It is a significant phrase to people who know that everybody from Stalin on down is paying lip service to freedom until its root meaning is no longer apparent. The term 'Freedom Under God' provides a means of identifying and separating conditions which indicate pseudo-freedom, or actual slavery, from those of true freedom." Citing an outpouring of support for the festivities, the committee resolved to make them an annual tradition…The entire nation, its members hoped, would soon think of itself as "under God."

And indeed, it did. The Christian libertarianism that propelled this religious rhetoric into American politics proved short-lived, but its slogans thrived long after it was gone. Ironically, language designed to discredit the federal government was soon used to sanctify it instead. Throughout the 1950s, a new trend of what the Senate chaplain called "under-God consciousness" transformed American political life. In 1953, the first-ever National Prayer Breakfast was convened on the theme of "Government Under God." In 1954, the previously secular Pledge of Allegiance was amended to include the phrase "under God" for the first time, too. A similar slogan, "In God We Trust," spread just as quickly. Congress added it to stamps in 1954 and then to paper money in 1955; in 1956, the phrase became the nation's first official motto. As this religious revival swept through American politics, many in the United States began to believe their government was formally and fundamentally religious. In many ways, they've believed it ever since.

Kruse's book, *One Nation Under God*, is such an essential resource for documenting the history and nature of the Faustian bargain between the American conservative clergy and big business that I have personally dog-eared almost every page of the text, each citation of which shares shocking and disturbing revelations of "the woman riding the beast" (to coin an image from the Book of Revelation) that set the table for the rise of what became known as the "Religious Right" in the latter part of the century, and thus I will mention just a few of the additional details from its text concerning this early period in Fifield's era. There he notes that eighteen months prior to James Fifield's fateful proposal at the December 1940 National Association of Manufacturer's national meeting, NAM president H.W. Prentis, head of the Armstrong Cork Company, had given a speech to the U.S. Chamber of Commerce which was said to have "electrified" the crowd, in which he had first made the claim that to defeat the impact of the New Deal in public relations, religion must be employed, saying that "Economic facts are important, but they will never check the virus of collectivism; the only antidote is a revival of American patriotism and religious faith."[112] Subsequently, his address at the 1940 NAM conference was broadcast live over ABC and CBS radio, where he reiterated his position. Kruse adds that Fifield and his business peers further argued that "the welfare state was not a means to implement Christ's teachings about caring for the poor and the needy, but rather a perversion of Christian doctrine," and as far as being in concert with the religious teachings of Christ, "nothing better exemplified such values, they insisted, than the capitalist system of free enterprise" (p. 7).

Not long after assuming the role of pastor in Los Angeles, Fifield became very wealthy as his church became the largest Congregational church in the world, and "the church of choice for Los Angeles' elite," with a reporter noting that "its roster read like the *Wall Street Journal*," with its board including the real estate magnate and publisher of the *Los Angeles Times*, the president of Cal Tech, mining magnate Harvey Mudd, insurance company heads and Albert Hawkes, who became head of the U.S. Chamber of Commerce and a U.S. senator, with the Los Angeles mayor and cinema producer Cecil B. DeMille also attending (p. 9). Kruse describes the mansion in the chic part of town that Rev. Fifield acquired to entertain these elites, employing a butler, chauffeur and a cook, during the latter part of the Depression (p. 10). He was known as a theological liberal, saying that reading the bible was "like eating fish—we take the bones out to enjoy the meat. All parts are not of equal value," and dismissed the many passages of the New Testament about wealth and poverty, rather working to reconcile Christianity and capitalism (p. 20). He also stated he acknowledged the personal monikers of "The Thirteenth Apostle of Big Business" or the "St. Paul of the Prosperous" (p. 11). Kruse notes that in December 1939 Fifield ran a full page ad in the *Los Angeles Times*, noting that the New Deal posed a dire threat to the American way of life, and it was the duty of clergymen to save the nation's soul. In their crusade against the wanton growth of government, the church would find natural allies in corporate America, stating in his ad that "Goodness and Christian ideals run proportionally high among businessmen. They need no defense, for with all their faults, they have given America within the last decade a new world-high in general economic well being" (p. 11). *He made this public statement as America was just trying to come out of a decade of the Great Depression.*

To further his agenda, he founded Spiritual Mobilization in the spring of 1935, along with President Cowling of Carleton College, and Prof. Hocking of Harvard, with the intention of empowering clergy nationwide to resist "pagan stateism" (pp. 11–12). He used Spiritual Mobilization to spread his political speeches from his pulpits nationwide, decrying the "grievous sin" of the New Deal state, which had meddled in the affairs of businessmen, accusing the President for "the willful or unconscious destruction of thrift, initiative, industriousness and resourcefulness which have been our best assets since the Pilgrim days." He also spoke of personal acquaintances who have "lost their ideal, their purpose and their motive through the New Deal's destruction of spiritual rootage," adding in another tract that "Every Christian should oppose the totalitarian trends of the New Deal," further adding that "the way out for America is not ahead but back" (p. 12). These pamphlets drew the attention and respect of former President Herbert Hoover, a pro-business leader who had been blamed for leading America into the Great Depression. In October 1938 Fifield sent out a tract to *over 70,000 ministers*, as a call to resist Roosevelt and his jobs and assistance programs to help the one third of Americans that had been out of work, which was met with approval by Hoover (p. 13). Ironically, Roosevelt's attempt to rein in spending to balance the budget (a pipe dream for conservative politicians for generations) caused the economic recovery to stumble, and the growing international conflict made the election of 1940 overshadowed by it, rather than economic issues. Fifield tried to rally clergy to resist America entering World War II, but to no avail (p. 14).

During the war period Fifield was able to coerce almost two million Christians to sign an official pledge (after being bombarded with newspaper ads) to fight "pagan stateism," and defend the freedoms in various sectors of society, including "free enterprise." As the war closed, he resumed his direct fight against the New Deal, with additional conservative figures in politics, business and religion, with the advisory panel including past presidents of the Chamber of Commerce, a leading Wall Street analyst, Dr. Norman Vincent Peale, an economist with the American Banking Association, a congressman, and college and seminary presidents, all to fight the New Deal provisions of job assistance and other federal aid for the poor and disadvantaged (p. 14). Senator Albert Hawkes warned that the jobs and other assistance for out-of-work citizens from the New Deal led him to say that "one can only conclude that there is the objective of the assumption of greater power and control by the government over individual life. If these policies continue, they will lead to state direction and control of all the lives of our citizens. That is the goal of Federal planners" (p. 15). *Seventy-five years later, did his dire prophecy come true?*

This same Hawkes arranged a meeting with leading industrialists in December 1944 at New York's Waldorf-Astoria to help underwrite the Spiritual Mobilization agenda, securing funds from Harvey Firestone, and other industrialists the attendees could contact (p. 15). However, his most important patron he secured was J. Howard Pew, president of Sun Oil (Sunoco) and founder of the Pew Charitable Trust and the Pew religious study and polling operations, all of which are very influential within the Christian community and society at large today. Pew was known as a typically dour Calvinist Presbyterian, and *was unsure of Fifield's belief in the divinity of Christ, but it didn't matter, because their shared belief in the messianic role of big business was common* (p. 16). Kruse writes that "During the 1930s, Pew had emerged as the voice of conservatism in corporate America, holding prominent positions in industrial organizations such as NAM and, more notably, serving as a driving force behind the Liberty League" (p.16) (a precursor anti-New Deal, pro-business public relations group to Spiritual Mobilization that was easily "outed" by the public and press as a big-business "front," and thus lost credibility and influence, according to Kruse). Pew warned Fifield in 1944, during possibly the most intensely war-focused period of the U.S., with the nation focusing on foreign affairs while all able-bodied Americans were on the battlefield or working in building war machines, that "the New Deal is in a much stronger position than it has been for the last several years. It is my judgment that within the next two years America will determine whether our children are to live in a Republic or under National Socialism; and the present Administration is definitely committed to the latter course." He further lamented that since his "character assassination" during the Liberty League fiasco, he would not be able to publicly lead it (p. 16). (The Liberty League was accused before Congress by American war hero Gen. Smedley Butler of being part of a 1933–34 fascist overthrow of Roosevelt (coined the "Business Plot"), and asking him to lead it, with his testimony being verified by Congress in their report and evidence they had collected.)

Kruse notes that "NAM had been making direct appeals to ministers for years, targeting them with outreach campaigns and mass mailings in hopes of swinging them over to industry's side" (p. 17). Pew then employed manufacturer's rep and GM consultant (and New Deal opponent) Alfred Haake to help Fifield make a real plan of action for the clergyman "storm troopers" they had been assembling nationwide, rather than expecting Fifield's supporters to each find their own way of coming to the aid of big business (p. 17). He reported back to Pew, after consulting clergy that had reviewed Fifield's materials, who demonstrated that at the time some clergy still had some discernment ability (unlike many of them today), when the clergy told him that "The careful preparation and framework for the meetings to which we are brought is too apparent. We cannot help but see that it is expertly designed propaganda and that there must be big money behind it. We become easily suspicious" (p. 17). Haake recommended to Pew that clergymen must feel like they are directly threatened by the New Deal as well, by propagandizing them that the New Deal was all about the glorification of the State and a "denial of God," which would "threaten their calling" (and thus livelihood), and if they bought that message, the clergy would become participants in fighting it (pp. 17–18). Haake thus signed on to become director of the Chicago office, as they began to build an organization of clergy-activists, securing eighteen hundred "minister representatives" by September 1945 (a month after the war) in all forty-eight states, with high numbers of Protestants (including many Methodists, Baptists, Presbyterians and Lutherans) (p. 18).

In May 1946 Senator Hawkes arranged for Fifield to meet with prominent businessmen in New York, including the vice chairman of General Motors, Dupont executives and others (including those involved in a pro-business think tank), to form a Businessmen's Advisory Committee for Spiritual Mobilization to raise large sums of money (pp. 18–19). By February 1947, Fifield was giving guidance to his now-10,000 minister-representatives on defeating the New Deal, arguing that government growth had crippled individual initiative and also personal morality, saying that "It is time to exalt the dignity of individual man as a child of God, to exalt Jesus' concept of man's sacredness and to rebuild a moral fabric based on such irreducibles as the Ten Commandments" (p. 19). *Not only does he steer the clergy, and through them, society to the "yoke" of the Mosaic Law from which Christ died to free us, but also contorts government's actions at the time to find the massively unemployed honorable work and the dignity it provides versus idleness on the street corners (and the crime, substance abuse and family disruption they cause), into a vice that somehow threatens man's "sacredness" and the "dignity of the individual man as a child of God." Their alternative, evidently, is for such unfortunate souls for which they hold contempt to totally "fend for themselves" as the "law of the jungle," including the "natural selection" of those (and their dependent families) who would be doomed by such lack of intervention. It thus serves as a godless naturalism that not only Darwin, but also radical libertarian Ayn Rand could smile about, as well as the business and financial community who would not be inconvenienced by their part in bankrolling it—at least, until they need more cheap labor in the future.*

As a result, ministers began to request copies of Friedrich Hayek's *The Road to Serfdom* (essential reading today in libertarian circles, including amongst many Christians and widespread in its citation in alternative and "patriot" media today) and anti-New Deal tracts by Herbert Hoover which were advertised by Spiritual Mobilization, as they distributed them to their parishioners and preached sermons based upon these principles, and found means to network with similar-minded individuals. Around this time (1947), Spiritual Mobilization held their "Perils to Freedom" sermon contest, awarding $5,000 in prize money for sermons espousing unshackling business to their congregations, *with participation by 24,000 clergymen.* This led to the pleased corporate backers doubling their investment in Spiritual Mobilization, raising money from their companies, and securing donations from across the corporate world (p. 20). *Notice that there was no agenda for these clergymen to share with their flock pertaining to eternal life for the listeners, executing the Sermon on the Mount commands of the Kingdom of Heaven, nor even closer relations with God. That was not the financial agenda of the corporate sponsors backing this initiative (which eventually trained and fully saturates the Religious Right leadership today), which despises government and any assistance to the unfortunate or "safety nets," promotes privatization of all societal functions to for-profit corporations, opposes any regulations of business as to fraud, full disclosure, consumer harm or exploitation or worker rights and safety, or pollution or environmental damage that harms the property and physical well-being of others who do not profit from such exploitation.*

Pew himself secured donations from hundreds of corporations, including General Motors, Chrysler, National Steel, Firestone, Sun Oil, Gulf Oil, Standard Oil, Colgate-Palmolive, US Steel and National Cash Register and many others, telling them that clergymen were largely ignorant on economic matters and thus giving biblical credence to "socialistic" assistance for their fellow man, but that much had been accomplished in educating them and still had to be done, and that funding the movement should be priority to fellow corporations *"because recent polls indicated that of all the groups in America, the ministers had more to do with molding public opinion"* (pp. 20–21) (emphasis added). By at least 1948, parts of the press were getting wise to their deceptive game, *The Nation* writing then that "With the 'Save Christianity' and the 'Save Western Capitalism' chants becoming almost indistinguishable," no one knew who was funding the operation, with Fifield only having said that "non-ministers who have a common stake in the American and Christian traditions cannot contribute service, but that it was only natural that they give substance instead" (p. 21). Republic Steel came to the defense of Fifield, with the former having fought hard against the New Deal's expansion of labor rights, such as emanating from the 1937 "Memorial Day Massacre," when ten striking workers were gunned down by policemen outside one of their factories, stating that "Our company has supported his Crusade, generously, for years" (p. 21). Afterwards, the Spiritual Mobilization board doubled the amounts they would receive from corporate donors (p. 22).

Kruse asserts that *"these businessmen were alarmed less by the foreign threat of the Soviet Union and more by the domestic menace of liberalism*, which had been recently reinvigorated by President Truman's surprising reelection in 1948," adding that Fifield's private correspondence with his corporate funders made it clear that *"the main threat to the American way of life, as they saw it, came from Washington, not Moscow"*; Pew responded that he was concerned of such matters, including the "socialization of security" (p. 22) (emphasis added). By 1949, Spiritual Mobilization launched *The Freedom Story*, a fifteen-minute radio story (on over 800 radio stations by 1951), and commonly given free airtime by stations to meet their "public service requirements" (with the influence of Republic Steel) (pp. 22–23). More importantly, Spiritual Mobilization launched a new monthly magazine entitled *Faith and Freedom*, using famous libertarian economist authors, while advertising itself as being created by ministers for ministers, with the tactic of stimulating self-discovery of their "truths," *while portraying those who disagreed with them as immoral* (pp. 22–24). In the periodical Fifield condemned "socialistic laws" such as minimum wages, price controls, Social Security pensions for the elderly, unemployment insurance, veteran's benefits, and such, as violating "the natural law which inheres in the nature of the universe and is the will of God" (p. 25)—*that is, Darwin's law of "survival of the fittest."* The magazine also denounced the Social Gospel and any expansion of state welfare programs, calling it of "pagan origin," and calling it "socialized covetousness, stealing, and the bearing of false witness" (p. 25). The magazine also featured Reconstructionism founder Rousas Rushdoony, who compared the American welfare state to what he saw on the Indian reservation.

In the spring of 1951, the leaders of Spiritual Mobilization got the idea to host a series of national events near the Fourth of July around the theme that has now become a mantra—"Freedom under God," forming a Committee to Proclaim Liberty. Although it had a spiritual emphasis, most of the planners were corporate, not religious, such as Pew, and the heads of Hilton Hotels, General Motors and Chrysler, and also included Herbert Hoover and General Douglas MacArthur, as well as entertainers such as Bing Crosby, Cecil B. DeMille, Walt Disney and Ronald Reagan (p. 27). Fifield's influence was felt in the formation of the Freedoms Foundation (p. 69), as the Eisenhower administration was extremely supportive of such direct propaganda efforts of "civil religion." Eisenhower also supported token displays such as putting "In God We Trust" on the currency and "under God" added to the Pledge of Allegiance, and promoting generic (from a Protestant perspective) prayers in school and Bible reading, which would split America's religious community a decade later. Movie producer Cecil B. DeMille (who intended his *The Ten Commandments* blockbuster movie to be a propaganda piece to further the aims of movements like Spiritual Mobilization, and who came out against unions in his testimony before the House Un-American Activities Committee) became a close ally of Fifield, attending his church and speaking there, praising him and Spiritual Mobilization, and told the eighteen hundred attendees and radio listeners to join Fifield's crusade (pp. 140–141). Later DeMille even offered a Paramount screen test for Billy Graham, promoting it publicly to raise Graham's profile (p. 141).

Speaking of Rousas Rushdoony, the Reformed Calvinist who founded the Christian Reconstruction movement to resist the coercion of the public via participatory socialism for the general welfare, *to be replaced by a forced coercion of the public by the old Mosaic Code (including its prescriptions for the stoning of disobedient children and wives)*, and *being a cornerstone in establishing the American homeschooling community*, he constructed a theological foundation of Christian libertarianism alongside and supplementing Fifield, with his son-in-law Gary

North providing further underpinnings not only to home schooling, but more so the promotion of the Austrian libertarian economic model.

A biography of Rushdoony by author Michael McVicar, Asst. Professor of Religion at Florida State University, entitled *Christian Reconstruction—R. J. Rushdoony and American Religious Conservatism*,[113] also includes significant passages of Rushdoony's intersection with Fifield and Spiritual Mobilization at a critical point in his philosophical formation. He explains that Fifield and Spiritual Mobilization "influenced several generations of American Christians and helped create a political and religious environment in which it has become common sense to suggest that theologically conservative Christians are also economically and politically conservative. He revolted against the New Deal and succeeded in creating an intellectual foundation for a small cadre of thinkers and activists who were eager to reinterpret capitalism in terms of Christ's Gospel" (p. 50). He notes that the *Faith and Freedom* newsletter, which described itself as "a voice of the libertarian," reached as many as 50,000 pastors and ministers by the mid-1950s, and was led by James C. Ingebretsen, a former Latter-day Saint, and not only included articles by libertarian academic and ideological legend von Mises, but also "atheist anarcho-libertarian Murray Rothbard," as well as "British writer and philosopher Gerald Heard, who was the confidant and spiritual guru of popular novelist Aldous Huxley [author of the dystopian *Brave New World*, and the psychotropic-promoting *The Doors of Perception*] and an early LSD enthusiast" (pp. 51–52). He adds that "More often than not, the publication's self-identified libertarian authors completely avoided any discussion of religion in their articles....*Faith and Freedom's* provocative journalism moved many pastors to embrace SM's anti-tax, non-interventionist, anti-statist religio-economic model" (p. 52).

He notes that Rushdoony began receiving *Faith and Freedom* while still serving as a young man as a missionary on an Indian reservation; *Faith and Freedom* "insisted that clergy see government as a problem, not a solution. Rushdoony shared this sentiment" and began contributing articles to the newsletter, where he argued that *Faith and Freedom* needed to attack the Christian church as a whole, observing, as was his wont, that it was not Calvinist enough, arguing that "the American republic was the product of two streams of thought, classical liberalism...and Calvinism," adding that "the Calvinist objection [to collectivism and stateism] needs stating too." This participation led to him being invited to an SM (Spiritual Mobilization) conference at Carleton College, leading him to make key future contacts with the leading libertarian activists, including representatives of the William Volker Charities Fund, "a secretive philanthropic charity" (p. 53). There he announced his desire to publish a periodical like *Faith and Freedom*, but with more of a focused theological, and sectarian Calvinist/Reformed bent (p. 53). Throughout the 1950s and up to 1962, the Volker Charities Fund underwrote the Carleton College symposium on behalf of Spiritual Mobilization, keeping Rushdoony in the spotlight along with other anti-stateism, libertarian and conservative activists (p. 59).

So who was this wonderful Protestant minister, James Fifield, whom we can thank so much for restoring our societal belief in America's global destiny "under God," carried out by its "anointed" national leadership (and sold to the public by its wealthiest corporations and robber barons), as many such as myself have been taught by our Religious Right leadership and role models for generations? *He must have had a pronounced Godly wisdom and inspiration by the Holy Spirit to lead such a mass revival such as many so crave today, right?* Well, in terms of his less-public beliefs and attitudes toward "others" as evidence of such "abiding" with Christ, it turns out he is not much different in general mindset than many of our Religious Right leaders today. As one example, the *Jewish Telegraphic Agency* (JTA), the news wire of the international Jewish community, reported[114] in 1951 that

> Rev. James W. Fifield Jr., minister of the First Congregational Church and leader of "Spiritual Mobilization," was severely criticized here for a radio broadcast in which he stated "it was a matter of historical record that Benjamin Franklin denounced the Jews at the Constitutional Convention in 1787." A demand that he should publicly apologize for spreading anti-Jewish fraud was addressed to Rev. Fifield by I. Benjamin, Los Angeles member of the national commission of the Anti-Defamation League of B'nai B'rith. "Anyone professing a familiarity with America and its history would know, from the most cursory examination of the public record of Benjamin Franklin, that this speech could not be genuine," Mr. Benjamin said. Expressing "terrible shock" that Rev. Fifield could give credence to a proved forgery, the Anti-Defamation League leader called his attention to articles and statements by the *Saturday Evening Post*, the Franklin Institute, and *Liberty* magazine, all of which carefully documented the fact that this alleged "speech" by Benjamin Franklin was originally made up in its entirety to serve anti-Semitic purposes....It was Nazi Propaganda Minister Josef Goebbels who invented this "speech" as part of his campaign against the Jews.

So this is a ringleader of the Christian/big business leadership we look to, to set us straight on our "true" national spiritual history…some things never change.

The mighty Mises Institute, founded in 1982 by the popular Lew Rockwell and originally housed at Auburn University, might be considered the "home" of at least American libertarianism; they host a large number of the original *Faith and Freedom* newsletter/journals from 1951–60 on their website in their entirety.[115] Perusing one such newsletter, from April 1954 and available at their site,[116] it can be seen stated on the inside cover that

> *Faith and Freedom* is a voice of the libertarian—persistently recommending the religious philosophy of limited government inherent in the Declaration of Independence....Freedom under God is in the interest of every man of faith....A Communist, Socialist, Fascist or other authoritarian government is always such an enemy; and *a democratic government espousing a paternalistic philosophy straightway becomes such an enemy.* As the journalists of Spiritual Mobilization, our editorial policy is based on a profound faith in God, the Author of liberty, and in *Jesus Christ*, who promoted persuasion in place of coercion as the means for accomplishing positive good. Our credo is the long-standing credo of Spiritual Mobilization: Man, being created free as a child of God, has certain inalienable rights and responsibilities; the state must not be permitted to usurp them: it is *the duty of the church to help protect them.* (emphasis added)

Given the presence of Ingebretsen in the leadership of this organization (particularly considering the very disturbing information we shall learn about him in the next chapter), it is surprising that that they can give *a pseudo-theological emphasis on Jesus Christ in this statement.* Beyond emphasizing the slogans we have documented from them of limited government and Christian religion in the Declaration of Independence (which, beyond the Preamble, only lists the grievances of *insufficient governance in the colonies,* and that *not featuring colonialist representation,* as opposed to an opposition *to all central governance*) and use of the loaded term "Freedom under God," it is interesting to observe that *the editors associate "democratic governments espousing a paternalistic philosophy" with Communism, Socialism and Fascism and being fellow "enemies of the people."* While it emphasizes a lack of coercion (as good libertarians) for accomplishing positive good, it also says that the church has *a responsibility to protect the rights of men from the State; not only is this not elucidated in scripture as a "duty" of the Church, but one should also ask, by what means should "the Church" accomplish this goal? Should the pulpits be turned into political lecterns, or other more "hands on" means, and why should they be "carrying water" for the political ideological goals of the libertarians?*

In the next chapter we shall learn far more disturbing details about the other major characters connected to *Faith and Freedom* and Spiritual Mobilization, which would cause one to greatly doubt the "Christian" motives and agenda with which they sought to influence clergy (to in turn influence their flocks) across America. However, before we close this discussion we should mention another organization similar to Spiritual Mobilization, but with a primary benefactor whose largesse led to its impact on conservative Christians in America. A 1990 *New York Times* obituary[117] for Howard E. Kershner states that "Mr. Kershner was at various times a newspaper editor and publisher, a real estate operator, builder, manufacturer and author. In 1939 he retired from active business and spent the rest of his life pursuing causes in which he believed," working with Quaker relief agencies to feed children on both sides of the Spanish Civil War, and as a vice president for Save the Children Federation and serving in Europe, as well as raising money for UNICEF and being a founding member of CARE. In addition to that commendable work, importantly "In 1950 Mr. Kershner organized the Christian Freedom Foundation, edited its fortnightly journal, *Christian Economics*, and wrote a column, 'It's Up to You,' which was *printed in 225 daily and 425 weekly newspapers*. From 1967–1973 he was a lay preacher for the Congregational Church in Los Angeles" (emphasis added)—*the very same church that Rev. Fifield had pastored previously*. They add that "He was awarded the Order of Leopold by the Belgian Government and the Order of Merit by the International Union for the Protection of Children, and was a member of the French Legion of Honor. He wrote several books, including 'The Menace of Roosevelt and His Policies,' published in 1936; 'Quaker Service in Modern War' (1950) and 'God, Gold and Government' (1956)."

According to a 2017 press release[118] by the First Congregational Church of Los Angeles—the same church for which both Fifield and Kershner served as pastors—was observing its 150-year anniversary in 2017, as "the city's oldest Protestant Church and long considered one of the most important churches in Southern California." Given the commitment of both men to combat the "social gospel" and programs to assist the afflicted or destitute, it is ironic that the church also mentions the event "recognizes *our deep commitment to education and social justice throughout our history*" (emphasis added). It is further ironic that the front page of the church's own website[119] states that "First Congregational Church of Los Angeles is a progressive, positive, and open church with a strong arts and music culture. We welcome and celebrate those of different faith traditions, cultural backgrounds, and sexual orientations....we celebrate compassion, diversity and inclusivity...we are called to open the doors of our church as wide as God's heart. Our values of faith, rooted in the life of Jesus, continue to be forged by the contemporary issues of our time....we celebrate the many diverse religious voices in our city, even as we seek to embody the spirit of Jesus by loving our neighbor as ourselves"—*the latter statement "flunking" many of the Darwinian self-centered precepts of the "Christian libertarian" message of Fifield and Kerschner.*

The Mises Institute website also hosts a lengthy paper written about "The Importance of Christian Thought for the American Libertarian Movement," which includes further details about the pertinent work of Kershner and his allies and sponsors, and can be currently read online.[120] There author Haddigan writes that "Spiritual values were the predominant justification for espousing a libertarian viewpoint before 1971, and continue today to provide the founding convictions of many American libertarians and conservatives....A case can even be made that Christian libertarianism forms the foundation of any claims for 'American Exceptionalism'. And as a body of political thought, largely as a consequence of the pressures exerted upon individual freedom by New Deal liberalism and events of the early cold war, Christian libertarianism received its fullest exposition in the 1950s and '60s" (pp. 1–2). He adds that

> One of the distinguishing features of the conservative intellectual movement after 1950 was the financial backing it attracted from businessmen in the United States. Either through individual donations, or the establishment of think tanks and foundations, industrialists provided the finance needed to spread the conservative message to a wider audience than before. One of the most, if not the most, generous of these donors was the retired Pennsylvanian oilman, J. Howard Pew. With a gift of personal stock from his company Sun Oil he established the Christian Freedom Foundation (CFF) in May 1950. Because of his personal religious beliefs Pew desired that all his philanthropic activity remained anonymous, and as a result he allowed the story to circulate that the CFF was organized and founded by Howard E. Kershner; the retired Quaker businessman who became the first President of the new Foundation, and editor of the organization's 4-page bi-weekly paper *Christian Economics*. The two men's correspondence, however, reveals that the CFF was Pew's idea, and that after consultation with Rev. Norman Vincent Peale in the fall of 1949, he invited Kershner to become the President of the new organization.

> In a 1961 letter to a friend (at which point he had spent *nearly $2.7 million on his organization*) Pew explained why he had started the CFF in 1950. He stated that in 1946 and 1947, as Assistant Chairman and

then *Chairman of the Public Relations Committee of the National Association of Manufacturers* (NAM), he had commissioned an opinion poll to determine *why businessmen were so distrusted by the American public*. And why, in general, capitalism was under attack. He was surprised to find that respondents named their ministers as the most influential molders of public opinion, and "shocked," that "in those tests it came out the Protestant churches were doing more to promote socialism and communism than any other group." As a consequence, Pew related, he "started a paper to educate ministers" in correct principles. And for the next twenty years Pew's paper, *Christian Economics*, was *sent free to every minister in the United States, approaching at its peak a circulation of 200,000.* (emphasis added)

What the ministers received was a paper that promoted the idea that the free market economy is implicitly sanctioned, but not specifically endorsed, by lessons contained in the Bible. God gave us the way, the Ten Commandments, by which to live a moral life. Unfortunately, the "original sin" of mankind meant individuals tried to circumvent the Divine law, and only the threat of harsh punishment by an earthly authority prevented the strong from enslaving the weak. In effect, individuals were coerced to obey God's plan for His creation through fear of the consequences. The crucial development came, for the Christian libertarian, when Jesus wrote the desire to follow voluntarily the Ten Commandments into the heart of mankind. Jesus gave us the choice, the individual freedom, to believe in Him and his message, or to reject Him. And as no manmade authority can intervene in that decision, the most important an individual can make, then no earthly authority can intervene in an individual's free agency in those parts of their life—economic, political, or religious—where mankind attempts to be a good Christian and live according to the laws revealed in the Bible. Thus, Government is a "necessary evil," as Thomas Paine once argued, limited to the police powers of preventing the unregenerate from injuring the "life, liberty and property" of their fellow citizens. When the State arrogated powers to itself more than those basic functions it became the "enemy" of the Christian libertarian, interposing governmental regulations between an individual and their God. (pp. 5–7)

Let's take a moment to sort out what this libertarianism-proponent author is really saying, from the facts expressed and by "reading between the lines," and trying to decipher the intended purposes the Christian libertarians are trying to use the Bible for, in convoluted fashion, versus a plain reading of history, reality, and a plain-sense reading of scripture, as we covered earlier in this book. It can be seen that the highly unpopular and marginalized view of unvarnished libertarianism (not the aspects of free association, and self-determination when not infringing on the rights of others that are rightfully espoused and laudatory, but rather unfettered markets that provide no protections for individuals or small businesses, the celebration of selfish indulgence and opposition to organized labor, environmental, consumer and worker safety protections, and any assistance to the most destitute, disabled or elderly) would not be taken seriously by most Americans of even the most modest of morality, if not bankrolled by Big Business. *In fact, Big Oil (including "Big Energy" like the Koch Brothers) almost singlehandedly seems to have kept not only libertarianism afloat, but also Billy Graham (see: Sid Richardson) and much of the Religious Right, although one should not discount the huge financial role of others like Rev. Moon and the Unification Church (as told in the next volume) and the "widows' mites" confiscated by the televangelists and newsletter alarmists.* Related to that, another certainty is that Big Business does not invest in anything without an agenda, and that will eventually be one that ultimately enriches their own pockets and those of their henchmen.

It is clear here that Pew's recognition that the people had "gotten wise" to their Industrial Age/Gilded Age "robber baron" exploitation that had led the country into the Great Depression, and urban squalor and mass-production servitude (to be only remediated by the meager resources of the Christian Social Gospel "do gooders"), and that more clergy were getting back to Bible-based advocacy and ministry to the poor, widow, orphan and "stranger" and had an effective moral "bully pulpit" (literally and figuratively), required his fellow aristocrats throwing their "thirty pieces of silver" at tempting Judas's in the clergy in a manner they knew could buy their support, and help in "sacredizing" their big business, common man-exploiting agenda with a veneer of Bible imagery. The "communism and socialism" the Big Business/NAM people thought the clergy promoted were radical ideas like worker rights and union/collective bargaining, worker safety, education for all, consumer protections and the like, which to them were dangerous ideological concepts.

Their "veneer of Bible imagery," masquerading as a theology, had the gall to suggest that the Bible "endorsed" unregulated "free markets," when (as we have seen) the Bible is chock full of admonitions from God Himself that the rich and merchants will consistently exploit the poor and vulnerable in the marketplace, with "dishonest weights and measures," and drain the poor man's vitality by dragging him into court in legal expenses, or throwing him into "debtor's prison," for which those in power, and the people who tolerate it and have a say, will be held accountable by Him. Their system glorifies the "rich man" of whom Jesus Himself says is hard for him to enter into the Kingdom of Heaven. The libertarian focuses, obsesses and fetishizes on property, wealth, assets and possessions, "tearing down barns to build new ones," while Jesus says they are liabilities that can keep us out of the Kingdom, like the Rich Young Ruler. The people who bankroll the libertarian industry are primarily concerned with minimizing taxes, regulations to protect consumers, workers and the environment that will impact their profit line, and government referees in the marketplace between the wealthy, their marketers, Madison Avenue advertisers, public relations groups and lawyers, and the poor individual consumer or worker that has just enough dough for the end of the month, however they thinly disguise their motives to the gullible public by emphasizing "personal freedom and liberty" and characterized by a noble individual fighting the government "system"—in fact, a "freedom" to be swindled, fooled, cajoled, threatened and sued into compliance, if they wish to feed the family that month.

They accept their well-funded assertion that "the government" is the enemy—the same one that Jesus paid taxes to without reluctance and told His disciples to do so, did not resist or rebuke, and which protected the Apostle Paul from Jewish mobs, fed Jacob and his sons, provided a decent life to exiled rebellious Jews in Babylon and the poor in their old homeland. We all know the evils of corrupt government officials and laws, and the duty to our neighbors to resist them when we are given such rights and duties as citizens (which the same Christians often neglect to do, such as over slavery in America), but nowhere does the Bible express righteous, law-abiding government as inherently evil, and in fact, we are told to obey them whenever possible to advance the Gospel. The taxes Jesus and Paul paid to pagan Rome built and maintained the roads, and their security, that were used to spread the Gospel to the uttermost parts of the Earth. These Babylon-gospel "great merchants" are trying to get Americans to not only resist paying the compulsory taxes-without-representation that Roman subjects and Christians through the ages willingly paid, but even resist taxes *for which they directly participate in the selection of representative-proxies to make such determinations on their behalf, with the ability to quickly replace them if they are dissatisfied.*

Many Americans find this "no tax," no-regulations message quite seductive, although they were raised in a blessed era of public schools they could attend (even if their family was poor), public assistance if their family went through a tough spell (or strike pay if pertinent), a network of roads to travel, conduct business, vacation and visit friends and relatives, parks to enjoy nature (including national parks), and libraries to learn and experience the world, *without recognizing that someone paid for all that.* They do not realize that if they lived in the "libertarian dream" existing up to the dawn of the Twentieth Century, most of them would not have achieved any appreciable education, denied proper nutrition or healthcare with high resultant mortality, and likely worked in a mine or sweatshop for endless hours until they died an early death from overwork, black lung, asbestos, workplace accidents, malnutrition or inadequate health care, *unless they were the few that were rich enough to afford it*—libertarian "blessings" they all missed because of some infernal "do gooder" Social Gospeller, who strode into the dangerous and sickening filth of the urban decay and began to minister to the wretched there. This was the world that the overwhelming number of the peoples of Europe (and later United States) lived under, during the entire "Church Age," while they were largely "in charge," both by way of their Christian kingdom leaders and their church and Christian populace sitting on the bulk of their nations' wealth. *If they did not eradicate poverty and suffering with their Industrial Age wealth and "Protestant Work Ethic" for two thousand years of Christian rule and cultural dominance, why would we believe the libertarians that they would suddenly do it now, if the secular government would only "get out of the way," instead of the latter having to fill a void of compassion and intervention that the Christian community largely failed to meet, like the religious leaders who stepped aside around their wounded kinsman, that only the heretical Samaritan would dare assist?*

The idea that Jesus died on the cross and preached a Kingdom of Heaven so that people could resist any collective assistance for the poor or needy and only grudgingly pay for soldiers or policemen (which some libertarians even complain about that), when we know that God will judge the nations and its rulers (even supernatural ones) for neglecting the weak and vulnerable, is the height of blasphemy, particularly when these agendas violate one of the two primary Laws which Christ says still applies, and for which the libertarian so strenuously rejects—the Golden Rule. They scapegoat "the government" as the only source of coercion, without acknowledging its primary role as society's collective coercive counterbalance to the coercive power of wealth in the marketplace, the workplace, the ballot box and the courts against the poor, the commoner/peasant, the stranger and the weak, "unconnected" and otherwise exploitable, and have hoodwinked much of the public to adopt such clouded and one-sided views. Most sadly, this includes even much of the Christian leadership and populace that people used to look up to as their advocates and friends, and even with the myriad of Biblical admonitions (from the Bible they say they believe "sola scriptura," and will defend its inerrancy) that warn them against such.

The author Haddigan adds that

> Kershner wrote the editorials for *Christian Economics*, and had an initial writing staff of two economists, George Koether and Percy E.

Greaves, who received instruction from Ludwig von Mises in the correct economic principles to explain to ministers....And, for the next twenty years, Kershner and a succession of staff and guest writers (including von Mises, Hayek, Haake, and Roepke) consistently defended that laissez-faire position in relation to the eternal principles contained in the Bible. The CFF urged a return to...the abolition of the welfare state and a return to the voluntary charity impulse that glorified the word of God, and the repeal of the Sixteenth Amendment which, with the establishment of the income tax, had made the State the arbiter of an individual's conscience when it came to the distribution of property. (p. 7)

The "voluntary charity impulse" does not "glorify the word of God," anymore than deciding on a whim on whether to obey the Sabbath Years or Years of Jubilee would not "glorify" the Mosaic Law, but rather gives an opportunity for the individual to get the public "praise amongst men" for their demonstrative and conspicuous individual gifts to the needy, strolling out of their limousines to briefly salve their conscience with a public donation to the wretched folk that they otherwise avoid, only when they feel the whim or need to do so, which even via their foundations creates "good public relations" that might offset their misdeeds and public recognition of their malevolence in the marketplace. The Christian libertarians writing in these publications also said that the Constitutional Amendment authorizing an income tax should be repealed "because it violated the First Commandment. By forcing citizens to pay tax to finance the welfare state the Federal Government replaced God as the keeper of man's conscience," calling it "the plan for human salvation inaugurated by Christ" (p. 8). *Note that they have no problem with the government collecting revenue to keep a large national defense—even ones of a nature or scale that would be offensive to many citizens—but resents funds being used to help people in desperate need; if reliance on "men's conscience" would have been adequate for the task over the last few millennia, there would be no widespread need of assistance that the government would need to address, nor the Sabbath years and Years of Jubilee if the Jews' conscience had led them to look out for their neighbors themselves, and not need to be enforced by their own government.* The author notes that "Kershner believed the Jews of the Old Testament had obeyed the letter of the Ten Commandments" (p. 9); his faulty theology neglects to note that they were not called to obey the "Ten Commandments," but rather all 613 statutes of the Mosaic Code; this included the essential practice of the Sabbath years and Years of Jubilee, for which their neglect caused them to be sent into Exile, as God attests in scripture and we have documented. They note that Jesus did not force compulsion to good deeds, so neither should the government; *they do not note that Jesus did not reprimand the Roman soldier for forcibly asking a citizen to carry his goods, and rather Jesus told the citizen to carry them the "extra mile"; in any case, the needs of the poor and destitute must be met, as God expects, whether the person purported to follow God chooses to follow his conscience or not, while the "Christian libertarian" would not mind if some people fell through the cracks, because the more important issue to them is ideological purity, which does not put food on the desperate mother's table.* They further claim that with a mankind guided by the Golden Rule (which somehow they think the libertarian lack of all regulation will somehow produce such virtue in humans), a man "can no longer exploit and enslave his fellows," because they don't want to" (p. 9); *remember, this teaching was funded by one of the biggest members of "Big Oil," and must be interpreted in light of his track record.* In 1957 Kershner said at the Grove City College commencement that "socialism is anti-God," and referred to the "sin of socialism" (p. 9); *this may be surprising news to the many Protestant Christians who live in the many Western European nations who practice a high degree of socialism (even providing state funds for Christian "state churches"), whose societies exhibit a higher degree of universal compassion and far higher levels of happiness and lifestyle satisfaction in polls than in the United States. It should be noted that no actual Bible verses were cited in any of these libertarian arguments, either, much less entire passages of Bible texts, to support their assertions.*

Kershner does not mind imposing government's will on those outside U.S. borders (even though they should also be subject to such human rights of freedom), making no hesitation of engaging the Communists' military and involving themselves with third parties in aiding them "in throwing off their galling yoke," whether or not they have chosen such government themselves. He further asserted that communism should be contained militarily when "it involved the prestige of the United States," and had no faith in the peaceful negotiations and war-avoidance of the United Nations, with their literature declaring that the "UN is mainly a device for spreading socialist tyranny" (p. 10). Haddigan adds that Kershner's journal *Christian Economics* did not show as much fear of international Communism as it did of the National Council of Churches (NCC), and rather said the church should teach that if you worked hard, you would not be poor (p. 10); they did not want pulpits to comment on political or economic social issues when influenced by their fellow churchmen (i.e., those with no profit motives) in the NCC (with them being "sowers of discord"), but rather wanted them to use the *Christian Economics* journal, written by big businessmen and their representatives, as an alternative source of information for sermons on "Christian economics" (p. 11).

Haddigan states that with journals like *Christian Economics* and *Faith and Freedom*, "ministers of American churches were to comprise an essential part of the vanguard of the conservative counterrevolution. A counter-revolution in that ministers would shepherd their flock back to an understanding of the Christian roots of political liberty that had infused colonial Americans, and inspired them to overthrow the might of the British Empire in the original Revolution" (p. 20). Articles by individuals like Rev. Edmund Optiz were warning of preachers preaching the social gospel as a pretext for setting up a socialist government in the U.S., with the fear at the time of embedded Communists in the clergy, as the deepest spiritual threat that he attempted to persuade fellow clergy; *we will see that this man had no compunction about taking LSD or talking to spirits from the beyond, and did not see that as nearly the threat as pastors who suggested Christ's example that "blessed are the poor" should lead to an emphasis on their care, government-wise or however, or that workers' rights and safety should be a concern.* Articles run at the time in these journals for clergymen in the 1950s were those such as "Our Pink-Tinted Clergy" ("with the aim of a secret core in their midst to destroy religion") and "Reds in Our Churches," proclaiming clergy-led humanitarian movements as "Communist fronts" and adding to the general hysteria of mutual distrust between fellow ministers of the Gospel (p. 21).

Haddigan also mentions Presbyterian Rev. Carl McIntire, and his weekly paper *Christian Beacon* (which started in 1936), who explained that his American Council of Christian Churches was to call "God's people back to the liberty, the individualism, the rights of private property, and the blessings of free enterprise in America" (p. 22). McIntire further explained that "the Christian religion does lay down in the most specific manner the fundamental principles which undergird our free enterprise, capitalistic order" (p. 22). He also started the *20th Century Reformation Hour* in 1955, as well as pamphlets (p. 23), and argued that it was the duty of ministers "to remind their congregations of the Christian sanction of individual freedom untrammeled by interference from the State, and to 'take the initiative in re-establishing in the minds of men everywhere *the validity of profit*... and, above all, the defense of the individual in his right to enjoy the fruits of his own labor' " (p. 23) (emphasis added). *This raises the question: why did a minister of the gospel find it such an imperative to spend so much time and money convincing Christians—rather than concerning the biblical emphases on the Great Commission and soul-winning—the critical importance of the "validity of profit" and keeping their money?* McIntire states that it would be difficult for "the capitalistic order" to "withstand the advances of the Marxist philosophy," *which seems to be rather curious if the former is naturally so much better than the latter.* He paints a picture of immediate American peril from Marxism within, the reason being that Americans are "too downright lazy to think," and their "thinking in many cases is being directed along socialistic or collectivistic lines" (p. 23). *I don't perceive myself as "too lazy to think," but I wonder what it makes me if I don't buy all of the arguments guys like McIntire makes (themselves devoid of detailed scriptural justification), and then lay out my objections in several hundred pages, most of which are Bible passage-based.*

The author notes that the Institution of American Democracy estimated that the 1965 incomes of the *20ᵗʰ Century Reformation Hour* was over $3 million dollars—*in 1965 dollars*—and the John Birch Society, over $4 million (pp. 25–26). The author also mentions in closing a 1964 letter from a business associate of oil tycoon Pew, imploring him to desist from financing "fascist" organizations, such as the John Birch Society (p. 30). He also cites as a footnote a speech Pew gave at the first meeting of the Christian Freedom Foundation (CFF) of Kershner's that he bankrolled, in April 1950, in which he stated "in Washington there are many politicians who will tell you that I am an economic royalist—some who contend even that I am Fascist," and cited a 1947 work entitled, "Nazis Parading on Main Street," that detailed Pew's contributions to anti-New Deal groups like the Liberty League and Sentinels for the Republic (p. 30). The American Liberty League comprised top officials of Dupont, General Motors, and top politicians in additions to Pew, and which was implicated in the "Business Plot" to overthrow Roosevelt in 1934 with 500,000 World War I veterans, to be led by Marine General Smedley Butler (who heroically turned in the plans to Congress, and who thus verified the claims). The Sentinels of the Republic fought against child labor laws and business regulations (in the guise of stopping the "growth of socialism"), also supported by Sloan of General Motors, Irenee du Pont, and Pew; the 1936 Black Commission in the Senate found that the Sentinels were anti-Semitic and claimed of a "Jewish threat" to the United States, talking of "old-line Americans" that wanted a Hitler.

The famous (and often seen on television) historian Allan Lichtman gives additional details on such related figures in his 2008 book, *White Protestant Nation*, of which Google Books has uploaded abbreviated sections of it online.[121] There he notes that Sunoco CEO J. Howard Pew made "substantial contributions" to libertarian journals *The Freeman*, Spiritual Mobilization, the Foundation for Economic Education, books and films, and "a project of the National Industrial Conference Board for 'an authoritative treatise [to] define liberty in spiritual terms as stemming from the teachings of Jesus' "(p. 173). More importantly, he adds that Pew was financing a Christian right group, the Christian Freedom Foundation, which he founded in 1950 in collaboration with the Reverend Norman Vincent Peale. The foundation sought to reach "as large a number of ministers as possible who will subscribe to the general concept of freedom in all its parts, *which of course comprehends economic freedom as well as the others".* Howard Kershner, a conservative journalist, became its first president. Anti-pluralist white Protestant clergymen held every board position. The foundation's biweekly magazine *Christian Economics* stood for *"free enterprise—the economic system with the least amount of government and the greatest amount of Christianity".* Pew and his family paid to distribute *Christian Economics* to *nearly a hundred thousand Protestant clergymen,* few of whom paid the yearly voluntary fee of one dollar. At its peak in the early 1960s, the magazine also had a circulation of about an *equal number of laypersons.* The Pews covered most of the foundation's *$430,000* first-year deficit and kept it breathing for *more than twenty years with average annual donations of about $300,000.* Pew monitored the contents of *Christian Economics,* sometimes disputing Kershner's views....Like Leonard Read, Kershner said, "The message of Jesus applies to *economic law* as well as to moral law—they both are God's law" (pp. 173–174) (emphasis added)

Lichtman also provides data and insight on a number of other related figures within the selection of pages that Google Books has excerpted. He notes that oil tycoon Pew also had an agenda to control the public's concept of big business and unregulated markets not only through the nation's pulpits, but also academia and institutes of higher learning and classrooms as well. He writes,

In higher education, conservatives hoped to reassert orthodoxy in economics and culture by *replacing academic freedom with the corporate model of control by managers and board members.* "The Board of Directors lays down the policy in a corporation," wrote J. Howard Pew. "In a college, the Board of Trustees should lay down the policy and all the *members of the faculty should carry out that policy."* At his personally financed Grove City College, Pew said, "'Chapel is compulsory, Bible is taught; *academic freedom as practiced is not tolerated."* Princeton alumnus and industrialist J. P. Seiberling joined other executives in urging universities to *cease* the "teaching of socialism under the protection of *so-called 'academic freedom',"* and to "begin to educate young people into *American concepts and American ideas"* that were not "watered down by foreignisms, including internationalism." (p. 153) (emphasis added)

The latter is an example of a corporate-operated knowledge and information community, and society at large—the libertarian ideal. The 2010 doctoral dissertation[122] of Darren Elliot Grem at the University of Georgia cites pages 215 And 216 of Lichtman's book, noting that Billy Graham petitioned Pew to fund his new pet project, *Christianity Today*, quoting that "Apparently convinced by Graham's hard sell, Pew pledged $150,000 and assured Graham and other members of the founding committee that he was 'prepared to underwrite the costs for the first year— so that in any event there will be no problem as to the organization expenses'," and added that *"To keep up impressions that CT was a popular magazine disconnected from corporate interests, Pew funneled the money through Harold Ockenga's church fund and the BGEA [Billy Graham Evangelical Association], both of which then made a direct donation to CT,"* as well as the backer of hard-core libertarian groups, The Volker Fund, and shoe magnate W. Maxey Jarman of Nashville in similar fashion (p. 65–66) (emphasis added). Lichtman's book also notes that "Graham assured the tycoon that the editors were not 'going to allow anything to appear in the magazine that will conflict with our views on economics and socialism' or contradict 'our basic policies' hammered out at board meetings. Henry agreed: 'We are sure that at bottom our politico-economic ideals are so largely one' " (p. 217), which Grem also cited. Grem also wrote that articles in *Christianity Today* "lauded Austrian economists like Friedrick von Hayek and monetarist economists like Milton Friedman, insisted on 'voluntarism and [the limitation of] government to a police function,' criticized the 'pay-offs, threats, blackmail, violence and disruptions' of labor unions, pushed for the replacement of 'inherently anti-Christian' forms of 'welfare-stateism' with voluntary charity and personal philanthropy, and warned that public welfare programs 'saps individual initiative, increases the size and cost of sustaining bureaucracy [and]...at least assures some form of totalitarian control that spells the death of democracy' " (p. 67).

Lichtman also notes that Pew's Pew Charitable Trust also funded Doug Coe and what was called his "secretive Fellowship Foundation, informally known as 'the Family'," as its budget topped one million dollars by the late 70s, sponsoring prayer groups throughout the top tiers of government and the National Prayer Breakfast, and conducting covert international diplomacy through its privately connected government officials and connected figures, as its budget swelled to exceed $10 million by the start of the twenty first century (p. 342). Lichtman also briefly discusses Spiritual Mobilization, with its own internal studies stating that "Spiritual Mobilization as a movement is mistrusted by most of the ministers as *a possible fascist movement, using the church as a front behind which to save the entrenched employer interests, and BIG BUSINESS"* (emphasis added)—*a tacit admission by their own findings that correlates with the views expressed in this work*—and that "In turn, businessmen feared that a contribution to Spiritual Mobilization was 'sure to be dubbed 'propaganda' and business will be charged to have ulterior motives in attempting to sell the American Way of Life through Ministers," according to the Sylvania president (p. 162) (emphasis added).

Lichtman also mentions another wealthy "oilman" funding the libertarian and conservative front that most people are not aware of—"Oilman William F. Buckley Sr."—the father of conservative icon and East Coast stuffed-shirt aristocrat William F. Buckley Jr. (p 152), who stated that "capital" [i.e., the "captains" of capitalistic industry and finance] must be "interested in upholding our institutions," otherwise "it is too much of a task for the rest of us to do the whole job." Lichtman adds that William Sr. envisioned a political career for his son, to combat conservatives types he identified, such as "the Young Republican Club (which I [Sr.] understand is dominated by radicals, mostly Jews)" (p. 209). Buckley Sr. raised his children in Mexico, South America, London, Paris and the United States, sending the children to private schools. When he migrated to Mexico in 1908, Buckley Sr. represented U.S. and European oil companies as a lawyer there, and became president of a local oil company. He also was appointed a legal counsel by Mexican President Huerta, *who himself had instigated a coup and assassinated the prior president and other top officials, leading a brief brutal regime until he abdicated, fleeing to the U.S. until he was caught brokering a deal with German intelligence to arm him to overtake Mexico again, and in turn help Germany in a war against the U.S.* Buckley then leased oil lands in Mexico, and was offered to be the civil governor of Veracruz by President Wilson as the U.S. was occupying it. He later formed a lobby group to permit Americans to own Mexican land and oil rights that their 1917 constitution forbade, causing him to be expelled by Mexico, moving on to cut deals with oil companies in Venezuela, and then Israel, Guatemala and other countries.

Lichtman also briefly discussed Reverend Carl McIntire, who founded the hard right American and International Councils of Christian Churches, his political lobbying organization, his monthly publication *Christian Beacon*, and his radio show, *The Twentieth Century Reformation Hour*, which began in 1955, airing on more than 600 stations (p. 196). McIntire brought within his ranks preacher Billy James Hargis and his Christian Crusade organization in the early 1950s, the latter having claimed that his helium balloons with mini Bibles flown over the Iron Curtain had helped inspire the Hungarian people to revolt. The Crusade included a *Christian Crusade Magazine*, other literature, radio and television broadcasts, and training schools for Christian conservatives (p. 196). By the late sixties, Hargis was bringing in more than a million dollars a year and his broadcasts aired on 500 radio and 250 television stations, although "In the 1970s his enterprises would crumble after he admitted having sexual relations with male and female students at a college he'd founded" (p. 197). Another one of McIntire's protégés was Fred Schwarz and his Christian Anti-Communism Crusade, teaching how "liberal theology" was connected to Communism, with his 1961 event at the Hollywood Bowl featuring Ronald Reagan, John Wayne, Jimmy Stewart and others, as millions watched on television, sponsored by Richfield Oil, Schick, and Technicolor. Lichtman adds that *McIntire also mentored a young minister named Francis Schaeffer, whose work inspired many evangelicals in the 1970s, and who served as the foreign secretary of the American Council of Christian Churches until breaking with McIntire in 1956* (p. 197). McIntire was a separatist, fundamentalist Calvinist Presbyterian known for outrageous stunts such as pursuing the building of a full-scale Noah's Ark or Temple of Jerusalem, or operating a seaborne pirate radio station, but was combative and lost all his vast religious empire before his death.

According to the obituary of Hargis in the London *Guardian* newspaper,[123] like many other press accounts, the IRS removed his religious organization's tax exemption because of its overt political emphasis, and noted in 1976 that *Time* magazine reported that two students from his American Christian College who married alleged that both discovered that each had lost their virginity to Hargis, while a "number of male choir members accused him of coercing them into sex, justifying his seductions by quoting the example of David lying with Jonathan," allegations which Hargis said were due to Communists and Satan conspiring against him, but he was inevitably forced to resign from the college; they also note that in his 1985 autobiography, *My Great Mistake*, he wrote that "I was guilty of sin, but not the sin I was accused of." The highly-regarded monthly magazine *This Land,* specializing in the greater Oklahoma region, reported in a 2012 investigative work on Hargis[124] that the FBI sought Hargis in connection with the 1959–60 bombings in protest of the desegregation of Little Rock (AR) schools, adding that "According to FBI special agent Joe Casper, Hargis was planning to bomb the Philander Smith College in Little Rock soon. The preacher had recently met with two other bombing suspects at a Memphis restaurant." They noted his pro-segregation sermons, and affiliation with the pro-segregation Maj. Gen. Edwin Walker, who was in command of the Arkansas Military District in Little Rock; Hargis preached that the entire civil rights movement was a communist plot, while Walker began interacting with the John Birch Society, who proposed that President Eisenhower himself was a Communist. While deployed and commanding U.S. troops in Germany, Walker began intensively programming them with Bircher materials, to the approval of the Pentagon, until his anti-government materials were exposed by the press. President Kennedy warned that such people "equate the Democratic Party with the welfare state, the welfare state with socialism, and socialism with communism. They object quite rightly to politics intruding on the military—but they are anxious for the military to engage in politics." He was relieved of his command and in turn Walker did not recognize the presidency of Kennedy as legitimate nor his position as Commander in Chief, and resigned.

Hargis was nominated to be president of We, the People in 1959, which held its first "T-Party" in 1962 to end the 'taxes, treason and tyranny" of the left. Hargis stepped down from the presidency to make way for Ezra Taft Benson, "who referred to America's South as 'Negro Soviet Republic'," and who later served as president of The Church of Jesus Christ of Latter Day Saints. The FBI questioned Hargis about the Little Rock bombings and continued to monitor him, while he called the NAACP a communist plot, and in his book *The Negro Question: Communist Civil War Policy*, he stated that segregation was "one of God's natural laws," and called Martin Luther King a communist-educated traitor and "Uncle Tom for special interests." Hargis and retired Gen. Walker then began a speaking tour together, as Walker soon thereafter ran for governor of Texas, with the financial support of oil man H. L. Hunt. Walker then tried to stop the attendance of a black man at the University of Mississippi; in the resulting riot six federal marshals were shot, and Walker was arrested for sedition and insurrection against the U.S. in 1962. The all-white jury in Mississippi later decided not to indict Walker, not calling in the key black witnesses. Hargis and Walker resumed their speaking tour, "Operation Midnight Ride" (sponsored by the Ku Klux Klan in South Carolina and Arkansas), as "Hargis told *The New York Times that most of his funding came from oil companies*" (emphasis added). In Los Angeles the John Birch Society presented Walker with a plaque calling him the "greatest living American." In 1963 Lee Harvey Oswald fired into Walker's home, barely missing him. By November 17, 1963, Hargis, Walker and George Wallace were speaking in Dallas, in opposition to Kennedy, with Walker running ads denouncing him then in the *Dallas Morning News*; the president was assassinated there five days later. They add that "Not long after Hargis' scandal, General Walker fondled an undercover policeman in the restroom of a public park in Dallas and was arrested for public lewdness. Twice, Walker pleaded no contest and paid a fine." President Reagan returned

Walker to an active status in the Army (at age 73), allowing Walker to enjoy full military benefits.

Another major work that further confirms many of these aforementioned statements of fact with additional source material, as well as adding additional details, is the book *The Conservative Press in Twentieth Century America*, excerpts of which are also available online at Google Books.[125] In a chapter entitled, "Christian Economics, 1950–1972," they note that J. Howard Pew "served nearly forty years as chairman of the United Presbyterian Foundation, devoting much time and energy resisting the social action movements within his denomination and in the National Council of Churches," and that "Pew, who never served in any official capacity in CFF [Christian Freedom Foundation] but nevertheless ensured its financial viability, intended to use *Christian Economics* as the primary weapon in his ideological struggles, and he shared with Kershner the role of ideological guardian of the journal. But he was also instrumental in establishing and financing *Christianity Today* as another weapon for his fight" (p. 164). They add that "Just as CFF provided an institutional base and tax-exempt status for *Christian Economics*, which incurred most of the costs and also provided most of the organization's visibility, so Pew contributed money while Kershner contributed his journalistic experience. Through CFF, Kershner made contacts with numerous other conservative organizations, and he gave them access to the pages of *Christian Economics*. This organizational cross-fertilization exposed a large number of the clergy to the appeals of ultraconservatism during the 1950s and 1960s," with spokesmen of the Christian Anti-Communism Crusade and the John Birch Society finding "a positive reception in the pages of *Christian Economics*," while Kershner lectured at places like Harding College and Pepperdine University (p. 164).

They write that the $430,000 provided to CFF in its first year from "cash donations and stock transfers from Pew family trusts," and averaging $300,000 annually for almost twenty five years, also paid for "Sermonettes" to nearly 1,500 churches and for the production of newspaper columns and *Howard Kershner's Commentary on the News*, a fifteen-minute program carried by more than 150 radio stations (p. 165). They quote him as explaining that, regarding *Christian Economics*, "our main drive is to set forth the errors of Socialism and to show the soundness of free market economics" (p. 165), and that "Socialism—Welfare Stateism—is a reversal of God's plan for man" (p. 166). They add that within *Christian Economics* Kershner "praised Senator Joseph R. McCarthy (R, Wisconsin) and the John Birch Society," with in-church social action movements as "essentially Marxist," calling his fellow Quakers that "Socialist Society of Friends," and "defending the apartheid of Rhodesia and South Africa, as well as racial segregation" (p. 165). He told a correspondent that "the best authorities agree that the Negro race is some 300,000 to 400,000 years behind the white race in its evolutionary development" (p. 165). They write that "Interviews conducted by Opinion Research Corporation with 311 Protestant ministers in Philadelphia, Cincinnati and Atlanta in 1953 indicated that 15 percent of the respondents relied 'heavily' on *Christian Economics* for information about social, political, and economic issues," and that "Eighty-eight percent of the ministers receiving *Christian Economics* said they read it regularly or occasionally" (p. 166). *The data in this book you are reading show that ideological media outlets targeting conservative Christians and clergy, funded by big business and other backers of questionable agendas, did not originate with the Christian Broadcast Network, Sean Hannity or Fox News, but the latter modern examples build on their legacy, with the same messages, techniques and agendas.*

They continue to state that "Kershner moved to California, where the Reverend James W. Fifield, Jr., of the First Congregational Church of Los Angeles, and former head of Spiritual Mobilization, secured an appointment for him in his church as minister of applied Christianity. In the spring of 1967 Kershner moved the editorial office of *Christian Economics* to Los Angeles and found renewal in the conservative environment of Fifield's church," stepping away from CFF in the early 1970s after the death of Pew, as CFF began to pursue a more youthful audience (p. 167). In 1971, its new publication, *For Real*, was advertised as a Christian "underground newspaper" (funded by corporate America, of course) that "aimed at high school and college students, and claiming a circulation of more than 100,000" (p. 167). They also add that Richard DeVos, the founder of the Christian multi-level marketing business Amway and father-in-law of Trump's Secretary of Education Betsy DeVos, "and a group of fellow conservatives acquired control of CFF in 1975, and Ed McAteer, formerly a district sales manager for Colgate-Palmolive Company, became a field representative and seminar organizer for CFF the following year" (they also note that McAteer "became a catalyst for organizing the New Right Among evangelicals and fundamentalists....Later he was instrumental in bringing [Howard] Phillips together with fund raiser Richard Viguerie and evangelist Jerry Falwell to found the Moral Majority," and that "McAteer followed that by establishing the Religious Roundtable in 1979") (p. 167).

The book editors and writers also briefly write about *Christianity Today* and their patron Pew, and how, as what is considered as the more moderate "neo-evangelical" main party organ, they too promoted a pro-business "Christian libertarianism" within their pages, including showcasing Kershner himself as one of their voices. They note that in a 1966 article, "Howard Kershner argued that Jesus had commanded Christians to go into the world and preach the gospel, but that did not mean involvement in the Peace Corps or civil disobedience" (p. 174). Not surprisingly, given their flagship figurehead Billy Graham and his close association with powerful figures including President Nixon and other presidents, *Christianity Today* boldly defended President Nixon and his innocence during Watergate, until it became laughable to do so, then applauded President Ford for pardoning him so his crimes would not be brought to justice (p. 175). They have traditionally praised libertarian stalwarts Friedrich Hayek, Henry Hazlitt and Milton Friedman; in the 1958 article, "Christian Approach to Economics," Irving Howard of the Christian Freedom Foundation (CFF) argues for capitalism and argues that "*inequality in wealth is part of God's providence or plan*," somehow relating to the Garden of Eden, thus "*restricting freedom or demanding equality would be contrary to God's principles for the world and thus immoral*," and "limit government to a police function" (p. 176) (emphasis added).

L. Nelson Bell wrote in *Christianity Today* (CT) in 1968 that enlisting the power of the government leads "straight to the concept of a socialistic state" (p. 176). They cite CT editorials against organized labor, arguing that "labor forces illegitimate restrictions on capital and gets its way through government coercion" (p. 176). Another editorial in 1958 characterized the "pay-offs, threats, blackmail, violence and disruption" as major characteristics of the labor movement, while not reporting on abuses within the ranks of management (p. 176). Other proposals within its pages called for the replacement of "welfare-stateism" with voluntary church welfare and philanthropy, with a 1960 editorial claiming that welfare programs were "inherently anti-Christian," and in 1974 that "the welfare state saps individual initiative, increases the size and cost of sustaining bureaucracy" and "assures some form of totalitarian control that spells the death of democracy" (p. 176).

It should be no surprise that the Central Intelligence Agency maintained files on the influential *Christian Economics* periodical; a number of links to their recently declassified files on the subject "Christian Economics" can be found in their "Reading Room" online.[126] In one entry labeled "Christian Economics" which appears to comprise a short article from the periodical and republished by the Clovis, NM *News-Journal* newspaper in 1954 (declassified in 2000), entitled "Soft Thinkers," author "Allen W. Dulles, Director, Central Intelligence Agency" complained that "neutrals and soft thinkers are often a greater danger than avowed communists," and focused on "front" organizations Soviet Russia funded to "conceal the real purpose of the communist conspiracy." He reiterated that "Today it is not the open communist, the admitted follower of Marx and Lenin, who is likely to trip us up. It is the neutralists, the soft thinkers, *the agrarian reformers, the welfare staters*, and collectivists who merely decry the methods, but are blind to the aims of international communism" (emphasis added). Allen Dulles should know a lot about "front organizations"—he formed an innumerable amount, including the "Mighty Wurlitzer" of U.S. media control using "Operation Mockingbird," and CIA assets Paley and Luce as heads of CBS and *Time* respectively that were taking orders from Dulles and the CIA directly to provide news to the *American public* that only the CIA approved, as an *official "psy-op" on their own citizens that paid their salaries.*

A lengthier entry in the CIA records is an actual copy of *Christian Economics* from 1960, which was declassified and approved for release in 2004.[127] In its "Voice of the Editor" (presumably Kershner), entitled, "The Marxian Trend," it lamented a pay raise for federal employees—*their neighbors who raise their families on lower to middle-income pay to help run their federal courts, inspect their food, repair their highways and railroads, keep airplanes from crashing, and the like*. They associate such with "pork barrel" spending, along with "welfare handouts for Social security beneficiaries and numerous other segments of our population." They say that others want on the "gravy train," and that sadly "their pleas *appeal to the sense of justice of the American people* and are granted" (emphasis added)—*a "sense of justice" (including economic varieties) these libertarian business barons hope to eradicate from the public conscience.* They say our nation had become "a nation of thieves" (such as by receiving biennial pay raises, as opposed to CEOs whom we know work for free for the benefit of society). They say it is "covetousness" and "There is no foreseeable end to this practice short of ruinous inflation and bankruptcy." *I for one believe in fiscal responsibility (both in government and in our homes), and in balanced budgets, which will require both drastic reductions in high-end "pork barrel" spending in defense (that benefits only a few), and tax rates restored for the affluent to historical norms, but these "Christian" visionaries use the most disrespectable and ugly means to make such cause, and for all the wrong reasons and for the wrong people. In terms of the imminent "ruinous inflation and bankruptcy," that may overtake us eventually (all while still paying low taxes by the wealthy), but in terms of the accuracy of their vision in 1960 of "imminent," fifty-nine years later we are struggling under the "ruinous" rate of almost two-percent inflation, and government wages have not risen in real dollars, or for all of Americans, for that matter; only the disparity in the income and assets of the top one percent and the remaining ninety-nine, and skyrocketing deficits along with reduced upper-tier taxes are becoming "ruinous"—a "mission accomplished" for these libertarian advocates for the deserving "achievers"—i.e., society's aristocrats.*

Their fear is that this trend "will reduce us toward a basis of equality wherein gifted men and women are not rewarded in proportion to their exceptional abilities....No society can long endure which denies to its exceptionally creative people sufficient reward to stimulate them to their best endeavors." *So is giving federal workers a few percent in cost of living raises going to deny the "gifted" their ability to receive their largesse? And by the way—does not the term "gifted" suggest to some degree, while all should be rewarded to some level for exceptional dedication and work, ingenuity and vision, that at least some of their abilities are a "gift" from God for all our mutual benefit, and not just for their excessive enrichment? Most of their "gifted" sponsors received their wealth via inheritance and such.*

The author's ingenious, virtuous and visionary answer to the gall of federal workers desiring a few percent cost of living raise to keep up with inflation, is that "public employees should receive rather less than the normal scale available to private employees. If they should feel aggrieved by reason of this fact, the remedy is always to seek employment in privately owned industry [like real virtuous people do] or in the professions and as managers of small businesses." These inadequately-intelligent and inadequately-wise libertarians such as this column's author should have recognized that due to the "law of the jungle" laws of "supply and demand" in the "free markets," their recommendation will cause a refusal of qualified people to be so abused in these essential jobs, or it will attract lesser-capable or dedicated people, further adding to the public dissatisfaction with the performance of government agencies. The author adds that with the employer, "Whatever they are willing to pay is the just and proper wage for him to receive," and that "there is less temptation to covet." *The goal appears to be to pay the bare minimum—even though the one on the losing end is part of the national collective that is deciding to pay himself the poverty wage. Does this system at large reduce the "temptation to covet" of the robber baron corporate CEO, owner, Wall Street hedge fund speculator or mine owner, whose financial means of their worker or customer is theirs for the taking? When the overwhelming majority of society does not have enough assets to survive a month, is there a "fair" and "free" negotiation going on for "fair wages" for them with the establishment that will hold out until somebody "breaks" in desperation, like the Dust Bowl migrant workers?*

The main article of the edition published by these "Christian leaders" is "Who Will Rescue the Colonies?," by a worker for the U.S. House of Representatives. It pines for the days when the Western powers exploited the "savage" Africans as their colonies, raping their lands of valuable raw materials, and using their veritable (or real) slave labor. They lament that "Nineteenth century colonialism is dead and gone, yet news dispatches from the Congo recount the emergence of primitive savagery over large areas which had been moving prudently toward civilization for almost a century." They note that fourteen new African nations will join the United Nations in 1960, "but nowhere in that stricken area is there a cultural foundation adequate to support law and order, the historical cornerstones of freedom under law," blaming the Communists for stirring "defamation" against "Western colonial administration." They write that "After 1918 *colony* suddenly became a bad word over vast reaches of the earth—a term of opprobrium and irrational hatred." They write that "Capital has a real function in national development, and we do not escape the underlying economic realities of colonial relations merely by parroting the Kremlin slogans of hate and vituperation against *investor nations*" (emphasis added). They add that "Before communism began to call the tune in the 1920s, the strong nations assisted the weak; and the weak gradually became stronger— and eventually free. Today, that entire concept of history has been blacked out by a world smog of hateful propaganda against colonialism....there are still many things primitive nations might learn from the *cultural centers of civilization*." *I wonder if the author would consistently apply his logic and condemn the unlawful rebellion of the British nations in the New World against "Christian Britain," which resulted in a bloody civil war?*

Other articles in the same periodical edition recommend dealing with foreign economic competition by further decreasing worker wages (with no mention of decreasing corporate profit targets or executive pay). The "Sermonette" in the edition (evidently intended to provide the "Gospel to the poor," as Christ announced when starting His ministry) noted, aside from a single generic Bible verse, that "when men become accustomed to living from subsidies, bounties, long-continued charity or any means of sustaining themselves by the effort of others, they lose confidence, integrity, courage, initiative and independence....[and] seeks more and more to cast the burden of his life upon his neighbors, the taxpayers. Herein lies the soul-destroying evil inherent in any type of collectivism, call it socialism, fascism, communism or welfare stateism...that which teaches him to obtain as much as possible of his living from the labor of others is from Satan." On the front page they did announce their survey of ministers nationwide, revealing that all but 43 of the 1,961 ministers replying to a "test mailing" received *Christian Economics*, with roughly 40 percent reading it regularly, and almost half finding it "very useful" or "fairly useful," and 43 percent "were in general agreement with the views expressed in *Christian Economics*, and another 32 percent agreeing half the time, causing them to declare that "the freedom philosophy as expounded in CHRISTIAN ECONOMICS finds increasing acceptance." However, with all the letters from pastors included that extolled the virtues of the periodical, they did include a letter from a "Rev. Paul W. Lindau" of Iowa, who wrote, "I WISH to thank someone for sending CHRISTIAN ECONOMICS to me *as it given me a bit of insight into the imaginations of the human mind. Any similarity between the views generally expressed in CHRISTIAN ECONOMICS and the Gospel of Jesus Christ are the result of sheer rationalization and I would appreciate it if you would remove my name from the list*" (emphasis added). *All this thought-provoking content (and much more) was derived from a single four-page bulletin.*

Kershner's influence still extends today; one web page[128] still online at the time of this writing appears to be connected to an organization that somehow affiliates itself with "The Emmaus Walk," a spiritual event that is widely acclaimed by a wide array of Christian communities, but unknown as to its affiliation here, but features a talk of Howard Kershner *from a 1966 edition of Lutheran Digest*, entitled, "The Future of the Welfare State." It is "classic Kershner," stating up front that "The welfare state is based on the concept that some have a right to more than they produce," as they "live by the sweat of the brows of other people," and based upon "coveting" and "stealing." As those who "disregard the Commandments of the Almighty do not long continue to prosper," he adds that "No welfare state has ever been able to produce as abundantly as the states that have a free economy. The welfare state and free enterprise are therefore in conflict with each other. They cannot permanently exist side by side. One will conquer and the other will disappear....We must stop misinterpreting our Christian religion." *I don't know if the single mother who left a wife-beating husband with her kids (or lost one due to his death), or lost their legs or eyes due to injury or by birth defect, or succumbed to mental illness or other medical conditions, focused on "covetousness" or exploiting the "producers" when they asked for immediate help to help feed their children through the end of the month, while the libertarians have their intellectual debates over how to make these elderly and infirmed into good entrepreneurs and Wall Street speculators—something "respectable," and that God could respect.*

We'll now share some additional data from this period that reflects a small part of the scope of financial investments that prominent businessmen and their businesses have made in some of the most iconic evangelical ministries, or those that are lesser known, yet by their personnel and amount of funding, are immensely influential behind the scenes. The academic journal document site JStor offers (for online readers with free accounts) read-only access to a paper publishing the findings of a study commissioned by the World Student Christian Federation in July 1980. The paper, "Whose Gold Is Behind the Altar? Corporate Ties to Evangelicals,"[129] begins by stating that religious nonprofit organizations exhibit a surfeit of financial data, or means to identify individual donors, due to the lack of requirements to file such data with regulatory agencies (which makes such organizations ripe for abuse), and thus is typically only gleaned from scant public sources, and at best a gross underestimate. They focused on evangelical organizations with membership or constituency of 100,000 or more, or annual revenues of $2 million or more, which comprised a total of 28 organizations to focus on in their study. They note that a church does not have to file an IRS Form 990 financial disclosure, as do other tax-exempt organizations, and do not even have to inform the IRS as to their existence.

They identified more than $20.5 million given to 18 of these organizations from 1975 to 1980. They note that *three quarters of the total ($15.5 million) came just from the individual Nelson Bunker Hunt alone* (with most going to Campus Crusade), with the remaining funds coming from 37 foundations and individuals. Of this remaining amount, most of it went to the Fellowship of Christian Athletes, Garden Grove Community Church (of Robert Schuller), Oral Roberts Evangelical Association, Billy Graham Evangelical Association, Young Life, Intervarsity Christian Fellowship, and the Christian Anti-Communism Crusade (pp. 63–64). They write that "Among the most notable donors are the Pew Family interests (divided among five foundations and trusts), with a combined total of over $1 million" in 1980 dollars over the period, and adding that "The Pew Family has been a long-time contributor to numerous ultra-conservative causes" (p. 64). Ironically, they also note that a large sponsor to groups such as Campus Crusade, the Church League of America, and the teetotaler Baptist Jerry Falwell's Moral Majority is the *Coors beer brewery family.* The Billy Graham Association is similarly funded by the Mormon Marriott family, and other groups by the notorious William Randolph Hearst (p. 64). They note that all these evangelical organizations are interconnected with common staff and representatives, forming a "complex web." The authors write that the data suggest that "the work of these evangelical groups must be seen in a partisan relationship with the wealthy elite" (p. 64). They observe that the evangelical organizations of the "Right Wing" who promote economic conservatism are "closely tied with very powerful corporate interests, such as the Joseph Coors family, the Pew family, the leaders and owners of Amway Corporation, Fluor Corporation, Rockwell International, and others" (p. 65).

A lot of evangelicals (particularly those who come from a Baptist (like myself) or other fundamentalist culture, for whom drinking was considered spiritually perilous) do not realize that a major financial backer that makes their favorite Christian political activist organization (promoting traditional family values and units) financially viable *is a major beer brewer.* In 1988 *The*

Los Angeles Times did a profile[130] on its leader at the time, Joseph Coors, and the Coors family. They begin by quoting Joseph's son Jeff, who had just taken the helm as president, who stated that while the press made his family "Cinderella-like" and "all lovey-dovey" and "all these smiling faces...[and] what a wonderful family," he wryly notes, "And my father has a mistress all the time!" They do confirm that "Dad just ran out on Mom, after 48 years, for a younger woman, and has gone off to live in the lazy, hazy climes of Northern California wine country." They also acknowledge that "for better than a decade, Coors has been the company Americans most love to hate: boycotted by organized labor, racial minorities, women, gays, students, teachers and countless other special-interest groups. And the Coors family itself has been routinely denounced as racist, sexist, union-bashing, right-wing fanatics." They further state that in son Jeff's eyes, "Joe Sr. is an adulterer and, therefore a sinner, along with homosexuals, gluttons, blasphemers, murderers, liars and a whole bunch of others. All five of Joe Coors' sons, inspired by their mother, Holly, 67, are self-described, 'born again' Christian fundamentalists. Hard core...The oldest son, Joe Jr., 45, for instance, even lists 'Biblical Prophecy' as a hobby...on his company resume, the whole family is awaiting Armageddon, which Joe Jr. believes will occur around the year 2,000."

They point out the family fighting to keep union organizers from their workers, as the only non-unionized brewery in the nation, and mentions its quiet manufacture of military weapons technology (for example, my office cohorts worked with Coors in developing military aircraft armor). They note that regarding recent Coors chief Joseph Coors, "a longtime personal friend of Ronald Reagan's," that "Over the years, he's also contributed to almost every right-wing cause of any consequence, from the John Birch Society to the Heritage Foundation, to wars against the equal rights amendment and the Nicaraguan Sandinistas. Most recently he wound up center stage at the Iran-Contra hearings, after personally donating a $65,000 airplane to the Nicaraguan 'freedom fighters'." His assistant at the helm, brother Bill Coors (both brothers having recently become billionaires by 1988), told Denver-area black businessmen in a speech in 1984 that "slave traders had done them all a favor by dragging their ancestors to this great country in chains. Likewise, Coors had added, descendants of Mexican 'wetbacks' should also give thanks that they got here, even if they had to swim the Rio Grande." Regarding the brewery operations, they write that "Especially controversial was a polygraph test Coors administered to all prospective employees, probing into everything from weekend drug habits and marital infidelities to homosexual activities. And, for all its national notoriety, Coors stubbornly clung to that test until only two years ago." They do acknowledge the tragedies the Coors clan has experienced, such as "The misery Bill Coors endured when it became clear, more than three decades ago now, that his first wife was an alcoholic; then, the awful suicide of his oldest daughter five years ago, when she leaped to her death from a New York City high-rise, leaving a husband and babies behind....And, going way back, everybody still speculates about whether it was really an accident, when the senior Adolph fell to his death from a Florida high-rise in 1929, at age 82, or another Great Depression suicide," or when Joe's "fourth son, Grover, now 38, became a temporary hippie, hiding out in California with his LSD, long hair and, even destroying his draft card."

They quote Chairman of the Board Bill Coors, who defends alcohol by saying that it was cigarettes, and not alcohol that killed his first wife (while disputed by his second), and states that "Beer is a *food* product, it's actually good for you....there's a growing body of clinical evidence that people who use moderate amounts of alcohol enjoy a better degree of health than those who abstain....you can reduce your health risk by (consuming) an alcohol equivalent of about two or three cans of beer a day." Bill reiterated on the day of the interview that he was glad blacks were brought to America in chains, because it was for their "own good" and they have "cashed in," where there was "economic opportunity" and anyone can start a business. Brother Joe then chimed by noting that Sen. Edward Kennedy was "a common murderer" and then railed against American Indians, saying that "Indians chose to stay on the reservations, versus becoming Americans! And now they're upset that the government didn't give them more money!" Regarding Joe, they mention that "Years ago, his nominations by both Presidents Richard M. Nixon and Gerald R. Ford to sit on the Public Broadcasting Corp. board were killed in a Senate committee after furious debate over his right-wing politics. But even more personally hurtful, he says, was his failure to get former Atty. Gen. Edwin Meese III's previous job as White House counselor to Reagan in 1984. Coors was high on the list of candidates being considered," to which he and family members blame Nancy Reagan, although Reagan appointed Joe's ex-wife Holly as "Ambassador of the Americas." *This is what the wealthy candidly sound like in their personal circles, and they see nothing wrong in their condescension and do not hide it.*

The 2003 London *Guardian* obituary[131] for 85-year-old Joseph Coors, called "Joseph Coors—The man who bought the White House for Ronald Reagan," also fills in some additional aspects of the patriarch and scion of right-wing causes. They write that he was "one of the ultra-conservative businessmen who, for all practical purposes, bought the White House for

Ronald Reagan in 1980." They write that "The two men first met in 1967 after Reagan, then governor of California, had become the darling of the Republican right for his unswerving support of Senator Barry Goldwater's presidential campaign. Coors, whose grandfather founded the business in 1873, had long supported extreme rightwing causes; *even his elder brother William described him as 'a little bit right of Attila the Hun'* " (emphasis added). They add that "After Goldwater's crushing defeat by Lyndon Johnson in 1964, he was looking for another reliable candidate to pursue his political and business agenda. Richard Nixon, an obvious frontrunner, had blotted his copybook through his readiness to deal with Nelson Rockefeller, the moderate Republican governor of New York, who was viewed as a class traitor by Coors and his associates." Together with a cabal of other capitalists, "they arranged for the Coors company to sponsor Reagan's political radio shows, which deployed his undoubted presentational skills to a national audience. *Coors then donated $250,000 as seed money for the Heritage Foundation*, a conservative Washington think-tank that generated many of Reagan's campaign ideas—and persuaded him to adopt the Star Wars anti-missile system once he got to the White House. *Coors supported the foundation for years with an annual subsidy of $300,000.* The initial outings for his new candidate came in 1968, when Reagan unsuccessfully challenged Nixon for the Republican presidential nomination. Another attempt followed in 1976 but, in the aftermath of the Watergate trauma, the Republican faithful opted for Gerald Ford" (emphasis added). They continue:

> Meanwhile, Coors had more immediate business problems at home in Colorado. Among the byproducts of his vast beer output were the toxic aluminum tailings left over from the production of the cans. A regional agreement prevented the movement of this waste across adjacent state borders, so Coors set up the Mountain States Legal Foundation, headed by James Watt, a local lawyer, to fight the environmental constraints in the courts. In the lead-up to the 1980 presidential race, Coors and his associates used every possible loophole to pour money into Reagan's campaign....Reagan's victory duly brought rewards to the Coors group. They became highly influential members of his kitchen cabinet and secured, among many other appointments, the job of secretary of the interior for James Watt. He immediately chose Anne Gorsuch, a Colorado legal acolyte, as head of the environmental protection agency [and mother of Trump Supreme Court nominee Neil Gorsuch], and, with absolutely no experience in the field, she embarked on the dismantlement of many laws covering toxic waste disposal.

For all Coors's backstairs influence, however, Gorsuch's appointment became a political disaster. She ran afoul of both Democratic and Republican politicians as voters howled about the renewed pollution threats to their localities. Her fate was sealed when the US justice department claimed that her administrative actions had raised serious conflicts of interest. After 22 calamitous months, Reagan was forced to sack her. James Watt attempted to carry on the Coors agenda but, after falling foul of Congress through his extraordinary political insensitivity, was also forced to quit. In the end, a score of the appointees pushed on to the administration by the Coors group were criminally convicted for their part in the environmental fiasco. Coors's business career suffered similarly. The federal trade commission won a case against him for illegal practices, including price-fixing and the unlawful limitation of competition. In the 1970s, he decided to bar trade unions from his plants, a move that precipitated a 20-month strike. The company eventually won, but then suffered a 10-year boycott of its beers by outraged members of the AFL-CIO confederation.

In 1987 *The Chicago Tribune* detailed how Joseph Coors worked with CIA Director Casey and Oliver North to go around U.S. law and congressional directives to secretly get money to the hard-right Nicaraguan contra rebels.[132] They write:

Former National Security Council aide Oliver North and fundraisers for Nicaraguan rebels worked out a "one-two punch" aimed at wealthy potential donors that netted millions of dollars for the contras, according to testimony at a congressional hearing Thursday. Beer executive Joseph Coors said that in June, 1985, he asked CIA Director William Casey how to get money to the contras—at a time when Congress had banned U.S. government aid—and Casey replied, "Ollie North`s the guy to see." Coors was one of three contributors to testify at the joint House-Senate committee hearings into the Iran-contra affair. The scenarios outlined by all three had several variations—in one case, a promise of a meeting with the President for those who gave more than $300,000—but all included North, a Marine lieutenant colonel....William O`Boyle, a private investor from New York...and Coors, vice chairman and director of the Adolph Coors Co. and a resident of Golden, Colo., said North told them the contras urgently needed an aircraft known as a Maule, which cost $65,000. O`Boyle said he gave $130,000 for two such planes in March, 1986, and Coors said he gave $65,000 for one in August, 1985. Coors said North provided him with an account name and number in Switzerland and he sent the $65,000 to that account to be used to buy the plane. The account was in the name of Lake Resources Inc., a company owned in part by retired Air Force Maj. Gen. Richard Secord, a major figure in both the covert sale of U.S. arms to Iran and the supplying of money to the contras. Last fall, Coors said, North "showed me a picture of what he said was my plane." Asked about Secord`s testimony that, essentially, assets in the Lake Resources account belonged to Secord and not the contras, Coors said he was "surprised and shocked." "I didn't give this money to Gen. Secord," he said. "I gave it to the freedom fighters".

O`Boyle said that at a meeting with North on April 29, 1986, the National Security Council aide described to him a secret plan for the contras to take over in Nicaragua with U.S. assistance. O`Boyle, who said his security clearance was last validated in 1965, said North told him, "You can't tell this to anybody"....On Capitol Hill Thursday, House Speaker Jim Wright (D., Tex.) said it was "increasingly evident" that laws, including the two-year congressional ban on military aid to the contras, "were systematically violated by members of the executive branch of the government." Retired Maj. Gen. John Singlaub, another witness at the hearings Thursday, said that while he conducted most of his fundraising efforts for the contras openly, he also worked with North on clandestine efforts. He said that on one occasion he offered to serve as a "lightning rod" to help conceal from Congress and the news media the existence of covert efforts to secure contra funding by North and Secord.

Oliver North, appearing in testimony in full military uniform and portraying himself as patriotically "following orders" and also doing what was right in his own eyes, knowingly defying laws of the nation intentionally via deception, to secretly work with the Israelis to sell forbidden weapons to the Iranians who had just held American citizens hostage and were under embargo, while his secretary shredded all damning documents, was convicted of crimes, but set free on a technicality of his immunity deal. He now appears annually on the Fourth of July at a prominent local evangelical church to speak at their "God and Country"-styled mega events, reflecting his "patriotism."

Returning back to our journal paper on the corporate funding of evangelical "ministries" (circa 1975–80), the authors write that "Campus Crusade has grown to be a huge organization with widespread domestic and international activities. It is well-funded through Bright's major corporate connections, and is strongly political. Over the last decade it has experienced substantial growth, from an $8 million budget in 1968, to $18 million in 1972, and more than $30 million in 1976. In 1976, the full time staff numbered 5000 in 82 countries," and headlined by major contributions by the Pew and De Vos families (p. 67). They add that "In 1977, [founder Bill] Bright launched the one billion dollar campaign, 'Here's Life' " to train 5,000,000 persons from 50,000 churches by 1980, and "By 1980, the campaign had succeeded in raising $170,000,000 and had extended its billion dollar deadline to 1982" (p. 67)—*now that's a lot of clout and influence, in worldly financial terms*. The authors also give a few examples of Campus Crusade's political emphasis, such as Bill Bright's endorsement of the martial law government in South Korea, saying that "There is no religious repression here. It is only political, and I believe it is a good cause....those in prison are involved in things they shouldn't be involved in," and the emphasis of their recent "Washington for Jesus Rally" to "overcome U.S. military weakness, inflation, and general economic disintegration", while the "Here's Life" campaign was to use "local prayer groups, Bible Study meetings and Sunday schools to create a grassroots constituency to elect right wing congressional candidates," with groups provided a copy of the book *One Nation Under God*, for the study of "Christian economics" (p. 68).

The book argues that the most important occurrence since the birth of Jesus was the formation of the United States, and that free enterprise system is a "manifestation of the Christian idea"; its author is a Director of the National Association of Manufacturers; the authors note that "The 'Christian economics' platform included the abolition of minimum wage, the institution of right-to-work laws, and increased military budget, a balanced federal budget, and the elimination of taxes used for social reform purposes" (p. 68). Bright explained in 1975 that there was "the very real possibility of a foreign power taking over our nation, and the fact that our economy could collapse." The Campus Crusade materials with it also included a book on 'winning elections" and "congressional voting records" on "free competitive enterprise," with "correct votes" as listed were "for decreased Food Stamp benefits," and such. The main financiers of this work were Amway chief Richard DeVos (also head of the Christian Freedom Foundation (CFF), the publisher of *Christian Economics*, at the time), and others. Only organization representative candidates who chose Ronald Reagan over Republican Nelson Rockefeller were chosen to represent Campus Crusade in each congressional district (p. 69). Another group sent 120,000 pastors in 1976 a letter urging them to buy Bill Bright's pamphlet, *Your Five Duties as a Christian Citizen*, showing how Christians could "take over" local voting precincts (p. 69). After much of these works were exposed by the Christian *Sojourners* publication, much of it was shut down, or went underground. Meanwhile, "Here's Life" raised more than $170 million by Spring 1980, with Nelson

Bunker Hunt, "a John Birch Society Council member," having donated $10 million and made chairman of its Financial Controls Committee, as Hunt was able to raise $20 million more from several hundred businessmen at a 1980 retreat, including Pepsico, Coors, Mobil Oil and Coca-Cola (p. 69). The authors also mention Jerry Falwell's "95 Theses for the 1980s," including No. 16, in which "the free enterprise system of profit be encouraged to grow, being unhampered by any socialistic laws or red tape" (p. 70). *The authors point out that the endorsements and political voting positions virtually always agree with positions taken by the Chamber of Commerce.*

The authors also point out the emerging power of the burgeoning religious broadcasting and media empire—*just as cable TV was starting, and before the advent of the universal reach of the Internet.* They note that the National Religious Broadcasters (NRBA) stated then (in 1980) that its 900 member TV and radio organizations reached 129 million listeners and viewers in the U.S. each week, with 1,400 of the nation's 8,000 radio stations being owned by NRBA members, with a new radio station each week and a new TV station each month, and with religious broadcasting being a $1 billion a year industry (p. 70)—*in 1980 level of technology and reach, and in 1980 dollars.* They show the top five televangelists bringing in from $30 million to $60 million each in 1979, and another five at $13 million to $25 million (p. 70). They note that Pat Robertson's Christian Broadcasting Network (CBN) was "the largest supplier of 24-hour cable programming in the world" (p. 73).

The authors conclude by noting that secular Right Wing political activist insiders pursued fundamentalists and evangelicals because "they found in the evangelical movement a potential constituency for their formerly unsellable economic program—a program that historically has lacked popular support because it simply goes against most people's interests"; in turn, "The conservative Christian leaders have likewise benefited, gaining political sophistication as a result of this alliance with the Right" (p. 76). Interestingly, they quote a 1980 Gallup poll that noted that "only 13.3% of the *born-again respondents* said they like Reagan 'very much'," and that they felt that drug abuse and alcoholism were issues that were the biggest threat to the welfare of the family, while *homosexuality and abortion were at the bottom of the poll's numbers of their concern* (p. 76); *obviously, this cartel of Religious Right leadership and Big Business had to use the latter's big dollars, and the public platforms (local and national) and sacred privileged position of public trust of the former to perform a "psy-op" on America's evangelicals to push them into beliefs and actions against their very instincts.* The authors note that the implications of their findings then in 1980 would obviously raise questions of "the meaning which Christianity will take in the future"; *at the time of their writing, at the dawn of the modern Religious Right, they would have no idea of the extent of its impact on America and the world, and the worldview and personal spiritual concepts of evangelical Christians and their reputations in the eyes of their fellow citizens, culminating in the Trump-evangelical axis in recent years.*

A similar data report available online[133] for right wing organizations (both religious and secular), using the very limited reported data available that obviously cannot reflect covert contributions (and therefore also a gross underestimate), for 1962 shows a top recipient (in 1962 dollars) is Carl McIntire's *20th Century Reformation Hour*, pulling in over $1.1 million in 1962 dollars, with the John Birch Society close behind with about $1 million, Billy James Hargis *Christian Crusade* with $775,000, and Dr. Schwarz's Christian Anti-Communism Crusade at $725,000. Curiously, the less extreme-religious, pro-business groups, such as Kershner's Christian Freedom Foundation, had fallen out of the top ten from 1958 to 1962, although the overtly racist Citizens' Councils of America and Christian Nationalist Crusade (under racist and Holocaust denier Gerald L. K. Smith) were still on the top tier list, as well as the Liberty Lobby, with most of them being tax-exempt. By 1963, the annual income of the *Twentieth Century Reformation Hour* had risen to $1.7 million in traceable income (p. 8) (added to the overwhelming amount of untraceable income, such as advertising in organization periodicals, gift subscriptions, etc.). The report give large tables of the top corporate heads, foundations and financiers funding these racist, anti-Semitic and other hard-right top national organizations profiled (p. 11). The report also notes that the rate of increase of giving to these top hard-right organizations was increasing at a rate of 17 percent per year (based upon the small amount they could trace through public sources), judging from the eight-year data collection trend line they constructed (p. 17). A "supplement" to this report in 1967 showed that these groups' funding increased by another 40 percent in the two years from 1963 to 1965 (p. 25); the John Birch Society alone had grown from $1.6 million to $4 million (p. 28), with $5 million in 1966, and $3.1 million for the *20th Century Reformation Hour* (p. 28).

To put these numbers in perspective, a web-based calculator[134] that can convert prior-year numbers into inflated "2019 dollars" reveals that one dollar in 1962 (from this report) would equal $8.50 in 2019; thus, all the numbers just cited in the last report from 1962 should be multiplied by 8.5 to be relevant to current days in equivalent dollars. Similarly, the 1966 data should be multiplied by 7.92, and the 1980 estimates from the earlier report by 3.11.

As a last comment on the organizations cited from this period, there is a quotation that was reportedly said by popular Baptist theologian and leader

Dr. Adrian Rogers that places such data into perspective. The popular website "Liberty Tree"[135] asserts that it is taken from his 1984 sermon, "God's Way to Health, Wealth and Wisdom," and in his 1996 book, *Ten Secrets for a Successful Family.* They claim that it circulated in anti-Soviet literature in the 1960s, and was in the 1958 Congressional Record as having been originally added by Congressman Bruce Alger. *It sounds like the identical statements used by James Fifield, Jr. and Howard Kershner in their "Christian Libertarian" publications time and time again,* and comprises the following:

> You cannot legislate the poor into freedom by legislating the wealthy out of freedom. What one person receives without working for, another person must work for without receiving. The government cannot give to anybody anything that the government does not first take from somebody else. When half of the people get the idea that they do not have to work because the other half is going to take care of them, and when the other half gets the idea that it does no good to work because somebody else is going to get what they work for, that my dear friend, is the end of any nation. You cannot multiply wealth by dividing it.

According to this source, the origins for this quote was not Rep. Alger; they claim it at least goes back to one of the figures in the report just cited, "Gerald L. K. Smith, who had written them first in his magazine, *The Cross and the Flag*...Rogers was essentially quoting Smith at the time." This 1964 report by Group Research, Inc. just cited describes Smith and his organization, the "Christian Nationalist Crusade," in the following way: "The principal organizational vehicle of long-time anti-Semite Gerald L. K. Smith...Smith's magazine, *The Cross and the Flag*, is the official publication of the Crusade and the Crusade's first 'principle' is listed as: 'Preserve America as a Christian Nation, being conscious of the fact that there is a highly organized campaign to substitute Jewish tradition for Christian tradition' " (p. 21). *The New York Times* published the following 1976 obituary about Smith[136] (excerpts which follow):

> Gerald L. K. Smith, the right-wing Arkansas preacher who once backed Gov. Huey P. Long of Louisiana for President, died today of complications from pneumonia. He was 78 years old. Mr. Smith was with Long when he was assassinated in 1935 and cradled the dying' Governor in his arms. He delivered the oration at the grave. Throughout the 1930's and 40's he was known for his opposition, over the radio, to President Franklin D. Roosevelt and was the founder of the Christian Nationalist Crusade, a strident right-wing

anti-Communist organization. Mr. Smith also delivered his anti-Communist views in his monthly magazine, *The Cross and the Flag*, in lectures and anonymously in 200 small newspapers. Although he was proud of being a purveyor of anti-semitism and other forms of religious and racial bigotry, Gerald L. K. Smith often expressed regret that "so many millions of my fellow Americans just don't like me."

Mr. Smith, whose career as a master extremist began in 1934 and continued until his death, seemed mystified that, because he was anti-black, anti-semitic, anti-Catholic and pro-Fascist, he was shunned by many persons he would have liked to know. *"There is nothing worse, nothing more deadly," he said in an interview a few years ago, "than never getting to talk to anyone but people who agree with you."* Mr. Smith, who H. L. Mencken called "the greatest rabble-rouser since Peter the Hermit," talked to the people who agreed with him on the platform and through the mails. Followers of his Christian Nationalist Crusade paid more than $325,000 in 1967, long after he had reached his peak of power, for his pamphlets and books that excoriated "the Jew-nited Nations," "black savages ruining our cities" and scores of other targets. From his Crusade headquarters in Los Angeles, he bombarded the faithful… (emphasis added)

Mr. Smith, who started out as a penniless fundamentalist minister in the Middle West, managed to acquire sumptuous homes in Los Angeles, Tulsa, Okla., and Eureka Springs, Ark.; a collection of antiques with an insured value of $500,000 and his own printing plant to turn out his monthly magazine, and other literature labeled by his critics as "hate mail." Some of the critics were convinced that such financial rewards were his chief justification for devoting most of his life to the organized promotion of hatred. The record is clear, that before the 1930's he held views and spoke out on injustices suffered by the poor, but he later seemed to take an ideological about-face.

Gerald Lyman Kenneth Smith, who was born Feb. 27, 1898, in Pardeeville, Wis., was the descendant of four generations of hellfire-and-brimstone fundamentalist preachers.…Gerald was a champion debater as a boy and once won an elocution contest for his rendition of William Jennings Bryan's "Cross of Gold" speech.… When he was 19 years old he received a "call" to the ministry, and as was the custom then, and to some extent now, in fundamentalist sects, he ordained himself a minister of the Disciples of Christ denomination. In 1922…Mr. Smith was given the pulpit in the Seventh Christian Church in Indianapolis. He became so popular as an orator that several churches vied for his services, and he finally, in 1928, moved to the fashionable King's Highway Church in Shreveport, La. There he met Huey P. Long, then a lawyer, who was to push Mr. Smith into the national limelight. In those days, Mr. Smith might have been called a leftwinger. He discovered what he called 'grave social injustices' in Shreveport, and he became a social reformer, even working as a union organizer. On one occasion, Mr. Smith found that Shreveport real estate men, in anticipation of the Home Owners Loan Corporation Law, designed to help homeowners pay off their mortgages, planned to foreclose on $1 million worth of homes. He went to Mr. Long, who had become Governor…Mr. Smith hitched himself to Mr. Long's fast-ascending star.

At one point during the war, *The Cross and the Flag* was listed by the Justice Department as a propaganda vehicle for alleged seditionists. Mr. Smith, however, at least temporarily desisted from printing and uttering any more praise of Adolf Hitler. "I'm a bad, bad fellow," Mr. Smith told an interviewer in 1944. "I'm an isolationist. I'm the organizer and leader of the America First party. Oh, I'm a rabble-rouser. Put that down—a rabble-rouser. God made me a rabble-rouser…of and for the right." The America First Party ran Mr. Smith for President in 1944, but he failed even to get on the ballot in most states. Mr. Smith dropped the party and, in 1947, organized the Christian Nationalist Crusade with the cooperation of several "rightist" groups. The Crusade was to remain Mr. Smith's principal organization, although he operated under several fronts, such as the Political Tract Society, the Midwestern Political Survey Institute and the Western Hemisphere Committee Against Communism.

The platform of the Christian Nationalists called for the deportation of Zionists, the dissolution of all "Jewish Gestapo organizations," "the forced shipment of blacks to Africa and the liquidation of the United Nations." All these remained Smith goals, in addition to about 40 others, some of which were, in Mr. Smith's words: "To fight the mongrelizers…the preservation of our Christian faith against the threat of Jew Communism…restore the right of Christian prayer in public buildings…expose and fight the black Plague." In recent years Mr. Smith trained his oratorical and pamphleteering guns on "our impotent, insipid and cowardly Congress" for its passage of civil rights legislation and on many occasions demanded that "the pro-criminal, pro-Communist, pro-pornographic Supreme Court must be impeached." Individuals were not spared in *The Cross and the Flag* or other Smith publications. In 1950, Mr. Smith led an unsuccessful campaign to prevent Anna M. Rosenberg's appointment as Assistant Secretary of Defense for Manpower. "Keep the Zionist Jew Anna Rosenberg from becoming the dictator of the Pentagon," he warned his followers. Mr. Smith was also active in efforts in 1952 to prove that the Republican Presidential candidate, Gen. Dwight D. Eisenhower, was a "Swedish Jew" and thus unfit for public office.

...Up to his death he continued to tell his supporters, estimates on the number of whom varied wildly, *from 200,000 to 5 million*, that "there is a premium on my head; I weep for America." And his presses continued to produce what he proudly called "200,000 pieces of propaganda a day." Gerald L. K. Smith was a thoroughgoing extremist and didn't care who called him one. He had his own formula for winning followers in his specialized field, which he characterized thus:

"Religion and patriotism, keep going on that. It's the only way you can really get them heated up....Certain nerve centers in the population will begin to twitch— and the people will start fomenting and fermenting, and then a fellow like myself... will have the people with him, with hook, line and sinker. Then I'll teach them how to hate!" (emphasis added)

The "Holocaust Encyclopedia" online provides a "Holocaust Denial Timeline," and stated that in 1959, "American clergyman Gerald L. K. Smith's antisemitic publication, *Cross and the Flag*, claims that six million Jews were not killed during the Holocaust but immigrated to the United States during World War II," as well as citing a similarly corporate-funded organization mentioned in the previous reports, noting that in the 1950s Willis Carto and the Liberty Lobby began advocating for a "racially pure" United States and blaming Jews for its problems, and adding on the "timeline" that "The Liberty Lobby begins to publish Holocaust denial literature in 1969."[137]

The Wisconsin Historical Society fills in more details on Smith, in the Winter 2002–2003 edition of its *Wisconsin Magazine of History* journal.[138] There they write that

Journalist William Bradford Huie wrote of Smith in the 1930s: "The man has the passion of Billy Sunday. He has the fire of Adolf Hitler....He is the stuff of which Fuehrers are made." "Before a live audience," another journalist wrote, "he makes Father Coughlin seem somewhat less articulate than a waxworks." He was, said Huey Long, "the only man I ever saw who is a better rabble-rouser than I am." H. L. Mencken, who in his long journalistic career had listened to orators from William Jennings Bryan to Franklin Roosevelt, wrote: "Gerald L. K. Smith is the greatest orator of them all, not the greatest by an inch or a foot or a yard or a mile, but the greatest by at least two light years. He begins where the best leaves off." (p. 19)

They note that as a young man Smith became sympathetic to progressive viewpoints, following Wisconsin's progressive governor Robert LaFollette, and his anti-monopoly crusade and defense of "the little man" (p. 22). In 1918, at the age of nineteen he became a pastor at a Church of Christ, quickly rising through the ranks with his excellent oratorical skills, but relocated to Shreveport when his wife fell ill to tuberculosis. There he met the famous Louisiana politician "Kingfish" Huey P. Long, a governor, Senator and "the most powerful politician in Louisiana's history" (p. 23). He became devoted to him when Long saved some of his parishioners' homes and businesses, as Smith actually did ecumenical work then with a local rabbi, to the point of visiting each other's congregations. They note that "From an early age, Smith had displayed symptoms of a bipolar disorder, prone to episodes of manic energy and frantic work, followed by relapses into periods of depression and withdrawal," and before his marriage "he had suffered two nervous breakdowns" (p. 23). They add that "His hatred of Jews and other minorities seems to have arisen more from a generalized authoritarian personality than from any specific incidents with minorities in his formative years. In addition, his fervent Christianity inclined him to view Jews as the enemies of Jesus" (p. 24). His support of politician Long and his radical liberal agenda alienated him from the wealthy and conservative board members of Smith's church, leaving in seven months after his arrival before he was fired, and he never returned to the pulpit."

They state that "It was in the early 1930s that he began to nourish secret fascist sympathies, which grew more pronounced as he aged. In January 1933 he wrote to a certain Hugo Fack, who had traveled to Germany and there met the leaders of the new Nazi government." Smith wrote to him: "I am anxious to get in touch with his Honor, Adolf Hitler, but knowing that you are recently removed from Germany, before doing so I desire your opinion of conditions in that country. They look good to me. Can you give me a code for getting in touch with Herr Hitler or one of his representatives in America?" (p. 24). They also write that "Just after quitting his Shreveport church, *Smith found himself attracted to the native Nazi William Dudley Pelley and his paramilitary Silver Shirts. Pelley, a religious mystic who claimed to have died, gone to heaven, and returned to North Carolina, planned to overthrow the American government.* Smith started a march up the Mississippi Valley to join him, writing: 'By the time you receive this letter I shall be on the road to St. Louis and points north with a uniformed squad of young men composing what I believe will be the first Silver Shirt storm troop in America.' The rendezvous never materialized. Few recruits swarmed to Smith. Disappointed, discouraged, he returned to Shreveport."

Huey Long offered him a job, as Long was planning to challenge Roosevelt for the presidency in 1936, where "The focus of his appeal was a plan to confiscate millionaires' incomes and redistribute them to the masses. It was an attractive program to many in the depths of the Great Depression, when Americans were turning to strange messiahs and desperate schemes. Demagogic and impractical, Long's approach was nonetheless clever and strategic. Smith was to be its chief advocate, touring the nation to organize local units of the Share-Our-Wealth Society" (p. 24). He enjoyed rallying people with his speeches and signing them on to this scheme, as he later used this growing mailing list, as "targets for additional propaganda." He said his program under this plan was to "impeach traitors (including FDR), deport Jews and blacks, repeal the income tax, outlaw communism, and make America, capitalism, and Christianity synonymous" (p. 24). This all came to an end when Long was assassinated in September 1935 (and they allege that Smith thought that the assassin was a Jew, when he was actually a Catholic), and gave his funeral oration at the state capitol for 150,000 people (p. 24). Smith then turned to Dr. Francis Townsend, who offered unemployed people over 65 years of age two hundred dollars a month, which had to be spent each month, to be financed by a national sales tax, called the Townsend Recovery Plan (p. 24)—*sounding like a real precursor to Social Security*. Smith got involved in his organization, and they were joined by Father Charles Coughlin, the Catholic priest *who more people listened to on the air than President Roosevelt*, organizing into the Union Party for the 1936 presidential election. While Smith and Coughlin were considered the most eloquent public speakers in the nation but having no credible candidate standing, they chose a surrogate as their candidate. Smith's anti-Communism oratory even then electrified the crowds, causing the cynical H. L. Mencken to marvel at how he agitated the crowd (p. 25).

After finishing with that crowd of 9,000, he later did the same with 8,000 of Coughlin's crowd at his convention of the National Union for Social Justice, as both became jealous of being upstaged and raised the rhetorical ante; it was not long before Smith decided he could accomplish things on his own. The historians then write that

On October 20, he announced that he was creating an independent movement to "seize the government of the United States." Townsend responded, "If the press reports concerning the fascist action of Gerald L. K. Smith are true, then I hereby disavow any connection that Mr. Smith may claim in the organization of the Townsend National Recovery Plan. I am against fascism." The sponsors of the Union Party gave up before the vote. Coughlin found Smith frightening….In the election of 1936, Roosevelt was reelected in a landslide. [Union Party candidate] Lemke won only 891,858 votes—less than 2 percent of the total—and carried no states…The Union Party never offered another candidate. (p. 26)

Smith then settled into Detroit, and *befriended Henry Ford*. Ford told Smith he would make a great president, and Smith ran for Senate in Michigan in 1942, finishing second in the Republican primary, then ran in the general election as a write-in, finishing last. They note that then "he turned to red-baiting and anti-Semitism. He credited Ford with revealing the connection between communism and Judaism. 'The day came when I embraced the research of Mr. Ford and his associates,' he wrote, 'and became courageous enough and honest enough and informed enough to use the words: 'Communism is Jewish'." They add that he began publishing a monthly periodical, *The Cross and the Flag*, in 1942, and *maintained it for thirty-four years, reaching twenty-five thousand subscribers, along with writing more than five hundred tracts, pamphlets and books* (p. 26). They opine that "He was a propagandist, not a scholar, living in a mental world inhabited by stereotyped villains and invidious conspiracies. He read only to confirm his prejudices, not expand his horizons" (p. 27). He also founded the political action group the Christian Nationalist Crusade in 1942, raising money by direct mail, and was criticized for accepting money from Fritz Kuhn, leader of the German American Bund. His annual revenues from mail solicitations grew from around $80,000 in the 1940s to $275,000 in the 1960s, becoming a millionaire in the process, investing much into his travel, books and tracts. Amongst his enemies, he often referred to President "Roosenfelt," and saying "We're going to get that cripple out of the White House," and was confident they would oust him by 1940; he even hated Truman worse (p. 27). They write that he said that President "Johnson was 'guilty of murder, homosexuality, a wide variety of perversions, thievery, treason, and corruption.' Nixon was a 'super-beatnik who seems to be a cross between Elvis the Pelvis and Franklin D. Roosevelt.' George Wallace of Alabama was more to his taste but *insufficiently militant on the race issue*. Wallace wanted to segregate blacks; Smith wanted to deport them. Still, he called Wallace 'the most Christ-like man I know' " (p. 27). He moved around, eventually to Los Angeles in 1953, but

> in the 1960s he rejuvenated and reoriented his career by constructing what he termed his "Sacred Projects" in the Ozark hamlet of Eureka Springs, Arkansas....In 1966 he constructed and dedicated the "Christ of the Ozarks," a seven-story cross-shaped rendition of Jesus—half as tall as the Statue of Liberty and twice the size of the well-known "Christ of the Andes" in South America. The statue, which still stands in Eureka Springs, weighs 340 tons; the face is fifteen feet high, and the hands are seven feet long. Smith thought it was more beautiful than the sculpture of Michelangelo and predicted that it would last a thousand years....In 1968 Smith began staging a Passion Play in an amphitheater carved into the side of a mountain outside Eureka Springs. Performed on a four-hundred-foot street of Old Jerusalem, it includes 150 actors and actresses nightly, illuminated by powerful colored spotlights, miming a script broadcast over a stereophonic system. The cast includes live sheep, goats, donkeys, Arabian horses, pigeons, and camels. The two hour play drew more than 28,000 spectators the first year in a 3,000-seat theater. By 1975 the theater expanded to a capacity of 6,000, and more than 188,000 attended the play, making it the largest outdoor pageant in America. (pp. 27-28)

While Jews complained about its anti-Semitic nature, Smith retorted that it was "the only presentation of this kind in the world that has not diluted its content to flatter the Christ-hating Jews." By reviving their economy Smith became a local hero, as hotels, restaurants and other entrepreneurs moved in, and by 1975 Eureka Springs was the leading tourist community in Arkansas. They also write that "He planned to construct a Disney-like replica of the Holy Land, including the Sea of Galilee, the River Jordan, and scenes from the life of Jesus. Visitors could even be baptized in the river. Smith's new Holy Land, slated to cost $100 million, provided inspiration for other religious entrepreneurs....However, only the Great Wall of Jerusalem had been completed in 1976 when Gerald L. K. Smith died" (p. 28).

They conclude by writing that "Smith was buried at the feet of the 'Christ of the Ozarks,' an appropriately gaudy memorial. He went to his grave unrepentant. His Sacred Projects represented only an alteration in direction, not a change of heart or a renunciation of Jew-baiting. Through the last four decades of his life he had continued to publish *The Cross and the Flag* and write inflammatory tracts. His Sacred Projects had brought him a veneer of respectability but not peace of mind, and at his death he was still consumed by hatred and bitterness. The *Arkansas Gazette* concluded his obituary with these words: 'To have the power to touch men's hearts with glory or with bigotry, and to choose the latter, is a saddening thing'." This journal paper also has a couple of interesting photos of Smith and intriguing captions as well. One shows him speaking on stage during his 1942 senatorial campaign, promising to end rationing and provide tires for everyone, and said that friend Henry Ford was making a synthetic tire that could provide abundant tires, but that Roosevelt was keeping from the public (the photo showing him demonstrating a tire on the stage) (p. 25). Another shows Smith on stage beside a painting of Washington, holding a strange flag with American stripes, a British Union Jack field and with an eight-pointed star on top. The caption reads that "Smith holds a flag representing the *so-called British-Israel movement. According to Smith, Jews masterminded a plan to force the United States back into the British Empire. The flag he brandishes would replace the American flag as America once more became a colony*" (p. 23) (emphasis added).

There is more to the Gerald H. K. Smith story. Another story from *The New York Times* in 1972[139] describes the unique hippie community in the Ozarks town of Eureka Springs, Arkansas, and their interactions with Gerald H. K. Smith and his wife, who had settled there. It says the Smiths moved there in 1964, and "First they built a 70-foot statue of Jesus on a mountain overlooking the town. Then they opened a Passion play portraying the last week of the life of Jesus, performed in a huge outdoor theater with permanent sets that depict Jerusalem's famous places. They have added a 'Christ Only Art Gallery' and a 7,300-volume Bible Museum. This spring, they started work on a $10-million, 167-acre model of the Holy Land." They add that "The Smiths and their 'sacred projects' became targets of criticism from many who disapproved of Mr. Smith's long crusade against what he calls 'the international Jewish conspiracy.' Nevertheless, the Passion play, the statue and the rest became popular tourist attractions, and are the town's largest economic asset. The Smiths estimate that a million people see the 'Christ of the Ozarks' statue every year. The Chamber of Commerce says tourism has increased 42 per cent over last year's rate. Deposits in the bank have doubled in four years. Real estate values have risen sharply and there are virtually no vacant commercial buildings." They add that in recent years (from 1972) hundreds of the hippie "longhairs" started settling in the town, adding that "virtually all of them earn money to support themselves. These may be the strangest freaks in the nation—they have developed a work ethic."

They add that "Thanks partly to a social event, Mr. Smith and the longhairs have finally achieved an uncertain detente. He had been fairly openly disdainful of them, and would *order his driver* to speed up to hurry past groups of them on the street. Then came the Smiths' 50th wedding anniversary on June 21" (emphasis added). He invited everyone in town to the reception, "even to the humblest citizen", but "to be safe, however, they had two policemen and a private guard on hand when the 426 guests arrived. The guests included the Mayor and the actor who plays Jesus in the Passion play, as well as former Gov. Orval E. Faubus." However, about 15 "longhairs" also showed up, stating, "Who could be more humble than us?" They write that

> Mr. Smith was so pleased with their behavior and with *Down Home's* [the town hippie underground newspaper] report that he wrote a letter of thanks to the paper. "As one who has been misunderstood and misrepresented down through the years," he wrote, "perhaps I am in a better position to understand others who are the victims of those misrepresentations better than might he expected." Interviewed in his home recently, Mr. Smith said that most of the longhairs were "sincere people who are at peace here." Five or 10 might have "villainous motives," he said, but "you can find more bad people than that in the back of a saloon every Saturday night." The longhairs are equally tolerant of Mr. Smith, although they have little use for his ideological views or his "sacred projects." "I can't forgive him for putting up such a bad piece of art," Gary Eagan, a young ceramics artist and owner of the Spring Street Pottery, said yesterday, referring to the statue of Jesus that loomed in the distance from the back of his studio. "It looks like a milk carton with head and arms. But I'd be the last person to try to run Smith out of here. There's room for everybody. He doesn't interfere with my Pottery. If I'm going to be free in this town, certainly he has to be free".

It sounds like Jesus came to Eureka Springs to stay (via the humble outreach of some "long hairs" who the Religious Right would cringe about and denounce), for "He whom the Son sets free, is free indeed," and not by some libertarian definition of "liberty." And by "Jesus," I don't mean a big tall statue of Jesus that looks like a "milk carton with head and arms."

As I concluded the research and documentation on these "gentlemen," I saw mention a few times of a 1953 reference book that some saw as definitive of the era of these demagogues and their "golden age," entitled *Apostles of Discord*, by Ralph Lord Roy. I afterwards chanced across a used copy of such which I was fortunate to obtain, since it contains a wealth of further information on these men and their hijinks, and other collaborators in their deeds and likeminded figures that fostered anti-Semitism and racism, *amongst the clergy and Christian followers specifically—all in the name of Christ.* While the 1953 timeframe of this work misses much of the development of events (both personally for these men, and nationally and globally) in the decades ahead, *it is an "eyewitness account" of these men, in "real time" when their deeds, and the "red scare," racism and the Roosevelt-Truman-Eisenhower controversies were well underway, and it supplies further details that historians decades later tended to miss, as well as verifying the more salacious details of these figures we have documented.*

Regarding its author, a 2002 article in the *Hartford Courant* newspaper[139] about his "fourth retirement" from pastoring notes that "He has picketed with Martin Luther King Jr., been arrested during the civil rights movement, written a nationally bestselling book and traveled across the globe. Yet these are only some of the accomplishments of the Rev. Ralph Lord Roy in the last 50 years. After serving as minister of 10 churches, Roy, 74, is retiring from First & Summerfield United Methodist Church." He earlier transferred from Columbia Law School to Union Theological Seminary (having "felt the call" to pastor). They add that "Roy was swept up in the civil rights movement in the 1960s, along with many other northern clergymen who joined a group called the Congress of Racial Equality, or CORE. In May 1961, the U.S. Supreme Court ruled that segregation on interstate travel was illegal. A group known as the Freedom Riders tested whether this ruling was actually being enforced. As part of this group, Roy was paired with an African American minister on the bus, to eat with and stay with in hotels." He described instances where southern restaurants would suddenly close when they arrived ("for cleaning"), but when they would wait until it reopened, they would be arrested for illegal assembly. They add that "The following August, he participated in a picket at the White House, in an effort to persuade President Kennedy to release from jail Martin Luther King Jr., with whom Roy said he had lunch many times. Later, Roy said he helped organize a large group of northern clergymen to join a protest in Albany, Ga., after receiving a letter from King urging him to become involved. The protesters were subsequently arrested, Roy's second arrest in two years. 'It was the largest group of clergy ever arrested,' Roy said." They noted that "Prior to 1970, when Roy was assigned to a church in Clinton [North Carolina], he had worked solely in New York with chiefly African American congregations." They also write that "Along with his work as a clergyman, Roy has written three books, one of which, *Apostles of Discord*, was a national bestseller. 'I look back at it with some chagrin,' Roy said. 'I don't see how it became a bestseller.' He has also written newspaper columns, as well as occasionally doing radio shows. Roy said he discusses a wide variety of topics including inspirational themes, the crisis in the church and politics.

'I've always been interested in politics, but I have to be careful because I don't believe in using the pulpit to advance politics,' he said."

The cover of the book itself has endorsements of famed theologian Reinhold Niebuhr ("Ralph Roy has performed an important task in his careful analysis....This book is a rather sobering reminder to us all that the worst corruption is a corrupt religion"), National Council of Churches chief Bishop Oxnam ("An extraordinarily valuable piece of work"), Henry Smith Leiper ("False piety, like false patriotism, shields many a scoundrel. This careful study exposes some of the worst groups of hate-mongers in contemporary America"), Herbert Philbrick ("*Apostles of Discord* clearly demonstrates the need for every layman and leader to re-examine and reaffirm the deepest roots of his spiritual beliefs, lest he be victimized by the extremists, both right and left, who are today successfully masquerading behind the clerical cloak and theological terminology"), and others. Within its Preface, Roy expresses the sincere concern that in his detailed documentation of the extremist groups within American Christianity and its media on both extremes, he might unfairly castigate sincere conservatives or liberals that do not hold bigoted or other dangerous views, or unfairly take the most egregious examples out of context. He might also reveal that some parties cavort with these "agents of discord" while not fully realizing their motives. He expressed an intention of revealing to them the dangers of their ways, but also desiring not to paint all of Protestantism with the reputation of these bad players, and rather to accomplish a constructive good. He admits his status as a Republican of centrist tendencies, but provides extensive coverage of Christian subversives (what he calls the "underground," although operating publicly) on both the Hard Right *and Communist infiltration as well*, with the range of racist, bigoted, anti-Semitic, Communist-sympathizing and anti-immigration and isolationist values and statements all fully documented, as well as "Christian libertarianism."

Roy notes that at the time of the 1952 national election, "Nearly all extremist groups in the country appropriated General Douglas MacArthur as the symbol of their cause, and sought to spur a country-wide attempt to sabotage the national tickets of both major parties. One of their weapons was an assemblage of third parties designed to counter the 'Jew-control' of the Republican and Democratic organizations," as in 1948, "The Protestant underworld inaugurated the 'Stop-Ike-the-Kike' campaign," with the aforementioned Rev. Gerald L. K. Smith noting the description of Eisenhower as "the terrible Swedish-Jew" from his West Point yearbook, and a chart showing Roosevelt's "Jewish ancestry."[140] *Younger readers should be aware that Gen. MacArthur was in command of all U.S. forces in Asia in World War*

II, and in command of the U.N. armies in Korea in that conflict, and willing to defy the commands of President Truman and the allies and continue to attack North Korea (and the likelihood of nuclear war with both the U.S.S.R. and China), with a belligerence that required his dismissal, but the admiration of American extremists and war hawks.

He adds that "a number of hyper-conservatives met in early August to nourish the Constitution Party, a splinter fringe born in New York City in early spring [1952] to work for the nomination of MacArthur. The new group elected as co-chairmen Percy L. Greaves, consulting economist of the Christian Freedom Foundation (publishers of the *Christian Economics*)...and Mrs. Suzanne Silvercruys Stevenson" (p. 21). Smith told his followers that "We propose that the great White Christian vote shall be the new balance of power in American politics...in many states our vote will be the determining factor in November and by 1954 we will be the most vital political entity in the United States" (p. 23), organizing the Christian Nationalist Party and getting MacArthur on the ballot in fourteen states. Smith later feared that with their failure, widespread conscription (the "draft") would occur and cause the "repeal of the McCarran immigration act so that 20 million Jews and colored will be dumped on American shores. *They proposed to see to it that never again will the great white Christian majority population of America be able to express majority power" (p. 24)—sounding much like the Trump campaign and followers today.*

Another key evangelical figure (and "apostle of discord") of the era that Roy documents (that has not been covered to date) is Gerald Winrod. Importantly, they note that "Winrod launched *The Defender Magazine* in April 1926," with circulation of 40,000 by 1934, and 100,000 by 1937, and with its low cost (fifty cents to a dollar a year) "helped spread its message among lower economic groups" (p. 27). He adds that "Winrod has never held a pastorate," with his secretary noting that "The entire United States and Canada are his congregation," as Winrod reported that a "rapidly developing cooperation of Catholics and Jews is gaining control of the American government" (p. 28). Winrod cited the *Protocols of the Learned Elders of Zion* forgery, and went to Germany in 1934 at the invitation of a Nazi propagandist to "study social, political, moral, economic, and prophetic trends" and meet the pro-Nazi church; he returned to the U.S. and destroyed his critical works about Hitler, and "began to praise the Nazi regime" and deny persecution of Jews there (p. 29). He then became involved with pro-Nazis, including Elizabeth Dilling, Robert Edward Edmondson and E. N. Sanctuary, who were all put on trial for sedition later, and he also sought allies amongst the American clergy (p. 30). In 1938 he ran for the Senate in Kansas, with a platform of "states rights, private enterprise, 'Americanism' and isolationism, saying, 'Let's keep Christian America Christian' "; in his divorce trial his wife alleged under oath that he expected to be a "nominal head of the country when the revolution came and that he wanted to take me to a secret hideout so I could be protected when the government should close in on him," as "Every evening at home, by the radio, the children were taught that everything Hitler did was right and that everything England and France did was wrong," and he began to organize a series of "Prayer and Prophecy Conferences" in 1940, featuring other nationally-known "apostles of bigotry" (p. 32).

With *The Defender* continuing to spout the pro-Hitler line, Winrod became known as the "Jayhawk Nazi" (as a Kansan), and was indicted three times for sedition, in 1942, 1943 and 1944, the latter with twenty-nine other Nazi sympathizers cooperating with members of the Nazi Party, but was set free from prosecution when the judge died (p. 33). By 1950 he claimed *more than a quarter of a million people read his monthly magazine,* then *in its twenty-fifth year of publication,* and built a publishing business with money raised from fundraising letters sent to his "Dear Christian Friends"; by 1950 his "business" was *bringing in more than a quarter of a million dollars annually, in 1950 dollars* (p. 34). Most importantly, he was enriched by advertisements by *Christian publishing houses* in his racist, anti-Semitic magazine, such as the *famous publisher Zondervan of Grand Rapids—who cares about morals when there's a big market to reach there, right? Don't be surprised—look at the overwhelming bulk of "pious" Christians who put Donald Trump into office to fatten their 401Ks.*

Regarding Gerald L. K. Smith, Roy also confirms that in 1933 he left his Shreveport pastorate "to join the Silver Shirt storm-troopers of William Dudley Pelley," who in turn "introduced Smith to the racist-nationalist fringe"; he adds that "Before World War II, he [Pelley] flooded the United States with seas of anti-democratic and anti-Semitic literature" (p. 60). He notes how this son of a Methodist minister gained national attention when *American Magazine* printed "Seven Minutes in Eternity," an "account of how Pelley's spirit supposedly left his physical body and soared to other worlds to converse with the dead" (p. 61). Interestingly, Pelley moved to Asheville, North Carolina to open Galahad College "for the study and advancement of 'Christian Economics'" (p. 61). On January 31, 1933, the day Hitler officially took over Germany, "Pelley dramatically organized his Silver Shirts, sometimes called the *Christian American Patriots, a group that one time claimed more than two million members"* (p. 61) (emphasis added). Also, "In 1936, under the slogan, 'For Christ and the Constitution,' Pelley established the Christian Party and nominated himself for President," with the platform, "I promise to defranchise the Jew by Constitutional Amendment, to make it impossible for a Jew to own property in the United States…to limit Jews in the professions, trades, and sciences by license according to their quotas of representation in the population" (p. 61). Pelley was jailed for sedition in 1942, finally being paroled in 1950, and Roy writes at that time that "Today he bombards ministers with cultist propaganda published by his Soulcraft Press, Inc., in Noblesville, Indiana" (p. 61).

He writes that "When Pelley's power grab failed, Smith switched over to Huey Long," and after his death to Father Charles Coughlin, pre-war leader of the Christian Front to eradicate Jews; by 1937 Winrod made Smith famous to the readers of *Defender Magazine*, as Smith "wanted to frighten the middle and lower strata into the extreme rightist camp, as Hitler had done in Germany" (p. 62)—*and Donald Trump did in 2016, along with the statistical group he bragged about on television—the "poorly educated."* Smith warned followers on the radio that if they didn't get behind him, there would be a Bolshevik revolution in America, while he defended a "White Christian America"; meanwhile, his periodical *The Cross and the Flag* "was listed by the Justice Department as a propaganda vehicle for alleged seditionists" (p. 62). Smith renewed his efforts to launch a "great nationalist party" after the war, and in May 1946 he brought together "a score of important nationalist leaders in the hope of uniting some sixty-eight extremist groups under his leadership," including Kenneth Goff of Christian Youth for America, Frederick Kister of the Christian Veterans of America, Larry Asman of the Christian Veterans Intelligence Service, Jeremiah Stokes of the Salt Lake City Pro-American Vigilantes, and others, organizing the Christian Nationalist Crusade, which also used "front groups" like the Patriotic Tract Society, the Midwestern Political Survey Institute, and the Committee of California Pastors, amongst others, with Winrod in alliance with Smith until their break in 1947 (p. 63–64). Smith also began the Christian Nationalist Party for him to head their ticket for the 1948 presidential elections, with their platform calling for the "deportation of Zionists, the dissolution of all 'Jewish Gestapo Organizations,' the shipping of Negroes to Africa, and the liquidation of the United Nations," and asking the question, "Shall the lovers of Jesus Christ or the enemies of Jesus Christ determine the destiny of America?" (p. 65).

Depending upon the estimates of Smith or other sources, his circulation of his *The Cross and the Flag* periodical (started in 1942) ten years later was from 25,000 to 90,000 (p. 65). The main points he drove home in his 32-page publication included "The preservation of our Christian faith against the threat of Jew Communism, a conspiracy to abolish Christian civilization and the church of Jesus Christ," "The preservation of our national sovereignty against the Jew-financed plot for World Government," "the preservation of our racial self-respect against a campaign to mongrelize our race and mix the blacks with the whites," and "The preservation of our national tradition threatened by the immigration flood," as Smith claimed that he distributed a million pieces of literature monthly on such themes to receptive Christian audiences, including items such as "Roosevelt's Jewish Ancestry" and "The Negroes Place in Call of Race" (p. 66). *While tens of thousands to hundreds of thousands of patriotic conservative "Christians" enthusiastically received and were conditioned or reinforced in those views by Smith's media products and those of allies, then in the "good old days" of the pious 1950s, with the exception of the Jewish connection (removed by Zionist influences within conservatives, apart from the "alt right"), it looks like many of the same positions are retained by conservative media and its supporters in the Christian community today.* Sounding like today's conservative Christian media (particularly what lands in my email in-basket), as one example in 1947 Smith warned in his Nationalist News Bulletin another anecdotal tale, short on verification but long on innuendo and demagoguery, that "Reports coming out of Atlanta indicate a complete breakdown in law and order. Citizens are buying their own private guns to protect themselves from rapists and robbers…private citizens do not feel safe to walk on the street day or night" (p. 68).

Another financier of the Christian Nationalist Crusade that Roy identifies is "George W. Armstrong, millionaire octogenarian of Natchez, Mississippi" (while noting that "The Armstrong fortune, sometimes estimated in the scores of millions [in 1950 dollars], came from steel, oil, and southern plantations," and being the son of a Methodist minister), through his "Judge Armstrong Foundation" for "charitable, religious and educational undertakings." Smith gave Armstrong the 1953 "Henry Ford I, Memorial Award," and described him in *The Cross and the Flag* as "one of the few great businessmen of responsibility who have been unafraid to attack and expose the political program of international Jewry," and who targeted then the Federal Reserve Board and with "his fierce hatred for the New Deal and his gradual acceptance of crude racism" (p. 79). *In recent years groups of similar perspectives marched (or goose-stepped) through Charlottesville, VA with torches and brandishing swastikas and weapons and chanting, "The Jews Will Not Replace Us," and they were able to incite violence and kill a young woman counter-protestor, and being described by the President as part of the "good folks on both sides," with the full endorsement and defense of the bulk of American evangelicals.*

Another influential figure was Southern Methodist University (SMU) professor (and Baptist) John O. Beaty, whose book *The Iron Curtain Over America* was described as "the most extensive piece of anti-Semitic literature in the history of America's racist movement," quoting from the libertarian periodical *The Freeman* and similar sources (pp. 84–86). Even the famed Hollywood gossip communist Hedda Hopper, with a readership of thirty-five million, called the book "the most revealing and frightening book that's come to my desk in ages" (p. 89). Roy also documents senior Christian leaders of various denominations who sent the book en masse to their clergy underlings, one warning them of "the anti-Christian and the anti-American 'conspiracy' in our beloved country" and imploring them to pass on the book and its contents to their flock and acquaintances, and telling them that "A Christian patriot has paid for these books" (p. 90). Roy disclosed that "The 'Christian patriot' who footed the bill turned out to be J. Russell Maguire of Greenwich, Connecticut, who has amassed millions from oil and manufacturing (Thompson sub-machine guns, electrical equipment, etc.)" (p. 90). It should be noted that the clergyman who had sent out the aforementioned endorsement to Episcopal clergymen and chaplains nationwide, "on the stationery of the Military Order of Foreign Wars of the United States, of which he is Chaplain," later apologized to recipients of the book, saying that "I was persuaded to do this, although I had not previously read the book," having been told that it dealt with the "threat of Communism," and admitted that "I now find that I was misled," and that the book "attempts to engender religious hostility," for which he apologized (p. 90). *It is commendable that he bravely extended his apology (possibly to save his damaged reputation), but how could such a senior Christian leader be so naïve and reckless as to endorse a book he never read, given his enormous spiritual influence? Sigh—here, well into the Twenty-first Century, it seems like some things never change.*

Roy also has a section on another prominent national "prophet of discord" with a national Christian media footprint—Carl McIntire, president of the International Council of Christian Churches and editor of the weekly *Christian Beacon*, and author of profoundly influential books such as *Twentieth Century Reformation* as well as *Modern Tower of Babel*, and a member of the Independent Board of Presbyterian Foreign Missions and other Presbyterian leadership positions (p. 187). He was part of a fundamentalist branch of the Calvinist Presbyterian leadership, along with the prominent Princeton Presbyterian professor J. Gresham Machen, who left to found the fundamentalist Westminster Seminary. They founded their own rogue mission board to select fundamentalist missionaries, until the Presbyterian Church USA told them to stop their rebellion, leading to resistance and a clerical trial, convicting McIntire specifically on acts in contravention of church government and violation of ordination vows, leading to his expulsion and that of others (p. 188). Machen then founded the Orthodox Presbyterian Church, and eventually McIntire split off again to form his own

Bible Presbyterian Church and Faith Theological Seminary (p. 189). McIntire would later found the American Council of Christian Churches, with support from senior Christian leaders such as the religious-survey editor of the *Sunday School Times*, and Dr. William Houghton, president of the Moody Bible Institute in Chicago (p.180). Roy also reiterates our earlier data that *Francis Schaeffer—who many view as the most important and influential Christian philosopher of the Religious Right of the Twentieth Century and beyond—was a "fellow traveler" with McIntire in these views and in some ways a protégé, whom McIntire described as a "brilliant and consecrated young man"* (p. 216) and who was the first graduate of McIntire's Faith Theological Seminary, although McIntire and Schaeffer fell on the opposing sides of a later denominational split again in the late 1950s.

Another author of the period who pushed a pro-business message to clergy very effectively, as well as warning of "a socialist revolution" and warning that famous clergy (such as Reinhold Neibuhr and E. Stanley Jones) who sought the well-being of the underclasses were part of it, was John T. Flynn, whose book *The Road Ahead* "by early 1953 sold almost a million copies, of which over 725,000 were distributed through the Committee for Constitutional Government," who "considered this economic treatise the 'greatest book of our time' " (p. 232). Roy adds that "In 1941, the Committee was reorganized and chartered as 'an educational, non-profit, eleemosynary corporation" to "uphold constitutional government and the system of free enterprise," that "prides itself on maintaining one of the most extensive lists of Protestant ministers in the country," with its chairmen including the "publisher of the Gannett newspaper chain" (now the largest U.S. newspaper publisher, including the national newspaper *USA Today*) and Norman Vincent Peale (p. 232). Roy also notes that Peale, who many have seen in days past as "America's pastor" and rival for that position with Billy Graham, as well as author of the societally-significant *The Power of Positive Thinking* in 1952, "exploited his ministerial position to disperse extreme political and economic theories," adding that "In 1944, for instance, he boosted—through mailings to Catholics and Protestants—a book [called *For Americans Only*] which tried to establish parallels between Franklin Roosevelt and Adolf Hitler," and which called his presidency a "dictatorship," and said that "the New Deal had harmed churches because high taxes [to help the out of work and destitute] cut church revenue" (p. 233). Peale told Protestant ministers that *For Americans Only* "is a stirring, factual and enlightening discussion of the dangerous trends toward collectivism in the United States," and recommended the Committee for Constitutional

Government send it to their 62,000 Protestant members on their list for a price of $15,000 (p. 233).

Another colleague typical of the era was Wisconsin Power and Light publicity agent Verne Kaub, who founded the American Council of Christian Laymen in 1949 to confront socialism in churches, and was known for writing and distributing the leaflet, *Jesus Was A Capitalist*, teaching that "Jesus worked with his father in the construction business" in the glorious age when "there was no labor union to meddle with prices and wages," and also wrote *Collectivism Challenges Christianity*, which taught that America was founded on Christian principles, which led to private enterprise" (pp. 244–245). He also taught that a long list of famous "subversive" church leaders that are part of "God-hating, un-American organizations" include famous missionary and author E. Stanley Jones, and others (p. 246). Even the Methodists, the largest single Protestant denomination in America at the time, got in on the act. Roy writes that "A Conference of Methodist Laymen was convened in Chicago in July 1935.…Its leaders, including many prominent bankers, contended that ministers should 'preach the gospel' and leave social, political, and economic problems to those who understood them" (p. 310)—*that can be either good or bad advice, depending upon the situation.* Rembert Gilman Smith wrote *Methodist Reds* in 1936 (being distributed amongst groups of the American Legion and Daughters of the Revolution, as well as bishops and ministers), and who recommended that that every parish appoint a "Vigilante Committee…to discover any literature or influences apt to undermine the loyalty of our children and youth to the Constitution, to warn the Church of them, and to propose prompt measures of resistance" (pp. 332–333). Another Methodist pastor-publisher, Blake Craft of Georgia, was disturbed by the Methodist affirmation of universal brotherhood, addressing it in his work *The Preservation of the Integrity of the Races*, promoting white supremacy in saying that "God designed it…I do not believe that God in His creative processes happened to smear a little black by mistake on some primitive man from which sprang the Negro man," and warned that "Mongrelization would mean the destruction of a cherished race-history" (pp. 334–335).

Roy devoted an entire chapter to the topic, "God and the 'Libertarians'." He writes that "a network of powerful religio-economic forces hopes to identify the same religious faith with materialistic 'libertarianism'—a kind of *economic royalism* dedicated to the extreme view that no positive governmental action of any kind is justified" (p. 285) (emphasis added). He adds that "These groups are well financed by big industry, endorsed by influential, sincere citizens, and intent on establishing a firm alliance between Protestant piety and unrestrained economic individualism" (p. 285). He says they "are not truly conservative" but rather "'reactionary'—eager to return to the nineteenth century rampant individualism that long since has been outdated by the increasing complexities of modern society. The doctrinal *laissez-faire* ["hands-off" approach of government towards business and the economy] which they profess is as much an enemy of reputable conservatives as it is of those who hold liberal economic views. In fact, in this naïve trust in the perfect working of an unchecked natural order are the seeds of social irresponsibility—and even anarchy" (p. 285); *well said, Brother Roy, well said.* He says he concentrates in this chapter on "the current attempt to inundate Protestant ministers and laymen with free literature popularizing this 'reactionary' point of view" (p. 285).

He briefly speaks of Spiritual Mobilization, noting its claimed membership of 17,000 "representatives" amongst the clergy, while 100,000 clergy and laymen receive *Faith and Freedom*, which is "conspicuous for its intellectual façade" (p. 286). He also notes its select advisory committee included J. C. Penney, the department store magnate, as well as Norman Vincent Peale, although they "have no function other than add their prestige" (pp. 286–287). He also announces that Rev. Kenneth W. Sollitt of First Baptist Church in Mindota, Illinois won the big cash prize for the 1951 "Independence Sermon Competition" held by Spiritual Mobilization (which was sponsored again in 1952), and Sollitt's articles began to appear in *Faith and Freedom* (p. 287). He also notes that from 1937 to 1942 Spiritual Mobilization was receiving "a substantial sum" from Fifield's own wealthy First Congregational Church, receiving gifts of up to $12,500 from corporations by the 1950s, and such contributors as Pew of Sunoco and the presidents of Gulf Oil, Chrysler, National Steel, Republic Steel and others also conducting fund raising for its budget (p. 288). Roy writes that "Spiritual Mobilization's rank and file have been depicted as 'Protestant priests of mammon,' 'benefactors of the rich and powerful,' and allies of groups and individuals that 'nestle on the fascist fringe' " (p. 289). He notes that Spiritual Mobilization launched *Truth in Action*, a bimonthly "sent free to 100,000 clergymen and designed as 'a forum for high level controversy.' It tends to dismiss the most serious charges against it as communist-inspired" (p. 289). He adds that "In February 1952, Theologian Reinhold Niebuhr spoke out against Spiritual Mobilization's 'political program,' which he called 'identical with that of the National Association of Manufacturers, to which it adds merely a prayer and religious unction' "; in response, "Edmund A. Optiz, a Unitarian clergyman and regional conference director for Spiritual Mobilization, engaged Niebuhr in a brief duel in the columns of *The Reporter*, biweekly journal of liberal political opinion. 'First,' contended Opitz, 'we have no political program' " (p. 290). *Opitz will be discussed in further detail, and his intriguing role with these characters, in the following chapter.*

We have already mentioned the disclosure by Jewish agencies concerning Rev. Fifield's anti-Semitic comments. Roy further states that author Carey McWilliams wrote in *The Nation* in 1948 and "accused Fifield of using his pulpit to promote prejudice against minorities in the Los Angeles area," citing Fifield's statements of being against "the efforts of minorities to push in where they are not wanted...we do not intend to turn the town over to Jews, Mexicans, and Negroes," and he alleges that Fifield had expressed approvals of restrictive covenants and other forms of segregation, while opposing fair-employment legislation, the Genocide Pact, and the Universal Declaration of Human Rights (pp. 290–291). In response Spiritual Mobilization's vice-president Ingebretsen accused the author of lifting the quotations indiscriminately from their contexts, and characterized him as a "known Communist sympathizer"—*a popular smear at the time to divert the public from the facts of assertions raised and to impugn the whistleblower, much like people might be labeled "liberal" today to dismiss any accusations (even when accompanied with hard evidence) to discourage serious consideration by conservative Christians and others.*

We all have seen in life how it is common how the well-to-do (including ambitious "wannabes" who cavort with them), behind the walls of their gated communities, have a condescending and contemptuous view of whoever they view as underclasses—not just the poor in general (and many working-class), but others they automatically assume to be either "leeches" on the economy, and/or just of low class, "peasant" tastes and "vulgar" lifestyles, merely breeding and consuming with their simple ways. Of this caste they usually include immigrants, and other minority religions and ethnicities, and particularly the African American community. We see these types of people publicly at times, such as Los Angeles Clippers owner Donald Sterling, who was exposed of having segregationist views (even criticizing his young mistress of physically appearing alongside Magic Johnson), and similar statements of his about other African-American superstars (earning him a lifetime NBA fine), as well as similar actions against minority tenants in his portfolio of building projects, including statements alleged in lawsuits wherein he stated that "Hispanics, smoke, drink and just hang around the building," and that "black tenants smell and attract vermin".[141] Of course, the best recent example is our current President, with a record of historical government rulings against the racist practices and policies of the rental properties owned and operated by he and his father, and his campaign and presidency statements against "rapist and murderer" Mexicans, people from "shi_hole' countries," and many other examples.

Similarly, Roy notes that in December 1952, Rabbi Julius Nodel of Temple Beth Israel in Portland, Oregon, expressed his opposition to Fifield and his cohorts and reflecting the fears of many Jews and "Negroes," asserting that "Their spirit is antithetical to religion; there is nothing spiritual about them....Thousands of gullible followers are deriving sadistic pleasure at having their pet prejudices repeated and a few vested interests capitalized," followed by evidence of instances of Fifield's antagonism towards minority races and religions (p. 291).

Roy quotes Fifield's statement of his program for America: "First, we must see to it that no more socialistic laws are passed. We must stop the granting of special privileges to any group....Our second step is to get rid of the socialistic laws we now have. This requires that we take away special privileges from groups who now have them," and notes that "the 'socialistic laws' that Fifield wants repealed" include "laws, national or statewide, providing for social security, a minimum wage, old-age pensions, veterans' benefits—in fact, welfare legislation of any kind," as he also "opposes effective international cooperation," and sees "the 'social gospel' is a key scapegoat" (p. 292). Roy also notes that Fifield gave enthusiastic endorsement to the red-baiting crusades of Senator Joe McCarthy (p. 293). He concludes by saying that "Spiritual Mobilization claims that it has had a marked influence upon the economic and political thinking of clergymen in the United States. In 1949 Fifield conducted a survey which allegedly proved that 64.2 percent of Protestant ministers were opposed to 'New Deal philosophy' and other types of 'collectivism'. This he contrasted with sentiment in 1934, when, according to Fifield, 82.4 percent of the ministers were for the New Deal 'or some other impractical idealism,' " while, based upon a recent (early 50s) poll of 2,000 pastors by *Faith and Freedom*, they allege that "more ministers are interested and active for our ideals today than at any time since we started," with 65 percent alarmed at big government (pp. 293–294).

Roy also briefly writes about another similar group we have covered—Howard Kershner and his *Christian Economics* publication. Roy claims that "More than 175,000 Protestant clergymen in the United States and a growing list of laymen regularly receive *Christian Economics* free of charge," and they also provide, free of charge, "speakers or radio discs for use by churches, radio stations, youth groups and other organizations interested in promoting the views of the Christian Freedom Foundation," and he also notes that "one of the most effective devices for reaching laymen—a technique developed during the past months—is the sending of free reprints to ministers for weekly insertion in their church bulletins" (p. 294). He also notes that "Working with Kershner in the New York office is Percy L. Greaves, the Foundation's consulting economist and former aide to a number of ultra-conservative interest groups and Congressmen," and who established the Foundation for Freedom, Inc.; Roy adds that "The Foundation lasted only long enough to publish *Operation Immigration*, a Greaves pamphlet on proposed legislation for displaced persons," where Graves warned that "if we Americans open our doors to the 'dregs of Europe,' our standard of living will be lowered and our moral leadership undermined," and he made it appear that only "undesirables" were being brought in as "displaced persons" (i.e., refugees) (p. 295)—*does this sound familiar to our recent presidential administration?* Both Greaves and *Christian Economics* fought the nomination of candidate Eisenhower, whereas General MacArthur (who directed Gen. Patton to fire on and kill protesting World War I veterans) was hailed as "a statesman of the highest order," and "More than fifty clergymen—many of them distinguished—serve on the Foundation's board of directors, including Norman Vincent Peale (p. 296).

Christian Economics occasionally included negative letters amongst its many supportive clergyman letters in its periodical; Roy quotes one Vermont preacher writing that "Your paper would be honest at least, and not deceive so many gullible clergymen, if you rightfully called it 'Big Business Propaganda' "; Kershner himself suggested that 60 percent of such letters exhibited strong approval, and 20 percent sharply critical; Peale himself wrote in the "Letters to the Editor" that "I read *Christian Economics* with great interest and consider it the soundest and best paper of its kind" (p. 297). Roy asserts that their definition of "socialism" was welfare legislation of any kind, and breaks two of the Ten Commandments by "forcibly taking the wealth of the more enterprising citizens for distribution to others" (p. 297).

Roy also discusses Leonard Read's Foundation for Economic Education (a long-time, lasting foundational organization of libertarian ideological promotion as a "think tank"), noting that Read was a "member of the advisory committee of Fifield's Spiritual Mobilization" (p. 299). He notes that the Foundation (FEE) does not seek a mass audience, with a small mailing list of 25,000, along with volume purchases by companies and individuals, and with donations from companies like B. F. Goodrich, Chrysler, Du Pont, General Motors, U.S. Steel, the Volker Fund and the like, and reaches the clergy through its own columns within the pages of *Faith and Freedom* and *Christian Economics*, and he quotes the "religious spokesman" of the Foundation as saying that each of its senior staff is an active church member (p. 300). He writes that FEE believes that government is the "enemy of the people," and that state administrators are a "professional criminal class" (p. 301). Roy writes that they believe that "'God's Law' is the same as 'natural law,' which is the same as '*laissez-faireism*,'" and that "To let 'natural law' take its course is to do the will of God. Whenever man interferes with 'natural law' through economic regulation, he is fighting against God. *Laissez-faire* capitalism arises directly from the Christian faith" (p. 301). *I would assert (and have asserted) that this view is no different than the atheistic, Darwinistic "survival of the fittest," and is no sign of "civilization," whose quality is marked by how well it values and cares for its weakest.* He says that they claim that "There is no middle ground between 'libertarianism' and communism," with the former exhibiting no public post offices, no public highways and no public schools, or otherwise being guilty of aiding "godless, materialist communism" (p. 302).

Another way that Roy asserts the "buying" of clergy through its senior leaders was the founding of the National Council of Churches in 1950, with Presbyterian and Sunoco founder J. Howard Pew as the chairman of its "sponsoring committee," including Harvey Firestone, heads of General Mills, DuPont, Standard Oil, General Foods, and Charles Wilson of General Electric (p. 302). Pew was reportedly treated like royalty at the inaugural convention, and escorted to the platform, where he denounced the destruction of "Christian liberty"—which he associated with economic *laissez faire*, and "exhorted his hearers to make the church a bulwark of freedom as defined in the 'libertarian credo,'" and "mentioned the role which he and his colleagues proposed to play in formulating policy in areas in which they had 'special competence and interest'" (p. 303). Roy notes that the Federal Council of Churches had resisted alliances with big business and other special interest groups for a generation, but for the National Council of Churches, Pew became its fundraiser, first in beginning to secure an additional $600,000 to support it, as "the oil magnate began to define the functions of his [layman's] group," including the *review rights to the senior clergy group's pronouncements and publications* (p. 303). Roy notes that Pew had been a heavy contributor to the activities of many apostles of discord," and also states that Carl McIntire "once solicited $50,000 from Pew to finance one of the divisive 'missionary' jaunts to the Far East," and is a major funder of Spiritual Mobilization and the Christian Freedom Foundation, underwriting a major share of the latter's budget (p. 304). Roy states that "*J. Howard Pew has probably been the major force behind the current revival of the archaic economic thought of the late nineteenth century. Through these 'non-partisan' educational fronts, he effectively promotes his own ideology*" (p. 304) (emphasis added). Pew also played a major role in soliciting funds by his "personal emergency appeals" to other corporations, with "over a thousand of them" placed on the list of contributors (p. 304).

Roy summarizes by stating that "What does this power struggle mean for the future of social concern among the Protestant churches? Most churchmen hope that the representatives of moneyed interests—sincere though their antiquated views may be—will be converted to less extreme views. But Pew is not surrendering" (p. 306). The famed theologian Reinhold Neibuhr wrote that "There are indications that a long period of 'creative tension' between the clerical leaders of American Protestantism and the American business community is coming to a close with the triumph of the business community over the churches" (p. 306). To this, Roy asks, "Will Protestantism retrogress to its nineteenth-century alliance with economic privilege, when its social theories echoed the heartless notion of 'survival of the fittest'—which too often meant the exploitation of the 'have-nots' by the 'haves'?" (p. 306). He writes (*remember—back in 1953*) that

> The "libertarians" aim to mold public opinion their way, and they view the churches as desirable instruments through which to propagate their antiquated views. They hope to convince churchmen that all welfare legislation is "tyrannical," "socialistic," and "un-American"....Those who oppose social security, pensions for the blind and aged, veteran's benefits, laws to protect laborers from abuse and farmers from disaster, and every other legal expression of humanitarian concern—including public schools, parks, and libraries—will want to join the "libertarians" in their campaign to turn back the clock....There is grave danger, however, that by vague and emotional appeals to "freedom under God"—channeled through mass media that only big money can afford—Protestants will be lulled into complacency, while aggressive "libertarians" try to rob the nation of its cherished inheritance. (pp. 306–307)

The reader might shrug their shoulders now, after having endured an extended chapter of information concerning this myriad of corporate-sponsored and paid "Christian libertarian" leaders and their expansive mass-media outlets from a generation ago or more, and wonder how these little-known figures are worthy of concern and "all the fuss" in terms of "wasting time" in reviewing their old exploits in detail. *The key point for the reader to grasp is that these figures performed a successful "psy op" on hundreds of thousands of clergymen, and the many-fold more in their pews or spheres of influence. They trained (and let's say it—"brainwashed") many of our older pastors today, by repeated messaging and overwhelming media exposure and control, and those pastors or seminary and Christian school professors who trained today's pastors or their mentors, and the leaders throughout today's Christian media.* This fundamental understanding of Christian duty and culture, extending across the Religious Right bulk of American Christianity that transcends denominational lines, comprising "free" (i.e., unregulated) enterprise and privatization, and a distrust of government and the poor and immigrant as "moochers" and unworthy of emergency assistance except on the occasional whim of well-to-do citizen, *was inherited without question, and collectively assumed as a "presupposition" with negligible vetting by God's revelation via Christ, and His mouthpieces the Apostles and the Old Testament prophets (which this book attempts to remedy, as a remnant of other "voices crying in the wilderness" in the days of wealth-obsessed pre-Exilic Israel, the days of Jesus and the Church Age since the days of Calvin's Geneva "Protestant Work (wealth) Ethic" tried to do in their days).* The perceptive reader of this chapter will have also observed that this indoctrinated contempt of "the stranger" and the poor, and glorification of wealth and the wealthy, *leads such propagandists and their followers to eventually cavort with their natural allies that are often openly "anti-Semitic," and definitely racist and xenophobic, and sometimes just blatantly Nazis, fascists or those sympathetic to them.* While we have shown here that these historical groups defended their "Christian (i.e., White European) America" klan and its culture and its women from the non-white "barbarians," with justifications from their "Christian Economics," *today the Religious Right aligns with the "Alt Right" and Charlottesville, Stephen Miller and their President against the "rapist and murderer" immigrants, arrested citizens our President tells police to rough up, and those from "sh-thole countries" (according to the President), and against Antifa (i.e., blacks) and the "socialists."* We will hear more about the hidden agenda and lifestyles of those in the Fifield and *Faith and Freedom* circles in the next chapter, *and in the next volume we will see that this underground operation continues with new names in the last generation and today, and even has a modern, little-known but even more powerful "Fifield" as the Christian-Big Business "Pied Piper" within the very halls of the White House today.* However, now we will briefly mention a few last words concerning the modern influence of one of the most fascinating and enigmatic rogues we have discussed—*the blatant Nazi William Dudley Pelley of the "Christian Party" and Silver Shirts stormtrooper fame.*

The online "Extremist File" on "John de Nugent" at the Southern Poverty Law Center website[142] explains that "John de Nugent is a prolific writer who has worked with numerous hate groups including the neo-Nazi National Alliance and the Holocaust-denying *Barnes Review*, and individuals like Willis Carto, the anti-Semitic founder of both the *The Barnes Review* and the now-defunct Liberty Lobby" (*Carto and the latter organization having been mentioned for its large fund-raising, support and influence previously*). They write that

"De Nugent has run for elected office, and has even vowed to one day become president....de Nugent is particularly anti-Semitic, *believing that the Jews are, along with nefarious space aliens, intent on exterminating the Aryan race.*" They include referenced quotes from de Nugent, such as "the Jews now misrule our beloved country of America, bringing it down by huge bribes, media brainwashing and blackmail of our officials, and police, and military officers both high and low. And worst of all, *by a national network of organized pedophiles, child molesting and child-murdering adults....The Jews of today descend from the Neanderthals, an animalistic, borderline-psychopathic and brutish clan* who then became the roving *apiru,* from which comes the word 'Hebrews'....*They even practice incest on their own children, making them into inbred psychopaths,*" and "The day will come when non-white Dems permanently get a lock on the White House, Congress, Supreme Court and the governorships and state legislatures, *then they will disarm the Whites and kill the men, boys, and older women, keeping the pretty younger women alive for rape*" (emphasis added). In a 2013 interview "he describes *finding a small portrait of Adolf Hitler in his grandmother's house as a child and being strangely compelled by the image,*" and as a student at Georgetown University "he discovered a passage from Hitler's *Mein Kampf,* which spoke to his own frustrations during the 1970s." They add that at that school he participated in a "*[s]torm troop demonstration in full uniform, with swastikas, brown shirt, black pants and motor cycle helmet—the uniform of the NSWPP [National Socialist White People's Party] storm troopers*" in 1979, *while he was serving in the Marine Corps. (since 1976), with his commanding officers merely reassigning him,* until he left the military in 1983. They add that "From 1981 to 1984, de Nugent worked in the National Alliance under William L. Pierce....the Alliance was a neo-Nazi organization that grew out of the National Youth Alliance, *itself an offshoot of both the American Nazi Party and the NSWPP.* Pierce is infamous for authoring *The Turner Diaries....*a race-war novel that *in effect calls for violent overthrow of the United States government, extermination of all Jews, 'race-mixers' and others....[it's] been the inspiration for numerous acts of white supremacist and other radical violence, including Timothy McVeigh's deadly 1995 Oklahoma City bombing*" (emphasis added).

De Nugent's own website features him wearing a "Georgetown" shirt, in front of a Nazi SS "Black Sun," *with the U.S. Marines logo on the other side,* and in 2015 lists an article of his tribute to William Dudley Pelley.[143] There, he writes that "The admirable Pelley proved 70 years ago that *no non-fanatical, moderate anything (religion or political party) can succeed in America....*What the Jews and Muslims have is a true cult. And they are kicking our ass....*The fanatics rise to the top, and elbow aside the moderates, who lack energy and fight....*At a National Alliance convention in the 1980s I met one of Pelly's valiant old

Silver Shirts, a gent in his 80s, quite a man still" (emphasis added). He then follows with a lengthy article by an "A. V. Schaeffenberg," entitled, "The Life of William Dudley Pelley," of which the following are excerpts:

> Outside of infrequent, fleeting references to him in a few histories of the Depression Era, there are no books about his dramatic life; not even any newspaper or magazine articles. His photograph cannot be found outside the pages of *The New Order*, nor any *photographs of his tens of thousands of followers, even though both his image and theirs dominated newsreels and publications of the time*. His speeches are unobtainable even though *they were heard by millions, sometimes over national-wide radio broadcasts*....Sinclair Lewis wrote a full length novel, *It Can't Happen Here*, based on his life....[Pelley's] books entered college curricula in the forefront of modern American literature. Yet, no college course in Great Books today features any of his titles. He was one of the most important creators of the silent film....Despite the man's undeniable impact on his times, his name has been thoroughly expunged from contemporary history....his only biography was written eighteen years ago, an obscure university thesis...
>
> [With] the diplomatic rank of "consular courier" conferred upon him by the United States government, he shipped out for Russia in early 1918....He learned first-hand that communism was not an ideology, *it was simply the organization of the worst criminal elements led by Jews to destroy Gentile society*....Pelley made his report to Representative Louis F. McFadden of Pennsylvania in 1920. The politician was so alarmed at what he heard, he personally read aloud the *Protocols for the Learned Elders of Zion* on the floor of Congress....Pelley was introduced to a Justice Department official and Robert Sharp, chief of State Department intelligence. They told him his experiences were entirely born out of their abundant files on Jewish agitation in Russia and the United States....he was hired as a screenwriter at M.G.M. and Universal Studios. He worked furiously, turning out scripts for the leading motion pictures of the day. He even scripted a film version of his own short story, *The Shock*, which was an instant hit....he soon became one of the most respected and highest paid writers in Hollywood. In the words of his biographer, his esteemed screen plays..."helped to establish Lon Chaney's reputation and forged a friendship between the two men"....He was favorably compared to F. Scott Fitzgerald and regarded as at least the equal to Sinclair Lewis.
>
> At the height of his career's success...on May 29th, 1928, he was suddenly and unexpectedly confronted by a deeply moving personal

experience. He wrote about it in *My Seven Minutes in Eternity*, which sold 90,000 copies....Whatever happened to him, it appears to have been *not unlike the vision a young Hitler had of his life when, as a 15 year-old student in Linz, Austria, something in a performance of Wagner's music showed him a glimpse of his future mission.* Such...*usually occurs to revolutionary personalities of a high order*....He studied *Mein Kampf* and *wondered if the principles so clearly laid out therein could be applied in the United States.*...Adolf Hitler was elected to power on January 30th, 1933....The very next day, Pelley founded the Silver Legion, regarded by most historians as the first genuine National Socialist-style organization in the United States....From its inception, *its thrust was the attainment of political power, to someday become the U.S. government and establish a folkish state based on the fundamentals of Mein Kampf....he loved the Swastika symbol and understood its pan-Aryan significance*....[but] instead of the old Hooked Cross, he chose the letter "L" as the symbol of his new organization....[that] stood for *Love of the Aryan Race, Loyalty to the American Republic, Liberation from Jewry* and, of course, the Silver Legion itself....For the next nine years, it was to be seen by *millions of Americans, carried into vicious street battles and hoisted over every state in the Union.*...The members of the Silver Shirts were by no means armchair revolutionaries, but *tough street fighters.*...Many [Legionnaires] were also *ex-serviceman*, betrayed veterans of the phony "War to End All Wars"....By 1936, he was a nationally-known public figure, who had already addressed hundreds of thousands of farmers, students, housewives and, *most usually, unemployed people all across the country.*...[those who] viewed the world with increasing sullenness *during this highly successful Jewish Depression*...[Roosevelt's] election bid increased Silver Legion membership three-fold and won some important figures, including *George van Horn Moseley, a retired general in the U.S. Army, Congressional Representative Jacob Thorkelson, Charles A. Lindbergh, Jr., and Walt Disney. All of them attended his public rallies and some shared the podium with the Chief.*...his biographer wrote, *"Pelley looked forward to a World Axis, centered in an Aryanized Washington and made secure at either end in Berlin and Tokyo"*.... As the 1940 presidential election approached, the Silver Shirts, *now 100,000 strong* (House Committee on "Un-American" Activities, Special Committee, 1939), were being taken very seriously by F.D.R....The Silver Shirts joined up with the *American-German Bund, the Ku Klux Klan and numerous other patriotic organizations*, large and small, united in mobilizing mass-opposition for peace....He also lived long enough to witness the rise of *George Lincoln Rockwell's American Nazi Party*, a phenomenon that offered him deep comfort: *Someone was carrying on the fight he began thirty years before.* (emphasis added)

De Nugent adds that whites "will never support their own heroes **unless a fanatic religion remolds their minds**...It means we need a fanatic, organized religion, but one better than what Pelley tried to launch. His stuff was good but too esoteric" (bold original). De Nugent also shows pictures of Pelley and troopers in Silver Shirt regalia, as well as ads on his site for the new news site *The Epoch Times*, "Third Reich art," South African whites sites, the "International Association for Near Death Studies" and UFO researchers, the Russian "news" site *RT*, and of course—*Infowars. We will review more of Pelley's esoteric, New Age "post-Nazi" spiritual pursuits in Volume 3.*

Given the cynical "Faustian bargain" the various elements of the Religious Right, including mainline Protestant, Catholic and even Jewish elements along with Christian evangelicals, have made since the early twentieth century with big business and their agenda of unregulated and unimpeded capitalism and free markets, it is not surprising that members of the younger generation, even as their forbearers in the earlier Sixties who trod before them (whom Religious Establishment standard bearer Billy Graham labeled as Communists "giving aid and comfort to the enemy" for opposing the Vietnam War and supporting civil rights, thus cementing the "Generation Gap"), don't feel compelled to "feed the beast" with their income to promote the big-business, anti-public assistance positions of their parents' religious institutions.

In November 2016 *The New York Times* reported[144] that, although religious institutions are still the largest recipients of charity donations, receiving 32 percent, or $119.3 billion of the giving of Americans in 2015, *that is down from about 50 percent since 1990, and has been "in steady decline for some time."* They do note that from (ironically) the Pew Research Center in 2014, 23 percent of Americans say they are not affiliated with any religion, up from 16 percent in 2007. One cited religious leader said that young people now give in "expressing their commitment to core values and their obligation to sustain those in need," and as such, giving to religious institutions is not "automatic." A spokesman for the National Council of Churches stated that "In the past, there was a general sense that the church was a trustworthy institution," and that even if people disagreed with the positions of their church institutions on issues such as civil rights, they would say that "This is my church, and this benefits the community, even if I disagree with its stand on civil rights." Now, when they disagree strongly, they tend to donate to other venues of service. They also note that giving has not declined within the Islamic Church, because "it is an essence of being Muslim," and "they want to change the narrative" concerning a religion that has been defined by outsiders solely in terms of terrorism. *Well,*

I am glad at least one religion in America recognizes that what they invest in and the values they demonstrate to society by their investments reveals the inner nature of their faith in God, and know that it might be effective in recruiting new converts. However, the trend in the younger adherents in diverting donations away from their religious establishments that violate their principles even extends to the Mormon church.

How long will the American church rely on this association with big-business and other institutions of Establishment power and authority in this society, and continue to "eat their seed corn" and see more and more of the next generation leave in disgust (because of their own conscience and commitment to being their "brother's keeper" in terms of social progress, and as "keepers of the Garden" in terms of sustainability and environmental protection), and thus rely on the dwindling landed gentry of the older generation (many of whom are already fiercely reliant on the social programs of Social Security and Medicare), and the few churches who may keep the doors open with the trusts from a few wealthy benefactors? Whatever the scenario, I am certain they will blame their demise on everyone around them, including those "lazy socialist kids" or other leftists, the gay community or the enemy *du jour*, rather than see the source of their demise in their nearby mirror, and in their ability to look so "unlike Jesus."

Regardless of the waning societal influence and political clout of the Religious Right, and the inevitable jilting of their interests by the amoral, self-absorbed agenda of a Wall Street who will seek new mistresses with unspent dowries, the Religious Right figureheads nevertheless will continue for some time to cling devotedly to the fond memories and interests of their capitalistic lovers, singing its praises as if it will return to again sweep them off their feet. As one example, Joseph Farah and *World Net Daily*, a model example of a Religious Right party organ and propaganda tool, recently earned yet another "creative writing" award for exhibiting the audacity of declaring that the suffering of Mary, Joseph and baby Jesus was due to excessive government interference, taxation, and even lax immigration policies (?)—all classic tropes of capitalistic talking points, to further promote the interests of for-profit big businesses unregulated by the public sector as to its predatory practices, or its exploitation of labor and natural resources, as the real "savior" of an ever-privatizing society. He also shows how well he has embraced and embodied the original principles of Rev. Fifield, his Spiritual Mobilization and the National Association of Manufacturers who bankrolled their creation. In December 2018 he writes[145]:

...Jesus, Joseph and Mary were no more refugees in Israel than those who have been illegally crossing the southern U.S. border for far too long....But think about what prompted their journey from Nazareth. It was a tax imposed by the Roman authorities....In other words, those responsible for making this pregnant young woman take the long march to Bethlehem were like other tyrants of the past—people who wanted to live in a borderless world, with them in charge.... Notice how many times the subject of taxes comes up in that first section of the Christmas story....They had to file the equivalent of their 1040 form. It ought to be referred to as "the Long March to Bethlehem" because of its familiarity with the forced population movements of so many modern-day tyrannies—all leftist, all "progressive," all globalist and all border-haters. Jesus' birth was marked by the first world tax....This was a government operation all the way....Joseph and Mary were not "homeless," as some of the modern, big-government shakedown artists suggest....Government is not your friend; it is the enemy of freedom. Government is not Santa Claus; it is the Grinch. Government is not your servant; it tends, all too often, to be our master. Government seldom helps people; it often enslaves them....Even back then, 2,000 years ago, government was often heartless and cruel....That's why the only kind of government the left hates is that which is limited, that which is accountable, that which has borders, that which is (the new dirty word) "nationalist"...In the meantime, the only king we want is Jesus.

It is true that within the pages of the Bible, it often illustrates, documents and warns of kingdom leaders that become tyrants, governments that become tyrannical, and even citizenry that comes to actually love subjugation to such autocratic leaders, and their pride when witnessing the conquests of their sovereign will over their neighbors. They thus claim for themselves a license for clannish pride, lack of compassion for the welfare of their neighbors, and personal greed for unregulated or restrained economic exploitation of their vanquished neighbors, or even their own communities and populace, amongst those disadvantaged by poverty or lack of societal clout. The Bible also warns the leaders of Gentile nations that they will be judged by the morality they already know in their hearts and communally, even if not constrained by the 613 ordinances of the Mosaic code, and in particular their accommodation, if not outright encouragement, of economic exploitation in the scales of the marketplace, or otherwise amongst the poor, widows and strangers who do not find justice in the courts, and the greed that does not allow the excess blessings of abundance to be shared liberally with those less fortunate.

The "rub," I believe, is that while in the "olden days" of yore, one could argue that such autocratic rulers—king, emperor or despot—would be held accountable by God in the Last Day if not before, in these modern days of "self government," the citizenry—that means you and me—will be held accountable by God on these matters, based upon who we select to administer the kingdom as our proxies. That means that we cannot simply slough off our responsibility to our neighbors, or to "be our brother's keeper," when the crown of government falls collectively on all our brows, as a shared duty of responsibility. Declaring government as merely "evil"— and indeed the era of all earthly governments will pass one day—is to not only shirk our God-given responsibility to assist in the governing process as self-governing citizens (both a blessing and responsibility given to us by God in our generation and locale), but *also to fail to rightfully exploit the government to provide blessings to its citizens within the jurisdictions God has established for it, and to be "salt and light" to encourage its noblest practice and reflect a generous and merciful society by example, and to hold it accountable in its duties to the vulnerable as God has assigned it.* The conservative Western, libertarian Christian has in essence turned over the keys of societal governing, in effect, to the "Great City Babylon" operated by the tight fist of the "great merchants of the earth," who regulate society themselves by their sculpting of the marketplace, labor environments, and the redistributing of the world's wealth from the common folk to the ever-growing vaults of the ultra-rich.

The contempt for earthly governance, as exhibited by Joseph Farah in the example above and by most conservative Christians today, as groomed by their handlers (or Pied Pipers) in talk radio and cable news, and in preference for Wall Street and Madison Avenue in taking the dominant role in fashioning our nation, society and communities, in essence shows the cynicism for Master Christ and the governments whom He told His followers to pay taxes to and render to while in this world as pilgrims. This mindset reminds oneself of the servant given one talent (which themselves are much like the resources we are given to bless society, both individually and in collective actions through our church fellowships and even the government who has been established by God to govern in this age), in the Gospel parable of the talents. While this parable can be applied to a number of scenarios in this life and in the Kingdom of Heaven, I believe its principles also apply in general to how we "invest" the resources God has given us to do His work in society, *as a reflection of what we think about Him.*

The servant who took his one talent and buried it, rather than investing it, justified his acts to the Master *by the servant's perception of him*, in telling him that "Master, I knew you to be a hard man, reaping where you did not sow and gathering where you scattered no seed. I was afraid, and went away and hid your talent in the ground" (Matt. 25:24–25, NASB). This view of God as the Old Testament "fire on the mountain," a fierce, transcendent "Wizard of Oz"-type that cultivates a "Sinners in the Hands of an Angry God" reputation, as our Religious Right heroes such as famous Reformed (Calvinist) Puritan preacher (and slaveholder) Jonathan Edwards would suggest, leads one to not only think that God will be unreasonable in assessing our good works done by ourselves and our local church fellowships, but *also our duties as citizens through the institutions of self government He has established for us.* Rather than focusing their zeal toward merely rooting out corruption within earthly government and holding it accountable with the tools before us, exposing it through the mass media now available to us, and promoting transparency and ethical government policies and administrators on our behalf, *they rather hold in total contempt the entire Biblical institution of earthly government God has instituted over us,* and any efforts by it, righteous or otherwise, to promote justice as is its biblical mandate— including economic justice and restraining the economic exploitation of those vulnerable to such, as God instituted in His own designed government in ancient Israel, and what He says He will judge other Gentile governments about. This "fear" exhibited by the unfaithful servant is a common paranoia of distrust not only in and about any specific government in general (and not confined to specific unethical leaders*), but for the entire institution itself, and thus the God who established it.*

While it is reasonable (and indeed essential) to hold a government accountable for waste, fraud, corruption, and initiatives that do not advance the well-being of all in society (including kickbacks and tax breaks to big businesses and lobbies that bankroll the campaigns and pockets of politicians and the out of control "war machine" that only benefits defense contractors), *it is not warranted to "bury in the ground" your funds and valuable resource of personal involvement (to otherwise be used in taxes which Jesus has already validated as a necessary part of society, even in totalitarian ones like imperial Rome), as an expression of total contempt for the institution, which otherwise could fulfill government's part of God's role in producing as just a society as is possible in this fallen world before His return.* In exchange for the servant's hoarding of his resource and not investing it in his community, the Master referred to him as a "wicked, lazy servant," and acknowledged that it pertained to the servant's perception of him, saying that "you knew that I reap where I did not sow and gather where I scattered no seed" (Matt. 25:26).

The Master then notes that even if the servant had not invested the talent in speculative, long-range entrepreneurial investments like the other servants, he could have at least invested it in the "bank," with guaranteed "interest" (v. 27). Obviously, Jesus was not referring to a regular bank in the sense of what He wanted His followers to use, but rather the institutions that one knows will produce a "return" of good works; of course our local church can be a likely conduit for such, but God-ordained governments can also be such a venue, if we stay engaged to influence its allocation and unique role as a coercive force to preserve justice, including economic justice. This coercive force, which the Church itself is not supposed to exhibit (although it sinfully has in its shameful past), is a power lawfully given to governments by God (as well as by those so governed, according to our Founding Fathers of our nation), if it is *used as a coercive force to restrain other societal coercive forces that would otherwise harm us,* either as a total collective, or minorities of some sort or those most vulnerable in our midst (like the "stragglers in the herd"). These dangerous coercive forces are not only outside armies that can overrun our villages, or armed bandits that can rob and terrorize us, but also *controlling "money changers" and powerful banking and "great merchants of the earth" as the Bible calls them, who can buy armies or thugs to enforce their will on us, or merely control our lives by making us debt slaves, controlling wages and prices of essential goods, or even the availability of essential commodities, as the Bible clearly shows in the Book of Revelation.*

God also expects us, as "our brothers' keepers," to look out for our neighbors *even when they might be too intellectually challenged or naïve to understand when they are being exploited by the financial community, Madison Avenue or other powerful forces*; indeed, God reproved "God's man" the prophet Jonah for being uncaring about the pagan Ninevites, whom God acknowledged were not just pagans, but also "cannot discern between their right hand and their left hand," and, as a "raging tree hugger" and "animal rights fanatic" Himself, God also showed concern for the "much cattle" who were endangered there, unlike the representative of God (Jonah 4:11). In the famous passage within Romans 13, Paul acknowledges that "rulers," or government, can have a useful role, even in his era of autocrats that ruled through most of recorded history, "for rulers are not a terror to good works, but to the evil…for he is the minister of God to thee for good…for he is the minister of God, a revenger to execute wrath upon him that doeth evil….For this cause pay ye tribute also: for they are God's ministers, attending continually upon this very thing. Render therefore to all their dues: tribute [i.e. taxes] to whom tribute is due; custom to whom custom; fear to whom fear; honour to whom honour" (Rom. 13:3–4, 6–7).

Of course, throughout history we have seen despotic corruption and evil doing, and sometimes God's people have had to pay the price for defying rulers by refusing to renounce God or break His commands, or (however not enough) standing up for the weak outside their ranks that are subject to persecution. However, in general God does not want us to pick fights with our authorities, particularly in terms of their attempts to restrain evil that could be applied to us by other armies or other violent force, or even the economic variety, and to pay the taxes involved for them to accomplish these missions. To perpetually denounce governments as evil in concept because they use funds to help or protect other people, or to restrain those who coerce others by various means, is not supported in the Bible; in fact, Jesus repeatedly demonstrated a willingness to pay tribute or taxes as a way of life, even in an imperial government, in which He or His Christian followers could have no political influence, while keeping a primary focus on Kingdom of Heaven activities. For those of us who have been specially blessed to live in a participatory democracy or republic, the responsibility further falls upon us to assist the government in this role, and help it determine what are the hidden coercive forces in the society and how to restrain them and look out for those "who do not know their right hand from their left," and also to use all legal powers at our disposal to confront its misuse by government officials. We must also pledge not to grow weary and "check out" from the frustrating and exhausting process of holding powerful societal forces and government officials accountable, but also working to restore a healthy, and one might even say, a *progressive* improvement in the institutions and processes based upon lessons learned, as a further responsibility for a Christian *tasked with using every means* to "bless" their neighbors, and be "salt and light."

In closing, this chapter should remind us that (a) libertarian thinking, with its value of self-determination and free association, exhibits many merits for a Christian, particularly those of us originating from the Radical Reformers such as the Baptists and Anabaptists and Mennonites, with their commitment to the "priesthood of the believer" and autonomy of the local church, (b) however, it also has its prominent "dark side" for Christians and other moral persons, with its common fundamental emphasis upon selfishness and lack of duty to its neighbor, which is actually a Luciferian and anti-Christ trait that is at least acknowledged by some of its figureheads such as Ayn Rand, (c) its emphasis on economic thinking, with "free markets" and lack of regulations, to the point of despising citizen government itself, even when the individual or minority is protected by a Bill of Rights (the *real* contribution of the United States to world civilization), while also ignoring the age-old coercive power of established capital and wealth over the marketplace and society that citizen-defending government was intended to counterbalance, which creates a plutocratic totalitarian state but is the primary influence on the broader conservative community, (d) it is a minority view in its extreme forms but is bankrolled by Fortune 500 corporations, tycoons and banking interests, in a semi-covert fashion, and (e) it has had a significant role in conditioning and, in effect, brainwashing the major portion of the Religious Right leadership and community for generations, using pseudo-religious media outlets like *Faith and Freedom* or *Christian Economics* and related organizations, ignoring the primary passages of scripture relating to emphasis on care for the poor in the Old Testament and collective societal well-being in the Kingdom of Heaven, and rather created a selfishness and marketplace-based value system in Christian trappings, as its wealthy benefactors recognize the merits of bamboozling the largest organized (but most gullible) segment of society in the evangelical and other conservative church communities to achieve their political and social agendas.

Thus, the ability to manipulate the masses of American Religious Right citizens did not originate with Sean Hannity, Fox News, Rush Limbaugh or even Jerry Falwell or Pat Robertson, but was built on a foundation of other Big Business-bankrolled front media outlets, from the anti-New Deal assistance for the poor and unemployed of the 1930s, through the anti-Communism-dominated 1950s. Of course, in propagating the "leaven of the Pharisees" of dismissing concerns about the "little people" (*anawim*) and rather holding the destitute to blame for their plight (asking, "Who sinned— this man or his parents?" (John 9:2)), emphasizing the pursuit of wealth (and a society structured to favor those most obsessed with it) and its possession being a sign of God's endorsement, and a general propagation of an elitist/elect worldview of a "chosen people," with a yet higher religious "super-elite" leadership, is it not surprising that the older *Beacon* and *Defender* outlets, like *Faith and Freedom, Christian Economics,* and modern day Religious Right-friendly talk radio and cable news, *also exhibit the old Pharisaic racism and anti-immigrant views that complement this greedy, self and Mammon-centered Babylonian worldview?* The real question now arises—how will a Twenty-First Century American follower of Christ tangibly respond to such revelations, and what are their duties and obligations?

In the next chapter we will see and give some examples how some of the "sages" advising the Christian clergy and flock within these periodicals (and their fellow travelers) have little-known spiritual understandings and agendas that are not recognized by their rapt readers, but *hopefully will be of great concern to them, once exposed.*

BABYLON'S GNOSTIC SORCERERS THAT HAVE INFLUENCED OUR SHEPHERDS

Verily, verily, I say unto you, He that entereth not by the door into the sheepfold, but climbeth up some other way, the same is a thief and a robber. But he that entereth in by the door is the shepherd of the sheep....And when he putteth forth his own sheep, he goeth before them, and the sheep follow him: for they know his voice. And a stranger will they not follow, but will flee from him: for they know not the voice of strangers... I am the door: by me if any man enter in, he shall be saved, and shall go in and out, and find pasture. The thief cometh not, but for to steal, and to kill, and to destroy: I am come that they might have life, and that they might have [it] more abundantly. I am the good shepherd: the good shepherd giveth his life for the sheep. (John 10: 1–2, 4–5, 9–11)

The Christian community had a problem with "bad shepherds" and "strangers" whispering into the ears of Christians—sometimes within their own ranks and by church leaders—ever since the early Church was founded. In Christ's own warnings to seven representative churches in the Book of Revelation, mere decades after His original departure and the establishment of the church at Pentecost, He spent much of the brief guidance He gave in these letters in addressing heretics they were already dealing with in their midst, including false apostles and Nicolaitans (Ephesus), false Jews and the "synagogue of Satan" (Smyrna and Philadelphia), the doctrine of Balaam (preaching for hire) and Nicolaitans (Pergamos), and prophetess Jezebel and the "depths of Satan" (Thyatira). The apostles and other epistle writers wrote to various churches, warning them about the perpetual battle in exposing a large array of false teachers in each community, even including "they which creep into houses, and lead captive silly women laden with sins, led away with divers lusts, ever learning, and never able to come to the knowledge of the truth" (2 Tim. 3:5–7), and those "whose mouths must be stopped, who subvert whole houses, teaching things which they ought not, for filthy lucre's sake [money]" (Titus 1:11).

However, two major sources of such errant teaching for which the Christian community seemed to be vulnerable were the Judaizers and the Gnostics. The Judaizers must have appealed to fleshly pride of being exclusively the "children of God," as evidenced by their ritual separateness and elitism over others, and righteousness by good works. Alternatively, the Gnostics appealed to the fleshly sin that Eve succumbed to in the Garden by Satan, who promised an experience where "your eyes shall be opened, and ye shall be as gods, knowing good and evil," and knowing man's desire to "make one wise" (Gen. 3:5–6), defying the spiritual experience restrictions God had wisely placed on these neophytes, who were well "out of their league." This pride of spiritual magnification by an independent inward search for "wisdom" which God had purportedly kept hidden or "occult," apart from God's outward and selective revelation, as a means of transcendence and "godhood" as an alternative form of salvation, has always been an alternative seduction to Christians, apart from the legalism of the Judaizers. The epistles of 1 Corinthians, 1 John and Colossians allude to their influences in those communities that the writer addressed, predominantly their insistence on the evils of the physical state and thus the denial of Christ as God in human flesh, or crucified on the cross, or the need for physical purity and the assurance of a physical resurrection. Because this latter heresy has its nature in the beliefs of the recent historical figures we have mentioned as having influence on Christian leaders, such as in the pages of *Faith and Freedom* and with other libertarian leaders, we will briefly explain some facets of Gnosticism further, and then keep it in mind when exploring in depth the true spiritual underpinnings of these figures of influence to Christians, and those in their circles who influence them.

The 1976 book *A History of Heresy*, by the British Oxford-educated Quaker, David Christie-Murray, has a section on Gnosticism. He points out the origin of their name being derived from the Greek word for knowledge, *gnosis*, as "Gnostics claimed to have a secret knowledge that was the key to salvation."[146] He writes that "Their beginnings preceded Christianity by many years," and "the problem which concerned all Gnostics was the reconciliation of the existence of evil with God who is good," and thus "since God is good and the material world is evil, he cannot have created it" (p. 21). He clarifies that they believed that God was a "First Father or Principle, eternal aeon," who created other spiritual beings, often paired in sexes (usually personifications of fundamental virtues, like Love or Patience, and even Christ and the Holy Ghost), numbering up to thirty, and who deteriorated in perfectness the farther they "emanated" from Him by breeding newer pairs, the last being Sophia (Wisdom), who in lust bred the most imperfect Demiurge (p. 21). This last figure (or his son, Yahweh from the Bible, in some systems), not only created a corrupt physical world and mankind for which he held in contempt, but also was ignorantly unaware of the higher Aeon divine figures, and thus thought he was the only God of the universe (which is their explanation of the self-omnipotence of what they viewed as the mean-spirited God of the Old Testament). In fact, in 1 Timothy 1:4 Paul tells church leader Timothy to "neither give heed to fables and endless genealogies, which minister questions, rather than godly edifying which is in faith," and told church leader Titus in Titus 3:9 to "avoid foolish questions, and genealogies, and contentions and strivings about the law"; in both cases, the Greek word for "genealogies" (*genealogia*, Strongs G1076), is explained as "the orders of aeons, according to the doctrine of the Gnostics" in *Thayer's Greek Lexicon*, which were the "genealogies" of spirit beings born from higher order *aeons*, which the Gnostics would debate as to their proper order, *as nauseum*, in their culture.

Importantly, Christie-Murray points out that a central premise of Gnosticism is that "Christ came to bring *gnosis*," and that in addition to the base fleshy passions and corruptions the Creator God Demiurge/Yahweh had created man from, Sophia had also secretly infused a higher spiritual essence—a "spark of the divine"; they also believed that most men had no such spiritual element, "and would be annihilated" (p. 22). They also saw the body as an "earthly prison," and to pass the various evil gods/demons that controlled the outer planets between us and the True Source, man would have to obtain the gnosis (occult knowledge) of the names of these entities and proper password at each stage to control them and pass by (the same teaching as in Isis worship and Egyptian and Babylonian Mystery religions, the Kabbalah/Merkabah element of Orthodox Judaism, and even Western Freemasonry (in a way)), incorporating "whatever there is of truth in all religions" (p. 21). He adds that in the Gnostic system, "Salvation was not by mere faith and love but by revealed speculative knowledge, *esoteric intuition* or by *magical rites*, instruction and *initiation* (p. 21) (emphasis added)—*the latter "magical rites" and "initiation" often performed with the drug-induced pharmakeia element of sorcery; remember the phrases in this sentence throughout this lengthy chapter.* He adds that "The heart of Gnosticism was mystery, free spirit from matter," and that "In Christian Gnosticism knowledge was supposed to come from oral teaching of Jesus, which was never committed to writing (p.

21). He writes that "There were three stages of Gnostic development. The pre-Christian drew its inspiration from Greek, Jewish and eastern sources. In the second stage, a still mainly heathen Gnosticism used Christian ideas to fill up the gaps....The third stage presented Christianity modified by Gnosticism to make it acceptable to religious-minded, intellectual pagans, and in this form was heretical and a real danger to orthodox Christian belief" (p. 21). He writes that

> Gnosticism, though beginning before Christianity, had early connections with it. Dositheus, said to have been a disciple of John the Baptist and therefore a contemporary of Jesus, was a Gnostic. He inspired Simon Magus, regarded by some Samaritans as "that power of God which is called the 'Great Power' " (Acts 8:10)—that is, the chief emanation from the Deity and thus entitled to divine worship....Simon is shown in Acts as a Christian believer, baptized by Philip and reacting humbly when reproved by Peter for trying to buy the gift of the Holy Spirit with money. But he reneged, for though not necessarily a full-blown Gnostic himself, the patristic writers regarded him as the father of heresy, the begetter of several Gnostic systems and the first to combine Gnostic elements with Christianity. He was the reputed author of the Gnostic work called *The Great Revelation*, of which fragments remain....according to Justin Martyr, writing about a century later, he went further, claiming to be the first or supreme God....Irenaeus wrote of him: "This man, then, was glorified by many as if he were a god; and he taught that he himself had appeared among the Jews as the Son but descended in Samaria as the Father while he came to other nations as the Holy Ghost. One of Simon's disciples was Menander. He practiced magic, for Gnosticism was theurgical as well as theological....his disciples, Basilides and Saturninus, both developed their own versions of the creed. (pp. 24–25)

These teachings began to assert that "Jesus was not crucified but that Simon of Cyrene, who was compelled to carry the cross, was transfigured into the likeness of Christ and was crucified instead. Jesus was given the appearance of Simon and, standing by, laughed at the mistaken Romans and Jews" (p. 25). *This teaching, adopted by many major Christian heretical groups and even Islam, not only makes Jesus look cruel, but also strips away from Christianity its most essential and defining element—the vicarious atonement of Christ on the cross for the sins of mankind, restoring their fellowship with the Father, and the eternal symbol of the Church itself as the symbol of its redemption.* Christie-Murray notes that "A very early heresy, [early church teacher] Jerome wrote that it came into vogue 'while the apostles were still surviving, while Christ's blood was still fresh in Judea, the Lord's body was asserted to be but a phantom'; and in John comes the assertion that 'every spirit which acknowledges that Jesus Christ has come in the flesh is from God, and every spirit that does not thus acknowledge Jesus is not from God' (1 John 4:2)" (p. 25). He writes that "The Nicolaitans mentioned in Revelation (2:6, 15) as hated by God may not be the same as the sect condemned by the patristic writers a hundred years later. If they were, their heresy was the common Gnostic condemnation of the Creator God of the Old Testament"; other Gnostics taught that those who did not ascend spiritually "were doomed to reincarnation" (p. 26).

Of the spiritual classes of men, they taught that the lowest, the "pagans," were materialists, while "others called psychics have a soul and believe in the Demiurge, but are unaware of the spiritual world above—these include the Jews and the ordinary Christian churchgoers. Those who are spiritual are open to the promptings of their guardian angel who accompanies them throughout their lives, reveals gnosis to them...History is a necessary progress from materialism and paganism by way of religion and ethics to spiritual freedom gained by gnosis" (pp. 28–29). They add that "When every spiritual being has received gnosis and become aware of the divinity within himself, the world-process will end" (p. 29). Christie-Murray adds that "Even after its disappearance as organized sects during the fifth century, Christian Gnosticism has continued as a strain of thought in much speculation since" (p. 30).

Stephan A. Hoeller, director of the Gnostic Society of Los Angeles "and a leading figure in contemporary Gnostic activities" and author of a number of Gnostic historical books and its connection to Carl Jung, wrote a sympathetic explanation of the belief in the book *The Inner West—An Introduction to the Hidden Wisdom of the West*. His succinct description of this belief system is that "Gnosticism is the teaching based on Gnosis: the knowledge of transcendence arrived at by way of interior, intuitive means," and "rests on personal experience."[147] Hoeller states that "The Gnosticism with which we are most familiar flourished among Christian sects in the first few centuries of the Christian era," and notes that most of what we used to know about them were from the "heresiologist Church Fathers of the second through fourth centuries, C.E.," which were "authors entirely hostile to the Gnostics (Irenaeus, Hippolytus, Tertullian, Epiphanius)," and who taught that it was a "Christian heresy," or a "deviant and corrupted form of the 'real' or mainstream Christianity," or "Paganism with a Christian coating" (p. 43)—*this would likely be because of their use of common Christian words such as "Christ" or "salvation," albeit with different meanings that could confuse gullible Christian inquirers, as is common with the New Age movement today.* He asserts that these views were "demolished" by nineteenth-century German scholars, who claimed that they were merely just other competitive varieties of Christianity at the time, albeit "far less rigidly monotheistic," and with a "feminine emphasis" that "may have had a relation to Egyptian or Greek goddess worship" (p. 43). He also notes that a "Pagan variant of Gnosticism, called Hermeticism, existed side by side with Christian Gnosticism," with possible influences from Persia, India and elsewhere in Asia, as well as Hinduism and Buddhism, noting that "these great Eastern traditions recognize a form of Gnosis, called *Jnana* in Sanskrit, which is regarded as a salvific form of enlightening knowledge," and even of "Jewish historical provenance" and associated with "Jewish Chariot-mysticism" [Merkabah] and the origins of Kabbalah," according to the Nag Hammadi library discovery (p. 44).

Hoeller summarized Gnosticism, in his view, as "a Jewish esoteric spirituality that assumed a Christian form after the coming of the Christian dispensation," which was "subsequently repressed by a self-declared orthodoxy," while early Gnostic literature asserts that their beliefs were taught by Old Testament figures like Adam and his son Seth (p. 45). He says that the Gnostic believes that "the world was flawed because it was created in a flawed manner," and humans are "strangers living in a world that is flawed and absurd," and rather than other religions that believe that "humans are to be blamed for the imperfections of the world" such as the Fall, Gnostics believe that "this interpretation of the myth is false. The blame for the world's failings lies not with humans, but with the Creator," thus with monotheistic faiths, "this Gnostic position appears blasphemous," although the author asserts that "it is in fact the most sensible of all explanations" (pp. 46–47). Hoeller affirms that "The basic Gnostic myth has many variations, but all of these refer to Aeons, intermediate deific beings who exist between the ultimate, True God and ourselves," and that one of them, Sophia, birthed the Demiurge, who created a corrupted world such as himself and being unaware of his own created origins, "imagined himself to be the ultimate and absolute God," and whose name means, "half-maker," who does not recognize the other divine half in humans, known as the spiritual "divine spark" connected to yet higher powers, which many are ignorant of possessing (p. 48). He also confirms that that the "psychic" amongst humanity "mistake the Demiurge for the True God" and have no awareness of higher spirituality, and as humanity progresses from materialism to "liberating Gnosis," that "This kind of evolution of consciousness was envisioned by the Gnostics, long before the concept of evolution was known" (p. 49).

Although Gnostics often have viewed Jesus as a principal "savior," Hoeller clarifies that *"Gnostics do not look to salvation from sin (original or other), but rather from the ignorance of which sin is a consequence.* Ignorance—*whereby is meant ignorance of spiritual realities—is dispelled only by Gnosis,"* brought by Christ and "Messengers of Light," and "It is *not by His suffering and death but by His life of teaching and His establishing of the mysteries that Christ has performed His work of salvation"* (p. 50) (emphasis added)—*a key distinction from historic Christianity that today's practicing Christians must never forget.* He adds that "Gnostic salvation may easily be mistaken for an unmediated individual experience" (p. 50), while (in a very important understanding of the free-wheeling "spirituality" of the Sixties) "morality therefore needs to be viewed primarily in temporal and secular terms; it is ever subject to changes and modifications in accordance with the spiritual development of the individual" (p. 51) and that "it falls to the intuition and wisdom of every individual 'Gnostic' to distill from these principles individual guidelines for personal application" (p. 52). Hoeller also shows the close connection of the psychological philosophies of Carl Jung and his perceived psychological relevance of Gnostic insights and the Nag Hammadi library discovered in the 1950s, as this ancient teaching prefigured and clarified "the nature of Jungian spiritual therapy" (p. 53), and concluded that "The Gnostic worldview is experiential and based on a certain kind of spiritual experience in Gnosis" (p. 54).

This Gnostic worldview, that man is in an absurd, illusory world for which he rightfully does not understand or fit in, and that some will achieve "gnosis" of a higher, truer reality above it and try to ascend, has proliferated our culture in myths that is now its common means of disseminating its beliefs, even in modern entertainment like *The Matrix* movies, or even *The Truman Show*. For some reason many Christians through the ages have been seduced by such beliefs, with its promises of "deeper knowledge or wisdom" and obtaining "self divinity" above the Creator ("what some call the deep things of Satan" (Rev. 2:24, ESV)), and today is no exception. A perceptive reader will not only recognize the worldview just considered and its terminology as being basically coincident with the New Age Movement, but while portions of the mystical Christianity tradition associated with the recent "Emergent Church Movement" might possibly have some merit for a mature believer, many of its elements would have similar perceptions as well. *For all readers, please take note and remember all of the specialized terms used in this brief description of Gnosticism, such as "intuition," "inner knowledge," "self-divinity" and "initiation" into deeper spiritual truths that transcend the physical realm, exhibiting either extreme asceticism and physical mortification, or the opposite of libertine "free love" and moral latitude (both of which debase and disregard the importance of the physical body and its functions), and even the assistance of theurgic, entheogen drugs as shamanic sorcery pathways for communication with higher beings. Also remember its contrast and contempt for the "offense of the cross" and the finished work of Christ, and the latter's acknowledgement of sin and atonement as the sole work of God rather than man (as opposed to the "evolutionary spiritual ascent of man"). We will now see repeatedly that they are the beliefs of the men we have met so far (and their prominent "fellow travelers") who have influenced libertarian thought and "Big Business," including the "Christian" forms as taught to hundreds of thousands of clergy via Faith and Freedom and other media "organs."*

Let's now consider a couple of interesting gentlemen that were colleagues of Fifield's and mentioned in Kruse's book and other references we have cited—one of which who served as his executive peer and successor at Spiritual Mobilization, and another who was one of the most popular and eclectic contributors to the spiritual content of its influential journal, *Faith and Freedom*, and both of whom had an incalculable spiritual, philosophical and intellectual influence on a critical mass of our nation's pastors at the time, and the generations of other clergymen as well as parishioners they themselves have trained.

The biography of the aforementioned James C. Ingebretsen on an online site listing his collection of working papers kept at The University of Oregon library archives[149] notes that

> James Ingebretsen was born on November 21, 1906, in Salt Lake City, Utah. His father, a lapsed convert to Mormonism, practiced law in Utah. The Ingebretsen family enjoyed considerable affluence and James benefited from this. In the late 1920s, he attended Stanford University and graduated magnum cum laude in 1930. During the Great Depression, he attended Stanford University Law School; then, practiced corporate law in Los Angeles. The Second World War brought Ingebretsen to Washington, D.C., where he served as counsel for the Los Angeles Chamber of Commerce. In 1942, he received the distinction of being appointed General Counsel and Director of Governmental Affairs for the Chamber of Commerce of the United States....In 1945, over the opposition of waterfront labor unions, L.A. Mayor Fletcher Bowron appointed Ingebretsen to the board of Harbor Commissioners.

> Given that Ingebretsen did not experience the Great Depression as most Americans did, it may not be surprising that he became an opponent of Franklin Roosevelt's New Deal programs. Ingebretsen's

opposition was channeled in large part through his participation in the Spiritual Mobilization (SM) organization....Ingebretsen served as the Society's general council and as an executive vice-president before agreeing to head the organization in 1954, at the height of the country's anti-communist crusade. Later in life, Ingebretsen expressed doubts about his spiritual commitment to SM; nevertheless, he remained at its helm until 1961 when the organization was disbanded.

Ingebretsen's spiritual misgivings with SM stemmed in part from a life-changing event that occurred in New York City in 1955. Ingebretsen experienced a "spiritual awakening" at age forty-nine that prompted him to interrogate the meaning of his life. Ingebretsen decided that hearing the voice of his dead infant daughter meant he needed to attain spiritual balance in his life. He took the name Kristifer and said that he dedicated his life to changing the world through inner, spiritual refinement. A friend, Gerald Heard, became central to this transformation. A philosopher, scholar, and close associate of Aldous Huxley, Heard guided Ingebretsen in meditation and "attunement," and he introduced Ingebretsen to his own variety of spiritual libertarianism. Heard guided Ingebretsen in "wayfaring," a method of individual spiritual development intended to bring about liberation and positive change in the world.

Ingebretsen credited Heard with being his "soul guide," yet Ingebretsen also drew on other belief systems. Ingebretsen said he wanted to merge "Eastern and Western" beliefs in his spiritual study and practice. He did so by studying with Wen-Shan, Ira Progoff, and Pir Vilayat. Ingebretsen adopted Tai Chi Ch'uan from Wen-Shan; he learned about "the deep, personal psyche" from philosopher and mystic Ira Progoff; and he learned Sufi'ism from Pir Vilayat. Ingebretsen became a Sufi cherag and was initiated into the seventh degree of Ancient Chisti Order. Between the late 1950s and the 1970s, Ingebretsen drew from other thinkers and mystics and their ideas including Shibayama Roshi (hatha-yoga), Virginia Warner (Tai Chi Ch'uan), Harry Butman (Congregationalism), Darrell Miya (Advaita philosophy and Zen instruction), Alan Watts (philosophy), Robert Gerard (psychology), Joseph Campbell (mythology), Peter Drucker (business management), Dane Rudhyar (astrology), J. Krishnamurti (religious philosophy), and Douglas Johnson (psychic).

Ingebretsen's personal spiritual journey drew from many different people and ideologies, and he gave in return. In 1957, he purchased land in San Jacinto and began a spiritual retreat center called Academy of Creative Education (ACE), later known as Koan of the

Cross. Ingebretsen hosted retreats that brought these spiritual instructors together to think and teach. He also offered them grants and legal advice and he managed their business affairs. Soon after meeting Pir Vilayat, Ingebretsen helped incorporate a U.S. Sufi Order and he served on its governing board. Ingebretsen's patronage extended to numerous foundations with which he was involved including the Foundation for Social Research, the Blaisdell Institute for Advanced Study in World Culture and Religion (at Claremont College and associated with Heard), Dialogue House Associates, Mid-Life Opportunities for Renewal Experience (started in 1974), the Gnostic Society, and [occult philosopher Manley P. Hall's] Philosophical Research Society (which published his autobiography).

Ingebretsen identified the purpose of his life to be his personal spiritual development. This orientation merged his spiritual seeking with his libertarian philosophy. Ingebretsen wanted to document his own spiritual journey in order to offer his experience as a model for others to follow. Consequently, he wrote his autobiography and collected a considerable amount of documents related to his life—which he donated to the University of Oregon Special Collections beginning in the 1980s. Despite the many twists and turns in Ingebretsen's spiritual life, he remained committed to spiritual and ethical libertarianism throughout his life. Thus, his papers offer a unique contribution to the University of Oregon's special collections pertaining to libertarians and conservatives.

Ingebretsen's active involvement in spiritual change and research organizations declined in 1976 when he developed health problems and began to lose his sight. He recounted that he used his blindness as an opportunity to further self-examination. He focused inward even more following the death of his wife Dorothy (nee, Dorothy Blanche Hitchcock). He also began to write and to compile documents associated with his life. In the 1980s he wrote, with Sondra Till Robinson, *Primordia: A Glimpse of Hermes*, and he completed his autobiography, *Apprentice to the Dawn*, prior to his death in 1999. His autobiography was published in 2003.

The university archive page adds that "In conclusion, the latter portions of the collection emphasize various forms of 'growing-edge spirituality' (a term coined by Gerald Heard) that frequently conjoin Western Gnosticism and Jungian analytical psychology. A related strength is the collection's focus on the nexus of science and spirituality. The (now defunct) journal, *Growing Edge*, is one testimony both to this synthesis and to the seminal role played by Heard in Ingebretsen's development." The web page[150] of Ingebretsen's own *Apprentice of the Dawn* autobiography further adds that

Ingebretsen was fortunate to have already made the acquaintance of the writer and thinker, Gerald Heard, who guided him through the first months after his awakening....His search for spiritual knowledge, which began with his background in Christian teachings, soon expanded to encompass Eastern religions, several forms of meditation, and various experiments with Heard and others to achieve a more profound understanding of divine energies and their interplay with human consciousness. In 1957, Ingebretsen purchased a 270-acre property located in the foothills of Mount San Jacinto in southern California, which he eventually operated as a retreat center known as Koan of the Cross. Five years before the founding of Esalen, Koan of the Cross was a gathering place for dozens of inspiring and gifted teachers from all over the world in a variety of spiritual, religious, psychological, and cultural disciplines. These teachers included such luminaries as Joseph Campbell, the famous writer on mythology; the philosopher, Alan Watts; Dane Rudhyar, a composer and astrologer; and the religious philosopher and educator, J. Krishnamurti....In 1974, after fire and floods had ravaged the land at Koan of the Cross, Ingebretsen sold the property and returned to live full-time in his home on the Palos Verdes Peninsula near Los Angeles....He continued to explore the meaning of several myths while evolving his daily "attunement" practices, his techniques for staying in touch with the divine forces which had entered his life in 1955.

On his page describing his autobiography,[151] it further adds that "Along the way he participated in early experiments with LSD." The Foreward[152] to the book at his website also notes that he "experienced a well-nigh classical conversion experience (*metanoia*) at a Salvation Army chapel in 1955," and that "He became an associate of Manly Palmer Hall, and corporate counsel of the Philosophical Research Society," but while at "the summit of his power," it notes that "Overnight he almost completely lost the sight of both of his eyes." The website's "Links" page[153] includes "The Gnostic Society" and Manly P. Hall's (author of the mystical *The Secret Teachings of All Ages* and *The Secret Destiny of America*) "Philosophical Research Society."

Possibly the first political and academic conservative/libertarian organization of the Twentieth Century in America was the Intercollegiate Studies Institute. According to their explanation of their purpose on their website, entitled "About ISI",[154] it explains its formation in 1953 and first leader, the famous William F. Buckley, Jr., with its "core beliefs" of "Limited Government," "Individual Liberty," "Personal Responsibility," "The Rule of Law," "Free Market Economy" and "Traditional Values," the latter embracing the "values, customs, conventions, and norms of the Judeo-Christian tradition," and the dependence of the new President Reagan on the leaders trained by the organization. A webpage of the organization's journal, *First Principles*, with a descriptive entry on "Spiritual Mobilization" (S.M.),[155] adds further details on Ingebretsen's tour at the helm of the organization, adding that "During its heyday in the critical decade of the 1950s, S.M. underwent a dramatic mutation when S.M.'s new president James C. Ingebretsen (1906–99), an influential Los Angeles libertarian lawyer, attempted to steer S.M. in new directions. First, he *emphasized libertarian political economy approaches*, going beyond Fifield's anticommunist focus. More importantly, he steered the organization toward *the emerging transformational human-potential paradigm formulated by Aldous Huxley's intellectual mentor, historian-philosopher Gerald Heard* (1889–1971). Though a generation in advance of their time, Ingebretsen's ideas marked a historic watershed that distinguished two different approaches to the libertarian theory of social change. Spiritual Mobilization dissolved soon thereafter in 1961" (emphasis added).

Speaking of Gerald Heard, the June 1956 edition of SM's *Faith and Freedom* newsletter, which can be reviewed online,[156] exhibits its veneration of Gerald Heard in its feature story by Associate Editor Thaddeus Ashby, "Exploration into Gerald Heard." (The inside cover confirms the position of James C. Ingebretsen as President, and James Fifield, Jr. as Chairman, with Thaddeus Ashby as Associate Editor; it mentions at the time its current circulation of 22,256, with their radio program *The Freedom Story* on over 400 stations, and their newspaper column *Pause for Reflection* in nearly 400 newspapers.) The article begins with a statement at the top that gives a mystical foundation for the discussion in the article, *in a journal which is intended to provide a Christian witness for its audience of Christian ministers:*

> Wanted: Ministers, psychiatrists, artists, laymen, to embark on a dangerous voyage to the beyond which is within. You may encounter terror and confusion. More awful than the voyage of Columbus, this one seeks an undiscovered treasure island of ineffable riches Within your Self. Pilot: Gerald Heard. Destination: Unknown.

The article quotes Aldous Huxley, the author of the famous dystopian novel *Brave New World* (in which the masses are drugged into stupor, while the elites rule), and author of the 1954 book (written two years before this article) *The Doors of Perception*, describing his own experiences in ingesting psychedelic substances (later that year ingesting them alongside Heard), who reportedly said that "Gerald Heard is that rare being—a learned man who makes his mental home on the vacant spaces between the pigeon-holes." They quote "poet-philosopher Christopher Isherwood" as saying that "I believe he has influenced the thought of our time to an extent which will hardly be appreciated for another fifty years." They note psychologist and author Dr. W. H. Sheldon as saying that "Gerald Heard may well be the best informed man alive." To the question whether Heard is religious, the article cites the following theologians, which was meant to impress the clergy readers as to Heard's religious credentials:

> You learn that he was on his way toward ordination in the Episcopal Church. What do preachers think of him? You find that Willard L. Sperry, former Dean of the Harvard Divinity School, said: "Gerald Heard…feels deeply the spiritually poverty stricken state of our modern world, and our need of a rebirth of personal religion….His indubitable intellectual skills are supplemented by a touch of authentic saintliness which gives to what he says the authority of the prophet…." And from the Reverend John Haynes Holmes, author and lecturer, you hear: "Gerald Heard is a scientist, seer, and a saint. The combination is impressive."

When Heard was asked, "What sort of Christian are you?" He reportedly replied that "My book, *Training for the Life of the Spirit*, is drawn largely from the Christian sources I most admire. I admire the neo-Platonists, St. Augustine, Francois de Salles, Catherine of Genoa, and William Law. I am not a Modernist because the Modernists don't take a sufficiently spiritual or psychological view. I believe in miracles and the Inner Light." The author notes that Heard was once the science commentator for the British Broadcast Corporation (BBC), causing famous author H. G. Wells to comment that "Heard is the only man I ever listen to on the wireless. He makes human life come alive," and then came to America in 1937, supposedly being offered the chair of Professor of Anthropology at Duke University, and also lecturing on sociology. He then settled in California, and had turned out thirty books by that time. The article author then attended one of his local lectures, noting that "You're surprised to see so many *celebrities, artists, film technicians and engineers*. What's the common denominator that pulls *capitalists, publishers, psychiatrists, actors, writers together*, binding Philistia to Bohemia?" (emphasis added). The author notes what appears to me to be his signature of the many "name-dropping" incidents Heard does in citing diverse thinkers and commentators, weaving together a storyline of some murky philosophy, when he surmises, "From all the quotations Heard gives you, and the way he relates them, you begin to see an outline of a map to guide your inward exploration. *'The Kingdom of Heaven is within you.'* 'There is a sun imprisoned in your Self.' Of this treasure to be mystically found in one's Self, Heard replies that 'The poets and prophets have always known about it. The mystics, the saints and the poets do not contradict each other. Now the scientists, psychiatrists, the physicists, chemists and brain surgeons are discovering it. I find these discoveries most exciting. The scientists are waking up to the power within the soul'."

Author Christopher Isherwood, present at the lecture, confirmed that he and Aldous Huxley "owed a great debt" to Heard and that Huxley's message changed after having met Heard, while he said of himself regarding Heard, "He helps me relate everything to a larger plane. He does it indirectly. By talking. He has been constantly talking for eighteen years, has spoken to psychiatrists, industrialists, the top communicators in every field…He is one of the most influential people (subtly influential) alive….he is interested in absolutely everything—(including suspect topics) and he has an impact on everything." When asked what were the "suspect topics" he was referring to Heard about, he replied, "For example, *take flying saucers*…Heard wrote a book about them called *Is Another World Watching?*," and referred to his writing on *Bridey Murphy—a 1950s woman who claimed to have been a 19th-century Irishwoman in a past life* (emphasis added). Isherwood also admitted the common criticism of Heard that he never completely answered questions, say that "It's maddening. He never answers in a simple, pat way that closes the subject. The soul of his talk is quoting. He always quotes some tiny, anomalous detail," and when asked if Heard actually contributes new ideas, he replied, *"It's not his ideas that are important. It's his state of mind. He's completely open"* (emphasis added).

The author notes Heard's numerous citation of Hindu and Buddhist sources, and asks Heard if he is truly a Christian or not, to which Heard replies that "What do you mean by Christian? Baron von Hugel, the eminent Roman Catholic theologian, said there were five Christianities, each formed to solve a contemporary need. *I don't believe that Christianity is finished. There is more revelation to come. Official, established Christianity proves that nothing fails like success…We need a contemporary Christianity"* (emphasis added). When the author told Heard it sounded like he was hedging his bet, Heard further replied, "Which would help you more? An easy answer, or an answer which asks you questions about yourself? Of course, you can find out what kind of Christian I am by reading *The Creed of Christ,* or *The Code of Christ.*" The author also cites Heard's detective novels, which somehow led Heard to supernatural stories, and the "terrors of the mind," which led to his pursuit of the "ecstasies equal to the terrors" in the mind, and a new type of religion as a result, and explained "Heard's attempt to combine religion with psychiatry," and possibly a "science of the soul," and developed a list of "break through books," which the author said were available from the Christian clergy publication *Faith and Freedom.*

He noted new breakthroughs in the science of the brain, and the discovery of new control centers, adding that, *"Manipulate these control centers, and perhaps you could manipulate the person"* (emphasis added). The author notes that these kinds of discussions at these lectures draw the rapt attention of audience members such as music virtuoso Igor Stravinsky, or William Mullendore, Chairman of the Board of the Southern California Edison Company (the local power company) [with Mullendore and his company being key figures in the "America Under God" campaigns of the mid-century]. When the article author asked Heard what his idea of "god" was, he replied, "God has but one purpose, to keep us pointed toward freedom....*Our great need is not for judges or dividers to redistribute property"* (emphasis added)—*a curious ending to an article and final statement by a man presumably consumed with esoteric matters, but certainly a central doctrinal message of the magazine's patrons and management, and possibly one "snuck in" on the enraptured listeners in Heard's lectures. Is Heard a deep thinker and uniquely spiritually-connected man with God, or a con-man that uses a never-ending flood of spiritual-sounding words and an agile ability not to be pinned down or give discrete findings that can be tested and verified, like many an Eastern religion charlatan in the same era and community (and pool of gullible devotees amongst the rich and poor) in Southern California—you be the judge.*

Regardless of Heard's consistently evasive answers as to his religious orthodoxy, the same edition of *Faith and Freedom* featured a routine article submission by Heard himself (a regular and featured contributor) regarding China's recent success on American prisoners in Korea with "brain washing," though not by the use of drugs. He notes that one-third of American POWs succumbed to their ideological techniques, amongst those of both high and low IQ, with those of strong religious convictions being the most resistant. He states that "Long ago, at the beginning of Christianity, its most powerful Propagandist, the Apostle Paul, told his raw recruits who were facing the unquestioned strength of the Roman Empire that they weren't fighting with flesh and blood-but against spiritual powers," and argues that the best institution to prepare our youth from Communism is the church and not the state (including military), because, in a statement showing a true libertarian unique contempt for the state, "The structure of the state, though we still call it free and democratic, is constantly coercive. It is government by threat," and the remedies should be transmitted by vision and example, not coercion. *Heard, and libertarians in general, are right in that the role of the State is to be coercive in matters to restrain others supposedly for the collective good or on behalf of innocent individuals (which will at times restrain the individualism of others as well as institutions that infringe on others). However, in their contempt for its particular coercive force, they ignore the competing coercive forces of Mammon and the wealth/financial class, both as collective institutions and individuals, using direct force in the marketplace or through proxies such as the media (or even pulpits) and even armies-for-hire, for which a properly-executed state can be a potential rival coercive force without a personal financial interest (at least ideally). It can thus create a "balance of coercive power" with other coercive forces, for the collective good of both rich and poor, powerful and weak—with the assistance, by testimony and by example and deed, of the (supposedly) non-coercive force of the church, and even other collectives of high moral character.*

The rest of the edition has articles promoting the libertarian philosophy, and book reviews of those such as Aldous Huxley's book *Heaven and Hell*, the 1956 follow-on book to his *Doors of Perception*, whereby he had moved on from mescaline to the more-potent LSD, and was attributing religious experiences such as in historical Christianity as due to tapping into parts of the brain via dietary restriction and the like, and now accessible by psychedelic drugs. The reviewer notes that Huxley points out the pursuit of the "visionary experience" of the inner mind, to which the reviewer observes, "How to get there? Huxley says certain ascetic practices lead you in that direction: meditation, stimulants like mescaline, the hypnotic trance, glittery objects and certain works of art." The review of the new book, *New Concepts in Healing*, notes that the author, British psychologist A. Graham Ikin, "agrees with Jung: The Protestant clergyman today is insufficiently equipped to cope with the urgent psychic needs of our age. It's high time the clergy and psychotherapists joined forces. The author focuses the spotlight on the minister as pastor—shows how psychotherapy can make this role more effective." Another review is of the new book, *Psychology and Worship* by author R. S. Lee, to which the review notes that "On the basis of Freudian psychology, Lee discusses the ordinary forms of worship, the habits and states of mind of the average good Christian. A minister might want to take a second look at his congregation through this window of psychology. Dr. Lee does and notes, for example: 'The hungry sheep look up and are not fed all too often because the pastor offers the desiccated and indigestible food of abstract dogmatics and moral theology'." Adding to this theme, their news section noted the recent meeting of the American Psychiatric

Association, and its presidential address, "Conflict and Cooperation Between Psychiatry and Religion," which called for intentional cooperation between both parties, and regular joint meetings in communities "for their mutual enlightenment." *This, from a newsletter for conservative Christian clergy.*

In addition to articles and book reviews extolling the virtues of Ludwig von Mises, Murray Rothbard and libertarian economics and unregulated ("free") markets, a good bit of the content, even looking back over half a century, can be seen as outright *weird.* A case in point is the piece entitled, "Letter From Peter" by Peter Crumpet (a pseudonym), which appears to be a piece of "gonzo journalism" for a religious publication, of a fictional writer sent to the "South to report on the progress of desegregation and to find out the farmers' reaction to what they call here Eisenhower's Slippery Parity Program," and his written report back to his superior, "Willie." It gives a stereotypical backward picture of rural South Carolina, and their full resistance and resentment of desegregation as a violation of "state's rights," and a "bitterness against Federal Government intervention in their private and State affairs," and is "not necessarily limited to the Negro issue." The article author also quotes the locals' frequent use of the "n-word" (in a backwards primitive English, like the "Lil' Abner" comic strip), while he observes that "The Negro farmhand here is a very stupid human being, at least three grades lower than the Negro in New York, and probably two grades lower than his white master in rural South Carolina," and stating of one nearby, "I don't think he understood more than a word or two of the conversation." He explained to the residents that the same federal government that would make them integrate their schools would also answer their request for price supports for their crops, which was a terrible thing of government control, on both counts, which seemed to get their respect, even getting an Eisenhower administration official to come explain it (presumably fictionally for the sake of the fable). *It is unclear if the article was intended to support local segregation as well as against subsidies to support libertarian principles or not, but it was highly disturbing and offensive, nonetheless.* The edition of *Faith and Freedom* also has a column by Rev. Fifield, mostly recounting his message of the ever-present menace of Communism overtaking America, and offers for his recent address—"Judaism vs. Zionism."

This is the publication that presumably was a major influence on the bulk and significant proportion of America's clergy through the 1950s; Christianity Today was not started as another periodical of broad clerical influence until later that year (1956), while Faith and Freedom had already indoctrinated a major portion of a generation of America's clergy (and those in turn they taught, in the church pew and in the seminary) for over five years beforehand.

More can be said about this enigmatic and significantly influential Gerald Heard. On the official website dedicated to Gerald Heard, a page[157] is present with excerpts of descriptions of Heard and interactions with him by his spiritual "disciple," Spiritual Mobilization President James Ingebretsen, from his autobiography, *Apprentice to the Dawn*. There, he writes:

> The Gerald to whom Ed Opitz had referred was Gerald Heard. Born in London in 1889, he had been educated at Cambridge and then worked in a variety of fields, including a stint on BBC radio as a science commentator and at Oxford as a lecturer. In 1937 he and his friend, Aldous Huxley, chose to emigrate to the United States, and both eventually settled in the Los Angeles area. Here, Gerald busied himself with far-ranging explorations into science, religion, and mysticism, finding much to appreciate in the wide array of cultures and ideas that had taken root in southern California. When I first met him, he was making his living as a speaker and had authored nearly thirty books. Ed Opitz had been responsible for introducing me to Gerald at a luncheon in New York shortly after I became president of Spiritual Mobilization (SM) in the spring of 1954. I knew immediately that I was in the presence of an expansive, deeply penetrating mind....Intrigued with Gerald's ideas, I attended several of his public lectures in Los Angeles.

> These talks stimulated me to approach Gerald about writing one or two essays in SM's monthly magazine, *Faith and Freedom*. I was delighted when he agreed. Gerald's first submission to *Faith and Freedom* in November 1954 was an article called "The Hunger We Have Not Stilled." In it, he advocated that those faced with moral questions needed to stop seeking recovery exclusively through psychoanalysis but turn also to a new form of religion which could provide humanity with purpose, awareness, and a capacity to appreciate human potential. As I sat awkwardly with Ed Opitz and his wife that evening, the conclusion of Gerald's article came back to me clearly. He had said that psychoanalysis was of use only if the patient can be brought within the contagion of one who has a whole conviction of purpose, of being part of a process whereby man is being brought to a new capacity for awareness. Man is approaching a new and wider focus of consciousness which the Hellenistic Greek of the Gospels calls "*metanoia*." We miniscularly mistranslate it by the word "conversion"....Gerald was calling not simply for a conversion of consciousness but for a psychological evolution, indeed a radical mutation of body and mind.

When I approached Gerald to share my startling spiritual awakening, I was not seeking a system of beliefs or set of practices nor a priest, guru, or mentor. Instead, I wanted and needed as much guidance as I was able to assimilate at any one time. I didn't know then that, like the cuckoo bird, Gerald was always willing to lay his eggs in any available nest! We began meeting every Monday morning for discussions that lasted for up to two hours....Gerald was slim—gaunt even—with haunting blue eyes and a curly, red-brown Vandyke beard and moustache....Gerald never answered questions directly and never closed a subject. Rather, nurturing a spirit of curiosity and wonder, he would usually respond to an inquiry with a quotation from a seemingly unrelated source....Without advocating one particular path, Gerald introduced me to a variety of methods of meditation....These efforts continued even after 1966, when Gerald suffered the first in a series of strokes which paralyzed his body and rendered him incapable of communicating....I had felt moved on the plane, in the aftermath of that glow, to compose a brief note to Gerald, now paralyzed and bedridden, and to tell him that perhaps his hopes for me to reach an additional stage of awareness had been realized. His longtime, devoted assistant, Jay Michael Barrie, who was caring for Gerald, replied on June 20, 1969....This was my final communication with Gerald before his death two years later, on August 14, 1971....prior to his death in 1971, he kept me informed of his public speaking engagements, his prolific output of books and essays, television and radio broadcasts, and research into psychedelics before a series of strokes left him unable to speak or write.

This same "Jay Michael Barrie" apparently maintains the Gerald Heard website, as well as an extended chronological biography of Heard. Regarding Heard's origins, Barrie notes[158] that

His boyhood years were unhappy, as his father, who often raged at the boy, subjected him to beatings. His older brothers teased him. Gerald's mother, Maud Jervis Heard, the daughter of Alexander Bannatyne of County Limerick, died when he was a child, and afterward the Rev. Heard remarried. Although his stepmother was fond of him (as he was of her), his excessive need for love made him emotionally vulnerable and overly responsive to the slightest show of kindness. This heightened sensitivity coupled with his uncommonly precocious mind made him an irresistible target of the sadistic teasing for which the English public-school boy is notorious. *Gerald finally learned to fend off the boys' attacks by keeping them absorbed in outlandish, outrageously unbelievable stories that he made up as he went along and which he recounted with such conviction that in the end he became a kind of bard who, so long as his tales could hold the attention and interest of his schoolmates, was left unmolested.* (emphasis added)

...his university years, 1908–1913, were spent at Gonville and Caius College at the University of Cambridge, following in the footsteps of his grandfather, father, and eldest brother....He remained there in residence on a scholarship doing postgraduate work studying theology as a candidate in preparation for Holy Orders and a career as an Anglican clergyman, but subsequently he never pursued ordination....He worked with Lord Robson for two years, having been rejected by the military on physical grounds, as he suffered from a back injury when dropped as a child [his brother died in Egypt in World War I]....From his youth on, it had been Heard's intention to follow in the footsteps of his paternal grandfather Rev. John Bickford Heard (author of a number of religious books), his father, and his eldest brother Alexander St. John Heard, and take Holy Orders in the Church of England. *However, such a probing mind as his, consumed with curiosity and with such a vast spread of interests, had been on a collision course with doubt as to many of the doctrines of Christianity from the time he was in his teens.*...The same reaction occurred with the Wright Brothers' historic 1907 flight, again initially dismissed by a doubting public. *The crash came at last in 1916. The result was a nervous breakdown.* After a long illness, Heard recovered to find that the young man who had wanted to be a priest-missionary had become a scientific materialist with a strong sense of social responsibility....During the time in Ireland he came to know well many of the notables of the time. George Bernard Shaw and his wife Charlotte, W. B. Yeats, Lord Fingall, George Russell, Colonel E. M. House, and Lady Gregory were some of those with whom Heard made friends. (emphasis added)

Barrie continues[159]:

He was reputed to read two thousand books a year and had an extraordinary flow of information about hygiene, sex, paranormal phenomena and the probable destiny of mankind....He published ten books in the 1930s. Because of Sir Julian Huxley's friendship and influence [brother of Aldous, grandson of "Darwin's Bulldog" Thomas Huxley, proponent of natural selection and eugenics, original director of UNESCO and, like Heard, suffered a nervous breakdown at a young age], he was brought in as literary editor of *The Realist*, a monthly journal of scientific humanism, during that periodical's short life of less than one year, from 1929–1930. There he worked with an editorial board composed of, among others, Arnold Bennett, Aldous

Huxley, Julian Huxley, Bronislaw Malinowski, H. G. Wells, and Rebecca West. Pacifists Heard and Aldous Huxley, associated with the Peace Movement, gave lectures in England in support of their cause in the mid-1930s, mainly at London's Peace Pledge Union, a major pacifist organization....*For ten years, from 1932 to 1942, he was active on the council and research committee of The Society for Psychical Research.* As mentioned earlier, in 1929 he published his second philosophical book, *The Ascent of Humanity*, an essay on the philosophy of history that was awarded the distinguished Henrietta Hertz Prize by The British Academy. For four years, from 1930 to 1934, he was the first Science Commentator for the British Broadcasting Corporation, commanding a large and regular listening audience with his fortnightly broadcasts. (emphasis added)

Barrie further continues[160]:

On April 12, 1937, together with his close friends Aldous and Maria Huxley, their then 17-year-old son Matthew, pianist/movie critic Christopher Wood, and Gerald Heard arrived in New York City on the S.S. Normandie. He had been offered the post of Chairman of Historical Anthropology at Duke University but decided, after delivering a series of lectures in that capacity for one term, that university life would be too confining for his curiosity-ridden mind... following a brief joint-lecture tour on world peace with Huxley—his participation in which was cut short by a broken arm—he settled in Southern California by early 1938....But it was in Hollywood where, in 1939, Heard met the aforementioned Swami Prabhavananda, founder of the Vedanta Society of Southern California, and began, under his guidance, the study and practice of Vedanta, which was to give him his final philosophical frame of reference. Referring to Heard's popularizing influence of Vedanta on Aldous Huxley, Christopher Isherwood, and other Western notables, mystery writer Ellery Queen wrote, *"Gerald Heard is the spiritual godfather of this Western movement"*....He also accepted that the nature of this Reality is essentially a mystery. That is, it cannot be understood through or grasped by rational processes; it can only be known through an immediate experience. He accepted further that this Reality was the first cause, the source of all the diversity that we seem to apprehend through the five senses, and which, pervading the diversity and containing it in itself, could be experienced...This self-perpetuating cycle of bondage to greed and the passions goes on and on, life after life according to Vedanta theory. [Note: these last statements should answer Heard's earlier interviewer in *Faith and Freedom* as to his Christian orthodoxy] (emphasis added)

In the final section of the latter life of Heard[161] on the site, Barrie adds that "he was celibate by choice for the latter several decades of his life." He noted his uncanny attractive pull on people, writing that "Most people, at first encounter, were drawn to Gerald Heard by an elusive but compelling attraction that he exerted, quite unconsciously, and by which even he was continually and genuinely puzzled. When asked after his passing what one word best described him, his personal physician instantly replied, 'Magnetism. Even when he was old, speechless, and at the point of death, he still had that magic 'something' which drew one to him'." He lists a long list of friends and admirers, including TV icon (and former *Tonight Show* host) *Steve Allen, Edwin Hubble*, Swami Prabhavananda, jazz great *Dave Brubeck, LSD researcher Dr. Sidney Cohen, actor John Gielgud*, author W. Somerset Maugham, *Alcoholics Anonymous founder Bill Wilson, and conservative leader and Time magazine publisher Henry Luce, and his wife, former congresswoman Clare Boothe Luce*, shown seated with him in 1962 (emphasis added). He also notes that "His 1950 book, *Is Another World Watching?—The Riddle of the Flying Saucers*, among the first full-length works on UFOs, was completed in three weeks," and that "His ideas on *sexuality, viewed as a force that could be harnessed for spiritual evolution* as outlined in 1939's *Pain, Sex and Time*, and his theories on *homosexuality as an evolutionary, spiritual phenomenon*, were maverick" (emphasis added); he also quotes an author who said, "Heard is sometimes championed as the first hippie on earth. He was known to affect long hair and denim and espouse mystical ideas in the 1930's." Barrie states on each of these pages that "Jay Michael Barrie (1912–2001) served as Gerald Heard's personal secretary, business manager and editor, associated with Heard from their meeting in December 1944 until Heard's death in August 1971," and that it was excerpted from Barrie's publication in *Parapsychology Review* in 1972.

One of the books that comes up in research on Heard, and his interactions with Aldous Huxley and even Bill Wilson, founder of Alcoholics Anonymous, as three men who experimented with LSD together, is the 2012 book *Distilled Spirits: Getting High, then Sober, with a Famous Writer, a Forgotten Philosopher, and a Hopeless Drunk*, by Don Lattin, which can be found online (in excerpted form) in Google Books.[162] The book, published by the University of California Press, and praised by one of these men's famous peers, comparative religions professor and author Dr. Huston Smith, gives a lot of salacious details of Heard and these men and those in their circle, with such details otherwise scattered about in various references. He talks about how Heard integrated himself in a circle of gay writers and poets in London, such as Christopher Isherwood, J. R. Ackerley and W. H. Auden, and described them as particularly promiscuous, with Ackerley's biographer writing of Heard that "Heard was particularly interested in homosexuality and spent much energy attempting to discover the psychological impulse behind buggery. Homosexual himself, he was also much taken up with the phenomenon of promiscuity and carried out an ad hoc field study amongst his friends, finding in Ackerley's circle a rich source of primary material" (p. 45). Lattin adds that

> Around this time Heard met a wealthy young dilettante called Christopher Wood. Wood, who was eleven years younger than Heard, was the heir to the British grocery fortune of Petty, Wood and Co....In 1929, Heard and Wood moved into an apartment together at 28 Portman Square in London's West End. They were a bit of an odd couple. Heard was interested in ideas and religion. Wood was a materialist and consumer of fine objects....Wood would become Heard's longtime companion and traveling partner. In 1937, the couple would come to America on the same ocean liner as Aldous, Maria, and young Matthew Huxley....Heard underwent a profound spiritual conversion in the early 1930s that inspired him to chart a new course in life, which included "renouncing sexual relations," said John Roger Barrie, literary executor of the Heard estate and the adopted son of Jay Michael Barrie. "After the conversion, everything changed....He embraced celibacy. He began practicing spiritual disciplines." (p. 146)

If this is true, then it would explain how Heard would be able to live in a fashionable part of Los Angeles with only the modest income from specialty books and an occasional lecture or two, even arriving before real estate there took off, as well as his life-long bachelorhood. This book contains much more data, including the involvement of Heard and Huxley with Alcoholics Anonymous founder Bill Wilson, as they introduced him to LSD, which Wilson wanted to try, to see if he could replicate the spiritual experience he had originally with the "Belladonna Cure" (using belladonna, aka nightshade, and another entheogenic deliriant herb henbane, which gives a sensation of flying, and some have asserted was conflated with myths of witches), which led to his original sobriety. A video of Gerald Heard talking to Dr. Sidney Cohen, who participated in many of these LSD experiments, is currently available on *YouTube*.[163]

Although these previous statements were taken from the abbreviated portions of Don Lattin's book *Distilled Spirits* that are available online via Google, I recommend that the interested reader obtain an actual copy of the fascinating book itself, for it fills in many more fascinating details about

Heard, Huxley, and even Alcoholics Anonymous founder Bill Wilson, and their circles. For example, Lattin notes that Heard inspired Michael Murphy, the co-founder of the famous Esalen Institute (which some view as the founding and central site of the New Age movement in the Big Sur area of California's coast), to found the entity after meeting with him (p. 2). Comparative religions scholar Dr. Houston Smith, author of *The World's Religions* (having sold more than 2 million copies since 1958), had read every book Heard had written, and during his Ph.D work, found Heard in Trabuco Canyon, which led to Heard introducing Aldous Huxley to him (pp. 2–3). Lattin also notes that Alcoholics Anonymous founder Bill Wilson was deeply involved with Heard, having met at Trabuco College in the 1940s and had a lifelong correspondence, and that "they even took LSD together. In fact, Gerald Heard was Bill Wilson's guide on Wilson's first LSD trip in the summer of 1956. Wilson didn't simply try LSD. He started a salon in New York City where he and a group of friends continued to investigate the spiritual potential of psychedelics….Huxley, Wilson and Heard thought LSD, used cautiously, could help some people deepen their spiritual lives" (p. 4). He notes that Wilson, who died in 1971, had founded AA as "one of the most successful *spiritual movements* of the twentieth century" (p. 6) (emphasis added); Huxley stated that Bill Wilson was "the greatest social architect of the twentieth century" (p. 7). Lattin adds that "Wilson's interest in the writings of Gerald Heard inspired him to seek out Heard during Wilson's first visit to California in the winter of 1943–44. Their friendship and spiritual collaboration continued over the next two decades. Wilson's practical, open-minded approach to religion helped change the way Americans envision the divine" (p. 6).

Regarding Heard's associate, *Brave New World* author Aldous Huxley, he writes that he died the same day as John F. Kennedy was assassinated in 1963 (the same day that prominent author C. S. Lewis also died, I might add), and experienced a "long, happy, and unorthodox marriage to Maria Nys, a bisexual born in Belgium," spending the last twenty-five years of his life in Southern California, and that "Heard was Huxley's best friend and one of his most important mentors," having met in London in 1929 and headed to the U.S. together in 1937 (p. 5). He notes that Heard wrote "pioneering articles on gay spirituality," and but that "the so-called godfather of the New Age Movement, was above all a mystic," and "laid the foundation for the human potential movement of the 1960s and 1970s" (p. 6).

Author Lattin admits that he and other children of the 1960s admired men like Heard, Huxley and Wilson because "We didn't want to worship

God. We wanted to *experience* God. Some of us wanted to *be* God. We were not interested in doctrine, dogma, or religious denominations. We wanted instant insight. We wanted to leave ordinary reality behind—to break on through to the other side—and there was no time to waste" (p. 7) (emphasis original).

He notes that "Aldous Huxley was born into a family with a legacy of doubt and disbelief," and his grandfather Thomas Henry Huxley, known as "Darwin's Bulldog" for not only working for Darwin but also being his staunchest public defender, had coined the term *agnosticism* and one "who engaged the religious leaders of his time in spirited public debate," and personally believed that any "gnosis" of the meaning of existence was unsolvable (pp. 11–12). He notes that Aldous and his brother Julian "were baptized in the Church of England and given just enough religious education so they might learn 'the mythology of their time and country' " (p. 12). While Heard suffered under the stultifying and brutal class culture of British schooling, Hattin notes that "Huxley was a big believer in the British boarding school," which kept children from their parents for most of the year, Huxley saying that they have "done much to accelerate the break-up of the family system in England," which Hattin says was "a welcome development in Huxley's view," as Huxley saw in the future a "decrease in the size and power of the family circle," as he wrote in his 1928 essay, *The Decline of the Family* (p. 37). By 1932 Huxley was also lamenting society's loss of its "secular faith," and in particular its "faith in democracy and individualism and personal liberty, and *faith in laissez-faire capitalism and unlimited competition*" (p. 83)—*the big business, libertarian principles of Huxleyian "dog eat dog" Darwinism that would have fit well within the pages of Faith and Freedom.* Even in the 1930s, Lattin notes that Huxley expressed an interest in drugs and altered states of consciousness, believing that such that people use such "stupefacients" because "they are bored with their surroundings and because they are bored with themselves," while it is common for one to "desire to transcend himself," saying that society needs to develop a wholesome substitute to addictive substances—*sounding like his own promotion of the stupefying drug "soma" to pacify and control the proletariat in Huxley's Brave New World, while having his own "psychedelic baptism" by the early 1950s* (p. 84).

Gerald Heard had a strict religious upbringing, which Lattin described as "abusive," with his father and grandfather being priests of Anglican evangelicalism, and Gerald reportedly beaten by his father, brothers and a drunken nursemaid (his mother died when he was four years old) (p. 14). He was then raised by his grandmother, a Christian fundamentalist who taught that "a child's will must be broken," with Heard later stating his grandmother's "belief in eternal damnation had a strong and painful presence on my early life" (p. 14). At school (when he wasn't being bullied), he loved science and the writings of H. G. Wells, while his father wanted him to become a minister, and he studied such at Cambridge for a time (learning Hebrew and the Greek New Testament), and later served on the council of the Society for Psychical Research there until he moved to the States in 1937 (p. 15). He had a nervous breakdown at the age of twenty-seven, on the eve of World War I, with his secretary later surmising that it occurred because Gerald was "on a collision course with doubt as to many of the doctrines of Christianity," changing his interests from the priesthood to scientific materialism with a social responsibility bent (p. 22). Lattin adds that "Another church doctrine that Heard may have struggled with was the church's condemnation of homosexuality, for Heard was also coming to terms with his own sexuality."

Heard's mental breakdown began in 1916, around the time he was introduced to the pleasures of bohemian London," including the Bloomsbury writers and artists (pp. 22–23), eventually meeting Huxley there in 1929, about the time he published *The Ascent of Humanity*. In London, he was introduced to the gay painter Glyn Philpot, who "shared his religious upbringing, his homosexuality, and his loquaciousness" (p. 44). Lattin notes that Heard then "met some of London's better-known gay writers and poets, including Lytton Strachey, Duncan Grant, Christopher Isherwood, W. H. Auden, E. M. Forster, and J.R. Ackerley, who worked with Heard at the BBC," as they "formed a raffish and intellectual circle," and as Heard adopted a " 'slyly exotic' type of dress," and were known as "a notoriously promiscuous lot." Around this time Heard met a wealthy young dilettante called Christopher Wood (pp. 45–46). Wood was an idle rich youth, and they moved in together, although "Heard underwent a profound spiritual conversion in the early 1930s that inspired him to chart a new course in life, which included 'renouncing sexual interactions'," as "he embraced celibacy" and "began practicing spiritual disciplines" (pp. 46–47).

Physical and emotional illnesses kept both Heard and Huxley out of World War I, and they both became Britain's leading pacifists leading up to World War II (p. 23). Although Aldous was battling depression, they both became activists in the Peace Pledge Union, "a British pacifist group that attracted more than a hundred thousand members in the mid-1930s" (p. 90). On the air together at the BBC, Heard and Huxley lamented that the Church had won its security from the deaths of a few thousand martyrs, and then forgot the power of passive resistance, with Huxley replying to Heard that "That's the trouble with organized religion. It provides so many justifications for violence. It is interesting to reflect that, as a matter of historical fact, humanitarianism has increased as organized religion has declined. For when you think you know the absolute truth is, you feel justified in forcing other people to agree with you" (p. 91). Such discussions were planned to be addressed further in their joint trip across America in 1937, in which Huxley also planned to pursue money in the writing of screenplays in Hollywood, as Heard planned to sell off properties in Nebraska and Wyoming he had inherited from an earlier employer (pp. 91–92). Lattin points out that Heard was trying to get Huxley to leave Europe with him as soon as 1933, as Hitler was taking the chancellorship, with Heard "advising us all to clear out to some safe spot in South America or the Pacific Islands before it's too late," according to a letter from Huxley (p. 92). For a road trip across the country, they procured a Ford, which Lattin found ironic since "Henry Ford had been depicted as the Antichrist in *Brave New World* (p. 92) (he adds that the book "envisions a nightmarish future in which Henry Ford is worshipped as God and his assembly-line innovations are used to produce test-tube babies programmed for the seamless operation of an authoritarian state. Any hints of social dissent or spiritual exploration are kept in check by sexual freedom, hypnotic drugs, and mindless entertainment" (p. 95)).

Heard had a motive in this trip also related to his pursuit of parapsychology even at this time, as "Heard, an avid follower of the latest research into psychic phenomena, wanted to visit the Duke University parapsychology lab of professor J. B. Rhine, who was conducting eyebrow-raising experiences in telepathy and extrasensory perception" (p. 92). Heard did not receive the professorship at Duke University he expected to receive as a further pretext for his trip; Lattin opines that "Heard's interest in spiritualism and the academically suspect field of parapsychology may have worked against him, or perhaps there were rumors about his sexual orientation" (p. 93). Eventually the Huxleys and Heard stayed for the summer and fall of 1937 in the mountains of Taos, New Mexico in the austere cabins of the ex-wife of author D.H. Lawrence and their lawyer, *while Huxley's wife complained of the lack of servants there.* Huxley's writing there connected the freedom of amoral sexual relations and lifestyle with the libertarian economic and political philosophies (and its foundations of the meaning of life), writing, that "For myself, no doubt, *for most of my contemporaries, the philosophy of meaninglessness was essentially an instrument of liberation. The liberation we desired was simultaneously liberation from a certain system of morality. We objected to the morality because it interfered with our sexual freedom; we objected to the political and economic system because it was unjust*" (p. 103) (emphasis added). He added that "The chief reason for being 'philosophical' was that one might be free from prejudices—above all, prejudices of a sexual nature...the desire to justify a certain sexual looseness played a part in the popularization of meaninglessness" (p. 103).

When Huxley and Heard finally made it California to stay in the fall of 1937, Huxley described the area that one could view as the West Coast "Burned Over District"—a birthing ground of weird yet influential spiritual movements—writing to a friend in England that in California "almost everything is happening—movies, astronomy, sweated labour in the fields, philanthropy, scholarship, phony religions, real religions, all stirred together in a vast chaos in the midst of the most astonishing scenery, ranging from giant sequoias and rock peaks to date palms and red hot deserts" (p. 106). He described the Hollywood scene as "the strangest variety of people—the movie world in its own little suburb of Hollywood...with its fearful Jewish directors, and the actors, and the film writers, who make more money than any other kind of author and are generally speaking not authors at all" (p. 107). The Huxleys became friends with Charlie Chaplin and Greta Garbo (p. 108), and soon were signed to lucrative screenwriting contracts (p. 109), writing screenplays for *Pride and Prejudice, Jane Eyre*, and others (pp. 110–111). Garbo and wanted to meet J. Krishnamurti—the Indian philosopher whom the occult Theosophical Society had promoted as the world Messiah, but the role of which he eventually rejected, as he set up his retreat center in Ojai, California, about an hour north of Los Angeles, and he began interacting with Heard and Huxley in 1938, becoming close friends (p. 112). Lattin also tells of a legendary October 1939 "picnic" in the remote Hollywood hills, involving the Huxleys, Greta Garbo, spiritual messiah/swami Krishnamurti (and his mistress/devotee Rosalind Williams Rajogopal), Charlie Chaplin and wife Paulette Goddard (who brought champagne and caviar while Krishnmaruti's entourage brought vegetarian food), writer and Huxley/Heard friend Christopher Isherwood and Bertrand Russell, which led to their trespassing and crawling under a fence, and being confronted by a sheriff who refused to believe they were celebrities (pp. 114–117). Huxley and Krishnamurti remained staunch pacifists even as Hitler invaded Poland in the fall of 1939. On *BBC Radio*, Huxley declared that

> For noncombatants, war actually makes life seem more worth living...The first condition of war is that the population of the planet should be divided into organized groups, and that each individual should be conscious of his own group's separateness from and superiority to all other groups. Today these potentially war-making

groups are nations. *Nationalism can be made to yield the individual immense psychological satisfaction. There is the satisfaction, to begin with, of feeling yourself at one with your fellows. This is intensified almost to ecstasy during war. By means of propaganda and patriotic display, it can be kept at a very high pitch even in times of peace. The dictators of modern Europe are all past masters at keeping it perpetually simmering, almost at boiling point...*Like war itself, *nationalism justifies the individual in giving expression to those antisocial impulses and emotions which he has always been taught to repress. The patriot is allowed to indulge with good conscious in vanity and hatred. Vanity in regard to his own group, hatred in regard to all other groups.*" (pp. 113–114) (emphasis added)

Meanwhile, in the late 1930s and early 40s Heard was focused on his inward journey, living in a shack with minimal food consumed and with hours of daily meditation; Huxley's wife drove him around because he refused to drive or own a telephone, as he got into the Hindu Vedanta Society there and its leader, Swami Prabhavananda, who had a "defining impact on Heard, Huxley, and the metaphysical intelligentsia gathering around them in Hollywood" (with their writing for Vendata publications and speaking at the Vendata Temple in Hollywood) (pp. 125–127). His predecessor Vivekananda came to Chicago in 1893 to represent Hinduism at the World's Parliament of Religions, "one of the watershed events in American religious history," which first brought Eastern thoughts to America, and words like *yoga, Zen* and *nirvana* (pp. 127–128). He stayed with an American acolyte in 1900 in California for six weeks, who became the main patron of the Vedanta movement in California, and later hosted Swami Prabhavananda, who was assigned from Calcutta to found missions on the Pacific coast, and allowed the use of their home for the movement (p. 129). Their large Temple was dedicated in 1938 as Heard and Huxley were arriving, both being initiated in the movement, with Heard particularly concentrating on the practice, and Isherwood becoming a lifelong disciple (p. 130). Eventually Heard had enough of the hypocrisy of the swami, and resigned himself to form his own ashram and commune, known as Trabuco College in a desolate area of the California wilderness (p. 136).

Alcoholics Anonymous' Bill Wilson was sixteen months younger than Huxley, and six years younger than Heard, and raised in a strict home in Vermont, with his father a drunk and woman chaser, with his parents divorcing and abandoning him to his grandparents, while his mother took his sister, which devastated him (p. 15). He grew attached to a girl at a boarding school, but her unexpected death caused another crisis in Wilson's life, ending his interest in Christian activities there, and later stating that her death "erased any vestiges he might have had of belief in God," describing himself in later years as an atheist or agnostic (p. 16). Hattin notes that Wilson confessed in 1954 that "He was not a faithful husband. There were other women, younger women, before and after he sobered up. Bill seemed to have persuaded himself that his affairs were psychologically justified," claiming that his wife always saw herself as a mothering figure" (p. 54–55). During the time of Roosevelt, Wilson was another figure who "thought the New Deal was a socialist conspiracy" (p. 55). Lattin notes that the location where Wilson eventually "saw the light" and became sober was the Towns Hospital, where its founder, Charles B. Towns, was known as "something of a quack," as developer of the "Towns-Lambert Cure" (p. 56), or also known as the "Belladonna Cure." He describes that in the treatment patients "were given hypnotic drugs," then "a series of potions to induce the 'puking and purging' stage of treatment; however, the centerpiece was the 'Belladonna Cure,' comprising "a cocktail of herbs, bark, and berries that included two deliriants, *Atropa belladonna* and *Hyocyamus niger*, also known as deadly nightshade and insane root, respectively," and given to them regularly their first two days (p. 56).

Wilson's last visit there was in December 1934, with the Treatment inducing a state in which Wilson said that "suddenly, my room blazed with an indescribably white light. I was seized with an ecstasy beyond description. Every joy I had known was pale by comparison...Then, seen in the mind's eye, there was a mountain. I stood upon its summit where a great wind blew. A wind, not of air, but of spirit. In great, clean strength it blew right through me" (p. 56). While others have described Wilson's experience as a sensation of "flying," and Wilson inquired during his spiritual experience if this was the "god of the preachers" (p. 68), there may be another explanation for the experience he had. The latter root chemical *Hyocyamus niger* is also known as "henbane," and as one of the folk religion root ingredients (along with belladonna/nightshade, and wolfsbane) traditionally associated with witchcraft, and part of what they used as the famous "flying ointment" that legends associated with their flying on broomsticks. One journalist from *The Atlantic*[164] cited numerous historical experts and sources, documenting that these hallucinogenic balm mixtures caused severe illness if ingested, but could achieve their effects without deleterious impact if applied as a balm and contacting the mucus membranes. According to historical records, *this was accomplished by applying the balms to broomsticks, and straddling them between the legs*, while other historical accounts described the sense of flying when being exposed to the concoction.

Other biographers of Wilson point out even more intriguing aspects of his spiritual views and experiences, and how they had an impact on what

Alcoholics Anonymous became and remains today. As one example, his biographer, Susan Cheever, the award-winning author of the 2004 book *My Name is Bill: Bill Wilson—His Life and the Creation of Alcoholics Anonymous* and a specialist on books of alcoholism, addiction and treatment, wrote what she intended to be a respectful and affirming treatment of a man she admired. For example, on a page[165] on her website that describes her reason for writing the book, she writes that

> About five years ago *Time Magazine* asked me to write a profile of Wilson, the cofounder of Alcoholics Anonymous. I was amazed to find that although there had been some books about Wilson including his own and his wife Lois' autobiographies, there had never been a proper, fully documented biography. Bill Wilson is one of the most influential thinkers of the 20th century, a man who founded a movement which changed all of our lives. I felt he deserved the best biography I could write. I began the book respecting him as a teacher and a writer. By the time I finished that respect had doubled and redoubled. I hope that my book does justice to this extraordinary man and gives some sense of his amazing life story.

However, being a well-respected biographer, she was bound to objectively and unapologetically write about all aspects and data concerning his life, "warts and all," even including some of the more curious aspects of his lifestyle and spiritual views. Selected sections of her biography of Wilson can be viewed online at a Google Books page,[166] which displays pages 202 to 206 of her chapter, "The Spook Room," which actually begins on page 201 and extends to page 209. Fortunately, the popular religious news site Beliefnet has posted what appears to be the entire contents of the chapter "The Spook Room"[167] of Cheever's book (upon perusing the contents of both sources). The excerpted passages from this posted chapter that are pertinent to our interests, with details of the unorthodox spiritual pursuits of Wilson and his compatriots as also documented by other biographers, comprise the following:

> ...Catholicism fascinated him [Wilson]. His spiritual adviser, Father Ed Dowling, was a devout Roman Catholic, and although Bill had stopped going to church in a formal way when he left the Congregational Church of his boyhood, he had become a Christian without a church. Nevertheless, Bill Wilson insisted that belief in God was not a prerequisite for membership in A.A....He was proud of the way the program had avoided associating itself with a specific God, limiting itself in the steps to what was called God as we

understood him....In the 1940s Bill met Monsignor Fulton Sheen, the popular Catholic radio host. Sheen, who later converted Clare Boothe Luce to Catholicism, was a man Bill Wilson could talk with. He began visiting Sheen for instruction every Saturday....Bill wrote letters to [Jesuit Father] Ed Dowling about the sweetness of Catholicism, and letters to Sheen laying out his questions.

Bill was also impressed by the story of Mary Baker Eddy, another New England teacher who had preached the connection of the soul and the body in an idea similar to those behind Alcoholics Anonymous. *Eddy also believed, as did Bill, that the living could communicate with the dead.* A powerful woman who had her epiphany after she fell on the ice of a New Hampshire lake and prayed herself back to health, Eddy's movement promoted the idea that all physical ailments were actually spiritual ailments and could be cured through prayer. "The thing that still irks me about all organized religion is their claim how confoundedly right all of them are," [Wilson] wrote to Bob E., an Akron A.A. member.

Bill's spiritual quest extended beyond organized religion. During the calm postwar years of the Truman presidency Bill and Lois, along with Anne and Bob Smith, continued *to investigate psychic and spiritual phenomena.* These days, psychic phenomena and the way people use to understand them and identify them are completely out of favor. For Bill Wilson and Bob Smith, though, *their investigations were part of a tradition of activity in rural New England at the end of the 19th and the beginning of the 20th century...Sometimes the Wilsons used a Ouija board...Lois and Bill, or two or three of the other participants, rested their fingers lightly on the board....On evenings when they decided to use the table instead of the Ouija board, they gathered around it, each person with their fingers resting lightly on the table's sharp edge. They dimmed the lights. Bill's voice would often ask the questions. "Are there any spirits in the room?" he would ask. "Are there any spirits who have a message for us?" Breathing slowed. The spirits seemed to gather in the room's dark corners, above the shelf where Bill's violins and musical instruments were kept....Then the people seated around the table would hear a soft, hesitant tap. Sometimes, if Bill had asked a direct question, the taps meant yes or no: one for yes and two for no. At other times the spirits had a longer message...In an evening the table might tap out a phrase or two. According to both Bill and Lois, on more than one occasion they succeeded in levitating the table a few inches off the floor.* (emphasis added)

*At other times the Wilsons and their guests experimented with automatic writing. Bill Wilson was very good at this. He would set a pen down on a piece of paper, close his eyes and wait for the spirit to guide his hand....*Lying there, he would receive messages, sometimes whole, as when he heard the *Reverend Dwight Moody* warning him against the past, and sometimes they would come to him letter by letter. *One evening the message spelled out appeared in Latin. Not knowing Latin, Bill took the message to John D. Rockefeller's associate Willard Richardson, who studied it and said it appeared to be an account of early Christianity in Italy. In Nell Wing's version of this story, Willard Richardson was in the room while Bill was receiving the message, and the Latin turned out to be a sermon written by St. Boniface.* "They were working away at spiritualism," says a friend who was often a visitor there. "*It wasn't just a hobby.*" On a visit to Nantucket in 1947…[Bill] was accosted by the shade of a Norwegian sailor, complaining that he saw people dimly and that when he spoke no one listened. The sailor was soon joined by the spirit of a man who introduced himself as David Morrow. Morrow told Bill that he had been killed with Admiral Farragut during the Battle of Mobile Bay. Then, as morning came and the kitchen grew brighter, he was joined by two other spirits: former whaling captains named Pettingill and Quigley. When Bill told this story at breakfast, he was met with friendly disbelief. People usually tried to humor Bill in order to avoid arguing with him. Later in the Wilsons' visit to Nantucket, they happened to be at the head of Main Street; there they saw a small Civil War memorial engraved with the name David Morrow. A subsequent visit to the Nantucket Whaling Museum confirmed that indeed Pettingill and Quigley had been the masters of whaling ships. (emphasis added)

Some A.A. members were disturbed by these psychic activities and by Bill's interest in the paranormal….Just as some A.A. members concluded that his depressions might mean that A.A. didn't work, they now decided that Bill's search for voices beyond the grave somehow cast aspersions on the program. Closer to home, the men who worked with Bill almost every day—sophisticated men and women who had come from fields like advertising and publishing—were concerned about Bill's activities in the spook room and on the living room couch at Stepping Stones. Some members thought the psychic activity Bill indulged in made him look crazy; others, who actually believed that he was able to summon spirits from another world, were afraid that he was speaking with evil spirits, or a hodgepodge of ghosts who would almost definitely give him bad advice or try to confuse him. One of the members of the Chappaqua A.A. group, Tom P., remembers that he and a group of fellow recovering alcoholics got so upset about Bill's spooking that they decided to do something about it….Another one of the men, Tony Guggenheim, wrote to a man they all respected—C.S. Lewis at Cambridge, England—to describe Bill and Lois's activities and to ask what he, Lewis, thought of them. Tom P. remembers that Lewis wrote back with total disapproval. "This is necromancy," he wrote. "Have nothing to do with it." Apparently, Bill's colleagues thought that an indictment from a man like Lewis would influence Bill to change his private beliefs. Apparently, they didn't know him very well.

...despite the controversy, they continued to communicate with spirits. In the evening, with a few friends, they would...arrange themselves around a table in the room at the back of the house, or in the wooden and upholstered chairs in the double-height living room in front of the big fireplace. Sometimes they would be joined by believing neighbors, sometimes by A.A. visitors from out of town, sometimes by one or two people from the office or one of the local A.A. groups. Their séances were never a secret. A quiet would come over them, almost as if they were conducting a group meditation....Then there would be an almost inaudible tap, or Bill's quiet voice would begin to form a letter.... They were in the presence of all their own dead, of Bill's cousin Clarence whose sad violin had been Bill's first fiddle, and the stern Fayette and Ella Griffith, of Lois's beloved mother, and her handsome father who read Swedenborg's teachings to his children in the Clinton Street living room, of all those who had passed on before them.

Wilson's real mentor or "sponsor" connected to Christianity well after his founding of A.A. was Jesuit priest Father Ed Dowling. A 1995 book by a fellow Jesuit priest, Robert Fitzgerald, *The Soul of Sponsorship: The Friendship of Father Ed Dowling and Bill Wilson in Letters*, details their communications and relationship on spiritual matters, with excerpts of the work available to review online via Google Books.[168] In the chapter entitled, "The Spiritual Exercises and the Traditions," He writes that Bill asked Dowling for a copy of *The Spiritual Exercises of St. Ignatius* (the founder of the Jesuits) to assist in developing A.A.'s book *The Twelve Steps and Twelve Traditions* (p. 55). In the 1940s Wilson wrote to Dowling, saying regarding his progress on the Twelve Steps and the Twelve Traditions that "I have good help—of that I am certain, both over here and over there," with Fitzgerald explaining that by "over there," he meant the "spirit world" (p. 59). Fitzgerald added that "It was, he said, the voice of Boniface, an apostle from England to Germany, Bavaria, and France, who reformed old church structures, and as bishop with powers from Rome, set up new monasteries and bishoprics," leading Fitzgerald to be surprised that he accepted help from a "dead bishop" (p. 59). Wilson wrote to Dowling that "One turned up the other day calling himself Boniface. Said he was a Benedictine missionary and English....I'd never heard of this gentleman but he checked out pretty well in the Encyclopedia. If this one is who he says he is—and of course there is no certain way of knowing—would this be licit contact in your book?" and also added that Boniface said he was "coming back to earth" (p. 59). Dowling responded that "Boniface sounds like the Apostle of Germany. *I still feel, like Macbeth, that these folks tell us truth in small matters in order to fool us in larger. I suppose that is my lazy orthodoxy*" (p. 59) (emphasis added).

In warning Wilson, Fitzgerald explains that Dowling was reflecting that "The otherworldly voices in *Macbeth* tempt Macbeth to power and the murder of the king, Duncan. *In the Spiritual Exercises, a person is to watch the beginning, middle, and end of a movement to discern whether the movement was from an evil or a good spirit*" (p. 60) (emphasis added). In Wilson's response letter in 1952, Fitzgerald notes that "Bill saw the need for caution in speaking with spirits from the otherworld....but did not want the Church to limit his conversations with the otherworld" (p. 61). Wilson wrote that "It doesn't seem reasonable to think that the Devil's agents have such direct and wide open access to us when other well-disposed discarnates including the Saints can't get through....I don't see why the aperture should be so large in the direction of the Devil and so small in the direction of all the good folks who have gone ahead of us. One can't blame the Church for being cautious but I do sometimes wonder if the view isn't rather narrow and even monopolistic. To assume that all communications, not received under Church auspices, are necessarily malign seems going pretty far....Without inviting it, I still sometimes get an intrusion such as the one I described in the case of the purported Boniface" (p. 61). Fitzgerald further clarified later that "Bill claimed he was helped in writing the *Twelve Steps and Twelve Traditions* by a psychic experience of an 11th century bishop, Boniface" (p. 81).

The key for Wilson associating his mystical experience with an encounter with the divine is the influence of several other men and their associated groups, including Dr. Bob Smith, Rowland Hazard and Ebby Thatcher. Lattin writes in *Distilled Spirits* that Hazard has his own beginnings in this quest at Calvary Presbyterian Church, in meetings held by a controversial organization that normally catered to the powerful and wealthy, known as the Oxford Group, and later as "Moral Rearmament," with Hazard himself hosting meetings for the group by 1934. Thatcher fed Wilson's interest in alternative religions when he gave to Wilson in the hospital, the day after his drug-induced mystical experience, a copy of William James' comparative religions book *The Varieties of Religious Experience* (p. 75). As a sign of the impact of this work on him, Wilson credited James, known as the "father of

American psychology," as the *real* "founder of Alcoholics Anonymous"; James himself had turned away from his father's Presbyterianism, to an old form of mysticism known as Swedenborgianism, which had much in common with spiritualism and likely a precursor of Theosophy and the New Age Movement, and these beliefs of a "God as we understand him" made its way into Wilson's tenets of "AA" (p. 76).

Author Lattin noted that while Wilson and his A.A. cohort Dr. Bob Smith were part of the Christian Oxford Group "Alcoholic Squad," "By 1938, they had split off from the evangelical movement. Forcing drunks to accept Jesus Christ as the personal Lord and savior was not working. Drunks needed only to find a higher power...Individual members could design their vision of the divine. God 'as we understand him' turned out to be the successful formula. In the spring of 1939, the fledgling fellowship published its founding text, *Alcoholics Anonymous*, known by AA members as 'the Big Book' " (p. 137). In 1939 *The Cleveland Plain Dealer* reported that its adherents "have an equally simple, if unorthodox, conception of God," which was based on "religious experience," and can come from "the Thomism of the Roman Catholic Church...the stern Father of the Calvinist. Or the great Manitou of the American Indian. Or the Implicit Good assumed in the logical morality of Confucius. Or Allah, or Buddha, or the Jehovah of the Jews," as well as "Nature" or even "It" (p. 138). *The Saturday Evening Post* looked into the movement in 1941, describing Wilson as "a very disarming guy and an expert at indoctrinating the stranger into the psychology, psychiatry, physiology, pharmacology and folklore of alcoholism," but they were eventually won over, with the positive piece resulting in its growth into a national movement (pp. 138–139).

Heard used the sales of the land he inherited in America from a former employer to build Trabuco College, starting in 1942, as a religious community to create "a new syncretism of Vedanta, Buddhism and some elements of Christianity," according to his letters, starting with twenty five acolytes at his isolated site in the Trabuco Canyon (p. 141). Heard thought that World War II would drive the world into another "Dark Ages" era, and that Trabuco would serve as an isolated monastery as such, to preserve learning (p. 142). There he taught that "you must become godlike. You will evolve into that divine manhood which is the purpose of life and the only hope of mankind," as Isherwood said that Heard at the time was going through "an anti-christian phase," as "he told me that he could never become a Christian, as long as the Church claimed for itself a monopoly of divine inspiration—which Hindus and Buddhists don't—and *as long as the crucifixion was presented as the inevitable and crowning triumph of Christ's life*" (p. 143) (emphasis added). At the time between both world wars, Heard was considered "one of the leading intellectuals in England and, later, in the United States," with his books reviewed by *The New York Times*, but Lattin acknowledges that "He was also something of a heretic" (p. 143). A Catholic periodical that sent a correspondent to the Trabuco site to investigate wrote that "Mr. Heard is leading a sect, a group, one of the many sprouted by the mystically fertile soil of California, and seems to be, perhaps unconsciously, founding, if not a new religion, then a new, modern brand of Gnosticism" (p. 143). As an example, at one time Heard was teaching there on "Dionysian spirituality," emphasizing "medieval Christian mysticism" and the writings of Meister Eckhart and works such as *The Cloud of Unknowing* (p. 144).

During these years Huxley wrote *The Perennial Philosophy*, on the common theme of the religions of the world; Lattin says that "For his research, Huxley dove deep into Heard's Trabuco library, studying saints and sages of the timeless past" (p. 152). There he writes that to connect with "the immanent and transcendent Ground of all being," one must become "loving, pure in heart, and poor in spirit...Why should this be? We do not know. It is just one of those facts that we have to accept" (p. 153). *What is so sad is that Jesus already explained all of that, because to commune with the personal Creator God of the Universe one must align themselves with those attributes that He chooses to comprise His personality, and it is also essential for an eternal Kingdom of Heaven to function in an eternally stable and healthy way, when filled by citizens who voluntarily agree to adopt these imperative life-sustaining attributes.* In the rising postwar materialism and consumer wealth of America, Heard could not maintain a sufficient body of fellow ascetic truth-seekers in this austere environment, and he signed over the Trabuco campus to Swami Prabhavananda and the Vedanta Temple in 1947, including his immense library of wisdom literature and mystical texts, becoming Ramakrishna Monastery in September 1947 (p. 154). Before it closed, Dr. Huston Smith, ordained minister in the Methodist Church, church leader in Monterey and author of *The World's Religions*, came to Trabuco, and coming across Heard's work he contacted him and met him in 1947 at Trabuco (p. 157). Decades later Dr. Smith told author Lattin that he now conceded "there was very shaky evidence to support Gerald's ideas," and "no evidence pointing to an evolutionary wave leading us all toward mystical consciousness" (p. 158). He did say that Heard "revolutionized my understanding" of other worlds, and by introducing him to Vedanta and a St. Louis swami, and if not for the latter, he "would have had no career in the world's religions nor have written a book by that name" (p. 159).

Trabuco, however, still left a mighty legacy. W.Y. Evans-Wentz of the Theosophical Society returned to Trabuco from the Himalayas with the *Tibetan Book of the Dead* for the library; first published in 1927, it fascinated Huxley, who passed it on to Timothy Leary, who used it as a guidebook on how to make an acid trip, which then inspired John Lennon to write the song "Tomorrow Never Knows" (p. 166). Michael Murphy used the Trabuco concept and Heard's ideas as a model for his Esalen Institute in Big Sur (p. 167). Wilson and his wife took a cross-country trip in 1943–1944, to see the AA community in California and also to get away from the pressures of the organization demands, and as a reader of Heard's work, came to his remote California commune at Trabuco College to meet him (p. 140). Although he lived in New York, he made at least three visits to Trabuco between 1944 and 1947 (p. 167). Visitors present there said that Wilson asked Gerald Heard on what direction he should take Alcoholics Anonymous, to which Heard recommended that it stay decentralized, and twelve-steps focused; Wilson had been familiar with Heard's writings from his publisher, and "Their first meeting at Trabuco was the beginning of a personal friendship and collaboration that would continue over the next two decades" (p. 169). Lattin also asserted that "There are many similarities between Heard's ideas and the principles outlined in *Alcoholics Anonymous* (the 'Big Book'), which was first published in 1939, and *Twelve Steps and Twelve Traditions*, another central AA text, released in 1962," both authored by Wilson and drawing on William James' *The Varieties of Religious Experience* and other works, while Heard's emphasis on prayer and meditation to lead to spiritual awakening found its way into the Twelve Steps book (p. 170). Lattin adds that "In his book, Wilson describes God as *he* understood him, as 'the ultimate Reality', a phrase Heard uses in his 1941 book *Training for the Life of the Spirit*," with both books stressing the surrender to a power "greater than ourselves" (p. 170).

In the early 1950s, Huxley read a paper by Canadian doctors Humphry Osmond and John Smythies in the *Journal of Medical Science* entitled "Schizophrenia: A New Approach," which compared the biochemical similarities between that mental illness and acute mescaline intoxication, and by 1953 Huxley was corresponding with Osmond about how mescaline might provide mystical enlightenment and "permit the other world to rise into consciousness" (pp. 183–184). Huxley coaxed Osmond to bring some mescaline from Canada for him to try it, which he subsequently did (p. 184). Lattin writes that "Bill Wilson had been sober for more than two decades when he had his first acid trip. Gerald Heard was his guide, joining Dr. [Sidney] Cohen for the session" (p. 190). Heard was not able to join Huxley for his first experience with mescaline in 1953, but he tried it himself months later. They soon moved on to LSD, and Lattin notes that "LSD changed Huxley and Heard, like it changes many who take it"; fellow British "psycho-naut" Alan Watts agreed to take psychedelics after seeing their response, and he noted "a marked change of spiritual attitude" in both men afterwards (pp. 190–191). Lattin writes that "Wilson had his first LSD session at the Los Angeles Veterans Administration hospital on August 29, 1956....Dr. Osmond thought LSD could be used to treat alcoholism...it might terrify drunks into changing their ways," but he later perceived that it was "insight, not terror that LSD sessions were helping provide to alcoholics" (p. 191). He adds that "Wilson was nervous about taking LSD, so he turned to his most-trusted advisor. He asked Gerald Heard to be his guide, a role in which Heard accompanied many others in the early years of the psychedelic movement," four years before Timothy Leary took his first "trip" (p. 191).

It is important to understand that the first promoters and importers of vast shipments of the dangerous drug LSD to proliferate it throughout large portions of the public were not the hippies and "radicals," but rather the "establishment"—not only its "covert guardians," the CIA, but in particular the psychiatric community, academia, and surprisingly the most conservative and libertarian Fortune 500 CEOs and captains of industry (for their own agendas of further exploiting a work force and occult interests), a full decade before young people ever heard of it (although a few of its proponents later to the youth, like Ken Kesey, were doped up at least partially unwittingly by the "establishment" in murky trials to set them on that course). Regarding getting others to try LSD, Lattin writes that "Heard turned on *Time* publisher [and arch-conservative, anti-communist patriot] Henry Luce and his wife, Clare Boothe Luce; Jesuit theologian John Courtney Murray; and William Mullendore, the chairman of the board of Southern California Edison [the main regional power company]. He also inspired Dr. Oscar Janiger, a Los Angeles psychiatrist who turned on Cary Grant, James Coburn, and Jack Nicholson," with Janiger writing that "It was the philosopher Gerald Heard who introduced me to psychedelics....He told me that the emergence of LSD in the twentieth century was simply God's way of giving us the gift of consciousness. He believed that LSD was a device for saving humanity from Armageddon" (pp. 191–192). Lattin adds that

Heard was the man who turned on Myron Stolaroff, a Silicon Valley pioneer who went on to introduce to LSD many of the other engineers and business people who launched the personal computer revolution [Apple's Steve Jobs and other key figures would later confess how LSD helped inspire them in their seminal contributions in the field]. Stolaroff met Heard at a series of Bay Area spiritual retreats in the 1950s known as the Sequoia Seminars. At first, Stolaroff couldn't understand why a famous mystic like Gerald Heard would need to take a drug to find God. But Heard was so enthusiastic about LSD that Stolaroff took his advice and made an appointment to see one of the most mysterious men in the early history of the psychedelic era, a secretive Canadian businessman named Al Hubbard. In April 1956, Stolaroff, an executive with the Ampex Corporation, which popularized the first tape recorders, was baptized into the LSD church at Hubbard's Vancouver apartment. Stolaroff returned to Silicon Valley to become one the region's first LSD evangelists, resigning from the Ampex board in 1961 to found the International Foundation of Advanced Study, which sponsored research to see if LSD could be used to inspire creative thinking. According to some observers of the era, psychedelic drugs fueled the burst of engineering and business genius that inspired Silicon Valley. (p. 192)

Much more on the mysterious Hubbard, Stolaroff and other figures, whom would later provide a key advisory role to the Billy Graham Association and other evangelical leaders with their long-range "wisdom" for the future and mankind's spiritual development, will be explored in much greater detail in Volume 3 of this book series. Lattin continues:

...it all started with Gerald Heard, who would soon set his psychedelic sights on another adventurous businessman—Bill Wilson. In the summer of 1956, Heard was working with Dr. Sidney Cohen at the VA hospital in Los Angeles. Wilson had been battling his depression and was unsure how he'd react to such a powerful psychotropic agent....Cohen, one of the leading researchers in the field, would supervise the session, and Heard would be there as Wilson's spiritual guide....By the time Wilson came to Los Angeles for his LSD session, he had developed a close relationship with Heard. Letters they exchanged from the late 1940s to the early 1960s document that friendship. They helped each other through painful bouts of depression. (pp. 192–193)

The recurring depression periods of Heard and Wilson, like many "visionaries" of humanity in the arts, music, film and literature, makes one wonder why they thought they had the "answers" for what "ills" society and solutions for humanity's malaise. Lattin quotes a letter from Wilson to Heard in 1957, in which he writes, "I am certain that the LSD experience has helped me very much. I find myself with a heightened color perception and an appreciation of beauty almost destroyed by my years of depression" (p. 183).

Wilson thought Heard should turn Trabuco into an institute for the study of psychic phenomena; Lattin writes that "Setting up a research center at Trabuco to document and prove that psychic activity is real, Wilson wrote, 'would place a truly hot blow torch against the scientific and theological icebergs that seem to chill that field. Maybe that's an idea for Trabuco' " (p. 193). In a letter from Heard to Wilson in 1950, Heard told him about new research in "telepathic linkage," and they also had a *shared interest in flying saucers* as well as psychic phenomena (p. 194). Heard's own pioneering book on the subject, *Is Another World Watching? The Riddle of the Flying Saucers*, was published in 1950, where Heard suggests that Mars was populated by giant, super-intelligent bees, in which he writes, "It is difficult to resist the conclusion that Mars is ruled by insects" (p. 194). *This bizarre concept for modern sensibilities is disturbingly close to that postured by famous screen writer Nigel Kneale and the equally famous Quatermass and the Pit series for BBC Television in 1958 (and a major influence on Stephen King and John Carpenter), and as the 1967 film Quatermass and the Pit (or Five Million Miles to Earth in the States). Heard's interest in bees is reflected in his 1941 novel A Taste for Honey, which was made into the British horror movie, The Deadly Bees.*

Lattin's own sources corroborate others we have covered that document the Wilsons' obsession with occult practices like séances. Lattin quotes the memoir of Wilson's own personal secretary, who writes, "In the early forties, Bill and Lois often held meetings—or 'spook sessions', as they termed them—in a small bedroom at Stepping Stones [the name for the Wilsons' home in Bedford Hills, New York] for *A.A. friends, a couple of Rockefeller people*, and even some Bedford Hills neighbors frequently participated in these sessions and experienced unusual phenomena" (p. 194) (emphasis added). He also notes that "John D. Rockefeller Jr. was an early AA patron, and some of his operatives worked closely with Wilson in the early years in New York" (p. 194).

By 1954 their major shared interest was psychedelic drugs, and one letter by Wilson to Heard at that time suggests that Wilson was invited to a mescaline session that year with Humphry Osmond and Aldous Huxley (it also mentioned Bill's recounting of a "saucer account" as "an unusually clean-cut sighting") (pp. 194–195). Osmond's account of turning Wilson on to drugs twenty years earlier was given in an address by him to the Esalen Institute in May 1975, stating that "Later on Bill got extremely interested and took LSD with Sidney Cohen in Los Angeles" (p. 195). In another letter from Wilson to Heard in 1950, Bill reported the psychic abilities of his sister

Dorothy Strong, saying his sister had begun channeling messages from Camille Flammarion, a deceased astronomer and spiritualist [and member of the Theosophical Society], in which the spirit sometimes referenced Heard, and Wilson acknowledged that his sister had experienced "a bad crackup" and "extreme emotional difficulties" three years earlier, but had emerged with "psychic talents" (p. 197). Heard responded to the letter within days, suggesting that he, Huxley, Wilson and Wilson's associate Tom Powers get together for a foursome séance to "explore—both for the insane and the so-called sane—the border country of psychical research of which you know so much" (p. 197). Wilson also wrote to Heard in 1956 about getting with the Huxleys at the home of David and Lucille Kahn, a wealthy couple who were involved with Wilson's LSD sessions, and who were followers of the famous psychic (and "Sleeping Prophet") Edgar Cayce, and shows how the interest of Wilson, Heard and Huxley in psychic activity led them to be interested in psychedelic drugs; it also notes his reading of *Heaven and Hell*, Huxley's second drug experience book after *The Doors of Perception* (p. 197).

Heard's notes of witnessing Wilson's first LSD experience at the VA hospital in 1956 have survived. Betty Eisner, another LSD-investigating psychologist involved with Cohen and these players, wrote that "Alcoholics Anonymous was actually considering using LSD," saying that alcoholics in the program "need a spiritual experience" (p. 198). Bill's wife Lois also participated with LSD. There were also seen letters between Wilson and Dr. Sidney Cohen from 1956–61 in the files of the Stepping Stones Foundation Archive, including Wilson's request to Cohen of "the desirability of omitting my name when discussing LSD with A.A.s." Wilson told Huston Smith that his LSD experience was "a dead ringer" of his first experience with the 'Belladonna Cure" in Towns Hospital in 1934 (p. 199). Wilson had hoped that his LSD experience would wean him off the one addiction that he could not kick—cigarettes—but it did not, and ultimately he died from that addiction (p. 204).

Wilson did say months later that the LSD experience "has done a sustained good," in a 1956 letter to Heard, and he further formed an experimental group in New York for LSD that included Catholic priest Father Ed Dowling and Eugene Exman, the religion editor at Harper and Brothers (p. 205). Meanwhile, Heard was hosting his own LSD gatherings in the Santa Monica home of Margaret Gage in 1957 (where Heard lived for a time); a participant and resident at the property said that "Gerald got Dr. Cohen to give LSD to lots of famous people, not just to Bill Wilson and the Luces. John Huston [the film director] and Steve Allen [the television show host] took LSD at Margaret's house" (p. 205). Lattin writes that "Wilson thought LSD could help cynical alcoholics undergo the 'spiritual awakening' that stands at the center of the twelve-step work....Wilson defended his LSD use and psychic experimentations in a long letter written in 1958—a statement that shows how his enthusiasm for the drug caused him to ignore its dangers"; Wilson even turned on Huxley to another drug—leukoadrenochrome (pp. 206–207). However, the Alcoholics Anonymous World Services 1984-published book, *Pass It On*, stated that "As word of Bill's activities reached the Fellowship, there were inevitable repercussions. Most A.A.'s were violently opposed to his experimenting with a mind-altering substance. LSD was then totally unfamiliar, poorly researched, and entirely experimental—and Bill was taking it" (p. 206).

As we documented earlier from a book by another Jesuit priest, Lattin also confirms that "Father Dowling, the Jesuit priest who had known Wilson since the early 1940s, and who participated in at least one of the early LSD sessions in New York, was initially as enthusiastic as Wilson, but would later warn Bill to be more careful with the drug," and "also inspired Wilson to take another look at Christianity, especially at its long mystical tradition. In the 1940s, Wilson met regularly with Dowling and Monsignor Fulton Sheen, the popular Catholic radio host," but Wilson did not become Catholic "because of his lifelong distrust of organized religion," as Wilson and Dowling exchanged letters on the subject from 1958 until 1960, the year Dowling died (p. 207). Lattin also confirms that "Dowling replied [to Wilson] by urging Wilson to proceed with caution, and even suggested the devil might be working through LSD," noting Saint Ignatius' caution that "It is the mark of the evil spirit to assume the appearance of the angel of light" (p. 208).

As the 1960s rolled around, both Huxley and Wilson were corresponding with the 1960s icon of drug promotion, Timothy Leary, extolling the virtues of the psychedelics (pp. 216–217). Lattin notes that "Huxley thought LSD should be carefully given to a select group of intellectuals, artists, and opinion leaders who would gradually influence the direction of the culture"—*i.e., the "elites," ala the converse of Brave New World*—and wrote to Humphry Osmond that the subject should only be discussed "in the relative privacy of learned journals, the decent obscurity of moderately highbrow books and articles" (p. 217). Leary's recklessness of distribution and guidance to youth would lead LSD to be banned in 1966, although Lattin points out today "the use of Ecstasy (MDMA) to treat returning Iraqi and Afghan war veterans suffering from post-traumatic stress disorder" (p. 218). He notes that Huxley prophesied that "Biochemical discoveries will make it possible for large numbers of men and women to achieve a radical self-transcendence and a deeper understanding of the nature of things," as Huxley and Heard laid the groundwork of the "human potential movement," which was built on at the Esalen Institute at Big Sur as well as "growth centers" nationwide, and noting the movement's roots in the humanist ideas of *T.H. Huxley* and psychology of William James (p. 218) (emphasis added). *Importantly, he writes that Huxley's and Heard's "fascination with psychic activity and paranormal phenomena in the 1930s and 1940s would later find expression in the so-called New Age movement of the 1970s and 1980s. That movement's emphasis on spiritualism and 'channeled' teachings can be traced back to the Theosophical Society of Helena Blavatsky and Annie Besant, but Heard and Huxley helped keep those ideas alive in the middle decades of the twentieth century" (p. 218) (emphasis added).* He adds that "Huxley laid out the ideas that would become the human potential movement in a series of lectures he gave in 1959 at the University of California, Santa Barbara" (p. 219).

Lattin notes that eventual Esalen founders Murphy and Price met Heard and were forever changed; when they put on their first seminar series there in 1962, Gerald Heard was invited to stay and lectured on "drug-induced mysticism," while Huxley supplied Sandoz Labs' LSD for Michael Murphy's first LSD trip in Mexico in 1962, although in subsequent LSD experiences they became more painful, but nevertheless, Esalen continues on successfully today (p. 220). Lattin adds that in the 1960s and 70s Esalen attracted psychologists, spiritual teachers and such, and there they were offered "the religion of no religion" (p. 222).

On the day that Huxley died—the very day President John Kennedy was shot, one of the most unforgettable days in the American psyche, as well as the death of Christian intellectual icon C. S. Lewis—he directed his wife to administer intravenously his last LSD hit in his final hour, while his medical staff stayed transfixed to the television coverage of the assassination, with his wife sending family members and Wilson a letter detailing how he left the world (p. 231). Heard began the 60s by releasing a trilogy of record albums about death, which taught about the soul surviving bodily death (p. 232). Heard also served as a spiritual guide to former congresswoman Clare Boothe Luce and her *Time* magazine publisher Henry, initiating both of them into LSD use, and providing guidance for her on into the 1960s, as her ambitious nature dealt with the loss of a child in the mid-1940s, turning to religion and psychotherapy (p. 233). Over the years, Heard and his friend and caretaker Jay Michael Barrie vacationed with the Luces, and by 1959 Heard introduced them both to an LSD encounter; Heard later wrote to Clare that "This [LSD] is the free gift of God which He may mediate through them and they themselves may receive from Him as His supreme reward" (pp. 233–234). The Luces in turn provided financial assistance to them, and Clare set up a foundation funding studies in Christian mysticism after Heard began to have strokes in 1966 (p. 234). Lattin notes that under the name D. B. Vest, Heard "contributed to the early gay liberation movement with a series of articles on the evolutionary and spiritual significance of homosexuality" (p. 234). Heard eventually died in 1971 at the age of eighty-one (p. 235).

The author, Don Lattin, writes that he meets in a group that includes Christian "centering prayer" mysticism, along with Zen Buddhism, Taosim and other syncretic faiths, in essence building a "god as we choose to understand him." He shows that this is indicative of society at large today, which rejects what they see as the hypocrisy and detached nature of organized religion (*an attitude with which one could sadly understand, if not agree with, based upon the data revealed in this book series*). He quotes polling data from 2008 and 2009 revealing that 57 percent of "evangelical Christians" believe that there is more than one way to enter heaven, and that "*two out of three Americans expressed belief in or reported having experience with at least one of the following spiritual concepts or phenomena: reincarnation, astrology, 'spiritual energy,' yoga as spiritual practice, the 'evil eye,' making spiritual contact with the dead, or consultation with a psychic*" (p. 213) (emphasis added). He adds that the personal identification of "no religion" was the only demographic group to grow in every state within the last eighteen years, and between 1990 and 2008 nearly doubling from 8 percent to 15 percent; three-quarters defined their spirituality as personal and individual versus in terms of organized religion and church doctrine, with one-third defining themselves as "spiritual but not religious," according to Gallup (p. 214). It also found than 80 percent of Americans saw God "everywhere and in everything," as opposed to "someone somewhere," with other data suggesting that "the number of people who believe the Bible is the literal word of God has 'dropped remarkably since the 1960s'," and by 1984 one in three Americans had switch religions or denominations (p. 214).

Lattin claims concerning this trend and theme that "It's not about believing in God as much as experiencing the power of the divine. It shows a deep mistrust of religious hierarchies.…It's about stress reduction, not salvation.…It's as much about feeling good as about being good"; Lattin also notes that in the three decades since LSD emerged in the 1950s, "*more than twenty-three million Americans tried LSD*" (p. 215) (emphasis added). *These trends suggest that our acknowledgement of the corruption and bad teaching from national Christian leaders seen in this book series (all volumes), and bad thinking and lack of obedience to the Kingdom principles by the rank-and-file Christians, and their lack of expression of Christ's love in their communities, is indeed "serious business," and a major setback to the advance of the Kingdom through the Church, within the spiritually confused, seeking "perishing" populace they were specifically sent to "rescue."*

Gerald Heard's pen name for his many popular fictional novels was H. F. Heard. One of those books was titled, *The Black Fox*. In a capsule of the book storyline by its publisher,[169] it reveals his adept knowledge of the darker world of religion as part of his vast compendium of spiritual knowledge. They write that

> Canon Throcton is a brilliant scholar, but the men of the Church can't bring themselves to trust him. His devoted study of Hebrew and Arabic has drawn him far from their intellectual center, and his interest in the obscure writings of the Middle East verges on heresy. Canon knows his brothers in the cathedral don't take him seriously, but he doesn't care. A great and terrible power hides within him, and he'll unleash it even if it destroys the Church, the town, and everyone he holds dear. When a junior colleague is elevated above him, Canon reaches into his darkest volume of forbidden lore and tries his hand at black magic. It works better than he ever could have dreamed. His enemy is destroyed and Canon feels the tug of unimaginable power. He's taken the first step along the road to damnation—and soon he'll burn. *The Black Fox* is English gothic at its best, a story of weird fiction steeped in author H. F. Heard's *unparalleled knowledge of world religion. Never before had black magic been written about with such deep understanding,* and never since has it been more terrifying. (emphasis added)

Rhea White, Ph.D, was Editor-in-Chief of the *Journal of the American Society for Psychical Research and Exceptional Human Experience*, and gave a paper at the 1982 conference of the Academy of Religion and Psychical Research, and published in the Proceedings in 1984 (pp. 56–69), entitled, "Gerald Heard's Legacy to Psychical Research,"[170] and which can be found on the Gerald Heard website. The paper is effusive in praise of Heard in his role as the centerpiece and foundational member of the psychical research community, and makes some curious observations of his activities and interests, such as, "His most intensive studies were involved with *mediumship*, and with Theodore Besterman (1933) he published a brief account of an attempt to measure the direct-voice phenomena of the *medium Mrs. Gladys Osborne Leonard*. Elsewhere he wrote about the history and development of *mediumship* (Heard: 1929, 1932a, 1937b, 1944a, 1944b, 1950, 1954, 1955)" (emphasis added).

Other sources provide more information on the forgotten activities and associates of the close circle of Fifield, Ingebretsen, Heard and their assistants at Spiritual Mobilization and *Faith and Freedom*, including Southern California Edison Corp. chief William C. Mullendore, and fellow libertarian founding father (and head of the largest branch of the U.S. Chamber of Commerce in Los Angeles), Leonard Read, who was also the founder of the Foundation for Economic Education (FEE), one of the first modern libertarian institutions. At the helm of the Los Angeles branch of the U.S. Chamber of Commerce (consistently the largest lobbyist in America), and with the pro-business mission to fight labor reforms and wage increases, and promote deregulation and off-shore business practices, Read was however more fully convinced of the nefarious nature of the public jobs and welfare assistance of the New Deal in 1933 by way of his interactions with Mellendore, and the preaching of Fifield, as an attendee of his church. Eventually founding the FEE, he regularly interacted with and was influenced by libertarian icon and author Ayn Rand, whose "Objectivism" philosophy became something of a cult amongst its followers in the eyes of many, with its emphasis on personal selfishness and lack of accountability to others, eschewing help for the disadvantaged, and draconian actions for those who stood in their way in terms of foreign policy, with an unabashed self-centered belief system probably rivaled only with Satanism in its self-glorification. This was explained in a brief biography article of Read by Rev. Edmund Optiz, another member of their inner circle, in a 1998 edition of *The Freeman* journal operated by Read's FEE, which is currently available online.[171] In addition to the above facts, it adds his starting of Pamphleteers, Inc., "a small group of friends of liberty within the Chamber orbit who, in their 'ninth-floor underground,' occasionally chipped in to print short works that otherwise might be neglected, like Rose Wilder Lane's *Give Me Liberty* and Ayn Rand's *Anthem*."

In an interview Read gave in 1975 for *Reason* magazine, which is also available online,[172] it notes that Read has stated in his publication that he believes that man's earthly purpose is based upon a basic premise of several assumptions, which include the following: "...my first assumption is the primacy and supremacy of an Infinite Consciousness. My second assumption is also demonstrable. While difficult, it is possible for the individual to expand his own awareness, perception, consciousness. My third assumption is a profound belief that the intellect—one's mind—is independent; that is to say, it is not subordinate to the organic matter of which one's body is composed. An inference from this belief is a conviction of the immortality of the human spirit or consciousness." *For a Chamber of*

Commerce, pro-business libertarian, the terms of these statements seem to reflect the influence of Heard, or Heard's proxies like Mullendore. Read added that "everything in life, from a blade of grass to the blink of an eye to a galaxy, is mystery....sometimes I'm called a mystic or neomystic by reason of believing that there's something over and beyond my mind." He said the incidents that led to him being the first publisher of Ayn Rand's book *Anthem* was that "Bill Mullendore and I were at her home for dinner one night," and he told her that he had read all of her books, but this one had not been accepted for publication in the U.S., to which he compelled her to let him read it, and wrote the foreword to the book.

A 1946 letter from Rand to Read at his FEE headquarters, available online at Read's FEE website,[173] is an example of their regular correspondence. In it, Rand gives an impression of her and Read together fighting an insurmountable battle in league against conservatives, many of whom are actually "pinko" Communists in disguise. She closes the letter in her characteristic acerbic manner by writing, "...whenever you have a chance to discuss the situation of intellectuals with any of your big business backers, you must drive relentlessly, at every opportunity, toward the goal of having them use their influence to clean up the Republican newspapers and magazines of their filthy load of pinks, and to hire the writers of our kind. That should be your purpose. That is the purpose for which I will fight by your side with everything I've got. Your fighting 'ghost,' Ayn."

The archives of William Mullendore's papers at the University of Oregon[174] further add that Mullendore was asked to be Assistant Secretary of Commerce to Herbert Hoover from 1922 to 1923. Concerning the Southern California Edison Company (the local power company), they note that he was president from 1945 to 1954, and chairman of the board from 1954 to 1959. It also notes that he helped to found the Foundation for Economic Education (FEE) in 1946 alongside Read, as the western states Chambers of Commerce supported its formation as they "resolved to create a united front," *evidently using the FEE as a front for big business interests*, and solicited the support of it from Henry Ford II and others. The archive adds that "The Mullendore Papers consist largely of nearly 2,000 letters covering the years 1945–1968. Lengthy dialogues are maintained with conservative theoreticians, economists, authors, publishers, and political leaders, including...William F. Buckley Jr....Ayn Rand...and Leonard Read. Other notable correspondents include...E. F. Hutton...*Gerald Heard, Henry Regnery, and Whittaker Chambers*" (emphasis added) [Regnery was the founder of the arch-conservative publishing house *Regnery Publishing*, and Chambers was a former Communist spy].

Speaking of *Reason* magazine, this background will help us to understand some of the eyebrow-raising historical assertions made by *Reason* senior editor (and former employee of the Cato Institute in the 1990s) Brian Doherty in his 2007 book, *Radicals for Capitalism: A Freewheeling History of the Modern Libertarian Movement*, concerning some of these secondary figures we have just briefly profiled. David Boaz, the Executive Vice President of the preeminent libertarian "think tank," the Cato Institute, wrote on their website[175] that *"Radicals for Capitalism* is going to be the standard history of the libertarian movement for years to come." With that in mind, Google Books provides access to excerpts of the book,[176] such as

> The FEE/SM scene was made up of men who had climbed to the highest reaches of American business and society. They were aware, acutely and sometimes painfully, that they were an embattled minority. Some were certain that civilization as they valued it was descending into a Dark Age that might be frightfully long, even endless. For that reason, perhaps many of these men were riven with deep spiritual dissatisfactions, possessing a yen for mystical enlightenment that went far beyond the standard Protestant Sunday School varieties of their era....Spiritual Mobilization head Fifield didn't seem to have these tendencies. He retired from active leadership in SM in 1954 and handed the reins to high-powered L.A. lawyer (and one of Read's partners in Pamphleteers) James Ingebretsen....Despite being president of an explicitly religious libertarian organization, Ingebretsen believed "that religion was balderdash." He wasn't particularly disturbed by apparent hypocrisy. "I didn't come to Spiritual Mobilization as a minister: I came as a lawyer and a libertarian. Fighting the forces that wanted to abolish the free enterprise system was my mission, not promoting Christ!" (pp. 274–275)

> Correspondence with his libertarian friends indicates that this cosmopolitan atheist politico had occasional yearnings for a mystic's life....But as he confided decades later in his memoir, he was not ready to feel repentance and grace overtake him in the battered Salvation Army church he dropped into on a mysterious whim during a business trip to New York. Later that night, he was similarly surprised to see Jesus appear out of a mosaic at St. Patrick's cathedral—a rather angry Jesus....Ingebretsen decided he was possessed by the spirit of a dead daughter, Kristi. He adopted a glyph as his new identity, which in English would be pronounced, "Kristifer"....Shortly thereafter during a meeting at the home of a Spiritual Mobilization funder, he scrawled "Kristifer" in large letters

on his host's table, where he usually collected the small signatures of famous guests....Spiraling into what felt like insanity, Ingebretsen called on an old colleague from Spiritual Mobilization, Edmund Opitz, a Unitarian minister who was working with Leonard Read at FEE. Opitz was at a loss when he heard the story of possession and rebirth and told Ingebretsen that what he needed to do, in the midst of this apparent super-accelerated spiritual evolution, was to talk to their friend Gerald Heard. (pp. 275–276)

Leonard Read was the first of the libertarian circle to know of Gerald Heard. Read was a general devotee of semi-popular metaphysical literature, and Heard purveyed such literature in the 1950s....Heard became Ingebretsen's guide through his strange new mystic dispensation—and led him far beyond the set free market frontiers of what Spiritual Mobilization and the libertarian movement had been. Read had questioned his membership on the Spiritual Mobilization advisory board...but Read was in many ways a spiritual leader in the psychological-mystical trends that overtook Ingebretsen, his mentor Mullendore, and *Faith and Freedom* editorial staffer Thaddeus Ashby [note: the earlier interviewer of Heard] (veteran of stints with Rand and the Hoiles newspaper chain...). (p. 276)

Read was an early surfer of an interesting cultural wave, one that has not traditionally been associated with ex-chamber of commerce men running a "far right" propaganda outfit....gaseous spirituality, *since the days of Madame Blavatsky and Anne Besant in late Victorian times, if not before, was often a preoccupation of the well-to-do leisure class....and Read and his pals followed this tradition.* Leonard Read had long been an eager spiritual seeker, and it was he who discovered and loved the writings of Gerald Heard. But he did not hoard those spiritual resources, always turning his old mentor Mullendore on to his latest metaphysical conjectures and guides. Even before his weird conversion experience Ingebretsen was often involved in spiritualist discussions through Reverend Edmund Opitz as an intermediary. The exact lines of influence are difficult to untangle, but all these men shared many interests in libertarianism and other subjects, and corresponded tirelessly. So now James Ingebretsen, a respectable lawyer and linchpin of a religious libertarian advocacy group, was a new man with a new identity. At Opitz's recommendation, he turned to Gerald Heard to shepherd him through his unexpected spiritual rebirth...Amongst the "astonishing number of people" who adored Heard were libertarian activists Mullendore, Read, and Ingebretsen." (pp. 276–277)

The man dazzled them. Heard was given a regular column in *Faith and Freedom*, and an entire issue was dedicated to Heardianism. Read, after going to a Detroit area meeting where Heard did his thing (Heard was hosted by FEE trustee and Chrysler executive B. E. Hutchinson, through a local Episcopal parish), told Mullendore that "I agree with everything you say about Heard"....A yearning for larger meaning, a wider understanding, an expanded consciousness consumed these men—lawyer Ingebretsen, private utility chairman and union buster Mullendore, world-changer-through-self Read....A general desire to not just understand politics, not just their own business, but the very nature of reality consumed them; and being political radicals who were unhappy with the standard varieties of their time, they tended toward spiritual radicalism as well....Read's sense of the divine was vague and gaseous. Although Read and FEE have kept a reputation as a beachhead of traditional religiosity and morality in a sometimes antinomian and libertine libertarian movement, Read's sense of religion was more mystical than Christian. He once wrote to R.C. Hoiles [newspaper chain owner], "I assume you consider the Bible as much and as little an authority as I do. What then is authority? Where does it reside? In my case it is my own judgment, the results of my own free will." He was no atheist or materialist but far more a seeker of spiritual truth than someone confident he had found them in a Western tradition. (pp. 277–278)

Read was not unique in this among his libertarian friends. Hoiles [whose national newspaper chain featured hard-core libertarian editorial views] was fascinated with Krishnamurti, and other FEE board members along with Read found theosophists and metaphysicians from Rudolf Steiner to Alfred DeNouy to Stewart Edward White and Franz Winkler endlessly worth delving into and contemplating. Mullendore was Read's special spiritualist buddy....But the libertarian businessman/intellectual circle found their personal guru in Gerald Heard. Read introduced Heard's writings to Mullendore. Read had met Heard personally in New York in 1951. But Mullendore, Ingebretsen, and others took off running with him, since they lived in Southern California where the wizard also resided. They began hosting Heardian meetings at Idyllwild, a wooded retreat in the mountains east of Los Angeles. The cream of the libertarian movement went for weekends to listen to Heard talk on evolution of the spirit, to encourage quiet meditation....*In the mid-1950s, they all would gather at the Bohemian Grove, a secretive nature retreat for the wealthy and powerful in Northern California. They'd kibitz with Herbert Hoover and Henry Hazlitt....wondering how far consciousness and spirit and energy can evolve and grow. [Bohemian Grove is known for annually hosting*

Presidents, ex-Presidents, international heads of state and captains of industry (even today), and although secrecy and security is a premium, several journalists have confirmed the rumors of their bizarre, elaborate sacred mystery plays in the woods in front of a large stone owl idol, performing a mock sacrifice of a human effigy by throngs of torch-bearing, hooded cloaked figures, including celebrities, known as the "Cremation of Care"—I am not making this up.] (emphasis added) (pp. 278–279)

Gerald Heard, along with his friend Aldous Huxley and another friend, UCLA medical researcher Dr. Sidney Cohen, was not just a leading metaphysician, but also one of the leading Los Angeles evangels for mescaline and later LSD. Heard seems to have played a similar role in the lives of his new libertarian friends, especially Mullendore, Ingebretsen, and Thaddeus Ashby, the former Hoiles employee then working for *Faith and Freedom* (Ingebretsen in his memoir admits to only one Heard-hosted LSD session, but Ashby was by the end of the 1960s writing guides to lovemaking on mushrooms filled with hippie language derived from *Stranger in a Strange Land*, the successful novel of another libertarian hero, science fiction writer Robert Heinlein). It is widely whispered in the libertarian community that Read joined his friends in acid explorations; it is worth noting that Read goes out of his way to deny this in his journals. In 1962, Read had his own mystical experience, undrugged…Mullendore found LSD a fascinating tool, talking of its wonders like a true utility man: "LSD steps up our voltage and frequency. To use the new vision thus made available one must be able to 'plug in,' 'get in tune'—to 'harmonize' with this new environment which LSD opens for us to 'correspond with'." Mullendore's son-in-law, Louis Dehmlow, was a huge LSD enthusiast by the early 1960s….Dehmlow failed to get Ayn Rand to say any good words about Heard. [Libertarian icon Murray] Rothbard found that "I…have never been able to read a Heard article through. On the rare occasions when I have, I've never been able to find a point, or any sort of concrete addition to knowledge…" (pp. 279–280)

Ingebretsen and Optiz started a Heardian spiritual self-awareness group called the Wayfarers, which they convinced Spiritual Mobilization's board to finance. More and more of Ingebretsen's energy went into promoting Heard….To the decidedly unmetaphysical Rothbard, Heard's influence "spread…like a miasmic blight, sapping both the will and the rationality of libertarians." The anarchist William Johnson was squeezed out of his editorship of *Faith and Freedom* in the heyday of Heardianism, as one prominent libertarian maintained, for "refusing to genuflect to the east whenever

Gerald Heard waggled his beard"....as Ingebretsen's interests shifted toward the Heardian realm, he gave *Faith and Freedom* an antiunion focus....He named Edward Greenfield as new editor, a Presbyterian preacher from Princeton, Indiana, famous for his union-busting exploits....Spiritual Mobilization petered out in 1961....Ingebretsen shifted his attention toward being a full-time New Ager, convinced he was a hermetic avatar of sorts after his "Kristifer" experience. (p. 281)

Doherty's book *Radicals for Capitalism* also contains additional information on Spiritual Mobilization and its principals, only available in the book itself, as well as a treasure trove of data on Ayn Rand and other leaders in the libertarian movement, which will be covered in the next volume. Regarding Spiritual Mobilization, Doherty emphasizes that "Leonard Read and his FEE crew and their general universe of funders and supporters saw this pamphleteering group of libertarian outreachers to Protestant clergy (and to those who listened to Protestant clergy) as one of their most significant peers. But few, among even the highest echelons of active movement libertarianism, remember Spiritual Mobilization today."[177] He opines that "Part of the reason may be a residual aftereffect of Ayn Rand's fiercely atheistic legacy to the movement. She laid brick after brick on a mighty wall of separation between libertarianism and religion. But Spiritual Mobilization, which reached more people with more radical libertarian ideas than any other group in the late 1940s and early 1950s, was an explicitly religious educational group" (p. 271). He writes that *"Members had their hands in the pulpit as well as all available media"* (p. 271) (emphasis added).

He notes that "Spiritual Mobilization advised its flock to judge every political candidate or government action against a checklist of criteria," which included those such as "Does it (the program, platform, or act) encourage the Christian principle of love or the collectivist principle of compulsion?" (p. 271)—*translated, does it pursue Biblical-styled economic justice, as we have documented in this book, or promote the well-to-do to give to the desperate poor on their own whims and moods?* It also asks, "If it proposes to take the property or income of some for the special benefit or use of others, does it violate the Commandment: 'Thou shalt not steal'?", and "Is it necessary to use the compulsion of political means in this instance, or could the ends be accomplished by Christian cooperation and non-political voluntary associations?" (p. 272). *The answer to the last litmus test is theoretically the latter option, but what does history tell us about relying fully and exclusively on the individual fickle charitable impulses of those whom God has blessed, often without their deserving such status or privilege, and their resultant control over the fate of the less fortunate? For many years I believed this utopian position, but in this two-thousand-year era dominated by a prosperous and technologically advanced Christian society as well as sustained and widespread poverty, inequality and suffering simultaneously, this laissez faire, "every man for himself" mindset that has dominated most of the era has produced the prosperity disparity of "Dickens' London," dominated by the charity (or lack thereof) of the "Ebenezer Scrooges'" of the business and capital classes (and their Christian communities in league with them) more than anything else.*

Doherty notes that Leonard Read was a member of Fifield's First Congregational Church in Los Angeles while he ran the local Chamber of Commerce. He notes that the founding of Spiritual Mobilization was spurred on by the resolution of the meeting of the General Council of the Congregational and Christian Churches in 1934, which called for the abolition of America's "destructive" free enterprise system, which Fifield saw as the evil "social gospel/social action" philosophy (p. 272). He adds that "a trio of financiers from the Spiritual Mobilization/FEE world—J. Howard Pew, Jasper Crane, and B E. Hutchinson of Chrysler—were high-level players on the National Lay Committee, a group of businessmen in the 1950s who fought a rear guard (and ultimately failed) action against the socialist trends they saw taking over American clergymen and churches" (p. 272). Spiritual Mobilization's *Faith and Freedom* newsletter emphasized that "socialism had crept into American life before FDR," *while not emphasizing foreign enemies*; within its pages Leonard Read argued on the Korean War that "I have yet to find a single person who is in favor of this present war, which is to say, I have yet to find an individual who is anxious himself to give up home, family, fortune, and even life, shoulder a gun, and go forth to kill Chinese" (p. 273). *Faith and Freedom* also ran a regular column by libertarian icon Murray Rothbard, although to allay concerns of his libertarian financial underwriters the Volker Fund and to preserve his own academic reputation as an economist, he bravely wrote under the pseudonym "Aubrey Herbert," and basically served as the magazine's Washington editor (p. 273). As far as its opposition at the time, Doherty notes that the 1953 book called *Apostles of Discord* said Spiritual Mobilization promoted "a kind of economic royalism dedicated to the extreme view that no positive government action of any kind is justified" (p. 273). The CIO labor organization called Fifield "a neo-fascist enemy of organized labor and the New Deal," while Spiritual Mobilization wrote pamphlets "distributed in bulk to churches across the country" (p. 274).

Leonard Read was not so bashful in publicly expressing the mysticism he felt was an important part of the libertarian message of this cabal of ideological promoters. His 1962 book *Elements of Libertarian Leadership* (1962) extolled a theological "Creative Force" that mystics like Rudolf Steiner said could be mastered by those with the proper spiritual disciplines. These daily "disciplines" of mind and subconscious control that Read would recommend, to somehow form the crux of the development of the successful libertarian individual and society, seemed to comprise the self-affirmations and mental conditioning akin to the "New Thought" spiritual movement of "mind over matter," promoted by Norman Vincent Peale and other "self-help" religious and secular leaders, the televangelist and faith healer celebrities, modern occult movements like "The Secret," and many popular evangelical leaders (like Joel Osteen) and mega-church leaders today. Read recommended lengthy periods of daily focused meditation on objects ("to free one from exterior influences like traditions, social positions, professions, nationalities"), *to do things ritually daily that have no purpose like walking around the perimeter of a room*, thinking of events in one's life to determine a hidden instructional guidance and message in them (with Read using a supposed legend from Jesus that actually comes from Zen Buddhism), and then warns that "No one should even consider these exercises who is not temperamentally and spiritually ready and determined to become an improved person, *at whatever cost...*To 'toy' with these untapped and potentially powerful forces within one's own person is actually dangerous" (p. 283). Lattin adds that "Yes, this is the work of a man whose organization was more commonly concerned with wage and price supports, tariffs, taxation, union perfidy, the provision of public services, and other mundane matters" (p. 283)—*yet feels the need to employ subliminal mind control techniques, rather than mere superior logic and reasoning.*

Another distinguished scholar who added further details and corroboration of some of these provocative facts is Dr. Eckard V. Toy, Jr. In a paper in the Spring 2014 edition of the *Oregon Historical Quarterly* journal, affiliated with the Oregon Historical Society, entitled, "Eckard V. Toy, Jr.— A Tribute," with its abstract available online,[178] it notes that Dr. Toy earned his Ph.D. in American History from the University of Oregon, with his 1959 Master's thesis, *The Ku Klux Klan in Oregon: Its Charter and Program*, relating to much of his research. They note his "teaching at several universities in the Midwest and on the Pacific Coast." In a 1980 edition of the *American Studies* journal (sponsored by the Mid-America American Studies Association and the University of Kansas College of Liberal Arts and Sciences since 1959, and merged with American Studies International (itself a part of the American Studies Department at George Washington University)), they feature Dr. Toy's paper, "The conservative connection: the chairman of the board took LSD before timothy leary"; this paper can be currently read in its entirety online.[179] There he writes that

In January of 1959, slightly more than a year and one-half before Timothy Leary would have his initial psychedelic experience, the chairman of the board of Southern California Edison Company casually informed a friend: "My LSD experience went off very nicely. There was nothing drastic about it in the sense of it being at all sudden or shocking or so strange as to be fearful....I am convinced that this drug is a real tool for exploration of consciousness. It holds great promise and as I reflect upon the experience I become more enthusiastic about it." William C. Mullendore took LSD-25 three more times during the next four years, each experience binding him closer in his intellectual apprenticeship to the English-born novelist, lecturer, and philosopher Gerald Heard. Acting as master to novice, Heard introduced Mullendore to LSD as he would later introduce Henry and Clare Boothe Luce [ultra-conservative publisher of *Time* and his congressman wife] and other business leaders, Hollywood celebrities, and artists to the drug. (p. 65)

The author concedes that "a discussion of conservatives and hallucinogenic drugs may even seem to be a contradiction in terms," but that "earlier assumptions about the influence of drugs in modern American society have been dramatically altered by revelations about experiments conducted by the Department of Defense and the Central Intelligence Agency during the 1950s and 1960s. Equally obscure but perhaps less surprising were the numerous experiments conducted independently by researchers and intellectuals during those same years" (pp. 65–66). He adds that Aldous Huxley's article "Drugs That Shape Men's Minds" even appeared in the October 18, 1958 issue of the *Saturday Evening Post* (p. 66). He notes that although the contribution of these libertarian pro-business ideologues was more obscure historically in comparison to 1960s youths, "In part, the obscurity was self-imposed, since government researchers generally conducted their experiments in secret and intellectuals like Heard chose to propagate their ideas among a *carefully chosen clientele, aiming at an elite rather than at the masses*," although researchers "identified Gerald Heard as one of the principal contributors to a counter-cultural tradition in the United States" (p. 66) (emphasis added).

He adds that when Heard and Huxley emigrated to the U.S. from England in 1937 to avoid war service, their first stop at Duke University also included a visit to parapsychologist J. B. Rhine (a pioneer of parapsychology and ESP research), followed by a visit to a home of mysticism, Taos, New Mexico, before arriving in California in the spring of 1938, joining "a large colony of their fellow countrymen who were a significant part of the growing movie industry" (p. 67). Toy also adds when his pet project Trabuco College failed, Heard "became dependent on the good will and the devotion of a small number of wealthy patrons" (p. 67). He notes that the paths of Heard and Huxley crossed again, "when Dr. Humphry Osmond, another English expatriate conducting medical research in Canada [and known for inventing the word, "psychedelic"], introduced the pair to mescaline within a few months of each other in 1953" (p. 67). He also notes that during the 1960s he "worked with Dr. Sidney Cohen in *introducing corporation executives, actors, and artists to LSD-25 and other hallucinogens*" (p. 67) (emphasis added). Toy states that in Heard's book *The Five Ages of Man* (1963), he refers to the use of psychedelics as an "initiation" into true awareness, and Heard later wrote that Huxley referred to their use as a "sacrament," but Huxley confessed to Dr. Osmond that both he and Heard "don't have visions with the eyes closed, show no signs of psi" (p. 68). He adds that they initially interacted with Timothy Leary but lost respect for him, and "they appealed to an older, established generation and were less inclined to seek publicity" (p. 68).

Toy then discusses Heard's actions as part of "The Wayfarers," "an inner circle of the principal sponsors of Spiritual Mobilization" [SM], as they were not fully satiated with the anti-New Deal and anti-Communism emphasis of it at the time, and, "under the spell of Gerald Heard, established The Wayfarers in 1955," including James C. Ingebretsen (president of SM), Leonard E. Read (president of the Foundation for Economic Education (FEE)), the Unitarian minister Rev. Edmund Optiz, and Southern California Edison head Mullendore (p. 68). Their original choice of name, Orpheus Fellowship, was rejected by Ingebretsen because he considered the title "too pagan," and while it "resembled the Oxford Group in its psychological impact and in its techniques, deviated significantly from orthodox Christian theology" (emphasis added) (p. 69). They note that The Wayfarers held retreats from the summer of 1955 to the summer of 1959 in numerous places, such as Idyllwild, California, and even Lexington, Kentucky (p. 69). He explains that, "Conservative in politics and economics, The Wayfarers were both angered and frightened by apparent trends toward socialism in American society" and "sought to transcend traditional Protestantism and the New Thought techniques of the positive thinkers," while "some of The Wayfarers embraced new forms of harmonial religion and esoteric philosophical beliefs; a few, Mullendore, for example, experimented with drugs and psychic phenomena," while "Ingebretsen and Mullendore became more deeply absorbed in his [Heard's] teaching" (p. 69). Eventually, Heard severed his official ties with the group, and according to his secretary and companion Michael Jay Barrie, this was to "*avoid identifying Heard too closely with Spiritual Mobilization,*" and Ingebretsen decided to work with Heard in his spiritual studies using psychedelics with Dr. Sidney Cohen outside of official channels, because some of the clergymen connected with or following Spiritual Mobilization might find it "*controversial*" if they knew (emphasis added) (p. 69).

Mulledore's motivation was largely his pessimism (some might say paranoid and conspiratorial) over what he saw as the future path of the country, when Eisenhower was chosen over conservative Robert Taft in the 1952 Republican nomination, and while being a conservative Republican and "moderately devout United Presbyterian," he sought solace in Heard's teaching and in LSD (p. 70). Toy notes that beyond Mullendore's lengthy term at the helm of Southern California Edison, and service as Hoover's secretary at the Secretary of Commerce position within the Harding administration, he was also director of North American Aviation, Union Pacific Railroad and a Trustee of Mutual Life Insurance Company of New York, and "*a prominent member of San Francisco's exclusive Bohemian Grove Club*" (emphasis added) (p. 70). He also observes that he was "a communicant of the Wilshire Presbyterian Church of Los Angeles," and maintained his church affiliation "even though he personally rejected 'total reliance upon the infallibility of the Bible as interpreted by Calvin, Knox and Puritans,' simply declaring, 'I am a member of the Presbyterian Church, but I cannot go along with much of their dogma…' " (pp. 70–71). In his speeches, he declared that the beginning of the end of America and Western Civilization began with the New Deal, with the "final blow, the death knell" with the Republican nomination of conservative/centrist Eisenhower, stating that it showed a pattern of "the rise and fall and the dominance of the *stupid mass man…*" (p. 71) (emphasis added). In turn, in 1955 Mullendore praised Heard as "the greatest scholar with whom I have ever come into contact, a truly great historian and psychologist, and a man of deep spiritual insight," which was echoed by Read (pp. 71–72); by 1957, Mullendore confessed to Ingebretsen that "these sessions with Gerald Heard have made the greatest contributions to my perception and understanding which have been made from any single source in my lifetime" (p. 72).

Soon thereafter, Mullendore wrote an article for the winter 1959–1960 issue of *Modern Age*, entitled, "Our Tragic State of Confusion: A Diagnosis," in which he bemoaned the state of Western life, and confessed that "our crisis is spiritual, not economic" (p. 72). Importantly, Toy adds that "*In September, 1959, several months after his initial experiment with LSD* and shortly after he had completed his article for *Modern Age, Mullendore joined a small group of thirty to thirty-five persons from the Los Angeles area who had been invited to Robert Welch's first meeting to organize the John Birch Society on the Pacific Coast,"* and told B. E. Hutchinson, *former treasurer of Chrysler Corporation, who was also a Wayfarer and fellow Trustee of Spiritual Mobilization and the Foundation for Economic Education (FEE),* that Welch—later known to be one of the most extreme yet influential hard-right firebrands of conspiratorial theories, such as the whole civil rights movement being merely a communist front—*"has a good balanced viewpoint of our entire situation, and I was particularly pleased that he emphasizes the spiritual and moral aspects,"* and that *"I could find nothing to disagree with in his presentation of the facts and his analysis of the meaning of those facts"* (emphasis added) (pp. 72–73).

Mullendore still lamented, after the 1960 presidential election, that "it was indeed a blessing to have had a man of the stature of Herbert Hoover as the last President of the Republic," while he "became more obsessed with internalizing the human struggle," and "LSD was one means to that end" (p. 73). Ingebretsen's Foundation for Social Research provided $15,000 in funds for Heard and Jay Barrie for their "Growing Edge" research, along with Sidney Cohen, and he adds that "Robert Greenleaf, executive of the American Telephone and Telegraph Company [AT&T], who had also taken LSD under Heard's guidance, was instrumental in gaining support for Heard from the Parapsychology Foundation" (p. 73). Meanwhile, Toy notes that "Mullendore rejected conventional religion because 'the ministerial frame of reference holds the mind closed to the cosmos as offered by LSD' " (p. 74).

Importantly, Foy adds that "For a brief time during the early 1960s, Mullendore was a missionary for LSD. In the casual atmosphere of the Bohemian Grove in California, where influential businessmen and politicians shared the fraternal bond of the good outdoor life, the wonders of the psychedelic experiments were a topic of discussion in Mullendore's camp. His favorable experiences outweighed the criticism leveled at Timothy Leary, and some of the businessmen were attracted by *the drug's potential for positively influencing personality and increasing efficiency"* (p. 74) (emphasis added). He later stated that "Communion or correspondence with Cosmic Consciousness—as in the LSD experience—is the supreme need of man" (p. 75). Foy adds concerning Mullendore that he was at the pit of despair for humanity by 1964, and "a conversation with Gerald Heard convinced him that mankind was rapidly approaching a new evolutionary stage and might not survive the crisis in consciousness," while Ingebretsen added that "some of his sources, such as the prophets and seers among the American Indians and astrologers, assure him that the BIG SHOW starts either at the end of 1964 or in 1965" (p. 75)—*sounding a lot like the evangelical Bible prophecy teachers as read and heard on TV.* Toy concludes by quoting Mullendore from the late 1960s, after the focus on LSD had moved from the conservative elites such as himself to the common people and youth, who said, *"What a shame that [LSD] is so easily manufactured and has fallen into the hands of the dope peddlers, the ignorant youthful 'Hippies' and the like"* (p. 76) (emphasis added).

Leonard Read and his Foundation for Economic Education (FEE) organization have archived some portion of Mr. Read's journal notes over the decades. One particular online entry shows his journal notes from July 1954.[180] That monthly entry basically comprises his non-stop mission to raise money from big business sources and captains of industry—the pursuit thereof the bane of non-profits, as well as politicians—but the bulk of it comprises the step by step experiences of his visit that summer to the otherwise highly-secretive "Bohemian Grove," where the most powerful men in the world from industry and government meet, outside the eye of the public and press, and carouse and scheme in debauchery, bizarre pagan-styled annual ceremonies, like the "Cremation of Care" mock human sacrifice before a towering stone owl and cloaked and hooded torch-bearing figures. It also features other fraternity-styled skits and complex plays featuring ample "stag party"-like debauchery and male cross dressing (including many prominent politicians and celebrities), all in an atmosphere of non-stop drinking and foreign policy talks and private networking under the massive redwoods, staying in rustic but opulent tribal lodges that are often multi-generational in membership, including Richard Nixon, Ronald Reagan, the Bush family and foreign dignitaries and industrialists. Sometimes important business and other initiatives are discussed there, even though the old maxim "Weaving Spiders Come Not Here" emblazoned everywhere is supposed to discourage such activity amongst the debauched fraternal fellowship—such famous planning including the critical design meetings of the atomic bomb, with even the original United Nations delegates being brought to the Grove, as I have documented elsewhere. Although such discussions are discouraged, such a concentrated assembly of the most powerful figures from business and government on earth provided an irresistible opportunity for Read to network, persuade prominent figures and garner financial and connection support for his fledgling FEE operation, as his detailed notes attest.

It begins with a telephone discussion that appears to involve J. Howard Pew (of Christian philanthropy, such as the Pew Charitable Trust, and Pew polling on religious issues, as well being president of Sunoco), with later citations of financial checks coming from him. Amongst his "random thoughts," Read writes, "The progress of society does not appear to be a part of the Grand Design. *Society, the mass, is but the spawning supply from which a few partake of the evolutionary process. Most of humanity, like cats, dogs, apes, and the like, are but evidence of the evolutionary surge that didn't make the grade*" (emphasis added). He also mentioned his guests that drop in, including libertarian economics icon Ludwig von Mises, as well as his riding in the back of a Cadillac and using a new-fangled car phone to make contacts; some of the contacts, affiliated with the United Fruit Company of the "banana republics," lamented the current unrest in Guatemala due to the "Commies," with wall-to-wall descriptions of the five-star restaurants Read frequented nightly.

The majority of the nineteen-page monthly journal comprised his detailed itinerary while at Bohemian Grove. At his arrival he was joined by Mullendore, and subsequently joined the "Lost Angels" camp, which he says was "one of more than 130"; he insinuates that his visit is costing his buddy Mullendore a hefty sum, and points out every detail of the rustic buildings and the amenities, noting one of the outdoor dining rooms (in addition to those at each of the individual camps) "that will seat perhaps 1,140," and that "The liquor flows free, no account being kept of what one consumes. They all inhale the stuff." He described the thousand or so around the evening campfire, while Bing Crosby's guitarist played, adding that "there is, however, a spiritual quality about this place and gathering that I cannot yet describe." He also mentioned watching "the Low Jinks and I mean low—bawdy as the devil, well-staged, very large cast, good acting, lyrics and music, all composed of Bohemians," and attended a Bohemian talk about "the problems of US helping Latin America." Read also mentioned that a guest can only be invited twice, and the waiting list to join is decades long. He discussed walking to the various camps, such as Cave Man, where "the Chief resides" (aka former President Herbert Hoover). He noted that the other stories heard there are "fitted for men only in ribald mood," and then came back home, to host the "head of a small Methodist college." In his narrative of meetings, it was apparent he was able to secure large sums of money and support from the captains of industry there for FEE and their journal *The Freeman*, while many of the Bohemians identified themselves as *Freeman* readers and supporters already. *It could be seen to be an ideal place for the financial and well-bred elites of society, the "survival of the fittest" of social and economic evolutionary processes, as a libertarian ideal of social stratification and plutocracy.*

In the last lengthy chapter we identified and described the capitalistic "captains of industry" that, in their mission to counteract the Social Gospel and New Deal agendas of not ignoring the destitute and disadvantaged, providing modest means to provide for their basic essentials and a modicum of decency, and a path to sharing a small piece of the wealth of the fruit of the God-blessed land, led them to hook up with their "messiah" in Rev. Fifield, arguably the first "prosperity gospel" preacher in the "unique" cultural climate of Southern California, using the National Association of Manufacturers to nail their theses there on the "Wittenberg Door" of a "Christian libertarian" theology of unbridled "Great City Babylon" capitalism, unfettered by environmental or worker safety responsibilities, and a lack of social responsibility towards the victims of that system, or that of the biologically or socially fallen world.

Many henchmen helped Fifield, both from the CEOs in their paneled board rooms and oil tycoons in their steer horn-festooned Eldorados, and "gurus" of unknown origins, beliefs or agendas. Their deep pockets and profit-motivated zeal led to their widespread proliferation throughout much of our nation's pulpits and from there to the minds of the majorities of Americans sitting before those pulpits, exploiting the unparalleled moral and psychological influence of these clergymen, as "men of God" who spoke the words of Deity. The flock itself was unaware of its intentional programming, or even the cash awards their clergy were receiving for being Big Business' "Johnny Appleseed." This little-known era was successful in building what we know in the last generation as the "Religious Right," and the political change of course and impact in the ballot box that has impacted almost everyone I know here in the Bible Belt. The other collateral beliefs often found with the "elitist/elect" and separatist mindset commonly inherited from their Calvinist/Presbyterian and general fundamentalist doctrinal legacy, including anti-Semitism or hatred of those of other religions and cultures (like they hold towards Muslims today), anti-immigrant (ironically held by people all of an immigrant heritage themselves) and racist views, and sympathy for authoritarian (even fascist) modes of strong-handed and merciless rule, found means to piggyback onto these movements via radio and periodicals like *The Defender* and charismatic firebrand media figures. *All of these views support the cause of Ayn Rand/libertarian/Darwinist Big Business capitalists—the creation of the Great City Babylon—and their means to exploit or eradicate all but the most financially-productive "Kings of the Hill"—a teaching most condemningly espoused by those paid mouthpieces of the "leaven of the Pharisees" who claim to speak the words of Christ and the teachings of the Kingdom of Heaven.*

Within the pages of *Faith and Freedom* and similar periodicals of unparalleled impact on the American Christian culture were subversively positioned spiritual "gurus" of unknown origins and agendas, to influence and brainwash a generation of our church's leaders, to in turn brainwash subsequent generations in the pulpits or in the Christian schools and seminaries. In this lengthy chapter we have exposed what made these influential gurus "tick," like Gerald Heard. These figures in turn were influenced, bolstered and supported, and thereby indirectly influenced our clergy as well, by famous controversial figures our Christian leaders would never claim or perceive as influences themselves—men such as the atheist but supernaturally inclined (including the use of sorcery-based *pharmakeia)* Aldous Huxley, who foresaw a dystopian world of a drugged and stupefied populace, but ironically pursued such a state in reality for the elites only. Their other colleagues left an indelible mark on others on the margins of America's Christian community, such as Alcoholics Anonymous founder Bill Wilson—a man whose "system" has undoubtedly helped untold numbers in some way in resisting the bonds of one particular addiction, much like the pagan folk-religion entheogen and hallucinogenic herbs that triggered his spiritual "experience," but a man who whose own teachings could not break the bonds of his other addictions to infidelity, nicotine, and a true addiction to necromancy and consulting of spirits, and even drug-based sorcery. Such was commonly known and documented by his inner circle, nevertheless creating a pseudo-religious cult as a legacy, albeit offering some stability for the destitute, as most cults do. Speaking of drugs, we have seen that the conscious-altering LSD was not the reckless plaything of immature young people, but established by the "respectable" big business leaders who pretended to be respectable Christians, but scoffed at its basic tenets in their own correspondence, and intending to keep their sorcerer toys solely for the elites.

We will conclude this lengthy volume with some chapters that place these revelations back into a spiritual and Biblical framework, and consider how this understanding might motivate us to some positive changes to better be "salt and light" in the fields of America where we are now planted, in the "days assigned to us."

THE BIBLICAL VIEW OF CAPITALISM'S NATURE, POWERS AND ITS DESTINY

The online site of the *Merriam Webster Dictionary*[181] defines "capitalism" as "an economic system characterized by private or corporate ownership of capital goods, by investments that are determined by private decision, and by prices, production, and the distribution of goods that are determined mainly by competition in a free market." The online entry of the *Encyclopedia Britannica* on "Capitalism"[182] states that "Capitalism, also called free market economy or free enterprise economy, economic system, dominant in the Western world since the breakup of feudalism, in which most of the means of production are privately owned and production is guided and income distributed largely through the operation of markets." They add that

> Although the continuous development of capitalism as a system dates only from the 16th century, antecedents of capitalist institutions existed in the ancient world, and flourishing pockets of capitalism were present during the later European Middle Ages....The feature of this development that distinguished capitalism from previous systems was *the use of accumulated capital to enlarge productive capacity rather than to invest in economically unproductive enterprises, such as pyramids and cathedrals.* This characteristic was encouraged by several historical events. *In the ethic fostered by the Protestant Reformation of the 16th century, traditional disdain for acquisitive effort was diminished, while hard work and frugality were given a stronger religious sanction. Economic inequality was justified on the grounds that the wealthy were more virtuous than the poor.* Another contributing factor was the increase in Europe's supply of precious metals and the resulting inflation in prices. *Wages did not rise as fast as prices in this period, and the main beneficiaries of the inflation were the capitalists. The early capitalists (1500–1750) also enjoyed the benefits of the rise of strong national states during the mercantilist era.*" (emphasis added)

Beginning in the 18th century in England, the focus of capitalist development shifted from commerce to industry. The steady capital accumulation of the preceding centuries was invested in the practical application of technical knowledge during the Industrial Revolution. The ideology of classical capitalism was expressed in *An Inquiry into the Nature and Causes of the Wealth of Nations* (1776), by the Scottish economist and philosopher Adam Smith, which recommended leaving economic decisions to the free play of self-regulating market forces....The policies of 19th-century political liberalism included free trade, sound money (the gold standard), balanced budgets, and *minimum levels of poor relief. The growth of industrial capitalism and the development of the factory system in the 19th century also created a vast new class of industrial workers whose generally miserable conditions inspired the revolutionary philosophy of Karl Marx...* In the decades immediately following World War II, *the economies of the major capitalist countries, all of which had adopted some version of the welfare state, performed well, restoring some of the confidence in the capitalist system that had been lost in the 1930s. Beginning in the 1970s, however, rapid increases in economic inequality* (see income inequality; distribution of wealth and income), *both internationally and within individual countries, revived doubts among some people about the long-term viability of the system. Following the financial crisis of 2007– 09 and the Great Recession that accompanied it, there was renewed interest in socialism among many people in the United States, especially millennials* (persons born in the 1980s or '90s), a group that had been particularly hard-hit by the recession. (emphasis added)

Tied to the understanding of the phenomena and impact of "capitalism" in world history is the creation and impact of the entity known as the "corporation." In its entry on the subject,[183] the online *Encyclopedia Britannica* explains that "the corporation is distinguished by a number of characteristics that make it a more-flexible instrument for *large-scale economic activity*, particularly for the *purpose of raising large sums of capital for investment*. Chief among these features are: (1) limited liability, meaning that capital suppliers *are not subject to losses greater than the amount of their investment*....(3) juridical personality, meaning that *the corporation itself as a fictive 'person' has legal standing and may thus sue and be sued, may make contracts*, and may hold property in a common name; and (4) indefinite duration, whereby *the life of the corporation may extend beyond the participation of any of its incorporators"; and thus to continue to collect, hoard and expand over the generations.* It mentions the prior existence of guilds and companies representing universities and even monasteries, and English corporations from the 16th century that were chartered by the crown, and adds that "The fusion of the two forms took place incrementally over the first two-thirds of the 19th century in Great Britain, the United States, France, and Germany with the passage of general incorporation laws." They add that

> the construction of railroads—a matter of pressing national importance for all industrializing nations in the late 19th century— required large sums of capital that could be secured only through the corporate form and, in fact, only with many innovations in the development of financial and debt instruments….the railroads made possible…an enormous expansion of existing industries (notably steel and coal) that the corporate form alone could support. By the final third of the 19th century, the last legal obstacles to the corporate form had been removed, and the ensuing period (c. 1870–1910) saw an unprecedented expansion of industrial production and the concomitant predominance of the corporate form.

However, they add that "Large industrial corporations such as the Standard Oil Company and the United States Steel Corporation came to exercise monopolistic powers in their respective economic spheres, often apparently at the cost of the public interest. U.S. President Theodore Roosevelt sought to curb this concentration of corporate power in the early 20th century, urging the enactment of antitrust legislation aimed at preserving competition." They add that "As corporations increased in size and geographic scope, control of the enterprise by its nominal owners, the shareholders, became impossible when the number of shareholders for the largest companies grew to the tens of thousands and as the practice of proxy voting (i.e., the voting of shares of absent stockholders by management in the annual shareholders' meetings) was legalized and adopted. Salaried managers came to exercise virtually proprietary discretion over the corporation and its assets."

In 2008 I was contacted by Christian book publisher Tom Horn to write the last remaining chapter of an anthology book he was publishing, entitled, *How to Overcome the Most Frightening Issues You WILL Face This Century*, which he published the following year. As the last of twenty authors selected, I was assigned the uninspiring "dregs" of a topic, entitled, "Fuel and Food Shortages," of which I had little to no expertise unlike the other topics, and for which required a "crash course" of study, including the Biblical antecedents for a Christian-themed book. I was tasked with writing on this topic—one for which I had shown little interest—at possibly a providential time. Up to that time, in the midst of the seven-year production of my *Future Quake* radio program for which I had gained some notoriety, I had been in previous years a proud, card-carrying, *Fox News*-watching Christian conservative, serving in my conservative denomination church weekly and whenever the doors were opened (and I still do, by the way), with a keen interest in Bible prophecy and Zionism, having spent my career working with the war fighters in the U.S. Air Force as a civilian scientist, followed by a period as an intellectual property entrepreneur, working hand in hand with venture capitalists and small technology businesses. By this time, my business pursuits were winding down, and the radio show production and its associated research served as a dawning of a process of my asking hard, overdue questions of my Bible Belt Christian cultural assumptions (while living in a hard "Red State" community), with time available to dig into scripture deeper, as well as the work of others outside my culture, for which the Internet Age, despite all its dangers, provided me sudden access (in truth, these questions began in the 2005-06 time frame as I began to be exposed to guests and new data). Thus, the few years leading up to this assignment prepared me to look at the spiritual implications of the economic effects on society in a fresher (and more disturbing) light.

Fortunately, I was asked to write on this bland topic at the time of the 2008 economic collapse later known as The Great Recession, the wake of which is still felt amongst citizens and businesses alike today. It was largely seen by experts in hindsight as a crisis begun by unregulated investment banks, easy credit and high-risk "liar loans" with little due diligence to verify incomes, and the associated "bubbles" in stock and real estate valuations that heretofore had been foreseen to "never end." It was a time when both competing U.S. political parties and their presidential candidates came together to authorize taxpayer-funded bailouts of the handful of investment banks deemed "too big to fail" as the result of their foolish, greedy investments that would otherwise have ended their misdeeds by a true unregulated market. A few of them (such as Lehman Brothers) were chosen as "sacrificial lambs," while the others with similar reckless behaviors went unpunished, and the politically-influential Goldman Sachs cemented its position as king of the investment banks. Other major retail giants and other businesses that were icons of the American public went bust as massive layoffs occurred, the stock market plummeted, and stability took years to restore, with the impact of the lost wealth and unemployed earnings period still lingering with many today. It was also the time when a major automaker (General Motors) was saved by politicians and public debt, after having let others fail, and the unions refused to compromise but rather relied on President Bush's promises of taxpayer bailouts, rather than wisely and opportunistically purchasing the beleaguered automaker outright to make it employee-owned; the government also became owners (and loan guaranteers) as the world's biggest "slum lord" over a large portion of the nation's defaulting real estate loans. This created an era of Internet-fueled paranoia and fear of the value of currency, bonds and stock aside from gold, to a level not seen since the Great Depression, which served as a backdrop of relevance to the topic.

The lengthy chapter I submitted to publisher Horn included a lengthy discussion of the great periods of economic distress in world history where shortages of food or other staples led to extreme measures by governments or others in power, including widespread starvation, migrations of people, and even civil or regional wars. In some cases, like the Great Irish Potato Famine, the Irish people starved while having an abundance of potatoes in harvest, but their farm owners (most foreigners, or corporations) saw greater profits in selling them off their shores. In almost all cases, the powers with access to true assets of value in time of crisis, be they governments, noblemen or other corporate entities, used such temporal crises (such as famine) to extract all other items of normal and future wealth at fire-sale prices from the citizenry, who did not have the capital to ride out the crisis, nor the right types of assets or wages for the times, and thus lost everything to the entities armed with superior capital, becoming debt or full-blown slaves to them, having surrendered their money-making assets, tools, land and eventually themselves and their own labor.

I began by noting that such a scenario is described in spades within the pages of the book of Genesis, concerning a clearly-described incident within its pages that, if taken at face value, would otherwise spoil the traditionally spotless public reputation of one of the most heroic figures of the Old Testament—Joseph, son of Jacob. Any attendee of children's Sunday School or Vacation Bible School would know of his virtues of maintaining his ethics even when tempted by Potiphar's wife and subsequent imprisonment, his prior betrayal by his brothers, and his diligent trust in God until he was elevated to second in command in Egypt, the greatest empire in the world at the time, and his eventual reunion with his Hebrew brethren and his role in their deliverance from famine after their sojourn of desperation there. In fact, the event that led to Joseph's elevation by Pharaoh was his interpretation of Pharaoh's dream of an upcoming famine crisis after a few years of future prosperity, as well as the wisdom Joseph provided to secure provisions during times of plenty to ride it out, which not only protected the kingdom, but further empowered it over that region of the world otherwise not so prepared. However, it also briefly recounts the not-so-inspiring side effects to the public at large when a power with economic resources to ride out crises can exploit the opportunity to confiscate the entire wealth and vitality of its subjects and citizens.

I began by reciting Joseph's recommendation to Pharaoh after his interpretation of his dream, for his officers to confiscate twenty percent of the harvest during the upcoming seven years of plenty, to be then sold back to the Egyptian people, and ultimately to other people from the region who came to Egypt, as recounted in Genesis 41. No mention is made in the text if the officers paid the Egyptian farmers for the twenty percent confiscation, or merely took it as a form of tax; regardless, *it does make clear that the government sold it back to the very people who grew it, at a price of their asking.* Furthermore, it states that the government sold the precious grain from the Egyptian people not only to them, but also to the rival nations nearby, depleting their wealth, but obviously at a price the Egyptian people could no longer afford, particularly since their wealth collapsed, which made the provisions even scarcer for the Egyptian people who grew it, and thus more valuable and harder to obtain. As I point out in my chapter, Joseph was even able to manipulate the outsiders when they were his family, "detaining them or dismissing them at his leisure, since the Hebrews and other starving people simply had no other choices".[184] I also noted that when Joseph told Pharaoh that the food should be gathered and "kept" in the cities, the Hebrew word for "keep" (*shamar,* Strong's Hebrew Lexicon H8104), is often used to "keep guard over" (as the New American Standard version translates it here), such as its use to describe the "flaming sword" that "guards" the Tree of Life in the Garden; this would imply that he foresaw the need to protect the stockpiles from hungry citizens later, as even wealthy landowners and corporations have done in times of need throughout history.

I then reviewed the darker elements of this incident, as recounted in Genesis 47, the narrative passage of which I recite here in full:

> And Joseph gathered up all the money that was found in the land of Egypt, and in the land of Canaan, for the corn which they bought: and Joseph brought the money into Pharaoh's house. And when money failed in the land of Egypt, and in the land of Canaan, all the Egyptians came unto Joseph, and said, Give us bread: for why should we die in thy presence? for the money faileth. And Joseph said, Give your cattle; and I will give you for your cattle, if money fail. And they brought their cattle unto Joseph: and Joseph gave them bread [in exchange] for horses, and for the flocks, and for the cattle of the herds, and for the asses: and he fed them with bread for all their cattle for that year. When that year was ended, they came unto him the second year, and said unto him, We will not hide [it] from my lord,

how that our money is spent; my lord also hath our herds of cattle; there is not ought left in the sight of my lord, but our bodies, and our lands: Wherefore shall we die before thine eyes, both we and our land? Buy us and our land for bread, and we and our land will be servants unto Pharaoh: and give [us] seed, that we may live, and not die, that the land be not desolate. And Joseph bought all the land of Egypt for Pharaoh; for the Egyptians sold every man his field, because the famine prevailed over them: so the land became Pharaoh's. And as for the people, he removed them to cities from [one] end of the borders of Egypt even to the [other] end thereof. Only the land of the priests bought he not; for the priests had a portion [assigned them] of Pharaoh, and did eat their portion which Pharaoh gave them: wherefore they sold not their lands. Then Joseph said unto the people, Behold, I have bought you this day and your land for Pharaoh: lo, [here is] seed for you, and ye shall sow the land. And it shall come to pass in the increase, that ye shall give the fifth [part] unto Pharaoh, and four parts shall be your own, for seed of the field, and for your food, and for them of your households, and for food for your little ones. And they said, Thou hast saved our lives: let us find grace in the sight of my lord, and we will be Pharaoh's servants. And Joseph made it a law over the land of Egypt unto this day, [that] Pharaoh should have the fifth [part]; except the land of the priests only, [which] became not Pharaoh's. Gen. 47:14–26

I noted that "through Joseph's actions, the government had a corner on the one asset with any value under those extreme conditions. They were then able to name their price in terms of money or coin in exchange for the essential asset. In the process, they accumulated the bulk of the nation's coinage, and thus the ability to purchase the other now-devalued assets still owned by the populace" (p. 249). I add that "The verse says then that the money 'failed' in the economy (some alternative translations say that all the money was spent)—presumably a collapse of the currency of some form…not only in Egypt, but in Canaan as well. Therefore, the people came again to their government for solutions, in essence a 'bailout' of free food and necessities in a welfare-type program" (p. 249). However, I point out that "the government officials themselves determined that there were indeed assets that were of value to the government (at least that they could secure to exchange for assets of value to the government later, even if they couldn't use them now). Those assets were their cattle, which also included their flocks, horses, and burden animals such as asses, in exchange for one year's supply of bread"(p. 249). I noted further that "We can see a vicious cycle further developing in which the people were now giving up the equivalent of their future 'seed corn' by 'hocking' the very tools they would use to generate income and produce further food, and by sacrificing their sources of meat, milk, and 'horsepower' to pull plows, tread grain, and transport crops to the market"; I state that "Inevitably, the people would return needy again the second year (it is ironic that the government supplied them only a single year's food, even though their data suggested the famine would be far longer)" (p. 249).

I noted that whether the government had paid for the twenty percent of the "bumper crops" or just took them by eminent domain, the "current market value would have been greatly reduced at the time due to the ample supply, [and] the government would have procured it at token prices, if any....the resource-depleted people must then sacrifice their very land and their own freedom as a last attempt to obtain one more year's worth of food (note that a citizen's forfeiture of private property is in essence the equivalent of indentured servitude anyway)" (p. 250). I observed that "It is cruelly ironic that the government then supplied seed for planting—the very asset that could have preserved the citizens' long-term security and independence earlier. But this time, it was to be used on land recently confiscated by the government, using government-confiscated tools and work animals to be produced by government-owned people! Presumably, the famine must have stabilized to a point that the proper seed, land, and tools could produce new crops, but the real damage to the citizens had already been done" (p. 250). I further state that "The government then flexed its totalitarian muscles by forcibly relocating people to the teeming, overcrowded cities, where they could be better controlled, presumably placed in austere communal housing with minimal real estate 'footprints' " (p. 250). I write that

> The most tragic portion of the Genesis narrative is the response of the government, via Joseph, which acknowledged and announced its role as savior of the people, while "generously" letting the people keep eighty percent of the product of their hard work although the government acknowledged their right to one hundred percent of "their" assets. In turn, the broken, disillusioned, and brainwashed citizenry thanked the benevolent government for "saving their lives" and letting them keep any portion of their labors, even though such governmental rights were obtained by exploiting and manipulating their own people under the guise of protecting them. This transfer of wealth and property to the state, and the precedents of heavy taxation, lasted for generations—long after the crisis had subsided. (pp. 250–251)

God must have seen this confiscation as ill-gotten wealth, and not merely "shrewd," because God certainly did not see it as "stealing" when He directed the Hebrews to purloin and pillage much of this wealth as they left Egypt in the days of Moses—maybe this was "back pay" for their wage-exploitation of the Hebrews, as well as the economic confiscation of the wealth of the region previously.

Some readers may look at these passages and their analysis and say, "Aha! The real culprit is the government itself, who is the real enemy of the people!" However, the cases of governments alone confiscating the entire wealth of a nation or kingdom are relatively rare in history, such as the Stalinist and Maoist governments in the twentieth century. However, for most of recorded history, the lines between the official ruling/royal/government class and the wealth class (call them "noblemen" with official peerage and lands, or "aristocrats"), begins to blur shortly after the formation of sophisticated forms of government and economic systems. One could even say that the wealth classes have more often controlled the government/royal class, than vice versa (and most often, they come from the same classes). In our era, they are recruited oftentimes from the same East Coast elite families (commonly idle rich with money made from Gilded Age robber barons, Prohibition smuggling, or modern oil and technology "gold rushes"), conditioned via military/boarding schools and Yale, and recruited for Washington political and intelligence leadership positions, and then return to Wall Street to profit from the largesse and friends they established from their time in office.

Certainly by the time of Babylon, ancient Greece and Rome, the wealthy aristocrats had a controlling influence, which continued in the feudal age, and more formally controlling the king through covenants like the Magna Carta. The rise of the Knights Templar independent banking empire scared the other power centers in the Church and royalty so much that they led an Inquisition to obliterate them (having already owed them much money), with the burgeoning medieval Jewish banking establishment coalescing into global powerhouses like the Bank of Rothschild (which used its wealth and control of media to create military crisis-and-"fake news"-fueled stock panics for its benefit), the rise of the fully independent "City of London" (led by banking oligarchs, and in essence totally sovereign), and the global investment banks and institutions such as the World Bank today. The foundation of the Federal Reserve in 1913 is a case in point of an entire global powerhouse nation and its government giving over its sovereignty and wealth to a relatively unknown cabal of bankers.

When one ponders the Bible narrative, as well as other details from the writings of Josephus or other ancient sources (including the Talmud) that may or may not be just legend, one could consider the original city of Babel on the plains of Shinar, purportedly founded by Nimrod as a place to organize the post-diluvian humanity into a congregated society that eventually challenged the heavens, as the place whereby tyranny and economic controls over wage-earners (slaves) began in earnest. It certainly was in play in the heydays of the great city Babylon, with writings of its sophisticated merchant systems, laws and accounting practices still preserved and built upon today, leading to unrivaled works of construction and magnificence, *and unparalleled suffering and enslavement.*

I noted in the same publication the hints in the New Testament concerning the continuous "sins" and exploitation of the peoples of earth by the merchant and money-class over history, and their proposed "crescendo" of domination leading into the End of Days, and their rapid judgment and fall. As an aside, after the famed "Letters to the Seven Churches," I see the next few chapters of the Bible's Book of Revelation as the narrative of a heavenly court under order, as a contrast to the Sanhedrin (seventy) judgment of Jesus on earth, where Satan as leader of the seventy rebellious "sons of God" over the nations passed judgment on the "son of God" who has identified Himself also as the "Son of Man," or man's representative, having sent out the seventy "Spirit-empowered" disciples previously to show that their current heavenly rulers were soon to be replaced. In this later case in Revelation, the trial is convened by the celestial Minor Sanhedrin of twenty four elders in the heavenly version of the Temple's Hall of Hewn Stones, which is called into order when the Judge appears—the Lamb, slain for the world—to pass judgment on Satan and his seventy Sons of God henchmen, and their earthly lackeys. The court then unseals each of the four indictments of the sins of the accused, before the court. The first seal reveals the "horseman" of a fraudulent "triumphant" church, armed with earthly weapons, "conquering and to conquer," with the crown of earthly government and forced violent theocracy, starting with Constantine and leading throughout the Church Age. The second seal reveals the violent institutional mass-murder known as war and plunder. The fourth seal reveals the inevitable pestilence, famine and ecological death in the wake of the human and spiritual actions of the first three horsemen, when the populace loses shelter, security, food, sanitation and other protections. However, the key "horseman" whose historic sins are unveiled for our discussion, is the third horseman, on the black horse. The narrative in Revelation describes it as follows:

And when he had opened the third seal, I heard the third beast say, Come and see. And I beheld, and lo a black horse; and he that sat on him had a pair of balances in his hand. And I heard a voice in the midst of the four beasts say, A measure of wheat for a penny, and three measures of barley for a penny; and [see] thou hurt not the oil and the wine. (Revelation 6:5–6)

In the earlier cited reference of my work, I described the significance of this imagery in the following way:

What have just been discovered by the author are the unique implications in the original language (Greek) of key words in these passages, which have been largely masked by the various English translations. First, please note the key word translated as "scales" in verse 5, which has been the most identifiable symbol associated with this passage. Through the years, countless pictures illustrating this passage have depicted a scale/balance-wielding horseman. However, a brief review of the Greek word *zygos*, from which the English translation "pair of balances" is normally employed, is revealed in Strong's reference (entry G2218) to primarily refer to a "yoke," such as "is put on draught cattle," "used of any burden or bondage," or "as that of slavery." A secondary reference is to a "balance" or "pair of scales." In fact, every other use of this word in the Bible is translated as a "yoke." The consideration of this device as a "yoke" is a much more enlightening translation, since it implies an economic "yoke" of slavery to debt and limited access to essential economic and other resources controlled by the evil entity who places the yoke. This picture is reminiscent of the scenario in Egypt where the citizens took the yoke of servitude to Pharaoh, using their own yokes that were then the property of the state in order to receive sustenance since they had no other assets by which to otherwise obtain essential goods. We see in the modern era these same activities by globalist groups like the International Monetary Fund, which burdens entire third world countries with deep levels of debt in exchange for bare essentials in a vicious cycle from which they cannot escape, even if their era of crisis was initially only temporary. In fact, John Perkins, in his shocking, best-selling 2004 book, *Confessions of An Economic Hit Man*, describes his duties on behalf of the IMF in such a role. The following excerpt of his concise description of this role exhibits disturbing parallels to the aforementioned passage in Revelation:

"Economic hit men (EHMs) are highly paid professionals who cheat countries around the globe out of trillions of dollars. They funnel money from the World Bank, the U.S. Agency for International

Development (USAID), and other foreign 'aid' organizations into the coffers of huge corporations and the pockets of a few wealthy families who control the planet's natural resources....They play a game as old as empire, but one that has taken on new and terrifying dimensions during this time of globalization."

This is a hauntingly plausible description of how the black horse (as in the black ink of economics—in fact, the Greek word *melas* used for "black" here was commonly used by the Greeks to particularly denote "black ink") can realistically control the fate of millions of humans, without guns or other coercion. One last comment regarding this verse is directed to the last Greek word *cheir* (Strong's 5495), translated as the word "hand," as the instrument of holding and controlling the yoke. One of the more intriguing historical definitions of this Greek word by Strong's is the phrase "symbolizing...might, power, activity, in determining and controlling the destinies of men." Many times in Scripture, it is apparent this word is used to describe the actions and ability of God himself, dependent upon the context present in the passage. But, in this passage in question, it is clear that it is used by malevolent forces for diabolical purposes. One might presume that the "balance" or "scales" translation might be more appropriate for this passage, given the further elaboration in verse 6, which states:

And I heard a voice in the midst of the four beasts say, A measure of wheat for a penny, and three measures of barley for a penny; and [see] thou hurt not the oil and the wine. (Revelation 6:6)

This can illustrate a picture of one "balancing" money and commodities in the pans of a scale, as one possibility, and that may indeed be the intended metaphor. However, the device known as a "yoke" in Scripture and in the ancient world was a device to join two entities together, such as two oxen. This understanding of their ancient procedures better illustrates the possible relationship Christ has to His followers when He says, "take My yoke upon you." Many have seen this as our installing the yoke of labor and servitude upon ourselves, with Christ behind the reins as the master directing from behind. However, it can also be envisioned as Christ applying the yoke on us, with Himself in the other side of the yoke, pulling as the lead ox. Because of this leadership role, He bears the brunt of the burden; thus, our burden is light in comparison. In fact, the previously discussed Greek word *zygos* for "yoke" is described by Strong's as "to join, especially by a yoke." Therefore, the "yoke" analogy can also be perceived as the joining of the value of money to precise quantities of critical resources such as food, under the control and whims of the "hand" wielding it, much like world bankers sometimes peg the value of currency to fixed assets such as gold, or in setting price controls, which can wreak havoc on the entire economies of countries and make large people groups rich or poor overnight at the determination of remote and dispassionate forces.

In the case of this passage, a "measure" (Greek *choinix*: an amount of food sufficient to sustain a man for a day (Strong's G5518) of wheat for a "penny" (Greek *denarion*: understood to be equivalent to a day's wages) and three measures of barley for a penny show that members of the populace will only be given a day's food for a day's work, with no other compensation for other needs implied. This illustrates the ultimate in irredeemable, irreversible dependency and servitude (no explanation is implied for the reason that three measures of barley are given; possibly it is less nutritious and requires more, or perhaps people are given weekends off after 'Barley Friday'!). Other basic needs may be met in government housing, or even internment camps, to meet catastrophic needs or merely for population control, albeit with the need for detainees to supply a full day's work to receive their essential food needs. This scenario is eerily akin to the Egyptians who lived in government-owned housing in the cities as they worked for the state in exchange for their minimal food needs.

The last portion of this verse exhibits a number of unremarkable words (in English); however, they yield a wide range of possible scenarios when considering the range of definitions of the original Greek words used (this author is not a Greek scholar, or even a linguist, so any assertions submitted here should be verified by diligent students of the Word). First, the phrase "[see] thou hurt" is a translation of the Greek word *adikeo*, which Strong's (G91) lists as having a range of meanings, such as "to act unjustly or wickedly, to sin," "to be a criminal, to do wrong," "to do hurt." In Revelation 22:11, for example, the word is translated as one being 'unjust'. Even more curious is the range of meanings possible for the Greek word *me* (Strong's G3361), translated in English as simply "not." It suggests possible translations such as "lest" or "God forbid"; it suggests "qualified negation" as opposed to "absolute negation," such as when the Greek word *ou* is translated as "no" or "not." Other meanings such as "unless" and "if not," among others, are also listed. Since this simple word has so many complex meanings, one must use extreme caution in committing to a single interpretation of this phrase, and it is prudent to consider a range of possible interpretations of how this passage could possibly be fulfilled. In modern vernacular, phrases such as, "God forbid they act unjustly with the oil and the wine," or "...unless they act criminally regarding the oil and the wine," are a few of a wide range of possible interpretations in the mind of this untrained linguist. The key point here is that one cannot confirm that the "wine" and "oil" will not be harmed or exploited in any case with absolute certainty, when considering only the range of interpretations of the Greek words used in this verse, regardless of the common English words chosen by modern translators.

Speaking of the "oil" and "wine," the Greek word used here (*oinos*, Strong's G3631) for the English word "wine" can pertain to the simple beverage known as wine, or as a metaphor of God's wrath, as it is used elsewhere in the book of Revelation. It is uncertain why this substance is chosen as a commodity in this reference, although it has been speculated upon by many. For example, maybe the totalitarian state will allow a form of "Victory Gin," as was available to the masses in the seminal book *1984* as a means of keeping the populace pacified, and their senses dulled. However, the findings are even more intriguing for the companion commodity translated in English as "oil," known in the Greek as *elaion* (Strong's G1637). This word is shown as representing a form of olive oil used for fuel oil for lamps, for healing the sick, and for anointing, but not for consumption. This particular word for oil is only used in Scripture for representing a fuel oil or as a medicine (as used by the Good Samaritan). This might imply that the substance is indeed heating oil, representing energy resources in general. If this is true, then determining the proper interpretation of the preceding phrase is paramount; it would hence reveal whether energy supplies might also be restricted and controlled alongside foodstuffs, or alternatively prevented from such manipulation. (pp. 256–260)

God's view of how He perceives the evolving and growing influence of the mammon/merchant juggernaut in controlling the fate and affairs of mankind in Revelation, is how the same book reveals the further nature, specific sins and mode of judgment of this "horseman," whose role in the deaths of man and creation was confirmed in the "Third Seal," in one of the last chapters and latter events in the historic narrative of this future era of judgment. I continue my analysis of Revelation 18 and the nature and fate of the "Great City Babylon" in the following excerpt I wrote from the previous citation from 2009:

These same diabolical characters are described in Revelation chapter 18, and are known as "Babylon, the Great City." I personally believe (at this time) that this passage describes the judgment and eventual, sudden downfall of the tyrannical economic institution that is described in the third seal (an unsealed indictment of sins, if you will), and which has been operating since the days of the Tower and the great kingdom of Babylon, being made manifest thence in numerous forms. Let's consider a number of the verses from this passage:

And he cried mightily with a strong voice, saying, Babylon the great is fallen, is fallen, and is become the habitation of devils, and the hold of every foul spirit, and a cage of every unclean and hateful bird. For all nations have drunk of the wine of the wrath of her fornication, and the kings of the earth have committed fornication with her, and the merchants of the earth are waxed rich through the abundance of her delicacies. And I heard another voice from heaven, saying, Come out of her, my people, that ye be not partakers of her sins, and that ye receive not of her plagues. For her sins have reached unto heaven, and God hath remembered her iniquities....Therefore shall her plagues come in one day, death, and mourning, and famine; and she shall be utterly burned with fire: for strong [is] the Lord God who judgeth her. And the kings of the earth, who have committed fornication and lived deliciously with her, shall bewail her, and lament for her, when they shall see the smoke of her burning, Standing afar off for the fear of her torment, saying, Alas, alas, that great city Babylon, that mighty city! for in one hour is thy judgment come. And the merchants of the earth shall weep and mourn over her; for no man buyeth their merchandise any more....and cinnamon, and odours, and ointments, and frankincense, and wine, and oil, and fine flour, and wheat, and beasts, and sheep, and horses, and chariots, and slaves, and *souls of men*. And the fruits that thy soul lusted after are departed from thee, and all things which were dainty and goodly are departed from thee, and thou shalt find them no more at all. The merchants of these things, which were made rich by her, shall stand afar off for the fear of her torment, weeping and wailing...For in one hour so great riches is come to nought. And every shipmaster, and all the company in ships, and sailors, and as many as trade by sea, stood afar off... saying, Alas, alas, that great city, wherein were made rich all that had ships in the sea by reason of her costliness! for in one hour is she made desolate. Rejoice over her, [thou] heaven, and [ye] holy apostles and prophets; for God hath avenged you on her. And a mighty angel took up a stone like a great millstone, and cast [it] into the sea, saying, Thus with violence shall that great city Babylon be thrown down, and shall be found no more at all....And the light of a candle shall shine no more at all in thee; and the voice of the bridegroom and of the bride shall be heard no more at all in thee: *for thy merchants were the great men of the earth; for by thy sorceries were all nations deceived. And in her was found the blood of prophets, and of saints, and of all that were slain upon the earth.* Revelation 18:2–5, 8–11, 13–15, 17, 19–21, 23–24 (emphasis added)

We see in the first verse that (a) the institution is known as "Babylon the Great"; (b) "devils" and "foul" spirits are behind its operations; (c) all nations, as well as individual world leaders ("kings") and merchants, have participated in her sins; and (d) the nations will also share in the wrath poured out on her. We see next a very important admonition: God's children should "come out of her" and "not be partakers of her sins" so they would "receive not of her plagues." The biggest question is this: How do we do this in a manner that God intends from this passage?...Does it mean that we get out of the world's financial, investment, and credit systems? If so, how do we do it? These things are the questions groups of Christians need to be discussing over coffee in homes and other venues. Are you affiliated with economic and financial groups that exploit other people by taking advantage of the poor or the third world, or that even practice predatory credit practices? Would God consider these things the sins Babylon will be judged about?

Further in this passage, it is clear that God sees these exploitative economic practices as sins that are important and grievous to the Lord. We also see that "the shoe will be on the other foot" as God issues a judgment of famine upon the nation that artificially created local famines to control others in the past. Notice here that the kings of the earth stand "afar off, for fear of her torment," yet they mourn over her destruction; they had "good times" with her and used her while it lasted (like a prostitute), but when she meets her end, they want to be far enough away that the sulfur and brimstone don't land on them....Men of evil are like this: They join together to pillage, exploit, and enjoy their plunder. But when the hard times come, they are nowhere to be found....Notice that the products Babylon was known to sell in the past included the "wine and oil" of Revelation chapter 6 and a host of nonessential but extravagant delicacies for the wealthy, as well as "the souls of men." That is what these wealthy cartels—particularly the ultra-wealthy, Rockefeller types who have no need for more money—really want to control. As the ultimate power trip, they want to manipulate people as they like, including their very basics of survival, as the third seal of Revelation 6, the indentured servitude of the citizens of Egypt in Genesis 47, and the generations of people in between imply.

All the merchants, including the international traders in ships, stand afar off, noting (a) how she had made them so wealthy, and (b) how rapidly she was destroyed ("within an hour"). I believe this destruction will be supernatural, physical, and clearly from God himself, but the way our current economic system is leveraged, with fractional reserve lending, one can see that even if it shakes financially, the whole system comes crashing down instantly, particularly if confidence in the artificial system is lost. While they are mourning, "heaven, the apostles and prophets" are told to "rejoice over her," because "God has avenged you on her." Later, this is explained because "in her was found the blood of prophets, and saints, and all that were slain upon the earth." I think this makes a point that the traditional conspiracy theorists make: that the wars of the world are typically fought for economic reasons and interests, and not for the reasons that kings tell their people to inspire patriotic fervor. The United States is not immune to this. We killed the Indians to get their valuable land for the railroads and settlers (and the British before that due to high taxes!), killed the Confederates to keep access to cheap raw materials (although some rightfully opposed slavery), killed the Spanish to obtain imperialistic lands far away for their economic and strategic value, and the list goes on and on.

Even the children of God have been killed for a number of reasons: they removed spirits from mediums who made money for their handlers; they did not provide money for the coffers of the institutionalized church; they did not cooperate with state power structures when their consciences forbade them; and they exhibited an air of even quiet rebellion that threatened the system (such as by merely refusing to briefly mention that "Caesar is lord"). From Rome to the modern day, "kings" have felt this rebellion might "catch on" with others and threaten their lucrative positions at the government treasuries. These latter concerns were the kinds of reasons the Pharisees arrived at with Roman leaders to squash Christ and His followers to maintain the status quo in the religious, political, and economic realms (I'm sure they never forgave Jesus for turning over the money changers' tables—where the presence of "Babylon" temporarily occupied and "conquered" the Temple in its own way). The end of this passage also says that "thy merchants were the great men of the earth," which we understand and have established are the true power brokers of this age, as opposed to kings—be it the Rockefellers, Rothschild, or the Morgans who have kept the nations and their kings on a leash for centuries. The passage also says that "for by thy sorceries were all nations deceived." God says that their seduction had a spiritual component, that it was a "sorcery" of some sort. Who knows what types of spirit communications these mysterious, powerful families conduct? In any case, entire nations in history were "deceived" by these economic power brokers, their motives, and how they had planned to enslave them. They possibly had spiritual help in their deceptions. (pp. 260–265)

In essence, one can view the establishment of "Babylon" as the "ground operations" of what I have coined the "Cosmic Rebels" of celestial beings who have defied their own Creator, either prior to the creation of the physical universe, in the days prior to the Great Flood by their unlawful habitation on earth, or the disobedience of the seventy "sons of God" who were signed administration over the seventy nations of earth with the first fall of the Tower of Babel, but who rather sought self-worship through idols and oppressed the poor, fatherless, afflicted, and needy, all through injustice, with their doom foretold in Psalm 82. Through Babylon they have enticed humans to assist them "on the ground," even though their agenda is to destroy the very mankind whom God has shown favor—shown by providing mankind their physical bodies and an environment to enjoy them, the mysterious ability of procreation, and the unique status of being granted redemption for sin, even by means of God Himself becoming a man, and mankind's representative "champion" as the "Son of Man," to the point of divine self-sacrifice. They have found mammon, or the economic means and material goods to grant men prestige, comforts, powers and even control over the environment and others, as a most successful means to secure their complicity; when that is not effective, they can otherwise corrupt, tempt, or even strike fear into men's hearts to coerce their assistance. "Babylon" represents the spiritual "organized crime" syndicate that has built a world system based upon greed and self-promotion, as ultimately Darwinistic vs. civilized and moral, and in direct opposition to the community need-centered focus of the Kingdom of Heaven, where each relies upon God as well as their neighbor to secure their own essentials and needs. "Babylon" has existed as a real place throughout history (even today), but it is much more than that—a system, a way of thinking, and a spiritual force that seeks to corrupt men (and women) by self-serving means that opposes God's Kingdom ways. It can tempt at times everyone reading this—*including this author.*

"Babylon" needed a self-centered, Darwinistic, competitive "survival of the fittest" economic system to enact upon communities, and ultimately the world system. That economic model would become what we now know as "capitalism," which may be their crown invention for subjugating the masses. It does so in a manner that can thrive even in modern eras of advanced education and communications, and in such a subtle and subversive way (as opposed to heavy-handed autocratic dictatorships, or totalitarian systems such as Maoism or Stalinism) *that the saints in Christ's church in the West can sing its merits (dismissing its faults yet emphasizing those of other systems), while ignoring the warnings of such a competitive, selfish and amoral system by God's Mosaic Law and Christ's teaching of the Kingdom of Heaven.*

By definition, as we saw earlier in this section, it derives its name from the reliance on private wealth, versus the collective resources of a community used for a shared mutual ends, as the "engine" that runs, and inevitably controls society. The very act of possessing capital or assets provides one possessing it the essential element to define the terms and rules in the marketplace, and ultimately every other part of society, over those who are smarter, wiser, more capable, harder working, innovative, creative, moral, noble, kind or ethical. I have seen this in spades in my own development of patented technologies, and the repeated reality that the venture capitalists or other investors control the entire process of innovation, and hoard also almost all of the largesse derived from it, even though they may have a terrible record of success, merely inherited wealth, bad management style, disreputable behavior, and/or no vision. This scenario is not just true in the technology fields; in the creative arts, such as the music industry and Hollywood, or other mass media, the "suits" define the game while they keep the profits, and stymie (and show contempt for) the best and brightest. The purest form of capitalism can be seen in the era of the "robber barons," where ruthlessness in the marketplace, or betraying and crushing worthy competitors became sport (and even seen by many as a virtue, as Ayn Rand might), along with providing horrible working conditions for wage earners and the slums they live in, while many of these heartless tyrants were seen as wonderful philanthropists, and some (such as Rockefeller, and many others in the oil industry) seen as "godly men" and role models, as their P.R. (public relations) firms successfully burnished in the minds of the public via the media, in distracting from their daily vices and evils on a vast scale.

In essence, capitalism functions on the old clichéd version of the "golden rule"—*that he who has the gold, makes the rules.* Never forget—even those of us who have survived and eked out lives (many very comfortable) in the business world, that the world of capitalism is committed, as its very nature, to serve private ends and benefits of its allied henchmen, not the public ends and interests of society; *you cannot change its nature or instinct, any more than having the leopard change its spots.*

A few words should be said about the other entity introduced in the beginning of this chapter in association with the concept of capitalism, that being the concept of the "publicly traded corporation." I think I could reliably say by beginning that, *"If capitalism is the religion of Babylon, then corporations are the chief priests."* Unlike humans, whom the founding fathers said were endowed by their creator with rights, including life and liberty, corporations are alien, artificial, man-made person-like golems or Frankenstein monsters without such virtues. Their limited liability to those they harm or offend permits the henchmen within it to stay hidden and out of reach, and unaccountable for their deeds (even if they suffer legal loss, they can always declare bankruptcy, form a new corporation and resurrect like Dracula); also like Dracula, their "life" can go on forever (some corporations in Sweden today go back to the 12th or 13th century), and thus they can play the "long game" and wait out any human resistance. Corporations are by definition amoral; they are to have no concern about their neighbors, only the shareholders (and the bigger the share they own, the more they care). Unlike some family owned businesses, they cannot find contentment in a fair profit; the only satisfaction is in profits that increase each quarter, otherwise the leadership is sacked. This leads to having the inevitable "hatchet man" hired to shore up flagging profits, by the ruthless cutting of staff to the bone, layoffs, reducing the quality of products and support, and seeking short term gain, but often ruining the hard-fought legacies and reputations of their own businesses. Their only real concern about the greater consequence of their deeds as corporation management and boards is if it ultimately hurts their near or future profits or share price, and any positive community deeds are for public relations purposes to improve sales, brand loyalty, avoid political backlash in taxes, levies or regulations, and to pacify workers to avoid collective bargaining; ethics never come into the mix.

Sadly most conservative Christians I have observed, in my experience and my earlier adult life, focus on and acknowledge the power and leverage wielded by governments and even armies, but do not understand the greatest earthly power of all—that of economic leverage, which can buy its own governments and armies at will, and how it vanquishes the illusory "freedom" of markets and "fair" trade, and regulates its own spheres of operation in the marketplace for its own benefit if not balanced by other collective forces, much less the spiritual implications of this reality. The power of capital to define all the terms in the marketplace means that when they seek workers to do their bidding (for their uncalloused hands are not geared for wielding a tool), their capital reserve means they can "wait out" a wage earner that has mouths to feed today, and thus has the leverage to negotiate a minimal wage—*in effect, conducting a military-siege style waiting game on the uncapitalized workers.* The never-ending greed and thirst for more by modern businesses—more profits, market share, capitalization—will lead to the inevitable Darwinistic "survival of the fittest" winnowing of the field of entities, and further centralizing of wealth into the hands of the ever-smaller few, as the earlier data we presented has confirmed for generations. Few politicians like Bernie Sanders have pointed this out; other historical figures like Karl Marx pointed out this throughout history, which helped make his convincing case (regardless of the veracity of his proposed "solution"). He witnessed the early Industrial Age's manufacturing capability providing a means of unending wealth for those with the capital to build factories, while workers were forced from sustenance farming to crowding in the teeming cities. *He saw the Church as largely aiding these aristocrats as they had the kings and czars before them—just as James Fifield and Ralph Drollinger (as we will see in the next volume) have done in recent days—and thus became hardened in his view of the Church as a stumbling block and co-exploiter of the working man, rather than his champion.*

Those with capital—call them the "wealth class," "bankers" or what have you—in reality do not compete with governments and armies for power in this world; *in actuality, they own the governments and armies, and replace them as needed.* Even armies can be procured through the politicians they bankroll, the defense industries they control, the media arms they own, or, more directly, by merely hiring their own mercenaries—*er, "security companies"*—like Erik Prince's Blackwater, or the goons hired by Rockefeller to kill and maim striking union workers before that; like the book of Revelation shows, these societal institutions do "prostitute" themselves to the Great City Babylon.

Capitalism can be seen to be defined as, in essence, a religion of "usury." "Usury" is ancient term, often talked about in the Bible, which describes it as *the making of money not by producing goods or improving them, but merely by possessing money itself, and holding it hostage from others who seek it to produce useful goods.* Many have been conditioned to believe that the term, in its negative sense in the Bible and elsewhere, merely refers to "excessive" interest on loans, the level of which remains undefined, but the term actually represents the collection of *any* interest upon the providing of capital, from the "haves" to the "have nots," with the goal of widening the gulf. *This is the heart of the principle of capitalism.* The Bible forbade Hebrews from usury, or charging interest from their own brethren, but *could* charge usury to foreigners. *This is because God knows that usury is a most effective form of inevitable confiscation of wealth from the debtor to the lender, and the inevitable real slavery it produces; it is a type of siege warfare that is seen to be acceptable against one's enemies or natural rivals, by defeating them by economic servitude, as I believe God was trying to illustrate.* I concede that my family invests in U.S. Treasuries, which charges a very small amount of interest to keep the U.S. from defaulting, which no one wants. The security sought from such a conservative (return-wise) investment is perceived to be derived from the faith and credit of the nation, to protect my household's assets in old age, such as those "secured" via Social Security, rather than in risky investments; one would like to think the assets of the nation back up such debt, *but in actuality the "printing press" of U.S. Federal Reserve to inflate dollars by raising rates and issuing more credit from thin air is the "real" security.* Debt does admittedly promote overspending and artificial standards of living, be it in mortgages and houses that are otherwise above one's means, or national budget deficits that would not be possible if balanced budgets were mandated; a more sobering and honest approach would be to raise revenue in real time via taxes, *but today's miserly and short term-focused citizenry would never agree to pay taxes commensurate with their expectations of services or lifestyle. The overwhelming up-front costs of (often unnecessary) wars were the original justification sold by the government (and defense contractors) to the public to justify this dishonest and destructive path.*

The world-famous and beloved English Christian philosopher G. K. Chesterton wrote an extended treatise on the subject in 1915, an era in which the robber baron/Industrial Age was still raging, and before the dawn of mass media and computers and Internet would give them new tools for manipulation of the public. Chesterton is considered one of the greatest, most heralded and influential minds of the Twentieth Century, proposing a philosophy, sociology and theology that were traditional Christianity at its core (what he considered "orthodox," as he veered from Anglicanism to Catholicism). Unlike Christian leaders today, his mind was so acute and insightful that he had no problem going toe-to-toe with the most influential secular philosophers of the era. The renowned secular/modernist intellectual philosopher "thinker" and playwright George Bernard Shaw (commonly considered to be the greatest British dramatist since Shakespeare), was a friendly rival or debater of his in the public sphere (as Christians then were educated and honest enough to interact comfortably and respectfully with secular thinkers, as opposed to being fearful of them after the 1925 "Monkey" Scopes Trial), and was known to have respectfully said of Chesterton that "He was a man of colossal genius." His 1925 Christian apologetic work *The Everlasting Man* was a primary influence on the intellectual author C. S. Lewis (having since eclipsed Chesterton in notoriety as a Christian philosopher and apologist in later generations) in converting from academic atheism to Christianity around 1930–31.

Economically, he expressed a model, hailed in Catholic circles, as a "third way" from capitalism and socialism (both of which he was wary), commonly known as "distributism." The *Merriam-Webster Dictionary* simplistically defines it as "the theory or practice of distributing private property (as land) to the maximum degree among individual owners."[185] In common practice, it espouses the decentralization of income-producing property into many hands, allowing the possession of capital, ownership and production means (including labor) into the same collective (the smaller the better as practical), preferring family businesses, then small collectives, guilds and cooperatives. It encourages individual effort, and the right to enjoy the "fruit of the land"; Chesterton laconically idealizes it as making available to every man "three acres and a cow."

His 1917 published anthology of essays, *Utopia of Usurers and other essays*, can currently be found online in public domain form at Archive.org, and read online or downloaded.[186] *Utopia of Usurers* comprises a 70-page essay, along with eighteen much shorter essays. He begins by saying there that

> ...we must hit Capitalism, and hit it hard, for the plain and definite reason that it is growing stronger. Most of the excuses which serve the capitalists as masks are, of course, the excuses of hypocrites. They lie when they claim philanthropy; they no more feel any particular love of men than Albu felt an affection for Chinamen. They lie when they say they have reached their position through their own organising ability. They generally have to pay men to organise the mine, exactly as they pay men to go down it. They often lie about their present wealth, as they generally lie about their past poverty. But when they say that they are going in for a "constructive social policy," they do not lie. They really are going in for a constructive social policy. And we must go in for an equally destructive social policy; and destroy, while it is still half-constructed, the accursed thing which they construct. (pp. 2–3)

Chesterton then warns about what future society will be like under "this paradise of plutocrats, this Utopia of gold and brass in which the great story of England seems so likely to end," and that "I propose to say what I think our new masters, the mere millionaires, will do with certain human interests and institutions, such as art, science, jurisprudence, or religion—unless we strike soon enough to prevent them" (p. 3). He adds that "Our merchants have really adopted the style of merchant princes. They have begun openly to dominate the civilization of the State, as the emperors and popes openly dominated in Italy," and as an example he shows how advertisers vulgarize art, and thus shame the artist, unlike the days of Michaelangelo with his wealthy patrons (p. 5). He further explains that before the Twentieth Century, "A fairly clear line separated advertisement from art," but that "the first effect of the triumph of the capitalist (if we allow him to triumph) will be that that line of demarcation will entirely disappear. There will be no art that might not just as well be advertisement" (p. 6), so that "the artist will work, not only to please the rich, but only to increase their riches; which is a considerable step lower" (p. 7). We can see that in the Hollywood movies that are produced today; it also afflicts the books published, music released extensively, television shows and all other art; *it is particularly true in the Christian sector, where music, books and movies fit within a very tight viewpoint that reflects that of their wealthy Christian or other corporate sponsors, and mostly praised on its ability to achieve widespread recognition and thus earn considerable money, although some are released to reflect the more extremist Christian views of eccentric individual or group benefactors, and non-profits for ideological benefits or long-term societal advances.*

Chesterton further clarifies that "no one who knows the small-minded cynicism of our plutocracy, its secrecy, its gambling spirit, its contempt of conscience, can doubt that the artist-advertiser will often be assisting enterprises over which he will have no moral control, and of which he could feel no moral approval," but that "He will be working to spread quack medicines, queer investments" (p. 7). Regarding politicians and their corruption with big business or specific ventures in earlier days, he laments that in his "modern era" (1917) "it has been increasingly true since, that the statesman was often an ally of the salesman; and represented not only a nation of shopkeepers, but one particular shop" (p. 13). Regarding the influence of the new rich business class within journalism he writes that "Literary men are being employed to praise a big business man personally, as men used to praise a king. They not only find political reasons for the commercial schemes—that they have done for some time past—they also find moral defences for the commercial schemers. They describe the capitalist's brain of steel and heart of gold" (p. 15)—*much like our top Christian leaders have beatified a real estate tycoon/scoundrel recently in America.* Just as these Christian leaders have been called compromised and opportunistic "court evangelicals" today, praising a leader devoid of character or ethics, including his dishonest avoidance of military service while criticizing the heroic reputation of POWs, Chesterton writes of his day of "all poets becoming court poets, under kings that have taken no oath, nor led us into any battle" (p. 17).

Chesterton notes than in our fairy tales, there is some hint of truth that the bad ogres or kings also tended to be magicians or wizards; similarly, just as with the "sorcery" used by the leaders of the Great City Babylon in Revelation 18 (evidently by means of marketing, psychology, public relations and mass media propaganda, and our food and pharmaceutical supplies as well as possible supernatural means), he notes of the businessmen of his day that

> Bad government, like good government, is a spiritual thing. Even the tyrant never rules by force alone; but mostly by fairy tales. And so it is with the modern tyrant, the great employer. The sight of a millionaire is seldom, in the ordinary sense, an enchanting sight: nevertheless he is in his way an enchanter. As they say in the gushing articles about him in the magazines, he is a fascinating personality. So is a snake. At least he is fascinating to rabbits; and so is the millionaire to the rabbit-witted sort of people that ladies and gentlemen have allowed themselves to become. He does, in a manner, cast a spell, such as that which imprisoned princes and princesses under the shapes of falcons or stags. He has truly turned men into sheep, as Circe turned them into swine. (p. 19)

Chesterton eloquently explains the incompetence in his day of the bigger near-monopolizing ("omnipotent") businesses, and "they will be even more incompetent when they are omnipotent," saying that "that is, and always has been, the whole point of a monopoly," adding that "It is only because it is incompetent that it has to be omnipotent" (p. 23). He makes a general point that "the reign of the capitalist will be the reign of the cad—that is, of the unlicked type that is neither the citizen nor the gentleman" (p. 25); *which is hard to relate to in these recent years of political experience, is it not?* He asserts that this may suggest why employers hate holidays or vacations. They concede that employees must rest each night to keep their work up, with minimal off-hours for eating and exercise, but "his whole mental attitude is that the passive time and the active time are alike useful for him and his business. His slaves still serve him in unconsciousness, as dogs still hunt in slumber," whereas "when you give a man a holiday you give him back his body and soul" (pp. 26–27). He explains that "This complete and reconstructed man is the nightmare of the modern capitalist. His whole scheme would crack across like a mirror….if once a plain man were ready for his two plain duties—ready to live and ready to die…The employers will give time to eat, time to sleep; they are in terror of a time to think" (p. 31). *I would add that Christians' embracing of status culture and materialism and consumerism feeds the capitalists' goal of spellbinding them into seeing the agenda of the employer and their coffers as the only agenda worth their own pursuit and unending attention, if not for loyalty, at least the concession that it is needed for those self-enslaved to their own covetousness for the* *"fine things of life" and status lifestyles.*

Chesterton notes that the major religions, and even Materialism and Atheism, are egalitarian in their positions on major issues (not dependent upon class or social standing), whereas "the capitalist really depends on some religion of inequality. The capitalist must somehow distinguish himself from human kind; he must be obviously above it—or he would be obviously below it....it is absolutely necessary for the capitalist to make a distinction between his wife (who is an aristocrat and consults crystal gazers and star gazers in the West End), and vulgar miracles claimed by gypsies or travelling showmen. The Catholic veto upon usury, as defined in dogmatic councils, cuts across all classes. But it is absolutely necessary to the capitalist to distinguish more delicately between two kinds of usury; the kind he finds useful and the kind he does not find useful" (p. 35). After giving several examples from his culture, he broadly claims that "Wait and see whether the religion of the Servile State is not in every case what I say: the encouragement of small virtues supporting capitalism, the discouragement of the huge virtues that defy it" (p. 37). He then explores the capitalists' exploitation of what he (and all scientists today) calls the "pseudo-science" of eugenics, which entailed the forced sterilization of the underclasses that were expensive to underwrite, presumably "for their own good," and other means of population sculpting. Commenting on the poor living environments of the underclasses, the corporations and eugenicists would note that "a rickety cradle may mean a rickety baby," and thus would not take the logical step of proving a better cradle, or money for it. However, Chesterton cuts to the core of what motivates the capitalist and makes him "tick"; he states that such assistance "means higher wages and greater equalization of wealth," but that, to their paid scientists' chagrin,

> More food, leisure, and money for the workman would mean a better workman, better even from the point of view of anyone for whom he worked. But more food, leisure, and money *would also mean a more independent workman*. A house with a decent fire and a full pantry would be a better house to make a chair or mend a clock in...than a hovel with a leaky roof and a cold hearth. But a house with a decent fire and a full pantry would also be a better house in which to *refuse* to make a chair or mend a clock...*and doing nothing is sometimes one of the highest of the duties of man*. All but the hard-hearted must be torn with pity for this pathetic dilemma of the rich man, *who has to keep the poor man just stout enough to do the work and just thin enough to have to do it*...there one day came into his mind a new and curious idea—one of

the most strange, simple, and horrible ideas that have ever risen from the deep pit of original sin. The roof could not be mended...without upsetting the capitalist balance, or, rather, disproportion in society; for a man with a roof is a man with a house, and to that extent *his house is his castle*. The cradle could not be made to rock easier, or, at least, not much easier, *without strengthening the hands of the poor household*.

...But it occurred to the capitalist that there was one sort of furniture in the house that could be altered. *The husband and wife could be altered*. Birth costs nothing....and the merchant need pay no more for mating a strong miner to a healthy fishwife than he pays when the miner mates himself with a less robust female whom he has the sentimentality to prefer. Thus it might be possible, by keeping on certain broad lines of heredity, *to have some physical improvement without any moral, political, or social improvement. It might be possible to keep a supply of strong and healthy slaves without coddling them with decent conditions*. As the mill-owners use the wind and the water to drive their mills, they would use this natural force as something even cheaper; and turn their wheels by diverting from its channel the blood of a man in his youth. That *is what Eugenics means; and that is all that it means*. (pp. 42–43)

Chesterton then plows a surprising field when he boldly asserts that, "If the capitalists are allowed to erect their constructive capitalist community, I speak quite seriously when I say that I think Prison will become an almost universal experience" (p. 49). *He seems to wax prophetic here, for in the poster-child of capitalism, the United States, this "Christian" nation imprisons more people than any nation on earth, including the most despotic tyrannies and totalitarian states like Red China and the Soviet Union*. He further states his vision, more accurate than his peer and rival H. G. Wells, when he adds that

It will not necessarily be a cruel or shameful experience: on these points...it may be a vastly improved experience. The conditions in the prison, very possibly, will be made more humane. But the prison will be made more humane only in order to contain more of humanity....We no longer lock a man up for doing something; we lock him up in the hope of his doing nothing. Given this principle, it is evidently possible to make the mere conditions of punishment more moderate, or—(more probably) more secret...capitalist society, which naturally does not know the meaning of honour, cannot know the meaning of disgrace: and it will still go on imprisoning for no reason at all. (p. 51)

Similar to our advanced "Christian" society as well, Chesterton saw in his "modern" and civilized Twentieth Century Britain a revival of old-fashioned corporal punishment and torture for adults. He writes that, "In spite of the horror of all humane people, in spite of the hesitation even of our corrupt and panic-stricken Parliament, measures can now be triumphantly passed for spreading or increasing the use of physical torture, and for applying it to the newest and vaguest categories of crime. Thirty or forty years ago, nay, twenty years ago, when Mr. F. Hugh O'Donnell and others forced a Liberal Government to drop the cat-'o-nine-tails like a scorpion, we could have counted on a mass of honest hatred of such things. We cannot count on it now" (pp. 61–62). *He might weep if he saw today's evangelicals supporting terrorizing torture today in the "War on Terror," led by two of "their" favorite presidents.*

Chesterton notes that the Socialists of his era made the mistake that the "problem" in society was the ownership of private property, as opposed to "property confined to the few" (p. 65); he adds that "The rich man today does not only rule by using private property; he also rules by *treating public property as if it were private property*" (p. 65) (emphasis added). He warns that "this unprincipled vagueness about official and unofficial moneys by the cheerful habit of always mixing up the money in the pocket with the money in the till, it would be quite possible to keep the rich as rich as ever in practice, though they might have suffered confiscation in theory" (p. 66). *This is possible since then for the wealthy and businesses to be in high tax brackets, but receiving lucrative government contracts or subsidies, or diverting assets to non-taxable entities, trusts and foundations.* Showing that the well-to-do politicians can assign the items of their lofty lifestyle to the public while not diminishing their lavishness one iota as its "caretakers," he warns that, if society is not careful, it will be directed to set itself up whereby every institution will be set up to benefit the "usurers," yet be given the ironic name, "Socialism" (p. 70). *Ironically, it would surprise many Western Christians who revere Chesterton and his Christian work that he frequently salutes the honesty, sincerity and integrity of Marxists in the following essays in this publication (admittedly before the Bolsheviks showed the corruption of their own brand), and concedes his own previous identity with Socialism, and appears to most criticize them only for their naïve idealism and use of scientific "big words" to combat the capitalists on their home turf, rather than use simple words that can be understood by the masses, are more cutting and effective, and reflect the poet's adeptness at striking truth into a situation.*

After having considered this treatise and other data and perspectives we have reviewed, a skeptical (particularly traditionally conservative) reader might understandably say that, if capitalism is so bad (a thought which is deemed traitorous by Westerners, and probably worthy of police surveillance), then what is so great an alternative? *It may well be true (emphasis on "may") that capitalism is the most practical economic system in a world of fallen people.* Certainly, noted historical utopian communities, even Christian ones, usually do not stay intact after a generation of collective mutual interest-based economies and lifestyles—either due to corruption (or often more likely) that the second generation does not buy into the unselfish aspects and demands of the community. However, a selfish, Darwinistic "survival of the fittest" approach that is the bedrock of capitalism will inevitably lead to competition, occasional war, the bloody, violent or barbaric "thinning of the herd" or the weakest, and *the ultimate centralization of all wealth into the fewest hands possible.*

The key to manage it (as much as possible, *if possible,* until our Lord returns and judges it) is to *first dispense with the myth held by the libertarian community (that otherwise espouses many genuine truths) and their less ideologically pure conservative/royalist/traditionalists, that unbridled capitalism is associated with "freedom" or "liberty"—at least that to be experienced by everyone. The thought being that a society with no rules will somehow produce widespread virtue and compassion, and those with economic power will somehow self-regulate based upon their own conscience, is a laughable myth that can only be sold by a wealthy, corporate-owned mass media (and their pulpits) to a mentally lazy, gullible, historically-ignorant and spell-bound public.* They will glorify a "freedom" from rules and government regulations, but will not concede the real reality—*that the marketplace will be regulated anyway—by the financial interests, for their own interests.* While a government can regulate the marketplace to purportedly represent the common interests of all citizens (if the citizens are vigilant enough to study and to hold their elected representatives accountable), the financial firm-regulated market will define rules, regulations, wages, interest rates, etc. in a way to further the accumulation of wealth into the hands of its corporations. Competition can provide some attempt to make the value to workers and consumers reasonable (for markets where the entry of new competitors is practical, and also not natural monopolies like utilities and others), and antitrust regulations (excoriated by conservative media and pulpits for decades) can try to control (feebly) the worst abuses, but a common business climate can always work around such influences for their own mutual interest, with "soft cartels," hidden and murky networks and political influence.

Words that are like music to the ears of conservatives, such as "privatization," such as that directed towards health care, social security and retirement, government services and even military, *are in reality the replacement of a non-profit system for the mutual benefit of all, with a for-profit system where extra funds are taken from citizens and transferred to the bankrolls of the few, and with motives of maximizing profits, not service.* It is hard to explain why taking part of citizens' money and giving it to someone as profit, *before even providing service*, will ultimately provide them with a better value, but the corporate-paid media has done an excellent job of selling it. Part of their job has been to sell the myth that for-profit companies hold geniuses in their leadership, who have made the world the Garden of Eden we have in America and the world. *What they have really shown is the ability to make ever-increasing profits for the few, keep wages the lowest possible (and sell it as a virtue), manipulate taxes to pay less proportionally than the average person, default on debt, pensions, bonds and creditors and class action lawsuits of those hurt by them, and otherwise escape accountability, while reducing quality of products and quality of work life, customer service and community responsibility.* This act of reason-defying "sorcery" was no better played than in the selling of a recent president to the public, as a real "poster boy" in reflecting their actual fidelity to the truth and to unselfish ideals—*or not.*

A capitalistic system can only be tamed (if at all possible) and kept from confiscating the wealth of those less powerful unless it is perpetually held in high suspicion—just like our elected officials—and kept evermore under investigation and accountability. It should expect and anticipate creative forms of corruption, with firm regulations that do not let them exploit those without the leverage of capital (such as workers or consumers), or exploit the tax code and kickbacks and lucrative contracts, or ever-accumulate wealth without any need to re-circulate it for the common good. Don't worry about offending the capitalists and big business, and driving them away with such an approach, which they will threaten to do; first of all, unlike your neighbors *they are not a real person whose feelings can be hurt or having the innate value of being in God's image; furthermore, whenever there is a dollar to be made (ethically or not), they will return in their never-satiated appetite for more wealth, regardless of the regulations present, for they have no other self-motivation or ability other than to confiscate wealth, and they will operate on as long a leash as is attached to them.* In other words, citizens should never turn their backs on the capitalistic beast, because its instinct is to "capitalize" on every opportunity, loophole, and sleight of hand to feed their hunger. It should be distrusted at every step, and multiple levels of safeguards and protective measures deployed to investigate its hidden deeds (which are bankrolled to use the most clever and amoral techniques and henchmen), expose its propaganda, and limit the extent of its exploitation and growth in wealth at the expense of the populace.

Remember—our Lord warned us! Remember how He treated the "den of thieves" set up in the Temple itself, and His "subtlety" in exposing them and how to remedy it! Most importantly, Christians have a primary role in reminding the public of this fundamental spiritual and physical risk and threat of the Great City Babylon, far beyond the typical lesser threats our

Christian leaders have normally raised funds to combat, be it backward masking on rock albums, whether people say, "Merry Christmas," or what our fellow citizens do in their privacy of their homes behind their shades. God made this threat a primary topic and issue from cover to cover in the Bible as He warned His people and the entire world throughout the ages, and it will be one of the last threats to the saints and the people of earth, for God to finally eradicate. *If Christians do not heed the call to "Get out of Babylon, and be not partakers of her sins," then who will sound the call, and can we expect the outside world to resist any better? Worst yet—are American conservative Christians actually a "stumbling block" in this important topic to society, by perpetuating this danger, minimizing it or even promoting it? Remember—the economic Babylon system and its model undergirds all the other activity of society, both global and local, and the issues of the home, foreign policy, immigration, speech, and societal ethics, and Christians should remember when analyzing these complex issues, to always "follow the money."*

Sadly, this "Great City Babylon" economic system, driven by amoral capitalism and the inhuman corporation, is what James Fifield in recent generations, and Ralph Drollinger today (as we shall see in the next volume), have sold to the Christian public as a sacred "brazen snake" for us to lift up as our divine savior, along with much of the American Religious Right. These same powers have bought the mass media empires, with its significant outlets only owned by a handful of corporations, as the means to "spread the gospel"—the Gospel of Hannity and *Fox News*, or the gospel of "conservatism"—to a devout Christian daily commuter or cable TV watcher. As I have previously pointed out, *the sheer number of hours in which they have the average Christian listener or viewer at rapt attention in their commuter car or kitchen table, as a captive audience speaking one-on-one to the driver or passenger, or even in the background in subliminal fashion as the listener multi-tasks in the car, work or at home, inevitably leads to the programming of the listener (and taking up its "talking points" and terminology like a rosary) that dwarfs any biblical sermon their pastor gives once a week.* It doesn't just stop at its direct glorification of the big business, low taxes, no regulation, no environmental protections, few worker rights and the like—it also promotes positions that indirectly support the big-business ever-increasing profits agenda—controlled immigration (allowing none that that need social assistance, but ample slave labor desired), big militaries (through which to sell lucrative defense contracts) and aggressive foreign policies (to plant American businesses overseas, and to protect them when the locals revolt), and similar issues for which there is a profit motive. *Every Christian becomes complicit in these Great City Babylon agendas when they feed into this narrative, and do not resist, nor awaken their brethren to the manipulation to which they are being bewitched.*

While I have tried to minimize the proportion of contents in this treatise dedicated to the even more controversial assertion of tying the strong advocacy of President Donald Trump by most evangelicals and the Religious Right to the bewitching and conditioning of the "gospel" ceaselessly preached by these media outlets, to ignore it would belie the most important and impactful current ramifications of this phenomena, and its impact on the poor, disadvantaged, immigrant, refugee, and even the working and middle classes. Make no mistake about it: *Fox News* and its talk radio henchmen have been chosen—by God, or by the Babylon financial interests, or maybe both—to sell Trump to the Religious Right as well as to the disaffected masses (many of whom have or will be hurt by Trump's policies such as in taxes, but are too simple or stubborn to understand or concede it). The official axis between the supposed independent societal "pillar" of the press they represent, and a controversial and minority-supported candidate and president, is indisputable, and *any viewer or listener should ask why such an unethical alliance and hard-core push for their support is warranted, and truly in their interests.* In March 2019 *The New Yorker* wrote[187] that *Fox News'* Sean Hannity's participation at an immigration rally held by the Trump Administration at the border, hugging the beleaguered Homeland Security Secretary and White House communications director (and former *Fox News* deputy) Bill Shine (whose family Hannity's family vacations with), reflected that prominent press outlet as crossing the line, to the point of observers quoted as referring to *Fox News* as "the closest we've come to having state TV." They also note the fact that it featured Hannity's seventh interview with the president, and *Fox's* forty-second, while Trump had given only ten to three other main networks combined, as Trump referred to *CNN*, to which it gave none, as "fake news."

They add that *Fox News* generates $2.7 billion a year, and regarding their relationship to Trump's followers, Prof. Hemmer at the University of Virginia calls them the "radicalization model" for the base. She notes that all day long Trump is retweeting headlines from the network, and while his press secretary Sarah Sanders has stopped having press conferences much less fielding questions, she has made around thirty appearances on "Fox and Friends" and "Hannity." Meanwhile, former *Fox News* chief Shine, who was implicated in their sexual harassment lawsuits (more for witting accommodation of the hostile environment versus harassment himself), was recently discovered in his financial disclosure forms of having *Fox* still paying him "millions of dollars since he joined the Administration." The article lists a long line of *Fox News* regular contributors who have filled senior cabinet level positions. Meanwhile, former Trump administration officials Hope Hicks and Sebastian Gorka are now affiliated with *Fox* (since my original drafting of this material, long-time Trump Communications Director Sarah Huckabee has also joined *Fox*); former *Fox* host Kimberly Guilfoyle is now dating Donald Trump Jr. They add that "Sean Hannity has told colleagues that he speaks to the President virtually every night, after his show ends, at 10 PM," with White House advisors calling him the "Shadow Chief of Staff." When Trump had a mid-term rally, he advertised Hannity as a "special guest," where he was called on stage and praised the President for "promises kept," and called all the other media covering the rally as "fake news," as Hannity and Shine shared a "high five at the end" (Shine earlier reprimanded Hannity for such a stunt when Shine was still with *Fox News*, after much public criticism, even though Shine had approved it previously). They add that the *Fox News'* motto "Fair and Balanced" was retired in 2017.

Meanwhile, they note that "*Axios* recently reported that sixty percent of Trump's day is spent in unstructured 'executive time,' much of it filled by television." Regarding the *Fox News* owner (and close Trump friend) Rupert Murdock, they write that "After Murdoch bought the *New York Post*, in 1976, he was introduced to Trump through a mutual acquaintance, Roy Cohn, the infamous legal fixer, who, as a young man, was Senator Joseph McCarthy's chief counsel." *Cohn is not only famous for ruining many, many lives in the Red Scare, but also is held as one of the most universally disliked men in generations; Trump allegedly selected William Barr as attorney general after proclaiming that he "needed to get a Roy Cohn."* During the debates Trump boycotted *Fox News* for a while because of too-tough questioning (even though they quote insiders who claim that *Fox News* gave Trump debate questions in advance), but eventually *Fox News* relented, after chief Roger Ailes called Trump to promise be more fair, according to Trump's tweets. When Ailes was forced out of *Fox* due to his repeated actions of sexual harassment, he joined the Trump debate team and began planning a joint business plan with Trump, for a *Trump TV* to rival *Fox*. They recount how a *Fox* reporter discovered about the Stormy Daniels affair and payoff before the election, but they refused to air it, until the *Wall Street Journal* did it after the election; the reporter was then demoted, sued the network and got a settlement, but under the guise of a gag order. Eventually, the Trump administration approved the sale of *Fox* to Disney, for seventy-one billion dollars, with the Murdoch family receiving two billion dollars and a major portion of the stock in the new company, with no antitrust concerns by Trump's Justice Department, even though the new company will account for half the box-office revenue in America, leading Trump to publicly congratulate him; his administration went to stop a similar merger between *CNN* and Time

Warner. *Fox* not only has a trance-like influence over the viewers; the article recounts how officials seeking to influence Trump would have *Fox News* schedule their spokesmen, to then influence Trump's views.

As of June 2019, President Trump continued his vendetta against Time Warner and *CNN*, saying in a public tweet that "I believe that if people stoped [sic] using or subscribing to AT&T, they would be forced to make big changes at *CNN*, which is dying in the ratings anyway. It is so unfair with such bad, Fake News!"; as President he tweeted a video in 2017 that showed him tackling and pummeling a person with a CNN logo superimposed over his head.[188]

As a Bible-believing Christian myself, I do sense and possibly concur with what many of Trump's Christian supporters assert—that God's hand may have been involved in his emergence—*but just not in the way they presume.* As I have said before on the record, I can foresee the possibility that God has allowed Donald Trump to ascend to the ultimate leadership position in this nation—with the conspicuous full-throated approval of most of the Religious Right leadership and 81 percent of evangelical voters, including well after his many despicable statements and decrees—*like a modern-day vulgar, profane and cruel Bar Kokhba, to expose what is really in the hearts and worldview of most of the professing Religious Right community, just like this historical leader did regarding his "pious" Jewish rabbinic supporters.*

It, in effect, may serve as the beginning of a formal, very public judgment of their ranks, and letting their sins reach full measure (as God is wont to do with those He has judged historically), and to make clear even to the dull-witted like myself, who was raised in their ranks, still believes the Bible they purportedly promote (while currently deprogramming myself from their views which do not comport with it) and the Christ and Kingdom message upon which is its focus, that *to "get out of Babylon" may mean to first get out of the Western Religious Right system that rides it like a Beast, but whose demise will likely be quick and sudden.* Will there now rise up prophetic "voices in the wilderness" from within their ranks, like John the Baptist, that will similarly tell the religious leaders of "God's people" that "the axe is laid unto the root of the trees" (Matt. 3:10)? Will the "finger of God" confront the powerful figures in our society, who are toying with the sacred relics of faith and mocking them while luxuriating in their confiscated wealth, and declare to them that "Thou art weighed in the balances, and art found wanting" (Daniel 5:27)?

THE FUTURE DESTINY OF AMERICAN EVANGELICALS IN THE TRUMP ERA AND BEYOND

29 AD:

...the chief priests and elders persuaded the multitude that they should ask Barabbas, and destroy Jesus...But they cried out the more, saying, Let him be crucified...Then answered all the people, and said, His blood [be] on us, and on our children. (Matt. 27:20, 23, 25)

2016 AD:

As their religious leaders persuaded their evangelical followers, they cried, "Let Donald Trump's reputation, character, values and deeds be on us, and our children, in the eyes of the lost souls around us!"

Given the embracement of the big business, financial industry and wealth class agenda, like a modern, Western embodiment of the biblical Great City Babylon, by today's Religious Right leadership and the overwhelming majority of its ranks, including its adoption of the former's values of unbridled capitalism and corporate power, immigration exploitation and control, minimal government and its regulations, low taxes, minimal public assistance to the disadvantaged, nor environmental protections or labor laws, and an aggressive foreign policy, as has been significantly documented in this work, we will now consider the implications of this "Faustian pact" between both parties to the professed mission of this segment of the American Church, and its success.

From this we may foresee the possible destiny of America's evangelical Christian community—one I was proudly raised in, and learned to accept both responsibility of my sin and the offer of forgiveness by my Creator by way the precious blood of our Lord Jesus. It provided me a culture of Sunday Schools, Vacation Bible Schools, choir specials, youth trips and lock-ins, and intimate conversations about finding purpose in life while following Jesus' footsteps, alongside young friends that became lifetime companions. It served me well into young adulthood, raising me to be faithful and responsible in service, reaching out to teach the younger while still growing in faith myself, making more lifelong friends, and meeting the love of my life in a Sunday night service. Adulthood brought more responsibilities behind the scenes, and even teaching adults on occasion. When I left my hometown to start my career as a single adult, a new church home became my local family, as we who were transplanted non-native residents there looked out for each other like real families. The same scenario applied when I moved again, this time with a spouse in tow, as we both settled in to a new "church family." It has been a special, blessed life of close relationships, phases of genuine revelation, growth and revival, opportunities to minister and even cry, and also a lot of fun and joy. I would wish it for anyone to experience.

Central of all in my experience and emphasis, both for myself and my "church culture," was the reality of the "born again" experience, and the primacy of sharing the Gospel, not through family birthrate growth and household and cultural pressure, sacraments and confirmation rituals, but by one-on-one "witnessing" of its message of deliverance. It sought willing, sober-minded "converts" in obeying the Great Commission mandate to "make disciples" and be "fishers of men," requiring the going through of the "highways and byways" of the world, amongst people very different than myself (with some in wretched states and despair from mental illness, addictions or regrets of past mistakes), in order to "rescue the perishing." I feel that the mission to this latter group, whom the capitalists, libertarians, elites and establishment (secular and religious) would perceive as the "burdens on society" (or worthy of eradication), was portrayed by Christ in his parable as being to those "both bad and good" (Matt. 22:10). They were also "the poor, and the maimed, and the halt, and the blind" (Luke 14:21) that the Lord invited to His supper, because the well-to-do were "not worthy" (Matt. 22:8), rather going to their "farm" or "to his merchandise" (v. 5), or having bought "a piece of ground" or "bought five yoke of oxen" (Luke 14:18–19) and more concerned with assets rather than the Lord's business. The former humble souls were "compelled" from the dangerous and seedy "highways and hedges" (Luke 14:23) by the Lord's servants (as I desire to be) to enjoy the Lord's pampering and celebratory blessings. *This central task is what made me an "evangelical" Christian by definition, and the focus of my community's priorities and identity as we also "abided in Christ," in contrast to self-serving agendas of societal power or even self-preservation from "persecution."* It also required that we love and empathize with the pitiful and wretched in their state, and proved that love in our assistance to them by helping them out of their "miry clay," not just with our message of future hope, but *with an immediate "helping hand"; the lack thereof impeding their ability to hear our message of spiritual deliverance.*

There was always a tension amongst those in our ranks who insist that we only stick to the message and its preaching, and away from any "social gospel" or "social justice," while others focused on it so much that they needlessly watered down the biblical doctrines of the Kingdom; still others emphasized "signs and wonders," healings and spiritual warfare as an identity and obsession, to demonstrate the reality of our message to others. *In contrast, the Gospels reveal that Jesus almost always conducted all three simultaneously, with each aspect giving legitimacy to the other facets or "legs" of the supportive "stool" of ministry.* As an example, once when Jesus was casting out demons, healing bodies and minds, and teaching the basic principles of the Kingdom, His disciples said the people were hungry, and *suggested sending them away to find fulfillment of that need elsewhere; in turn Jesus stopped His other ministering, and tasked His own disciples to "feed them!"* Jesus did not lecture the people then on their slothfulness or lack of preparation, *although we know that He, like Paul and the apostles and ourselves, knew the need to eventually disciple people into wise choices, self-sufficiency (when possible, while noting that early church leaders always expected to assume the duty to take care of the "widows and orphans" and their like, forever) and self-responsibility so they in turn can focus on helping others, and foster a culture of such mutual accountability, so to "sin no more" in that light.* When their bellies were full, the people could then focus on witnessing the love of Jesus and their followers in a tangible way by their service, and could concentrate on the Kingdom message. These own disciples of Jesus, who recommended "sending the people away," had been fed by their Lord when *they* were hungry, even when it led to Jesus being accused of "breaking the Sabbath" by the religious establishment in His zeal to meet their mortal needs.

I know that old people always worry that the world is going to pot, and the younger generation is going to ruin everything. As I am getting to be in that "older than average" time of life now (while still feeling like a fourteen-year-old and in my "awkward years" on the inside), I guess I have been feeling some of this for some time. I see church attendance slowly dwindling, peoples' connections to their fellow parishioners and depth of fellowship and service ever-more shrinking in breadth and depth, and an apparent lack of connection to "church life" and the commitments it needs, both spiritual and as a social community, as younger people today like to make their relationships distant (preferably online) and ad hoc, for just as long as something has their immediate attention and fancy. It will take very little to spook young people away from the church for good, and if they may want to retain some semblance of a corporate interaction with God, they may be satisfied with online forums, and streaming services. I know that many find intimate relationships and service opportunities in small groups and ministries within mega-churches, but my experience (in contrast to most of my interactions in small and medium-sized churches previously) in a mega-church setting always left me cold and aloof. I still find it to be very similar to watching services on TV, and one can easily remain free of entanglements with others there and of responsibilities of service, and easily slip out after (or before) the service benediction prayer. I have witnessed not only the flinging aside of a hymnbook culture that provided greatest comfort to me in my lonely hours and darkest days, but possibly also the deep roots and relationships centered on the neighborhood church.

One additional matter that unsettles me about this time versus the past history of such changes, is that I am *even more concerned about the generation that is older than me*. I know generations have long seen their elder generations as stodgy, non-progressive, stubborn, and judgmental (and defining and defending a rigid "establishment"), but I see deeper clouds of paranoia, hard hearts and lack of empathy than in previous generations—even in some of those still lingering from the "Greatest Generation" or "Silent Generation," who feel like they have uniquely "paid their dues," unlike others. Of course, we have witnessed the eras of their acceptance (and participation) in racist acts (with Klan membership deemed quite acceptable nationwide across all of America for eras in the Twentieth Century), and smaller acts of bigotry and heartlessness against blacks, Jews, Catholics, and immigrants, and a blind eye to the suffering of the poor and others, but I sense that at this time the resentment and lack of empathy of those less fortunate is far more strident and "in your face" like never before. Speaking of "in your face," the actions of these paranoid older generations that exhibit xenophobia and bigotry has been "in my face" for a number of years as I have been writing a book series on how American Christians are responding to the Muslim community in the age of the "War on Terror," and what it has revealed about their genuine spiritual life and acceptance of the principles of Christ. From that, I have to admit that, by and large, the picture is generally not very pretty.

This brings me to a "gut" feeling that I have had for some time—that the actions of my fellow Bible Belt peers in the Age of Trump has been the passing of a bar or "crossing the Rubicon," and entering an era of no turning back. This is much like when the Hebrews in the wilderness declined to enter the Promised Land due to fear and distrust, when the nation of Judah decided to ignore God's commands to repent and to submit to Nebuchadnezzar's yoke, when Israel lightly considered their high place altars and the threat of the Assyrians, when the Jews listened to their "fake news" from their religious leaders and publicly choose the patriot war fighter Jesus Barabbas over Jesus Christ, and when they again chose the profane thug Bar Kokhba to "Make Israel Great Again" after their Temple was gone, leading to their permanent diaspora. I hope I am wrong, and that this is merely a time of instability and "reset," with all forgiven eventually, but I am afraid that is wishful thinking. I thought that the selection of the loutish buffoon Trump would humble both the Republican Party and their "court evangelicals" as they were electorally routed, causing them some long-overdue soul searching, but God surprised us all. They believe it shows God's endorsement and blessing of their political agenda; I believe it is a sign of God's judgment, in that it "signifieth the removing of those things that are shaken...that those things which cannot be shaken may remain" (Heb. 12:27), i.e., that of an "unshakable" remnant. As I said on a radio show with friends, "I do believe that God is using Donald Trump....*to expose the spiritual bankruptcy of the Religious Right.*" Whether I am right or wrong (and this is all "much ado about nothing"), I am "confident of this very thing, that he which hath begun a good work in you will perform [it] until the day of Jesus Christ" (Phil. 1:6), and His will be finished on Earth, regardless. However, as with all the other seminal times in Israel's history, the question still remains—*when this shaking is over, who will be remaining?*

I have witnessed Christian leaders and their followers get all excited about all the great things they think Donald Trump could possibly do on their behalf, to bring about their agenda on the courts, not only to overturn Roe V. Wade, but to overturn the Johnson Amendment, to then let untold millions of political action committee money flow tax-free through church and Christian organization coffers, using the holy pulpit to promote the agendas of special interests, while sacredizing it by the use of scripture and Christian imagery. I have heard our top evangelical leaders like Jerry Falwell Jr. of Liberty University, Franklin Graham, Pastor Jeffries of First Baptist Dallas and numerous others refer to Trump as the "new Cyrus," or even "King David." Others say that he was anointed to fulfill Bible prophecy, by helping build the Temple in Jerusalem. The "Fireman Prophet," author of *The Trump Prophecies* (published by Christian publisher Tom Horn, and with a movie about his life recently in theaters in conjunction with Horn and

Liberty University), has not only supposedly foretold of Trump's election, but even explained that the Illuminati and Freemasons had used special electromagnetic frequency weapons to alter the DNA of people, to facilitate their opposition to Trump[189] (he also revealed that POW war hero Sen. John McCain was killed by a military firing squad for opposing Trump[190], rather than a mere brain tumor, as many of us gullible dupes believed). The most prominent aspect of Trump's evangelical supporters I have witnessed is their consistent and strident defense of his moral behavior, his cover-ups and lying about said behavior, his statements about women, minorities, white supremacists, immigrants, etc. ad nauseum, and his choice of shady bare-knuckles "Good Fellas" for his central cabinet posts—in other words, like a good Mafia "fixer" lawyer. *But what will they reap in return?*

These evangelical leaders, and seemingly most evangelicals really like to appear to be "winning" (more important than standing for what is ethical or of integrity), and have bet on and are riding a winning horse, but will he turn out to be the snake, riding across the river on a turtle or frog (I forget which) from the story Trump loves to tell at his rallies?

They envision their receipt of selfish, short-term material gains from him (like many other non-evangelical supporters, such as big business and Wall Street, with both focusing on monetary rewards to their 401Ks and profit sheets), while mortgaging their grandchildren's financial future in debt and physical well-being due to environmental disregard, and regardless of how his policies affect other minorities and vulnerable groups of all types, admittedly just like many of them conduct their personal lives. However, in regards to their "heavenly" calling of spiritual husbandry over their society, will they ultimately find that, like Esau, *they sold their "birthright" of the "high ground" of spiritual and moral heritage and example, as well as the care-taking of their society, for a mere "mess" of Trump porridge, thereby "despising" their birthright of societal spiritual guidance?*

One thing I hear almost no "Great-Commission evangelical" person talk about is, while they have gained some transitory influence and clout in Trump's court (or so they think), *do they ever look at things from a "Kingdom of Heaven" view, and see how their Faustian Bargain they struck with Trump, evidenced by their vote and vocal support for him and his views, will impact their "heavenly calling" to be "fishers of men" and to "rescue the perishing" by being "salt and light" in their society, in the eyes of the "white fields" of non-Christian Americans who are assessing their real sincerity, genuineness and love for their neighbors in how they are interacting and supporting Trump?* In Christ's parable of the "Great Commission, evangelical" invitation to the Kingdom feast, those He invited that were distracted by the Great City Babylon-business-financial affairs-conservative obsession on property/asset acquisition and their income generation (from property and oxen), *actually declined from participating*, leading the Master to then only invite "the poor, the maimed, and the halt, and the blind" (Luke 14:21). Religious Right leaders and their followers have been hoodwinked (somewhat willingly in many cases, for their own selfish interests) by the *Hannity*s and *Fox News*es and conditioned by them through countless hours of exposure, to think that these very types of people are the "lazy" exploiters and "burdens on society" seeking handouts, that instead need to "get right with God" and quit being such screw-ups in their lives (and in particular, not to expect any assistance from them). *In reality, Jesus says that these are the people who appreciate God's call, and will be the ones Jesus plans to spend eternity with in His Kingdom. Wouldn't it be wise for us to ingratiate ourselves to these people, to see if they invite us to join them at the Master's Table?* For the record, as mentioned before by me on the radio, in this "Faustian bargain" of Trump and evangelicals, *I am not sure which one is Faust, and which is the Devil—which is blinded by transient ambition, and which has the true rotten agenda.*

Considering this seemingly never-regarded aspect of how their very-public "Trump-ophilia" might impact their real calling that Christ left them here to perform for the Kingdom of Heaven, let's consider several segments of the "white fields" of souls to harvest in America by the preaching of the Gospel of Christ, and how they might respond to this Trump-glorifying, Babylon-supporting message now proclaimed by these self-professing "soul winners," given their public defense of Trump's overtures to these groups:

Women: Women comprise just over half of the population across humanity, but in terms of their rights and self-determination, throughout history they have been treated and experienced much more of the injustices that are common to a minority group. Jesus changed the historical culture of women within the religious world, by noticing them and their unique needs as individuals worthy of His time, and as joint participants in Kingdom work (to be accurate, there were "roles" for women in the pagan world as priestesses, temple prostitutes or diviners, but these were roles assigned to them by men, and no regard seemed to be given to their own spiritual needs or well-being). Jesus found the women to be the ones who anointed Him and comforted Him with perfume and oil for His sake, while the men sought merely to extract more wisdom or rewards from Him (such as prominent positions in the Kingdom). The women did the same act of devotion when His disgusting, shredded body was taken from the cross, when the men left Him and He could not even express thanks to the women, or give more. In turn Jesus appeared first to a dear woman friend, possibly because she and her friends did not forget the Lord, nor neglect to minister to His body after the "thrill" of His ministry was over for others. The Apostle Paul found the women in his ranks as indispensable fellow troopers and leaders in global Kingdom work that he relied upon, and leader Apollos was taught on the "more excellent way" of Christ by Priscilla. Church history is replete with giants of the faith such as missionary Lottie Moon, Corrie Ten Boom and many other women who did the "heavy lifting" of the Kingdom, usually while men stood around.

Today, evangelicals justify and excuse their figurehead leader who publicly in the media mocked fellow Republican female candidates and leaders because of their facial appearance or his definition of femininity (as reflected by his confirmed affinity for porn stars and Playmates). He makes fun of their menstrual cycles and moodiness, and brags of his ability to molest and fondle their most private areas because of his power and celebrity; he even assented on the radio as to his own daughter being a "fine piece of a_s," and that he would date her if he could. The porn stars and Playmates whom he originally denied affairs with (eventually proven by his own signed payoff and hush money checks) occurred while his own wife stayed at home with their newborn; he also bragged in the media of the best part of his beauty pageant sponsorship, in that he could go backstage and see all of them with no clothes on. In response, Religious Right leaders and their followers not only defend him, but see him as their leader and the "New Cyrus," and brag about his "faith." They say he is a new man now, but he publicly said he has nothing to ask God forgiveness for. *These positions of our religious leaders is the clearest testimony of their true beliefs regarding marital fidelity, sexual purity and morality (including ringleader Dr. James Dobson, whose "Focus on the Family" has made a fortune selling an opposite message for the common folk who, unlike Trump, cannot offer his types any power), regardless of the empty words and puritanical brow-beating they otherwise do, and even their condescending and debased value of women in general. Are women in society today motivated or inspired to pursue a Gospel that values them and their needs, and their potential to contribute and excel in the Kingdom, based upon the mouths and testimony of these witnesses?*

The Poor: Donald Trump, like the rest of the Religious Right and conservatives in general, see the "poor" or needy as no more than a drain on the profit margins and bank accounts of the more fortunate. They wish they would just go away, other than needing a vast pool of "slave labor" to work at below-living wages to maintain the ever-demanding increase in material standard of living of the rest, as judged by an ever-growing thirst for more consumer goods, prestige and status symbols and pampered vacation homes and junkets synonymous with "the good life" they deserve. At least Trump was clear in whose bidding he desired to serve, for all but the most densely undiscerning—*unfortunately the latter included most of my fellow evangelicals, although admittedly they may be blinded more by their selfishness and low character than true intellectual limitations.* Trump made clear who he was really serving in his first act as President, moments after his inauguration, when he signed his first Executive Order releasing financial advisors of consumers from the fiduciary duty to first act in the customer's interests, and thus could push bad financial products that enriched the trusted advisor with bigger commissions, and rewarded the financial firms offering defective products, to the detriment of the uninformed "mark" of the scam—*the consumer.* His tax plan was sold as a thinly veiled giveaway to corporations and the very rich, cutting their taxes almost in half, and removing valuable exemptions for the poor and middle class, and a throwaway finite standard deduction increase that is unusable for the vast portion of the public with a mortgage or charitable deductions that justify itemizing on their returns.

The massive deficits and debt the corporate tax cuts provide will be paid by future generations after his time, with the poor and middle class least able to shoulder it. His refusal to provide health care assistance to the lower income strata (as provided for under Obamacare) and desire to reduce entitlements to them to pay for the corporate tax cuts receives cheers from his Religious Right followers, and their leaders whose "ministries" are paid by billionaires and corporate donations. In the campaign, Trump bragged in press conferences about his electoral strength amongst the "poorly educated," saying "I love the poorly educated"—*he just doesn't "love" them so much as to "educate" them as to what is in their best interests or how they can be misled and exploited, rather desiring, in metaphorical terms, to "keep them on the plantation."* This view is supported by most of the rank-and-file evangelicals, which is why they didn't show up for the recent "Poor People's Campaign" marches nationwide, leading the secular moralists to fill the moral vacuum created there. *Will the vast and ever-growing sea of the "poor" and those clinging month-to-month to solvency respond to a gospel message by a Religious Right evangelical community with vast holdings of upper-scale church property and "Christian Life Centers" and other investments, not to mention its well-heeled leaders and parishioners themselves or the "prosperity gospel" hucksters so conspicuous on television, and who by their statements and deeds all see the less fortunate as parasites and lazy connivers? Will the needy trust evangelicals as "being their brother's keeper" like the Good Samaritan?*

Hispanics and Other Immigrants: Donald Trump opened his presidential campaign with his initial primary issue that the Mexicans crossing the U.S.

border were "rapists" and "murderers," saying that "they're [the Mexican government] not sending us their best folks," and that they were "tough hombres"; this inspired his initial proposals to completely close down the border, and to build a wall, that somehow Mexico themselves would "pay for." As president he did show his sensitivity to Hispanic culture by tweeting a picture of him eating enchiladas (the only thing missing was him wearing a giant sombrero and handlebar moustache). As president he also came up with a new "points-based" protocol to allow immigration, with the largest points given if they were Olympic athletes, had high education, or were very wealthy with a lot of money to invest; unfortunately the immigrants who risked their lives to find new hope in America (like the immigrants of past generations who built this nation, and fought in its wars) would have none of these (ironically, I thought this was supposed to be the "Home of the Brave," like those who risked their lives in their dream to live here, instead of the "Home of the Aristocrat"). He was found to employ illegal immigrants en masse in his own businesses, to give them below-market wages. These policies were some of the most popular as embraced by Religious Right evangelicals. *Will their contempt for those of Hispanic immigrant heritage help evangelicals to not only fulfill the Great Commission, but also at least maintain if not grow their ranks, in a nation where whites are declining and Hispanics will be the fastest growing group?*

Refugees: The other initial policy that was the beginning centerpiece of Trump's presidential campaign was his adamant refusal to let any immigrants of the Muslim faith to enter the country, and furthermore to stop any immigrants of nations were he thought trouble resided, regardless of the years of vetting by U.S. officials that currently goes on for these applicants. Although recent Muslim-blamed terror or violent attacks in the U.S. were not due to immigrants at all (consistent with data showing that immigrants have never been the source of domestic terror), Trump used some small-scale events as justification of his no-exceptions policies. This form of religious discrimination and bigotry has (not surprisingly) also been one of the most popular positions of the U.S. Religious Right and much of the evangelical communities. As I have documented extensively in my lengthy book series, *The Holy War Chronicles—A Spiritual View of the War on Terror*, the bulk of evangelicals and others comprising the Religious Right have chosen to ignore the mandate from their Lord to love, minister to, reach out and share the gospel with their Muslim neighbors—*whom the Lord may be sending to the West since cowardly Western Christians do not love them enough to risk taking the Gospel to Muslim lands, by and large*—and rather choose to demonize, slander and ostracize (and at times persecute themselves) such people seeking a peaceful new life, and avoid any contacts or understandings that might lead to further spiritual dialogue. *When Muslim immigrants, often fleeing persecution in their Muslim homelands and now free and open to learn the truth about real Christians and the beliefs, see this outright hatred in the name of "Christian" tribalism, should we expect their ranks to be interested in the gospel we purportedly exist to promote?*

African Americans: Trump and his slum-lord father Fred have long had a reputation in New York City in discriminating in their rental property by race, as attested to in court cases, such as that taken by the Department of Justice in 1973 when their rental agents were told by the Trumps to turn black applicants away (both Trumps were represented by attorney Roy Cohn, the notorious figure who was the attack dog of Senator McCarthy in the 1950s "Red Scare" hearings). Even historic American folk legend Woody Guthrie sang the blues of the Trump's poor housing in which he resided. When the "Central Park Five" (four of them African American, one Hispanic) were convicted of raping a New York jogger, citizen Trump got involved with full page ads calling for their execution immediately. When the real rapist later confessed and his personal evidence was proven on the victim, the innocent parties were released years later, but Trump refused to apologize, and suggested they were still guilty—a position he maintained later even during the election campaign. He has been accused of treating African Americans negatively by those who have participated in his television programs, and many assume racial bias was behind his leading role in disputing President Obama's birth certificate, long after it had been made public. One of his most notorious examples was his endorsement of the clearly-labeled and dressed Nazis that came to defend the Confederate monuments at Charlottesville, calling the crowds there "good people on both sides."

He was then noted as President in telling immigrants from Nigeria to "go back to their huts," and wanting to turn down their aid since they were one of many "shit hole countries"; he further explained in a staff meeting regarding Haitians that "They all have AIDs." In a 1991 biography, he was quoted as saying that he "hated" having "black guys" counting his money, and rather wanted "short guys wearing yarmulkes," and adding that "laziness is a trait in blacks"; in a subsequent 1997 interview, Trump stated that the information in the book was "probably true." He subsequently tweeted during the campaign that "the overwhelming amount of violent crime in our cities is committed by blacks and Hispanics." He explained his animosity for the Puerto Ricans who were devastated by Hurricane Maria by stating via tweet that "they want everything to be done for them." When Sheriff Joe Arpaio was sued by the Justice Department for racially profiling Latino inmates and mistreating them; he ignored their orders and was held in contempt by the court; in turn Trump pardoned him. However, in fairness Trump was shown equality in treating other races and ethnic groups; he accused rival Indian casino owners of "not looking like Indians" and then forming a "pro-family" group with Roger Stone to publicly portray Mohawk Indian casino owners as violence-prone, and accused an American-born judge of bias in an immigration case because of his Mexican heritage. Polls have shown that almost two-thirds of Americans believe he makes racist comments and respects white people more than other races. In all these incidents, the Religious Right has stood strong with Trump, and defended him. *Is it not amazing that very few black and other minorities are attending Religious Right-leaning churches, and few outside the church reached in minority communities, when they see the public positions of the Religious Right, and the history they have in our country that they've not denounced?*

Transgendered and Gay Communities: Donald Trump, not truly being a spiritual man, has not been as voracious a persecutor of those of alternative sexual preferences, compared to his Religious Right "Witchfinder Generals," but he did throw them a bone by randomly forbidding the presence of trans-genders in the military, by executive fiat, over the views and studies underway by senior Pentagon officials. My wife and I first met members of that community when we volunteered at a community radio station, and we found opportunities to minister spiritually and with healing and love, and were in turn blessed by the growing experience. Religious Right activists focus on the sexual identity issue not because it is the most egregious sin in the Bible or exhibits the most innocent victims (gossip, backbiting and unloving attitudes were shown to be the most damaging in the early church epistles), but because in cloistered, "White Bread" America it still retains a uniquely quaint and old-fashioned "yuck" factor in the Religious Right communities of the Bible Belt in comparison to other egregious sins, and beyond its spiritual aspects alone. This phenomenon allows the exaggeration of its emphasis as a "boogeyman" and a good fundraiser to raid the pockets of superstitious and paranoid "villagers" for whom such lifestyle practitioners are so exotic as to possibly be from Mars, since they mostly do not knowingly have contact with such people, but ironically certainly do with those of such persuasion who do not feel at liberty to reveal themselves.

In more reserved American Christian generations, the subject was not discussed much and such practitioners were at least pitied at worst, and usually left alone, except by boozy thugs in the streets; in the rise of the Religious Right in the early 1980s, the LGBTQ community quickly became American Christianity's "Public Enemy Number One." When the contempt the Religious Right community shows towards these dear people whom Christ died for even exceeds that of the overtly xenophobic and bigoted Trump, are we shocked that the inroads Religious Right Christians are having with those of non-traditional sexual inclinations in terms of spiritual dialogue and reconciliation are having limited success, if any at all?

As an example of my assertions, a June 2019 online article[191] by the Billy Graham Association's *Decision* magazine, entitled, "The Lie of 'Progressive Christianity'," reveals at its top a large overlay photograph of South Bend (IN) Mayor and 2020 major Democratic presidential candidate Pete Buttigieg—a publicly professing Christian, a military veteran, and…*a married gay man*. They began by focusing on his spiritual critique of the Religious Right's "favorite son," Mike Pence (whose real reputation many Hoosiers like Buttigieg know better than most, and as we will review in the next volume in detail), and make him the poster boy of a "progressive Christianity" that "denies the full authority of Scripture." They claim that his false Christianity allows him to "remain married to his male partner" (evidently instead of "putting his spouse away" and breaking a marital covenant, like Ezra recommended to the men of Israel, to get rid of their Moabitess wives and such—*women like Ruth*), with Calvinist Southern Baptist leader Al Mohler calling such "the root of all unfaithfulness," as a "sin that began in the Garden of Eden" (?). They stoke the paranoia by stating that progressives' goal "appears aimed at driving Biblical Christianity to the outer margins of society," and a representative of the "conservative Institute on Religion and Democracy" is quoted as saying that the religious progressives tend to "loath Western civilization and the idea of American liberty as exceptional"—*evidently these principles being the primary agendas of these conservative Christians (and what these folks are selling), and ironically a nationalistic message coming from "strangers and pilgrims on the earth" (Heb. 11:13) and citizens of a city "not made with human hands" (Heb. 9:11).* He laments that these dreaded reprobates "expect Americans to be uniquely altruistic and self-denying, unlike any other societies in the world."

In turn, Mayor Buttigieg has also expressed some views of his own spiritual critique of President Trump and his entourage—be they "court evangelicals," or other followers. In April 2019, he was reported[192] to say that "I'm reluctant to comment on another person's faith, but I would say it is hard to look at this president's actions and believe that they're the actions of somebody who believes in God. I just don't understand how you can be as worshipful of your own self as he is and be prepared to humble yourself before God. I've never seen him humble himself before anyone. And the exaltation of yourself, especially a self that's about wealth and power, could not be more at odds with at least my understanding of the teachings of the Christian faith." They note that Buttigieg also criticized the Democrats for shunning religion, stating in *The Washington Post* that "I think it's unfortunate [the Democratic Party] has lost touch with a religious tradition that I think can help explain and relate our values. At least in my interpretation, it helps to root [in religion] a lot of what it is we do believe in when it comes to protecting the sick and the stranger and the poor, as well as skepticism of the wealthy and the powerful and the established."

Minority Faith Communities: We already know of Trump's early slanderous statements about Muslims, and the inability to trust any of them, and their inherent violent motives—views he has not renounced during his time in office. We see him joyfully embrace Israeli Prime Minister Benjamin Netanyahu (Trump's father was a good friend of his, and co-operated in a bond fund in America to bankroll Israel's initiatives), but we must remember that Netanyahu is not really an authentic practicing religious Jew, and that roughly half of the Jews in Israel want him locked up for indictments of his corruption that only his minority-led election put on hold (with such indictments underway by the end of 2019), and they oppose his policies that Trump bolsters, as well as a good portion of American Jews. When the Charlottesville neo-Nazis loudly proclaimed, "The Jews Will Not Replace Us," Trump defended them as part of the "good people on both sides," and routinely re-tweeted material from their anti-Semitic websites. As far as smaller faith communities, Trump largely ignores them, while showing contempt for their ethnic or nationalistic heritage, such as in Africa. *With Christians encouraging him to take these stands, is it no wonder that the "evangelicals" are not longer largely successful in "evangelizing" these communities, even amongst disgruntled or seeking members of these faiths, when they see how these type of prominent Christian leaders and communities have such contempt and ill-intents for those of differing faiths in general?*

Those With Disabilities: When Donald Trump had Trump Tower built, he told the architect he wanted the braille code on the elevator controls removed, because "no blind people will be living here." When a known journalist that suffers from debilitating cerebral palsy asked him a pointed question, Trump responded by mocking and physically recreating his shaking tremor spasms and drawn up limbs, to the laughter of the Christian rally-goers in his audience. *Is there anyone else of the downtrodden that Trump has not attempted to offend, and when Christians do not publicly and pointedly denounce this, how can they say they are representing a Christ who embraced lepers and prostitutes, and whose heart was moved so much by the suffering of others that he stopped His teaching and activities to first address their needs?*

In essence, the Religious Right is continuing the age-old Western Christian conservative/fundamentalist "game plan" in their calling to reach out to a dying and hurting world with a saving message and hope, love and forgiveness they received while wretched and without hope themselves, using the old business adage that "the beatings will continue until morale improves"—if we keep ignoring their hurt, menace them and shame them, and slander them and their intentions and hearts, and otherwise show them no humble respect, eventually they will "see the light" and come to us (and the Lord) with open arms and groveling on their knees, seeing it as their own benefit! This must be the game plan of America's Religious Right in their "yoking" with Trump and his ilk (or worst ones that come after him), and "their blood (and Trump's 'virtues') will be on them and their children" spiritually. We will see in the future how successful that "game plan" is (unless they have really given up on the Great Commission, and rather prefer to be "hunters of men" rather than "fishers"), but if it is not (as I expect), and they even experience an expected over-corrected backlash in society, they will still not be able to look in the mirror, in circumspection and heart searching, to find probable cause, and rather chalk it up to another era of old-fashioned "Christian persecution."

I used to assume that these evangelical leaders and their followers merely winced and looked the other way when Trump bragged of molesting women, lying about his infidelities and other vices, his defense of white supremacists marching, his embrace (and publicly professed envy) of dictators, his mistreatment of women, his hurtful comments toward the disabled, POWs, immigrants and the like, and murky associations with disreputable figures in his campaign and administration, dangling pardons over them to keep their mouths shut, separating families at the border, and the like, and while yet embarrassed, still keeping their "eyes on the prize" of their political agenda. However, after I have witnessed over four years of their strident and unwavering defense of all his actions, and a refusal to call him to any account, I am starting to believe that they actually, not-so-secretly *like* all these things he does, otherwise they would speak up about it. I think they vicariously live through him as a vulgar, crass "guilty pleasure," a lifestyle which sadly we already see glimpses of in many Christian leaders behind the scenes when they are exposed in their own ministries from time to time. However, this time this devilish desire is shared with the rank-and-file Christians as well, who cheer at rallies when Trump calls to "Lock Her Up," or, regarding protestors, "beat the hell out of him" or to "hit him for me, and I'll pay your legal bills," and makes fun of a woman's looks who disagree with him, or other shortcomings of a person. *We are seeing the real person behind the mask of superficial piety on our Christian friends and neighbors now slipping from many of them before our very eyes. They stand with Trump because they like the way he does things, pure and simple, and they see no need to justify.* Like Young Goodman Brown, the title character of the short story of the same name by *The Scarlet Letter* author Nathaniel Hawthorne, who saw his fine Christian Puritan community religious leaders as upstanding stalwarts until he horrifyingly saw them under cover of darkness, participating in the most diabolical deeds and exposing their hypocrisy and duplicity, I also feel that "the scales have come off" my eyes and I see my evangelical "heroes," both national and local, in their true nature of anti-Christian convictions and agendas deep within their souls, to my grief.

I hope not to be too harsh, but I fear that God has exposed much of our Religious Right leadership, and their flocks, as to being spiritually shallow, duplicitous, double minded, and sad to say, possibly not even aware that they are not connected to the Vine, in many cases (I am to the point where I am not sure if many of these popular Christian leaders really believe in God or not, and thus not feel accountable to Him). *Otherwise, how do we explain the cognitive dissonance they display?* Again, this is NOT an indictment of Trump, who is merely being the same well-known *jackass* (for lack of a more descriptive term) he has always been known for. God appears to have certainly used him to expose the same traits in the self-righteous evangelical leaders (and many of their flock) who like to say (usually with great personal remuneration in turn) that they represent Him. It reveals a widespread spiritual and Biblical ignorance, and lack of understanding of spiritual mindedness and even common decency and civility, which we have been unwilling to admit is widespread within our own ranks, as a supposedly "superior" people necessary to play a role in "saving" others. *This is not a mere transient, debatable political disagreement; Trump indeed is so "unique" in action and tone, that in those who like his "style" and agenda, and relationship with others, it reveals their most foundational character traits, of who they think Jesus is, what the Kingdom of Heaven values, and what the Gospel is all about.* For those of my fellow American Christian brethren who are genuinely good in heart and loving of Jesus and what they perceive to be His teachings, yet live with the cognitive dissonance of not only the values of the profane and narcissistic Donald Trump, but also the selfish, Darwinistic self-preservationist priorities of Great City Babylon conservatism, *I believe it further supports my premise that the overwhelming exposure to conservatism's "Tokyo Rose" broadcasts by talk radio shows like Hannity and cable news outlets like Fox News are drilling into their brains a Babylon "gospel" that is far overwhelming any church and Bible teaching, as evidenced by their incessant recitation of a "rosary" of its talking points over the words of Jesus in every societal issue.*

One can empathize (a tiny bit) with the evangelical flock, like those followers Jesus called "sheep without a shepherd," when their top evangelical leaders wrap themselves in Trump values (or just acknowledge that his positions coincided with their original illicit views already). In October 2019 the Christian online news outlet *World Net Daily* reported[193] that Franklin Graham is calling on the nation to pray for Democrats in Washington to have a "change of heart" regarding impeachment, writing on Facebook that "The socialist Democrats' message to the United States of America is: 1. We're going to take your guns, and 2. We're going to impeach your president," and warned about a "conflict," or a "civil war," as the pastor of First Baptist Church of Dallas described it. Graham added that Speaker Pelosi is responsible for any "'constitutional crisis' based on unsupported claims that Trump colluded with Russia in 2016," and told "gay Christian" Pete Buttigieg that "it's up to God, not people, to define sin." *Let me ask you—does this sound like the tone, and agenda of the "weightier matters of the law" referred to by Jesus?*

A few days later the *Associated Press* reported[194] that this appeal of a Christian mandate to support Trump was under a long-running national tour entitled, Decision America (sounding like his father's historical programs for *soul-winning*), and they noted attendees (at a Decision event of 13,800) expressing fears that an impeachment might escalate such that we "could have a war...you just don't know. It's scary." They quote Graham telling the reporters that the evidence of Trump withholding critical military assistance to Ukraine on conditions of their producing evidence against his campaign rival is "a lot over nothing...It's going to destroy this country if we let this continue," and added that Trump should look for more evidence on Joe Biden's son Hunter, noting "the son's acknowledged drug addiction as a reason Hunter Biden is 'suspect'," and "it's probably worth looking into to see what Vice President Biden (did) at the time, what kind of promises he made to help his son with the Ukrainians." They close by noting that an August 2019 Pew study found that *77% of white evangelicals approved of Trump's performance, with the approval of weekly church attendees rising up to 81%.*

On the eve of the 2016 election, our pastor at our church rightly called for a prayer meeting, praying that the election and its impact would help promote a season of spiritual revival in our land. In my view, the election results, further reinforced by what has transpired since, has led me to believe that *it is the least likely to create any revival, at least in the short term, either in the "lost" society or the "spiritually confused" evangelicals who want to provide spiritual leadership to them.* I am more afraid that it actually signifies a time of *judgment*, not for the former group but rather the latter, "For it is time for judgment to begin with God's household" (1 Peter 4:17, NIV).

In closing I want to reiterate that these harsh words are in no way an indictment of Christ, the Apostles, the Gospel or their other writings, for their genuineness and relevance remain, and we need them now more than ever. But, one must ask as the smoke eventually clears, who will be remaining, standing here in America to represent their message and values, with relatively unspoiled reputations and thus societal credibility as evangelist messengers, in the aftermath? To do so, is it wise for the prudent to publicly distance themselves now from Trump and his values, before the "rats" flee the ship, as the rest of society has had enough of his cruelty and hijinks?

In other words,

> I tell you, he will see that they get justice, and quickly. However, when the Son of Man comes, will he find faith on the earth? (Luke 18:8, NIV)

> You hypocrites, rightly did Isaiah prophesy of you: "THIS PEOPLE HONORS ME WITH THEIR LIPS, BUT THEIR HEART IS FAR AWAY FROM ME. BUT IN VAIN DO THEY WORSHIP ME, TEACHING AS DOCTRINES THE PRECEPTS OF MEN." [i.e., conservatism and capitalism] (Matt. 15:7–9, NASB)

> But when he saw many of the Pharisees and Sadducees come to his baptism, he said unto them, O generation of vipers, who hath warned you to flee from the wrath to come? Bring forth therefore fruits meet for repentance: And think not to say within yourselves, We have Abraham to [our] father: for I say unto you, that God is able of these stones to raise up children unto Abraham. And now also the axe is laid unto the root of the trees: therefore every tree which bringeth not forth good fruit is hewn down, and cast into the fire. (Matt. 3:7–10)

Conclusions, Opportunities and Warnings for God's People in the West

I want to applaud the handful of readers who have exhibited the stamina (or foolhardiness, "rubber necker"-styled morbid curiosity to see how this "train wreck" work ends, or having little better to read or spend one's time) to withstand this lengthy tome by a first-time solo writer, as I attempt to "tie a bow" on and summarize the wealth of data and issues covered in this work. I am sure it is a small remnant of those initial readers who either got bored with a work longer than a Facebook post, or elected to heave it across the room when they encountered a topic or passage that incensed them (for, as I warned, "there is something here to offend everybody"). I assume that this remnant is a smaller "remnant" from those who have heard this book described by myself in media outlets or by others, and who for various reasons—due to lack of interest, suspicions of opposition to its premises, and other distractions—chose not to pick up the book and actually see the assertions I make, and the evidence I present to back them up, for themselves. I have convinced myself that this quest of writing from morning-to-night, seven day a week for years without compensation or feedback, digging up data, screening and sifting (probably not enough for most readers) data tidbits and mountains of books and articles, was intended for the tiny audience of people who still read books and care what is going on in the world and their responsibility to it, for I believe that they are the people who define or change the world we live in. I feel a duty to provide to them the findings I can uncover for their education, enlightenment and edification, including future generations who may find my works at the local flea market or yard sale one day, and possibly inspire them as well.

I will not subject you to an exhaustive list of the key areas and findings throughout this extensive work (you've been through enough, already), and many are somewhat summarized at the end of each chapter, but the following are a few of the major points we have explored and considered in this work, which many of you may have forgotten if you have been reading this at a leisurely pace (although "leisure" is probably not a word one should use with topics and material this heavy):

(1) I have asserted that our evangelical community has recently "crossed the Rubicon" in terms of its legacy and reputation (and focus) during the Trump era, although it has been building up for at least generations,

(2) "Trump Values" (which I would assert include conspicuous wealth as a sign of worth, braggadocio and swagger in style, confrontationalism, contempt for the poor, weak and stranger, and willingness to lie or deceive if it is justified by "winning" and protecting one's self and one's clan), have either directly influenced the Religious Right people that I observe around me, or merely reflect and have exposed what has been partially hidden in the hearts of the Religious Right Christians for a long time (particularly the older folk),

(3) As a result, and while being the primary foundation of Trump support and people like him in politics and even religious leaders, they have isolated themselves from everyone in society (aside from sympathetic groups like the white supremacists), and either pretend to not know it, do not care, or look to blame everyone but themselves, including the usual lineup of suspects—"liberals," socialists, secular humanists, etc.

(4) Because of this, they are in no position to perform the calling and mission they purportedly claim they received from Christ in the Great Commission, to be "fishers of men" and "rescue the perishing" by means of "unnatural" sacrificial love, acceptance and forgiveness, ministry to the destitute, a listening ear to those in crisis, and a gentle word of persuasion and putting others before themselves, as "salt and light" for others to witness with their own eyes the nature and love of Christ Himself, and the nature of the eternal Kingdom of Heaven that is now accepting new applications for residence, and never seem to consider the impact to this sacred calling in the brazen and uncaring public positions they espouse,

(5) The media outlets of Talk Radio, Cable News, the Internet and the like have become the most influential "preachers" and sermonizers by far amongst American citizens within the Religious Right, having certain narratives and values (being sold by the Big Business "wealth class" who bankroll these PR and propaganda outlets) drilled into their heads, sometimes for hours, every day on their commutes, at their desks, and at the dinner table, leading them to recite their "talking points" in regard to today's issues as opposed to the teaching of Christ and the Apostles in scripture, the latter which they may hear for thirty minutes in church once a week,

(6) I assert that the message these powerful national media outlets provide can be viewed biblically as no more than the values of the old "leaven of the Pharisees," as Christ Himself described it, coming from the descendants of today's Religious Right, having an outer cloak of piety and policing of others, yet inside motivated by mammon, greed, and lack of concern for the "lesser types" of society, along with a host of values from scripture I have documented,

(7) When comparing the positions taken on basic issues by *Fox News*, Sean Hannity and other talk radio and cable news celebrities and outlets, to the specific teaching of Jesus Christ and the Kingdom of Heaven, further amplified by the apostles and prophets in the Bible, we see that there is little to no overlap of perspective, giving American Christians a real choice today to decide "whom they will serve today,"

(8) We have extensively documented the modern era roots of this purchasing of America's conservative clergy and their flocks by Big Business and the banking and wealth class, in the 1930s in response to the New Deal and Social Gospel which aided common people with jobs, literacy, basic food and health needs, and the terrible reputation of business and banking after their greed had led America and the world economy into the Great Depression, and how the first "prosperity gospel" preacher, James Fifield Jr., and these big business types, including "Big Oil" leaders such as J. Howard Pew, successfully penetrated the minds of the widespread clergy ranks, and their flocks and ministers-in-training, for generations to come,

(9) We have seen that the spiritual advisors in the religious media used by these nefarious cabals often delivered unorthodox, even anti-Christian

spiritual beliefs like a "Trojan Horse" into the impressionable minds of an immature American clergy community, to the extent of even sorcery-type drug use as an entheogenistic, shamanistic portal for spiritual experience, which dismissed the Cross, the Atonement and Lordship of Christ, and often hatched in dark venues like Bohemian Grove,

(10) We have seen that what we now see as modern-day unbridled capitalism, as promoted by the libertarians and many conservatives, was foreseen and foretold by the Bible itself, suggesting its origins on the Plains of Shinar in Babylon, influencing all culture (including Israel), being the enemy of how God prescribed righteous nations to protect the weak and poor in the marketplace and courts and actively take scheduled steps to stop the concentration of wealth, resulting in God's decree that He would judge the heavenly powers who promoted such cultures, and a final, swift eradication of the Great City Babylon and its system so glorified and sanctified by the Religious Right today, and

(11) We have considered what the future destiny will be for America's Religious Right and evangelicals, galvanized by their allegiance to Donald Trump and those like him, just like the ancient Jews chose a path through the "patriotic" Jesus Barabbas and Bar Kokhba, who both promised to "make Israel great again," and what history and the Bible shows us will be their destiny, in terms of their utility to Christ and His mission to expand and advance the Kingdom of Heaven, and how their hateful views will impact their ability (if they even desire) to make disciples and be "salt and light," and the potential societal reactionary backlash that will also victimize gentler Christians who know better.

I feel the need to reiterate again to the confused reader who is not used to hearing such strong, pointed criticism of American Christian behavior and attitudes from a practicing Christian themself, that I am not suggesting that the entire Christian message is a fraud, or is to be rejected, because of what we may see as the blatant hypocrisy of many of its most vocal representatives. Rather, I take the extended effort to toil at an exhaustive effort such as this *in the defense of the reality and virtues of the classic Gospel message and its authenticity, by distinguishing it from a perverted version, the latter being repugnant to many people at arm's length from the Christian culture (or left it after refusing to tolerate its hypocrisy anymore) and the many who lamentably but understandably reject the legitimate "Good News" because of the ugliness of its misguided message bearers.* I believe that God loved the world so much that He sent His son to voluntarily make the ultimate sacrifice to make payment to the Serpent in securing our freedom from our choice of indentured bondage due to our sinful obedience to him, and to further honor justice by providing a personal offer of payment to God for our injustices each of us have done against His children and Himself (both aspects illustrated by the two sacrificial lambs offered for different roles in the Day of Atonement (Lev. 6:7–10, 20–22, 26)). It is the ultimate manifestation of free substitutionary mercy and forgiveness (and a divine love unparalleled in all other religious systems) for each of us, who can then not only experience communion with the One who made us and finally sense an eternal purpose we were given and have been seeking and a deeper identity our soul desires, but also a mission to extend that mercy and forgiveness and continue His example to "tear down walls" with our neighbors. (Although while Christ's work provides payment of the eternal consequences of injustices we commit to all who accept His offer, I believe that we still possess the duty to make atonement and restitution to those to whom we have been unjust (even as a society and in history, as well as personal) to prevent the temporal consequences of unresolved injustice, and to aggressively forgive those who have been unjust to us to release them from such as consequences, or as Christ taught us to pray, "forgive us our debts, *as* [generous or stingy] we forgive our debtors....For if ye forgive men their trespasses, your heavenly Father will also forgive you" (Matt. 6:12–14) (emphasis added).) It is a testimony of a death and resurrection verified by historical records, the eyewitness testimony of many, many witnesses who sealed their authenticity with their martyred lives, and an inspirational, healing message unmatched by any other spiritual or ideological movement ever devised. *That is the real message I bring, as I strive to remove any understandable stumbling blocks to the genuine gentle truth seeker, and to separate the charlatan from the "real thing," to facilitate their enjoyment of its satisfying answers and meaningful purpose to life, and a legitimate and reasonable hope that can extend beyond this life.*

I have also been told before, including in my radio days, that my focus on these unsavory aspects of hypocrisy and darker elements of duplicity can be a "downer," particularly for many Christians who are used to reading the "classic" and popular Christian inspirational books that avoid such divisive and controversial topics, and rather focus on "self help" and promote the self esteem of everyone, focusing only on upbeat, inspirational anecdotes and "feel good" stories. Believe me, I would rather be writing such uplifting and warm stories myself; I am mindful of an old Johnny Cash song (one of my favorites) entitled, "Man in Black" (often known as "Why I Wear Black"), which explained its purpose to remind folks of the easily-forgettable "beaten down," drug addicted and the traumatized soldier, and who said he'd "rather wear a rainbow every day". Some of those athletes who "take a knee" to remind their fellow citizens that we have a long way to go to meet our ideals are similarly viewed as "unpatriotic" rather than heroic encouragers of us to seek our best selves. Indeed, when one reads the books of the prophets, we see God's message not typically one of patting his people on their backs and telling them to feel real good about themselves. His word tends to praise the one on their knees, pleading for mercy like the publican in the Temple, or as God says, "Humble yourselves in the sight of the Lord, and he shall lift you up" (James 4:10), and "The LORD is nigh unto them that are of a broken heart, and saveth such as be of a contrite spirit" (Psalm 34:18). Many Christians today do not understand that one's consideration of one's shortcomings to the example of Christ is not "beating oneself up," but *rather a continual, lifelong aspiration to conform to Christ, while also being secure in the love and acceptance of our Lord.* Considering and discussing the shortcoming of one's own Christian ranks is not "going against one's team" nor setting oneself above one's peers, but rather *mutually exhorting each other to continuously improve ourselves with God's help to better resemble Christ in sober self-reflection, out of loyalty to Christ and in debt to those we are attempting to be "stepping stones" to reach with the Good News.* When we compare ourselves or our "klans" to the Cornerstone as the standard, *I assert that we are in effect conducting an act of worship of Jesus Himself.* I myself am a cheerful, joyful, active participant in the ministries of my local church, try to be a good friend, sibling and husband, and love joking and normally even being silly as a grown adult, *but as a serious Christian I feel a duty to uncover and consider unsavory matters that can impact our collective witness and fruit-bearing, and think many of you should, too, regardless of your own conclusions, because God's expectations of our Kingdom work is "serious business."*

Before I forget to remind the devoted reader as I proceed to finish up the comments in this volume, that believe it or not, *this lengthy volume is not the whole story on this matter I intend to tell*; in fact, it will comprise *three volumes*, the remainder which will follow and be published on the heels of this current work, and I encourage the interested reader to keep a lookout for their availability, to explore these issues on an even deeper level. The next volume will focus in depth on a few recent-generation examples of prominent, profit-focused "Babylon" entities that have bankrolled the Religious Right for the last few generations, with agendas that far depart from those espoused by orthodox Christian teaching, and reveal the degree to which our vaunted Christian figureheads will prostitute themselves in "shaking hands with the devil" under the rationale of the "ends justifies the means," but truly serves as an expose on their greed, avarice, cynicism and exploitation of

God's gullible sheep, as the "wicked shepherd." It will also focus on a modern day "James Fifield, Jr." that has used the same *modus operandi* to lift himself to the highest ranks within the Trump administration, in a "ministry" of similar Big Business agendas as Fifield's, but *including the Vice President, Secretary of State and other top officials within their operation.* The third volume will tread even stranger paths, deeply exploring a few prominent examples of how our most revered Christian leaders have been seduced by influencers and movements not dangling almighty dollars in front of them, but *actual foreign spiritual beliefs and anti-Christian agendas* who have roots in the earlier influences of Heard, Ingebretsen, Wilson, Read and the like, but have taken it to the "next level," involving necromancy and other forbidden spiritual pursuits, *with the willing acceptance by our Religious Right leadership.*

In terms of constructively processing the information in this book and the book series in general, I recommend using a protocol I follow for substantive issues and matters to think through, which I have given the acronym, K.U.W.—Knowledge, Understanding and Wisdom. I define "knowledge" as the accumulation of facts and information pertaining to an issue; I hope that the years of information I have collected, embedded in this volume and the links, serve as a good start for interested readers to begin their own search for information. Such data should be from quality sources (preferably from media outlets big enough that they must consider legal consequences and legal review in-house to affirm verifiable allegations and data), from diverse venues and perspectives, and with a reliance on historically significant investigative journalism outlets, as well as some good "gumshoe" investigation in online tax forms and archived websites. This knowledge, upon pondering it and looking for trends and relationships, should lead to an "Understanding" of how it all fits together, how the system functions, its significance (while discarding insignificant facts) and even its spiritual implications and reflections; I have added my "two cents" liberally throughout this work, and I invite you to do the same, augmented by new data and facts beyond this publication as they become available. "Understanding" the nature of the issue should lead a responsible citizen, particular a God-fearing one, to a duty to translate one's understanding into appropriate personal and collective actions to affect the system in a socially and spiritually beneficial way, the determination of such appropriate responses I define as "Wisdom." While I want to impress the view that all of us should feel a call to take pertinent steps to address these issues and not merely "hide our candle under a bushel," *this step may be the most complex, and will require a collective effort of sincerely concerned and open-minded citizens to make our society more loving, humble, thoughtful of others, contented and spiritually consistent.*

The following are some suggested approaches I might propose off the top of my head for readers to adopt to "up their game" and constructively address the facts and situations we have considered, for starters:

(1) Be mindful that our aggressive and paranoid words towards "outsiders" to our ranks, ethnically, religiously, ideologically or in social class, have a direct bearing on Christians' duty to be disciple-makers, and that "honey" draws more flies than "vinegar," as well as showing our love in action,

(2) Stop and listen to "outsiders" and the disenfranchised and minorities of various stripes and their grievances, rather than being defensive; They are all human beings like us and some of their accusations may be a stretch, but if we can "walk a mile in their shoes" and imagine the mindset and culture they have inherited, we may be able to have empathy, and in turn they will often be shocked at our genuine love and respect, and become mutual friends,

(3) Remember that the "Golden Rule" is always applicable and paramount in every circumstance, even amongst those outside the Judeo-Christian ranks, and since Jesus says that on it rests "all the Law and the Prophets," it trumps other less important spiritual issues and prescriptions, with the goal of focusing on what Christ calls the "weightier matters of the law"—justice, mercy and faith—as opposed to unconstructive and unedifying legalism,

(4) Please do not always assume that others who need some help, financial or otherwise, for a while are instinctively lazy or exploitative; not only may they be facing family, economic, health or psychological challenges you haven't faced, but also such help is usually temporary but critical during seasons of misfortune or challenge, and such mercy usually "comes back around,"

(5) Remember that addictions to drugs, alcohol, gambling, pornography and other "life controlling issues" are indeed a form of enslavement and bondage, so be gentle in judging those in the misery of its grip, even as they exploit others in their irrational greed and insanity, and realize that this issue poses a greater threat to our society than most of what the Religious Right fears, and thus should be of paramount

concern if we are to address poverty, violence, crime and the family unit,

(6) Don't be afraid to confront older people who are at the forefront at spreading paranoia and animosity to those on the fringes of society, albeit respond with respect; they may have fought in wars, raised generations and kept our churches funded and functional, but they still have their biases and blind spots, and while tact and gentleness are often the prescription, sometimes a direct confrontation of their un-Christ like manner, made plain to them, is the order of the day,

(7) To better augment your assertions of Christians "upping their game" in their loving interactions with their neighbors and giving them a helping hand, do your part for your own credibility by "standing on your own feet" and being self-sufficient whenever possible by your own diligent effort (just like Paul and his tent-making), to be taken seriously by those you are trying to persuade, which is hard to do when living in your parents' basement,

(8) Be involved in a local church (more than warming a seat on Sundays), and be vocal in small groups about the unloving tone of Christian figures nationally and locally (and even from those in your own congregation), and being willing to "swim against the tide" of pack-like thinking there and on blogs and places like Facebook, giving defense of the "scapegoat," be they a foreign person or immigrant, a Muslim, another political party, or those of different lifestyles,

(9) Spend some time at the local shelter, and learn the stories of people there, and how easily a missed paycheck or medical bills can send anyone there quickly, as well as addictions; while you're at it, keep an eye out for jobs for the folks you meet, and pray for what they ask you about,

(10) While making your belief foundation firm in your own studies, spend much of your time with people outside your spiritual "pack"—the kinds of people Jesus hung out with, and get to know them, listen to them, finds ways to be a good friend, and let them debunk many church misconceptions, and see them as real people with real spiritual and emotional needs, and worthy of defense,

(11) Read and study substantive writings outside your own historical and cultural mindset, and try to understand their arguments, whether you adopt them or not, but at least understand them and be open to prayerful enlightenment and reconsideration, and participate in discussions with those online or elsewhere in a respectful rather than condescending way,

(12) For goodness sake, please stop listening to the corporate-paid cable news and talk radio propaganda outfits (or at least hear from a plurality of voices), which we have seen violate most of our most basic Christian virtues, and peruse hard news or investigative journalism sources for verifiable facts, but put editorializing (even the subtle kinds in the words used to describe the facts and players) in a separate category of "To Be Verified,"

(13) Make book reading of serious issues a regular part of your lifestyle, and a little less entertainment or information from other forms—all data must be vetted, but books usually are well-referenced (except many in the Christian bookstore) and normally take a "long view" of topics rather than thirty-second sound bites or Facebook slogans; be careful to challenge assertions or the scope of data presented, and seek out material of contrasting views—this should be done concerning this book you are reading, in particular, and let your views rest upon a plurality of voices, or the greatest truthful fidelity,

(14) Always maintain a skepticism of information, and seek to determine the agenda of any work itself, and who is funding it—particularly if corporate or wealthy patron-funded, as are most think-tanks and non-profits, Christian or otherwise, and consider the data within a larger context of the views of other stakeholders to the matter,

(15) If you are a "good Christian boy or girl" like I always tried to be, don't take the opinion of anyone as "gospel," even if they are your local (or more so a national celebrity) Christian leader, or popular political or media figure; if you are a Christian, then all must conform to the views, commands and lifestyle of the Cornerstone, Jesus Christ, and they must all be carefully vetted against that standard, as we must remind ourselves that many of these national figures may be well-known, but they are still "strangers" in that we

do not know their true motives, or even the depth of their true relationship to Christ,

(16) Do not cower from critiquing these beloved religious, and even military or political figures, or even our own parents or family members at times, or feel guilty for being disloyal for even asking hard questions; God may be calling you to help spur or be part of a new revival or reformation, merely catalyzed by your boldness in asking worthwhile but unsatiated questions and claims,

(17) Do not carry "anyone else's water" or anything else in your "bucket" except Jesus Christ and His gentle and eternally-constructive ways; that excludes many things we have traditionally viewed as "sacred"—our family cultural views and pride, church denominational beliefs, pet doctrines, political ideologies and parties, or anything else, which must be tested firmly against the standard of Christ and His values, if we are to worship Him alone,

(18) Be wary when everyone in your circles are marching in the same direction, particularly to scapegoat or demagogue a people group, ethnic group, religious faction or other minorities, or to wage a "holy war"—"culture" or otherwise—as they rally the troops and whip them into a furor; remember the "two spies" Joshua and Caleb, and that even a "minority report" within God's people isn't always wrong, and look for the innocent Hagars and Ishmaels swept up in the wreckage of the grand crusades, and seek them and minister to them like Christ did Himself, and

(19) Spend every morning when you get up, every night you lay down, when on the bus or commuting, in the shower, or whenever you are in some "time out," asking the Lord if there is someone desperate who needs your help, a defenseless person slandered you need to boldly defend, a broken-hearted or lonely person you can encourage, a struggling person you can help meet their goal, or a position or movement you should support, or even start or lead, to "preach the gospel to the poor...to heal the brokenhearted, to preach deliverance to the captives, and recovering of sight to the blind, to set at liberty them that are bruised" (Luke 4:18).

The people vouched for in this work—the poor, the weak and ill, the disabled, the immigrant, the minority, the addicted—are strongly opposed by the Big Business system funding talk radio and cable news, and by much of the Religious Right, and all their Great City Babylon underwriters who see them as wealth-wasting parasites, and at best, a source of dirt-cheap labor to exploit. However, the Bible clearly shows that our response to these groups *has a direct bearing on our entry into the Kingdom of Heaven.* Ironically, these passages are not quoted by the pious Christian Republican party, who wears their evangelical *bona fides* on their sleeve, but rather by those "depraved" Democratic candidates in the debates, as to the motives for their policies and their impetus for public office, which causes the Religious Right to rage. Such a biblical passage, which unambiguously shows the preferential treatment Heaven gives to these *anawim* that Babylon hates, and the litmus test Jesus will use on those who interact with them, includes the following:

When the Son of man shall come in his glory, and all the holy angels with him, then shall he sit upon the throne of his glory: And before him shall be gathered all nations: and he shall separate them one from another, as a shepherd divideth [his] sheep from the goats: And he shall set the sheep on his right hand, but the goats on the left. Then shall the King say unto them on his right hand, Come, ye blessed of my Father, inherit the kingdom prepared for you from the foundation of the world: For I was an hungred, and ye gave me meat: I was thirsty, and ye gave me drink: I was a stranger, and ye took me in: Naked, and ye clothed me: I was sick, and ye visited me: I was in prison, and ye came unto me. Then shall the righteous answer him, saying, Lord, when saw we thee an hungred, and fed [thee]? or thirsty, and gave [thee] drink? When saw we thee a stranger, and took [thee] in? or naked, and clothed [thee]? Or when saw we thee sick, or in prison, and came unto thee? And the King shall answer and say unto them, Verily I say unto you, Inasmuch as ye have done [it] unto one of the least of these my brethren, ye have done [it] unto me. Then shall he say also unto them on the left hand, Depart from me, ye cursed, into everlasting fire, prepared for the devil and his angels: For I was an hungred, and ye gave me no meat: I was thirsty, and ye gave me no drink: I was a stranger, and ye took me not in: naked, and ye clothed me not: sick, and in prison, and ye visited me not. Then shall they also answer him, saying, Lord, when saw we thee an hungred, or athirst, or a stranger, or naked, or sick, or in prison, and did not minister unto thee? Then shall he answer them, saying, Verily I say unto you, Inasmuch as ye did [it] not to one of the least of these, ye did [it] not to me. And these shall go away into everlasting punishment: but the righteous into life eternal. (Matt. 25:31–46)

The malaise the American evangelical community finds themselves in today, in the decadent Donald Trump's hip pocket as "court evangelicals," seemingly paranoid and hating all others outside their ranks, can lead many sincere and thoughtful Christians, young and old, into a depressed spirit of mind, and feeling that things are too far gone, judgment is here, the Christian witness in America is shot, and therefore it is of no use to engage and attempt to repair the dikes and the breaches. However, there are glimmers of hope that a remnant, and even a few within the Christian leadership, are beginning to see the error of their ways, or are becoming bolder in their denouncements of the status quo. As an example, Chuck Baldwin was instructed at the Liberty Bible Institute, founded a Baptist Church that grew spectacularly over decades (even recognized by Ronald Reagan), with thousands of new converts documented, with Jerry Falwell, Pat Buchanan, Roy Moore, Joe Scarborough, D. James Kennedy, Janet Folger, Michael Peroutka, Alan Keyes and many other prominent people speaking from his pulpit, hosting a national radio show and newspaper column with numerous television appearances, serving as the State Chairman of the Florida Moral Majority, helping to get many presidential candidates nominated statewide, and was the 2004 Vice Presidential nominee and 2008 Presidential nominee of the Constitution Party, gathering more than 200,000 votes and being endorsed by Rep. Ron Paul, according to his website.[195] While I differ with him on a number of issues, I do respect, as an original member of the Religious Right "establishment," his willingness to change his mind in the face of the "writing on the wall" on many controversial issues, such as the forced yoking to the Republican Party and Christian Zionism, and has taken the heat and lost support for his evolving views, the following of which suggest that not just "yours truly" is concerned about the future direction of evangelicals, as Baldwin is another of a conservative Christian heritage like myself.

In February 2019, he wrote[196] that "The influence of America's evangelical churches has been in steep decline ever since the two administrations of professed evangelical Christian President George W. Bush at the beginning of this century. Again and again on my radio talk show and in this column, I tried to warn Christians about the way the Bush presidency was distorting Christ's teaching and how millions of our countrymen were being turned off to Christianity as a result. For the most part, of course, my appeals fell on deaf ears. But I Pollyannaishly thought we had seen the worst of it with Bush. Boy was I wrong! Donald Trump has taken up where Bush left off—in spades." He adds that "A *Christian Post* interview with former Trump White House aide Cliff Sims explores how the adoration heaped upon President Donald Trump by evangelical pastors is pushing millions of Americans into a repudiation of Christianity and causing mass acceptance of atheism and paganism (which are now at all-time highs in this country—and growing)." He quotes Sims from the *Post* article and references to it, who said "he fears Trump-loving evangelical leaders are turning an entire generation away from Christianity thanks to their embrace of an amoral president," and that "many people on Trump's faith advisory board are vicious social climbers who will happily knife one another to maintain their access to the president." Sims said that "I found some of the board to be mainly interested in maintaining their proximity to power, even to the point of trashing 'rival' faith leaders to keep them from threatening their own position close to the President." It notes that "Sims also reveals that he's worried about how the president's top evangelical advisers are affecting Americans' views of Christianity," quoting an author who stated that "The greatest single cause of atheism in the world today is Christians who acknowledge Jesus with their lips and walk out the door and deny Him by their lifestyle." To this, Baldwin adds,

> What Sims says absolutely resonates with me, because I saw some of this in my days with the Moral Majority during the Reagan/Bush I years. I watched evangelical leaders that I had respected and admired compromise virtually every great Christian principle that they professed to believe in order to sit at the king's table. What I witnessed then was but a precursor to what is happening today. That evangelical leaders could enthusiastically embrace and endorse a man (Donald Trump) who is every bit as immoral and corrupt as Bill Clinton stretches the imagination. Jerry Falwell Sr. went to war against Democrat Jimmy Carter—a professed born-again Christian who had taught Sunday School (and still does, by the way, at age 94) in a Southern Baptist church for decades, a man who had never cheated on his wife—because Carter granted an interview to *Playboy* magazine.
>
> Fast forward to 2016: Forty years after that [Falwell Sr.'s] press conference [denouncing Carter's *Playboy* interview], a very different scene unfolded. This one took place in New York and starred Jerry Falwell Jr., inheritor of the family business. Hours earlier, the younger Falwell had introduced the GOP presidential candidate Donald Trump to a massive gathering of Christian leaders, calling him "God's

man," anointed to lead the nation in turbulent times….As they celebrated back at Trump Tower, Falwell sought to document the occasion with a photo. The future president stood in the middle, flanked by Falwell Jr. and his wife, Becki….Falwell tweeted the photo to his 60,000 followers. There was just one hiccup: Lurking over Becki Falwell's left shoulder, framed in gold, was a cover of *Playboy*, graced by a bow-tied Trump and a smiling brunette covered only by his tuxedo jacket. Nothing, it seemed, could so neatly encapsulate the religious right's backsliding as Falwell Jr. giving a thumbs-up in front of the very magazine his father had singled out as symbolic of America's moral decay—while standing shoulder to shoulder with a man who had appeared in a softcore porno flick and who reportedly [committed serial adultery with a bunch of women] including a *Playboy* model and hardcore adult-film actress…Suffice it to say, Jerry Falwell Jr. and his fellow evangelical leaders who fawn over Donald Trump have deliberately decided to bury Biblical morality in favor of sitting comfortably at the king's table.

…Trump needs more illegal immigrants at America's southern border in order to rally his base for his "Finish the Wall" 2020 reelection campaign. You are reading it right. I am saying that Trump is deliberately trying to destabilize already unstable Central and South American countries in order to create tens of thousands of additional immigrants as a way to "prove" to his supporters that he needs to be reelected so he can finish his wall…Trump knows the fix is in. The Mueller probe is dead; the evidence is buried….Our judicial branch of government is being won over by the imperial presidency doctrine. Brett Kavanaugh is making sure of that. And our legislative branch of government has ceded so much unconstitutional authority to the President (any President) that current attempts to rein in the imperial presidency are all but futile. There is precious little standing in Trump's way now. *And the only people who refuse to open their eyes to all of the above are Jerry Falwell Jr. and his fellow evangelical pastors and their congregations. They are too busy fighting for position at the king's table. The rest of the country…can only assume (wrongly) that these warmongering, Zionist-fawning evangelicals are representative of Bible Christianity—and THAT'S why they are headed in the opposite direction by the droves. By their preoccupation with self-interest, personal ambition and infatuation with power, evangelicals are unwittingly pushing America toward atheism and paganism.* (emphasis added)

The libertarian argument, as we have documented, is that the government should not provide any assistance for those in dire and desperate need, because it is "stealing" from the well-to-do, and we should rather rely on the whims of the aristocrats and comfortable, and to when, if and the degree of assistance they decide to provide—*much like how they eradicated suffering and poverty in Gilded age America, or Dickens' London.* The Religious Right community, further catalyzed around Pied Pipers like James Fifield, Jr. and his Big Business financiers, "sacredized" this position as somehow being "biblical," in that professing American Christians will address the needs of poverty, illiteracy, health (mental and physical), safe housing, strong family units, substance abuse and life controlling issues, and can be relied upon to solve these issues without a government safety net, *while fighting their fellow Social Gospel Christian brethren who were trying to do precisely that; these positions of the Big Business libertarians and their Religious Right dupes will be explored in greater depth in Volume 2 of this book series, and the nature of their arguments and tactics.*

Of course, their arguments are all predicated upon the imperative that "God's people" actually "step up to the plate" and charitably provide the resources to accomplish this privately, and the Religious Right has a history of proudly "patting itself on the back" in viewing itself as the acme of the model of the "Christian nation" of virtue, regardless of what the rest of the world thinks. This includes the view of America being the most generous, domestically and throughout the world, even considering that God had blessed them with a largesse based upon His grace in protecting them from invasion and its infrastructure destruction, or modern-day civil war, and with bountiful natural resources. One might think with the massive Trump tax cuts, predominantly for corporations and the upper classes but with a little bit for the middle class, would bolster their argument that it would "free up" funds for people to address societal needs, apart from the "evils" of government intervention. However, recent data shows that utopian model to be a myth, and probably suggests a greater skepticism of the Trump-aligned religious community.

In June 2019 the conservative *Washington Times* reported[197] that the international Charities Aid Foundation performed a 2018 survey of 140,000 individuals from 140 countries, and found that American *charitable giving had declined 2 percent (adjusted for inflation) for the year,* while the School of Philanthropy reported *that 20 million fewer American households gave in 2018 than in 2000,* noting that declines in religious service attendance and giving probably correlate. The Charities Aid Foundation showed that the most charitable nations in terms of "helping a stranger" were the *Muslim Libya and Iraq,* with more than 80% saying they helped people they didn't know, while 60 percent of Americans donated time or money to help a stranger. They write that "Myanmar held the top spot on the five-year ranking of the world

Giving Index, *bolstered by Theravada Buddhism,"* while *the U.S. also receives its own aid from others, such as during Hurricane Katrina, when it received aid of medical kits, blankets and food rations* from Canada and *Afghanistan.* The U.S. often withholds international aid based upon political agendas, noting that "The State Department announced Monday that it would withhold $185 million in international assistance to the Central American 'Northern Triangle'—El Salvador, Honduras, and Guatemala—*until those countries stem emigration"* (emphasis added). When including time, money or assistance to a stranger, the top country for all three deeds was *Muslim Indonesia, where 59% of respondents did such, followed by the largely secular Australia and New Zealand.*

In recent days the Religious Right, under their man Trump, has been "feeling their oats" and think they can poke all their fellow citizens in the eye, and gloat over the temporal power and influence they think he has given them (rather than the reality of his merely pandering to them to get their voting bloc, in an even more exploitative and condescending way than the Republicans before him). They have participated in exploiting the extreme powers that prior interpreted law and the executive branch's own internal policies have awarded the presidency, intended to facilitate rapid response by the Chief Executive in times of emergency, but in reality providing—*assuming a rogue elected president would so choose to exceptionally abuse it*— an ability to pardon any henchmen who keep their mouths shut, an immunity from prosecution and the ignoring of subpoenas that Trump has used in a fashion to make any tin pot dictator green with envy. They have used their influence to provoke the executive branch to restrict those of other lifestyles who wish to practice such in peace but for which the Religious Right sees as their enemy, the predominantly Catholic immigrants, the poor and disadvantaged they would desire not to share their wealth with, and securing his promise to repeal laws like the Johnson Amendment, which would permit the free flow of political action money into our churches and pulpits. However, as a fellow "Bible-believing" Christian, I hate to tell them that "the times, they are a'changing." The rapidly changing society in which they are being surrounded by, *including their own children*, will produce a conundrum for them—necessitating they either change their attitudes (not the timeless principles of Christ, but the hateful and elitist cultural policing and elect ethnic heritage they focus upon), or they will rapidly become ever more irrelevant to the direction of society, blaming everyone but themselves, which would be a true shame. *Having grown up myself in their culture and also still clinging to their supposed Christian core beliefs, in the past I would have been too timid (and intimidated) to stand up to these brow-beating Christian leaders, but no more—they are the ones to be shamed, not those of us who are asking questions.*

As an example of how things are changing, in April 2019 the Gallup polling agency reported[198] that "Gallup finds the percentage of Americans who report belonging to a church, synagogue or mosque at an all-time low, averaging 50% in 2018. U.S. church membership was 70% or higher from 1937 through 1976, falling modestly to an average of 68% in the 1970s through the 1990s. The past 20 years have seen an acceleration in the drop-off, with a 20-percentage-point decline since 1999 and more than half of that change occurring since the start of the current decade." They add that "the decline in church membership is consistent with larger societal trends in declining church attendance and an increasing proportion of Americans with no religious preference," and add that "even those who do identify with a particular religion are less likely to belong to a church or other place of worship than in the past." They also note that "Since the turn of the century [2000], the percentage of U.S. adults with no religious affiliation *has more than doubled, from 8% to 19%*" (emphasis added). They write that "Religiosity is strongly related to age, with older Americans far more likely than younger adults to be members of churches," but "church membership has dropped among all generational groups over the past two decades, with declines of roughly 10 percentage points among traditionalists, baby boomers and Generation X" and with only 42% of millennials being members of churches (and 33% of them have no religious affiliation in 2019), although 62% of the Gen X predecessors were church members at their age. *Now, barely three-quarters of all Americans identify with any religion, lesser still identification with a specific church or mode of worship.* They also note that "Another obstacle churches face is Americans' eroding confidence in the institution of organized religion," and that "Americans have lost more confidence in it than in most other institutions," and that as a result "thousands of U.S. churches are closing each year."

In May 2019 *The Associated Press* and the University of Chicago published another poll[199] entitled, "Attitudes Toward Clergy and Religious Leadership," and found that "55% of adults say religious leaders have a positive impact on society, and 34% describe them as extremely or very trustworthy." This is contrasted with "teachers (84%), medical doctors (83%), scientists (80%), and members of the military (75%)." They add that "Few adults overall consult clergy or other religious leaders when making important decisions in their life." The actual 11-page report itself[200] further reveals, ironically, that the "positive value" numbers of clergy are far closer to *lawyers* (42%) and *business executives* (40%)—*two personas that many view para-church organization leaders and mega-church pastors functioning like in many ways.* In terms of the evangelical mission to be of "good report" towards nonbelievers as a means of being well-regarded and trusted "fishers of men," the report states that "Those with a religion are twice as likely to say clergy have a positive impact" (62% vs. 32%) (p. 2). They show that half of Americans believe that clergy are "selfish" (p. 3), and the more people go to church, the more they see clergy as "intelligent" or "honest"—*a disconcerting sign since church attendance is also rapidly declining.* Also significant is that amongst young adults aged 18–29—*our "future"—only 30 percent welcome the influence of religious leaders in their life*; and amongst the more "established" 30–44 year olds, it *only goes up to 44 percent.* As we have said, for evangelicals, who accept a divine mission to make converts and disciples, *their perception and reputation by outsiders has a direct impact on their sacred calling,* and data such as this (and our personal observations) show that *they have a MAJOR public relations problem, which their strident defense of a president who shows open contempt for all who are not wealthy, powerful or Caucasian is not helping their case at all.*

This change in population, and their view of religion, religious leaders and its culture and values, is also having implications on their and society's political and other cultural views. In August 2019 *The Wall Street Journal* reported[201] that "younger generations rate patriotism, religion and having children as less important to them than did young people two decades ago, a new *Wall Street Journal/NBC News* survey finds." They show that the value of "patriotism" drops from *just under 80% for the Boomer/Silent Generation to just above 40% by Generation Z/Millennials, and Religion/Belief in God dropping from about 66% to just above 30%.*

Younger generations have a general cynicism about the values of older generations, including the religious, military and political establishment, and the narrow classes, ethnically and economically, who are allowed to run the wheels of society and profit from it, and define its views on lifestyles and priorities; to them, Trump typifies the worst examples of what they detest (the "alt right" and white supremacists such as at Charlottesville and prevalent online and on *Breitbart* notwithstanding), as well as the Religious Right leaders and flock aligned with him who help defend and perpetuate the dominance of the "old guard" and white European superiority. They often "overreact," just like their older generation peers, and sometimes "throw out the baby with the bathwater" in their cynicism and zeal, but they have a genuine contempt for the powerful, influential and resourceful Religious Right leadership and community that targets their school friends and online communities. Sadly, the Religious Right community does not seem to possess the age-old Christian, biblical value of self-assessment and introspection, humbly seeking the "beam in their own eye" and "searching their hearts," blaming any public resistance to them not on a rejection of their broadly-recognized insensitivity and ugliness, but rather falsely on offense of "the Cross," Jesus Christ and the Gospel message, which is truly "good news" to all; *repulsed not even by their controversial social positions per se, but rather the ugly, harsh, accusing and hateful way in which they express it.* Scripture says pertaining to the parable of the Pharisee and publican praying in the Temple, that "He [Jesus] spoke this parable to some who trusted in themselves that they were righteous, and despised others" (Luke 18:9), and focused on the religious leaders. Even the Apostle Paul pointed out to one of his founded churches that they were good in acknowledging sin, but not in how they tolerated it in their own ranks while judging outsiders, and how their pious self-perception in the midst of it (rather than pointing out and dealing with corruption amongst their own) would *give ground for self-righteous pride to take root, and cause further loss of respect amongst the "Gentiles" (those outside the Church) they were called to recruit to the Kingdom of Heaven.*

When Paul confronted the Corinthian church of believers, he pointed out the rampant corruption *within their own ranks*, in their instance a case of sexual morality of a type that even outsiders of the church ("the Gentiles") found repugnant (1 Cor. 5:1). In addition to acknowledging the sin and the responsibility of the one who was engaging in the corrupt activity, Paul also pointed out *the pride of the congregation that harbored him and tolerated the behavior*, saying "you are puffed up, and have not rather mourned, that he who has done this deed might be taken from among you" (1 Cor. 5:2, NKJV). In fact, Paul recommended them to "deliver such a one to Satan for the destruction of the flesh, that his spirit may be saved in the day of the Lord Jesus" (v. 5). *In essence, his recommendation was to give the appearance of "letting the offender go" to twist into the wind and to let the sin come to full measure and its consequences, with the ultimate goal being that the painful, embarrassing and uncomfortable decline of the offender and those affiliated with them would be the best chance for the final redemption of the offender as opposed to their demise, just as the safest place for the redemption of Jonah was in the "belly of the whale," as opposed to the safe harbor in the boat.* Paul acknowledged that while he had told the Corinthian previously to "not keep company with sexually immoral people" (v. 9), he clarified that "Yet I certainly did *not* mean with the sexually immoral people *of this world*, or with the covetous, or extortioners, or idolaters, *since then you would need to go out of the world.* But now I have written to you not to keep company with anyone *named a brother*, who is sexually immoral, or *covetous*, or an idolater, or a reviler, or a drunkard, or an extortioner—not even to eat with such a person" (vv. 10–11) (emphasis added).

Many well-meaning Christians today who take God's Word and their faith seriously are trying to shield their children from the "world" by using

Christian schools (where I was taught during high school), or even more so, homeschooling children, keeping them engaged solely with other church youth and shoveling them into Christian Bible schools, in their vain goal of keeping their children out of touch with the world of which they are afraid. Sadly, I have observed in my Christian circles that the later in life that young people are exposed to others who are different or other ideas, the "harder their rebellion" when they finally are, and the less-equipped they are to deal with those who are different in a spiritually-healthy way. It is even sadder that such young people are often the most spiritually-grounded because of the active discipling of their parents at home, and thus the best instruments we have as the Church to fulfill the Great Commission and actually interact with others on the outside to fulfill our "real mission" to be "fishers of men." Paul makes it clear that such "scoundrels" of the world are those we should interact with in our evangelical mission (particularly adult Christians), while specifically avoiding such within our own ranks. *Meanwhile, such well-meaning Christians will often allow Christian leaders, both nationally and locally, to exhibit covetous and idolatrous behaviors to their children and within their homes in the "Christian" materials they view and read, whether "puffed up" with patriotism and promotion of big business free markets and wealth-obsession, or demonstrating a mistrust of the less fortunate and the God-installed governments meant to secure their legal and economic justice, and teaching such poison to corrupt our young with the materialistic idolatry their parents had adopted.*

While American Christians fight purported "culture wars" against such folks in the world, and pride themselves on their cultural separation from them—politically, socially and even geographically, *we see that they often tolerate and even celebrate such behaviors of greed, materialistic standards of wealth and status, and such values reflected in their priorities and their public associations, from their Christian leaders both national and local, and even their fellow parishioners, even if they just "look the other way" when these "heroes" engage in shameful immorality and other lifestyle actions and views, and sometimes even try to cover it up and hope the world doesn't notice.* Paul clarifies that it is not his business, or theirs as a church, to judge what the people *outside* the church do (because God will judge them), but *rather what those inside the church do* (vv.12–13). *With the Christian figures we have pointed out historically or implied in this volume, or more directly the modern Christian leaders we will identify in the next volume and their ilk, their corruption in "carrying the water" of big business and the well-heeled and securely established as reflected in the Great City Babylon, to the detriment of the needy, downtrodden, poor, minorities and others of the "anawim" ("lost and forgotten ones") whom God loves, needs to be publicly denounced by both honest Christian leaders and the average parishioners, and ostracized just as aggressively (if not more) than those caught in more salacious sexual misdeeds. Do we take their "sins" as seriously as God does, as His word shows clearly?*

Is there even something deeper Paul is trying to say in this passage? He first emphasizes that the church members themselves, and not the sexual offender, are "puffed up" (v. 2), and reiterates concerning the accommodation of the sexual offender in saying that "Your glorying is not good. Do you not know that a little leaven leavens the whole lump?" (v. 6). He adds that "Therefore purge out the old leaven, that you may be a new lump, since you truly are unleavened. For indeed Christ, our Passover, was sacrificed for us. Therefore let us keep the feast, not with old leaven, nor with the leaven of malice and wickedness, but with the unleavened bread of sincerity and truth" (vv. 7–8). Some will say that the "leaven" is the sin of the offender that is tolerated, and this could be spread like leaven. However, Paul clearly suggested that the church members themselves are "puffed up," and that of them, "your glorying not good," immediately followed by Paul's mention of the "leaven" analogy. So—could it be, the "leaven" refers to *their pride over the matter itself, and not the offender?* Some might easily think that such pride would be over their tolerance of the offender, which does not remedy the problem. *However, a "pride" can also arise from seeing oneself as superior to the offender, in a legalistic fashion. In fact, one could say that a legalist "needs" a "sinner" in their midst, by which to make their distinction of "superior status." As an example, the "Pharisee" in the Temple in Christ's parable needed the "publican" in his midst by which to draw a contrast; the Pharisees needed to keep a "woman caught in adultery" in their hip pocket to exploit for their own purposes to show Christ their devotion to the Law; the Puritan needed the witch or the Quaker kept around to show their own "high standards." The legalist in our own midst needs the "sinner" kept around to provide them fodder to express their piety; otherwise, people would begin to ask the legalist what they have to offer to truly advance the Kingdom of God. Even within the church, demagogues need their rivals to maintain their reason for existence, particularly when they depend upon mail-order contributions to keep their operations running, just like a "Cold Warrior" needs a local leftist, or the anti-sharia "warrior" a local Muslim.*

However, such status of being "puffed up" and "glorying" can apply to yet another aspect. Christians have evidently, since the days of the early Church in places like Corinth, and certainly today in America, liked to be "puffed up" and "glory" in their religious and moral superiority over "the world"—*the very world each church member came from as a base sinner themselves.* Rather than humbly ministering to the world as servants, they maintain an air of transcendence over their unwashed neighbors, often talking about the "wicked pagans" or "socialistic secular humanists" in their Christian media, pulpits, or local circles, and reveling in their latest sinful pursuits. They attempt to hold this over their communities as some means of justifying their own existence as "culture warriors" and moral arbiters of personal behavior, and by some baffling reason must think this will lead to greater soul-winning opportunities and a swelling of their ranks, since the Great Commission is a primary endeavor to which they have been called. To maintain this posture of superiority, they feel they must not acknowledge (if made public), or if necessary, cover up (if not yet known) any such foul, hypocritical misdeeds by those within their own ranks—particularly the "more presentable members" in Christian leadership. (I am not talking about private moral failings for which discreet remediation can gently deal with family considerations and privacy, but rather the blatant and/or public display of greed, arrogance or abuse that is not due to fleshly weakness, but is rather fundamental in mindset and spirit.) Their "glorying" in their collective superiority cannot seem to tolerate cracks in their posture by means of public admission of occasional failure, and even more damningly, their refusal to renounce it publicly and testify that it is unbecoming of a witness of Christ to the world. Their denial of such problems leads to the world itself finally identifying the corruption such as may have happened in Corinth, with the Church seen as covering up the offense, and any opportunity for innocent members of the Church to salvage their reputation to the community long passed. *They really think that pretending problems don't exist can somehow make them go away, even though history has told us that is not the case.*

Once the world has exposed it and it is undeniable, the church may lament the sinful behavior and situation, and privately wring their hands and grieve, and wonder how it will affect the church's reputation and members' morale, *but often they most importantly worry about the impact to the offering each week.* Denominations wielding authority over these Christian leaders will try to maintain clean hands, but usually it is found out that they knew for a long time but let circumstances fester because the offender was such a "cash cow" for the organization. When they are exposed by the world and things come apart, they will quickly change the conversation and eventually try to get the same charismatic figure back in the limelight as soon as the heat is off, so they can get back and spread the wealth.

Pertaining to our discussion in this book about the corruption of the Christian community by the wealth-community of Babylon and their values, most of us of any age under our belt have seen the opulent lifestyles of private jets, mansions and extravagant "good life" of top Christian leaders (somehow justified by a tortuous reading of scripture), led by Jim and Tammy Bakker and a myriad of televangelists and Christian cable networks, but even extending down to the local megachurch. Everyone who's "been around" will know that it's a matter of time before these people get exposed for tax evasion, money laundering or a host of other excesses that are greed-related, much of which other Christian denominational and media leaders long suspected or knew. When it falls upon the "world" to finally set the moral example and expose such malfeasance, rather than being quickly dealt with by the church itself as per Paul's prescription (at least by publicly denouncing it if other authority to act is not available), it not only fails to prevent the unavoidable and inevitable ends, *but it also makes the remaining church look to the world as complicit in the misdeeds or seen as being unconcerned when financial recklessness or vanity are expressed within their own ranks, and has a devastating effect on their witness to their outer world they are tasked with reaching.* To be fair, this problem not only extends to the church but also to other societal institutions, like the government, military and even the police, who when one of their own is exposed as rotten, will also "close ranks," forming a "thin blue line' of defense to protect the offender, and then wonder why the police has a bad reputation in many communities. *A true evangelical Christian and community must not only police unethical and insensitive financial behavior and covetous teachings within their own ranks, but also publicly denounce it when it is made public, because their duty to be "fishers of men" as representing Christ and His reputation demands it, and the world has a right to expect it, if we expect them to respect the gospel the Church preaches.*

The other big change in the middle and younger generations is a rejection of the taboos, not of sexual morality and lifestyles, *but those emanating from the sacrosanct, non-debatable political edicts and assumptions commonly associated with the conservative base of America and what they have traditionally conflated with patriotic, wholesome "American" values, such as the glorification of capitalism and unregulated markets, privatizing and the sanctity of the corporate and business world, and contempt for government regulation, economic justice and environmental protection.* For example, many older working-class Americans thought the "Great Capitalist" Trump would help them economically and lower their taxes, and that it's "taboo" to consider they may have been sold a bill of goods, given his campaign promises. However, in April 2019 *The Hill* reported[202] that "About two-thirds of Americans, 68 percent, say they paid the same or more in taxes for 2018 than the previous year, while less than a quarter said they paid less, according to a new Hill-HarrisX survey."

One of the biggest taboos, the bane of conservative discourse and the public menace that replaced the Cold War's communism, that being the dreaded "socialism," the source of all evils and the destroyer of worlds (according to big business paid media outlets), no longer cast a spell of fear on a larger segment of the younger generations, whether they understand the full ramifications of that form of civil order or not, but actually reflects the divide that existed generations ago, yet more polarized. In May of 2019 the Gallup polling organization also reported[203] that "While 51% of U.S. adults say socialism would be a bad thing for the country, *43% believe it would be a good thing.* Those results contrast with a 1942 Roper/*Fortune* survey that found 40% describing socialism as a bad thing, 25% a good thing and 34% not having an opinion" (emphasis added). They add that "Previous Gallup research shows that Americans' definition of socialism has changed over the years, with nearly one in four now associating the concept with social equality and 17% associating it with the more classical definition of having some degree of government control over the means of production," and that Democrats have viewed socialism positively since 2010, with 57% so inclined in 2018. In 2019, 29% of respondents said they believed that the majority of nations in the next fifty years would turn to socialism, whereas 14% of respondents in 1949 thought the world's nations would become socialist in the next fifty years. However, most still prefer the free market to have control over most areas of life versus the government, *except in online privacy and environmental protections.* They also add that "the April survey found that 47% of Americans say they would vote for a socialist candidate for president," while 58% would vote for an atheist, and 58% a Muslim president.

These changes in the attitudes of social and political policy are not just occurring in the United States, but are pervasive globally as well. In March 2019 *Reuters* reported[204] that "A strong majority of people in wealthy countries want to tax the rich more and there is broad support for building up the welfare state in most countries, a survey conducted for the OECD showed on Tuesday. In all of the 21 countries surveyed, more than half of those people polled said they were in favour when asked: 'Should the government tax the rich more than they currently do in order to support the poor?', with an average of 68 percent, the Organisation for Economic Cooperation and Development said." They added that "Higher taxation of the rich has emerged as a political lightning rod in many wealthy countries, with U.S Democrats proposing hikes and 'yellow vest' protesters in France demanding the wealthy bear a bigger tax burden." They write that

> The Paris-based forum's survey of 22,000 people about perceived social and economic risks also found deep discontent with governments' social welfare policies, which many people said were insufficient, the OECD said. On average, only 20 percent said they

could easily receive public benefits if needed while 56 percent thought it would be difficult to get benefits, the survey found. People were on average particularly concerned about access to good quality, affordable long-term care for the elderly, housing and health services. Not only did people say they were not getting their fair share given what they paid into the system, people in all countries except Canada, Denmark, Norway and the Netherlands did not think that their governments were heeding their views. "These feelings spread across most social groups, and are not limited just to those deemed 'left behind'," the OECD said in an analysis of the survey's results. *The feeling of injustice was even higher among the highly educated and high-income households*, it added. In light of the high level of discontent, a majority of people wanted their government to do more in all countries except France and Denmark, whose welfare systems are among the most generous in the world. Most people said the top priority should be better pensions, with 54 percent saying that would make them feel more economically secure. Healthcare followed in second place at 48 percent while nearly 37 percent were in favour of a guaranteed basic income benefit, which has attracted international interest from policymakers but has yet to be tried at the national level.

We see that the majority of the world's peoples—even the majority (but not electoral plurality) of Americans who voted in the last presidential and mid-term congressional elections—want a future modern society that pursues more egalitarian circumstances for peoples of all social standing, and basic protections and social benefits assured for their health, livelihood, infirmity and old age—*even the wealthy who can otherwise afford it, and those of traditional republican and Christian enlightened nations and societies*. However, simultaneously we see the rise in recent years of an old authoritarian streak, based upon nationalism and patriotism, worship of one's own culture and ethnicity, competition in the markets (as part of a fascist (meaning, "corporatist") revival) and on the battlefield, and value of a "strong hand" and fierceness, and lack of tolerance for stragglers and those too weak to contribute enough to satisfy the herd, or anyone whose views or values may differ. As I have written elsewhere, such an authoritarian "sphere of influence" exists in Putin's Russia, augmented by their "traditionalist" church the Russian Orthodox, who are spreading and funding their xenophobic and intolerant views of minorities or those not in lockstep, in the old Soviet satellite countries like Hungary, Poland and Ukraine, and in major Western "enlightened" nations through the National Front Party in France and the anti-immigrant and separatist Farange and Johnson movements in the UK, and the governing parties of Austria. All these

"Aryan"-sympathetic strong arm movements have found greatest strength and encouragement in the rise of Trump's America, and its Charlottesville marches, protestors beaten up at Trump rallies with the praise of Trump and the crowd, and threats of violence against immigrants at the borders and cages for children separated from their mothers. *Most of these movements find much of their strength from the power of their domestic conservative church communities.*

Frederick Kempe, the best-selling and prize-winning author and journalist, and president of the Atlantic Council, a think tank created to promote continued American and European cooperation in politics and economics, wrote in July 2019 on the *CNBC* website about these storm clouds that he sees brewing over the Western world.[205] He writes:

> Dangers are accelerating to the democratic ideals that the American Revolution inspired. If no unanticipated shock disrupts current trajectories—say a democratic uprising in China, a Russian regime change or, still significant, a Venezuelan dictator's decline—*autocratic powers will surpass democracies in their economic size and influence within the coming decade. And history has shown prosperity often precedes political dominance.* What's been broadly reported by now is that *global democratic freedoms are in their 13th year of decline*, a result both of surging autocracies like Russia and China, fraying freedoms in liberal democracies and Western complacency about both. "The overall losses are still shallow compared with the gains of the late 20th century, but the pattern is consistent and ominous," Freedom House reported in its 2019 assessment. Less recognized, but *perhaps ultimately more decisive, is that within five years at current trends autocratic countries will account for more than half of global income for the first time in more than a century.* That's based on an analysis of International Monetary Fund figures by political scientists Roberto Stefan Foa and Yascha Mounk. That would mark a stunning reversal in fortunes. Back in the 1950s and 1960s, when the Eisenhower and Kennedy administrations responded successfully to the pioneering Soviet launch of the Sputnik satellite, the *U.S. and its democratic allies in Europe and Japan were producing some two-thirds of the global economy.* As recently as 1990, countries rated "not free" by Freedom House accounted for *only 12 percent of global income. Now they produce a full third, matching the level authoritarian-run economies achieved during the rise of European fascism in the 1930s. That raises some unsettling questions.* (emphasis added)

How much of democracies' success came from the attraction of Western values like free speech and individual rights? *How much instead was a result of new democracies wanting to hitch their wagons to American and Western European prosperity and extract themselves from the bankruptcy of the*

Soviet and other, similarly constructed, state-controlled systems? It was certainly a product of both—but democracies will struggle more in a contest with autocracies if they produce less comparative prosperity over time. "If the West is to navigate this new world successfully, *it will need to understand how the scales tipped so rapidly from democratic dominance to authoritarian resurgence,*" write Foa and Mounck. They conclude the more important factor than weakening democracies has been the rise of "authoritarian capitalism." Previously, they write, autocratic regimes whose income increased substantially either stopped growing, like the Soviet Union, or became democratic, like South Korea, Spain, Portugal and Greece and other formerly military regimes…."But a growing number of countries have learned to combine autocratic rule with market-friendly institutions," write Foa and Mounck, "and they have continued growing economically well beyond the point at which democratic transitions used to occur." If there were any doubt that today's autocrats consider themselves locked in competition with liberal democracies—and believe they are winning—that was dispelled by last week's ground-breaking interview by Lionel Barber and Henry Foy of the *Financial Times* with Russia's Vladimir Putin…. Putin said "the liberal idea" had "outlived its purpose." Said Putin, "(Liberals) cannot simply dictate anything to anyone just like they have been attempting to do over the recent decades." (emphasis added)

Meanwhile, as of the end of 2019 (the time that I am completing this manuscript), the global "wealth gap" between the "haves" and "have nots" continues to grow, sparking widespread unrest. In October 2019 the *New York Post* reported[206] that in other places like South Korea, where special privileges for the rich in entering college also exist, "there are riots in the streets and demands for the president—who ran and won on abolishing income inequality…to resign." They add that "Chile is literally on fire, amid violent protests sparked after their billionaire president announced a subway fare hike. This is a country where the average income is $807 a month, a wage that has stagnated as the cost of everything else, from food to gas to electricity to mass transit, keeps going up," and quote residents who say their leaders are out of touch, as eleven people had died there in riots the last weekend. They add that "In Haiti, at least 18 people have died since riots and protests broke out six weeks ago. The precipitating event was a gas shortage," and quote residents there as saying, "We are in misery and we are starving….We cannot stand it anymore." They write that "More than 50 percent of Haitians live on about $2 a month. Tens of thousands of protesters are storming the rich, burning tires in wealthy enclaves. And it's not just the poor who are rioting—it's academics, businesspeople, artists, intellectuals. These protesters, too, want their president out. Beirut is burning, too, as are other areas of Lebanon, as protesters demand an overthrow of the government," with one there saying, "Sunni, Shia, Christian or Druze, it doesn't matter—our pain is one and the same." Meanwhile, they note in the U.S. "Forty percent of Americans don't have $400 saved in case of emergency. Last year, 68 percent couldn't afford a recreational activity—from a vacation to concerts to a professional sporting event to even dinner or a movie—for lack of funds. This year, *the Census Bureau reported that the gap between the rich and poor has hit its highest level in the 50-plus years since they began marking it... The average American can't afford to buy a house in 70 percent of the country."

Also in October 2019, the London *Guardian* newspaper reported[207] that "From Hong Kong to Chile, young people are rising up to fight injustice and inequality. Their elders should be grateful." They write of "large-scale street protests around the world, from Chile and Hong Kong to Lebanon and Barcelona," all led by young people, such as one that "swept away Sudan's ancient regime this year." They note that about 41% of the global population is aged 24 or under; in Africa, 41% are under 15, and in Asia and Latin America (where 65% of the world's population lives), it's 25%, the opposite of the developed countries, like in Europe, where 16% are under 15, but 18% are over 65. They write that "many current protests are rooted in shared grievances about economic inequality and jobs," including in Tunisia during the Arab Spring. They write that each month in India, one million more people turn 18 and can vote, while "In the Middle East and North Africa, an estimated 27 million youngsters will enter the workforce in the next five years. Any government, elected or not, that fails to provide jobs, decent wages and housing faces big trouble." The availability of Facebook and the Internet is amongst factors leading global young people to share a desire for human rights and a living wage, and to expect it, and "They appear less bound by social conventions and religion." Such a fight in Hong Kong is being led by the youth against the authoritarian Chinese. Those fighting such authoritarianism in places like Egypt, India, Russia and Palestine now all see themselves as having common cause, and are connected by the Internet. They add that "Another negative is the perceived, growing readiness of democratically elected governments, notably in the US and Europe, to lie, manipulate and disinform," but that "What helps protect us is the noisy, life-affirming dissent of the young." *My question is—is the Christian community of America equipped to handle these difficult and explosive developments in the days ahead, and lead the way alongside these youth, both spiritually and societally as their "brother's keeper," or will they just "get in the way" or add to the problem?*

My fellow American conservative evangelical Christians have focused on the mirage of economic prosperity and stock market increases they believe Donald Trump has brought, just like Hitler was popular early with German Christians because he "made the trains run on time" and revived their economy and nationalistic pride, while they casually ignore (or even defend) Trump's human rights abuses against immigrant women and children, and minorities of various stripes, and show of contempt for the less fortunate nations and peoples of the world. It will likely fall on the younger generations, most of whom are currently focused on their own self-centered entertainment and scrapping out a living (but with notable exceptions) and disillusioned with the establishment religious organizations and leaders, to be inspired to "man up" and "take up the mantle" to represent Christ and the Kingdom of Heaven in having compassion for their fellow man and showing them the reality of the Lord of deliverance, who cares about their needs, both earthly and temporal as well as spiritual and eternal, if the Western Church is to continue with its advancement of the Kingdom in a decaying world.

In contrast, the "Baby Boomers" today, as with the "Greatest Generation" or "Silent Generation" before them, need to ponder not only their own generation's spiritual reputation of representing the values of God towards the poor and the wealthy and their institutions, but also what kind of example they are setting for their children and grandchildren. Furthermore, they need to consider not only how their example and teaching will impact their own children's' reputations later in representing Christ, but also if their bad example will jeopardize the sensitive, justice-minded hearts of today's young people, who may second-guess whether they want to remain a part of a church for which they've lost respect. *Much data today seems to suggest that this is a real peril for the church of tomorrow.* For the younger reader here, it falls on you, while building on what legitimately comprises the firm foundations provided by your elders, to also accept the duty to correct the course where needed, elevating the poor, minority and disadvantaged as called for by God in both the Old and New Testaments, and not to commit the selfish and covetous sins of your Establishment elders.

Numbers 20 in the Bible tells the story of the wandering Hebrews who thirsted and accused Moses of taking them to the wilderness just to die of thirst. In essence they were a society of needy people, complaining and asking for a "handout." Moses was a governmental and spiritual leader of God's people who initially did the right thing, and took the problem of the material needs of his community first to the Lord, along with another religious and civil leader. They were showing that any real solution to the needs of the people would have to come from God's assistance. God in turn told Moses and Aaron to bring the people to a rock, and to speak to it for water to be supplied, as evidence to the people that God was their supplier (v. 8). However, rather than focusing on the needs of the destitute people and being a facilitator of God's blessing, Moses lost his cool with their complaining and their wanting of handouts, telling them, "Hear now, you rebels! Must *we* bring water for you out of this rock?" (v. 10) (emphasis added). Moses thus expressed his contempt for *his* having to solve the people's problem of destitution, and his "work" (in essence) for them to feed off of, *rather than acknowledging that God was the provider of all, rich and poor, and would provide when asked, with Moses as the privileged facilitator.* Rather than asking the rock for extra provisions for his community as God directed, Moses struck the rock twice—apparently trying to force the water out by his own "work" and merits, which he resented. The water then indeed came, because the people needed it and God would insure their provision, but He was not happy at what Moses had done to mistakenly portray God's resentment at meeting their needs as the destitute (even with them being complainers), and further suggesting that it came by Moses' own work.

In a similar manner, God expected the secure in the land of Canaan to practice the "Sabbath Years" and jubilees to be the privileged instruments by which God showed His love to the destitute, and to do it without resentment, and let it be from the wild vegetation grown and provided by God Himself, and not by their own hand. It also was an act of faith in and acknowledgment of a God that provided an excess to some, so to be in an enviable position of being given an ample harvest to share with those suffering from life's misfortunes, such as widowhood, orphan-status, physical ailment, old age, or *even mental or addictive bondage, and be an illustration that God provides His exclusive provisions to both the needy amongst the materially well-to-do, and the materially destitute, so both can glory in and praise God, and drop the walls of class and resentment.* If Cain had acknowledged his role as "his brother's keeper," *God's mission to restore the relationship between both brothers by remedying the spiritual misunderstanding present would have been accomplished.* God felt these consistent and regularly-scheduled acts of transferring God's blessings from the "haves" to the "have nots" were so essential to the spiritual welfare of His "holy nation" and its viability as a nation-state, that He *codified it in their very economic laws, with the enforcement of civil government* (not being a Temple or tabernacle-based ritual religious act and under the dominion of the priesthood), in an ordered and regularly scheduled process and not on the occasional whims of the well-to-do feeling the urge to be "charitable." Its ultimate enforcement, when they ignored and neglected it, was the warned destruction of the nation and dispersal of its people *before it completely self-destroyed the nation itself due to the concentration of wealth and inevitable revolution and complete slavery of the common folk*, which God backed up with action in executing the Exile, as the prophets had previously warned about.

It was a serious offense that Moses had conducted at the rock, and possibly even worse than these wretched complainers, since He represented God and fellowshipped with Him. Even though Moses talked with God "as a man talks to a friend," God said Moses' actions did not "hallow Me in the eyes of the children of Israel" to show He would provide for them, and "because *you* did not believe me" to produce the needs of the people when spoken to, *Moses forfeited the honor of leading the people into the Promised Land of abundance* (v. 11) (emphasis added). This place was then called "Meribah," meaning "contention" (v. 13). This did not just represent the contention of the people with God, but more importantly, *of "God's own representatives" with God*, and not using their position to be a conduit, with the assumption that God would freely provide *through them to the people*, but rather feeling they had to metaphorically and resentfully "strike" God to force Him to provide provision by their own work on the rock, and view Him as the "harsh master" of the paranoid man with one talent. *God was intended to be the source of meeting the needs of the needy in the community, but the civil leaders (Moses, not Aaron) were the chosen ones to cheerfully facilitate the process for God to do it by blessing all of society, and yet still let them see that their blessings came from God and not their leaders. Moses had a unique role of wielding the coercive power as their civil leader to provide provision to the needy, through which God was more than willing to do (as He pragmatically just wanted to see the people's needs met, as He did though civil authorities Joseph, Nebuchadnezzar, Cyrus and others), but he also represented God to the people, and thus had a chance to oversee their provision as a spiritual intercessor—both roles of which the otherwise humble and faithful Moses "flunked" on both counts.*

Thus, God would prefer to use His spiritual representatives—now the Church—to meet the material needs of the weak and needy in their societies, as Jesus charged His disciples to "feed them," particularly with the law supposed to be "written on their hearts." However, until they decide to fulfill that role, God is more than willing to use civil authority channels to meet immediate needs that cannot wait until His people "get their act together"—and it is doubtful they ever will, in "Christian nations" like America. The Christians here, who do not want to part with their excess big-screen TVs and upscale cars and time-shares and who resent sharing their blessings adequately with the "lazy parasites" like the poor, blind, aged and infirm (not even caring to know how much it would take, or the true extent of the need itself), are the real ones who have a "hang up" with God using any responsive channel, including the elected, representative civil government, in filling the void in the "compassion and mercy gap" to meet the immediate needs of the "anawim" to whom God's heart is devoted. They are just like resentful Jonah, the prodigal son's brother, and the field workers who saw the "late arrivers" getting comparable pay in Christ's parable. *In effect, they serve as a "stumbling block" to ministering to those in real distress, and for them to see their deliverance and love as coming from God, not just because they don't see the charity coming from the Christians' hands vs. government, but more so because they see themselves slandered by Christians publicly, as they resist any measures to help them societally, rather playing the "religion game" with them as hostages. More importantly, pertaining to the "evangelical mission," the "example" Christians set as models of God's perception of the weak and vulnerable it does not motivate them to consider Christ's offer of eternal forgiveness, restoration with God and deliverance. They are just like the spiritual ancestors the Pharisees, whom Jesus described in this way: "Woe unto you also, ye lawyers! for ye lade men with burdens grievous to be borne, and ye yourselves touch not the burdens with one of your fingers" (Luke 11:46).*

God never let the people forget about the sin of either the people or Moses that occurred there. When God took Moses onto Mount Arabim to see the Promised Land before he died, He reminded Moses again that He could not go because of Moses' own rebellion against God at Meribah (Numb. 27:14, Deut. 32:51). The Psalmist also reiterated the story, and the fact that the people sinned, which led to Moses sinning, when he states, "They angered Him also at the waters of strife, so that it went ill with Moses on account of them; because they rebelled against His Spirit, so that he spoke rashly with his lips" (Psalm 106:32–33).

So—could the needy and destitute of America be blessed by a Christian community that agreed to ask God to provide an extra financial and economic abundance that they could then cheerfully share with the needy, all in turn giving God the glory rather than their own generosity, and trusting God to provide the excess beyond the modest and non-materialistic lifestyle He intended for them, so they could bless others? If America's wealthy church of opulent buildings and property (and bank accounts) and their well-to-do parishioners with disposable income collectively agreed to provide their communities free health care, emergency shelter and food, and means to work and lay up for old age, and agreed to trust God to provide them sufficient income and a willingness to adjust to a lifestyle that would allow them to do so, would we have any problem then filling our churches? Would our churches, their testimony and the gospel they preach be so ill thought of in reputation as today? Considering our recent generations of Christians, it appears unlikely that the biblical template will ever be tried, but it is up to the new generation to decide if they want to put God to the test. They begin with a "clean sheet of paper" (albeit inheriting a tarnished church reputation in society they will need to repair), and could explore this concept (if they desired) in "laboratory incubators" of this principle in small communities, centered around the organizing principle of the neighborhood church, while also obviously deploying the immeasurable assets and organizing infrastructure of the democratically-elected civil government (through the fair and free deliberations with their fellow citizens) to meet the physical needs of their neighbors in concert if needed, and to not be so prideful as to envy or resist the assistance it can provide (such pride's only accomplishment being to punish the destitute), in the hope God's people eventually make its immediate emergency resources obsolete.

In fact, other biblical admonitions that cite this story and event do it as a context for the new generation of God-followers to not make the mistakes of earlier generations, *and this certainly applies to young followers of Christ in America today, as the crucial "crisis generation" deciding the destiny of Christian influence in the West.* In Psalm 95 the new generation at that time was given a warning, pronounced again verbatim to Christians in Hebrews 3, as they were told to their generation,

> Do not harden your hearts, as in the rebellion, as in the day of trial in the wilderness, when your fathers tested Me; They tried Me, though they saw My work. For forty years I was grieved with that generation, and said, "It is a people who go astray in their hearts, and they do not know My ways." So I swore in My wrath, "They shall not enter My rest." (Psalm 95:8–11)

If they decide to decline this challenge to enact true, humble spiritual leadership, and rather fall into the "old ways" of their Christian descendants of materialistic consumerism and the "sacralization" of it and the heartless Babylon system that indulges but inevitably destroys its practitioners, and holds God's dear *anawim* in contempt and hampers their needs being met, following the "broad way" the mass media (Christian and conservative) drones in their ears by big-dollar, business/financial paid mouthpieces today, then don't worry that Christ's mission and that of His real church will be confounded ultimately. Christ *will* "complete the good work," and His work eventually *will* be done "on earth as it is in heaven," but the consequences will be personal and specific to the perpetrators of all generations, and His accurate ledger may or may not result in judgment on earth for each, but it will at His *Bema* judgment of works, or the Great White Throne. As Christ expressed to "God's people" in Jerusalem, right after they rejected Him and His ways for a patriotic but despicable countryman to represent them in Barabbas (who promised to "make Israel great again"), and as He drug His beaten body through the streets as a rejected messiah, *a mere generation away from their own destruction via the city and Temple, and His rejection of them.*

But Jesus turning unto them said, "Daughters of Jerusalem, weep not for me, but weep for yourselves, and for your children." (Luke 23:28)

NOTES

Introduction

1. "AG James Secures Court Order Against Donald J. Trump, Trump Children, And Trump Foundation," New York State Attorney General Office (press release), Nov. 7, 2019, https://ag.ny.gov/press-release/2019/ag-james-secures-court-order-against-donald-j-trump-trump-children-and-trump.

2. Michael S. Heiser, "Deuteronomy 32:8," *Bibliotheca Sacra* 158 (Jan–Mar 2001): 52–74,https://faculty.gordon.edu/hu/bi/ted_hildebrandt/OTeSources/05-Deuteronomy/Text/Articles/Heiser-Deut32-BS.htm.

3. Jamie Hopkins, "Trump Signs memorandum Shelving Fiduciary Standard For Financial Advisors," *Forbes*, Feb. 3, 2017, https://www.forbes.com/sites/jamiehopkins/2017/02/03/trump-signs-executive-order-shelving-fiduciary-standard-for-financial-advisors/#2e5f01e65863.

4. "U.S. Population," Worldometers (website), accessed June 29, 2019, https://www.worldometers.info/world-population/us-population/.

5. "Exit Polling," *CNN Politics* (website), Nov. 23, 2016, https://edition.cnn.com/election/2016/results/exit-polls/national/president.

6. "America's Changing Religious Landscape," Pew Research Center (website), May 12, 2015, https://www.pewforum.org/2015/05/12/americas-changing-religious-landscape/.

7. Mark Joyella, "Sean Hannity Unrivaled As Fox News Posts 66th Consecutive Quarter at No. 1," *Forbes*, July 3, 2018, https://www.forbes.com/sites/markjoyella/2018/07/03/sean-hannity-unrivaled-as-fox-news-posts-66th-consecutive-quarter-at-number-one/#3c67f62536d2.

8. "Top Talk Audiences—April 2019," *Talkers* (website), http://www.talkers.com/top-talk-audiences/.

9. Top Talk Audiences—August 2018," *Talkers*, https://web.archive.org/web/20181022023243/http://www.talkers.com/top-talk-audiences/.

10. Georg Szalai, "SiriusXM Grows Subs, Earnings in Second Quarter, Raises Full-Year Targets," *The Hollywood Reporter*, July 26, 2016, https://www.hollywoodreporter.com/news/siriusxm-grows-subs-earnings-second-914582.

11. "Religious Practices and Experiences," Chap. 2 in *U.S. Public Becoming Less Religious*, Pew Research Center, Nov. 3, 2015, https://www.pewforum.org/2015/11/03/chapter-2-religious-practices-and-experiences/.

12. "7 Startling Facts: An Up Close Look at Church Attendance in America," *Outreach* (website), April 10, 2018, https://churchleaders.com/pastors/pastor-articles/139575-7-startling-facts-an-up-close-look-at-church-attendance-in-america.html.

13. "The Top 10 Most Popular Sites of 2019," *Lifewire*, June 24, 2019, https://www.lifewire.com/most-popular-sites-3483140.

14. "Top 15 Most Popular News Websites—June 2019," eBizMBA (website), http://www.ebizmba.com/articles/news-websites.

15. "Ku Klux Klan," *New World Encyclopedia*, accessed April 4, 2018, https://web.archive.org/web/20180404133624/http://www.newworldencyclopedia.or g/entry/Ku_Klux_Klan.

The Leaven of the Pharisees Ideology Explained

16. Daniel Alexander Hays, "'A Babe in the Woods?': Billy Graham, Anticommunism, and Vietnam," (master's thesis, Eastern Illinois University, Jan. 1, 2017), 123, https://thekeep.eiu.edu/cgi/viewcontent.cgi?article=3522&context=theses.

17. *Protocol Additional to the Geneva Conventions of 12 August 1949*, 8 June 1977, Article 56 ("Protection of works and installations containing dangerous forces"), accessed June 30, 2019, https://ihl-databases.icrc.org/applic/ihl/ihl.nsf/ 7c4d08d9b287a42141256739003e636b/f6c8b9fee14a77fdc125641e0052b079.

18. *The Nuremberg Trials: Trial Proceedings & Indictments*, The Jewish Virtual Library, accessed June 30, 2019, https://www.jewishvirtuallibrary.org/nuremberg-trial-proceedings-and-indictments.

19. Morgan Watkins, "Bevin: Blood of patriots may have to be shed," *The Courier Journal*, Sept. 13, 2015, https://www.courier-journal.com/story/news/politics/ky-governor/2016/09/13/bevin-blood-patriots-may-have-shed/90275284/.

20. *The Jewish Encyclopedia*, 1906, s.v. "Annas", http://www.jewishencyclopedia.com/ articles/1554-annas.

21. *The Catholic Encyclopedia*, s.v. "Annas", http://catholicencyclopedia. newadvent.com/cathen/01536a.htm.

22. *The International Standard Bible Encyclopedia, 1915 Edition* , James Orr, ed., s.v. "Annas", 137, https://books.google.com/books?id=Ows9AAAAYAAJ.

23. *The New International Encyclopedia*, Vol. 1, Second Edition (New York: Dodd, Mead and Company, 1923), 669, https://books.google.com/books?id=X-ujrIiwq5IC.

24. James Hastings, "Annas." In *Hastings Dictionary of the Bible*, Vol. 1, 100, https://babel.hathitrust.org/cgi/pt?id=uva.x000819095&view=1up&seq=120&size=12 5.

25. Pesachim 57a, *Koren Noe Talmud* ,William Davidson digital edition (Jerusalem: Koren Publishers, 2017), https://www.sefaria.org/Pesachim.57a?lang=bi.

26. *The Jewish Encyclopedia*, s.v. "Sadducees" (New York: *Funk & Wagnalls*, 1906), http://jewishencyclopedia.com/articles/12989-sadducees.

27. Josephus, *Josephus, the Essential Writings*, trans. and ed. Paul L. Maier (Grand Rapids: Kregel Publications, 1988), 276.

28. Philippe Bohstrom, "Archaeologists Uncover Life of Luxury in 2,000-year-old Priestly Quarters of Jerusalem," *Ha'aertz*, July 12, 2016, https://www.haaretz.com/ archaeology/priestly-quarter-of-ancient-jerusalem-found-on-mt-zion-1.5409239.

29. Michael Specter, "Tomb May Hold the Bones Of Priest Who Judged Jesus," *The New York Times*, Aug. 14, 1992, https://www.nytimes.com/1992/08/14/world/tomb-may-hold-the-bones-of-priest-who-judged-jesus.html

30. Aram Roston, "Exclusive: Trump fixer Cohen says he helped Falwell handle racy photos," *Reuters*, May 7, 2019, https://www.reuters.com/article/us-usa-politics-falwell-exclusive/exclusive-trump-fixer-cohen-says-he-helped-falwell-handle-racy-photos-idUSKCN1SD2JG.

31. Sarah Rodriguez, "Falwell Speaks," *The Liberty Champion*, March 8, 2016, https://www.liberty.edu/champion/2016/03/falwell-speaks/.

32. Bob Bryan, "The US national debt just pushed past $22 trillion," *Business Insider*, Feb. 20, 2019, https://www.businessinsider.com/trump-national-debt-deficit-compared-to-obama-bush-clinton-2019-2.

33. Ben Collins, "Student: Jerry Falwell Jr. Axed Anti-Trump Story from Liberty University's School Newspaper," *The Daily Beast*, Oct. 18, 2016, https://www.thedailybeast.com/student-jerry-falwell-jr-axed-anti-trump-story-from-liberty-universitys-school-newspaper?ref=scroll.

34. France Robles and Jim Rutenberg, "The Evangelical, the 'Pool Boy', the Comedian and Michael Cohen," *The New York Times*, June 18, 2019, https://www.nytimes.com/2019/06/18/us/trump-falwell-endorsement-michael-cohen.html.

35. Joe Heim, "Jerry Falwell Jr. can't imagine Trump 'doing anything that's not good for the country' ", *The Washington Post*, Jan. 1, 2019, https://www.greenvilleonline.com/story/news/2019/01/01/jerry-falwell-jr-cant-imagine-president-donald-trump-doing-anything-thats-not-good-country/2457767002/.

36. Christine Szabo, "Pastor expresses sympathy for church members 'hurt' by surprise Trump visit," *ABC News*, June 4, 2019, https://abcnews.go.com/Politics/pastor-expresses-sympathy-church-members-hurt-surprise-trump/story?id=63452430.

37. Heather Clark, "Jerry Falwell Jr. Deletes Crude Tweet Regarding David Platt's Explanation of Prayer Over Trump at Church," *Christian News*, June 6, 2019, https://christiannews.net/2019/06/06/jerry-falwell-jr-deletes-crude-tweet-regarding-david-platts-explanation-of-prayer-over-trump-at-church/.

38. Jerry Falwell Jr., Twitter, June 4, 2019, https://twitter.com/JerryFalwellJr/status/1136056209679822849.

39. Jerry Falwell Jr., Twitter, June 4, 2019, https://twitter.com/JerryFalwellJr/status/1136046428588040194.

40. David Fouse, "As a Liberty graduate, I am troubled by Jerry Falwell Jr.'s treatment of Russell Moore," *The Washington Post*, June 28, 2019, https://www.washingtonpost.com/religion/2019/06/28/liberty-graduate-i-am-troubled-by-jerry-falwell-jrs-treatment-russell-moore/?utm_term=.2f5caaae68ac.

41. Aram Roston and Joshua Schneyer, "Exclusive: Falwell steered Liberty University land deal benefiting his personal trainer," *Reuters*, Aug. 27, 2019, https://www.reuters.com/article/us-usa-falwell-trainer-exclusive/exclusive-falwell-steered-liberty-university-land-deal-benefiting-his-personal-trainer-idUSKCN1VH283.

42. Graham Gremore, "There's so much to unpack in this video of Jerry Falwell Jr. and his 'personal trainer'," Queerty (website), Sept. 3, 2019, https://www.queerty.com/theres-much-unpack-video-jerry-falwell-jr-personal-trainer-20190903.

43. Graham Gremore, "This flirty Instagram post between Jerry Falwell Jr. and his 'personal trainer' is probably nothing," Queerty (website), Sept. 4, 2019, https://www.queerty.com/flirty-instagram-post-jerry-falwell-jr-personal-trainer-probably-nothing-20190904.

44. Jerry Falwell, Jr., Instagram post, July 6, 2019, https://www.instagram.com/p/BzlJgSYFSW6/.

45. Ben Crosswhite, Instagram post, April 22, 2019, https://www.instagram.com/p/Bwkk9R7AgYB/.

46. Mark D. Griffiths, "The Psychology of Animal Torture," *Psychology Today*, Nov. 23, 2016, https://www.psychologytoday.com/us/blog/in-excess/201611/the-psychology-animal-torture.

47. Brandon Ambrosino, "'Someone's Gotta Tell the Freakin' Truth': Jerry Falwell's Aides Break Their Silence," *Politico*, Sept. 9, 2019, https://www.politico.com/magazine/story/2019/09/09/jerry-falwell-liberty-university-loans-227914.

48. Seth Browernik, "UPDATE: Rebuke to Jerry Falwell Jr.'s Comment to Politico's '"Someone's Gotta Tell the Freakin' Truth": Jerry Falwell's Aides Break Their Silence' Article," World Red Eye (website), Sept. 10 and Sept. 20, 2019, https://worldredeye.com/2019/09/rebuke-jerry-falwell-jr-s-comment-politicos-someones-gotta-tell-freakin-truth-jerry-falwells-aides-break-silence-article/.

49. Liberty University, Twitter, Sept. 10, 2019, https://twitter.com/LibertyU/status/1171557414698725376.

50. Bobby Ross, Jr., "Sorry, but Politico's long expose on Jerry Falwell Jr. lacks adequate named sources to be taken seriously," GetReligion.org (website), Sept. 9, 2019, https://www.getreligion.org/getreligion/2019/9/9/sorry-but-politicos-long-expos-on-jerry-falwell-jr-lacks-adequate-named-sources-to-be-taken-seriously.

51. "Omitted Statements of Liberty University Regarding Business Transactions Recently Questioned in Media," Liberty University (website), September 2019, https://www.liberty.edu/media/1617/2019/september/LU-RESPONSE.pdf.

52. Aram Roston and Joshua Schneyer, "Exclusive: Falwell blasted Liberty student as 'retarded', police chief as 'half wit' in emails," *Reuters*, Sept. 12, 2019, https://www.reuters.com/article/us-usa-falwell-emails-exclusive/exclusive-falwell-blasted-liberty-student-as-retarded-police-chief-as-half-wit-in-emails-idUSKCN1VX1QJ

53. Sarah Rankin and Alan Suderman, "Liberty's Falwell says he's target of 'attempted coup'," *Associated Press*, Sept. 10, 2019, https://www.apnews.com/01404d7b984b4010b08834459e4813f1.

54. Jenny Rose Spaudo, "Jerry Falwell Responds to Politico's 'Hit Piece' in Exclusive Interview: 'We Have Nothing to Hide'," *Charisma* (website), Sept. 12, 2019, https://www.charismanews.com/us/77985-jerry-falwell-responds-to-politico-s-hit-piece-in-exclusive-interview-we-have-nothing-to-hide.

55. Ben Finley, "Liberty students protest in wake of reports about Falwell," *The Associated Press*, Sept. 13, 2019, https://apnews.com/2af299bb899d4d6e8a65dd20d18a99a8.

56. Alex MacGillis, "Billion-Dollar Blessings," *ProPublica*, April 17, 2018, https://www.propublica.org/article/liberty-university-online-jerry-falwell-jr.

57. "Falwell is No. 2 in salary ranking," *Richmond Times-Dispatch*, Dec. 6, 2016, https://www.newsadvance.com/archives/falwell-is-no-in-salary-ranking/article_5d7ee779-e8fe-58fc-add8-ff72767efbc3.html.

58. Brad Tuttle, "Billy Graham Was One of America's Richest Pastors. Here's What We Know About His Money," *Money*, Feb. 21, 2018, http://money.com/money/5168865/billy-graham-net-worth-quotes-money-greed/.

59. Ela Teodosio, "Billy Graham Net Worth: Beloved Evangelist was Reportedly a Millionaire," *The Christian Post*, Feb. 22, 2018, https://www.christianpost.com/trends/billy-graham-net-worth-the-life-he-left-behind.html.

60. Tim Funk and Ames Alexander, "Franklin Graham takes pay he once gave up," *The Charlotte Observer*, Aug. 12, 2015, https://www.charlotteobserver.com/living/religion/article30505932.html.

61. David Roach, "SBC to unveil Billy Graham tribute sculpture at '06 meeting," *Baptist Press*, June 23, 2005, http://www.bpnews.net/21067/sbc%ADto%ADunveil%ADbilly%ADgraham%ADtribute%ADsculpture%ADat%AD06%ADmeeting2/2.

62. Michael Gryboski, "9-Foot Billy Graham Statue Move Delayed as Lifeway Blames Unforeseen Problem," *The Christian Post*, June 8, 2016, https://www.christianpost.com/news/billy-graham-statue-move-delayed-as-lifeway-blames-unforeseen-problem-164969/.

63. Rachel L. Miller, "Nashville," *Road and Travel Magazine* (website), https://www.roadandtravel.com/travel%20directory/Tennessee/Nashvillestory.htm.

64. J. Gordon Melton and Martin Baumann, eds., *Religions of the World: A Comprehensive Encyclopedia of Beliefs and Practices (Second Edition), Volume One* (Santa Barbara: ABC-CLIO, 2010), 234, https://books.google.com/books?id=v2yiyLLOj88C.

65. Adam Elihu Berkowitz, "Arab Emirates Bring Pagan War Goddess to UN," *Breaking Israel News*, Nov. 28, 2017, https://www.breakingisraelnews.com/98498/pagan-war-goddess-statue-unveiled-un-idol-worship-makes-global-comeback/.

66. "Parthenon and Statue of Athena," RoadsideAmerica.com (website), https://www.roadsideamerica.com/story/14603.

67. Richard Grigonis, "Nashville Parthenon (Nashville, Tennessee)," That's Interesting (website), Feb. 12, 2013, http://www.interestingamerica.com/2013-01-19_Nashville-Parthenon_by_Grigonis.html.

68. Stewart, John L., *The Burden of Time: The Fugitives and Agrarians* (Princeton: Princeton University Press, 1965), https://books.google.com/books?id=Gx7WCgAAQBAJ.

The Gospel of Jesus Vs. The "Gospel" of Hannity, etc.

69. Christopher Ingraham, "The richest 1 percent now owns more of the country's wealth than at any time in the past 50 years," *The Washington Post*, Dec. 6, 2017, https://www.washingtonpost.com/news/wonk/wp/2017/12/06/the-richest-1-percent-now-owns-more-of-the-countrys-wealth-than-at-any-time-in-the-past-50-years/.

70. Elena Holodny, "The top 0.1% of American households hold the same amount of wealth as the bottom 90%," *The Business Insider*, Oct. 23, 2017,

https://www.businessinsider.com/americas-top-01-households-hold-same-amount-of-wealth-as-bottom-90-2017-10.

71. Aimee Picchi, "World's richest 1% control more than half of all wealth," *CBS News*, Nov. 14, 2017, https://www.cbsnews.com/news/richest-1-percent-control-more-than-half-of-all-wealth/.

72. Rupert Neate, "World's richest 0.1% have boosted their wealth by as much as poorest half," *The Guardian*, Dec. 14, 2017, https://www.theguardian.com/inequality/2017/dec/14/world-richest-increased-wealth-same-amount-as-poorest-half.

73. Chuck Collins, "The Growing Hidden Wealth Problem," *The Huffington Post*, June 12, 2017, https://www.huffingtonpost.com/entry/the-growing-hidden-wealth-problem_us_593eb29fe4b094fa859f1a63.

74. "Global Inequality," Inequality.org, https://inequality.org/facts/global-inequality/.

75. "Part IV—Trends in Global Wealth Inequality," World Inequality Lab, http://wir2018.wid.world/part-4.html.

76. "Poor America: 40% of Americans Can't Afford Middle-Class Lifestyle," *Prison Planet*, May 21, 2018, https://www.prisonplanet.com/poor-america-40-of-americans-cant-afford-middle-class-lifestyle.html.

77. Taylor Telford, "Income inequality in America the highest it's been since Census started tracking it, data show," *The Washington Post*, Sept. 26, 2019, https://www.stamfordadvocate.com/business/article/Income-inequality-in-America-the-highest-it-s-14469954.php.

78. Alexandre Tanzi and Michael Sasso, "Richest 1% of Americans Close to Surpassing Wealth of Middle Class," *Bloomberg*, Nov. 9, 2019, https://www.bloomberg.com/news/articles/2019-11-09/one-percenters-close-to-surpassing-wealth-of-u-s-middle-class.

79. "Mission Statement," Liberty University (website), accessed July 3, 2019, https://www.liberty.edu/index.cfm?PID=6899.

80. "Ten Liberty University Distinctives" (April 23, 2015 archived copy, accessed July 3, 2019), Liberty University (website), https://web.archive.org/web/20150423145907/http://www.liberty.edu:80/index.cfm?PID=6909.

81. "Pat Robertson: Jews too busy 'polishing diamonds'," *Jewish Telegraphic Agency*, April 1, 2014, https://www.jta.org/2014/04/01/united-states/robertson-jews-too-busy-polishing-diamonds.

82. Aram Roston, "The Televangelist and the Warlord," *The Nation*, Aug. 11, 2010, https://www.thenation.com/article/televangelist-and-warlord/.

83. Christine Lagorio, "Pat Robertson Apologizes To Israel," *CBS News*, Jan. 12, 2006, https://www.cbsnews.com/news/pat-robertson-apologizes-to-israel/.

84. Kevin Drum, "How Much Do We Spend on the Nonworking Poor?," *Mother Jones*, Feb. 13, 2012, https://www.motherjones.com/kevin-drum/2012/02/how-much-do-we-spend-nonworking-poor/.

85. *Average Household Monthly Welfare Payment*, U.S. Dept. of Health and Human Services, accessed July 5, 2019, https://upload.wikimedia.org/wikipedia/commons/6/66/Welfare_Benefits_Payments_Graph.gif.

86. "Military spending in the United States," National Priorities Project, accessed July 5, 2019, https://www.nationalpriorities.org/campaigns/military-spending-united-states/.

87. "Federal Spending: where Does the Money Go," National Priorities Project, accessed July 5, 2019, https://www.nationalpriorities.org/budget-basics/federal-budget-101/spending/.

88. Brad Plumer, "Who Receives Benefits from the Federal Government in Six Charts," *The Washington Post*, Sept. 18, 2012, https://www.washingtonpost.com/news/wonk/wp/2012/09/18/who-receives-benefits-from-the-federal-government-in-six-charts/?utm_term=.a5f1b9efce5b.

89. Melissa Kearney, "Welfare and the Federal Budget," University of Maryland, July 25, 2017, https://econofact.org/welfare-and-the-federal-budget.

90. "Do You Qualify for Social Security Disability?," Disability Benefits Help, accessed July 5, 2019, https://www.disability-benefits-help.org/content/do-you-qualify.

91. "Eligibility for Food Stamps, or the Supplemental Nutrition Assistance Program (SNAP)," eligibility.com, accessed July 5, 2019, https://eligibility.com/food-stamps.

92. "Iowans off welfare, but still in poverty," *The Des Moines Register*, May 23, 2016, https://www.desmoinesregister.com/story/opinion/editorials/2016/05/24/editorial-iowans-off-welfare-but-still-poverty/84793168/.

93. John Beisner, "How much does welfare cost the average taxpayer?," *The Des Moines Register*, May 26, 2016, https://www.desmoinesregister.com/story/opinion/readers/2016/05/26/how-much-does-welfare-cost-average-taxpayer/84917512/.

94. Tim Worstall, "The Average US Welfare Payment Puts You In The Top 20% of All Income Earners," *Forbes*, May 4, 2015, https://www.forbes.com/sites/timworstall/2015/05/04/the-average-us-welfare-payment-puts-you-in-the-top-20-of-all-income-earners/#6a67a796316f.

95. "How Military Spending has Changed Since 9/11," National Priorities, accessed July 5, 2019, https://www.nationalpriorities.org/campaigns/how-military-spending-has-changed/.

96. Philip Bump, "Trump's 15,000 border troops would top the number stationed in 160 countries," *The Washington Post*, Nov. 1, 2018, https://pressfrom.info/us/news/offbeat/-206411-trump-s-15-000-border-troops-would-top-the-number-stationed-in-160-countries.html.

97. "U.S. Defense Spending Compared to Other Countries," Peter G. Peterson Foundation, May 3, 2019, https://www.pgpf.org/chart-archive/0053_defense-comparison.

98. Stephen Collinson, "Trump slams 'crazy, lunatic' constitutional amendment in midterm endgame," *CNN*, Nov. 2, 2018, https://www.cnn.com/2018/11/02/politics/donald-trump-immigration-midterms-missouri/index.html.

99. Martha C. White, "Slash Immigration, and GOP Is the Victim, Research Finds," *NBC News*, Aug. 15, 2017, https://www.nbcnews.com/business/economy/slash-immigration-gdp-victim-research-finds-n792821.

100. "US Merit Based Immigration," VISAGuide.world, accessed July 6, 2019, https://visaguide.world/us-visa/merit-based-immigration/.

101. "'This Time' *This is the Army* (Finale) 1943," *YouTube*, June 15, 2018, https://www.youtube.com/watch?v=LL1fVdyIlCw.

James Fifield Jr. and the Little Known History, etc.

102. Jonathan P. Herzog, *The Spiritual-Industrial Complex* (Oxford: Oxford University Press, 2011).

103. Martin J. Medhurst, "Eisenhower and the Crusade for Freedom: The Rhetorical Origins of a Cold War Campaign" *Presidential Studies Quarterly* 27, no. 4, (Fall, 1997), 646–661, https://www.jstor.org/stable/27551792?seq=1#metadata_info_tab_contents.

104. Stacey Cone, "Presuming A Right to Deceive: Radio Free Europe, Radio Liberty, the CIA, and the News Media." *Journalism History*, (Winter 1998/1999), http://media.leeds.ac.uk/papers/pmt/exhibits/1226/cone.pdf.

105. "Henry Ford II," Ford Automotive (website), accessed Feb. 9, 2019, https://web.archive.org/web/20121019192653/http://media.ford.com/article_display.cfm?article_id=3380%22.

106. "Past Leaders—Charles E. Wilson," GE (website), accessed Feb. 9, 2019, https://www.ge.com/about-us/leadership/profiles/charles-e-wilson.

107. Anthony Leviero, "President Proclaims a National Emergency; Auto Prices Rolled Back; Rail Strike Ends; Allies Give Up Hamhung; WU Rejects Truce," *The New York Times*, Dec. 16, 1950, https://web.viu.ca/davies/H102/Truman.national.emergency.Communism.1950.htm.

108. Paul G. Pierpaoli, *Truman and Korea: the Political Culture of the Early Cold War* (Columbia: University of Missouri Press, 1999), 50.

109. Michael J. Hogan, *A Cross of Iron—Harry S. Truman and the Origins of the National Security State 1945–1954* (Cambridge: Cambridge University Press, 1998), http://library.aceondo.net/ebooks/HISTORY/A_Cross_of_Iron__Harry_S__Truman_and_the_Origins_of_the_National_Security_State__1945_ndash_1954.pdf.

110. Alden Whitman, "Charles E. Wilson of G.E. Dies; Mobilized Industry in 2 Wars," *The New York Times*, Jan. 4, 1972, https://www.nytimes.com/1972/01/04/archives/charles-e-wilson-of-ge-dies-mobilized-industry-in-2-wars-charles-e.html..

111. Kevin M. Kruse, "How Corporate America Invented Christian America," *Politico*, April 16, 2015, https://www.politico.com/magazine/story/2015/04/corporate-america-invented-religious-right-conservative-roosevelt-princeton-117030.

112. Kevin M. Kruse, *One Nation Under God: How Corporate America Invented Christian America* (New York: Basic Books, 2016) 6.

113. Michael J. McVicar, *Christian Reconstruction—R J. Rushdoony and American Religious Conservatism* (Chapel Hill (NC): The University of North Carolina Press, 2015).

114. "Los Angeles Minister Urged to Apologize for Broadcasting Anti-Semitic Falsehood," *The Jewish Telegraphic Agency*, July 27, 1951, https://www.jta.org/1951/07/27/archive/los-angeles-minister-urged-to-apologize-for-broadcasting-anti-semitic-falsehood.

115. "*Faith and Freedom* 1951-1960," Mises Institute (website), accessed March 4, 2019, https://mises.org/library/faith-and-freedom-1951-1960.

116. *Faith and Freedom*, April 1954, https://mises-media.s3.amazonaws.com/FAF54-4_3.pdf.

117. Glenn Fowler, "H. E. Kershner, 98, A Longtime Worker In Children's Causes," *The New York Times*, Jan. 3, 1990, https://www.nytimes.com/1990/01/03/obituaries/h-e-kershner-98-a-longtime-worker-in-children-s-causes.html.

118. "First Congregational Church of LA Marks 150-Year History in the City" (press release), *PRN Newswire*, June 2, 2017, https://www.prnewswire.com/news-releases/first-congregational-church-of-la-marks-150-year-history-in-the-city-300467777.html.

119. "Welcome to First Church," First Congregational Church of Los Angeles (website), accessed Sept. 14, 2019, http://www.fccla.org/#christianity.

120. Lee Haddigan, "The Importance of Christian Thought for the American Libertarian Movement: Christian Libertarianism 1950–71," *Libertarian Papers 2 no. 14* (2010): 1–31, https://mises-media.s3.amazonaws.com/-2-14_2.pdf.

121. Allan J. Lichtman, *White Protestant Nation—The Rise of the American Conservative Movement* (New York: Grove Press, 2008), https://books.google.com/books?id=3q92ePfQDloC.

122. Darren Elliot Grem, *The Blessings of Business: Corporate America and Conservative Evangelicalism* (doctoral dissertation, University of Georgia, 2010), https://getd.libs.uga.edu/pdfs/grem_darren_e_201005_phd.pdf.

123. Michael Carlson, "Billy James Hargis," *The Guardian*, Dec. 9, 2004, https://www.theguardian.com/news/2004/dec/10/guardianobituaries.religion.

124. Lee Roy Chapman, "The Strange Love of Dr. Billy James Hargis," *This Land*, Nov. 2, 2012, http://thislandpress.com/2012/11/02/the-strange-love-of-dr-billy-james-hargis/.

125. George A. Lopez, Ronald Lora and William Henry Longton eds., *The Conservative Press in Twentieth Century America* (Westport (CT): Greenwood Press, 1999), https://books.google.com/books?id=Ioakmq8yxA4C.

126. "Christian Economics," Central Intelligence Agency "Reading Room" (website), https://www.cia.gov/library/readingroom/search/site/%22christian%20economics%22.

127. "Who Will Rescue the Colonies?," *Christian Economics*, Sept. 6, 1960, https://www.cia.gov/library/readingroom/docs/CIA-RDP88-01314R000100190044-7.pdf.

128. "The Emmaus Walk Presents 'The Future of the Welfare State'," The Emmaus Walk (website), accessed Sept. 17, 2019, http://theemmauswalk.tripod.com/futureofwelfarestate.html.

129. Deborah Huntington and Ruth Kaplan, "Whose Gold Is Behind the Altar? Corporate Ties to Evangelicals," *Contemporary Marxism*, no. 4, (Winter 1981/1982): 62–92, https://www.jstor.org/stable/23008556.

130. Bello Stumbo, "Brewing Controversy: Coors Clan Doing It Their Way," *The Los Angeles Times*, Sept. 18, 1988, https://www.latimes.com/archives/la-xpm-1988-09-18-mn-3400-story.html.

131. Harold Jackson, "Joseph Coors," *The Guardian*, March 18, 2003, https://www.theguardian.com/news/2003/mar/19/guardianobituaries.usa.

132. Janet Cawly and Nathaniel Sheppard, Jr., "Contributors Tell of '1–2 Punch' For Contra Aid," *The Chicago Tribune*, May 22, 1987, https://www.chicagotribune.com/news/ct-xpm-1987-05-22-8702070939-story.html.

133. "Finances of the Right Wing," Sec. 4 SPECIAL REPORT #16, Group Research, Inc., Sept. 1, 1964, 5, https://ia800801.us.archive.org/8/items/FinancesOfRightWingSeptember1964/Finances%20of%20Right%20Wing-September%201964.pdf.

134. "CPI Inflation Calculator" (website), accessed Sept. 18, 2019, http://www.in2013dollars.com/us/inflation/1962?amount=1.

135. "Dr. Adrian Rogers Quote," Liberty Tree (website), accessed Sept. 18, 2019, http://libertytree.ca/quotes/Adrian.Rogers.Quote.4152.

136. Albin Krebs, "Gerald L. K. Smith Dead; Anti-Communist Crusader," *The New York Times*, April 16, 1976, https://www.nytimes.com/1976/04/16/archives/gerald-lk-smith-dead-anticommunist-crusader.html.

137. "Holocaust Denial Timeline," *Holocaust Encyclopedia* (website), accessed Sept. 18, 2019,https://web.archive.org/web/20150412131846/http://www.ushmm.org/wlc/en/article.php?ModuleId=10008003.

138. Glen Jeansonne, "Gerald L. K. Smith—From Wisconsin Roots to National Notoriety," *Wisconsin Magazine of History*, Winter 2002–2003, 18–29, https://web.archive.org/web/20040612071644/http://www.wisconsinhistory.org/wmh/pdf/wmh_winter02_jeansonne.pdf.

139. Roy Reed, "Hippies and Gerald L. K. Smith Make Ozark Resort Town a Model of Coexistence," *The New York Times*, July 27, 1972, https://www.nytimes.com/1972/07/27/archives/hippies-and-gerald-l-k-smith-make-ozark-resort-town-a-model-of.html.

140. Robert J. Miller, "Pastor Retires for 4th Time," *Hartford Courant*, July 4, 2002, https://www.courant.com/news/connecticut/hc-xpm-2002-07-04-0207040293-story.html.

141. Ralph Lord Roy, *Apostles of Discord* (Boston: The Beacon Press, 1953), 13.

142. Nathan Fenno, "Clippers owner Donald Sterling is no stranger to race-related lawsuits," *The Los Angeles Times*, April 26, 2014, https://www.latimes.com/sports/sportsnow/la-sp-sn-donald-sterling-past-controversy-20140426-story.html.

143. "John de Nugent", Southern Poverty Law Center (website), https://www.splcenter.org/fighting-hate/extremist-files/individual/john-de-nugent.

144. John de Nugent, "William Dudley Pelly—proof that Americans will not rally enough even to the most heroic, charismatic and energetic political leader," John de Nugent (website), Jan. 31, 2015, https://www.johndenugent.com/william-dudley-pelly-proof-americans-will-not-rally-enough-even-heroic-charismatic-energetic-political-leader/.

145. Alina Tugend, "Donations to Religious Institutions Fall as Values Change," *The New York Times*, Nov. 3, 2016, https://www.nytimes.com/2016/11/06/giving/donations-to-religious-institutions-fall-as-values-change.html.

146. Joseph Farah, "Jesus Faced a Sword, Not a Cage," *World Net Daily*, Dec. 11, 2018, https://www.wnd.com/2018/12/jesus-faced-a-sword-not-a-cage/.

Babylon's Gnostic Sorcerers That Have Influenced Our Shepherds

147. David Christie-Murray, *A History of Heresy* (Oxford: Oxford University Press, 1976), 21.

148. Jay Kinney, ed., *The Inner West—An Introduction to the Hidden Wisdom of the West* (New York: Tarcher/Penguin, 2004), 42.

149. "James C. Ingebretsen papers, 1941–1977," Archives West (website), accessed Feb. 19, 2019, http://archiveswest.orbiscascade.org/ark:/80444/xv95777.

150. "About James C. Ingebretsen," *Apprentice of the Dawn* (website), accessed Feb. 19, 2019, http://apprenticetothedawn.com/aboutjci.html.

151. "About the Book," *Apprentice of the Dawn* (website), accessed Feb. 19, 2019, http://apprenticetothedawn.com/aboutthebook.html.

152. "Foreword," *Apprentice of the Dawn* (website), accessed Feb. 19, 2019, http://apprenticetothedawn.com/foreword.html.

153. "Links," *Apprentice of the Dawn* (website), accessed Feb. 19, 2019, http://apprenticetothedawn.com/links.html.

154. "About ISI," Intercollegiate Studies Institute (website), accessed Feb. 22, 2019, https://home.isi.org/about/about-isi.

155. John Cody "Spiritual Mobilization," *First Principles*, Intercollegiate Studies Institute (website), Dec. 13, 2012, https://web.archive.org/web/20171212224211/http://www.firstprinciplesjournal.com/print.aspx?article=116&loc=b&type=cbbp.

156. Thaddeus Ashby, "Exploration Into Gerald Heard," *Faith and Freedom*, VII, no. 10, (June 1956), https://mises-media.s3.amazonaws.com/FAF56-6_3.pdf?file=1&type=document.

157. James C. Ingebretsen, "Dancing in the Sky," Gerald Heard (website), 2003, accessed Feb. 23, 2019, https://www.geraldheard.com/writings-and-recollections/2017/8/2/dancing-in-the-sky.

158. Jay Michael Barrie, "II. Early Years," Gerald Heard (website), accessed Feb. 23, 2019, https://www.geraldheard.com/blog/2017/7/14/early-years.

159. Jay Michael Barrie, "III. A Psychological-Historical Tapestry," Gerald Heard (website), accessed Feb. 23, 2019, https://www.geraldheard.com/blog/2017/7/14/a-psychological-historical-tapestry.

160. Jay Michael Barrie, "IV. In America: Vedanta Society," Gerald Head (website), accessed Feb. 23, 2019, https://www.geraldheard.com/blog/2017/7/22/in-america.

161. Jay Michael Barrie, "VI. Later Years," Gerald Heard (website), accessed Feb. 23, 2019, https://www.geraldheard.com/blog/2017/7/22/later-years.

162. Don Lattin, *Distilled Spirits: Getting High, then Sober, with a Famous Writer, a Forgotten Philosopher, and a Hopeless Drunk* (Berkeley: University of California Press, 2012), https://books.google.it/books?id=xBIgjIfhN-gC.

163. "LSD and Bill Wilson, the co-founder of Alcoholics Anonymous," *YouTube*, July 31, 2012, https://www.youtube.com/watch?v=XeO2BOdmkEg.

164. Megan Garber, "Why Do Witches Ride Brooms?," *The Atlantic*, Oct. 31, 2013, https://www.theatlantic.com/technology/archive/2013/10/why-do-witches-ride-brooms-nsfw/281037/.

165. Susan Cheever, "How I came to write a biography of Bill Wilson," Susan Cheever (website), accessed Sept. 8, 2019, http://www.susancheever.com/my_name_is_bill__bill_wilson__his_life_and_the_creation_of_alcoholics_anonymous_87508.htm.

166. Susan Cheever, *My Name Is Bill: Bill Wilson—His Life and the Creation of Alcoholics Anonymous* (New York: Washington Square Press, 2004), https://books.google.com/books?id=laEa_0TiUnYC .

167. Susan Cheever, "The Spook Room," Beliefnet (website), accessed Sept. 8, 2009, https://www.beliefnet.com/entertainment/books/2004/03/the-spook-room.aspx.

168. Robert Fitzgerald, *The Soul of Sponsorship: The Friendship of Father Ed Dowling and Bill Wilson in Letters*, (Center City (MN): Hazelton, 1995), https://books.google.com/books/about/The_Soul_of_Sponsorship.html?id=RDDS2TzIN98C.

169. "*The Black Fox* by H.F. Heard," Mysterious Press (website), accessed Feb. 23, 2019, https://web.archive.org/web/20161017145839/http://mysteriouspress.com/products/suspense/the-black-fox-by-hf-heard.asp.

170. Rhea A. White, "Gerald Heard's Legacy to Psychical Research," *1982 Academy of Religion and Psychical Research* (Proceedings), 56–69, https://www.geraldheard.com/writings-and-recollections/2017/8/5/gerald-heards-legacy-to-psychical-research.

171. Edmund A. Opitz, "Leonard A. Read: A Portrait," *The Freeman*, 48, no. 9 (Sept. 1998),https://web.archive.org/web/20091222225834/http://www.thefreemanonline.org/featured/leonard-e-read-a-portrait/#.

172. Tibor R. Machan, "Educating for Freedom," *Reason*, April 1975, https://reason.com/archives/1975/04/01/educating-for-freedom/.

173. Ayn Rand, "August 1, 1946 Letter to Leonard Read," FEE (website), accessed Feb. 25, 2019, https://fee.org/media/4884/randthinkers.pdf.

174. "William C. Mullendore papers, 1930–1968," Archives West (University of Oregon), http://archiveswest.orbiscascade.org/ark:/80444/xv02410/.

175. David Boaz, "NYT Clueless on Libertarianism," Cato Institute (website), March 31, 2007, https://www.cato.org/blog/nyt-clueless-libertarianism.

176. Brian Doherty, Brian, *Radicals for Capitalism: A Freewheeling History of the Modern American Libertarian Movement*, Google Books, https://books.google.com/books?id=BOrT8tMMS5AC.

177. Brian Doherty, *Radicals for Capitalism* (New York: Public Affairs, 2007), 271.

178. "Eckard V. Toy, Jr,: March 19, 1931 – October 7, 2013," *Oregon Historical Quarterly*, 115, no. 1 (Spring 2014), 122–128, https://www.jstor.org/stable/10.5403/oregonhistq.115.1.0122?seq=1#page_scan_tab_contents.

179. Eckard V. Toy, Jr., "The conservative connection: the chairman of the board took lsd before timothy leary," *American Studies*, 21, no. 2 (1980), 65–77, https://journals.ku.edu/amerstud/article/view/2645/2604.

180. "Leonard E. Read Journal—July 1954," https://history.fee.org/media/4469/ler_journal_1954_07.pdf.

The Biblical View of Capitalism's Nature

181. "capitalism," *Merriam Webster Dictionary* (website), accessed May 27, 2019, https://www.merriam-webster.com/dictionary/capitalism.

182. "Capitalism," *The Encyclopedia Britannica* (website), accessed May 27, 2019, https://www.britannica.com/topic/capitalism.

183. "Corporation," *Encyclopedia Britannica* (website), accessed May 27, 2019, https://www.britannica.com/topic/corporation.

184. J. Michael Bennett, "Fuel and Food Shortages," in *How to Overcome the Most Frightening Issues You Will Face This Century* (Crane (MO): Defender Press, 2009), 247.

185. "Distributism," *Merriam-Webster Dictionary* (website), accessed May 31, 2019, https://www.merriam-webster.com/dictionary/distributism.

186. G. K. Chesterton, *Utopia of Usurers and other essays* (New York: Boni and Liveright, 1917), https://archive.org/details/cu31924013463207.

187. Jane Mayer, "The Making of the Fox News White House," *The New Yorker*, March 4, 2019, https://www.newyorker.com/magazine/2019/03/11/the-making-of-the-fox-news-white-house.

188. Craig Timberg, Taylor Telford, and Josh Dawsey, "Trump urges customers to drop AT&T to punish CNN over its coverage of him." *The Washington Post*, June 3, 2019, https://www.washingtonpost.com/business/2019/06/03/trump-urges-customers-drop-att-punish-cnn-over-its-coverage-him/?utm_term=.948f9161ccdf.

The Future Destiny of American Evangelicals

189. Kyle Mantyla, "Mark Taylor: Freemasons And Illuminati Are Using A Special Frequency to Change DNA And Make People Hate Trump", *Right Wing Watch*, Aug. 31, 2017, https://www.rightwingwatch.org/post/mark-taylor-freemasons-and-illuminati-are-using-a-special-frequency-to-change-dna-and-make-people-hate-trump/.

190. Kyle Mantyla, "Mark Taylor: John McCain Was Executed By A Military Tribunal," *Right Wing Watch*, Sept. 17, 2018, https://www.rightwingwatch.org/post/mark-taylor-john-mccain-was-executed-by-a-military-tribunal/.

191. Jerry Pierce, "The Lie of 'Progressive Christianity'," *Decision* (website), June 1, 2019, https://decisionmagazine.com/lie-progressive-christianity/.

192. Julio Rosas, "Mayor Buttigieg: It's Hard to Look at Trump's Actions and Think He Believes in God," *Mediaite*, April 3, 2019, https://www.mediaite.com/trump/mayor-buttigieg-its-hard-to-look-at-trumps-actions-and-think-he-believes-in-god/.

193. "Franklin Graham calls for prayer to 'change hearts' of Democrats," *World Net Daily*, Oct. 1, 2019, https://www.wnd.com/2019/10/franklin-graham-calls-prayer-change-hearts-democrats/.

194. Elana Schor, "Rev. Graham's tour evokes evangelical support for Trump," *Associated Press*, Oct. 4, 2019,https://apnews.com/5cfef4941efd4d23b06f7b4db8ca546a.

Conclusions

195. "Chuck's Bio," Chuck Baldwin Live (website), accessed Oct. 10, 2019, https://chuckbaldwinlive.com/About.aspx.

196. Chuck Baldwin, "Evangelicals Unwittingly Pushing America Toward Atheism and Paganism," Chuck Baldwin Live (website), Feb. 28, 2019, https://chuckbaldwinlive.com/Articles/tabid/109/ID/3848/Evangelicals-Unwittingly-Pushing-America-Toward-Atheism-And-Paganism.aspx.

197. Christopher Vondracek, "Americans robust charitable donors despite recent slip," *The Washington Times*, June 20, 2019, https://www.washingtontimes.com/news/2019/jun/20/charities-aid-foundation-survey-donations-decline-/.

198. Jeffrey M. Jones, "U.S. Church Membership Down Sharply in Past Two Decades," *Gallup* polling (website), April 18, 2019, https://news.gallup.com/poll/248837/church-membership-down-sharply-past-two-decades.aspx.

199. "Attitudes Toward Clergy and Religious Leadership," AP-NORC (website), May 2019, http://www.apnorc.org/projects/Pages/Attitudes-toward-Clergy-and-Religious-Leadership.aspx.

200. *Attitudes Toward Clergy and Religious Leadership* (report), The Associated Press-NORC Center (AP-NORC), May 20, 2019, http://www.apnorc.org/PDFs/AP-NORC%20Omnibus%20May%202019/APNORC_Religion_2019.pdf.

201. Chad Day, "Americans Have Shifted Dramatically on What Values Matter Most," *The Wall Street Journal*, Aug. 25, 2019, https://web.archive.org/web/20190825133907/https://www.wsj.com/articles/americans-have-shifted-dramatically-on-what-values-matter-most-11566738001.

202. Julia Manchester, "Poll: 68 percent say they paid same or more in taxes in 2018," *The Hill*, April 18, 2019, https://thehill.com/hilltv/what-americas-thinking/439552-36-percent-say-they-paid-the-same-in-taxes-in-2018-as-they-did.

203. Mohamed Younis, "Four in 10 Americans Embrace Some Form of Socialism," *Gallup* (website), May 20, 2019, https://news.gallup.com/poll/257639/four-americans-embrace-form-socialism.aspx.

204. Leigh Thomas, "People want higher taxes on rich, better welfare—21–country OECD survey," *Thomson Reuters Foundation News*, March 19, 2019, http://news.trust.org/item/20190319112743-3136f.

205. Frederick Kempe, "Democracies are on track to lose their global economic dominance as 'authoritarian capitalism' rises," *CNBC* (website), July 6, 2019, https://www.cnbc.com/2019/07/05/democracies-are-on-track-to-lose-their-global-economic-dominance.html.

206. Maureen Callahan, "The 'have-nots' of the world are over the wealth gap," *The New York Post*, Oct. 22, 2019, https://nypost.com/2019/10/22/the-have-nots-of-the-world-are-over-the-wealth-gap/.

207. Simon Tisdall, "About 41% of the global population are under 24. And they're angry…," *The Guardian* (UK), Oct. 26, 2019, https://www.theguardian.com/world/2019/oct/26/young-people-predisposed-shake-up-established-order-protest.

INDEX

ABOUT THE AUTHOR

J. Michael Bennett, Ph.D has a doctorate degree in Mechanical Engineering, and served for sixteen years as a team leader in technology development at the U.S. Air Force Research Laboratory, as well operating his own successful consulting and technology development business as an inventor, having received over twenty four patents on personal inventions now used in the military, commercial and transportation industries, with his work profiled in the *Wall Street Journal*, *Scientific American* and television programs on *CNN* and *PBS*. For seven years, he produced and hosted a radio program entitled *Future Quake* (as host "Doctor Future"), broadcast weekly on WRFN FM ("Radio Free Nashville") and then daily on the Christian radio station WENO, AM 760 in Nashville, TN, and worldwide via the Internet (with his shows currently archived at the show website, www.futurequake.com). He is a contributing author of the books *How to Overcome the Most Frightening Issues You Will Face This Century* and *Pandemonium's Engine* (both of Defender Publishing), and at any time is working on a number of new solo book projects. He has also been featured as a radio guest on programs such as *Coast to Coast AM with George Noory*, and as a keynote speaker on religion and spirituality at the 2008 United Nations and World Council of Churches-sponsored international conference entitled "Reconnecting Heaven and Earth in Spirit, Space and the Human Psyche," hosted by the United Nations NGO (non-governmental organization), The International Institute of Integral Human Sciences (www.iiihs.org). He was a researcher and on-camera host of the documentary, *Dark Clouds Over Elberton: The True Story of the Georgia Guidestones*. He also irregularly posts his musings on his blog site dedicated to Joshua and Caleb and other "minority views" of God's people, "The Two Spies Report" (www.twospiesreport.wordpress.com), and also hosts a site (www.mikebennettbooks.com) dedicated to news about his published works.

 **Akribos Press**

Akribos Press is an imprint dedicated to making available to the public opinions and perspectives, in well-researched, prepared and thoughtful forms, on matters spiritual, social and philosophical to which they have not been previously exposed, from authors with new voices and with fresh ideas that might not be appreciated, or left intact in their original nature by other publishing venues. "Akribos" is translated in English in Thayer's Greek Lexicon as "accurately" or "diligently," or as in the case of the King James translation of Ephesians 5:15, as "circumspectly." The goal is to publish narratives that exhibit the principle of "circumspectness," or the pursuit of holistically "looking at all sides" of a matter or issue, to discern the true nature of the circumstance. In fact, *Merriam-Webster* defines the term "circumspect" to be "careful to consider all circumstances and possible consequences: prudent." It appears to be related to the Latin word *circumspicere*—"to look around." Just as "first in" Special Forces may parachute or repel from a chopper into an open field behind enemy lines, looking in 360 degrees around them to quickly assess opportunity or danger, and friend or foe hidden in the brush, **Akribos Press** authors make efforts to look in directions that others might have missed, and digest the full measure of understanding on complex topics, or supplement them with missing intelligence data and uncovered relationships. This pursuit has an unabashed and essential philosophical and spiritual component, or as St. Paul wisely advised the Church at Ephesus,

See then that ye walk circumspectly, not as fools, but as wise, redeeming the time, because the days are evil. Wherefore be ye not unwise, but understanding what the will of the Lord is.
Ephesians 5:15–17

CPSIA information can be obtained
at www.ICGtesting.com
Printed in the USA
LVHW091756240521
688347LV00001B/5